Time Out

Brussels

timeout.com/brussels

Published by Time Out Guides Ltd, a wholly owned subsidiary of Time Out Group Ltd.
Time Out and the Time Out logo are trademarks of Time Out Group Ltd.

© **Time Out Group Ltd 2004**
Previous editions 1996, 1998, 2000, 2002

10 9 8 7 6 5 4 3 2 1

This edition first published in Great Britain in 2004 by Ebury
Ebury is a division of The Random House Group Ltd,
20 Vauxhall Bridge Road, London SW1V 2SA

Random House Australia Pty Limited, 20 Alfred Street, Milsons Point, Sydney, New South Wales 2061, Australia
Random House New Zealand Limited, 18 Poland Road, Glenfield, Auckland 10, New Zealand
Random House South Africa (Pty) Limited, Endulini, 5A Jubilee Road, Parktown 2193, South Africa

Random House UK Limited Reg. No. 954009

Distributed in USA by Publishers Group West
1700 Fourth Street, Berkeley, California 94710

Distributed in Canada by Penguin Canada Ltd
10 Alcorn Avenue, Toronto, Ontario, Canada M4V 3B2

For further distribution details, see www.timeout.com

ISBN 1-904978-15-0

A CIP catalogue record for this book is available from the British Library

Colour reprographics by Icon, Crowne House, 56-58 Southwark Street, London SE1 1UN

Printed and bound by Cayfosa-Quebecor, Ctra. De Caldes, KM 3 08 130 Sta, Perpètua de Mogoda, Barcelona, Spain

Time Out Guides Limited
Universal House
251 Tottenham Court Road
London W1T 7AB
Tel + 44 (0)20 7813 3000
Fax + 44 (0)20 7813 6001
Email guides@timeout.com
www.timeout.com

Editorial

Editor Peterjon Cresswell
Deputy Editor Lesley McCave
Consultant Editor Gary Hills
Listings Editors Alita Byrd, Wim Verhaeghe
Copy Editors Dominic Earle, Andrew Humphreys, Ros Sales
Proofreader Angela Jameson Potts
Indexer Jonathan Cox

Editorial/Managing Director Peter Fiennes
Series Editor Ruth Jarvis
Deputy Series Editor Lesley McCave
Guides Co-ordinator Anna Norman
Accountant Sarah Bostock

Design

Art Director Mandy Martin
Acting Art Director Scott Moore
Acting Art Editor Tracey Ridgewell
Acting Senior Designer Astrid Kogler
Designer Sam Lands
Junior Designer Oliver Knight
Digital Imaging Dan Conway
Ad Make-up Charlotte Blythe

Picture Desk

Picture Editor Jael Marschner
Deputy Picture Editor Kit Burnet
Picture Researcher Ivy Lahon
Picture Desk Assistant/Librarian Laura Lord

Advertising

Sales Director Mark Phillips
International Sales Manager Ross Canadé
International Sales Executive James Tuson
Advertising Assistant Lucy Butler

Marketing

Marketing Manager Mandy Martinez
US Publicity & Marketing Associate Rosella Albanese

Production

Guides Production Director Mark Lamond
Production Controller Samantha Furniss

Time Out Group

Chairman Tony Elliott
Managing Director Mike Hardwick
Group Financial Director Richard Waterlow
Group Commercial Director Lesley Gill
Group Marketing Director Christine Cort
Group General Manager Nichola Coulthard
Group Art Director John Oakey
Online Managing Director David Pepper
Group Production Director Steve Proctor
Group IT Director Simon Chappell

Contributors:
Introduction Gary Hills. **History** Gary Hills (*Off the rails* Leo Cendrowicz). **Brussels Today** Derek Blyth, Gary Hills (*Brussels tomorrow* Leo Cendrowicz). **Art Nouveau** Derek Blyth. **Cartoon Brussels** Peterjon Cresswell, Jonathan Murphy. **Where to Stay** Sue Heady. **Sightseeing** Gary Hills (features by Derek Blyth, Leo Cendrowicz, Peterjon Cresswell, Simon Cropper, Jeremy Duns, Gary Hills, John Miller, Norman Miller, Jonathan Murphy, Julius Stenzel, Craig Winneker). **Restaurants** Gary Hills. **Bars** Peterjon Cresswell, Gary Hills. **Shops & Services** Sue Heady, Anouk Vandeneijnde (*Rare junk, Good housekeeping* Jeremy Duns). **Festivals & Events** Gary Hills. **Children** Derek Blyth. **Film** Jonathan Murphy. **Galleries** Sarah McFadden. **Gay & Lesbian** Gary Hills. **Music** Mark English, Marian Hobbs, Julius Stenzel. **Nightlife** Gary Hills. **Sport & Fitness** Alita Byrd (*Purple reign* Leo Cendrowicz, Peterjon Cresswell). **Theatre & Dance** Gary Hills. **Trips Out of Town** Derek Blyth, Gary Hills, Peter Soetens (features by Derek Blyth, Simon Cropper, Jeremy Duns, Nico Favoreel, Sue Heady, Gary Hills, Norman Miller). **Directory** Alita Byrd, Gary Hills (features by Gary Hills).

The Editor would like to thank: Sophie Bouallegue (Belgian Tourist Office/Brussels & Wallonia), Philippe Guilmin and Gary Hills.

Maps by Mapworld, 71 Blandy Road, Henley on Thames, Oxon RG9 1Q, and JS Graphics (john@jsgraphics.co.uk).

Photography by Matthew Lea except: pages 6, 19, 21, 22 Corbis; pages 9, 11 AKG; page 12 Bridgeman Library; pages 17, 18 Hulton Archive; page 27 Moritz and Simon Architects; pages 75, 82, 84, 93, 102, 103, 144, 153, 197, 202 Hadley Kincade; pages 32 and 33 Hergé/Moulinsart 2004; page 92 Belgian Tourist Office/Brussels & Wallonia; pages 65, 125, 128, 129, 131, 133, 141, 158 Sarah Blee; page 134 National Genever Museum; page 150 Christopher Moore; page 166 Patrick Ward/Corbis; page 169, 170 Brussels Gewest/Tourism Flanders; page 179 Art Brussels; page 181 Baronian_Francey Gallery; page 190 Christopher Willibald Gluck; page 192 Eva Vermandel; page 202 Yves Boucau/AFP/Getty Images; pages 210, 211 Rosas, Herman Sorgeloos; page 213 Richard Pik/Royal Ballet Flanders; page 221 Antwerp, Ruben Shuis – Collections Management; page 245 Groeninge Museum; pages 262, 275, 277 Tourism Flanders; pages 267, 283 Belgium Tourist Office; page 271 World Pictures. The following images were provided by the featured establishments/artist: pages 198, 281.

Contents

Introduction

If Brussels was put in the therapist's chair, it would be reasonable to ask if it had an identity crisis. After all, it's the capital of Flanders, of Belgium and of Europe. It sits firmly in the Flemish north, but is a region in its own right, where the majority of residents speak French. Around 25 per cent of its inhabitants are expat foreigners, English is a lingua franca on the streets, so too is Arabic from the largely North African population. Crisis? What crisis? The truth is, Brussels takes the mix in its stride and pulls everything into an offbeat, almost bizarre sense of being.

Since 2000, when it was Cultural Capital of Europe, Brussels has found its way. Cleaned up, spruced up, a sense of purpose and a whole raft of social and inner-city regeneration projects have enticed people – particularly the young – back into town. Trendy areas such as rue Antoine Dansaert, St-Géry, Ste-Catherine and the canals offer loft space along with a sweep of bars and restaurants up to the Grand' Place and rue du Marché aux Charbon, offering a boozy nightlife that routinely turns into day. Walking is the best way to get around and feel the spirit of the place. And don't forget to look up – architectural gems sit above the ground-level shopfronts.

Brussels is a city that has a festival and a museum for everything, its showpiece theatres have been renovated, it remains a centre for dance and avant-garde performing arts, and its galleries heave with activity.

In contrast, the city lacks a river and cash machines. It's a bureaucratic nightmare, orientation is often difficult around the two-line metro system, driving is dire, dogs do their business wherever they want and there are still embarrassingly shabby streets. Rain and roadworks are common. And don't even think about pushing a pram around the uneven cobbles and high kerbs of the city centre. The eloquence of the centrepiece Grand' Place and belle époque architecture around it are the saving grace in a metropolis where post-war architecture was allowed to run wild, and the impersonal EU quarter thankfully sits in an area all of its own.

But none of this really matters. Brussels is roguish, cheeky, full of character. The locals are open and welcoming, with a nod to the traditional and a wink at the unusual. Irony is its strong suit. The city's restaurants are among the best in the world, as are its beers. In a world where globalisation has reduced much to blandness, the bars of Brussels are individual. The capital of Europe celebrates quirk. Brussels' artistic heritage is justifiably venerated – remember, you may be sitting in a bar where Magritte tried to hawk his paintings. Above all, Brussels is on a human scale; walking and taking it as you find it is the best way to allow it under your skin. You may well go home wondering what it was that made the trip so good, unable to put your finger on one single thing. So who's got the identity crisis?

ABOUT THE TIME OUT CITY GUIDES

Time Out Brussels is one of an expanding series of Time Out City Guides, now numbering more than 45, produced by the people behind London and New York's successful listings magazines. Our guides are all written and updated by resident experts who have striven to provide you with all the most up-to-date information you'll need to explore the city or read up on its background, whether you're a local or a first-time visitor. The guide contains detailed practical information, plus features that focus on unique aspects of the city.

THE LOWDOWN ON THE LISTINGS

Above all, we have tried to make this book as useful as possible. Addresses, telephone numbers, websites, transport information, opening times, admission prices and credit card details are included in our listings. And, as far as possible, we've given details of facilities, services and events, all checked and correct at the time we went to press. However, owners and managers can change their arrangements at any time, and often do. Many small shops and businesses in Brussels do not keep precise opening hours and may close earlier or later than stated here. Similarly, arts programmes are often finalised very late, and are liable to change. We advise you whenever possible to phone ahead and check opening times, ticket prices and other particulars. While every effort has been made to ensure the accuracy of this guide, the publishers cannot accept responsibility for any errors it may contain.

PRICES AND PAYMENT

The prices given in this guide should be treated as guidelines, not gospel. If they vary wildly from those we've quoted, please write and let us know. We aim to give the best and most up-to-date advice, so we always want to know when you've been badly treated or overcharged. Wherever possible we have factored in the sales tax (TVA), which many restaurants and hotels leave out of their advertised rates.

We have listed prices in euros (€) throughout, and we have noted whether venues take credit cards, but have only listed the major cards – American Express (**AmEx**), Diners Club (**DC**), MasterCard (**MC**), Visa (**V**). Many businesses will also accept other cards, including **JCB**.

THE LIE OF THE LAND

We have divided the city into areas – simplified, for convenience, from the full complexity of Brussels' geography – and the relevant area name is given with each venue listed in this guide. Wherever possible, a map reference is provided for every venue listed, indicating the page and grid reference for where it can be found in the street maps at the back of the book.

TELEPHONE NUMBERS

It is necessary to dial provincial area codes with all the numbers in Belgium, even for local calls. Hence all normal Brussels numbers begin 02, whether you're calling from inside or outside the city. From abroad, you must dial 32 (the international dialling code for Belgium) followed by the number given in the book – without the initial 0. For more information on telephones and codes, *see p301*.

ESSENTIAL INFORMATION

For all the practical information you might need for visiting Brussels, including emergency phone numbers and details of local transport, turn to the **Directory** chapter at the back of the guide. It starts on page 285.

LANGUAGES

Brussels is officially a bilingual city; street signs, tourist information and menus are given in French and Flemish, although the language used in the everyday life of the city is French. For this reason, and for brevity and clarity, we have used French for all official titles and addresses and in our street index. Be advised

that the language of Flanders is Flemish, and the default language is English. Locals in Antwerp, Bruges and Ghent will not take kindly to you trying to use French.

MAPS

The map section has an overview of Brussels and neighbourhoods, plus detailed street maps, a large-scale map of the centre, and a map of the metro network. The maps start on page 313.

LET US KNOW WHAT YOU THINK

We hope you enjoy *Time Out Brussels*, and we'd like to know what you think of it. We welcome tips for places that you consider we should include in future editions and take note of your criticism of our choices. You can email us at guides@timeout.com.

There is an online version of this guide, and guides to over 45 international cities, at **www.timeout.com**.

PASSIONATE ABOUT YOU.

We really look forward to welcoming you on board time after time - in fact, we really find it hard to say good-bye. Every flight, our team is committed to delighting you with our personal approach to service. And as one flight ends, we hope you'll be looking forward to the next. Just as much as we are. **flySN.com**

In Context

1958 World Fair in Brussels.
See p22.

History

From a muddy swamp surrounded by forest to the capital of
Europe enclosed by steel and glass.

When Julius Caesar arrived in what is now
known as Belgium in 59 BC, the area was
inhabited by Celtic and Germanic tribes who
had been drifting into the region since 2000 BC.
The Belgae, as the Romans called them, were
tough and resistant but were no match for the
formidable Roman army, which settled into
control of what it called Gallia Belgica, a useful
cushion between the Rhine and the provinces of
Gaul. The Roman settlements, therefore, were
largely in the south-east, though we know they
also used the coast for salt production, the
south-west for quarrying and the region near
Ghent for ironworks.

Brussels at this time simply did not exist.
The site was an inhospitable one, with marshy
flood plains from the multi-directional River
Senne making settlement difficult. Surrounding
the marsh was a vast forest, the Silva
Carbonaria (Charcoal Forest), which had
provided fuel and iron ore for weapons long

before the Romans arrived. The Forêt de
Soignes to the south-east of modern Brussels
is the last remaining remnant of what once
covered huge swathes of Gaul. The importance
of the forest as a source of fuel is still reflected
in Brussels street names such as rue du Marché
au Charbon and quai au Bois à Brûler.

THE FRANKS

The Roman empire in Gallia Belgica began to
founder in the third century AD, when the
Franks, a coalition of Germanic tribes, attacked
its northern borders. This was compounded by
constant flooding, an ongoing problem
throughout the history of the Low Countries,
and by the fifth century the Romans were gone.
From 350, the Franks were beginning to settle
into the more economically viable parts of the
region, but Gallia Belgica remained volatile as
waves of invaders passed through to continue
attacking the Roman armies in Gaul. These

invasions can be seen as the first stage in the process that was to lead to the deep linguistic division of present-day Belgium, since the northern areas became German-speaking, while to the south, Latin-based languages remained the dominant tongue.

The presence of the Franks in the Brussels region is unrecorded, though burial sites give evidence that they were around from the fifth century, and almost certainly using the tributaries of the River Senne as a trading post. The rest is largely conjecture, though it seems an early church was erected in the hamlet of Brosella, the first mention of the place now known as Brussels. The first extant documented reference to Bruocsella (dwelling in the marsh) dates from 695, when it was a stopping point on the trade route from Cologne to Bruges and Ghent.

> **'Ile St-Géry became the heart of the city; it still exists in the shape of place St-Géry, though the fortifications have given way to trendy bars.'**

King Charlemagne ruled from 768 to 814 and built an empire from Denmark to southern Italy, from the Atlantic to the Danube. When he died in 814, his sons and grandsons went to war over their inheritance. Eventually, in 843, the kingdom was split between his three grandsons following the Treaty of Verdun: Louis the German received East Francia, which roughly corresponds to Germany; Charles the Bald was given West Francia, which equates more or less to France plus Flanders; and Lothair received Middle Francia, or the Middle Kingdom. This was a thin strip comprising the land between the River Scheldt and Germany in the north, and stretching down to the Mediterranean.

Throughout the ninth and tenth centuries, the old Frankish kingdoms were subject to regular invasions by the Vikings, who took advantage of the power vacuum. There was a gradual disintegration of coherent central power and a rise of feudal domains. Flanders became one of the most powerful of all, and although it was theoretically ruled by the kings of France, the Flemish counts were virtually autonomous. Other fiefdoms were Liège, Hainaut, Namur, Luxembourg and Brabant.

Around 1000 a church dedicated to St Géry was erected on an island formed by the River Senne. This Ile St-Géry or Grand Ile was to become the heart of the city; it still exists in the shape of place St-Géry, though the early fortifications have given way to an agricultural hall and numerous trendy bars. Walk along the narrow street called Borgwal and you retrace the line of the original wooden palisades. Borgwal, therefore, could lay claim to being the oldest street in Brussels. From 1020, Brosella started to be mentioned as a port and in 1047 its ruler, Lambert II, Count of Louvain (Leuven), built a fort on Coudenberg Hill, overlooking the flood plains. The growing strategic importance of the Brussels settlement saw the erection of the first city walls over an 80-year period. Known as the *première enceinte*, or first enclosure, they were an impressive run of towers and gateways that kept the inhabitants in and the attackers out. All that is left of them now are a pair of isolated towers, including the Tour Noire, sandwiched between blandish modern buildings by place Ste-Catherine.

THE DUKES OF BRABANT

From 1106 the Counts of Louvain became known as the Dukes of Brabant, even though they continued to rule Brussels from the city of Louvain. They started to use the surrounding forests as hunting ground and the city soon started to spread out from the marshy valley of the River Senne into the hills and plateaux around it. The new city walls gave confidence to build grand stone houses, which are still reflected in central street names such as Plattesteen. Also at this time, Brussels became an important commercial centre, mainly for wool and cloth and, by the 12th century, Flemish cloth was being sold in France, Italy and England and the basis of an Anglo-Belgian trading partnership was firmly established. In 1282 there is first mention of the Drapers' Guild, something that indicated the importance of the cloth trade, and the future of Brussels itself.

The economic health of Flanders depended not only on the state of its relations with England and English wool imports, but also on Anglo-French relations, with Flanders often suffering from English reprisals against the French. Despite the fact that the Flemish counts were in the pockets of the French royals, the Flemish were often hostile to the French. On 11 July 1302, at the Battle of the Golden Spurs, the French knights suffered a shock defeat, the victorious Flemish collecting 700 pairs of spurs from the fleeing French. It was a milestone in Flemish resistance to the French. Consequently, the victory was hugely important in Flemish and Belgian consciousness (11 July is still a holiday in Flanders). The balance of the England-France-Flanders triangle became even more fragile in 1337, when the Hundred Years War began. At the start of the war, a Flemish landowner called Jacob van Artevelde led a rebellion in Ghent against the pro-French counts of Flanders, who fled to France. Flanders had been officially neutral, but van Artevelde actively allied it with the English.

During this time, Brussels continued to grow dramatically. Whilst Louvain/Leuven remained the capital of Brabant, the rulers were already receiving dignitaries in Brussels and the city's jurisdiction widened to take in places such as Schaerbeek and Ixelles. But in 1356, there was a power struggle between the daughters of Duke John III, resulting in a deadly battle won by Count Louis de Malle of Flanders. For the first time in its history, Brussels was ruled for a short while by the Flemish.

> **'The names of the gates are still with us, but only the Porte de Hal remains, a lonely Cinderella castle on a traffic island.'**

This brutal shock led the city elders to recognise the need for stronger defences and in 1357 construction began on a new set of walls, the *seconde enceinte*, or second enclosure. It was these walls that gave the centre of Brussels its pentagonal shape and which now provide the city with its inner ring road: le Petit Ring. The names of the gates are still with us: Porte de Namur, Porte d'Anderlecht and so on, but only the Porte de Hal remains, a lonely Cinderella castle on a traffic island.

THE DUKES OF BURGUNDY

A process of great cultural change began in the 1360s when Margaret of Malle, daughter of Count Louis de Malle, married Philip the Bold, Duke of Burgundy. When Louis died in 1384, Flanders and other provinces came together in a loose union under the authority of the Dukes of Burgundy. The key figure was Philip the Good (Philippe le Bon), grandson of Margaret and Philip the Bold. Having inherited Flanders, Burgundy, Artois and other provinces, he then acquired Brabant, Holland, Hainaut, Namur and Luxembourg through a combination of politics, purchase and military action.

Although the Dukes of Burgundy ruled for less than a century, the cultural changes during this period were significant. In addition to their ducal palace in Dijon, they had important residences in Lille, Bruges and Brussels. The court moved regularly between them, although from 1459 it was based mainly in Brussels. Keen to be viewed as equals of the French court, the Dukes of Burgundy initiated their own court

culture in the Low Countries, and were active patrons of the arts. Parades, tournaments, jousting and pageants were a major part of city and court life under the Dukes, as a means of displaying their power and wealth. This was also apparent in the great building works that took place. The first university in the Low Countries was founded in Leuven in 1425; work on Brussels' Town Hall, the dominant feature of the Grand' Place, started in 1402; and the awesome tower of Mechelen Cathedral was begun in 1452. In the arts, the best-known evidence of the Dukes' patronage is in 15th-century painting. The Brabant-born painter Jan van Eyck worked in Ghent and Bruges. Rogier van der Weyden worked in Brussels as the city's official painter. German artist Hans Memling settled in Bruges in 1465.

Although the textile industries were declining in the 14th and 15th centuries, mainly in the face of cheaper English competition, other industries were replacing them. Brussels was now producing tapestries, was becoming a centre for goldsmiths, and its first printing works opened in 1475. Brussels soon became the centre of Philip the Good's court and the Coudenberg Palace one of Europe's finest.

With the death of Philip the Good in 1467, the end of the rule of the Dukes of Burgundy was in sight. Philip was succeeded by his son Charles the Rash (Charles le Téméraire), who disliked Brussels and moved his court to Mechelen. There was no great grief when he was killed at the Battle of Nancy in 1477. He was succeeded by his daughter Mary, whose death five years later left the Netherlands in disarray. Mary had married Maximilian von Habsburg of Austria, and their son Philip was only four when she died. The Low Countries were then ruled by Maximilian for the next ten years, making them part of the Habsburg empire.

THE SPANISH NETHERLANDS

Maximilian's son Philip married Juana, the daughter of King Ferdinand and Queen Isabella of Spain. Their son Charles was born in Ghent in 1500 and, after an extraordinary series of premature deaths and childless marriages among the ruling families of Europe, he had inherited most of Europe by the time he was 20. He became Lord of the Netherlands in 1506 and King of Spain in 1516, and he was made Emperor Charles V of Germany when his grandfather Maximilian died in 1519. In this way, a native of Ghent came to rule the Netherlands, Austria, the Tyrol, Spain, Mexico, Peru, the Caribbean, Sicily, Naples and the German empire. Charles spent much of his earlier reign in Brussels and spoke both Dutch and French. While the connections with Spain

Abdication of **Emperor Charles V** in 1555.

were to prove quite disastrous in the future, Charles understood the Belgians well and he became a popular ruler and returned great wealth and prosperity back to Brussels, just as its fading medieval glories needed a kick-start.

> **'A man in Bruges had his hand and foot wrenched off by red-hot irons and his tongue ripped out, before being roasted over a fire.'**

At this time, Brussels had its new statement-piece Town Hall in place with its 90-metre (300-foot) tower (*See p10* **Crafty burghers**) and the palaces on the hill beamed prestigiously over the city. The first regular international mail service was set up in Brussels in 1520 by Jean-Baptiste de Tour et Taxis. Antwerp was even more prosperous than Brussels, as it was the crossroads of the trading routes between Spain, Portugal, Russia and the Baltic. Each day, some 5,000 merchants gathered in the exchange, and up to 500 ships came and went from the port.

Charles's reign saw the beginning of the Reformation, which would have devastating consequences for Europe. Lutherans from Germany extended their influence westwards into the Netherlands, while Calvinism spread northwards from Geneva. Although Charles was prepared to negotiate with Luther and his followers, he also would deal harshly with

Protestants, whom many considered heretics. The first Lutheran martyrs were burned in Brussels in 1523, and in 1550 Charles passed the Edict of Blood, which demanded the death penalty for all those convicted of heresy.

Charles abdicated in 1555, in an emotional ceremony at Brussels' Coudenberg Palace, and handed over the reins of the Netherlands to his son Philip, who became Philip II of Spain. Like his father, Philip inherited a collection of provinces in the Low Countries, rather than a nation. There was no common ancestry or language among the 17 provinces, and the French and Dutch language split was already patently evident.

The problems afflicting the Netherlands during Philip's rule were similar to those suffered under Charles: heavy taxation and the gradual spread of Protestantism. But whereas Charles had remained popular, Philip was never liked. He was Spanish by birth and sentiment, he didn't speak French or Dutch and he had little affection for his subjects in the Low Countries. He was also rather more hard-line in his defence of Catholicism than his father. In this he was aided by the Inquisition. Although the Spanish achieved the greatest infamy, their Belgian counterparts were hardly moderate. A poor citizen in Bruges who happened to trample on a consecrated wafer had his hand and foot wrenched off by red-hot irons and his tongue ripped out, before being slowly roasted over an open fire. Brussels' Grand' Place became a grisly home to executioners.

THE DUTCH REVOLT

Philip's troubles in the Netherlands started fairly quickly. He appointed his half-sister Margaret of Parma as regent, but power was mainly in the hands of two hated pro-Spanish councillors, Cardinal Granvelle and Count Berlaymont. Philip's most prominent opponents were Prince William of Orange, Count Egmont and Count Hoorn. In 1565 a group of nobles opposed to Philip formed the League of Nobles. Berlaymont referred to them disparagingly as 'ces gueux', beggars, and 'Vivent les gueux!' became their rallying cry. They objected to Philip's refusal to tolerate Protestantism, his attempt to centralise power, the heavy taxes imposed on the provinces, and the presence of Spanish troops in the Netherlands.

The spread of Protestantism was not confined to the League of Nobles. It burgeoned among the poor in the towns of Flanders, Brabant, Holland and Zeeland. In the 1560s Calvinist preachers attracted huge crowds, and part of their attraction to the poor was that they railed against the wealth of the Catholic Church. The preachers also criticised the imagery and art in the Catholic churches. In the Iconoclastic Riots of 1566, Calvinist mobs destroyed Catholic churches all across the Netherlands.

Crafty burghers

What is now the Grand' Place was a marshy area before the first market – the Nedermerckt, or lower market – began life around the present St Nicholas church in the 11th century. The current square was paved over in the 12th century and the first buildings appeared to the south and west of the square. Over time, the tangle of medieval streets around the Grand' Place became home to markets, traders and craftspeople (something that's still identifiable in today's street names). It's no wonder, then, that the powerful medieval guilds began to establish themselves on this square, the economic and spiritual focus of the city.

But the guilds were not just bodies of skilled craftsmen – they were a politically powerful mix of union, local magistrate and charity. What started out as an occupational organisation soon developed into something that stipulated work hours and conditions, lengths of apprenticeship and conditions of mastership. In Ghent the guilds built almshouses and charity was given to those in their professions who had fallen on harder times. But the guilds also had a political role: run by the wealthiest families, they were able to exert influence on the authorities of the time to further their own economic interests. This lobbying function allowed them to provide a counterbalance to aristocratic taxes, levies and trade restrictions and to fund small rebel armies to create popular unrest in the face of impositions. Guild militias even took part in the Battle of the Golden Spurs in 1302.

The powerful textile guilds were the most troublesome to the authorities, followed by the smiths, brewers, butchers and then the carpenters. As the textile industry declined and new non-guild industries developed, the guilds lost much of their influence and towards the end of the 16th century their great era was on the wane.

What we now see on the Grand' Place is a result of the guilds' irrepressible wealth and influence that was still in place after the French bombardment of Brussels in 1695. Over three days and three nights the French reduced medieval Brussels to rubble – on the Grand' Place only the tower of the Hôtel de Ville survived. It took the guilds only five years to rebuild their houses in the stunning baroque style that today makes the Grand' Place one of Europe's finest squares. As well as numbers, the houses were given names, something that provided them with the prestige they demanded.

Yet it was only in 1852 that a law was passed to protect the buildings, while the city agreed to pay for the upkeep of the façades in 1883. These days only one guild still occupies the same house it built for itself – the Brewers' House at No.10 (officially the L'Arbre d'Or, or the Golden Tree). The rest are occupied by bars, shops and restaurants, filled with tourists, although nothing can take away from their magnificence.

The Grand' Place continued as a fruit and vegetable market until after the war. There was also a caged bird market here until the 1990s, when it was deemed socially unacceptable. Today there is a small daily flower and plant market run by two families during the summer. Trams used to run through the square until the 1960s and, incredibly, cars were only stopped from driving through and parking in 1985. The medieval guilds would undoubtedly have had something to say about that.

In Antwerp, crowds attacked the cathedral with axes: they hacked up the Madonna, pulled down the statue of Christ at the altar, destroyed the chapels, drank the communion wine, burned manuscripts and rubbed the sacred oil on their shoes. They then did the same to 30 other churches in the city.

Philip duly appointed the Duke of Alva as new governor in the 17 provinces, and he arrived with an army of 10,000. One of his first acts was to set up the 'Council of Blood' (officially the Council of Troubles or Tumults). On 4 January 1568 alone he had 84 people executed on the scaffold. In March, there were 1,500 arrests, 800 of them in one day, and in June Count Egmont and Count Hoorn were beheaded in the Grand' Place. Their deaths marked the start of a full-scale revolt in the Netherlands that would last for 80 years.

Although Calvinism had first taken hold in the south, the southern provinces were now coming under the influence of the Counter-Reformation, and in 1579 the ten southern provinces formed the Union of Arras, accepting the authority of Philip, and Catholicism. The north's response was the 1581 Union of Utrecht, which was essentially a declaration that the seven northern provinces no longer recognised Philip's authority. By the end of the century the northern provinces had formed the Republic of the United Netherlands, also known as the United Provinces, while the southern provinces were known as the Spanish Netherlands, a split that became irreversible.

In 1598 Philip handed over his remaining territories in the Netherlands to his son-in-law, Archduke Albrecht of Austria. Philip hoped this might make reconciliation between the north and south possible. However, when Albrecht died without an heir in 1621 the provinces reverted to Spanish rule, although Philip's daughter Isabella remained governor until her death in 1633. Isabella and Albrecht maintained a lavish court, with court painter Peter Paul Rubens as its focal point.

They negotiated a truce with the Dutch in 1609, but it lasted just 12 years, and the war then continued until 1648. During its last phase, the religious gap widened between the two sides, with the United Provinces becoming more firmly Calvinist and the Spanish Netherlands in the grip of the Catholic Counter-Reformation. The war ended in 1648 with the Treaty of Munster, in which Spain recognised the independence of the north's United Provinces, with the agreed borders corresponding to the present-day Belgian-Dutch border.

In the second half of the 17th century Louis XIV of France had ambitions to dominate Europe at the expense of the Dutch, the English

Execution of **counts Egmont** and **Hoorn**.

and the Habsburgs. Spain's power had dwindled so far that it was no longer able to defend its territory. The late 17th century brought a succession of wars: the War of Devolution, the Dutch War and the War of the Grand Alliance, in all of which the Spanish Netherlands were either attacked or occupied. The ensuing peace treaties led to the territory of the Spanish Netherlands being whittled away, with France gaining Artois and Ypres.

Brussels was still producing a variety of luxury goods, including lace, tapestries and porcelain, both for export and for the nobles and merchants still living in the Spanish Netherlands. It was at this time, in 1695, that Louis XIV, unable to enter Brussels to claim the Spanish Netherlands, ordered the pointless bombardment of the city, destroying most of its medieval fabric. See p10 **Crafty burghers**.

THE AUSTRIAN NETHERLANDS

When Philip IV of Spain died in 1665 the Spanish throne passed to his sickly four-year-old son Charles. Despite two marriages, Charles II remained childless and for most of the 1690s he seemed to be teetering on the verge of death. Eager to fill a vacuum, the French, English, Dutch and Austrians manoeuvred over who would succeed him. By the time Charles II died in 1700, there were two candidates: Archduke

The signing of the **Treaty of Munster** in 1648. *See p11.*

Charles of Austria and Philip of Anjou, grandson of Louis XIV of France. Charles favoured the Frenchman as his heir and in 1701 the French Duke of Anjou entered Madrid as King of Spain. The French occupied Dutch-held barrier fortresses in the Spanish Netherlands, and the English and the Dutch declared war on France. The War of Spanish Succession lasted from 1701 to 1713 and was fought in Germany, the Netherlands, Italy, and Spain, as well as at sea. During the war, the Spanish Netherlands were governed by the French and the English. Peace was made at the 1713 Treaty of Utrecht and the 1714 Treaty of Rastatt. Philip of Anjou kept the Spanish throne, but the Austrians came away with the Spanish Netherlands, henceforth known as the Austrian Netherlands.

The main effect felt by the Austrian Netherlands during the first years of the 18th century was peace, for the country was no longer the prey of French armies. Only once during Austrian rule were the Netherlands invaded by the French, in 1744. Emperor Charles VI of Austria wanted his daughter Maria Theresa to inherit his empire, but the rest of Europe refused to accept this. France invaded and occupied the Austrian Netherlands until the Treaty of Aix-La-Chapelle restored Austrian rule in 1748 and gave the throne to Maria Theresa's husband, Francis I.

The real power, however, lay with Maria Theresa. Her rule, lasting until 1780, brought considerable economic renewal in the Austrian

Netherlands. This was partly a result of peace, and partly because of efforts by her governor, Charles of Lorraine, to build roads and waterways. There were also improvements in agricultural techniques, to the extent that the late 18th century was the only time in Belgium's history when it was self-sufficient in grain. There were also new glass, coal and cotton industries, which, unlike the trades that came before, did not revolve around the power of the guilds. Smaller industries – paper mills, sugar refineries and silk factories – also grew.

Cultural life developed, censorship was relaxed, French books circulated freely and bookshops were opened in the towns. There was a growing printing industry too. However, the Austrian Netherlands were scarcely at the fore of the Enlightenment, and rural culture still followed traditional values, with companies travelling around the countryside performing medieval mystery plays.

In 1731 the Coudenberg Palace burnt down after a fire in the kitchens. In 1740 work began on a new palace, the Palais du Roi, which is now the town residence of the Belgian royal family. The neo-classical place Royale and the Palais de la Nation, the seat of the Belgian parliament, were built in the 1770s and 1780s. In 1782, work started on the official residence of the Belgian royals at Laeken.

Maria Theresa was succeeded by her son Joseph II in 1780. His rule was more radical than his mother's. He immediately tried to modernise the country, closing monasteries and seminaries, taxing the Church and reforming both the judicial system and government administration. In 1781 he passed the Edict of Toleration, recognising religious freedoms. Joseph was loathed by the conservative Belgians, who saw their traditional privileges and vested interests threatened. The result was the Brabançon Revolution of 1789-90, involving all the provinces except Luxembourg. The rebels, led by a Brussels lawyer, wrote a new constitution inspired by the US Articles of Confederation and formed the Confederation of the United Belgian States. But the revolution collapsed into chaos as a result of the widening split between conservative and progressive rebels. Around 100,000 peasants, led by priests, marched through Brussels to protest against the progressives, many of whom were forced to flee to France. Austrian authority was restored in 1791, and when Joseph II died, he was succeeded by the liberal Leopold II, who had less enthusiasm for reform, preoccupied with events in other parts of his tottering empire.

FRENCH REVOLUTIONARY RULE

In 1792 the French declared war on Austria and Prussia, occupying the Austrian Netherlands and independent Liège. The French armies were initially greeted as liberators, but the welcome quickly faded, and when the loathed French temporarily withdrew from Brussels after a defeat in 1793, the people of Brussels ransacked the houses of pro-French families. When France reoccupied the Austrian Netherlands in 1794, tens of thousands of Belgians emigrated. The French exacted strict war levies and military requisitions and set up an *agence de commerce* to take anything from cattle to art back to France. Among their booty was Jan van Eyck's *Adoration of the Mystic Lamb*, now hanging in Ghent's cathedral, and they also confiscated the palace at Laeken. In 1795 the French absorbed the former Austrian Netherlands and set up a new administration. They abolished the former provinces and created nine new *départements*. Brussels itself became a departmental capital answering to Paris. Liège and the Netherlands were united for the first time, and the region was referred to by the French as *Belgique*.

The French passed laws suppressing feudalism and the guilds and from 1796 applied French law to Belgium. The Belgians accepted the occupation and annexation passively but unenthusiastically, and the French leaders complained of their apathy. The leading opposition to French rule came in 1798, after the French introduced conscription. There were riots in east and west Flanders and about 10,000 peasants formed an army in Brabant.

The uprising was soon crushed, brutally and bloodily, and hundreds were executed. The last five years of the century saw industry in decline, the depopulation of towns, new taxes, economic hardship, and organised gangs of robbers roaming the highways. Slowly, the French encouraged the growth of industries such as coal and cotton, which benefited from the new markets in France. The new industries were capitalist, funded by entrepreneurial nobles and traders who had bought former monastery lands cheaply. One of the notable beneficiaries of the French occupation was Antwerp, where Napoleon constructed a new harbour and port, which he described as 'a pistol aimed at the heart of England'.

He also made his mark on Brussels, ordering the city's old walls to be demolished and replaced with open boulevards. He bought the palace at Laeken as his official residence, but only used it occasionally before trading it for the Elysée Palace in Paris in a legal settlement with the Empress Josephine. French rule of the Netherlands came to an end in 1814, when Napoleon was forced to abdicate as Emperor of France, following his defeat at the Battle of Leipzig. His opponents (Britain, Prussia, Russia, Austria) recaptured Brussels in February 1814 and appointed a council of conservatives to govern the city. The council was very keen for Belgium to return to Austrian rule. In 1814 the Congress of Vienna began its work to break up and redistribute Napoleon's empire.

On his return from exile, Napoleon rounded up an army. The Congress of Vienna quickly condemned the landing and Europe prepared for war. The combined armies of the British, Spanish, Prussians, Austrians and Dutch numbered over one million men. Napoleon had gathered about 375,000 soldiers. The Duke of Wellington, commander-in-chief of the British, Hanoverians and Belgians, established his headquarters in Brussels. One of the legends of Waterloo is that Wellington was at a ball hosted by the Duke and Duchess of Richmond in the rue de la Blanchisserie when news reached him of Napoleon's approach on 18 June. The battle lasted for ten hours and 50,000 soldiers were killed. Napoleon escaped to Paris, where he abdicated and surrendered to the British. He was banished to the island of St Helena, where he died in 1821. *See pp16-17* **Where Napoleon met his demise**.

UNITY AND REVOLUTION

The Congress of Vienna redrew the map of Europe after Napoleon. One main dilemma was the Netherlands. The north had existed as an independent state since 1648, but the former Spanish and Austrian Netherlands had no tradition of independence and Congress was reluctant to create one. Austria had no desire to recover these provinces, and there was no question of their going to France. So what was to become of them? The Congress of Vienna opted to unite the Netherlands with the Austrian Netherlands and form the United Kingdom of the Netherlands, thereby creating a strong buffer between France and Prussia. It was a solution that few inhabitants had asked for, other than some Belgian entrepreneurs who saw that union with the Dutch might compensate for the loss of markets in France.

The United Kingdom of the Netherlands was created as a constitutional monarchy ruled by William of Orange. He was installed as sovereign prince on 31 July 1814, and declared king in 1815. As well as its 17 provinces, the new kingdom had two capitals, The Hague and Brussels. William I was eager to promote prosperity and unity, and although he succeeded in the former, he failed in the latter. The southerners found many reasons to resent the new state. The south of the kingdom was already industrialised and had become wealthy as a result. Although Brussels was joint capital, the new country was governed by a Dutch king, Dutch ministers and Dutch civil servants. Despite being more numerous and prosperous, the Belgians had little political power at the outset and gained little more over time.

Many Belgians took refuge in memories of the earlier grandeur of Antwerp and Brussels, regarding the Dutch as upstarts. There was also fury at the government's attempts to introduce Dutch as the standard language. This resentment was not confined to French speakers – those who spoke Flemish dialects also protested against the use of Dutch. Belgium's Catholics were opposed to the new government because it had declared religious freedom and removed the Catholic bias in the education system. Belgian liberals also opposed the new state, seeking freedom of the press and a less autocratic style of government. In 1828 Catholics and liberals formed an unlikely alliance, demanding that the Belgians, not the Dutch, become the dominant force in the Netherlands. The government did make concessions, repealing the language decrees in the south and guaranteeing freedom of education, but it would neither accept Belgian supremacy nor grant freedom of the press.

The winter of 1829-30 was severe and farmers suffered accordingly. In addition, overproduction in the industries of the south had caused wage cuts, bankruptcies and unemployment. Workers in both sectors were mutinous, and there were regular protests and demonstrations in Brussels. On 25 August 1830

an opera called *La Muette de Portici*, by Daniel Auber, was performed at Brussels' Théâtre de la Monnaie. Its subject was the Naples rebellion of 1647 and the opera had been banned since being written in 1828. During an aria called 'L'Amour Sacré de la Patrie' (Sacred Love of the Fatherland), liberals and students in the theatre started rioting, and then joined the workers who were protesting in the square outside.

This was the start of the Belgian Revolution. The Dutch government negotiated with the leaders of the revolution and there seemed a possibility of administrative separation. But William I prevaricated and the impatient and disillusioned rebels decided to go for secession. William sent 10,000 troops into Brussels at the end of September, and while the numbers were insufficient to crush the revolution, they were enough to inflame the southern provinces into joining the uprising. Belgian soldiers deserted their regiments, and William's troops were driven out of Brussels. A new government was rapidly assembled. On 4 October 1830 the rebels declared an independent state and provisional government; on 3 November they held elections for a National Congress. It met for the first time on 10 November and comprised 200 members, most of them intellectuals, lawyers and journalists. There were few representatives from industry or finance.

> '**It was sadly inevitable that the coalition between liberals and Catholics would be neither harmonious nor long-lived.**'

On 22 November the new Congress decided on a constitution. Belgium was to be a parliamentary monarchy and unitary state of nine provinces, with freedom of religion, education, assembly, press and language, and a separate church and state. On 3 March 1831 the Congress passed an electoral law defining the electorate, which consisted of about 46,000 men of the bourgeoisie. This meant that one out of every 95 inhabitants had the vote, a relatively high proportion – in France, it was one in 160.

The rest of the world soon recognised the new nation, and in January 1831 the Great Powers met in London to discuss the issue. Britain advocated the creation of a Belgian state, France and Germany agreed, and Belgium was recognised as an independent and neutral state. The decision on a new king was less easily reached, but eventually Léopold of Saxe-Coburg-Gotha was selected. He was related to the major European royal households, most famously as uncle to both Victoria and Albert. He took an oath to the constitution on 21 July, now Belgium's National Day. Shortly afterwards, the Dutch invaded Belgium, and this helped prolong a sense of unity among the Catholics and liberals. The Dutch beat the Belgian rebels at Leuven and Hasselt but then retreated on hearing reports of an approaching French army of 50,000. They did not recognise the new country until 1839. Léopold's resolve strengthened his popularity, along with his belief in the new constitution.

INDEPENDENT BELGIUM

It was sadly inevitable that the coalition between liberals and Catholics in the new state of Belgium would be neither harmonious nor long-lived. The political history of Belgium in the 19th century was of a tug of war between the two, the main bones of contention being the education system and the language split.

Belgium's history as a nation state began with the Catholics and the French speakers in the ascendant. The new constitution allowed people to use whichever language they preferred, but French was the language of the dominant class and was spoken in the courts, the education system (apart from some primary schools) and the administration. In the country as a whole, Flemish was more widely spoken, with 2.4 million Flemish speakers to 1.8 million French ones. The majority of the population was being governed in an alien language.

Intellectuals in Antwerp and Ghent soon began to resent the prevalence of French. In 1840 they organised a petition demanding the use of Flemish in the administration and law courts of Flemish-speaking provinces. Initially, the Catholics were dominant at most levels. Membership of monasteries and convents more than doubled during the 1830s and 1840s, and in 1834 a new Catholic university was founded at Mechelen, moving to Leuven in 1835. The Catholic Church also controlled much of secondary education. In 1846 the liberals held a congress in Brussels to clarify a political programme and to plan an election strategy. The Catholics did not organise themselves in the same way until the 1860s. Charles Rogier formed a liberal government in 1848, and the liberals governed, with a few gaps, until 1884.

Although Belgium lost the Dutch East Indies markets when it split from the Netherlands, there was industrial expansion from the 1830s, at a time when much of Europe had falling industrial prices. With its programme of railway construction, and large-scale investment in the coal, iron and banking industries, Belgium was the first country in continental Europe to undergo the Industrial Revolution. In Brussels the canal system was extended with the new Canal de Charleroi, and with it a whole new industrial complex was built on the western side of the city in Anderlecht, Forest and Molenbeek. It became known as Little Manchester. The king wished to keep his capital as a prestigious centre of commerce, banking and luxury goods rather than a hub of manufacturing. There were also political reasons: with economic problems across the country, an industrialised urban workforce was seen as dangerous. The Belgian Workers' Party was founded in 1885 and the Socialists would soon exert political influence.

Universal male suffrage was introduced in 1893 and in 1894 the Socialists gained their first parliamentary seats – but with the bulk of support in Flanders, the Catholics regained power until 1917. There had already been concessions to Flemish speakers, and the Catholics accelerated the process. Language continued to be a problem. There had been legislation introducing bilingualism in Flanders and strengthening the Flemish position in law and education, but the Flemings were still governed and tried in French. In 1898 Flemish was given official equality with French, though the electorate (only taxpayers could vote) was almost entirely French-speaking.

EXPANSION AND EXPLORATION

Despite constant dispute over particular issues, the Belgians did demonstrate a sense of unity in some areas of public life. Independence led to a building spree in Brussels. Among the earliest additions were the Galeries St-Hubert in the 1840s. These were followed by a spate of official buildings and commemorative projects as Belgium celebrated its own existence, culminating in the construction of the Parc du Cinquantenaire for the 50th anniversary exhibition. The Palais de Justice was completed in 1883 on the Galgenberg Hill, the site of the gallows in past times. The first railway station in Brussels opened in 1835 where Yser métro station now stands, with a line to Mechelen.

The main town-planning feat of the 19th century was the covering over of the River Senne. *See p64* **Hidden Brussels**. The river had become a repository for industrial and agricultural waste, including effluent from breweries and textile industries that had deliberately set up shop on its banks. Periodic cholera outbreaks led to an epidemic in 1866, when 3,500 people died. Rather than develop civil engineering schemes to clean up the river, the authorities decided on the more radical approach of a *voûtement*, or covering up. The idea was not just for sanitary reasons. Central Brussels was short of grand property in the

Where Napoleon met his demise

It is rare that the name of a battle evokes such strong feelings. Waterloo can be included with Hastings, Trafalgar and the Normandy landings as something that emphatically changed the course of history. Waterloo was also an extension to what was already happening among diplomats at the Congress of Vienna after the first fall of Napoleon. The redrawing of Europe was already well advanced, and Wellington's choice of the Mont St-Jean ridge had been selected long before as a defensive position should Napoleon ever escape from exile and stage a comeback. Which of course he did.

In February 1815 the exiled emperor landed in Cannes, immediately gathered a small army and headed to Lyon where he amassed troops. The great powers duly declared war. Brussels was chosen as the Allied base and from April, troops began to pour into the city.

Wellington (*pictured*) was commander of the English and Dutch army with Belgians and Poles in support. In reality, the army was ill trained and lines of command were not clear; they were also demoralised by poor conditions, knowing that their commanding officers were fox hunting in the forests and grand balls in the great Brussels houses. Wellington also knew that he was dependent on 120,000 Prussian troops to the east under Marshal von Blücher. Napoleon had the upper hand with his 125,000 battle-experienced men, loyal to their emperor. His strategy was simple: to stop the armies of Wellington and Blücher joining up.

On 15 June Napoleon crossed the border, took Charleroi and moved onwards to Brussels. This was Wellington's signal to mobilise the army and take up positions at the pre-planned Mont St-Jean. The next day Napoleon attacked Blücher's forces at Ligny and defeated them roundly. But it was here that he made an uncharacteristically crucial mistake; believing they were on the run, he failed to follow the victory through. He continued his march towards Brussels, aware that his men were suffering terrible conditions and that time was of the essence. On the same day, at Quatre Bras, on the Brussels-Charleroi road, the gauntlet was thrown down and Napoleon formally challenged Wellington. Positions were taken closer to the village of Braine l'Alleud than Waterloo, so the battle never actually took place there. Wellington's

headquarters were established at the Bodenghien Inn, while Napoleon commandeered Le Caillou farm to the south.

The night of 17 June teemed with rain but despite the mud and treacherous conditions the Allied armies established their positions on the ridge, while the French amassed across the valley a mile away. The following morning they could look directly at each other. The waterlogged ground put paid to Napoleon's plan to launch an early attack, and it wasn't until 11.35am that it was deemed dry enough for battle to commence. A massive artillery barrage engulfed the Allied army while Napoleon decided to send his less-than-competent brother, Prince Jerome, to head over and take the fortified farm of Hougoumont on the Allied left.

This was supposed to be a diversionary tactic to force Wellington to weaken his centre of defence of the stronghold, but the defenders held off the enemy. At 5pm, when the attack was abandoned, more than 3,000 French corpses were piled outside the farm's battered walls. In the meantime, Napoleon had learned that Blücher's troops hadn't been routed and were closing in. He sent 14,000 troops to prevent the Prussians reaching the battlefield. To force the battle, he then took the risky step of ordering a huge infantry assault on Wellington's left and the farm of La Haie-Sainte.

The arrival of the Prussians swung the battle in favour of the Allies. Wellington ordered his troops to pull back slightly from the ridge. Wave after wave of French cavalry attacks wreaked havoc on the Allies, but they refused to crumble. By 6.30pm the French flag was raised at La Haie-Sainte and the Allies were buckling under the pressure. It was then that the first Prussian troops arrived, and Blücher's troops began making inroads on the French right.

Napoleon threw every resource he had available into the battle in a last desperate attempt to snatch victory. At 7.30pm his beloved Imperial Guard entered the fray, but, bogged down in the heavy mud churned up by their own cavalry, they made easy targets. Onwards they marched, almost as far as Mont St-Jean, before being forced to retreat. By 8.15pm and the arrival of Blücher's entire army, Wellington rode up and down his lines, and urged his soldiers into a huge counter-attack. Gradually, French confidence evaporated and their troops fled. The Battle of Waterloo was over.

At 9.30pm Wellington and Blücher embraced at the Belle Alliance inn, just south of Waterloo. The victory despatch was sent from the village and, following the convention of the time, this was the name that was given to the battle.

Today Waterloo, about an hour by direct train from Brussels, has a modest scattering of tourist attractions set by the motorway to Paris. An all-in ticket of €12 allows access to the old quarters used by Napoleon and Wellington, the Waterloo Visitors' Centre and the mound. The most impressive sight is the view from the Butte du Lion, the huge monument built by the Dutch on the spot where the Prince of Orange was wounded. From this 226-step vantage point, the battleground seems remarkably small. The battle itself is re-enacted every five years – the next one is due in June 2005. Contact the Waterloo Visitors' Centre for details.

Musée Wellington

147 chaussée de Bruxelles, Waterloo (02 354 78 06/www.museewellington.com). **Open** *Apr-Sept* 9.30am-6.30pm daily. *Oct-Mar* 10.30am-5pm daily. **Admission** €5; €4 concessions. **Credit** V.

Napoleon's Last Headquarters (Le Quartier Général de Napoléon – formerly the Musée du Caillou)

66 chaussée de Bruxelles, Vieux-Genappe (02 384 24 24/www.pixelsbw.com/ 1815/caillou.htm). **Open** *Apr-Oct* 10am-6.30pm daily. *Nov-Mar* 1-5pm daily. **Admission** €2; €1.50 concessions. **No credit cards**.

Office de Tourisme de Waterloo

218 chaussée de Bruxelles, Waterloo (02 354 99 10). **Open** *Apr-Sept* 9.30am-6.30pm daily. *Oct-Mar* 10.30am-5pm daily.

Waterloo Visitors' Centre

254 route du Lion, Braine l'Alleud (02 385 19 12/www.waterloo1815.be). **Open** *Apr-Oct* 9.30am-6.30pm daily. *Nov-Mar* 10am-5pm daily. **Admission** *Combined ticket* €7.44. *25min film* €4.96. *Panorama de la Bataille* €2.73. *Butte du Lion* €1. Concessions available. **Credit** AmEx, MC, V.
One-hour walking tours (€3) of the battlefield are held on weekend afternoons in summer. Next battle re-enactment due in 2005.

19th century, and its tangle of streets resembled Bruges more than a major European capital like London or Paris. The *voûtement* gave the opportunity for grand boulevards, big hotels and Parisian-style apartment blocks for the wealthy. Property developers jumped on the idea. Above the *voûtement* appeared the boulevards Anspach, Lemonnier and Adolphe Max, achieving the required design, but never the social cachet. The city elders hadn't thought that wealthy residents would much rather buy grand houses in Ixelles and St-Gilles than live in close quarters to others.

The grandiose plans of Léopold II, who had succeeded his father in 1865, did not limit themselves to Belgium. As crown prince, he had looked around for suitable territories, and considered British-run Borneo, the Philippines, South Africa and Mozambique. Finally, he decided to grab a piece of the 'magnificent African cake'. Much of central Africa was still unexplored and in 1876 Léopold set up the Association Internationale Africaine with the help of explorer Henry Stanley. Although other European governments and the United States expressed qualms about Léopold's activities in Africa, he dismissed them sufficiently for the Berlin Declaration of 1885 to recognise the independent state of the Congo, with Léopold as

The greed of **King Léopold II**.

head of state. He referred to himself as its proprietor and ruled his new territory with absolute power and terror. Léopold's colonial adventures were to cast a dark shadow on Belgium's reputation. From 1895, when he started exporting wild rubber, it generated huge revenue, much of which was passed back to Belgium and used for massive public works such as the Musée Royal de l'Afrique Centrale at Tervuren (*see p102*). Local entrepreneurs, industrialists and engineers who grew rich on the Congo Free State could build themselves great houses in the extravagant art nouveau style, with little regard for the expense.

By the early 20th century, Léopold's policy of extracting maximum profit from the Congo, regardless of ecological and human cost, was exposing Belgium to international criticism, particularly from Britain. In 1908, the Belgian government forced Léopold to hand it over to the nation, and it remained a Belgian colony until independence in 1960.

WORLD WAR I

On its creation in 1830, Belgium declared itself perpetually neutral. But on 2 August 1914 Kaiser Wilhelm of Germany demanded that Belgium give its troops free passage on their way to invade France. Belgium had half a day to respond to the ultimatum, which it rejected.

On 4 August German troops entered the country, and the government took refuge in Antwerp. Seven hours later Britain declared war on Germany. By midnight, five different empires were involved in war. The Germans entered Brussels on 20 August. It was a strategic city for them, being a staging post between Aachen and the Western Front. English nurse Edith Cavell (*see p99* **Hidden Brussels**), who had stayed on in the city and was later executed by the invaders, said that conversations with the Germans revealed they were surprised to find themselves there, having believed they were marching on Paris. Once in place, the Germans demanded a massive war indemnity and huge amounts of food for the troops, meaning a real possibility of starvation for the locals. The situation in Brussels was saved by the Americans who organised the Commission for Relief in Belgium and set up charitable aid. The US ambassador, Brand Whitlock, became something of a national hero.

Yet Belgium suffered horribly in World War I. Snipers shot at the Germans and retaliation was brutal. At the village of Hervé, the Germans set an example. Within a few days, only 19 of the 500 houses were still standing, the church was in ruins, and the shattered village was littered with corpses. Other massacres occurred elsewhere: the Germans

French soldiers await transportation to Belgium at the start of **World War I**.

shot 110 people at Andenne, 384 people at Tamines, and 612 people, including a three-week-old baby, at Dinant.

By the end of September Antwerp was under siege and fell on 10 October, despite the arrival of British troops, including the poet Rupert Brooke, in a fleet of London buses. Half a million refugees left Antwerp, among them thousands who had fled there from all over Belgium. Some 1.5 million had already left the country, although many later returned. The government went to Le Havre, while King Albert I, successor to his uncle Léopold II, took up position with the small Belgian army in the north-west of the country. Known as 'le Roi Chevalier' (the Soldier King), he won acclaim from his people by fighting with his troops in the trenches alongside the French and British.

> **'700,000 Belgians were deported to Germany to work on farms and factories, including the burgomaster Adolphe Max.'**

The four-year German occupation had terrible consequences. A total of 44,000 war dead might be dwarfed by the losses of Russia and France, but 700,000 Belgians were deported to Germany to work on farms and in factories, including the burgomaster Adolphe Max. The economy was devastated. Belgium had once depended on other countries for its raw materials and its export markets, and it lost both. Much of its rail system was destroyed in an attempt to prevent the German invasion, agricultural production fell, and there was widespread poverty and hunger. Belgium was liberated in 1918, and until 1921 the leading consideration of the post-war governments was how to rebuild the country. It is estimated that its losses represented about one fifth of its national assets in 1914, and not all of them were recovered in war reparations.

The Germans had been pro-Flemish, and a small group of Flemish politicians had been enthusiastic collaborators. In 1916 the Germans had declared the University of Ghent Flemish-speaking. It reverted to French and did not adopt Flemish again until 1930. Having just recovered what they had lost after World War I, the Flemings made a series of language gains during the 1930s. In 1932 French and Flemish ceased to have equality in Flanders, where the official language now became Flemish.

The period immediately after World War I had been marked by brief political unity, as Catholics, liberals and Socialists worked together to rebuild the country. The unity quickly dissipated, however, particularly after the introduction of proportional representation. The first universal male suffrage elections without multiple votes for the bourgeoisie were held in 1919 (women had to wait until 1949), and they resulted in a series of coalition governments. Between 1918 and 1940 Belgium had 18 different administrations. After a slight recovery, the country slumped into depression in the 1930s. There was severe unemployment, social unrest and a move to the right. In the 1936 elections Flemish nationalist and right-wing parties in Wallonia and Brussels managed to make big gains, blaming the economic depression on the weak parliament, lack of strong leadership and the unions. Also, the Soldier King, Albert I, had died under suspicious circumstances in a rock-climbing accident in 1934 and his son, Léopold III, lacked the same charisma.

WORLD WAR II

After allying with France, Belgium reasserted its neutrality following the German invasion of Poland in 1939. It did little good. Hitler attacked on 10 May 1940. Showing opposite traits to his father, Léopold III surrendered after just 18 days. Much of the population was in support of Léopold's action, but the government itself was not. Believing that Belgium should commit itself to the Allies, it became a government-in-exile in Le Havre and then London.

Despite initially espousing a policy of normalisation, the Germans became more authoritarian during the course of the war, creating greater resistance. Belgium suffered

Off the rails

Eurostar travellers to Paris have to cross the city to connect with TGV services to the Alps or Mediterranean. Likewise, most arriving at London Waterloo then do battle with the city's transport. Travellers and commuters passing through Brussels, however, can delight in the fact that all trains conveniently pass through the three main stations of Nord, Centrale and Midi. The city can be traversed in less than ten minutes, half of Europe accessed, too, by a simple change of platform.

The reason is the Jonction Nord-Midi, a rail tunnel linking each hub, whose construction took more than a century from idea to implementation – and for which local citizens paid a high price. The city's unenviable reputation for thoughtlessly knocking down beautiful historic buildings and replacing them with faceless office blocks began with the rail tunnel, a project that ripped up the working-class heart of the city.

When the idea was first proposed in 1837, rail networks had developed independently of each other at disconnected stations at either end of the city. A link would transform Brussels into a regional rail hub, handling through-traffic across Europe. Similar ideas were proposed throughout the 19th century, inspired by Léopold II's grandiose vision of Belgium as a European power. Progress, though, was painfully slow. Frédéric Bruneel's 1893 underground plan took the line under the Botanical Gardens, the Cathedral and the church of Notre Dame de la Chapelle. It was eventually adopted in 1901, and construction began in 1911.

The work was scheduled to be completed in 1915, but World War I intervened. As the city focused on more immediate reconstruction,

new questions were asked about whether the link was worth it, whether it should be electrified, and whether the route should be changed. In 1935 these questions appeared resolved and the works restarted. Victor Horta was brought in to design a modern station above the Grand' Place. World War II brought progress to a halt.

After the war, Nord and Midi stations were rebuilt with new facilities. In between, a third station, the Gare Centrale, was created, according to the plans left by Horta before his death. Building the entire 3.5-kilometre (two-mile) rail link involved removing one million cubic metres of earth, placing 85 kilometres (53 miles) of reinforced concrete pillars, and using 42,000 tonnes of iron. By then, the work had destroyed 1,200 homes by driving a four-lane highway through the centre and completely dissecting the city. Thousands of poor families living in the old Mont des Arts district had been driven out, and the area rebuilt with the royal library and archives, the Cité Administrative complex and numerous museums. Churches such as the 15th-century Chapelle de la Maidelaine were completely knocked down and rebuilt elsewhere. Brussels truly earned its grim reputation.

The link was finally opened on 4 October 1952 by the young King Baudouin. Six days after its opening 1,140 trains and 135,000 passengers had travelled on this new route. By the end of the 20th century, 320,000 people were taking the train every day through the centre of Brussels. Meanwhile the city council was desperately finding ways and the wherewithal to install an urban rail network, similar to the RER in Paris, to ease the congested Nord-Midi link.

The signing of the **European Common Market** treaty in 1957. *See p22.*

the same problems as it had in World War I: deportations, forced labour, poverty and food shortages. In Brussels there was a Gestapo HQ in avenue Louise and the Résidence Palace in rue de la Loi was the Nazi administrative centre for Belgium. From 1 June 1942, Belgian Jews were required to wear the yellow Star of David. The Germans created a deportation centre in Mechelen and, between 1942 and 1944, sent 25,257 people from there to Auschwitz. Two thirds died on arrival. A network of Belgian resistance and opposition saved thousands of others from a similar fate. Concentrating on the children, Belgians from all classes and backgrounds risked their own lives by taking Jewish children into their families and creating new identities for them. In that respect, Belgium saved more Jews per capita than any other occupied country.

Belgium was liberated in September 1944 and one of the first tasks was to tackle the issue of collaboration. The war tribunals considered 405,000 cases, reaching 58,000 guilty verdicts, of which 33,000 were in Flanders. Then there was the behaviour of Léopold III. In a non-binding referendum, only 57 per cent voted in favour of his return (72 per cent in Flanders and 42 per cent in Wallonia), and when he did come back there were disturbances. In 1951, Léopold stepped aside in favour of his son Baudouin.

Even today, the issue of collaboration is sensitive. Up to 15,000 Belgians convicted of collaboration still receive reduced pension and property rights. In February 1996 a military court in Brussels reconsidered the case of Irma Laplasse, a Flemish farmer's wife who had betrayed resistance fighters to the Nazis in 1944. She was executed by firing squad in 1948. The court upheld her conviction, but ruled that the death sentence should have been commuted to life imprisonment. The judgement was met by protests from both sides. Concentration camp survivors and former members of the resistance and the Belgian secret army demonstrated to protest at any moves to rehabilitate collaborators. For its part, the far-right Flemish Vlaams Blok party campaigned for an amnesty for all those accused of collaborating, insisting that the tribunals were an attempt to victimise and repress the Flemish.

POST-WAR BELGIUM

World War II had made it clear that Belgium's traditional neutrality was untenable, and even before the war was over the government-in-exile set about rejecting the policy in favour of international alliances. It signed the Benelux Customs Union with Luxembourg and the Netherlands, abolishing customs tariffs and setting a common external tariff. Belgium became an enthusiastic participant in post-war international relations; as an export-driven economy it needed to belong to the growing international relations superstructure. Belgium was one of the first signatories of the UN Charter in June 1945, joining the Organisation

Attorneys of accused murderer **Marc Dutroux** face the media outside court.

for European Economic Co-operation in 1948. It also became a member of the Council of Europe and the European Coal and Steel Community, and the HQ of the European Economic Community (EEC) when it was set up in 1957. Brussels' hosting of the World Fair of 1958 allowed for rapid modernisation, the ring boulevards becoming a network of highways and tunnels. Brussels became the HQ of NATO in 1967, the same year that the EEC main offices of the controversial Berlaymont building were opened. Its vast structure typified the grandiose, impersonal quarter of steel and glass growing up around it, as the EEC took on more members. Officials and diplomats swamped the old Léopold quarter and created, in effect, two Brussels: an international zone around Schuman and the rest of the city.

During the EEC era King Baudouin became a respected and beloved monarch, concerning himself with the well-being of his subjects and social issues. A quiet, unassuming man, he is credited with preventing Belgium from splitting into two countries. He reigned until his death in 1993 and, being childless, his crown passed to his brother, the present King Albert II.

The Flemish-Walloon debate was initially dampened by the awkward question of Flemish collaboration, but from 1960 onwards the split over language and community deepened. The language barrier between French-speaking Wallonia and Flemish-speaking Flanders was formally created in 1962, leaving Brussels

officially bilingual. In 1965 the political parties split into Flemish and Walloon wings. Debate then focused on the constitution and the treatment of each community. The split was exacerbated by economic developments. Once an economic powerhouse because of its coal and steel, Wallonia declined, leaving Flanders to flourish in successful post-war industries such as telecommunications. The Flemings claimed their wealth propped up Wallonia, the Walloons that the government favoured the Flemings.

The Belgian government made a series of reforms, granting greater autonomy to each community and changing Belgium from a centralised to a federal state. There were prophesies of doom when King Baudouin died, but so far the country has not fallen apart and a new constitution was introduced in 1994. This created a new system of elected assemblies and governments representing Flanders, Wallonia and Brussels, and each language community. Brussels is an autonomous region governed by Flemish and French community parliaments and home to the national government.

Two events further galvanised the country: the massive public protests over the police handling of the Dutroux affair, in which an accused child murderer escaped detection and then, briefly after his arrest, from captivity entirely; and the marriage of the royal heir, Prince Philippe, to an ordinary Belgian citizen, in 1999. Unity and injustice always seem to bring out the best in Belgium.

Key events

EARLY AND MEDIEVAL HISTORY
57-51 BC Julius Caesar fights Gallic Wars.
15 BC Foundation of Roman Gallia Belgica.
5th century AD Collapse of Roman rule.
814 Death of Emperor Charlemagne.
843 Charlemagne's kingdom split between his three grandsons.
979 Official founding of Brussels (Bruocsella).
1041 Dukes of Brabant build palace at Coudenberg in today's Upper Town.
1302 Flemish army beats the French at the Battle of the Golden Spurs.
1337 Outbreak of Hundred Years War.
1348-9 Black Death in Flanders.

DUKES OF BURGUNDY
1369 Margaret of Malle marries Philip the Bold, Duke of Burgundy; they inherit Flanders, making it part of the Duchy of Burgundy.
1459 Philip the Good's court set in Brussels.
1467 Death of Philip the Good.
1477 Death of Charles the Bold.
1482 Mary of Burgundy dies and her husband Maximilian becomes regent.

THE SPANISH NETHERLANDS
1516 Maximilian's son Charles inherits Spanish throne and becomes Charles I.
1519 Charles inherits the Habsburg empire and becomes Emperor Charles V.
1555 Abdication of Charles V in the Netherlands in favour of his son Philip.
1565 Nobles in the Netherlands form the League of Nobles, opposing Spanish rule.
1566 Iconoclastic Riots spread from Antwerp.
1568 Execution of Counts Egmont and Hoorn and outbreak of the Revolt of the Netherlands.
1579 Southern provinces form Union of Arras, in support of Philip II and Catholicism.
1581 Northern provinces form Utrecht Union and declare independence from the Spanish.

COUNTER-REFORMATION
1598 Philip hands over the Netherlands to his son-in-law Archduke Albrecht.
1609-21 Twelve Year Truce between the Dutch and the Spanish Netherlands.
1621 Netherlands revert to Spain.
1648 Spain recognises Dutch independence in the Treaty of Munster.
1695 The French bombard Brussels.

THE AUSTRIAN NETHERLANDS
1701-13 War of the Spanish Succession.
1713 Spanish Netherlands pass to Austria in the Treaty of Utrecht.

1740-8 War of Austrian Succession.
1780 Joseph II becomes Emperor of Austria.
1789-90 Brabant Revolution against Austria.
1790 Austrian authority restored.
1792 France occupies Austrian Netherlands.
1795 Austrian Netherlands annexed into France and old boundaries abolished.
1798 French introduce conscription and Belgian peasants riot.
1814 Napoleon exiled; Congress of Vienna merges Belgium into the United Kingdom of the Netherlands.

UNITY AND REVOLUTION
1815 Napoleon defeated at Waterloo. William Prince of Orange declared King William I.
1830 Start of the Belgian Revolution.
1831 Belgium recognised as an independent state; Léopold of Saxe-Coburg-Gotha is king.
1848 First liberal government, after initial political domination by Catholics.
1885 Belgian Socialist Party founded.
1885 Berlin Declaration recognises Léopold II as head of state of the Congo.
1893 Introduction of universal male suffrage.
1898 Dutch given official equality with French.
1908 Léopold hands Congo over to Belgium.

BELGIUM IN THE WARS
1914 Germany invades Belgium.
1918 Belgium liberated by Allies.
1919 First universal male suffrage elections.
1940 Germany invades Belgium; Léopold III quickly surrenders.
1944 Belgium liberated; war tribunals set up.

POST-WAR BELGIUM
1948 Benelux Customs Union established.
1949 Women given the right to vote.
1950 Léopold III returns but stands down due to national unease over role in the war. His son Baudouin I becomes king.
1957 Brussels becomes the headquarters of the European Economic Community.
1962 French-Flemish language border set up.
1967 Brussels headquarters of NATO.
1970-94 Constitutional reforms change Belgium from a centralised to a federal state. Vast construction of the EU Quarter in the former Quartier Léopold in eastern Brussels.
1993 Death of Baudouin I; Albert II is king.
1996 Dutroux paedophile scandal.
1999 Grand state marriage of Prince Philippe to Belgian citizen Mathilde.
2004 EU expansion from 15 to 25 members.

Brussels Today

Signs of life in this urban enigma.

'The best thing about Brussels is that it is only three hours to Paris,' quipped Bill Bryson in *Neither Here nor There*. It's an old joke, but it's what many think about the city. Few include Brussels on a list of cool destinations. It's too much of a government town, too bourgeois to fire up the editor of a style magazine. Yet there are pockets of alternative energy in this city that are as interesting as anything happening in Paris or Amsterdam. The only problem is that it takes time to track them down.

No one – not even the Minister President of Brussels – will deny that some pretty hideous things have been allowed to happen in Brussels. The old medieval and 19th-century fabric of the city was ripped apart to create urban motorways, road tunnels, oppressive office districts, parking garages and – that ultimate symbol of naïve modernism – a heliport. What remained after the dust cleared was all too often a dismal mixture of boarded-up houses and wasteland piled with dumped television sets. Belgians often try to blame it all on Europe,

but the planning procedure is controlled by the communes, and the grim offices in the European Quarter were mostly built by the Belgian government using Belgian architects.

If anyone is to blame, it's King Léopold II, who used some of the money he made in the Congo on urban projects in Brussels. Some of his grand schemes augmented the city's beauty, like the avenue de Tervuren and the little cluster of exotic buildings in Parc de Laeken – but others left it devastated, such as the rail tunnel through the heart of Brussels (*see p20* **Off the rails**) and the Palais de Justice on the edge of the Marolles.

In recent years Brussels has undergone subtle changes. The drift towards federalism has helped, turning the city from a collection of 19 weak communes into a strong regional government with the power to determine its own transport, economic and urban policies. The government for the Brussels region has improved the quality of life by investing in public transport, cycle lanes and urban renewal. It has also brought new high-tech companies to a city that has lost almost all its old industries.

Brussels is also making an effort to tackle the blight caused by property speculators. In the bad old days, property barons would buy old houses and let them rot while waiting for the market to pick up, then tear the buildings down and put up cheap office buildings. The city has now slapped a big tax on empty properties, forcing many speculators to sell up. Investment has helped renovate downtown quarters such as formerly bleak St-Géry, whose main attraction used to be the launderette, but is now a fashionable café quarter.

> **'The law also raised the surreal prospect of George Bush being prosecuted in the Belgian courts for alleged war crimes in Iraq.'**

The city has also sunk considerable money into improving its museums: the **Musée des Instruments de Musique** (*see p71*) is now a combination of sophisticated scholarship and state-of-the-art technology; the once-dowdy **Musées Royaux d'Art et d'Histoire** (*see p82*) has made itself more visitor-friendly; and the **Musées Royaux des Beaux-Arts** (*see p71*) opened a stunning new wing in 2004, with new galleries, a museum shop, bookstore and restaurant. The **Palais des Beaux-Arts** (*see p71*), once a temple to staid bourgeois values, has been relaunched as the Bozar, a dynamic centre for exhibitions, film and music. Local cultural life has also been boosted by the opening of the **Flagey** centre (*see p88* **All aboard!**) in a landmark art deco building that has been boarded up for the best part of a decade. This inspired project has revitalised place Flagey in Ixelles, bringing a lively programme of movies, concerts and readings to a gloomy neighbourhood. Yet such is the political incoherence still blighting the city that the opening of Flagey coincided with the (ongoing) construction of a huge stormwater collector underneath the square. Anyone tempted to sit out on the new café terrace has to shout above the noise of bulldozers.

NEW POLITICS

Urban renaissance in Brussels received another boost in the elections of 2001, which marked the end of 40 years of increasingly smug Christian Democrat rule. The coalition government headed by Guy Verhofstadt was a mixed bag of Liberals, Socialists and Greens. It launched a series of progressive measures that were more in character with liberal neighbours the Netherlands, slapping sanctions on Austria for

allowing far-right politicians into government, legalising possession of cannabis and allowing gay marriages.

Some of these policies annoyed old allies like the US and Britain. Diplomatic relations became tense after an obscure 1993 law was brought into play, allowing Belgium to prosecute anyone suspected of genocide, no matter where it occurred. The law led to cases being filed against Ariel Sharon for Israel's treatment of Palestinians, but it also raised the surreal prospect of George Bush being prosecuted in the Belgian courts for alleged war crimes in Iraq. The crisis in Belgian-US relations became acute in early 2003 when Belgium joined France and Germany in opposing the invasion of Iraq, though the Belgian government subsequently repaired some of the damage by weakening the scope of its genocide law.

One of the oddest initiatives of recent years was the decision by François-Xavier de Donnea, the former Brussels mayor, to lower the height of 17 skyscrapers in the Brussels commune. He apparently wanted to remove all ugly buildings visible from the balcony of the town hall on Grand' Place, to end negative comments made by distinguished visitors. Three skyscrapers have already been demolished, and others are due to follow, though the hated Hilton tower does not feature on the list. Another radical move came in 2002, when the entire city was closed to traffic on European Car Free Day, 22 September. After years of cars dominating the city, this was a brave move, intended to show that Europe's capital could be an inspiration to other cities. Many grumbled, but the event was successfully repeated in 2003.

The city now has ambitious plans to make most of the historic centre traffic-free (following the lead of Ghent and Bruges) and to encourage more people to travel by bicycle. The opening of a dedicated cycle lane down the rue de la Loi in the summer of 2003 was something of a turning point, proving that the city government was genuinely committed to an alternative transport policy. Yet the chances of turning Brussels into Amsterdam seem remote, given that 300,000 commuters drive into the city every day, few of whom are willing to use two wheels.

BRUSSELS DC

François-Xavier de Donnea also came up with a proposal to rename the city 'Brussels DC'. The idea never got beyond the middle pages of *Le Soir*, but it was perhaps not as daft as it seemed. As the official capital of the European Union and the headquarters of NATO, Brussels is beginning to look a lot like the Washington of Europe. It has a massive diplomat presence, a flourishing subculture of 10,000 lobbyists, heavy police security (even for a modest demonstration by the Flemish Union of Pensioners), helicopters chugging over the rooftops, international hotels that are virtually empty at weekends, and 700 foreign journalists all trying to sex up stories on the reform of the Common Agriculture Policy.

Since starting out in a single office building on the avenue de la Joyeuse Entrée, the European institutions have steadily expanded their presence in Brussels. Today's European Union currently employs some 30,000 staff in the city, and occupies most of the office buildings around Rond-Point Schuman, including the controversial Berlaymont Building at 200 rue de la Loi. A presence in the European Quarter is increasingly becoming a must-have for international companies and non-governmental agencies. Charming old town houses that once contained a Belgian family are now carved up into offices for lawyers, lobbyists, journalists and interpreters. The non-governmental organisations based here range from Greenpeace to the European Chemical Industry Council. There are even organisations representing organisations, like the Federation of International Associations and the Union of International Associations.

'Brussels is a major building site as the property developers rush to meet the expected demand.'

The European presence has become vital for the economy of the city, but it has thrown up some major headaches for the authorities. After hard negotiations at the EU's Nice summit in 2000, the Belgian government persuaded leaders to stage all EU summits in Brussels, rather than in the country holding the six-month presidency. This sparked off a heated debate about a suitable location, with some politicians pushing for a separate site on the edge of town, while others (led by prime minister Guy Verhofstadt and Commission President Romano Prodi) lobbied for a site in the European Quarter, arguing that the EU had to be close to the people. Verhofstadt won the argument, and his government invested heavily in renovating the Résidence Palace, a former 1920s apartment complex, as a summit venue. While boosting the image of Brussels as capital of Europe, the summits regularly brings chaos to the European neighbourhood, since large areas are cordoned off by riot police, and heavy security checks are carried out on anyone on the wrong side of the barbed wire.

LOVE THY NEIGHBOURHOOD

Despite its international importance, and a supposition that the expat crowd dominates the inner-city housing mix, Brussels remains an urban enigma where old neighbourhoods sit resolutely amid new developments with their high-earning young professionals. It's almost impossible to categorise Brussels' residents. While many Belgians moved to the green belt in the 1960s and '70s, older generations continue to live in their lifetime apartments and the younger generation continue to move back in as they return to the city. This is mostly due to impressive efforts by the authorities to clean up their urban act and a new lifestyle afforded by the regeneration of St-Géry and Ste-Catherine. Here is a classic example of the young Flemish moving in to rent and buy ready-made flats, or taking over loft spaces to renovate themselves, often with handy subsidies from the Brussels Region. Prices remain cheap in London or Paris terms, though a 13 per cent property rise in 2003 made a noticeable difference to the market. A boom it may be, but prices are set to level out again as the rental market continues to dominate. Buying property in Belgium is not a cheap option, with a 12 per cent stamp duty putting off many expats who may not want to commit to the country for the long term.

The communes of Ixelles, St-Gilles and Etterbeek remain popular with the young European crowd, while expatriate families tend to prefer the gardens and well-schooled outer suburbs such as Uccle or Boitsfort. What the urban mix means is that there is a constant need for housing stock, especially as the ten accession countries join the EU in 2004. As a result, over 30,000 civil servants will need somewhere to live; Brussels is a major building site as the property developers rush to meet the expected demand. Still, it's not all bad news – ghettos are unlikely as newcomers will move into any gaps between traditional neighbourhoods and find a way to fit in rather than live in some ultra-designed quarter.

It is a familiar gripe of local residents that Europeans force up property prices, but much of the energy for urban regeneration has actually come from foreign communities in Brussels. The conversion of **La Tentation** (*see p133*) – an abandoned department store on rue de Laeken – was carried out by the Galician community in Brussels, while the Spanish region of Asturias has come up with an inspired plan to restore the art deco *La Socialiste* printing works opposite the **Centre Belge de la Bande Dessinée** (*see p34* **Brussels walks**). Without European input, Brussels would be quieter, but far less dynamic.

Brussels tomorrow

For the residents of Brussels, their city's vocation as capital of Europe can be perplexing. While various EU buildings sprawl across the Etterbeek commune east of the centre, those who are not inside the EU bubble often feel a deep sense of disengagement with the institutions, which can verge on resentment. For the Belgian state, having so many EU offices – and every European summit – in the city is an economic boon, but the government has belatedly recognised the planning failures that have prevented the EU Quarter from integrating into the surrounding local neighbourhoods. At the end of 2003 Prime Minister Guy Verhofstadt attempted to address this with an ambitious plan aimed at reinvigorating the once pretty Quartier Léopold, area of the steel-and-glass façades of today's EU Quarter.

The project (www.ombudsplanmediateur.be) was proposed by a Belgo-Spanish consortium and includes 133 separate proposals, calling for 1.3 hectares of new public space, the revitalisation of the Parcs Léopold and Cinquantenaire, 27,000 sq metres (290,322 sq feet) of shops and public facilities, and a new tram line running through the pivotal Maelbeek valley, whose new focus will be a dynamised place Jean Rey. The two poles of the area – north around the Berlaymont and Breydel buildings near place Schuman, and south at the European Parliament by place Luxembourg – will be linked by paved walkways. A new cultural centre will be set up on rue Van Maerlant, off rue Belliard, which will host a major European event in 2007/08 to coincide with the 50th anniversary of the Treaty of Rome, and presence of European institutions in Brussels. Among the long-term proposals, a metro line will connect Schuman, the underused Luxembourg station and the Gare du Midi by 2020.

Verhofstadt's new plan, presented to the public on a vast and confusing map across the lobby floor of the Résidence Palace in December 2003, is not without its critics. Most vocally, the local urban action group ARAU (*see p29* **Campaign trail**) has pointed out the vast cost of a new metro link, the lack of cohesion between the 133 proposals, and the need for consultation, not least with the respected ARAU itself.

Whatever happens, what is certain is that wheels are in motion to address the urban blight that is the EU Quarter. In a separate plan, a 6,000-sq metre (64,516-sq feet) space is being built next to Luxembourg station, provisionally earmarked for a Museum of Europe, to open in 2006. Needless to say, the city's ambitious projects haven't always gone as planned – repair work on the controversial headquarters of the European Commission, the Berlaymont, out of commission for 13 years, is running way past deadline into the summer of 2004.

Art Nouveau

Capital of sensual style.

The art nouveau architectural movement was born in 1893 in the suburbs of Brussels. Two houses built almost simultaneously a few blocks apart provided the inspiration for a style that spread to Paris, Barcelona and Glasgow. It flourished between 1893 and the 1910s, when Brussels was the scene for an extraordinary revolution in architecture.

Led by Victor Horta and Paul Hankar, dozens of architects in Brussels embraced a bold new style that used materials such as iron, stone and mosaic tiles in combination with motifs adopted from the natural world. Hundreds of private houses and a dozen department stores were built in this way. It was used in increasingly daring buildings by architects such as Henri van de Velde, Ernest Blérot, Gustave Strauven, Octave van Rysselberghe and Paul Cauchie.

ORIGINS AND DEVELOPMENTS

Most critics agree that art nouveau originated in England around 1890 in the Arts and Crafts movement. It became known as Jugendstil in Germany, Modernista or Modernismo in Spain, Stile Floreale in Italy and Sezessionstil in

Austria. Most sources trace the term to an interior design gallery in Paris, la Maison de l'Art Nouveau. The phrase was also used in the Belgian avant-garde publication *Art Moderne*.

The art nouveau style combined the linear patterns of the Arts and Crafts movement with curving motifs modelled on plants and flowers. It also borrowed heavily from Japanese wood prints, which melded angular shapes with the movement of flowing kimonos and trees. Blending traditional craftsmanship with contemporary style, art nouveau architects created a totally new form, concentrating on every detail down to doorknobs and window panes. The style is marked by sinuous lines, ornate cast ironwork, rounded windows, tiled floors, stained glass and winding staircases. Many houses incorporate murals in a distinctive traditional style known as sgraffito, in which the top layer of glaze or plaster is etched away to reveal the layer underneath.

Art nouveau became the preferred medium of free-thinkers and socialists, condemned by Catholics as a godless extravagance. It was embraced by an emerging middle class eager to break with old traditions. Clients included industrialists and engineers who had amassed enormous wealth in the Congo Free State, and who could commission at will. Victor Horta lavished attention on every detail. Many of his followers, such as Ernest Blérot, adapted the style for less wealthy clients who saved money by preserving a traditional Belgian interior.

> **'The most scandalous demolition was when Horta's Maison du Peuple was torn down to make way for a banal office building.'**

Over time the style gradually faded in favour of the more geometrical architecture of early 20th-century Vienna and Glasgow. Even Horta abandoned art nouveau, adopting a modern geometrical style when he came to design the **Palais des Beaux-Arts** (see p72) and the Gare Centrale. Yet there are still hints of art nouveau in his final buildings, suggesting that he never abandoned his love of organic curves.

By the 1960s hundreds of exceptional buildings were torn down, often replaced by unexceptional office blocks. In a relatively short period, the city lost most of its art nouveau shopfronts, almost all of Victor Horta's department stores, and a beautiful private home once owned by Blérot. The most scandalous demolition was in 1964, when Horta's famous Maison du Peuple was torn down in the face of widespread international protest to make way for a banal office building. Considered Horta's finest work, la Maison was a stunning glass and cast-iron palace with an auditorium, café and shops. Its remains were carefully numbered and stored in a cemetery, but much of the ironwork was lost. Some balustrades are now displayed in Horta metro station, and part of the building has been incorporated into a café in Antwerp.

After decades of indifference, the city now recognises its rich architectural heritage; surviving buildings from the art nouveau period are protected and put to imaginative new use. The most striking example is the **Musée des Instruments de Musique** (see p73), formerly the Old England department store. Designed by Paul Saintenoy in 1899, this fine structure of glass and swirls of wrought iron was restored and re-opened in 2000.

ART NOUVEAU BY AREA

There are about 2,000 surviving art nouveau buildings in Brussels, mainly concentrated in the 19th-century communes of Ixelles, St-Gilles and Schaerbeek. The streets of Ixelles are especially rewarding to explore, particularly around the Ixelles Ponds and the St-Boniface church. For a general amble, see p31 **Brussels walks**. The **TIB** tourist office (see p301) has maps showing important buildings. To get behind the façades, take one of the excellent guided tours organised by ARAU (see below **Campaign trail**), which give access to private homes that are usually closed to visitors.

Many important art nouveau houses were built on avenue Louise and in the nearby streets, including Horta's first art nouveau building, the Hôtel Tassel. Born in Ghent in 1861, Horta studied drawing, textiles and architecture before working under Alphonse Balat, the classical architect who designed the Serres de Laeken for Léopold II. In 1889 Horta won a commission to design a temple in the Parc du Cinquantenaire. Intended to contain Jef Lambeaux's large sculpture of the *Passions Humaines*, the project was never finished after the naked figures caused the building to be closed after three days. It is occasionally open

Campaign trail

The demolition of the Maison du Peuple (*see left*) helped spark the creation of the **Atelier de Recherche et d'Action Urbaines**, or **ARAU**, in 1969. Formed by a group of concerned citizens, the organisation set out to confront a city government callously neglecting its architectural heritage. The immediate aim was to save and renovate historic buildings, and fight against a policy that was turning large areas into barren office districts, dubbed 'Bruxellisation' by critics. The ARAU campaigns have brought new life to many areas of the city, including the Quartier Léopold, where the sprawl of EU buildings has created an urban nightmare.

As well as campaigning, ARAU runs guided tours. The most popular ones, covering art nouveau and art deco architecture, are held on Saturday mornings (€12-€15) from March to mid December, and take visitors around remarkable art nouveau interiors that are usually closed to the public. Other walking tours (€10) focus on particular districts or themes. Tours are usually in French, though regular English ones are scheduled. Book through the tourist office (*see p301*) or directly from ARAU (02 219 33 45, www.arau.org).

Contretype photo gallery. *See p31.*

to the public during the **Journées du Patrimoine** in September (*see p168*). The first commission Horta realised, the **Hôtel Tassel**, was built at 6 rue Paul Emile Janson for the professor Emile Tassel. The façade features stones of different colours, cast-iron railings, curved windows, stained glass and five small glass columns.

At the same time Paul Hankar was working on the **Hôtel Hankar** at 71 rue Defacqz, whose exquisite façade incorporates sgraffiti tiles by Adolphe Crespin. Hankar was strongly influenced by Henri Beyaert, for whom he worked at the start of his career. He built another art nouveau house at 48 rue Defacqz for the symbolist painter Albert Ciamberlani, easily recognised from the two large north-facing windows and the faded sgraffiti decoration. The house next door was also designed by Hankar but it has lost much of its art nouveau decoration.

Horta was commissioned to build several large department stores in **central Brussels**, but only one has survived. His last art nouveau commission before war-time exile in the US, the Waucquez, was built as a fabric warehouse, and later used as a department store. Abandoned for many years, it was lovingly restored to provide a home for the **Centre Belge de la Bande**

Dessinée (*see p34* **Brussels walks**). The modern Brasserie Horta in the main entrance has been designed in a style imitating art nouveau. Several art nouveau shopfronts were designed by Hankar in the centre of Brussels, but the only surviving example you can see today is at 13 rue Royale.

The streets and squares of **St-Gilles** are dotted with houses built by Horta and his followers. The most important is the Hôtel Horta at 25-26 rue Américaine, the architect's home and office. Now the **Musée Horta** (*see p91*), it has a stunning interior adorned with mosaic tiled floors, Asian tapestries and elaborate staircases. The place is maintained in immaculate condition and is bathed in a warm golden light on the gloomiest of days.

'Schaerbeek's faded glory has inspired many a grim comic-strip backdrop.'

The largest development of art nouveau houses in Brussels was built by Ernest Blérot in the rue Vanderschrick. The north side of the street is lined with tall houses decorated with an extraordinary variety of art nouveau balconies, small gables and bow windows.

The style gained a hold in **Schaerbeek** after mayor Louis Bertrand decreed it to be in favour. One of Horta's earliest works here was built for lawyer Eugène Autrique at 266 chaussée de Haecht. Horta accepted the job immediately, refusing any payment on condition that the money saved was devoted to a white stone façade. It is currently being restored by François Schuiten and Benoît Peeters, cartoonists for whom Schaerbeek's faded glory has inspired many a grim comic-strip backdrop. *See p36* **Brave new world**.

A number of interesting art nouveau houses were built in the elegant streets bordering the Parc du Cinquantenaire. The five-storey **Maison de St-Cyr** in square Ambiorix was designed in 1905 by the 22-year-old Gustave Strauven. With its narrow façade, ornate ironwork, intricate railings and round loggia at the top, it is one of the most striking buildings in the city. But, unlike a Horta house, this building is all surface decoration; the interior is divided up into conventional rooms.

A house built in the same year across the park reveals the beginning of a new geometrical style inspired by the Vienna Secession and the Glasgow School. The **Maison de Cauchie** on rue des Francs is decorated with gilded murals of beautiful women in long gowns, echoing the style of Gustav Klimt.

Brussels walks Art nouveau

This tour of the architecturally rich St-Gilles and Ixelles areas starts at the Nos.93 or 94 Lesbroussart tram stop by rue du Bailly. Here at No.224 avenue Louise is the **Hôtel Solvay**, built by Victor Horta in 1898. He was quite unknown when he designed this fine house of wrought iron and curvaceous stonework.

Back down avenue Louise, a left turn takes you down rue Paul-Emile Janson and Horta's **Hôtel Tassel** at No.6, built in 1893, when wrought iron was not used for family homes.

At the end of the street and right down to the end of rue Faider is **48 rue Defacqz**, built by Paul Hankar in 1897. Right along Defacqz is another Hankar house, his studio at **No.71**.

At the end of Defacqz, turn left down the chaussée de Charleroi; the next street on the left is rue Américaine, where Victor Horta built his home and studio (*see p91*) at Nos.25-26. Now the **Musée Horta**, it contains plans, photographs and architectural fragments.

Heading back down the chaussée de Charleroi/Brugmann, a left turn takes you to No.55, and a house called '**Les Hiboux**' (The Owls), built by Edouard Pelseneer in a curious art nouveau style. Next door the impressive **Hôtel Hannon** was designed by Jules Brunfaut in 1903 for an engineer who had made his name taking documentary photographs. It is now the **Contretype** photo gallery (entrance at 1 avenue de la Jonction; *see p182*).

Behind it, in rue **Félix Delhasse**, are two houses in the Glasgow style of Mackintosh, at **Nos.13-15**. Right along rue de la Glacière and left on to the chaussée de Waterloo brings you to **Horta metro station**, its artwork made of Horta's demolished works. Down the chaussée de Waterloo for 15 minutes, a turn into rue Vanderschrick reveals a row of art nouveau houses by Ernest Blérot. Here is the **La Porteuse d'Eau** (*see p141*) café, an old local done out in the style of Victor Horta.

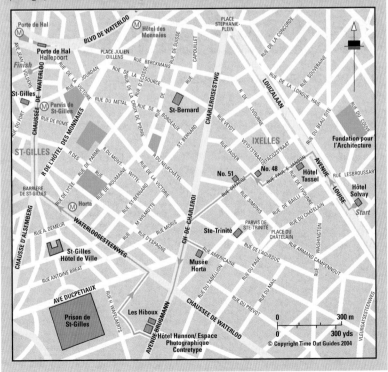

© Copyright Time Out Guides 2004

Cartoon Brussels

The city's most illustrious characters.

Belgium's cultural identity is tied with its most widespread artistic contribution to the outside world: the comic strip, or *bande dessinée (BD)*. Its figurehead, Tintin, is the country's most easily identifiable cultural icon. The bequiffed cub reporter shifts more postcards, T-shirts and books than anything else Belgian, pissing urchins included. Some 200 million Tintin albums have been sold around the world, more than half of them in French, the rest in Faroese, Tahitian and 50 other languages. Tintin has spawned more than 200 books, from simple biographies of his creator, Hergé, to obscure psychoanalytical textbooks using Tintin to elucidate theories about family relations.

Apart from these spin-offs, Hergé practically invented what Belgians refer to as the 'Ninth Art'. Before Hergé emerged, comic strips were a light chuckle. The father of the contemporary European comic book, creator of the clear graphic that would inspire the pop art of Warhol and Lichtenstein – Warhol would later return the favour with portraits of the Belgian

cartoonist – Hergé transformed the genre, heading a local cottage industry that has now gone global. Major Brussels-based studios accommodate design talent from Belgium, Holland and the francophone world, publishing houses churn out 40 million comic albums a year, while the tales of Tintin and other Belgian BD stars are animated for TV series or the cinema screen. In Brussels, as well as a museum dedicated to the genre (*see p34* **Centre Belge de la Bande Dessinée**) and 40 or more BD stores (*see p145*), downtown façades have been colourfully transformed into murals of cartoon characters. These murals compose the Comic Strip Walk, a tour of painted street corners (*see p34* **Brussels walks**).

The 75th anniversary of Tintin's first appearance in print is being marked in 2004. In addition, a clutch of yet more books, a specially minted €10 coin, and a set of stamps issued by the Belgian Post Office are accompanied by exhibitions. The foremost is 'Tintin et la Ville' at the Halles Saint-Géry (place St-Géry, 02 348 45 13), running until July 2004, setting the hero in his Brussels' context (the fictitious 26 rue du Labrador) and his urban travels: Moscow, Shanghai or the equally fictitious but quite wonderful Latin American capital of Tapiocapolis. The cosmopolitan nature of Tintin's adventures allowed Hergé to develop plot and a rich cast of characters, and raise comics from strips to stories; by contrast, today's best artists feel free to use real metropolitan settings to analyse Brussels' own urban landscape, in particular in Schuiten and Peeters' seminal *Brüsel*, from 1997. See *p36* **Brave new world**.

Tintin's own space at the Comic Strip Museum will be revamped and opened in May 2004, while London's National Maritime Museum hosts its 'Adventures of Tintin at Sea' exhibition until September. 2004 also sees the publication of *Tintin and the Alph-art*, the unfinished adventure Hergé was working on when he died in 1983. Previously only available as a collector's edition, the fragmentary sketches have been reformulated into a coherent story of opera, art forgery and assassination. A theatrical version of *Les Bijoux de la Castafiore* is being staged at Louvain-la-Neuve outside Brussels, where a long-awaited Tintin Museum is due to open in 2007 to coincide with the centenary of his creator's birth.

BACK TO THE DRAWING BOARD

When Georges Rémi (aka Hergé) was born to middle-class parents in Etterbeek in May 1907, the comic strip was in its infancy. A Swiss illustrator, Rodolphe Töpffer, had produced early narrated drawings in the 1830s, followed by a few French artists, whose work ran in occasional periodicals. By the late 19th century, American broadsheets were publishing a cartoon of vignette adventures; the French press ran the best ones, as well as work by native artists. In England, children's comics began to catch on.

The precocious boy scout Rémi, meanwhile, began to contribute drawings to the monthly *Le Boy Scout Belge*, and got a job at Catholic daily *Le Vingtième Siècle*. Finding a new character,

Totor, a precursor to Tintin, for *Le Boy Scout Belge*, he began to sign his name with his reversed initials, RG (*'er-gé'*). At *Le Vingtième Siècle*, he was in charge of its children's supplement, *Le Petit Vingtième*. Totor became Tintin, whose first published adventure 'In the Land of the Soviets' ran for two pages on 10 January 1929. Four months later the paper staged Tintin's triumphal return from Russia, in a stunt at Brussels' Gare du Nord; Tintin, played by an actor, and his small, white dog Milou (later known to English-speaking readers as Snowy), were swamped by their new-found fans. After a similar series of adventures in the Congo in 1931, the Gare du Nord was packed. In 1934 the stories were compiled into comic album books by Tournai publisher Casterman.

> ### 'With his own weekly comic, the foundation of the Hergé Studios and a film, Tintin had become a living legend.'

Until then, Tintin's adventures were simple, puerile even. The Soviets were firmly castigated for their communist ways, the native Congolese subjected to paternalistic colonialism. For *The Blue Lotus*, Hergé met Chang Chong-Yen, an emigré Chinese studying in Brussels, whose tales of the Japanese occupation of his homeland persuaded Hergé of the need for documentary research. Thereafter, whether it was Australia or the moon, Hergé would painstakingly refine each detail. A new clarity – of plot, dialogue and, above all, draughtmanship – came to light, the influential *ligne claire* that makes every box stand out and contribute to the overall narrative. Characters emerged, starting with Captain Haddock in *The Crab with the Golden Claws*, then Professor Calculus and the Thom(p)son Twins. With his own weekly comic in 1946, the foundation of the Hergé Studios in 1950 and a film adaptation in 1960, Tintin had become a living legend.

JOIN THE GANG

While their American, French and British counterparts used superheroism and sci-fi, Belgian cartoonists stuck to funny, character-driven everyday situations, in particular detective stories. Strong plot and dialogue kept the pages turning. Once Hergé had set the rules for content and continuity, Belgian artists could delve deep into their irreverent and surrealistic heritage, showcased by the seminal Marcinelle School. Based in the suburb of Hainaut, a new body of cartoonists sprang up with the now-legendary *Spirou* magazine, launched by publisher Jean Dupuis in 1938.

It was Dupuis who turned a hobby into an industry. An apprentice printer, he kept a foot-operated pedal press at home, printing leaflets and newsletters. His workshop extended to the parish press (at the same time that Hergé was working on *Le Petit Vingtième*), before he went

Brussels walks Comic strips

In 1991 local comic-book illustrators hit upon the idea of brightening up their city with a series of comic murals. Using original drawings by each artist, the group Art Mural created a series of 20 works; their number is slowly being added to. There are also underground stations gayly decorated with cartoon heroes (*see p75* **Hidden Brussels**), but the walking tour allows visitors to glimpse at grey streets they wouldn't otherwise venture down.

For a detailed outline of the six-kilometre (3.7-mile) route, follow the tour with a map (€1.25) from the tourist office (*see p301*). Walkers are first welcomed by a large statue of Franquin's error-prone Gaston Lagaffe, before being pointed to the nearby **Centre Belge de la Bande Dessinée**. Set on three floors of a beautiful Horta-designed former department store, the Comic Strip Museum greets visitors with a statue of Tintin, Snowy and the iconic red and white rocket they took to the moon. The Tintin collection, revamped for the 75th anniversary celebrations in 2004, is the highlight of the three-floor exhibition, which covers the history of comics and cartoons from Winsor McCay's early masterpiece *Gertie the Dinosaur* (1914) to the present day. (If you've kids in tow, beware that erotic works are featured on the third floor.)

The route runs to Willy Vandersteen's Bob and Bobette; Suske and Wiske, as they are known in their original Flemish, became the biggest post-war smash after Tintin. The walk then goes through the heavily muralled Ste-

Catherine and St-Géry quarters (including Sleen's Nibbs, *pictured*), passing Lucky Luke, before heading, via Edgar P Jacobs' Yellow M on rue du Petit Rampart, to a myriad of murals on and off lively rue du Marché aux Charbon. Notice, for example, Frank Pé's Broussaille at the top of the street. The trail winds through the Marolles (Hergé's wily Quick et Flupke on rue Haute in character with the area) right down to the Gare du Midi. Here you are ushered on to the Eurostar by Philippe Geluck's Le Chat and, fittingly, the figures of Tintin and Snowy on top of the Lombard Publications building.

Centre Belge de la Bande Dessinée

20 rue des Sables (02 219 19 80/www. brusselsbdtour.com/cbbd.htm). Métro/pré-métro Rogier/tram 92, 93, 94. **Open** 10am-6pm Tue-Sun. **Admission** €6.20; €2.50-€5 concessions. **No credit cards. Map** p317 D2.

on to launch weeklies for men, women and, in 1938, children. *Spirou* featured key artists such as (André) Franquin, creator of Gaston Lagaffe, and Peyo (Pierre Culliford), father of the Smurfs (les Schtroumpfs). Along with Jijé (Joseph Gillain) and Morris (Maurice de Bevere, creator of Lucky Luke), and EP Jacobs of the Tintin School, the quintet placed Belgian comic strips on to the world stage. Some would collaborate with staff of *Mad* and *Superman* magazines in

America, others helped with artistic development when Astérix creator René Goscinny set up *Pilote*, France's pioneering BD publication. Major cartoonists had their own studios, backed by a skilled labour pool of letterists and colouring artists. Dupuis, along with Casterman, became one of Belgium's leading publishers.

The 1960s and 1970s saw great changes in the industry. While Tintin and the Smurfs found fame as international TV stars, comic

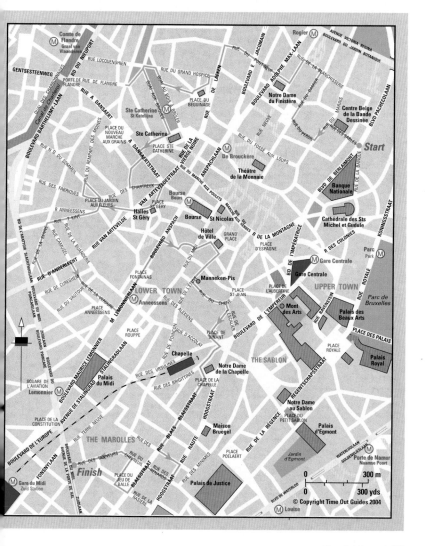

sales decreased as the animated versions became more popular. Artistic integrity was being sacrificed to the demands of commercial logic. Domestic Belvision became one of Europe's biggest manufacturers of televised animation. After boardroom disputes, Dupuis was swallowed into a publishing conglomerate. The *Tintin* comic folded in 1988. He and Snowy now sit atop the vast office block of Lombard Publications outside Midi station, as if to greet Eurostar travellers on their arrival to Brussels.

Comics began to appeal to baby boomers who had grown up with Tintin and Spirou, and now wanted something more adult, erotic even. Albums took the place of magazines. Casterman launched a new generation of

cartoonists with the series *À Suivre* in 1978, with contemporary themes for a more demanding readership. Its key *auteur* was François Schuiten, whose collaboration with Benoît Peeters gave rise to the Obscure Cities series, exploring themes of urbanisation gone mad and social isolation (*see below* **Brave new world**). Taking the peeling grandeur of Schaerbeek as their inspiration, Schuiten and Peeters redefined their native city, much as Hergé defined foreign climes for his readership. Their success illustrates that the Ninth Art can appeal to an adult readership and the television screen too. Schuiten's computer-generated TV series *Quarxs* found fans across the generational divide in the late 1990s.

Brave new world

The most successful and influential cartoonists of modern-day Brussels are school chums François Schuiten and Benoît Peeters. Schaerbeek-born Schuiten *(pictured)* does the drawings, Peeters writes the scripts. The inspiration for their work has been the grandiose urban development and brutal property speculation that has led the city of Brussels to repeatedly destroy its own past in the search for an elusively more beautiful future: *Bruxellisation*.

Their arrival on the scene in 1978 with Casterman's *À Suivre* was the biggest revolution in comic strip lore since Tintin, mostly thanks to their smash *Les Cités Obscures* (Obscure Cities) series. These 20 volumes reveal the fantastical feats of a group of 'urbatects' – Utopian city builders – in a parallel universe, where cities such as Pâhry and Brüsel bear strange resemblances to their more familiar names on the map, and architects like Eugen Robick find comparison with real-life counterparts like Victor Horta. Joseph Poelaert (designer of the actual Palais de Justice, and the Palais des Trois Pouvoirs, its twin in Brüsel) gets an imaginary biography, while Auguste Spanach resembles Jules Anspach, the real burgomaster who covered up the River Senne.

The mix gets more complicated when their dark cities intrude into our own; there's now a

real BD shop called **Brüsel** (*see p145*), and Schuiten and Peeters have been called upon to design stamps, exhibitions, public spaces and even two metro stations – the Arts et Métiers in Paris and Brussels' Porte de Hal.

Schaerbeek station plays a key role in *Brüsel*, one of the duo's most emblematic tales, and the commune's blend of broad avenues and narrow winding streets is an acknowledged influence on the series. Their real-life conversion of Horta's formerly derelict **Maison Autrique** at 266 chaussée de Haecht will open as a walk-through museum in the summer of 2004. (*See also p98*).

Where to Stay

Where to Stay

Weekenders of the world, unite!

The **Métropole**.
See p39.

Brussels is a business city, which is why it has far more hotels than most other cities of similar size. The EU capital welcomes a significant number of visitors on expense accounts with a range of swish lodgings in the three- to five-star category. You find a lot of uniform international chains, such as **Novotel**, **Hilton**, **Marriott** and **Sheraton**, plus a scattering of charming independents, like **Le Plaza** and **Métropole**. You'll also find that nearly all of the higher-bracket hotels offer bargain rates at weekends and in summer. Few cities cater so well for weekenders after a little comfort but not willing to pay top whack for it. Good hotels in lower price brackets are harder to come by, but the **Noga**, **Welcome** and **Saint-Michel** can all offer something special.

ALL SHAPES AND SIZES

Rooms tend to be of a decent size, but can vary greatly, not only between hotels but within properties. For the many hotels created out of townhouses, the rooms inside are usually more compact, although their high ceilings give an impression of space and period details often make up for the lack of elbow room.

PRICES AND CLASSIFICATION

In Belgium, hotel stars are awarded according to the quantity and type of services a hotel offers, rather than by the innate quality of the property. As a result, a nondescript hotel with a slew of services will have more stars than one with character that doesn't see the need for trouser presses and 24-hour room service.

We have classified hotels according to style and location, then by the cost of their cheapest double room: **Deluxe** (€250 or over), **Expensive** (€150-€249), **Moderate** (€90-€149) and **Cheap** (under €90). In addition, we have listed the best B&Bs and hostels. Most establishments will have no trouble in dealing with your enquiries in English.

All prices quoted below apply to rooms with a toilet and a shower or bath and include breakfast, unless otherwise stated. Some of the cheaper hotels often offer communal washing facilities, rather than en suite bathrooms, so be sure to check when booking.

Even if you're on a tight budget, don't completely rule out the smarter hotels – the upmarket chain hotels sometimes offer cheaper rates than the smaller independent hotels simply because they can afford to slash their rates. Traditionally, these cheap rates have been offered during weekends and the city's low season, ie July and August, although what appears to be an oversupply of hotel rooms has led to many hotels introducing what they call 'floating' rates, which effectively means that they set their rates according to demand: more demand, higher rates; less demand, lower rates. Only one thing's a certainty: two or three times a year when there's an EU summit meeting, hotels will charge rack (or official) rates – or close to them. For current prices, check the hotel websites or call **De Boek-MHR** (02 522 69 16, Mon-Fri 9am-9pm, Sat 11am-7pm).

Resotel (02 779 39 39/fax 02 779 39 00/www.belgiumhospitality.com, call centre open Mon-Fri 8.30am-6pm) is a free booking service for hotels in Belgium. The service negotiates rates with the hotels and can offer up 50 per cent off the rack rates. Alternatively, the **Belgian Tourist Information Office** (63 rue Marché aux Herbes, Lower Town, 02 504 03 90/fax 02 513 04 75/www.belgium-tourism.net) can send a list of Brussels hotels by post or email. Staff can also book hotels for you free of charge if you visit the office in person.

For travellers from the UK, a full list of hotels in Brussels is available from the **Belgian Tourism brochure line** (0800 954 5245).

Grand' Place & around

Deluxe

Hotel Amigo

1-3 rue de l'Amigo, Lower Town, 1000 Brussels (02 547 47 47/fax 02 513 52 77/www.hotelamigo.com). Métro Gare Centrale/pré-métro Bourse. **Rates** *Mon-Thur €475-€550 single; €500-€600 double; €790-€2,900 suite; weekend rates on request. Breakfast €20-€28.* **Credit** *AmEx, DC, MC, V.* **Map** p315 B3.
Hotel services *Bar. Business services. Conference facilities. Disabled: adapted rooms (1). Fax. Gym. Laundry. Lift. No-smoking rooms. Parking. Restaurant.* **Room services** *Dataport. Hairdryer. Minibar. Room service (24hrs). Safe. TV: satellite.*
The height of luxury, steeped in history and decked out *à la mode*, the Amigo accommodates pop stars and politicians alike. *See p40* **Jailhouse rocks**.

Métropole

31 place de Brouckère, 1000 Brussels (02 217 23 00/fax 02 218 02 20/www.metropolehotel.com). Métro/pré-métro De Brouckère. **Rates** *Mon-Thur €279-€379 single; €329-€429 double. Fri-Sun €119 single/double. €450-€750 suite.* **Credit** *AmEx, DC, MC, V.* **Map** p315 C2.
The Métropole deserves a mention simply because it is the grande dame of the Brussels hotel scene (it opened in 1895) and displays the most stunning architecture in its public areas, including its

renowned café (*see p130*). The French Renaissance main entrance leads into an Empire-style reception hall, with gilt flourishes, columns and impressive stained-glass windows. An original cage lift conveys guests up to rooms in the main building, which are disappointing by comparison and lack the luxury touches of other top hotels. The 1925 extension at the back of the building, however, does have some nice art deco fittings, and the massages in the in-house health centre are superb.
Hotel services *Babysitting. Bar. Beauty salon. Business services. Conference facilities. Fax. Laundry. Lift. No-smoking rooms. Restaurant.* **Room services** *Dataport. Hairdryer. Minibar. PlayStation. Room service (24hrs). Safe. TV: satellite.*

Le Plaza

118 boulevard Adolphe Max, 1000 Brussels (02 278 01 00/fax 02 278 01 01/www.leplaza-brussels.be). Métro/pré-métro Rogier or De Brouckère. **Rates** *Mon-Thur €435-€477. Fri-Sun double €125. €620-€897 suite. Breakfast (only incl in some packages) €18 continental; €27 buffet.* **Credit** *AmEx, DC, MC, V.* **Map** p317 C2.
Le Plaza, like the Métropole, is an independent hotel owned by a well-known Belgian family. Dating from 1930, the building was the headquarters of the Nazis and later the Allied Forces in the war, so the (now listed) structure was largely spared the bombing.

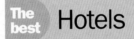

The best Hotels

For rooftop views
Try the moderately priced **Arlequin** (*see p41*) or top-of-the-range **Amigo** (*see p39*).

For fussy sleepers
The **NH Atlanta** (*see p40*) provides a choice of pillows.

For families
The spacious **Agenda Louise** (*see p51*) is most accommodating.

For historic detail
The authentic art deco **Crowne Plaza** (*see p46*) hosted Grace Kelly's wedding tour party; the **Métropole** (*see p39*) has an original cage lift from the 1890s.

For exotic decor
The **Welcome** (*see p43*) takes you round the world under one roof; the bar in the **Manos Premier** (*see p50*) displays decorative touches of Africana.

For gourmets
The upmarket Sea Grill fish restaurant in the **Radisson SAS** (*see p41*) boasts two Michelin stars.

The winter garden, which did suffer, was rebuilt and now houses the restaurant. The rest of the building, with original fittings (amethyst crystal chandeliers, Gobelins tapestry, marble bas-reliefs), has been restored to its old glory. The sumptuous rooms are decorated in shades of cream, beige and ochre, and an ornate Moorish-style theatre is used as a function room. The only drawback is the surroundings – the boulevard has more than its fair share of sex shops. **Hotel services** *Bar. Business services. Conference facilities. Fax. Gym. Laundry. Lift. No-smoking rooms. Parking. Restaurant.* **Room services** *Dataport. Fax. Hairdryer. Minibar. Room service (24hrs). Safe. TV: cable.*

Expensive

NH Atlanta

7 boulevard Adolphe Max, 1000 Brussels (02 217 01 20/fax 02 217 37 58/www.nh-hotels.com). Métro/prémétro De Brouckère. **Rates** *Mon-Thur* €150-€325 single/double; €275 suite. *Fri-Sun* €79-€114 single/double; €204 suite. Breakfast €15. **Credit** AmEx, DC, MC, V. **Map** p317 C2.

The Spanish NH Hoteles chain has been making huge inroads into Brussels and, at the last count, had five properties in the city. The Atlanta is its flagship. Housed in an elegant early 20th-century building, the hotel boasts modern, bright and cheerful

Jailhouse rocks

To wake up in a Brussels hotel with a hangover is not unusual. To wake up to find that the room service manager has popped out, umprompted, to the local pharmacy to buy you aspirin is quite special indeed.

It's this kind of service that inspired the local press to label the **Amigo** (*see p39*) Brussels' first six-star hotel when it saw the completion of its rather extensive refurbishment programme in May 2002. Of course, there's also the fantastic location, the local history associated with the place, and its stunning contemporary decor.

Just behind the Town Hall, the Amigo is the natural choice for heads of state, pop stars and politicians, for whom security is vital – a police station stands next door.

The hotel building was first mentioned in the city records in 1522, when the city council managed to buy it from a wealthy merchant family to turn it into a prison. The Spanish rulers confused the Flemish words for 'lock-up' and 'friend', and translated the latter into their own language. The name has stuck with it ever since.

In between then and now, the building has been razed at least twice, but parts of it still ooze history. The polished flagstones in the lobby were paving stones on the surrounding streets and are said to be 500 years old. The walls are adorned with beautiful 18th-century Aubusson tapestries and paintings of the Flemish and Italian schools.

The rest, however, is quite wonderfully contemporary, thanks to the €15 million refurbishment that took place following its purchase by Rocco Forte Hotels in January 2000. Sir Rocco's sister, Olga Polizzi, in charge of the redesign, created 155 elegant rooms and 19 suites, with the double rooms alone rumoured to have cost €30,000 each to decorate. Only the finest leathers, linens, silks and marbles have been used, and she has managed to incorporate a touch of Belgian flavour in each – Tintin prints and statues adorn the bathrooms, Magritte prints hang in the bedrooms.

The hotel's *pièce de résistance* is the top floor – and top bracket – Blaton Suite, named after the Belgian family who owned the hotel from 1957 until 2000. Larger than most one-bedroom flats in central London, it boasts its own kitchen, dining room, living room and a huge terrace with views over the rooftops. This, truly, is the height of luxury in Brussels.

decor, thanks to the Mediterranean influence. A terrace attached to the breakfast room offers great rooftop views, a real bonus in summer. The highlight, though, of any stay at an NH hotel is the excellent attention to detail: for example, you can choose the type of pillow you want.

Hotel services *Bar. Business services. Conference facilities. Disabled: adapted room (1). Fax. Gym. Laundry. No-smoking rooms. Parking. Restaurant. Sauna.* **Room services** *Dataport. Hairdryer. Minibar. Room service (24hrs). Safe. TV: cable.*
Other locations: NH Grand Place Arenberg, 15 rue d'Assaut, Lower Town, 1000 Brussels (02 501 16 16); NH Stéphanie, 21 rue Jean Stas, St-Gilles, 1060 Brussels (02 537 42 50); NH Brussels City Centre, 17 chaussée de Charleroi, St-Gilles, 1060 Brussels (02 539 01 60); NH Brussels Airport, 14 De Kleetlaan, 1831 Brussels (02 203 92 52).

Le Dixseptième

25 rue de la Madeleine, 1000 Brussels (02 517 17 17/fax 02 502 64 24/www.ledixseptieme.be). Métro Gare Centrale. **Rates** *Mon-Thur* €180-€400 single; €200-€430 double; weekend rates on request. **Credit** AmEx, DC, MC, V. **Map** p315 C4.

Le Dixseptième is a real gem: a boutique hotel with just 24 very individual rooms in a great location not far from the Grand' Place. Popular with business people looking for a hotel with a more personal touch during the week, the 17th is the ideal destination in Brussels for a romantic weekend – although it now faces competition from its recently acquired sister hotel Le Sablon (*see p45*). Twelve of the rooms are housed in the 17th-century building that was once the home of the Spanish ambassador, while the other 12, equally spacious but more prosaic, are in a new block to the back. There's a bar, beside the lovely period salon overlooking the inner courtyard where breakfast is served. Impeccable service.

Hotel services *Bar. Business Services. Conference facilities. Fax. Laundry.* **Room services** *Dataport. Hairdryer. Minibar. Room Service (24hrs). Safe. TV: cable.*

Hotel Floris Grand' Place

6-8 rue des Harengs, 1000 Brussels (02 514 07 60/fax 02 548 90 39/www.grouptorus.com). Métro Gare Centrale/pré-métro Bourse. **Rates** €204 single; €214 double; €263 mini-suite. **Credit** AmEx, DC, MC, V. **Map** p315 C3.

A small hotel (there are just 12 rooms lining one floor), the former Hotel Sema is housed in a building dating from 1821. Authentic old touches remain, such as the wooden beams, but this can make the place seem a little dark. The location, just off the Grand' Place, is both a plus and a minus: the Floris is conveniently central, on a cobbled street with shops and cafés a step away, but can be noisy if there's an event on in the square. The guestbook, however, testifies to the excellent staff and friendly service, so we're happy to recommend the place.

Hotel services *Bar. Fax. Laundry. No-smoking rooms. Safe.* **Room services** *Hairdryer. Minibar. Room service (24hrs). TV: cable.*

Radisson SAS

47 rue du Fossé aux Loups, 1000 Brussels (02 219 28 28/fax 02 219 62 62/www.radissonsas.com). Métro/pré-métro De Brouckère. **Rates** *Mon-Thur* €220-€245 single/double. *Fri-Sun* €134-€159 single/double. €1,450 royal suite. Breakfast (not incl in standard room Mon-Thur) €25. **Credit** AmEx, DC, MC, V. **Map** p315 C2.

Behind the art deco façade of the Radisson SAS lies a top-class business hotel with good leisure facilities and a well-earned reputation for great food. Choose from four different styles of room (Classical, Maritime, Oriental and Royal Club); all come with luxury fittings, wireless internet access as well as tea/coffee-making facilities, but you might also find the lovely little flourishes that set them apart – opt for a Maritime room if you prefer wooden rather than carpeted floors, for instance. You can indulge yourself at the fitness centre or at the Bar Dessiné, with Belgian cartoons on the walls and a superb selection of malt whiskies behind the bar. The hotel's Executive Chef is Yves Mattagne, who has earned two Michelin stars for the in-house Sea Grill (*see p110*), so expect to eat well.

Hotel services *Babysitting. Bar. Business services. Conference facilities. Disabled: adapted rooms (3). Fax. Gym. Laundry. Lift. No-smoking rooms. Parking. Restaurants (2). Safe. Sauna. Solarium.* **Room services** *Dataport. Hairdryer. Minibar. Room service (24hrs). TV: satellite.*

Moderate

Arlequin

17-19 rue de la Fourche, 1000 Brussels (02 514 16 15/fax 02 514 22 02/www.arlequin.be). Métro/pré-métro De Brouckère. **Rates** *Mon-Thur* €80-€105 single; €125 double; €150 triple; €165 quad. *Fri-Sun & July, Aug* €62-€73 single; €80 double; €95 triple; €110 quad. **Credit** AmEx, DC, MC, V. **Map** p315 C3.

The contrast between this modern, 92-room hotel and the little cobbled street on which it stands could not be more stark. The rooms vary in size (but are uniformly comfortable, bright and clean), and three of them, as well as the top-floor breakfast room, offer panoramic views over the rooftops. Internet rooms must be booked in advance and are only available on weekdays. The Athanor bar (*see p195 and p199*) on the ground floor hosts jazz concerts and other lively nightlife options lie nearby.

Hotel services *Bar. Conference facilities. Fax. Internet. Laundry. Lift. Safe.* **Room services** *Dataport. Hairdryer. Room service (24hrs). TV: cable.*

Saint-Michel

15 Grand' Place, 1000 Brussels (02 511 09 56/fax 02 511 46 00/www.accueilettraditiongrandplace.be). Métro Gare Centrale/pré-métro Bourse. **Rates** €113-€120 single with view; €65-€85 single back room; €133-€144 double with view; €99 double back room; €23 extra bed. **Credit** AmEx, DC, MC, V. **Map** p315 C3.

If you want to wake up, draw back the curtains and look out over one of Europe's most beautiful squares, then stay at the Saint-Michel. However, be warned that there's no double glazing, so if there's an event on in the Grand' Place you might not get the earliest of nights. Situated behind a picturesque façade on the south-eastern side of the square, the building (dating to 1698) belonged to the Tanners' Guild before becoming a private residence after the French Revolution and then a hotel. Breakfast can be served in your room or at La Brouette, a café across the square under the same ownership. **Hotel services** *Bar. Fax. Lift. Restaurant. Safe.* **Room services** *Hairdryer. Minibar. Room service (noon-11pm). TV: cable.*

Cheap

À la Grande Cloche

10-12 place Rouppe, 1000 Brussels (02 512 61 40/ fax 02 512 65 91/www.hotelgrandecloche.com). Pré-métro Anneessens. **Rates** €60 single/double with shower; €77 single/double with bath & shower. **Credit** AmEx, MC, V. **Map** p318 B4.
This renovated family-run hotel is located in a quiet square equidistant from Midi station and the Grand' Place, upon which stands the three Michelin-starred restaurant Comme Chez Soi (*see p108*). This nearby hotel is not quite in the same league, but the rooms are clean and fairly comfy. Each one has a queen bed: roomy for one, but a bit of a squeeze for two (the twin-bed rooms avoid the problem and are usually spacious). The cheaper rooms tend to have a small shower box, encouraging a swift dash down to a breakfast room overlooking the square. **Hotel services** *Fax. Internet. Lift.* **Room services** *Safe. TV: cable.*

Ste-Catherine & St-Géry

Expensive

Marriott

1-7 rue Auguste Orts, 1000 Brussels (02 516 90 90/ fax 02 516 90 00/www.marriott.com/brudt). Pré-métro Bourse. **Rates** *Mon-Thur* single/double €209-€239; €259-€289 suite. *Fri-Sun* €99-€139 single/ double; €205 suite. Breakfast (not incl in standard room) €25. **Credit** AmEx, DC, MC, V. **Map** p315 B3.
The Marriott is a relatively recent addition to the local hotel scene, having opened in October 2002. While the façade of the hotel is a beautifully restored remnant of the 19th century, most of the interior is completely new, creating a nice blend of original and modern. As you'd expect from an American chain, the rooms come fitted to a high standard, and include large beds and wireless internet access. The room decor is bright, but the bathrooms – in muted shades of beige – are a tad more relaxing. A nice touch is the free tea and coffee served in the ground-floor bar before 9.30am. An executive floor available for the business folk who need one.

Hotel services *Babysitting. Bar. Business services. Conference facilities. Disabled: adapted rooms (5). Executive Lounge. Fax. Gym. Laundry. Lift. No-smoking rooms. Parking (€27.50). Restaurant. Sauna.* **Room services** *Dataport. Hairdryer. Minibar. Room service (24hrs). Safe. TV: satellite.*

Moderate

Atlas

30 rue du Vieux Marché aux Grains, 1000 Brussels (02 502 60 06/fax 02 502 69 35/www.atlas-hotel.be). Pré-métro Bourse/métro Ste-Catherine. **Rates** *Mon-Thur* €105-€160 single; €115-€199 double. *Fri-Sun* from €79 single/double; €40 extra duplex/studio. Discount available for internet booking. **Credit** AmEx, DC, MC, V. **Map** p316 B3.
Behind the 18th-century façade of the Atlas lie acceptable rooms that teeter on the edge of sterility. Location scores highly here over style. It's near the trendy shops of rue Antoine Dansaert and the nightlife hub of St-Géry – book one of the five four-person split-level duplex rooms if you're making a party weekend of it. For an early night, book a back room overlooking the inner courtyard. A free drink is served to guests on weekday evenings. **Hotel services** *Conference facilities. Disabled: adapted rooms (1). Fax. Laundry. Lift. Parking (€10). Safe.* **Room services** *Dataport. Hairdryer. Minibar. Room service (7am-4pm). TV: cable.*

Noga

38 rue du Béguinage, 1000 Brussels (02 218 67 63/ fax 02 218 16 03/www.nogahotel.com). Métro Ste-Catherine. **Rates** *Mon-Thur, Sun* €80-€85 single; €100 double; €130 triple; €155 quad. *Fri, Sat & Aug* €65-€70 single; €80 double; €105 triple; €130 quad. **Credit** AmEx, DC, MC, V. Five per cent discount with cash payment. **Map** p316 B2.
Noga means star in Hebrew and this hotel, located on a charming and tranquil street in Ste-Catherine, lives up to its name. The atmosphere is friendly and delightfully kitsch, with nautical-themed knick-knacks in the airy public areas jostling for space with pictures of royals and assorted bric-a-brac. The rooms, which have showers but no baths, are a tad more restrained, but each is individual in its colour scheme and fittings. That said, you can pretty much guarantee they'll be bright, spacious and comfy. **Hotel services** *Bar. Bicycle rental. Billiard room. Fax. Garden. Internet. Laundry. Lift. Parking (€10). Safe.* **Room services** *Dataport. Hairdryer. Minibar. Safe. TV: cable.*

Welcome

23 quai au Bois á Brûler, 1000 Brussels (02 219 95 46/fax 02 217 18 87/www.hotelwelcome.com). Métro Ste-Catherine. **Rates** €85 single; €95-€115 double; €145 triple; €160 quad; €130 junior suite; €150 suite. **Credit** AmEx, DC, MC, V. **Map** p316 B2.
The typical 19th-century façade of the Welcome belies the guest rooms inside: each one is unique and has been decorated with genuine antiques and arte-facts to represent a different destination, among

them Bali, India, Japan and Morocco. Other options include the Tibet room, which has a small terrace and is filled with dramatic shades of red and black; the Congo room, with its safari hues and animal skins; and the Jules Verne room, which follows a round-the-world theme and boasts a large balcony overlooking place Ste-Catherine. The exotic interior, paired with the friendliness of the owners, the Smeesters, make this a great place to stay.

Hotel services *Bar. Fax. Internet. Laundry. Lift. No-smoking rooms. Parking (€10). Safe. Shuttle service.* **Room services** *Dataport. Hairdryer. Minibar (some rooms). Room service (6am-1am). Safe. TV: cable.*

Cheap

George V

23 rue 't Kint, 1000 Brussels (02 513 50 93/fax 02 513 44 93/www.george5.com). Pré-métro Bourse. **Rates** €64 single; €74 double; €84 triple; €94 quad. **Credit** AmEx, DC, MC, V. **Map** p316 A3.

Don't be fooled by the proud exterior of the George V, which was recently repainted, because there's nothing glamorous about the slightly tatty but clean interior. It's pot luck with the rooms, which vary between bright and morose, but everyone booking a single room gets a tiny bathroom. And we mean tiny. That said, the hotel is in a quiet location, fairly close to the fashionable shops and bars, and the option of triples and quads makes it an attractive deal for weekend parties.

Hotel services *Bar. Fax. Laundry. Lift. Parking (€7).* **Room services** *Dataport. TV: cable.*

The Marolles & Gare du Midi

Moderate

Agenda Midi

11 boulevard Jamar, 1060 Brussels (02 520 00 10/ fax 02 520 00 20/www.hotel-agenda.com). Métro/ pré-metro Gare du Midi. **Rates** €84 single; €97 double; €112 suite. **Credit** AmEx, DC, MC, V. **Map** p318 A4.

Most people wouldn't stay in the insalubrious area around the Gare du Midi out of choice, but if you find yourself forced to seek a bed for the night because you've missed the last Eurostar to London, you could do a lot worse than the Agenda Midi. With its welcoming bright yellow façade, it's not hard to find, and its rooms, though neither huge nor spectacular, are decorated with warm Mediterranean colours and have mosaic-tiled bathrooms. The town centre is easily reached by pré-métro – or even on foot, if you're feeling energetic.

Hotel services *Fax. Laundry. Lift. No-smoking rooms. Safe.* **Room services** *Dataport. Hairdryer. Minibar. TV: cable.*

Cheap

Galia

15-16 place du Jeu de Balle, 1000 Brussels (02 502 42 43/fax 02 502 76 19/www.hotelgalia.com). Métro/pré-métro Porte de Hal or Gare du Midi. **Rates** €57 single; €67 double; €90 triple; €113 quad. **Credit** AmEx, DC, MC, V. **Map** p318 B5.

The **Astoria**.
See p45.

The Galia is a simple, family-run hotel offering good-value accommodation overlooking the square where the flea market is held, making it the ideal place for bargain hunters to stay. The hotel is decorated with images of Belgian comic strips and the cheerful rooms are basic but clean and pleasant, with fairly large triples and quads available. The brighter front rooms are triple-glazed to block out the sound of the market and surrounding bars. An extension programme in 2005 will bring the total number of rooms to 40 and will also include a new brasserie.
Hotel services *Bar. Fax. Lift. No-smoking rooms (all).* **Room services** *TV: cable.*

Upper Town

Deluxe

Astoria

103 rue Royale, 1000 Brussels (02 227 05 05/fax 02 217 11 50/www.sofitel.com). Métro Botanique/tram 92, 93, 94. **Rates** *Mon-Thur* €180 single; €300 double; €490 suite; weekend rates available on request. Breakfast €25. **Credit** AmEx, DC, MC, V. **Map** p317 D2.
There's a real old-world charm to the Astoria, which was built in 1909 to welcome guests to the Universal Exposition that took place in Brussels the following year. It was then considered the height of luxury, with 'hot water everywhere, electric lighting and two lifts', the latter being extremely rare at the time. Now a listed building, the Astoria has wonderful high ceilings, stained-glass windows and a stunning glass roof in the lobby. The rooms (including some singles) may seem a tad faded, but somehow this only adds to the feeling of staying in a magnificent historical building. Furthermore, the neighbourhood is peaceful, the Parc de Bruxelles is nearby, and it's just a ten-minute walk from the centre.
Hotel services *Bar. Business services. Conference facilities. Fax. Gym. Laundry. Lift. No-smoking rooms. Restaurant. Safe.* **Room services** *Dataport. Hairdryer. Minibar. Room service (24hrs). Safe. TV: cable.*

Stanhope Hotel

9 rue du Commerce, 1000 Brussels (02 506 91 11/fax 02 512 17 08/www.stanhope.be). Métro Trône. **Rates** *Mon-Thur, Sun* €295 single; €325 double; from €615 suite. *Fri, Sat* €120 single/double; from €195 suite. Breakfast (not incl Mon-Thur, Sun) €24.50. **Credit** AmEx, DC, MC, V. **Map** p322 E4.
The Stanhope has almost doubled in size in the last two years, but that has not changed the calm and intimate atmosphere of the hotel. Book one of the original rooms, carved out of a row of elegant townhouses, if you want to stay in a room that evokes an idealised 19th-century English country home. But check into a new room if you prefer antique-style furnishings, but also want modern wooden floors and hi-tech bathrooms. More rooms will be created in the classified building that houses the hotel's new entranceway – given its stunning staircase and

beautiful architectural details, they're bound to be special. The hotel also has two elegant apartments for rent by the month, at €2,500 each.
Hotel services *Bar. Business services. Conference facilities. Disabled: adapted rooms (1). Fax. Garden. Gym. Laundry. Lift. No-smoking rooms. Parking (€18). Restaurant. Sauna.* **Room services** *Dataport. Hairdryer. Minibar. Room service (24hrs). TV: cable.*

Expensive

Jolly Hotel du Grand Sablon

2 rue Bodenbroek, 1000 Brussels (02 518 11 00/fax 02 512 67 66/www.jollyhotels.com). Tram 92, 93, 94/bus 27, 95, 96. **Rates** *Mon-Thur* €179-€209 single; €200-€270 double; €330-€440 suite. *Fri-Sun* €114-€135 single; €129-€159 double; €249-€349 suite. **Credit** AmEx, DC, MC, V. **Map** p315 C4.
Antiques hunters will enjoy at stay at the Jolly, on pretty place du Grand Sablon, site of the weekly antiques market. This leading Italian hotel chain prides itself on the location of its properties and the stylish decor of its rooms, which – in this instance – vary somewhat in size. Same flowery detail, though.
Hotel services *Bar. Business services. Conference facilities. Disabled: adapted rooms (2). Fax. Laundry. Lift. No-smoking rooms. Parking (€20). Restaurant.* **Room services** *Dataport (some rooms). Hairdryer. Minibar. Room service (6am-noon). Safe. TV: cable.*

Le Sablon

2-8 rue de la Paille, 1000 Brussels (02 513 60 40/fax 02 511 81 41/www.hotellesablon.be). Métro Gare Centrale/tram 92, 93, 94/bus 27, 95, 96. **Rates** *Mon-Thur* €144-€174 single; €188-€218 double; €209-€253 suite; €30 extra bed. *Fri-Sun* €102-€174 single; €112-€218 double; €209-€253 suite. **Credit** AmEx, DC, MC, V. **Map** p315 C4.
In the heart of the Sablon antiques area and just five minutes' walk from the Grand' Place, this intimate hotel of just 28 rooms and four suites is tucked away on a quiet cobbled street. Don't be put off by the modern façade – once inside you'll find another beautiful boutique hotel from the same family that owns Le Dixseptième (*see p41*). After a number of renovations have been completed in autumn 2004, expect elegant rooms of taupe and beige, or warm yellow and aubergine, wireless internet throughout, and a meeting room and sauna in the basement.
Hotel services *Babysitting. Bar. Business services. Conference facilities. Fax. Laundry. Lift. No-smoking rooms. Sauna.* **Room services** *Dataport. Hairdryer. Minibar. Room service (24hrs). Safe. TV: cable.*

Moderate

Du Congrès

42-44 rue du Congrès, 1000 Brussels (02 217 18 90/fax 02 217 18 97/www.hotelducongres.be). Métro Madou. **Rates** *Mon-Thur* €75-€100 single; €105-€160 double; €115 triple; €160 quad; weekend rates on request. **Credit** AmEx, DC, MC, V. **Map** p317 D2.

The four elegant townhouses that constitute the Du Congrès have been beautifully renovated to create a sleek, modern hotel with original fin-de-siècle features. Some rooms have high ceilings, a stunning fireplace and original cornicing, with a simple modern bathroom en suite. Others may not include as many authentic features, but what they lack in detail they make up for in space and/or tranquillity. This is particularly true of those overlooking or opening on to the back garden and split-level terraces, where guests can breakfast in summer. Guests at the one-star sister hostel Madou (45 rue du Congrès, 02 217 18 90) opposite can use the facilities here. Nearby, the two-star Sabina (78 rue du Nord, 02 218 26 37/ www.hotelsabina.be) is also in the same family.
Hotel services *Bar. Business services. Conference facilities. Fax. Garden. Laundry. Lift. Safe.* **Room services** *Dataport. Hairdryer. TV: cable.*

Place Rogier & St-Josse

Deluxe

Hilton Brussels City

20 place Rogier, 1210 Brussels (02 274 24 62/fax 02 203 43 31/www.brussels-city.hilton.com). Métro/pré-métro Rogier. **Rates** *Mon-Thur* €250-€350 single/ double; €445-€545 suite. *Fri-Sun* €130 single/double. Breakfast (not incl Mon-Thur) €26. **Credit** AmEx, DC, MC, V. **Map** p317 C1.
If you want the standard five-star Hilton, go to the Hilton Brussels on boulevard de Waterloo. If you prefer smaller boutique hotels (and lower prices), then head for the four-star Hilton Brussels City. This stylish modern property, which is housed in three buildings dating from the 1930s and still retains some of the original features (such as the art deco lights in the restaurant), offers a much more personalised service with the help of some of the best hotel staff in town. The rooms in the different buildings offer various configurations, but the decor remains the same and includes pale wooden floors and light-saving sensors. A modest fitness centre, sauna and steam room, plus a decent buffet breakfast, make this a great place to stay.
Hotel services *Bar. Business services. Conference facilities. Disabled: adapted rooms (4). Fax. Gym. Laundry. Lift. No-smoking rooms. Restaurant. Sauna.* **Room services** *Dataport. Hairdryer. Minibar. Room service (24hrs). Safe. TV: cable.*
Other locations: **Hilton Brussels** 38 boulevard de Waterloo, 1000 Brussels (02 504 11 11).

Expensive

Sheraton Brussels Hotel & Towers

Manhattan Center, 3 place Rogier, 1210 Brussels (02 224 31 11/fax 02 224 34 56/www.sheraton.be). Métro/pré-métro Rogier. **Rates** *Mon-Thur* €195-€410 single/double. *Fri-Sun* €105-€410 single/ double. Breakfast (not incl in some rooms) €22-€25. **Credit** AmEx, DC, MC, V. **Map** p317 C1.

With 533 rooms, Brussels' biggest hotel boasts 30 floors of spacious, elegant rooms with large beds and all the other comforts and services you'd expect from an American chain. Constant modernisation does mean a newly renovated lounge bar and 'smart rooms', an added perk for high-powered business types, amid the exclusive top five floors. Further draws include the panoramic vistas of the city from rooms on the upper storeys and the top-floor heated indoor swimming pool. The in-house Crescendo is a seafood restaurant of notable quality.
Hotel services *Bar. Business services. Children's room. Disabled: adapted rooms (30). Fax. Gym. Laundry. Lift. No-smoking rooms. Restaurant. Swimming pool.* **Room services** *Dataport. Hairdryer. Minibar. PlayStation. Room service (24hrs). TV: cable.*

Moderate

Crowne Plaza

3 rue Gineste, 1210 Brussels (02 203 62 00/fax 02 203 55 55/www.crowneplaza.com). Métro/pré-métro Rogier. **Rates** €125-€375 single/double; additional €25 triple. Breakfast (not incl in some rooms) €25. **Credit** AmEx, DC, MC, V. **Map** p317 D2.
The Crowne Plaza dates back to the Belle Epoque, but its heyday belongs in the 1930s and, as a result, the overwhelming design influence is art deco. When the hotel was renovated in 1998, great effort went into preserving its architectural heritage while improving the levels of comfort and services. As a result of this revamp, some of the rooms here are original (with a decor that feels somewhat dated), while others are imitation art deco (and have a whiff of the chain hotel about them). If you want to splash out, book the hotel's pride and joy: Grace Kelly's wedding tour suite. Centrally situated between the Lower Town and the Gare du Nord.
Hotel services *Babysitting. Bar. Business services. Disabled: adapted rooms (15). Fax. Gym. Lift. No-smoking rooms. Restaurant. Sauna.* **Room services** *Dataport. Minibar. PlayStation. Room service (24hrs). TV: cable.*

EU Quarter & Montgomery

Expensive

Dorint

11-19 boulevard Charlemagne, 1000 Brussels (02 231 09 09/fax 02 230 33 71/www.dorint.com/ brussels). Métro Schuman. **Rates** *Mon-Thur* €210-€290 single/double. *Fri-Sun* €79-€98 single/double; €475 junior suite. Breakfast (not incl Mon-Thur) €7 continental; €24 buffet. **Credit** AmEx, DC, MC, V. **Map** p321 F4.
There are two sides to the Dorint. On the one hand, its location in the heart of the EU district, its rooms (each with a desk and internet connection) and the slick efficient staff mark it out as a business hotel. On the other hand, the modern architecture, spa and

The **Manos Premier**. *See p50.*

arty streak give it a certain funkiness. What makes the hotel really unique, though, is the photography collection that adorns the walls of the rooms and the basement Zoom Gallery, with some 450 images from photographers across the EU. In the main, the hotel strikes the right balance between business and pleasure, although leisure visitors may find it a little out of the way. For business travellers, the Dorint also runs a building with 12 apartments nearby, ranging in size and prices of €1,900-€5,500 by the month.
Hotel services *Art gallery. Babysitting. Bar. Business services. Conference facilities Disabled: adapted rooms (1). Fax. Gym. Laundry. Lift. No-smoking rooms. Parking (€15). Restaurant. Sauna. Solarium. Steam bath. Sun terrace. Whirlpool.* **Room services** *Dataport. Minibar. Room service (24hrs). TV: cable.*

Montgomery Hotel Brussels
134 avenue de Tervueren, 1150 Brussels (02 741 85 11/fax 02 741 85 00/www.montgomery.be). Métro Montgomery. **Rates** *Mon-Thur, Sun* €360 single; €380 double; €520 suite. *Fri, Sat* €140 single; €160 double; €260 suite. Breakfast €20. **Credit** AmEx, DC, MC, V.
The Montgomery is a lovely small – and smart – hotel in an upmarket residential area, beside a métro station six stops from the city centre. The rooms are all beautifully decorated in three versions of an English country style, but come equipped with all the latest gadgets, including wireless internet access and DVD players (DVDs can be borrowed from reception). As most guests are here on business, the restaurant only opens on weekdays. So although it's a peaceful and elegant place to stay, if you like to be at the heart of the action, go elsewhere.
Hotel services *Bar. Conference facilities. Gym. Lift. Laundry. No-smoking rooms. Parking (€15). Restaurant. Sauna.* **Room services** *Dataport. DVD. Fax. Hairdryer. Minibar. Room service (24hrs). Safe. TV: cable.*

Moderate

Hotel Monty
101 boulevard Brand Whitlock, 1200 Brussels (02 734 56 36/fax 02 734 50 05/www.monty-hotel.be). Métro Montgomery. **Rates** *Mon-Thur* €85 single; €110 double. *Fri-Sun* €75 single; €90 double. **Credit** AmEx, DC, MC, V.
The Hotel Monty opened its doors in December 2002, setting out its stall as the first design hotel in Brussels. Located in an elegant 1930s townhouse, and a standard hotel in a previous life, it has been transformed by Thierry Hens' mix of modernity and tradition, and sparkles with contemporary items of classic design by Philippe Starck and Charles Eames, with grey and red decoration throughout. The 18 rooms are simple but stylish, with en suite shower rooms, and guests seem happy to mingle around the breakfast table in the reception area. Relaxing and informal, it has a front terrace and courtyard garden, as well as a fashionable lounge

which adds a welcome touch of home – especially when juxtaposed with the sterility of the EU façades nearby. Boutique at €100 a night? Yes, please.
Hotel services *Bar. Business services. Fax. Garden. Internet. Laundry. No-smoking rooms.* **Room services** *Dataport. TV: cable.*

Ixelles

Deluxe

Conrad Brussels
71 avenue Louise, 1050 Brussels (02 542 42 42/fax 02 542 42 00/www.conradhotels.com). Métro Louise. **Rates** €140-€595 deluxe; €165-€620 superior; €190-€645 executive; €240-€695 junior suite; €1,500 executive suite; €3,500 royal suite; €40 extra bed; cheapest rates usually available Fri & Sat. Breakfast (not incl Mon-Thur) €30. **Credit** AmEx, DC, MC, V. **Map** p319 C5.
Some would say there are only two five-star hotels in Brussels: the Conrad and the Amigo (*see p39*). It's certainly hard to fault the quality of the Conrad's decor (renovated in 2002 and 2003), even if it's not to everyone's liking. The service is perfect, perhaps too perfect, with rooms tidied at annoyingly frequent times of the day. Room service, though, is tailor-made: you can choose exactly which ingredients go into your sandwich, salad or main course. To work off that in-bed brunch, head down to the basement and the Champneys fitness centre (*see p206*). Given all the swank – flunkies in top hats, chandeliered reception area the size of a small airport – it's no surprise that the Conrad is set on the smartest shopping street in town. The only real criticism: it can feel a little soulless in its pursuit of excellence.
Hotel services *Babysitting. Bars (2). Beauty salon. Business services. Conference facilities. Disabled: adapted rooms (2). Fax. Gift shop. Gym (€17). Laundry. Lift. No-smoking rooms. Parking (€14). Restaurants (2). Sauna. Spa. Swimming pool.* **Room services** *Dataport. Hairdryer. Minibar. Room service (24hrs). Safe. TV: satellite.*

Hotel Bristol Stéphanie
91-93 avenue Louise, 1050 Brussels (02 543 33 11/fax 02 538 03 07/www.bristol.be). Métro Louise. **Rates** *Mon-Thur, Sun* €325-€375 single; €350-€400 double; €375-€425 triple; €600 junior suite; €850 executive suite; €990 full suite. *Fri, Sat* €115-€165 single; €140-€190 double. Breakfast (not incl Mon-Thur, Sun) €25. **Credit** AmEx, DC, MC, V. **Map** p319 C5.
There's something distinctly old-fashioned and unappealing about the brocade upholstery and deep blues, reds and gold in the entrance of the Hotel Bristol Stéphanie, but once you get past the lobby things improve. In this Norwegian-owned establishment, there's a Scandinavian slant to the decor in the restaurant and some of the suites. One is done out in kitsch chalet style, another has a nautical theme and has a balcony and sauna. Also note the upmarket location and in-house swimming pool.

Centre Vincent Van Gogh. *See p52.*

Hotel services *Bar. Business services. Conference facilities. Disabled: adapted rooms (2). Fax. Gym. Laundry. Lift. No-smoking rooms. Parking (not for standard rooms) €25. Pool. Restaurant. Safe. Sauna.* **Room services** *Dataport. Hairdryer. Minibar. Room service (24hrs). TV: satellite.*

Hyatt Regency Brussels – Barsey

381 avenue Louise, 1050 Brussels (02 649 98 00/fax 02 640 17 64/www.brussels.hyatt.com). Métro Louise then tram 93, 94. **Rates** *Mon-Thur €257-€557 single/double; €407-€557 suite. Fri-Sun €97-€117 single/double. Breakfast €22.* **Credit** AmEx, DC, MC, V. **Map** p324 E8.

This lovely luxurious boutique hotel recently gained its fifth star – quite right too. As soon as you walk in the door, you know you're somewhere special. The interior was designed by Jacques Garcia, of Paris's Hôtel de Costes fame, who created an opulent reception area in his signature rich red with Napoleon III-style furnishings and neo-classical relief work, and 18th-century prints on the walls. The restaurant (with occasional DJs) and rooms are similar in style, exuding a warmth and intimacy that makes the Hyatt a perfect winter hotel. And then there's also the courtyard terrace, making it a perfect summer residence as well. The only downside is the location: at the leafier end of the avenue Louise, it's quite a hike from the centre, though not too far from Brussels' luxury shops.

Hotel services *Bar. Business services. Conference facilities. Fax. Garden. Internet. Laundry. Lift. No-smoking rooms. Parking (€20).* **Room services** *Dataport. Hairdryer. Minibar. Room service (24hrs). Safe. TV: satellite.*

Manos Premier

100-106 chaussée de Charleroi, 1060 Brussels (02 537 96 82/fax 02 539 36 55/www.manoshotel.com). Métro Louise then tram 91, 92. **Rates** *Mon-Thur €285 single; €310 double; €460 suite; €25 extra bed. Fri-Sun €110 single; €110 double; other weekend & summer rates on request.* **Credit** AmEx, DC, MC, V. **Map** p319 C6.

With its ivy-clad front, dotted with fairy lights, there's something undeniably romantic about the Manos Premier. It's a converted townhouse with just 50 rooms, so when you step inside you feel like you're entering someone's home (which is not surprising, since it's been run by the same Greek family for the more than three decades). While the rooms are certainly comfortable and elegantly fitted, with antiques and Louis XVI-style decor, the hotel's real attractions lie elsewhere. The Kolya restaurant, open for lunch and dinner, has a lovely conservatory; there's a great African-themed bar with striped carpets, curvy velvet armchairs and leopard skin, and the spacious, terraced garden is a real oasis of peace. There's even a fully equipped gym. The icing on the cake, however, is the magnificent, Moorish-styled hammam, with a jacuzzi and sauna. The hotel's plainer, four-star sister, the Manos Stéphanie, is located along the street.

Hotel services *Babysitting. Bar. Conference facilities. Fax. Garden. Gym. Jacuzzi. Laundry. Lift. Parking (€7). No-smoking rooms. Restaurant. Safe. Sauna. Steambath.* **Room services** *Dataport. Hairdryer. Minibar. Room service (6am-11pm). Safe. TV: cable.*

Other locations: **Manos Stéphanie** 28 chaussée de Charleroi, St-Gilles, 1060 Brussels (02 539 02 50).

has acquired a fair amount of decorative features in that time. Every room is crammed with antiques, kitsch holiday souvenirs and what look like jumble sale buys, while plants and flowers spill out from balconies and bathrooms. Nothing is standard: not the decor, the room sizes or the amenities – two of the 11 rooms have no en suite facilities. Smokers and noisy young people not welcome. Check-in is from 11am to 10pm, and cash payments are preferred. **Hotel services** *Fax. Garden. Internet. No-smoking rooms (all).* **Room services** *TV: cable.*

Rembrandt

42 rue de la Concorde, 1050 Brussels (02 512 71 39/ fax 02 511 71 36/www.hotel-rembrandt.be). Métro Louise then tram 93, 94/bus 71. **Rates** €40-€60 single; €65-€85 double. **Credit** MC, V. **Map** p319 D6.
There's something rather quaint about this one-star hotel, with its two cats, a reception that closes at 10pm and a breakfast room filled with twee china ornaments and gilt-framed still lifes. The rooms are similarly homely, with high ceilings, flowery wallpaper, old dark wood furniture and framed prints on the wall. Not all rooms have en suite, and those that do are often separated by only a flimsy partition – but at these prices it would seem rude to complain. **Hotel services** *Fax. Lift.* **Room services** *Dataport.*

Moderate

Agenda Louise

6-8 rue de Florence, 1000 Brussels (02 539 00 31/ fax 02 539 00 63/www.hotel-agenda.com). Métro Louise then tram 93, 94. **Rates** *Mon-Thur* €87-€104 single; €99-€116 double; €111-€128 suite; €12 extra bed; weekend rates on request. **Credit** AmEx, DC, MC, V. **Map** p319 C6.
The Agenda Louise started a renovation programme in 2003, refurbishing one floor at a time. As a result, where once all the rooms had kitchenettes, some now have a large desk instead to accommodate the growing number of business visitors. With its quiet location just off avenue Louise and clean and spacious rooms, the hotel is popular with families. A nice touch in each room are the framed photos of Brussels and the accompanying book giving details of the subjects in the pictures. **Hotel services** *Fax. Garden. Laundry. Lift. No-smoking rooms. Parking (€6). Safe.* **Room services** *Dataport. Hairdryer. Minibar. TV: cable.*

Cheap

Les Bluets

124 rue Berckmans, 1060 Brussels (02 534 39 83/fax 02 543 09 70/www.bluets.be). Métro Hôtel des Monnaies. **Rates** €40-€57 single; €53-€81 double; €20 extra bed. **Credit** MC, V. **Map** p318 C6.
Les Bluets is as colourful as the couple who run it: an eccentric Belgian/English lady and her Colombian husband. It is set in a building dating from 1864 but has only been a hotel for 30 years, and

B&Bs

B&Bs in Brussels (also known as *maisons* or *chambres d'hôtes*) are traditional in that they involve staying in someone's house – it's not a euphemism for a cheap hotel. Be prepared to respect the owner's foibles and accept that hotel-style services are not on offer. A B&B stay here is therefore more suited to the less frantic traveller, rather than the boozy weekender. The appeal lies in the chance to stay with Belgians, often eager to regale you with insider tips.

Bed & Brussels

02 646 07 37/fax 02 644 01 14/www.bnb-brussels.be. **Rates** *Per night* €35-€71 single; €55-€95 double. *Per week* €205-€405 single; €316-€545 double. *Per month* €438-€974 single; €675-€1,314 double. **Credit** MC, V.
B&Bs throughout Brussels can be booked at this friendly agency.

Chambres en ville (Philippe Guilmin)

19 rue de Londres, 1050 Brussels (02 512 92 90/fax 02 502 41 01/www.chez.com/chambreenville). Métro Trône. **Rates** €50 single; €80 double; €15 supplement for one-night stay. **No credit cards**. **Map** p322 E5.
There's no better endorsement for a place than word of mouth, and most of Philippe Guilmin's custom comes via recommendations. You could easily walk past the ordinary front door, behind which lies a very attractive, good-value place to rest your head.

The sympathetic, erudite and English-speaking Guilmin is hospitality itself, his handful of rooms all individually decorated and boasting spacious en suite bathrooms. They feature stone or stripped wooden floors, high ceilings and windows (so they're naturally light), wall hangings and homely touches such as fresh flowers. The large breakfast table is often shared with Guilmin's cosmopolitan and friendly clientele – middle-aged academics, art historians, Brussophiles – pleased with the proximity to the restaurants of Ixelles, the palaces of the Royal Quarter, a métro station, and peace and quiet.

Phileas Fogg

6 rue van Bemmel, 1210 Brussels (02 217 83 38/ mobile 0495 22 09 85/www.phileasfogg.be). Métro Botanique or Madou. **Rates** €60-€100 single; €65-€120 double; €85 2-person suite; €120 4-person suite. **Credit** MC, V. **Map** p320 E2.

When seasoned traveller Karin Dhadamus decided to settle back home, the natural thing for her to do was to open a B&B. In her lovely townhouse you'll find three large double rooms (two with a shower actually in the room, one with an en suite bathroom), one twin room and one less remarkable basement suite. The pick is the Blue Room, which has a quite amazing modern chandelier, a luxurious Philippe Starck bathroom and a large bamboo terrace. In the rest of the house, a mix of antiques, modern Belgian artworks and fairy lights add a delightfully quirky touch. Be warned, though, that there's also the house dog to contend with. A number of apartments are also rented out on a more long-term basis.

Hotel services *Fax. Garden. Hammam. Internet. Laundry. No-smoking rooms (all).* **Room services** *Hairdryer.*

Youth hostels

There are three hostels in Brussels belonging to Youth Hostelling International and one 'youth hotel', also non-profit-making. They tend to have a maximum stay of a week, although this is sometimes negotiable.

YHI hostels require a membership card purchased in your country of residence. (If you don't have one, you will be charged an extra €3.50-€4 per night.) It's also advisable to book through www.hostelbooking.com, as this guarantees that your bed will be kept longer than usual (so you can arrive later in the day). The use of bed sheets is compulsory, rental usually included in the price, but at the **Centre Vincent Van Gogh** you can bring your own or use your sleeping bag. Prices quoted below include breakfast and are per person:

Bruegel (YHI)

2 rue du St-Esprit, Lower Town, 1000 Brussels (02 511 04 36/fax 02 512 07 11/www.youthhostels.be). Métro Gare Centrale. **Rates** (incl sheet rental) €25 single; €20 double; €16.75 4-person room. **Credit** MC, V. **Map** p315 C4.

This hostel is set on a pleasant church square near the Sablon, a short walk from the Gare Centrale and the Grand' Place. Another plus is the recent renovation programme, removing the 12-person rooms and introducing a chill-out area for every floor (the first floor also having a TV). On the downside, it's the only hostel to impose a curfew (1am), but the basement bar stays open until the last person goes to sleep, so there's always time for a nightcap.

Hostel services *Bar. Disabled: adapted rooms (4). Internet. Lift. Lounge. Luggage storage. No-smoking rooms (all). Safe. TV.*

Centre Vincent Van Gogh (CHAB)

8 rue Traversière, St-Josse, 1210 Brussels (02 217 01 58/fax 02 219 79 95/www.ping.be/chab). Métro Botanique. **Rates** €26.50 single; €20 double/triple; €15.50 4-person room; €14 6-person room; €12 8/10-person room; €3.75 sheet rental (optional). **Credit** AmEx, DC, MC, V. **Map** p320 E2.

This may be the largest hostel in town, but it's still advisable to book a month in advance (especially in holiday season), because it's used by school groups visiting the European Parliament. Housed in two facing buildings, the hostel has clean, bright and modern rooms, some split-level with en suite bathrooms. Public areas include a bar (open from 6.30pm), with snacks and board games, and a farmhouse-style kitchen for self-catering. Nearby is the cheery Jacques Brel (30 rue de la Sablonnière, Upper Town, 1000 Brussels, 02 218 01 87/www.laj.be/en/hostels/brussels_brel.htm), with the attraction of a roof terrace in summer.

Hostel services *Bar. Billiards. Fax. Garden. Internet. Kitchen. Laundry. Luggage storage. No-smoking rooms (all). Safe. TV. 24-hr access.*

Sleep Well Youth Hotel

23 rue du Damier, Lower Town, 1000 Brussels (02 218 50 50/fax 02 218 13 13/www.sleepwell.be). Métro/pré-métro Rogier or De Brouckère. **Rates** €26.50 single; €23.75 double; €21.25 triple; €19.25 4-person room; €17.75 6-person room; €15.75 8-person room; prices decrease after 1st night; €3.75 sheet rental (obligatory for 1st night). **Credit** MC, V. **Map** p317 C2.

This 'youth hotel' feels a lot less institutionalised than youth hostels. Although the basic formula is still bunk beds in bare rooms (adapted for disabled use), an on-site tourism adviser, comfy armchairs in the communal areas and a comic strip mural in the lobby are bonuses. The location also scores highly: it's pretty central, just behind the main shopping street of rue Neuve and a five-minute walk to the Grand' Place. Be advised that guests must be 35 years or under, although this rule doesn't apply to the Sleep Well's new wing. This is more akin to a traditional hotel, and here the more cheerful rooms have en suite showers, with en suite baths a luxury in the triple rooms.

Hostel services *Bar. Billiards. Disabled: adapted rooms (all). Guided tours. Internet. Lift. Lounge. No-smoking rooms (all). Restaurant. TV: cable. 24hr-access & reception.*

Sightseeing

Features

Introduction

A metropolitan mish-mash of masterly art and absurd artefacts.

The finest sight in all Brussels – the **Grand' Place**. *See p58.*

Planning a trip to Brussels does not involve compiling a long list of must-sees. There's only one major set piece, the magnificent **Grand' Place**, surely one of the finest town squares in the world. From here, elementary footwork will take you around this surprisingly compact city – but you'll only get truly under its skin by visiting neighbourhoods rather than buildings, mixing with residents in bars and restaurants (there are few tourist-only places) and allowing yourself to become part of the all-encompassing Brussels experience. Putting a finger on what exactly constitutes that experience is not easy but most visitors come away from Brussels with a warm feeling of well-being.

First, some bearings. Central Brussels is cleanly sliced into a **Lower Town** and an **Upper Town**, both enclosed by an inner ring road known as the Petit Ring. This neatly follows the line of the old city walls, historically punctuated by gates (*portes*), although the only one still standing is **Porte de Hal** (*see p89*). The Lower Town radiates from the Grand' Place, though the historical heart is actually the little enclave of **St-Géry** where the very first wooden fort stood. **Ste-Catherine** is the old port area, now tarted up and filled with fish restaurants; alongside, the arterial boulevard Anspach leads down to the grim, soulless marshalling yards of the **Gare du Midi**, the initial interface with the city for Eurostar arrivals. Don't despair, it does get better.

The Upper Town is built atop and on the sides of a steep hill. This is posh Brussels, home to royalty, state institutions and fancy art collections. Dividing Upper and Lower, a grey frontier of boulevards – de l'Empereur, de l'Impératrice, de Berlaimont and Pachéco – that follow the route of the railway below ground linking Brussels' three main train stations. This civic route-making project flattened entire neighbourhoods (*see p20* **Off the rails**) but it helped to reinforce the distinct personalities of the two halves of the city.

Nestling around the Petit Ring are the seven inner *communes* or boroughs, each with their own characteristics and atmosphere: the **EU Quarter**; **Ixelles**; **St-Gilles**; **Anderlecht**; **Molenbeek**; **Schaerbeek** and **St-Josse**. *See p57* **By area**. Beyond that, the posher suburbs, and beyond that – forest or the wide flatlands of Flanders. You can be in open countryside within 20 minutes.

Travel within and between these communes can be marked by low or little street lighting, precious few ATMs and street signs in two languages: Tree Street becomes rue de l'Arbre Boomstraat. Ironically, the only area where you're guaranteed to get confused is the EU Quarter of tabloid lore, a city within a city whose expat workers live a protected life, and where locals rarely venture. Emerging from Schuman metro station is the stuff of sci-fi nightmares – no wonder there's a 133-item proposal on the table to integrate the area back into the city: *see p27* **Brussels tomorrow**.

So, what will you love about Brussels? Well, while the city can be grey by day, wait until darkness falls. The restaurant scene is legendary, something even the French begrudgingly admit. It's also one of Europe's piss-up places *du choix*, particularly with the ever increasing numbers of hen-nighters – although the shrieking crowds are easily avoided if you go native and calmly bar-crawl through to the wee hours and an early-morning Duvel in a corner café.

Will you love the architecture? Yes and no. Despite some fine set pieces and manifold signs of urban renovation, Brussels still has a shabby, neglected air in parts. It doesn't help that no two houses are exactly alike. This is partly due to the fact that Brussels was built in the main by private citizens, without the interference of town councils. The 19th-century city fathers often deliberately encouraged chaotic streetscapes by organising façade competitions. The disorder is exacerbated by a quirky Belgian law that allows architects to sue for plagiarism. The result is urban chaos, with neo-Gothic next to Victor Horta's innovative art nouveau; a nine-floor apartment building towering over a three-storey town house, and a petrol station next to a 17th-century coaching inn. The only period when Brussels was planned on a grand scale was during the reign of Léopold II. He was behind Joseph Poelaert's **Palais de Justice** (*see p77*), avenue Louise, the **Mont des Arts** (*see p71*) and the broad, tree-lined **avenue de Tervueren** (*see p102*).

You can't climb to the top of the Hôtel de Ville or the Cathedral, but Brussels does offer plenty of other vantage points for panoramic views:

Abbaye de la Cambre
The south side of the avenue de Mot offers a Breugel-like view of the abbey and gardens. *See p89*.

Atomium
Puzzling view of the Mini-Europe theme park from the top sphere when it re-opens in 2005. *See p96*.

Basilique du Sacré Coeur
Sweeping view of northern Brussels from the dome of this enormous art deco church. *See p95*.

Belgacom Balloon
Ten minutes over Brussels for €10. Contact 02 201 30 30, www.aerophile.com.

Hilton Hotel
The Hilton's rooftop restaurant on the boulevard de Waterloo overlooks the Upper Town. *See p46*.

Inno car park
Church domes and cathedral towers seen from the rooftop car park of this landmark department store on rue Neuve. *See p146*.

Musée de l'Armée
Unexpected view of the EU Quarter from atop the Arc de Triomphe, accessed from the museum – upon entering, turn left, head behind two stuffed horses and take the lift to the top. *See p83*.

Musée des Instruments de Musique
Splendid view of the royal palace and the Upper Town from the rooftop restaurant terrace. *See p74*.

Musées Royaux des Beaux-Arts
Unexpected panorama of the Lower Town and the city beyond from the upper level of the department dealing in 19th-century art. *See p74*.

Place Poelaert
Fascinating view of the Marolles and the northern skyline from the square beside the **Palais de Justice**. *See p77*.

The flamboyant Gothic splendour of **Notre-Dame au Sablon**. *See p77*.

The horror of post-war property development is still evident throughout Brussels, where characterless boxes replaced terraces of townhouses with little regard for the human condition. You only have to try walking by the Centre de la Monnaie shopping centre on a windy day to see how thoughtless it all was. Such was the blight that *Bruxellisation* has become the international shorthand for bad urban planning. Even now, *façadisme* describes the practice of removing a building's guts and leaving only its frontage. Yet you can find good

interpretations of every trend here, from the Italian-Flemish baroque of Grand' Place to the Parisian-style central boulevards.

But back to sightseeing. Brussels has a museum for everything – from chocolate to drains, from comic strips (*see p34* **Brussels walks**) to the Flemish Masters. Many of these are housed in very fine buildings indeed, such as the **Palais des Beaux-Arts** (or 'Bozar'; *see p72* **A new broom at the Bozar**), the **Musée des Instruments de Musique** (*see p74*) and the Léopold monuments in the **Parc du Cinquantenaire** (*see p82*). Do see the **Manneken-Pis** (*see p62*), good for a laugh, if only a quick one. You might want to wander along the glorious **Galeries St-Hubert** and you'll not want to miss the **Atomium** (*see p96*), though it's being revamped during most of 2005. Nearby, you can tour the royal parks and palaces of leisure zone **Laeken** (*see pp96-7*). Lovers of the quirky will find solace and joy in the museum homes of **Victor Horta** and **René Magritte** (*see p93* **Magritte's Brussels**).

Meticulous planners or the just plain fortunate may find themselves in Brussels on a celebration weekend, in which dour teenagers are forced to dress as hapless 15th-century peasants and parade through the streets, or

Brussels card

Introduced in 2003, the laughably good-value Brussels Card (02 548 04 71, www.brusselsmuseums.be) gives access to 30 museums and free city transport over three days for €30. It's available from the **TIB** tourist office (*see p301*), major hotels and participating museums.

A revised version incorporating new venues should be introduced in October 2004, valid until December 2005.

when there's a concert on the Grand' Place, ice-skating in Ste-Catherine or a troupe of transvestites in the incomparable **L'Archiduc** (*see p134*). Soon after the bar's dawn closure, you may find yourself picking among the bric-a-brac in the morning **flea market** at place du Jeu de Balle (*see p153* **Good housekeeping**) or later on shopping for antiques in the Sablon or designer frocks in rue Antoine Dansaert (*see p67* **Fashionably late**).

Whatever you do, you'll punctuate it all with a coffee, a beer, a pit-stop at any one of scores of idiosyncratic bars. Have lunch. Take your time, all afternoon if you want. Slowly but surely the Brussels effect will creep up on you.

Guided tours

ARAU

Highly recommended architectural tours of the city (www.arau.org), offering access to private houses closed to the public. See *p29* **Campaign trail**.

De Boeck's Sightseeing Tours

8 rue de la Colline, Lower Town (02 513 77 44/ www.brussels-city-tours.com). **Tickets** €13.50; €12 concessions; €9 children. **Credit** AmEx, DC, MC, V. **Map** p315 C3.

Three-hour coach tours in English – usually three a day – covering the main sights, with a short walk at the Grand' Place, Laeken, Sablon and the EU Quarter. Pick-up is from the Grand' Place. The hop-on hop-off Visit Brussels Line allows 14 stops over a 48-hour period for the same price.

By area

Greater Brussels is comprised of 19 municipalities, or communes. The areas listed below border the city's medieval walls: the ring road that follows the city's medieval walls:

EU Quarter & Etterbeek

The steel and glass of the EU institutions, bordered by old townhouses. See *pp78-83*.

Ixelles

Divided by swanky avenue Louise into a grand if bland western half, and an arty, ethnic eastern half. See *pp84-89*.

St-Gilles

Plenty of greenery and the odd art nouveau gem. See *pp89-91*.

Anderlecht & Molenbeek

Sleepy industrial districts by the canals, an area once known as Little Manchester. See *pp92-95* Anderlecht & the West.

Schaerbeek & St-Josse

Faded grandeur sits amid urban gloom, dotted with pockets of Turkish and North African communities. At the southern edge, huge five-star hotels. See *pp98-100*.

Sightseeing

Every dog has a contribution to make to daily life in downtown Brussels.

The Lower Town

As grand and yet as gritty as it gets.

The **Grand' Place**.

The Lower Town is the spiritual heart of the Brussels. It falls into three main areas: the **Grand' Place & around** (a tourist showcase based on medieval and 19th-century street plans, with a bland commercial area to the north, and a tangle of streets of quirky boutiques and bars to the south); revamped **St-Géry** and **Ste-Catherine**, the adjoining quarters the other side of arterial boulevard Anspach, full of restaurants, chic bars and hip designer stores; and the shabby **Marolles**, the authentic working-class area stretching from the slopes of upmarket Upper Town Sablon to the grim underpasses and concrete wastes of the Midi railway estuary.

Grand' Place & around

Map p315

The Grand' Place is Brussels' outstanding set piece. Victor Hugo first described it as 'the most beautiful square in the world', a sentiment still valid today, particularly now that UNESCO has named it a World Heritage Site. The Place has always been the focus for the social and cultural life of the city, whether as a medieval market, a parade ground, a place of execution, a concert venue or, until the 1980s, a short cut for traffic and a car park for coaches. Now a pedestrian zone, it changes colour and character according to season: flower-strewn in summer, fairy-lit for Yule. It is the starting point for any tour of the Lower Town, with the tower of the **Hôtel de Ville** (Town Hall; *see below*) as its distinctive landmark. Completed in 1448, this magnificent Gothic edifice is the mayor's official seat and home of the **TIB** tourist office (*see p301*).

The houses on the square were once made of wood until the French bombardment of 1695 (*see p10* **Crafty burghers**), which destroyed 4,000 buildings and flattened the Place, all except for the tower of the Hôtel de Ville, which was used by the gunners to take aim. Under the command of the mercantile guilds, the square was rebuilt in under five years, in stone, with fine bronze and gold detail. While each building is unique, the whole is impressively homogeneous, with a nod to Italian baroque (introduced to Flanders by Rubens) and all perfectly adapted to fit the small plots of land. As each guild jostled for influence, it branded each house with individual markings and a name (although some pre-date the guilds and their activities). The following are among the most spectacular:

Nos.1-2 Au Roi d'Espagne, also the bakers' guild, now a pub (*see p131*). The Spanish king is Charles II, whose bust is on the front façade.

No.3 La Brouette (the wheelbarrow). The tallow dealers' guild, with a statue of patron St Gilles above the door.

No.4 Le Sac (the sack). The joiners' and coopers' guild, with a carving of a man diving into a sack above the door.

No.5 La Louve (the she-wolf). The archers' guild, with a phoenix at the top to symbolise the building's two burnings and rebuilds.

No.6 Le Cornet (the horn). The boatmen's guild, with a façade designed to resemble the stern of a galleon.

No.7 Le Renard (the fox). The haberdashers' guild, with a female statue representing each of the world's continents.

No.9 Le Cygne (the swan). The butchers' guild. Marx and Engels (who wrote the Communist Manifesto in Brussels) drank in a bar here and the house witnessed the birth of the Belgian Workers' Party.

No.10 L'Arbre d'Or (the golden tree). The brewers' guild, and the only building still under guild ownership. Note the hop plant detail above. It houses the modest **Musée des Brasseurs Belges** (*see p61*).

Nos.24-25 La Chaloupe d'Or (the golden galleon, now a brasserie) and **La Maison des Tailleurs** (the tailors' house). The tailors' guild is topped by St Boniface holding a symbolic pair of scissors.

No.26 Le Pigeon (the pigeon). The artists' guild. Victor Hugo stayed here in exile in 1852.

No.8, L'Etoile (the star), was knocked down in 1850 to accommodate tourists. Burgomaster Charles Buls was so incensed he had it rebuilt over an arcade which now shelters the much-caressed recumbent figure of Everard 't Serclaes, the guild leader who fought off a Flemish attack on Brussels in 1356. Soldiers from Gaasbeek tore his tongue out, prompting locals to destroy Gaasbeek castle. Stroking his worn limbs is meant to bring good luck.

On the east side of the Place is a terrace of six houses with a single façade, designed by Willem de Bruyn in 1698. The grouping is known as the House of the Dukes of Brabant because of their sculptures on the front. The Brussels *commune* has recently bought two – one (No.13) currently the modest **Musée du Cacao et du Chocolat** (*see p61*) – and intends to convert them into apartments and a new exhibition centre.

Facing the Hôtel de Ville is the Maison du Roi, which houses the **Musée de la Ville de Bruxelles** (*see p61*); the highlight here is the costume collection of the Manneken-Pis.

The patron saint of merchants is **St Nicolas**, whose church (*see p61*) – the oldest in Brussels – stands off the Place by the Roi d'Espagne on rue au Beurre. Diagonally opposite is the **Bourse**, the old Stock Exchange. This grand, neo-classical building boasts a decorative frieze by Carrier-Belleuse, with statues by Rodin adorning the top. Underneath, in Bourse metro station, is the hands-on **Scientastic Museum** (*see p173*), bringing science alive for children. Flanking the Bourse are two classic cafés, the **Falstaff** (*see p127*) and **Le Cirio** (*see p126*).

Hôtel de Ville

Grand' Place (02 279 43 65/tourist information 02 513 89 40). Pré-métro Bourse/métro Gare Centrale. **Open** *Guided tours* (in English) 3.15pm Tue; 3.15pm Wed. Apr-Sept also 10.45am and 12.15pm Sun. **Admission** €3. **No credit cards. Map** p315 C3.

Work on this superb edifice, adorned with sculptures, took 50 years. The left wing (1406) was built by Jacob van Thienen and, for balance, a right wing was later introduced by an unknown architect. The old belfry was too small for the new structure, so Jan van Ruysbroeck added the splendid 113m (376ft) tower, an octagon sitting firmly on a square plinth. In 1455 a gilt statue of St Michael slaying the drag-on was erected at its pinnacle. The tower seems to unbalance the rest of the building and legend has it that, in despair, the architect climbed to the top of his masterpiece and threw himself from it. This is unlikely; the reason for the imbalance is that the left wing is smaller than the right in order to preserve the street pattern. You can't climb the tower, but a series of elegant official rooms can be visited on the guided tour. The most flamboyant of them is the 18th-century Council Chamber, awash with gilt,

Sightseeing

Londoners take when they go out.

London

EVERY WEEK

tapestries, mirrors and ceiling paintings. Brussels' only secular Gothic building, the town hall is still in practical use as the seat of the Mayor of Brussels and is also the official venue for many marriages. What a place for a wedding.

Musée des Brasseurs Belges

10 Grand' Place (02 511 49 87/www.beerparadise. be). Pré-métro Bourse/métro Gare Centrale. **Open** *Winter* 10am-4.30pm Mon-Fri, noon-4.30pm Sat, Sun. *Summer* 10am-5pm daily. **Admission** €4. **No credit cards**. **Map** p315 C3.

Run by the brewers' confederation, this permanent exhibition displays traditional techniques plus a new high-tech brewing centre.

Musée du Cacao et du Chocolat

13 Grand' Place (02 514 20 48/www.mucc.be). Pré-métro Bourse/métro Gare Centrale. **Open** *Winter* 10am-5pm Tue-Sun. *Summer* 10am-5pm daily. **Admission** €5. free under-12s. **No credit cards**. **Map** p315 C3.

Founded by Jo Draps, a third generation Belgian chocolatier, the museum traces the history of chocolate from its discovery by the Aztecs, through its arrival in Europe, and on to the development of the praline and other Belgian specialities.

Musée de la Ville de Bruxelles

Grand' Place (02 279 43 50/www.brucity.be). Pré-métro Bourse/métro Gare Centrale. **Open** 10am-5pm Tue-Sun. **Admission** €3. **No credit cards**. **Map** p315 C3.

Constructed in the 13th century and thrice rebuilt, the Musée de la Ville is known in Dutch as the Broodhuis (bread house), a more accurate title since it was owned by the bakers' guild. Shored up after 1695, it was left to crumble until mayor Jules Anspach decided to rebuild it in fashionable neo-Gothic style in 1860. A museum since 1887, it now houses a somewhat dowdy collection of paintings, photographs, documents, tapestries and models that chronicle the history of Brussels. You'll find enlightening sections on the bombardment of 1695 and Léopold II's ambitious building programme, but the dizzying impression is one of constant invasion. The museum also contains the vast wardrobe of the Manneken-Pis (amounting to some 600 costumes, of which around 200 are on permanent display) plus some impressive paintings, including Pieter Bruegel the Elder's *Wedding Procession*.

St-Nicolas

1 rue au Beurre (02 513 80 22). Pré-métro Bourse. **Open** phone for details. **Map** p315 C3.

Founded in the 11th century, this calm model of medieval sanctity survived the 1695 bombardment. Its curved shape follows the old line of the River Senne and has tidy little houses (now shops) built into its walls. A dark, Gothic interior features a strangely out-of-place model showing Brussels in supposedly happier medieval times. It is currently undergoing renovation until 2006 – services are being held at churches nearby.

Hôtel de Ville courtyard. *See p59.*

Ilot Sacré

Just north of the Grand' Place is the **Ilot Sacré** (Holy Isle), saved by locals, and now one of the Lower Town's liveliest areas. At the time of the World Expo of 1958 city authorities were looking to redevelop the streets here to ease the traffic flow. Shopkeepers in the neighbourhood were outraged and the plans were axed. After the Expo, the authorities decided to create seven protected 'isles' with stringent planning rules to protect their identity. Thus in 1960, the Ilot Sacré was created. It's an evocative medieval tangle of small streets, devoted almost entirely to restaurants, many of which entice tourists with stupendous displays of fish and seafood reclining on mountains of ice. Rue des Bouchers is the main thoroughfare with the street names around it appetisingly evoking the Middle Ages, with the likes of rue des Harengs (Herring Lane) and rue du Marché aux Herbes (Grass- market). Butchers' Lane is still full of original houses with stepped gables and

The **Manneken-Pis**.

wooden doors mostly dating from the 17th century. At the end of the street, near No.58, a narrow passage leads to the **Résidence Centrale**, a modern development in olden style with tranquil courtyard and an elegantly modish bronze fountain. Not so elegant is **Jeanneke-Pis**, the female counterpart to the Manneken (*see below*), made in 1985 to raise money for charity and who squats in nearby impasse de la Fidélité. Petite rue des Bouchers is more of the same brash restaurants, but it was here at No.30, that La Rose Noire jazz club gave Jacques Brel (*see p100* **Brel's Brussels**) his first success in 1953. The renowned Théâtre du Toone (*see p63* **Talk of the Toone**), a puppet theatre and café, is in an alley off here in a building put up a year after the bombardment.

In contrast to the bustle of medieval markets evoked nearby, glass-covered **Galeries St-Hubert** suggests the seeds of the modern mall. Europe's oldest glass arcade was designed by JP Cluysenaar and opened by Léopold I in 1847, at the time, as Karl Marx cynically observed, of a potato famine. It still sparkles, equalling the glitter of the jewellery shops that it harbours. Set out in three sections (galeries de la Reine, du Roi and des Princes), it also houses keynote cultural venues such as the **Arenberg Galeries** (*see p177*), a fabulous independent art-house cinema currently fighting for survival, the **Théâtre Royal des Galeries** (*see p211*), with a Magritte fresco on the ceiling, and the recently reopened **Théâtre du Vaudeville** (*see p190*), which boasts a fine pedigree as a cabaret and concert venue. Restaurants such as **Ogenblik** (*see p108*) and cafés such as **Mokafé** (*see p130*) exude the splendour of their surroudings.

By the arcade's southern entrance stands busy place d'Agora, an oasis of waiting taxi cabs with a small craft market on most days. It's marked on most maps as place d'Espagne, which is, strictly speaking, the desolate area behind with the giant statue of Don Quixote looking over the old town.

South of the Grand' Place

The south side of the Grand' Place is quieter, characterised by idiosyncratic shops and odd vendors of strange plastic figures. Follow the crowds from the square, past the lace and tapestry shops into rue de l'Etuve, and you come across the **Manneken-Pis**, famous as a national symbol but eternally disappointing as a tourist spectacle, though you wouldn't believe it when you see the crowds. Like the *Mona Lisa*, it's so much smaller than you expect but the boy is fortunately elevated on a baroque pedestal to give him some grandeur. Around

Talk of the Toone

In December 2003, José Géal ceremoniously passed the crown of Toone puppet master down to his son Nicolas. With this, the future of Brussels' most traditional form of entertainment is assured.

Eight generations of puppet masters link back to the Toone's origins in 1830. The city once had hundreds of such theatres, where you could see satirical, bawdy variations of the shows the well-heeled were watching on the big stage. Only the Toone remains. Nestled in a third-storey attic on the petite rue des Bouchers, in the Ilot Sacré, it's a must-see for anyone seeking true understanding of this small and cynical country.

Here you can catch five shows a week, in French, English, German, Italian and *Bruxellois*, the old Brussels dialect. On the three-metre-wide stage, metre-high wooden mannequins costumed by top designers act out comedy and drama, hand-guided by six assistants. Nothing, from bloody battles to sex, is off limits, but it's never obscene, so as with *The Simpsons*, kids and adults see two different shows.

Nicolas, aka Toone VIII, reads all the parts, dishing out the sarcastic ad libs, tricks all learned from his 73-year-old father. José, a national icon, in his beret and goatee, took over Toone in 1963 by choice, not by birth. A classical actor, he wanted to save the theatre, centuries old but at that point, homeless. 'All that was left were 125

puppets,' he says. He bought a crumbling 1696 brick house, renovated the ground floor and began to put on shows. Moved by what he calls 'a crazy stubbornness', Géal worked furiously to produce snappy shows and promote his craft. Word got around, crowds started coming, and then visiting dignitaries.

Mayors gave Géal more keys to the city than he could carry. The building was listed. Bizarre prize-winning pianist Pierre-Alain Volondat gave up recording and touring to play the piano at Toone. Its bar (*see p131*) became almost as popular as the theatre it served. Upstairs, shows are invariably a 200-seater sell-out, and in any case, as a national treasure the Toone gets oodles of subsidies. In a Schaerbeek workshop, a staff of three works full time on promotion, preserving archives and making puppets, churning out characters to add to the 1,300 that range from Aladdin to Hitler.

Nicolas studied classical theatre at the Brussels conservatory, and shares his father's cynical sense of humour, especially about anything political. Don't be surprised to see Islamic fundamentalists turn up in *Faust*, Herod's men sing German war songs in the Nativity or George Dubya cameo in *Hamlet*.

Toone
21 petite rue des Bouchers (02 217 27 53). Pré-métro Bourse. **Open** & **tickets** vary. **No credit cards. Map** p315 C3.

him, gated railings, only opened by the person whose sole job it is to dress him in his various costumes: Euro-jogger, Santa Claus, a condom on World AIDS Day, and so on. A framed sign gives a calendar of upcoming costume days. The current statue was made in the 17th century by Jérôme Duquesnoy. Stolen by the British in 1745, then again by the French in 1777, it was smashed by a French ex-con in 1817, who got life for doing so. It's origins are unknown, though it is naturally endowed with local myth as well as a never-ending pee.

Up the hill, on the Vieille Halle aux Blés, is the **Fondation Internationale Jacques Brel** dedicated to the famed chanteur (*see p100* **Brel's Brussels**), while rue de l'Etuve, which runs south from the little micturitor, is Brussels' main thoroughfare for bars, with one in almost every building. Perhaps the loveliest of the Lower Town's half-dozen churches also stands here: **Notre-Dame de Bon Secours**.

Notre-Dame de Bon Secours

Rue du Marché au Charbon (02 514 31 13). Prémétro Anneessens. **Open** 9am-5pm daily. **Services** 11am Sun. **Map** p315 B3.
Built in the late 1600s, this baroque masterpiece, designed by Jan Cortvrindt and Willem de Bruyn, is a superb example of Flemish Renaissance style.

North of the Grand' Place

After the building over of the River Senne (*see p64* **Hidden Brussels**), much of the historic heart of the city was lost when straight avenues and formal squares were constructed between the Gares du Nord and Midi. Distinguished architectural ensembles included place de Brouckère, whose grandeur – and fountain – gave way to build the metro station. Although home to the classy **Hotel** and **Café Métropole** (*see p39* and *p130*), it's now just a traffic intersection overshadowed by the awful Centre Monnaie mall. It overshadows the neo-classical opera house **Théâtre de la Monnaie** (*see p190*) behind it, built in 1819. As well as historically significant (in 1830 it staged the opera which led to the uprising for Belgian independence; *see p14*), the venue is worth visiting for its ornate interior. Sadly the exterior has been ruined by what seems like a shed attached to its roof to house the mechanicals. Behind the opera in rue Léopold is the house where artist Jean-Louis David was exiled.

Arrowing north from the plaza in front of the theatre is gaudy rue Neuve. It could be any high street in any town, a crowded, pedestrianised stretch of brand names culminating in the ugly shopping centre, **City 2** (*see p143*). It's hard to

Hidden Brussels The River Senne

It takes a while for visitors to realise what's missing here: a river. No bridges or left bank, no waterside cafés or boat trips. In fact there *is* a river, only it runs lazily underground. The Senne flows for 100 kilometres (60 miles) from Hainaut province, before entering a tunnel by the Gare du Midi. From here it runs underground until it reaches Laeken and flows north towards Mechelen to join the River Dyle. Flow is the inoperative word, for it is the sluggish nature of the river which sealed its fate in central Brussels.

Old pictures offer an idyllic scene: old houses and footbridges reflected in the still waters, an air of calm and tranquillity. The reality is that the river was an open sewer and a repository for industrial and agricultural waste, including effluent from breweries and textile industries. The problem continued to grow, ultimately resulting in the awful cholera epidemic of 1866 that killed 3,500.

Rather than an engineering scheme to clean up the river, it was decided to be more radical and so the idea of a *voûtement* or cover-up was proposed. This allowed for a grand

sweep of tree-lined boulevards above, with hotels and Parisian-style apartment blocks for the wealthy. Boulevards Lemonnier, Anspach and Adolphe Max duly appeared on top of the covered river.

Currently in central Brussels, the banished Senne can only be seen in one lonely spot, a courtyard through the gates of 23 place St-Géry, but as more and more waterfront cities reinvent themselves – Glasgow, Bilbao, Antwerp – an action group, Les Fous de la Senne, has been campaigning for stretches of the river to be reopened – especially once a sewage treatment centre is open in 2006. Their aims are not as overly ambitious as they first seem. In December 2003, fish were spotted near Lembeek, the first ones seen in the river for a decade. With more local groups joining the campaign and a willingness from the Brussels authorities to restore the centre to its former glory, anything is possible. So the Senne may finally re-emerge with a new lease of life and the inhabitants will be able to drink a beer safely by the riverside rather than be poisoned by it.

Ste-Catherine.

believe that here was the site of the Duchess of Richmond's ball on the eve of Waterloo (*see p16* **Where Napoleon met his demise**) – although the airy **Notre-Dame du Finistère** does provide some architectural relief. Near it is the place des Martyrs, with a monument to the 445 revolutionaries who gave their lives for Belgium in 1830. It was a cobbled ruin until the Flemish authorities took the initiative to restore some buildings as government offices. Their French counterpart then responded by renovating another part of the square. It is lined with fine neo-classical buildings, including the impressive **Théâtre des Martyrs** (*see p210*). Around the corner is one of Brussels' most popular museums, the **Centre Belge de la Bande Dessinée**. Located in a beautifully restored Victor Horta department store (whose ground-floor café can be entered without a ticket), it features a revamped Tintin section to coincide with his 75th birthday celebrations, as well as lesser-known Belgian comic characters – many of whom are featured on vast murals in the comic strip walking tour of the city (*see p34* **Brussels Walks**).

Running parallel to rue Neuve is the grand boulevard Adolphe Max, with stunning buildings if you look up beyond the ground-level shops. To the north the boulevard peters out into brash sex shops and hostess clubs.

Notre-Dame du Finistère

Rue Neuve (02 217 52 52). Métro/pré-métro De Brouckère or Rogier. **Open** 8am-6pm Mon-Sat; 8am-noon, 3-6pm Sun. **Services** 9.15am, 12.10pm, 5pm Mon-Fri; 4.30pm, 6pm Sat; 9am, 11am, 4pm, 5.30pm Sun. **Map** p317 C2.
Largely built in the early 18th century, on the site of a 15th-century chapel, the church's baroque interior features a stupendously over-the-top pulpit.

St-Géry & Ste-Catherine

Maps p315 & p316

Restaurants, bars and churches are the key features of sassy St-Géry and former quayside Ste-Catherine, two small, self-contained quarters across boulevard Anspach from the Bourse. Both neighbourhoods have recently undergone major renovations, turning what was once shabby into a likeable but somewhat sanitised version of their former selves.

St-Géry is centred on the square of the same name, composed of a slew of designer bars built around the grand **Halles St-Géry**, a former covered market now a large bar and exhibition space with a nightclub in the basement. St-Géry was given the kiss of life by entertainment mogul Fred Nicolay (*see p139* **Right said Fred**), who set up a string of trendy cafés and bars and spread word of a scene. On summer nights the busy terraces of Nicolay's bars, which include Mappa Mundo and Zebra, create a Mediterranean atmosphere around the square.

The former desolate inner-city quarter was ripe for modernisation, especially given that it borders chic **rue Antoine Dansaert** (see p67 **Fashionably late**), the city's fashion centre and heart of the Flemish revitalisation of the area (the reopening of the Beursschouwburg theatre is a recent example; see p210). It has led to an influx of young professionals, media types and the gay community, with the result that St-Gèry is deemed the only place to live or be seen.

By contrast, set around the quays of the old harbour, where a thriving traffic of fishing boats was grounded with the filling in of the Senne in 1870, Ste-Catherine still feels like a port. Fountains and paved walkways now cover what locals (but not maps) refer to as the **Marché aux Poissons**, the Fish Market, either side of the metro stop. Hosting, indeed, a fish market once a week, lined with fish restaurants lit up with vast red neon lobsters – and turned into a market and giant outdoor skating rink over the Christmas period (see p169 **Christmas on ice**) – Ste-Catherine is dominated by its namesake church (see below). The belfry of an earlier (13th-century) Ste-Catherine is nearby, as is the **Tour Noire** (Black Tower), one of the few remaining remnants of the first city wall, rescued from demolition by Mayor Charles Buls.

Beside the church, **place Ste-Catherine** has been completely rebuilt, losing some of its old character, but no one bemoans that it is no longer a car park. On the contrary, since the restorations a small vegetable market has returned, as has the oyster man. A little further away but still in the neighbourhood are the churches **Notre-Dame aux Riches Claires** and **St-Jean-Baptiste au Béguinage**. The latter was once the centre of Brussels' largest *béguinage*, a charitable community for single women, founded in the 13th century.

In tandem with picturesque slices of history, the knock-on effect of St-Gèry has crossed over into Ste-Catherine; everyday Belgian bars, cafés and shops are becoming interspersed with minimalist chic. A classic example is **De Markten** (see p133) on rue Vieux Marché aux Grains, an old refurbished building with a café on the ground floor and a new Flemish arts centre above. The square out front is packed with drinkers and diners and live sound stages in the summer. But turn in to rue de Flandre and once again you are presented with an image of how things used to look: traditional restaurants (such as **Le Pré-Salé**, see p110), quaint old shops selling caged birds, bridal gowns, bakeries and triperies.

West of central Ste-Catherine on the edge of town is all that remains of the river, the **Canal de Charleroi**, a thin stretch of water running north-south. Along bankside boulevard Barthélémy, an art-gallery complex (see p179) housing **Kanal 20** has tried to boost an urban revival in this forgotten quarter, although activities around the former customs building Tour et Taxis further north show more promise: see p94 **On the waterfront**.

Notre-Dame aux Riches Claires
23 rue des Riches Claires (02 511 09 37). Pré-métro Bourse. **Open** 4-6pm Sat; 9.30am-2pm Sun. **Services** 9.30am, 11.30am Sun. **Map** p316 B3.
A charming asymmetrical structure built in 1665 and probably the work of Rubens' pupil, Luc Fayd'herbe. It reopened in 2000 after renovation.

Ste-Catherine
Place Ste-Catherine (02 513 34 81). Métro Ste-Catherine. **Open** 8.30am-5pm (summer until 6pm) Mon-Sat; 9am-noon Sun. **Services** *Chapel* 8am. *Church* 10am. **Map** p316 B2.
Almost as unkempt as its surroundings (and with an ancient pissoir built between the buttresses), Ste-Catherine was designed in 1854 in neo-Gothic style by Joseph Poelaert, and almost became the stock exchange before opening as a church in 1867. The interior is arched and graceful, cathedral-like in its proportions, with blue and yellow glass windows. One treasure is a 15th-century statue of a Black Madonna and child, supposedly rescued from the Senne after being thrown in by angry Protestants.

St-Jean-Baptiste au Béguinage
Place du Béguinage (02 217 87 42). Métro Ste-Catherine. **Open** 9am-5pm daily. **Services** 5pm Sat; 10am, 8pm Sun. **Map** p316 B2.
One of the best examples of Flemish baroque architecture in the city, this large church, attributed to Luc Fayd'herbe, has a fluid, honey-coloured façade. Its light-filled interior has a beautiful pulpit and 17th-century paintings by Theodoor van Loon.

The Marolles

Map p318
The Marolles is Brussels' resolutely working-class district, a tatty but durable resistance to urban expansion and standardisation in the 19th and 20th centuries. While you do still see washing lines strung between dilapidated buildings, a gradual gentrification is tangible. The area is now an incongruous mix of shabby shops, gentrified antique boutiques and interior design palaces. The population is largely immigrant with some nouveau-riche interlopers and a few deep-rooted locals who still speak odd words of Marollien, the fantastically rude dialect which is a mélange of world languages. At night, the Marolles restaurants take over as

Fashionably late

Twenty years ago rue Antoine Dansaert was a rather run-down cobbled street whose grand, fin-de-siècle façades were growing old disgracefully while locals scutted along them for late-night groceries or videos. Then a small shop selling outlandish clothes came along and changed everything. Sonja Noël's ground-breaking **Stijl** (*see p149*) opened in 1984, selling clothes by graduates from the fashion wing of the Antwerp Art Academy: the Antwerp Six. A few artists in the locality welcomed the new arrival with open arms.

Within weeks, Jean-Louis and Nathalie Hernant had reopened the classic art deco jazz bar **L'Archiduc** (*see p134*). Artists and artisans had a place to hang out. Stijl's unexpected success led to more cutting-edge boutiques opening, and the area began to take on a distinctly Flemish feel. Next door, the **Beursschouwburg** (*see p210*) was staging performance art, bringing Bruxellois from across the city, attracted as much by the new galleries and restaurants as by anything happening on stage. Dansaert was Brussels' chic epicentre of creativity.

All this time later and Stijl and L'Archiduc are still there, weathering the rapid and regular changeover of shopfronts. Current highlights include **Nicolas Woit** (*see p149*), whose shop is like a traditional dressmaker's from the 1950s, and knitwear queen **Annemie Verbeke** (*see p149*). A new addition is **Kartell** (No.3, www.kartell.it), 300sq m of the Italian furniture firm's trademark bold and translucent plastic interior décor. The street is a gold-mine for accessories, such as the wares carried at the art deco store run by architect and fashion designer Pili Collado, **Les Précieuses** (*see p155*), or **Christa Reniers**' jewellery (*see p155*) at No.29. There's eyewear at **Théo** (*see p164*), exotic footwear at **Hatshoe** (*see p155*) and finely made hats at **Christophe Coppens** (*see p155*), round the corner at rue Léon Lepage.

Eateries still abound. New hit **Comocomo** (*see p115*) lines up with fancy Moroccan **Kasbah** (*see p116*) and New York-style **Bonsoir Clara** (*see p116*), launched by leisure impresario Fred Nicolay, the man who is almost single-handedly responsible for the regeneration of nearby St-Géry, and whose latest venture **De Walvis** (*see p134*) at the dark, canal end of Antoine Dansaert looks set to open up that unchartered stretch. *See also p139* **Right said Fred**.

Even at the Bourse end, it's still the kind of street where you'll find a laundromat sitting happily beside an architects' office – a living example of Brussels' appealing, lucky-bag vibe. Elderly Turkish men stroll along, seemingly impervious to the hipper-than-thou browsers of avant-garde design.

Enjoy these traces of the old Antoine Dansaert while they last. In five years, they'll be gone, and much here will be as mundanely mainstream as rue Neuve.

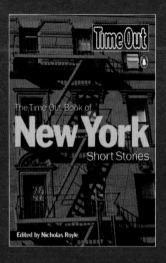
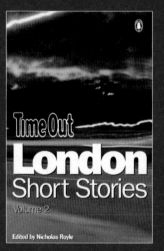
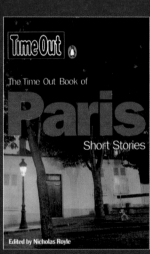

Baudelaire's Brussels

In the mid 19th century, a handful of the most notable names in French literature spent time in Brussels. It became known as 'la lune de Paris', such was its satellite status. Fleeing censorship or creditors, most writers found misery. Verlaine was imprisoned after shooting Rimbaud after an argument on the Grand' Place; Victor Hugo spent many a depraved, guilt-ridden weekend here.

Charles Baudelaire took out his misery in two of the most bilious hatchet jobs carried out on any country. In *Pauvre Belgique* and *La Belgique déshabillée*, Belgium is excoriated. On Belgians: 'a whistling people, like sottish birds'. Their eyes: 'clueless, wide, stupid, boggling'. Their women: 'flat-footed, with elephant legs'. Their food: 'disgusting and simple'. Their beer: 'urine'. The weather, the poor grasp of French, the mercantile mindset, even the black soap Belgians used to wash the pavements: it all stank.

Baudelaire had moved to Brussels in April 1864, hoping to deliver lectures on literature and art, cut a deal with a Belgian publisher and give his French creditors the slip. He stayed at the now defunct Hôtel du Grand Miroir, rue de la Montagne near the place d'Espagne. The lectures, after initial success, foundered (no thanks to a slip about loss of virginity that appalled his audience); the publisher ignored his overtures, and his health, never robust, declined – as did his view of Belgium. He would wander madly up and down the Galeries St-Hubert. So why didn't he leave? Partly because his hotel debts kept him prisoner; partly because he knew the French shared most of the traits of the Belgians. On 2 July 1866, when bundled on to a train bound for France, he was paralysed and speechless; four months previously, he had suffered a stroke at the Eglise Saint-Loup in Namur. He died in 1867.

the shops close; trendy drinkers still congregate in the Sablon before making their way down the hill to eat, or move on to Brussels' top techno spot **The Fuse** (*see p199*). As they tip out at daybreak, and the market sets up, so the cyclical life of the Marolles starts all over again.

The name derives from an order of nuns, the Mariam Colentes (devotees of Mary) who lived in a convent on the corner of rue Montserrat and rue des Prêtres; now all that is left as a reminder is a statue of the Virgin in rue Prévoyance. The area stretches haphazardly from the slopes of the imposing **Palais de Justice** (*see p77*) down to the Gare du Midi. To the east it runs up against adjoining Sablon, up the hill and upmarket. A public lift – and slow improvement in antique shopping down below – now link the Upper and Lower Towns.

At the north end of the district is place de la Chapelle where **Notre-Dame de la Chapelle** (*see below*) stands, built in an interesting mix of styles. The church is widely known as the burial place of Pieter Bruegel the Elder but he is, in fact, buried elsewhere. The confusion arises from a memorial plaque laid by his son in the fourth chapel. The house where Bruegel lived is nearby at 132 rue Haute, the 16th-century **Maison de Bruegel**. Although it doesn't contain any of the artist's works or artefacts, it's open to groups by written request. The artist would have drawn inspiration for his peasant feasts and skating crowds from the life around him. Short, narrow streets proclaim

their roots: rue des Orfèvres (Goldsmiths' Lane); rue des Tonneliers (Barrelmakers' Lane) and rue des Ramoneurs (Chimney Sweeps' Lane).

Running south from place de la Chapelle are the parallel rues Blaes and Haute. Some say the ladder of narrow streets between these two are all that's left of true Marolles but rue Blaes wasn't built until 1852.

Midway along Blaes is **place du Jeu de Balle**, Marolles' epicentre, where a daily flea market is surrounded by earthy bars and cafés. Although you'll still see a few toothless locals jigging to the accordion playing on a Sunday, these days tipplers are more likely to be shoppers back from a browse in the local bric-a-brac shops. (*See p153* **Good housekeeping**.)

The burial of the Senne saw much industry move out of the centre, and the Marolles was left to rot. Thousands of homes were destroyed to make way for the railway (*see p20* **Off the rails**) and Palais de Justice. The railway arches now provide space for energetic **Recyclart** (*see p200*), an urban regeneration project with a remit of culture and community care.

Notre-Dame de la Chapelle

Place de la Chapelle (02 512 07 37). Pré-métro Anneessens/bus 20, 48. **Open** *June-Sept* 9am-4pm daily. *Oct-May* noon-4pm daily. **Services** 4pm Sat; 8am, 10.30am, 4.30pm, 6.30pm Sun. **Map** p315 B4.
A rare mix of styles: part of the chapel dates from the 12th century, the transepts are Romanesque and the nave 15th-century Gothic. Most of the paintings inside date from the 19th century.

The Upper Town

Royal Brussels beside swanky Sablon.

Ever since the 11th century, when Lambert II built his castle on top of Coudenberg (Cold Hill) to escape the murky River Senne, the ruling classes have surveyed their subjects from the heights of what is now called the Upper Town. The grand buildings with their neo-classical façades and the palaces and parks still speak of wealth, power and high culture and remain home to royalty and government, as well as the city's most important museums. From the Cathédrale to the Palais de Justice, via rue Royale and impressive royal squares, the Upper Town stands solid and proud. Even its steep drop to the Lower Town is impressively studied, whilst its gentler descent to the south is softened by the smart, sophisticated Sablon.

Royal Quarter

Maps p315 & p317

Ten minutes' walk uphill from the Grand' Place stands the **Cathédrale des Sts Michel et Gudule** (*see p73*). While isolated from the city by the modern buildings that crowd it, it's easy to imagine the Cathédrale dominating the medieval skyline, a constant reminder to the

hapless Bruxellois of the power of the church. In 1999, after a restoration of the exterior and interior was completed, it hosted the royal marriage of the heir apparent Prince Philippe to Princess Mathilde. As the scaffolding came down, the façade and towers (by Jan van Ruysbroeck of Hôtel de Ville fame) emerged gleaming. To the left and rear is rue du Bois Sauvage where, between Nos.14 and 15, stands a solitary scrap of the old city wall.

Walk up the steep hill and you come to the determinedly straight **rue Royale**, the main artery of the Upper Town, punctuated at one end by the Palais de Justice and at the other, by the Church of Ste-Marie. This is the 'royal route', linking the Royal Palace in Laeken (*see p96*), where the royal family live, with the Royal Palace off place Royale, used for state ceremonies but unoccupied. The king is driven along it most days. Tourists can jump on any No.92, 93 or 94 tram and let it take them up and down the stately road with as many stop-offs as they like for the hour validity of a normal ticket.

Running alongside rue Royale is the 18th-century **Parc de Bruxelles**. Laid out in classic French style, the design of its avenues is based on a Masonic pair of dividers. Throughout are strange classical statues, armless, but with toes peeking out the bottom. You'll notice that some also have their noses missing – it was believed Lord Byron was responsible for this vandalism, but eventually the Austrian Count Metternich owned up to the not so statesman-like behaviour. The park was once a chic strolling ground, although in the revolution of 1830, its avenues ran with blood. These days it's full of joggers and office workers on their lunch breaks. It also makes the perfect setting for the chocolate box **Théâtre Royal du Parc** (see p211).

At the park's northern end stands the Belgian parliament building, the **Palais de la Nation**, graced by a lovely 18th-century façade by Guimard, the architect responsible for the homogenous nature of the area, while at the southern end is the king's starkly imposing official residence, the **Palais Royal** (see p76), It's never been much in favour with the royals who prefer the airiness of Laeken (see p96) and the flag only flies on the rare occasions when the monarch is home and on official duties. It is open to the public in the summer. At the western end of the palace is the Hôtel Belle Vue, built as a swanky hotel in 1777. It was Wellington's headquarters at the time of Waterloo but now houses the **Musée de la Dynastie** (see p73), where memorabilia, documents and photographs chronicle the short history of the Belgian monarchy since 1831. Directly behind the palace is the narrow rue Brederode, where Joseph Conrad visited the Congo Trading Company in 1889; it remains as creepy today as when it was first described in his *Heart of Darkness*.

West of the Palais Royal lies the graceful **place Royale**, built over the site of the 15th-century Coudenberg Palace; its name is remembered in the church of **St-Jacques-sur-Coudenberg** (see p76) at the top of the square. The statue here is of Godfroide de Bouillon, who led the successful first Crusade in the 11th century; he remains victoriously unaware of the trams circling beneath him. From here, you get one of the best views in Brussels, looking directly down to the Grand' Place. Underneath the streets are some remains of the original **Palais Coudenberg** (see p74), which burned down in 1731 when a fire started in the kitchens. When the square was rebuilt under the orders of Empress Maria Theresa, the ruins were buried for cost reasons and forgotten about until the 1930s. They were re-exposed in 2000 during major renovations and – in typical Brussels style – were subjected to plans for an underground car park. Mercifully intact, they are now open to the public.

At the western corner of the place Royale are Brussels' two major art galleries, the Musée d'Art Ancien and the Musée d'Art Moderne which, linked by an underground passage, together make up the **Musées Royaux des Beaux-Arts** (see p74). This huge, outstanding collection, covering the Masters to surrealism, has been considerably embellished by an impressive new wing opened in December 2003.

Downhill from the place Royale on rue Montagne de la Cour are two architectural landmarks. The first is one of the great triumphs of art nouveau in the city: the spiky and curly Old England department store, long shuttered up but open from 2000 as the **Musée des Instruments de Musique** (see p74). It's one of the most distinctive and best-known buildings in Brussels. Further down the street, as it sweeps right into rue Ravenstein, is the red-brick, gabled **Hôtel Ravenstein**. This 15th-century building, the only significant survivor from the old Coudenberg quarter, was the birthplace of the ill-fated Anne of Cleves, fourth wife of Henry VIII.

Descending Ravenstein, to the left is the classic shopping arcade **Galerie Ravenstein**, now sadly faded and echoingly empty. To the right is the main entrance to the city's recently revived cultural centre the **Palais des Beaux-Arts** aka the 'Bozar' (see p72 **A new broom at the Bozar**) and, alongside, on rue Baron Horta, is the **Musée du Cinema** (see p73 and p178), both a film museum and working picture house. From here, you can climb the steps back up to rue Royale, or take the steep descent down Ravenstein to the **Mont des Arts**, a 1950s piazza that joins the Upper and Lower Towns.

Sightseeing

Sunday's best

Weekends on the Mont des Arts have improved dramatically with the introduction of a Sundays-only combined museum pass and Sunday cultural events for all age groups. The pass gives admission to seven key museums (including the **Musées Royaux des Beaux-Arts**, **Palais des Beaux-Arts** and **Musée des Instruments de Musique**) and is €11 for adults, €5.50 for teenagers and free for under-13s. In addition, concerts, films and activities for kids has seen families flock back to the Mont des Arts in droves. Tickets and details (02 507 84 32, www.montdesarts. be) are available all week from the office of the Palais des Beaux-Arts (see p72 **A new broom at the Bozar**).

A new broom at the Bozar

The Palais des Beaux-Arts used to be a stuffy cultural institution in a moribund neighbourhood. Not any more. Since Paul Dujardin took over as director in January 2002, the centre has been given a complete makeover. False ceilings have been ripped out, original features restored and even the cumbersome old name has gone, replaced by the cutesy contraction 'Bozar'.

The idea for a Palace of Culture was first mooted by King Léopold II. Searching around for legitimate causes to launder his Congo wealth, he had the idea of a 'Mont des Arts', where all the arts in the city would be concentrated. At the time much of the city was already being ripped up to build a new north-south rail link (*see p20* **Off the rails**), so losing another old quarter in the name of progress was no big deal. The site on the edge of the Upper Town was cleared and ready by 1910, but then war broke out and everything was put on hold until the economy picked up again. The building was designed by

Victor Horta, but long after he had given up his curvaceous art nouveau style in favour of the fashionable new art deco. When it eventually opened in 1928, the Palais des Beaux-Arts was the leading architectural feat of its day – the first building in the world designed specifically as a multi-purpose arts centre. Under one roof, it contained a sumptuous oval concert hall, a theatre, exhibition galleries, a bookshop, café and restaurant. It was the setting for surrealist exhibitions, an annual antique fair and the Europalia arts festival. Jacques Brel played his last concert in Brussels here.

Dujardin has taken the Beaux-Arts by its tatty ear and dragged it into the 21st century. The previous collection of loose-knit artistic organisations, each with their own management styles and archaic outlook, hummed and hawed about change, but now they hum along in some sort of harmony, which helps return the Beaux-Arts to its original multi-purpose ethic. A year-round programme of music, art, theatre, dance, film and literature sets Dujardin's sights firm on achieving a mission he likens to London's Barbican Centre. Add to that his commitment to attract a wide and diverse public (the initiative for the Mont des Arts Sunday pass and programme comes from the Bozar; see *p71* **Sunday's best**) while remaining at the forefront of top-drawer European culture, and it's clear the new Bozar now packs a cultural wallop unmatched elsewhere in Brussels.

Palais des Beaux-Arts (Bozar)

23 rue Ravenstein (02 507 84 86; tickets 02 507 82 00/www.pskpba.be). Métro Gare Centrale or Parc/tram 92, 93, 94. **Open** 10am-6pm Tue-Sun. **Admission** varies. **Credit** AmEx, MC, V. **Map** p317 C/D4.

It's flanked on one side by the **Palais du Congrès**, on the other by the **Bibliothèque Royale de Belgique** and adjacent **Palais de Charles de Lorraine** (*see p74*), and on both by skateboarding teenagers. Recently the introduction of an all-in museum pass and kids' events on Sundays has seen the staircased piazza become a major part of a Brussels' family weekend: *see p71* **Sunday's best**.

Cathédrale des Sts Michel et Gudule

Place Ste Gudule (02 217 83 45/www. cathedralestmichel.be). Métro Gare Centrale or Parc/ tram 92, 93, 94. **Open** 8am-6pm daily. **Services** 7.30am, 8am, 12.30pm Mon-Fri; 4pm, 5.30pm Sat; 10am, 11.30am, 12.30pm Sun. **Admission** €1; *Crypt* (by appointment only) €2.50. **No credit cards.** **Map** p315 C3/p317 D3.

Dedicated to the male and female patron saints of Brussels, St Michel the better known, Ste Gudule more popular in local lore. Her symbol is a lamp, said to be blown out by the devil for her devotion, but relit when she prayed. The cathedral stands on the site of a Carolingian-era chapel on the Treurenberg (Hill of Sorrows) which gained importance when Lambert II decided to move the saint's relics there from St-Géry. The current Gothic building (replacing a second church that had been built in 1072) was begun in 1226 and completed in 1499, with later chapel additions in the 16th and 17th centuries. The Cathédrale's darkest moments were mass defacement in 1579 perpetrated by Protestant iconoclasts and in the late 18th century when French revolutionary armies largely destroyed the interior along with priceless works of art. The renewed interior is splendidly proportioned and happily retains a host of treasures. Most impressive are Bernard van Orley's fine 16th-century pictorial stained-glass windows in the transepts, and the 13th-century choir. Inside and out were heavily renovated in the 1990s when remnants of the 11th-century Romanesque church were unearthed in the crypt.

Musée du Cinéma

Palais des Beaux-Arts, 9 rue Baron Horta (02 507 83 70/www.cinematheque.be). Métro Gare Centrale or Parc/tram 92, 93, 94. **Open** 5.30-10.30pm daily. **Admission** €2. **No credit cards.** **Map** p317 C4.

This modest but fascinating museum traces the early days of cinema, particularly the main inventions that led to the discovery of cinematography by the Lumière brothers. It's still used as a working cinema, with piano accompaniment to silent films in the two projection rooms. *See also p178.*

Musée de la Dynastie

7 place des Palais (02 511 55 78/www.musbellevue. be). Métro Gare Centrale or Trône/tram 92, 93, 94. **Open** 10am-4pm Tue-Sun. **Admission** €3; €2 concessions. Combined ticket with Palais Coudenberg €5; €4 concessions; free under-12s. **No credit cards.** **Map** p319 D4.

Along with chronicling the Belgian royals, this museum has become of wider interest since the Fondation Baudouin installed an exhibition on the life of the popular last king, including his office and relics of his childhood. It's all rather voyeuristic, which makes it bizarrely irresistible.

Time for some culture at the **Mont des Arts**. *See p71.*

Musée des Instruments de Musique

*2 rue Montagne de la Cour (02 545 01 30/www.mim.
fgov.be). Métro Gare Centrale or Porte de Namur/
tram 92, 93, 94.* **Open** 9.30am-5pm Tue-Fri; 10am-
5pm Sat, Sun. **Admission** €5; €3.50 concessions;
free after 1pm on 1st Wed of mth. **Credit** MC. V.
Map p315 C4.

Designed by Paul Saintenoy in 1899, with curving
black wrought-ironwork framing large windows,
the former Old England department store emerged
a century later – and after a decade of restoration –
as a museum housing a 6,000-strong collection of
instruments (the world's largest), of which 1,500 are
on display at any one time. Look out for the bizarre
saxophone types dreamed up by the instrument's
inventor Adolphe Sax. There are concerts in the 200-
seater hall (*see also p187*), and the top-floor restaurant offers excellent panoramic views of the city.

Musées Royaux des Beaux-Arts

*3 rue de la Régence (02 508 3211/www.fine-arts-
museum.be) Métro Gare Centrale/tram 92, 93, 94.*
Open *Museum* 10am-5pm Tue-Sun. *Café/restaurant*
9am-6.30pm daily. **Admission** €5; €2-€3.50
concessions. **Credit** AmEx, MC, V. **Map** p315 C4.

The most conspicuous of many recent upgrades of
Brussels' cultural institutions is the transformation
of its Fine Arts Museum, freshened up on the outside and vastly enlarged and improved within. The
collection covers the art of the Low Countries over
the past six centuries, from masterworks by Rogier
van der Weyden, Hans Memling and Pieter Bruegel
the Elder to a great spread of Belgian surrealist

work. A new wing carved out of two landmark
buildings (art nouveau and neo-classical) adjacent
to the museum contains a bookstore, sleek café and
upscale restaurant, all accessible from the street.
Indoors, a vast swathe of new gallery space has permitted the rehanging of the museum's marvellous
collection of 17th- and 18th-century Flemish paintings, now exhibited in superior numbers, cleaned
and restored. A colossal gallery, the Patio, has been
created for the display of a rare suite of eight vast
Renaissance tapestries made in Brussels. After 30
years of work, the museum is looking like the world-
class repository of art that it always promised to be.

Palais de Charles de Lorraine

*1 place du Musée (02 519 58 07/www.kbr.be). Métro
Gare Centrale/tram 92, 93, 94.* **Open** 1-5pm Tue-Fri;
10am-5pm Sat; 10am-5pm first Sun of the month.
Admission €3; €2 concessions. **No credit cards**.
Map p315 C4.

Also known as the Museum of the 18th Century, and
opened to the public for the first time in 2000, five
themed salons document the time when Charles of
Lorraine was governor-general of the Austrian
Netherlands. Visit for exhibits on Charlie boy, music,
science, cartography and the art of table-setting.

Palais Coudenberg

*Entrance through Musée de la Dynastie, place des
Palais (02 512 28 21/www.coudenberg.com). Métro
Gare Centrale or Trône/tram 92, 93, 94.* **Open** *Oct-
Mar* 10am-5pm Tue-Sun. *Apr-Sept* 10am-6pm Tue-
Sun. **Admission** €4; €3 concessions. Combined
ticket with Musée de la Dynastie €5; €4 concessions;
free under-12s. **Credit** MC, V. **Map** p315 D4.

A crafty nose job at the **Parc de Bruxelles**. *See p70.*

Hidden Brussels Underground

Below Brussels there exists a parallel universe, one that lives amid the stations of the city's metro system.

Almost every human need, from food and drink to carnal desires, not to mention artistic and spiritual fulfilment, can be satisfied below street level at one metro station or other. To start with breakfast, just about any of the main stations can provide a pain au chocolat or croissant. Later on, drop by **Schuman** station, where you can linger over a three-course meal in a full restaurant setting.

This being Brussels, there is no shortage of beer. Many underground bars are hangouts in their own right: the ones by the foot of the main staircases at **De Brouckère** and the **Gare Centrale** deserve special mention. Some set up little bistro tables along the walkways as if it were the Champs-Elysées. In **Madou** station, the tables are decked out with umbrellas.

The stations feature a lot of art, some of it interesting enough for a sightseeing visit alone. Delvaux, Hergé and Horta are all here: Delvaux's 13-metre mural *Nos Vieux Trams Bruxellois* in praise of the urban transport of his childhood is on display at **Bourse**; Hergé drew 150 characters from Tintin's adventures at **Stockel** station shortly before his death; and fragments of Horta's art nouveau buildings are built into **Parvis de St-Gilles**. More unusual but equally noteworthy are

Jean-Paul Laenen's photo mural *Metrorama 78* in **Aumale** station, and Roger Somville's psychotropic graffiti illustrating *Our Times* in **Hankar**. Four new murals were added at the start of 2004 – a full list can be found at www.art-public.com/caid.

Sports fans will enjoy the new **Eddy Merckx** station in Anderlecht, and the racing bike 'the Cannibal' he used to set the world one-hour record in 1972. For music fans the choice of destination is not so easy. Once bored with the piped tripe at every station, you could try the Manhattan Disco in **Maelbeek** – however, be warned, it's a striptease bar.

After that last diversion a trip to the **Rogier** or **Madou** stops may be required. Both feature fully fledged churches, complete with priest, nun and confessional. The chapels are tucked among the other storefronts, but you can't miss the burning candles and religious iconography. Père Christian Haudegand presides over mass in Rogier's Chapelle de Ste Rita on Thursdays at 5.30pm and in Madou's smaller Chapelle Notre-Dame de l'Unité every day at 12.30pm. Rogier's has the added attraction of a tanning salon.

For architecture, **Saint-Guidon** may be a bit tattered around the edges, but it's a swooping, circular wonder – which would recall Saarinen's famous TWA terminal at JFK airport in New York, if only JFK had the same smell of waffles.

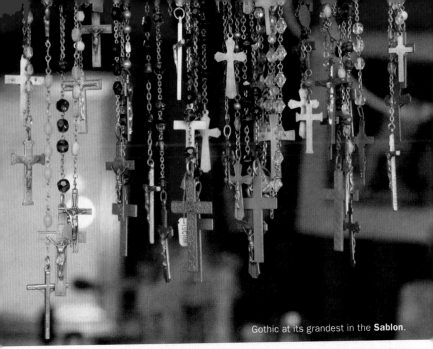
Gothic at its grandest in the **Sablon**.

Begun in the 11th century and enlarged by Philip the Good in the 15th century to become one of Europe's finest palaces, the Coudenberg was razed by fire in 1731. Built over to create the place Royale, the Coudenberg was excavated in recent times to allow visitors a glimpse of its glory. The most impressive sight is the Aula Magna, a huge reception chamber with a capacity of 1,400, used by Charles V in 1555 for his farewell address. In its day, the palace was large enough to host indoor jousting tournaments. There are also the remains of a chapel, cellars and rue d'Isabelle, where Charlotte Brontë once lived at No.32; the royal quarter is described by her in *Villette*.

Palais Royal

Place des Palais (02 551 20 20/www.monarchie.be).
Métro Trône/tram 92, 93, 94. **Open** Late July-early Sept Tue-Sun; phone for details. **Admission** free.
No credit cards. Map p321 D4.
The current, charmless building is an amalgam of styles created originally by Dutch king William I, remodelled in 1825, and again in 1904. As this is a residential palace, there's nothing much of historic interest here, so don't expect to see a fur wrap thrown casually over a Louis XV chair. But it's good for a nose and to see a classical interior.

St-Jacques-sur-Coudenberg

1 impasse Borgendael, place Royale (02 511 78 36/
02 502 18 25). Métro Trône/tram 92, 93, 94. **Open** 10am-5.45pm daily. **Services** 5.15pm Tue-Thur; 9am, 9.45am (English), 11am Sun. **Map** p321 D4.

This church was built in 1775 to resemble a Roman temple (although an incongruous belltower was added in the 19th century) giving it a strange Pilgrim Fathers-New England sort of look. The interior is as peculiarly imposing as the exterior and you can imagine that it served perfectly as a temple of reason and then as a temple of law when Brussels was under the sway of revolutionary France, before being returned to Catholicism in 1802.

Sablon

Maps p315 & p319

Stroll on south past the Musées Royaux des Beaux-Arts and you come to upmarket and sophisticated Sablon. The local landmark is **Notre-Dame au Sablon** (*see p77*), probably the loveliest Gothic church in Brussels. Across busy rue de la Régence from the church is **place du Petit Sablon**. Its centre is taken up by a small park, whose railings, by art nouveau architect Paul Hankar, are divided by 48 columns, each with a statuette representing one of the ancient guilds of Brussels. Its chief dedicatees are the 16th-century counts Egmont and Hoorn (*see p11*), executed on the Grand' Place in 1568. At the top end of the square stands the **Palais d'Egmont**. Begun in the 16th century, it was enlarged in the 18th century and had to be rebuilt at the start of the 20th after a fire. It is now used for receptions by

the Ministry for Foreign Affairs and it was here that Britain, Ireland and Denmark signed their entry to the then EEC in 1972. The rooms are superb, but only the gardens are open to the public. There you'll find a statue of Peter Pan, a copy of the one in Kensington Gardens.

Behind Notre-Dame is the **place du Grand Sablon**, a major square lined with glitzy restaurants and high-price antiques shops. Small independent art galleries and some of Brussels' best chocolate shops (*see p158* **Sweet success**) complete the picture. At weekends, an antique market adds colour to the foot of the church. Grand Sablon is full of life and verve, although it is always bisected by cars and buses, and there remains an inappropriate car park at its centre. This doesn't stop the magic of white lights at Christmas or numerous festivals.

At the lower end of rue de la Régence stands the unloved (by critics and criminals) **Palais de Justice**, completed in 1883 by Joseph Poelaert, Léopold II's favoured architect. It was the death of him, brought about, it was said, by a witch from the Marolles in revenge for the site's 3,000 demolished houses. The steps are a perfect stage for demonstrations, and the terrace is ideal for panoramic views. You can take either the lift or steps down to the more endearing streets of the Marolles. The public are allowed into the main hall – a free municipal lift drops you next to the Palais entrance.

Notre-Dame au Sablon

3B rue de la Régence (02 511 57 41). Métro Porte de Namur/tram 92, 93, 94. **Open** 9am-7pm Mon-Sat. **Admission** free; guided tours available on request. **Map** p319 C4.

Recently spruced up, Our Lady of the Sablon was built in the 15th and 16th centuries on the site of a 14th-century chapel that contained a statue of Mary shipped in from Antwerp on account of its supposed healing powers. A carving of the boat can be seen in the nave but the statue was demolished by Protestants during the iconoclastic riots. The statue's arrival is still celebrated in July's Ommegang procession (*see p168*). The current impressive structure boasts stunning 14-metre (46-foot) high stained-glass windows.

Palais de Justice

Place Poelaert (02 508 64 10). Métro Louise/tram 91, 92, 93, 94/bus 20, 48. **Open** 8am-5pm Mon-Fri. **Admission** free. **Map** p318 C5.

The largest of Léopold II's grandiose projects, this intimidating colossus of 26,000sq m caused the demolition of 3,000 houses and demise of its architect Poelaert, driven mad by his need for symmetry. Few critics agree on its style even today. The exterior is supposedly Assyro-Babylonian, though it is truly a mish-mash of styles that has led to ridicule over the centuries. The interior is equally imposing – and flawlessly symmetrical – with magisterial statues of Demosthenes and Cicero, and an echoing waiting room, the Salle des Pas Perdus (Hall of Lost Steps). Kafka would have loved it.

EU Quarter & Etterbeek

Greenery and glass make unlikely bedfellows in the capital of Europe.

Art nouveau attractions at the **Maison de Cauchie**. *See p83.*

In the 1960s, an attractive 19th-century quarter around the Rond-Point Schuman was torn down to allow the construction of office buildings for the burgeoning European institutions. In the 1980s, the once lively Quartier Léopold suffered a similar fate since the European Parliament complex was built, partly on the site of an old brewery. Most Bruxellois are appalled at the damage that has been done to the fragile urban fabric of their city, with shiny glass and steel office blocks next to boarded-up houses and tracts of wasteland taken over as car parks. But things are changing. Prime Minister Guy Verhofstadt has embarked on a major plan to link the EU institutions by a series of footpaths and cycle trails. Already, a former car park has been turned into the attractive place Jean Ray, the abandoned Van Maerlant chapel has been converted into an EU library, and a new park has been set next to the Charlemagne building, itself restyled by Helmut Jahn. (For more on the future city, *see p27* **Brussels tomorrow**.)

Even so, it will be years before the scars have healed and, with EU expansion, finding space is one long struggle. While the needs of locals are set against the Eurocrats', the sweep of Brussels from east of the Petit Ring to the Fôret de Soignes remains a mix: elegant squares are overlooked by tower blocks, art nouveau treasures sit alongside glass edifices, rows of terraced streets are girdled by stately parks. This is Brussels at its most fractured.

EU Quarter

Maps p320 & p322

The EU quarter is a series of office and policy-makers' buildings linked by streets that echo an older Brussels. The area has long been the focus of attentions of urban heritage action groups who refer nostalgically to pre-EU days when it was the lively Quartier Léopold, with its characteristic local bars and beautiful houses. Patches of these still exist but as the heritage activists lament, the heart has been torn out. Recent times have at least seen a more decisive architectural style, and many of the heavy grey office blocks are being replaced by more daring sculptured buildings which may one day be seen as standard bearers of their time.

A good starting point is to take the métro to Schuman. Exiting on to Rond-Point Schuman your attention is snagged by the (in)famous **Berlaymont building**, a star-shaped symbol not just of the EU, but of the bureaucratic nightmares associated with it. This was the original home for the European Commission until 1991, when it was deemed too dangerous because of its outrageous asbestos content. It would have been cheaper to pull it down, but local disquiet – yes, the locals learned to love it – and its tricky foundations, meant renovation was the only option. After years under white plastic, it is now a gleaming, state-of-the-art smart building, which more or less breathes for its computerised self. Late and hundreds of millions over budget, it is now due to open in mid 2004. Word on the street is that no one wants to move back in.

Opposite the Berlaymont is the **Justus Lipsius building**, opened in 1995 for the Council of Ministers. Its frontage of pink granite and fluttering flags will be familiar as the backdrop to countless newscasts as it's the place where the world's media gather on high days. Since the decision was taken to hold all EU summits in Brussels, this little corner can be security-cordoned for days, which is not

something that endears the EU to locals. By 2010, these summits will be switched to the **Résidence Palace** nearby (*see below*).

Away to the south, shining like a Crystal Palace in the distance, is the **European Parliament** (opened in 1998). It is known locally as the 'Caprice des Dieux' (Folly of the Gods), which strangely enough is also the name of an identically shaped supermarket cheese. The best view of this undeniably impressive set of buildings is from the attractive but unexceptional **Parc Léopold**. Briefly the site of a zoo, this was one of the world's first science parks in the late 19th century and it's still dotted with impressive research institutes. One of the park's public attractions is the **Institut Royal des Sciences Naturelles** (*see p81*), famous for its dinosaur skeletons and the robotic wonders of 'dinamation', a hit with kids. Across the street is the **Musée Wiertz** (*see p82*), home and studio of the oddball 19th-century artist of the same name.

Turn right out of the park and you'll come to **place Jourdan**, a slice of Brussels life, lined with bars and restaurants in the old style. The queue here is for the most famous *friterie* in town, **Maison Antoine**: *see p117* **On the move**. Turn left out of the park and you'll see

Hidden Brussels The ring of spies

The greatest spy of all time was not a suave British agent with a girl on both arms and a fondness for Martinis. Leopold Trepper was a burly, middle-aged Polish Jew selling raincoats in Brussels.

With the rise of the Nazis, Russia placed spies across Europe to monitor the situation. Trepper was sent to Brussels in 1939 as 'Jean Gilbert', director of a company manufacturing raincoats, with its modest headquarters at 101 rue des Atrébates in Etterbeek. He used the business as cover for his trips around Europe to meet agents. At its peak, the network numbered 117 agents strewn across the continent.

The Nazis referred to this spy ring as Die Rote Kapelle (The Red Orchestra), because agents relayed their information to Moscow via radio transmitters known as 'music boxes'. Their own agency, the Abwehr, tried to track down these radio operators, or 'musicians', with its direction-finding units, but all to little avail.

In 1941, Trepper's agents succeeded in informing Moscow of Hitler's plans for the invasion of Russia. Stalin chose to ignore the

evidence. After the invasion went ahead, Moscow put pressure on agents to send more information. Operators began transmitting all night, giving the Abwehr more time to locate them. On 14 December 1941, they tracked the messages to rue des Atrébates. German agents surrounded the house and three adjacent buildings also being used by the Orchestra. The greatest spy ring in history was blown. The Red Orchestra was silenced.

Trepper himself had an exceedingly lucky escape. He turned up in the middle of the raid and claimed to be a street vendor. He then fled to Paris, where he was apprehended a year later while sat in a dentist's chair. The Nazis made him send back false messages to Moscow but he managed to escape again and find his way back to Russia – where Stalin threw him in jail for treason. He wasn't freed until after Stalin's death. He moved to Israel, where he died in 1982.

Today 101 rue des Atrébates is a private residence but a commemorative plaque honours the men and women who once furtively slunk in and out of here, risking their lives to defeat the Nazis.

Inside the EU

Even for insiders, the European Union can be hellishly complex. Brussels, the shorthand for EU bureaucracy, is a mesh of institutions and procedures rather than just one single voice.

The **European Commission** has the sole right to initiate legislation across the 25 member states. It administers the EU's annual budget of €100 billion: it can instruct farmers what shall be planted and the prices we pay for the food. In charge are one commissioner for each country, aided by 20,000 civil servants in offices all around Schuman métro. The EC President, elected every three years, sits in the Breydel building (corner of rue Belliard/avenue d'Auderghem), but is due to move to the refurbished **Berlaymont building** (200 rue de la Loi; see p79) when it is ready in the summer of 2004. External Relations services are in the Charlemagne building (170 rue de la Loi), others are scattered further out of town in Evere (Foreign Aid) and Beaulieu (Economics).

The Commission's initiatives can only become law if agreed by the national governments, who meet in the **Council of Ministers**. This is the real decision-making body: it consists of member state representatives, plus its own secretariat and the EC President. Membership changes according to the agenda; for farming, agriculture ministers will attend, for general affairs foreign ministers, and four times a year heads of state meet in the European Council, the so-called summit meetings. As of 2010, these summits will be staged in a new wing of the **Résidence Palace** (see below).

Ministers' meetings will continue to take place in the **Justus Lipsius building** (175 rue de Loi; see p79), also housing the 3,000-strong Council secretariat.

Although the above meetings are closed to the public, each institution arranges group tours for ten people, bookable three months in advance. Contact www.europa.eu for details. Tours also take place on open day, the nearest Saturday to May 9, Europe Day.

The **European Parliament** (pictured) brings a measure of democratic control and accountability to the other institutions. It is the only EU institution to debate in public. Visits here last between one and three hours, including a general introduction, and are at 10am and 3pm Mon-Thur, 10am Fri. Contact the Parliament Visitors' Service (02 284 34 57) for details. The EP's 732 members directly represent EU citizens, and elections are held every five years. MEPs divide their time between their home country and the parliament offices in Brussels and Strasbourg. The Brussels building (rue Wiertz) is where they hold political group meetings and committee meetings – most plenary sessions take place in Strasbourg. Originally given just a consultative role, the parliament now holds co-legislative powers with the Council of Ministers in many areas.

Brussels is also the home of the **Economic and Social Committee** (2 rue Ravenstein) and the **Committee of the Regions** (92-102 rue Montoyer), the consultative assemblies that represent the unions and business, and local and regional authorities.

---

the back of the **Résidence Palace**, a superb honey-brick art deco block built originally as an apartment complex in the 1920s, complete with a pool, theatre and roof garden. It was later the Nazi administrative headquarters. It now houses the International Press Centre, and Europe's largest press pack. A new, yet-to-be-built wing – the subject of an ongoing architectural competition – will stage EU summits from 2010: see above **Inside the EU**.

Circling south of Parc Léopold then following the train tracks north brings you to the busy **place du Luxembourg** and the old Luxembourg railway station booking hall. The station became a key chapter in the saga of resistance to development when squatters moved in to protest its demolition. To no avail: the bulldozers have since moved in, wiping

away the old billiard room and the waiting room and with them a cherished piece of urban history. The remaining booking hall looks like a bad tooth, although there are plans to scrub it up as a Euro-info centre. Plans are also in place for a possible Museum of Europe on the site. Meanwhile the square itself has kept much of its old charm, though the cafés and restaurants lining it are of the bland, universal type to meet the needs of their Eurocrat punters.

North of place du Luxembourg are two major roads, rue Belliard and rue de la Loi. Scoot over them and through the area beside Maelbeek metro station, known as the Maelbeek valley (the Maelbeek is a tributary of the River Senne). Currently a wasteland, the locality is set for regeneration: see p27 **Brussels tomorrow**. Running parallel to rue de la Loi is the more

pleasant rue Joseph II with rows of terraced townhouses punctuated by the odd ugly office building. Near its Petit Ring end is the **Musée Charlier** (*see p82*), home to a rather unusual collection of art and furniture.

Back east along **rue du Marteau** – a charming street full of eclectic architectural styles – is **square Marie-Louise**. It has a fanciful pond frequented by waterfowl and is flanked on two sides by rows of charming fin-de-siècle houses, each one tall and narrow but otherwise unique. East again, along avenue Palmerston (named after the British PM, who early in his political career had been a supporter of independence for Belgium; a blue plaque marks where he lived), is **square Ambiorix**, its grassy expanse surrounded by lovely art nouveau houses. To the south, rue Archimède is alive with restaurants (*see p121* **Little Italy**); to the north-east slopes **rue des Confédérés** where WH Auden spent five months in 1938 'bathing and café-crawling': *see p83* **Auden and Isherwood's Brussels**.

Institut Royal des Sciences Naturelles

29 rue Vautier (02 627 42 38/www.naturalsciences. be). Métro Trône/bus 34, 80. **Open** 9.30am-4.45pm Tue-Fri; 10am-6pm Sat, Sun. **Admission** €4; €3 concessions; free under-5s and after 1pm 1st Wed of mth. **Credit** MC, V. **Map** p322 F5.

The Royal Natural History Museum contains one of the world's finest collections of iguanodons as well as a deep-sea diving vessel that plunges down to see a scrap between a sperm whale and a giant squid. These now vie for visitors' attention with the sumptuous new Arctic and Antarctica Room.

Under lock and key – the **Pavillon Horta**.

Musée Charlier

16 avenue des Arts (02 218 53 82/www.musee-charlier-museum.be). Métro Arts-Loi or Madou/bus 29, 63, 65, 66. **Open** noon-5pm Tue-Sat. **Admission** €5. **No credit cards. Map** p320 E3.

Guillaume Charlier was an active figure in Brussels in the early 1900s, when he was taken under the wing of Henri van Cutsem, a patron of the arts. Charlier moved into van Cutsem's house, the site of the museum, where he hosted concerts and salon discussions. The house, whose interior was redesigned by Horta, is filled with tapestries, furniture and works by Ensor, Meunier and Charlier himself.

Musée Wiertz

62 rue Vautier (02 648 17 18/www.fine-arts-museum.be). Métro Trône/bus 34, 59, 80. **Open** 10am-noon, 1-5pm Tue-Fri and every 2nd Sat & Sun. **Admission** free. **No credit cards. Map** p322 F5.

Antoine Wiertz (1806-65) painted vast canvases of the most gruesome subjects: biblical and mythical scenes with gratuitous violence thrown in. Well regarded in his time (not least by himself – he put his own work on a par with that of Michelangelo and Rubens), Wiertz persuaded the state to buy him this house and studio in return for inheriting his works when he died. The museum contains 160 works and makes for an unusual, if not bizarre diversion. These days most locals only know Wiertz as the name of the road that runs between the parliament buildings.

Parc du Cinquantenaire

Map p323

If it's overblown and neo-classical in Brussels, it's probably the work of Léopold II. The king had 300 labourers working day and night to complete the massive **Arc de Triomphe** that stands at the centre of the largest, most impressive and best-known of the Brussels city parks. The overdrive was an attempt to meet the deadline of Belgium's 50th anniversary, celebrated in 1880. In the event, construction was not completed in time and the Arc had to be substituted by a wooden stand-in for official ceremonies. It was only completed in 1910, a year after Léopold's death. Hugely impressive in scale, it is a monument that singularly fails to stir the emotions – a reflection perhaps of Léopold's own failed ambitions of glory.

Either side of the central Arc grand colonnades front wings that house three very different museums. The northern wing is home to the **Musée Royal de l'Armée et d'Histoire Militaire** (*see p83*), which provides an enjoyable retro journey for military buffs; the southern wing is shared by **Autoworld** (*see p83*), which is one of the world's most prestigious collections of motor vehicles, and the **Musées Royaux d'Art et d'Histoire** (*see p83*), which represents one of the world's largest collections of antiquities.

In the north-west corner of the park, the unexpectedly neo-classical and austere **Pavillon Horta** is an early piece (1889) by the architect who was later to become synonymous with art nouveau in Brussels. The real interest, however, is inside with Jef Lambeaux's luxuriant reliefs *Les Passions Humaines*. Unfortunately, for reasons of economy the pavilion is kept locked. On the south side of the park, on avenue des Nerviens, is the **Centre** d'art contemporain (see p182), devoted to modern Wallonian art, while nearby, on rue des Francs, is the **Maison de Cauchie**, art nouveau home of painter Paul Cauchie.

Also on the east side of the park, built by Léopold II to link it with his African Museum at the other end, the avenue de Tervueren begins its long run out of the city flanked by impressive fin-de-siècle houses. Ahead stands a statue of Field Marshal Montgomery calmly observing the square that bears his name; pick up the No.44 tram to **Tervuren** (see p102) here.

Autoworld

11 parc du Cinquantenaire (02 736 41 65/www. autoworld.be). Métro Mérode or Schuman/bus 22, 27, 80. **Open** *Apr-Oct* 10am-6pm daily. *Nov-Mar* 10am-5pm daily. **Admission** €5; €2-€3.70 concessions. **No credit cards. Map** p323 H4.
The venue for Belgium's motor show since 1902 (!), this is one of the most extensive auto museums in Europe. Starting from 1886, it traces the development of the car through myriad incarnations.

Maison de Cauchie

5 rue des Francs (02 673 15 06). Métro Mérode/bus 22, 27, 80. **Open** 11am-1pm, 2-6pm 1st weekend of mth and by appointment. **Admission** €4. **No credit cards. Map** p323 H5.
Entirely refurbished in 2001, the former home of painter and architect Paul Cauchie was built in 1905 in the twilight of Brussels' art nouveau period. It shows the influence of the Vienna Secession with it geometric shapes – the guilded mural of the lovely maidens in long gowns is slightly reminiscent of Gustav Klimt and was designed to be an advertisement of Cauchie's art.

Musée Royal de l'Armée et d'Histoire Militaire

3 parc du Cinquantenaire (02 737 78 11/www.klm-mra.be). Métro Mérode or Schuman/bus 22, 27, 80. **Open** 9am-4.45pm Tue-Sun. **Admission** free. **No credit cards. Map** p323 H4.
A recent revamp has added a new department covering international conflict from 1918 to the present day – The European Forum on Contemporary Conflicts – interlinked with counterpart museums in Berlin and Russia. The display of the 1830 Belgian uprising and the hangar filled with aircraft from two world wars are also particularly striking.

Musées Royaux d'Art et d'Histoire

10 parc du Cinquantenaire (02 741 72 11/www. kmkg-mrah.be). Métro Mérode or Schuman/bus 22, 27, 80. **Open** 9.30am-5pm Tue-Fri; 10am-5pm Sat, Sun. **Admission** €4; €3 concessions; free 1st Wed of mth. **Credit** V. **Map** p323 H5.
The antiquity department has a huge collection of artefacts from the ancient worlds of Egypt, Greece, the Near and Far East, and pre-Columbian America. Other collections include European art from the Middle Ages, art deco glass and metalwork, lace and 18th-century carriages.

Auden and Isherwood's Brussels

In 1938, poet WH Auden lived in Brussels for half a year. He stayed at two addresses in what is now the EU Quarter: 83 rue des Confédérés and then 70 square Marie-Louise. He wrote a raft of poems during his stay, including 'Brussels in Winter' and 'Gare du Midi'. One of his most famous works, 'Musée des Beaux-Arts', was inspired by a visit to the museum of the same name, where he saw Bruegel's *Landscape with the Fall of Icarus*.

Although the poem is about the mundanity of tragedy, Auden had a fairly uneventful stay in the Belgian capital – apart from a dose of the clap picked up from a local boyfriend he called 'Petit Jacques'.

The same cannot be said of his friend, the novelist and playwright Christopher Isherwood. Isherwood is usually associated with Berlin but in the late 1930s, he lived in Brussels on four separate occasions. While in Berlin, he had fallen in love with a 17-year-old German, Heinz Neddermeyer. When Hitler introduced conscription in 1935, the two fled.

A colleague suggested buying Belgian nationality for Heinz and so the two set off on a merry dance around Europe trying to obtain the necessary paperwork. When in Brussels Isherwood and Heinz stayed at a second-floor apartment at 22 boulevard Adolphe Max, where their doddery landlady slept in the kitchen. But Heinz still hadn't got the requisite documents. In a bid to resolve the issue, Heinz travelled to meet a lawyer at a Belgian consulate over the German border; there he was arrested by Gestapo agents as a draft-evader and sentenced to six months' imprisonment, a year of hard labour and two years in the army. Isherwood was condemned in absentia for 'reciprocal onanism'.

Two years after this drama, Auden moved to Brussels. Isherwood joined him at his square Marie-Louise residence. With war looming, the two decided to leave Europe altogether. On 18 January 1939, Auden and Isherwood left Brussels, returned to England, and boarded a ship bound for New York.

Sightseeing

Ixelles & St-Gilles

Brussels at its diverse best.

Local cheer around friendly **St-Gilles**.

Sightseeing

Ixelles and St-Gilles summarise the diversity of Brussels in a way that other *communes* can't. Each offers the cachet of upmarket inner-city living, a robust restaurant and nightlife scene, glitzy shopping and tree-lined avenues and parks. Then come the contrasts. The African quarter in Ixelles, the Matongé, has a buzz of its own that's a far cry from the glitzy boutiques just a short wander away. *See p87* **African Brussels**. St-Gilles, which is home to some of the city's most stunning architecture and best addresses, has thriving North African and Spanish communities. These contrasts mean that both areas open a wide window into what living in Brussels is really about.

Ixelles

Maps p319, p322, p324 & p325

The Bois de la Cambre is Brussels' answer to Central Park. It's a vast wooded parkland on the edge of the city centre that was originally part of the wild and greater Fôret de Soignes. In 1859 construction began on a grand, broad avenue – the avenue de la Cambre – giving the citizens in the centre of town easy access to the wide, open, green spaces beyond. In 1864 Léopold II decreed that the new avenue should be named after his eldest daughter, Louise. Around avenue Louise grew Ixelles.

Beginning at **place Louise** on the Petit Ring (the Palais de Justice behind you), the top end of the imperial avenue has human proportions. Top-notch shops and galleries line each side, although the portentously named **Galeries de la Toison d'Or** (Golden Fleece Galleries) are more of a mixed bag with everyday shops nestling in amongst the jewellery and fake fur. Two small pedestrianised streets, **rue Jordan** and **rue Jean Stas** are full of small restaurants, mainly Italian and seafood, and in the summer the terrace tables are packed with chattering shoppers.

As soon as you reach **place Stéphanie** (the younger sister of Louise, married to Crown Prince Rudolf, who was later found dead with his mistress at Mayerling) the reality of the avenue hits home: there are double-lane highways on each side of a central tree-lined reservation, itself squatted by tram tracks. Scale and traffic render the pedestrian insignificant – and don't even think about trying to cross the road.

By far the best way to experience avenue Louise is by tram; any one will take you from place Stéphanie right down to the Bois. Along the way keep a look out for the Horta-designed **Hôtel Solvay** at No.224, built for the son of an industrialist: *see p31* **Brussels walks**. The 33-year-old Horta was given free rein to produce a work of fluid, intricate, symmetrical lines, with gigantic windows and imaginative use of stone. At **No.453** what is now a high-rent apartment block was the Brussels HQ of the Gestapo in the war. The worst of atrocities took place in its cellars until in January 1943 Belgian pilot Jean De Selys Longchamps, flying with the RAF, detached himself from his squadron and flew his plane directly into the building. There's a small memorial to him opposite the building.

It's worth hopping off the tram halfway down Louise, where down a sidestreet off to the east is the **Fondation pour l'Architecture** (*see p89*), a centre for architecture, urban planning and landscape gardening, whose own bookshop features models of local buildings. Opposite you'll find the **Musée d'Archives d'Architecture Moderne** (86 rue de l'Ermitage, 02 649 86 65), an old Masonic lodge with exhibitions of neglected local architects.

At almost the same point on Louise but west of the avenue, just a short stride down rue du Châtelain is **place du Châtelain**, ringed with trendy but affordable restaurants and managing to maintain a neighbourhood feel despite throngs of bright young things turning up for its buzzy nightlife. There's an excellent **food market** on the square every Wednesday afternoon. **Rue du Page**, which runs south-west off Châtelain, has some of Brussels' most enduring restaurants, while the small square of **parvis de la Trinité**, north-west of Châtelain, is an assemblage of graceful houses around a lovely church, which looks as if it might belong somewhere in Latin America.

Further south, after avenue Louise makes a slight swing to the right to home in on the Bois de la Cambre, one block west on rue de

Hidden Brussels Audrey Hepburn

A plaque on a grimy Ixelles townhouse facing a cheap hotel is testament to the unlikely linkage of inner-city Brussels to Gigi, Eliza Doolittle and Holly Golightly. Here, on 4 May 1929, in rue Keyenveld, Audrey Hepburn was born. (A rue Audrey Hepburn in Jette, in furthest north-west Brussels, was named shortly before her death.)

She had a curious parentage – even her exact christened name(s) are a matter of dispute, although Audrey is generally agreed to be her Christian name. Her father was Joseph Anthony Hepburn-Ruston, an Anglo-Irish banker, and her mother was divorced Dutch baroness Ella van Heemstra, whose family sold their ancestral home to the former German kaiser. Her parents had attended Nazi rallies during the 1930s, and after their daughter was born, Hepburn-Ruston began spending more time in London with Hitler sympathisers running a pro-Nazi news agency.

After Ella discovered him in bed with little Audrey's nanny in 1935, he left for good, leaving no forwarding address. It was a moment Audrey called the most traumatic in her life: 'I was destroyed,' she said, 'and cried for days and days. I worshipped my father and I missed him terribly from the day he disappeared.'

Her father was later imprisoned in Britain for his Nazi sympathies. What actually happened to him during that time is not clear, possibly because British records relating to wartime internment without charge or trial were destroyed. Insecurity would haunt Audrey throughout her adult life.

After her mother took her to the Dutch city of Arnhem, the Nazis invaded. Audrey acted as courier and performed in underground concerts to raise funds for the local Dutch Resistance. She worked as a nurse at a hospital which took in wounded during the battle that would later be re-enacted in the film *A Bridge Too Far*, and she later refused a role in *The Diary of Anne Frank* because of the grief she saw in Arnhem.

After the war, Audrey went to a London ballet school, before going on to model and getting bit parts in British films. In 1953, an Oscar-winning performance with Gregory Peck in *Roman Holiday* shot her to world fame.

She died 40 years later, after a glittering career in film and charity work for UNICEF. After two failed marriages, her constant companion in later years was Robert Wolders, a Dutch actor who had lived through similarly traumatic experiences while growing up in Holland through World War II.

Market at **place du Châtelain**. *See p85.*

l'Abbaye is the **Musée Constantin Meunier** (*see p89*), with more than a quarter of the artist's prolific output, while a small garden to the east is home to the **Abbaye de la Cambre** (*see p89*), which dates back to the 12th century. The Bois de la Cambre itself is described in the **Green Brussels** chapter: *see pp101-3.*

CHAUSSEE D'IXELLES

For a grittier take on Ixelles make your way east from avenue Louise to Porte de Namur (one stop on the metro) where the twin chaussées of Wavre and Ixelles fan out. Between the two, spreads the Matongé, a predominantly Congolese area, but there are also Indians and North Africans, and the quarter's colourful shops and cafés are a welcome change from the blandness of avenue Louise. *See p87* **African Brussels**. At the centre are **rue Longue Vie** and **rue de la Paix**, the former a gaudy, paved strip lined with bars and restaurants that gradually become more upmarket the closer you get to **place St-Boniface**. A centre for classy nightlife, the square is somewhat incongruously signposted by the blackened, sinister, turreted church of St-Boniface.

Further south, halfway down chaussée d'Ixelles, the uneven square of **place Fernand Cocq** is an attractive evening option, with half a dozen lively bars. In summer, when customers sip their drinks outside, the square mutates into a Mediterranean terrace, looked over by the Riviera-styled **Maison Communale** at the far end. Surrounded by gardens, this large, pleasant building belonged to the violinist Bériot and his Spanish wife, the famed and exalted singer La Malibrán, who bought the house as a monument to their newly-wed love.

As it slowly meanders southwards, chaussée d'Ixelles becomes sparse and dark, dotted with the occasional bar or low-range retail name. There is one notable bright spot, just off the chaussée up steep rue Van Volsem, and that's the **Musée Communal d'Ixelles** (*see p89*), an art museum in a former abattoir which is renowned for the quality of its exhibitions.

The chaussée ends at the **Etangs d'Ixelles** (Ixelles Ponds), pretty in spring and summer with ducks and fishermen. It's not quite the tranquil locale that it once was though, not since the rebirth of **Flagey** (*see p88* **All aboard!**). When it was completed in 1938 the ocean-liner-profiled building was the world's most advanced communications centre. Its moment passed however, and the place fell into disrepair. It was quite literally left to rot through most of the 1990s. Its recent revival as a studio, concert venue (*see p189*), cinema (*see p178*) and stylish bar, **Café Belga** (*see p138*), has brought thousands down to this once dark, forgotten corner of Ixelles. Talk of a new happening quarter, however, is premature – in true Belgian style, the reopening has coincided with major roadworks all round the square, which is being dug up for major repairs to the flood-prevention system. A quiet drink on the Belga terrace, or feeding the ducks at the lake, will be accompanied by loud drilling until 2005.

Near the southern end of the ponds is the wonderful and intelligent **Musée des Enfants** (*see p172*). The guiding principle here is hands-on. There are art and puppet workshops, and the activities are completely revamped every three years so that children don't tire of the place. But be aware that labelling is in French and Dutch only. East of here is the bilingual university, the French side being the ULB and the Flemish the VUB. They are both enclosed by boulevard du Triomphe within a pleasant campus. This is a lively area, with a swathe of bars and restaurants along the chaussée de Boondael, between the university and the Abbaye de la Cambre, particularly near Ixelles cemetery. **Le Tavernier** (*see p141*) is a fine example of bar guru Fred Nicolay (*see p139* **Right said Fred**) being able to site the right place at the right time.

Further south extend the leafy expanses of Watermael-Boitsfort and the Forêt de Soignes: *see pp101-3* **Green Brussels**.

African Brussels

Brussels has no Chinatown or Slav-style Brighton Beach but it does boast a winningly vibrant bit of Africa. Known as the Matongé, it takes its name from an area of Kinshasa in the Congo and sits between chaussée d'Ixelles and rue de Trône. It's a mix of bright colours and gentle decay far removed from the bland glitz of nearby avenue Louise.

This Africanisation of Ixelles began in the early 1960s, when a wave of students came to Brussels after the independence of the former Belgian Congo. Congolese intellectuals gathered in clubs such as the Les Anges Noirs and bars around Porte de Namur métro. This became the jump-off point for the Matongé.

These days the epicentre of the Matongé is the **Galerie d'Ixelles**, the arcade that links chaussées de Wavre and d'Ixelles. The gallery's two sides take their names from Kinshasa's two main streets of Inzia and Kanda-Kanda: Inzia is filled with snack bars; Kanda-Kanda with hair-product shops. Packed hairdressers double as social centres. African fashion boutiques peddle opulent *bazin* (wraps).

Shipping agents bundle up boxes destined for the homeland. Wanly lit grocers sell foodstuffs that more than justify their *produits exotiques* tag: 'Makelele,' says one shopkeeper, holding up a dried grasshopper, 'African caviar!'

Also here is **Musicanova**, one of Europe's best-known African music shops and record labels. Outside, locals wash down fiery chicken piri-piri and *chikwangue* (chewy yam dumplings) with giant bottles of Jupiler beer.

Busy by day, the Matongé really comes to life at night. The main drag is **rue Longue Vie**, a pedestrianised section of street between chaussée de Wavre, and rue de la Paix, crammed full of raucous bars and restaurants. Most are Central African, interspersed with a few Portuguese and Indian. All offer chilled beers, spicy meats and most open late. Grilled gazelle or *ndole* (meat-and-dried-fish stew) are served in places on rue Francart, named simply after their owners: Chez Mère Rose, Chez Ida.

More mainstream fare is on offer at nearby **L'Horloge du Sud** (*see p139*), an easy introduction to African cuisine and music.

All aboard!

Now simply 'Flagey' after the eponymous square it faces, the Institut National de Radiodiffusion (*pictured*), or INR, was designed in the 1930s by Joseph Diongre and soon became the flagship of Belgian media. 'Flagship' is the appropriate term, as the distinctive round tower jutting above the roof gave the INR its nickname: *Le Paquebot*, or 'steamship'.

Behind the fancy art deco façade was some serious engineering. The largest of its broadcasting and concert halls, Studio 4, could seat over 300 and accommodate the largest symphony orchestras. A grand piano could be rolled on and off stage on its own section of podium. The microphones were mounted on movable ceiling tracks (thus keeping them out of the musicians' way). Heavy double doors and partitions blocked the cobblestone rumble of trams and traffic outside. The acoustics were simply world class.

Le Paquebot contained a superb 80-seat concert hall (Studio 1) for chamber formations, whose octagonal columns could be easily rotated for reflective or absorbant surfaces, according to the type of ensemble. A cafeteria overlooked the Ixelles ponds and on the square, L'Antenne and Le Concerto cafés thrived on the mini industry the INR generated.

When national radio expanded into television, bigger quarters were required. The new RTB-BRT building on boulevard Reyers was built in distant Schaerbeek to meet demand. With the move of administrators and technicians to Reyers, the musicians (now split down linguistic lines) had Le Paquebot to themselves.

In the 1990s, dangerous levels of asbestos were discovered in the building, just as a budgetary crisis made repairs impossible. The musicians were ejected and the building put up for sale. As no buyers were forthcoming, Le Paquebot was left to sink.

Finally, a private consortium bought the tatty building for a fraction of the original asking price and began the long process of remodelling and restoration. In addition to refurbishing the main studios and the façade – historic landmarks – the consortium has also broadened Flagey's appeal: there's now a **cinema** (*see p178*) in the old Studio 5, and enough studio space elsewhere to stage festivals such as classical's **Ars Musica** (*see p166*) and major film seasons (*see p176*). On the ground floor is now the spacious **Café Belga** (*see p138*) with a cool buzz until 2am; next door, Le Varietés restaurant offers quality fare until midnight.

With the major repair to underground flood defences turning the square outside into a huge building site for the foreseeable future, it is too early to see whether the relaunch of Le Paquebot will pull its neighbourhood along with it – what is clear, though, is that Brussels has a most dynamic contemporary arts centre in the former gloomy wasteland of southern Ixelles.

Abbaye de la Cambre

*11 avenue Emile Duray (02 648 11 21). Tram 23,
90, 93, 94/bus 71.* **Open** 9am-noon, 3-6pm Mon-Fri,
Sun; 3-6pm Sat. **Admission** free. **No credit cards.**
Map p325 E/F9.

Founded in the 12th century by the noble Gisèle for
the Cîteaux Order, the abbey was badly damaged
during the Wars of Religion and was rebuilt in the
16th and 18th centuries, although the 14th-century
church attached to the abbey survives. It's all set in
elegant French gardens, alongside the National
Geographical Institute and an exhibition centre.

Fondation pour l'Architecture

*55 rue de l'Ermitage (02 642 24 80/www.
fondationpourlarchitecture.be). Tram 81, 82, 93, 94/
bus 38, 54, 60.* **Open** noon-6pm Tue, Thur-Sun;
noon-9pm Wed. **Admission** €6; €5 concessions. **No
credit cards. Map** p319 D7.

This converted pumping house should be the first
port of call for anyone interested in Brussels' architectural heritage. Exhibitions are varied and well put
together, with models, photos, videos and furniture,
and there is a first-class bookshop too.

Musée Communal d'Ixelles

*71 rue Van Volsem, Ixelles (02 515 64 21/www.
musee-ixelles.be). Bus 38, 54, 60, 71.* **Open** 1-6.30pm
Tue-Fri; 10am-5pm Sat, Sun. **Admission** €6.20.
Credit AmEx, DC, MC, V. **Map** p322 E6.

This excellent little museum, founded in 1892, is well
known for its exhibitions of mainly modern art. Its
permanent collection features local artists Magritte,
Delvaux, Spilliaert and Van Rysselberghe, plus original posters by Toulouse-Lautrec. Two wings blend
perfectly for a well-lit and interesting space.

Musée Constantin Meunier

*59 rue de l'Abbaye (02 648 44 49/www.fine-arts-
museum.be). Tram 93, 94/bus 38, 60.* **Open** 10am-
noon, 1-5pm Tue-Sat, every other Sun. **Admission**
free. **No credit cards. Map** p324 E8.

The home and studio of the 19th-century Belgian
sculptor and painter has more than 170 sculptures
and 120 paintings (of an output of 800), the best
known being his bronze figures of workers. Meunier
began painting religious scenes, but turned to sculpture inspired by social realism: farmers, miners and
workers heroically labour in grim surroundings.

St-Gilles

Maps p320 & p324

The neglect around the Gare du Midi aside, St-
Gilles is one of Brussels' most beautiful
residential areas. It's built on a hill that climbs
roughly north to south. As altitude increases,
the changes are subtle but significant. Terraces
of rooming houses and tacky shops slowly give
way to terraces of well-groomed, middle-class
townhouses, culminating in the magnificent
belle epoque and art nouveau mansions located
around avenue Brugmann.

A good starting point for any exploration is
the 14th-century **Porte de Hal**, down on the
Petit Ring, the sole surviving medieval gate of
the many that once studded the old city walls.
Nineteenth-century additions give it the
appearance of something fit for Cinderella,
though in reality it's more of a Sleeping Beauty.
The gate has been used as a prison, a toll booth,
a grain store and a museum, but other than
playing host to temporary exhibitions it is now
left empty most of the time. Mercifully, a tunnel
redirects traffic underground so the gate rests
in relatively peaceful gardens.

Running south from the Porte is chaussée de
Waterloo. Its lower end is uninspiring, though
the local Spanish community have peppered it
with cheap (but not necessarily cheerful)
restaurants. For the real St-Gilles, you need to
head uphill toward the main square, the **parvis
St-Gilles** which, like the neighbourhood in
general, is quiet with a contemplative air –
except for the bustling market on Sunday
mornings. This is very much a residential part
of town and if you move away from the main
thoroughfares, you are in small, quiet streets,
most with their own bars and local shops.

Further up the hill, beyond the **Barrière de
St-Gilles**, where several large avenues
converge on the charming little square and zip
off again in all directions, the richer St-Gilles
appears; the houses are truly monumental,
although the traffic and trams cutting through
their midst do detract from the grandeur.

Visible to the south of the Barrière,
occupying a commanding position at the head
of avenue Dejaer, is St-Gilles' **Hôtel de Ville**,
an impressive 19th-century building in French
Renaissance style. Designed by Albert Dumont
in 1900-04, its most arresting features are the
frescoes on the ceiling above the main staircase
and in the Marriage Room. Behind this bit of
civic monumentalism, on rue de Savoie, is the
old bar **Chez Moeder Lambic** (*p141*), worth a
visit or even a peek through the window.

St-Gilles' high point was at the end of the
19th century when a few wealthy men
commissioned fabulous art nouveau residences.
With their swirling, daring lines and elaborate
friezes, the houses appear flamboyant and
insouciant beside their more stalwart
neighbours. Most of these are to be found in the
area south of the Barrière de St-Gilles and east
of the immense Prison de St-Gilles. Most are,
sadly, closed to the public, but one striking
exception is architect Victor Horta's own house,
known as **Musée Horta** (*see p91*), at the heart
of the art nouveau area in rue Américaine.

The prison itself is remarkably harmonious
with its genteel surrounds, with fairly low walls
and bisected by pleasant avenue de la Jonction.

Espace Photographique Contretype.

At the head of the avenue, by the junction with avenue Brugmann, is the art nouveau Hôtel Hannon, built in 1902 by Jules Brunfaut. Today it functions as the **Espace Photographique Contretype** photo gallery, which is also open to the public: *see below and p182*.

The area's art nouveau heritage is more fully explored elsewhere in this guide: *see p31* **Brussels walks**.

To the west of the prison extends the easily accessible greenery of the Parc de Forest and Parc Duden: *see p101-3* **Green Brussels**.

Espace Photographique Contretype

1 avenue de la Jonction (02 538 42 20/www. contretype.org). Tram 81, 90, 92/bus 54. **Open** 11am-6pm Wed-Fri; 1-6pm Sat, Sun. **Admission** €2.50. **No credit cards**.

Jules Brunfaut built this house in art nouveau style for the industrialist Edouard Hannon, a keen amateur photographer. His photos are on display, along with other works by photographers in residence. The interior features light, lofty salons and a staircase with a vast fresco by PA Baudouin. Stripped of its original furniture, the house has the echoing impersonality of a grand showpiece studio.

Musée Horta

25 rue Américaine (02 543 04 90/www. hortamuseum.be). Tram 81, 82, 91, 92/bus 54. **Open** 2-5.30pm Tue-Sun. **Admission** €5; €3.70 concessions. **No credit cards**. **Map** p324 C7.

Horta built this house in 1899-1901 as his home and studio. The exterior is plain enough, and is nothing compared with the Hankar-designed house round the corner in rue Defacqz. This external reticence is fairly typical of an architect who was Belgian enough to want to keep his delights hidden away indoors. The interior is astonishingly light, graceful and harmonious. It was clearly designed as a place to live in; there's no attempt to dazzle, startle or disturb, as there is in other art nouveau elsewhere. The attention to detail is simply astonishing and every functional element, down to the door handles, is designed in the fluid, sensuous architectural style Horta helped create. The staircase and stairwell are particularly breathtaking: an extravaganza of wrought iron, mirrors and floral designs, topped by a stained-glass canopy. But a word of warning: the museum is quite often crowded and even Horta's wonderful staircase loses its appeal when you have to queue ten minutes to climb it. You'd be better off visiting on a weekday.

Sightseeing

Van Damme's Brussels

Jean-Claude van Damme, the Muscles from Brussels, is a product of the school of hard knocks: Ixelles. Hollywood's all-action hero, Jean-Claude Camille François van Varenberg, was a shy kid, buried deep in comic books – in particular *The Silver Surfer*. His father, a florist, ran a shop in avenue Buyl, in the same grim neighbourhood as Jean-Claude Camille's school in the chaussée de Boondael.

'I was born skinny, and I was laughed at in school. I had glasses and a lisp,' admits the man who today can crack walnuts between his buttocks. When he was 12, his father took him to the nearest karate school.

'He was weak, short and wore glasses,' says Claude Goetz, his karate teacher, a burly man in his sixties who now runs the **Golden Club** gym in place du Châtelain (*see p206*). 'But he was keen to learn.' Goetz put the boy onto a rigorous regime that set him on his way to a pumped-up physique.

But van Damme wasn't all muscle. While working at the florists', the teenager noticed an older woman who ran a ballet school in town; he enrolled. Her name was Monette Loza, and she had appeared on French TV with Jacques Brel. 'I had no idea Jean-Claude was the van Varenbergs' boy', recalls Loza. 'But he was extraordinarily flexible. I thought to myself: "At last! Someone I can make into a dancer." "I don't want to be a dancer," he told me, "I want to make lots of money."

'Jean-Claude would come to my class, then head off to the gym,' remembers Loza. The determined van Varenbergs' boy was also in love with his ballet teacher. 'I was 16, and she must have been 40,' says JC, 'But she was as fit as any 18 year old.'

Van Damme kept up the ballet for five years, but left school and set up his own gym in Brussels, The California. In 1981 he moved out to Los Angeles and adopted the name van Damme, after the name of the entrepreneur from whom Goetz bought the Golden Club.

In 1986, after five years of dead-end jobs, van Damme seized his moment. He spotted influential action-film producer Menahem Golan leaving a restaurant in Beverly Hills, and he aimed a 360-degree kick at him, stopping a hair's breadth from Golan's face. Golan asked him to come by the next day. The meeting led to van Damme's first hit film, and a string of others followed. The puny boy with the glasses had become a movie star.

Van Damme's career has since dipped, his last films going straight to video. He's often seen in Belgium – his fifth and most recent marriage took place on the Belgian riviera.

Anderlecht & the West

A mixed bag of attractions and canalside development.

Basilique du Sacré Coeur. *See p95.*

The grey districts of **Anderlecht**, **Jette**, **Molenbeek** and **Koekelberg** are unlikely but rewarding destinations for the adventurous visitor. Separated from the city centre by a thin strip of canal, part of this former industrial zone is soon to undergo major redevelopment. *See p94* **On the waterfront**.

In the meantime, two sights attract tourists across the water: the bizarre **Basilica** in Koekelberg and the **Musée Magritte**, set in an anonymous terraced house in Jette – his home and studio. *See p93* **Magritte's Brussels**.

Anderlecht

Enter the word 'Anderlecht' into an internet search engine and the first 30 entries refer you to RSC Anderlecht, Belgium's biggest football club (*see p205* **Purple reign**). The *commune* appears to have a modest self-image, allowing the **Vanden Stock stadium** in Parc Astrid to be its most prominent asset. Match nights bring the area to life and the football bars along avenue Théo Verbeek pack with fans.

Most days, though, Anderlecht is sombre. At its Midi end, station developments encroach on what were once grand boulevards of upper

middle-class living. Muddled streets of run-down neighbourhoods finally give way to green space, punctuated by café-lined squares such as place de la Vaillance. But this is Brussels and, even in Anderlecht, surprises abound.

Anderlecht is a rough translation of 'love of Erasmus', after the great humanist who lived here for only five months but whose influence on the Low Countries can still be felt today. The **Maison d'Erasmus** (*see p94*), where he stayed, is now a quiet sanctuary amid the daily grind of inner-city life. It was also a sanctuary for Erasmus, recuperating at Canon Pieter Wijchman's house De Swaene (the Swan), now a museum of his work. The atmosphere has changed little over the centuries, though there were plans to demolish the house in 1920.

The majority of sights in Anderlecht are near St-Guidon métro station. Leaving the station, you see the beautiful Gothic **Collégiale des Sts Pierre et Guidon** (*see p93*), gracefully aloof from the shopping arcade. Behind is the 17th-century **Béguinage de l'Anderlecht** (*see p93*), now a museum. *Béguinages* were lay sisterhoods whose members lived in religious communities, unbound by vows. Their charity work was prevalent across the Low Countries.

Back east, the seedy area towards the station is dotted with odd attractions. The local abattoir houses a crazy, tacky **market** (24 rue Ropsy Chaudron, open from 7am Fri-Sat), with anything from plastic mosque alarm clocks to cheap electronics, and mountains of melon and tomatoes. Renovation here until 2011 should not distract visitors from its bizarre charms, more akin to North Africa than Europe. Opposite, the **Brasserie La Paix** (49 rue Ropsy Chaudron, 02 523 09 58) has been serving honest Belgian fare since 1888. Nearby, on rue Gheude, is the **Musée Bruxellois de la Gueuze** (*see p94*) at the brewery of the same name.

Off rue Émile Carpentier stands the moving **Monument aux Martyrs Juifs**; on its side are the names of 23,838 men, women and children taken from the Nazi collection point in

Mechelen and sent to concentration camps between 1942 and 1944. Not one survived. Nearby, the **Musée de la Résistance** (*see p94*) illustrates some of the secret history of Belgium's World War II experience.

Béguinage de l'Anderlecht
8 rue du Chapelain (02 521 13 83). Métro St-Guidon. **Open** 10am-noon, 2-5pm Tue-Sun. **Admission** €1.25. **No credit cards**.
Founded in 1252, this convent consists of four modest 16th-century houses and a garden. The museum documents and evokes the life of the *béguinage*.

Collégiale des Sts Pierre et Guidon
Place de la Vaillance (02 523 02 20). Métro St-Guidon. **Open** 9am-noon, 2-5pm daily. *Services* 8.45am Mon-Fri; 6pm Fri; 4.30pm, 6pm Sat; 9.30am, 11am, 5pm Sun. **Admission** free.

Sightseeing

Magritte's Brussels

It is hard to imagine the cream of Belgium's famous surrealists meeting every Saturday at an astoundingly ordinary house, where their emblematic figure René Magritte lived and painted for 24 years – but here at 135 rue Esseghem, Jette, the more subversive Belgian branch of the Paris-born movement would convene. Here was, in effect, the spiritual home of surrealism.

Today a museum (*see p95*), Magritte's salon still has the same sky-blue walls and fireplace of *La Durée Poignardée* – although none of the paintings are original. This inappropriately bourgeois location of faceless terrace suburbia is fabulously Belgian, too. None of the overblown, egg-topped pseudo-monstrosity of Dalí's Figueres. For Belgians – who took to surrealism like ducks to water – preferred to disturb convention from within. René and wife Georgette led lives as quiet as their neighbours, the artist painting in his suit and bow tie, his wife and dog pottering about the garden. The downtown cafés he frequented – the **Greenwich** (*see p135*), the **Cirio** (*see p126*) and **La Fleur en Papier Doré** (*see p127*) – are quiet and sedate. All is how it should be. Or is it?

Magritte's work challenged banality. The pipe that is, in fact, a pipe. The faceless bowler-hatted man. It undermines our ideas of everyday objects. It didn't follow the dictat of André Breton's *Surrealist Manifesto* of 1924 by simply interpreting the psyche. Sure, Magritte and his friend and fellow traveller, writer and theorist (and founder of the Belgian communist party) Paul Nougé formed the

Brussels group soon after the Breton declaration, and in 1926 Magritte took Georgette to Paris, but he fell out with Breton over bourgeois attitudes. The couple returned to mundane life in mundane Jette.

And when they got a little money, where did they move to? Grey old Schaerbeek, boulevard Lambermont, then rue des Mimosas. As Magritte said in 1938, 20 years after the war whose horror on Belgian soil inspired the movement in the first place: 'Surrealism is revolutionary because it is relentlessly hostile to all those bourgeois ideological values that keep the world in the appalling condition in which it is today'.

Founded before the 10th century, the current Collegiate Church is late 15th-century Gothic. Inside, a long altar is illuminated by light filtered through the stained-glass windows; below is one of the oldest Romanesque crypts in Belgium.

Maison d'Erasmus

31 rue de Chapitre (02 521 13 83). Métro St-Guidon. **Open** 10am-noon, 2-5pm Tue-Sun. **Admission** €1.25. **No credit cards**.
The house where Erasmus stayed is a small, well-preserved, red-brick seat of learning set in a shady garden. A museum, it contains first editions of his *In Praise of Folly* and *Adages*, and letters from Charles V and Francis I. There are also his portraits by Dürer and Holbein, and a medal by Cellini.

Musée Bruxellois de la Gueuze

56 rue Gheude (02 521 49 28/www.cantillon.be). *Métro Clemenceau/pré-métro Lemonnier.* **Open** 9am-5pm Mon-Fri; 10am-5pm Sat. Last entry 4pm. **Admission** €3.50. **No credit cards**. **Map** p318 A4.

Enjoy a tasting tour around Brussels' last working brewer of Gueuze, the unusual beer fermented naturally in Anderlecht's gloomy climate.

Musée de la Résistance

14 rue van Lint (02 522 40 41). Métro Clemenceau. **Open** 9am-noon, 1-4pm Mon, Tue, Thur, Fri. **Admission** free.
Members of Belgium's resistance put together this striking collection of original documents relating to their struggle in the war years.

Jette & Koekelberg

The large, anonymous *commune* of Jette is set between the western canal districts and **Laeken** (*see p96*). Its very anonymity made it the perfect home for that most respectable and bourgeois of surrealists, René Magritte. The equally anonymous house where he lived with his wife and muse Georgette between 1930 and

On the waterfront

Situated beside the docile Willebroek Canal, Brussels' port area is dominated by factories, breweries, railway yards and industrial quays. Not much reason to go there, you might think, but that could soon change. The huge **Tour et Taxis** complex (3 rue Picard, Molenbeek, 02 420 60 69, www.tourtaxis.be), considered one of the finest industrial heritage sites in Belgium, is being carefully redeveloped to provide offices, a museum, exhibition space, new housing and perhaps even a cultural venue. The project is part of a broader development plan for the grimy canal quarter.

The iron and glass warehouses, customs sheds and marshalling yards were built in 1904 on land owned by the Tour et Taxis family, who founded Europe's first postal service in the 16th century. After the site closed down in the 1980s, ideas were put forward for the abandoned buildings (a music venue, an EU summit site, a European school) but nothing was done. Meanwhile, the abandoned buildings offered a raw post-industrial backdrop for off-beat events like the annual **Couleur Café** world music festival (*see p187* **The best Fests** *& p196*).

1954 opened as the **Musée Magritte** in 1999, and is an essential stop for anyone with more than a passing interest in the artist (*see p93* **Magritte's Brussels**). The Magrittes lived only on the ground floor (although they also used the garret; the first and second floors were occupied by others), and it has been restored to as authentic a condition as possible.

The tiny bordering commune of Koekelberg houses Brussels' most bizarre and overblown church: the **Basilique du Sacré Coeur**. The panoramic view from the dome is fantastic.

Basilique du Sacré Coeur

1 parvis de la Basilique (02 425 88 22). Métro Simonis. **Open** Church *winter* 10am-5pm daily; *summer* 8am-6pm daily. Dome *winter* 10am-4pm daily; *summer* 9am-5pm daily. **Admission** *Church* free; *dome* €3. **No credit cards**.

Commissioned by Léopold II in 1905, this vast structure, an extraordinary mix of Gothic and art deco with a lit-up cherry-coloured crucifix on top, took seven decades to finish. Inside, the honey-coloured brick enhances a clean-cut but soaring style.

Musée Magritte

135 rue Esseghem (02 428 26 26/www. magrittemuseum.be). Métro Bockstael/tram 18, 19, 81, 94. **Open** 10am-6pm Wed-Sun. **Admission** €6; €5 concessions. **No credit cards**.

Magritte's house is a fittingly bizarre monument to the artist. The window and fireplace in the front room appear in numerous Magritte paintings, but perhaps the most surprising discovery is the tiny back living room where he executed hundreds of his works, despite the lack of light due to the tall wall outside the window. Magritte built himself a studio in the garden but never used it, preferring the comfort of the house. The first and second floors are now taken up with an excellent display of letters, photos and other personal artefacts, together with a smattering of original works by Magritte and his circle.

Now there's a plan to create an entire new city neighbourhood on the site. It's being financed by property developers, which should set alarm bells ringing in Brussels, given the destruction already done by private capital. But the people behind Project T&T promise high-quality development. They've brought in the American architectural firm HOK to draw up a sensitive plan for the site, with public amenities such as a park, open-air arena and modern apartments. The success of the scheme depends on a new tram link, a bridge across the canal and other public works.

Work is already well advanced on the conversion of the huge brick and iron Entrepôt Royal warehouse into a business centre, and the massive iron and brick warehouse known as Building B has been restored as a striking exhibition centre. In early 2004 the annual Brussels Antiques Fair moved to this new venue after almost half a century at the Palais des Beaux-Arts. But any major changes elsewhere won't start happening until planning permission for the other sections has been granted, which won't be until late 2005 or 2006 at the earliest.

Sightseeing

Laeken

Leafy suburb of pleasure grounds and royal gardens.

Laeken stretches over a huge green area some distance north of the centre, divided into a royal estate and residence, and the public leisure complex of Heysel. It seems an unreal, artificial city hovering outside Brussels proper, pieced together by jigsaw designers. Each of its main sights are in themselves worthy of a visit; they just make unlikely neighbours. Here you will find the national stadium, the Atomium, theme parks, a multiplex cinema, the Royal Palace and two Léopoldine follies. It's easy to reach by metro (Heysel), or for a more interesting ride, by the 18, 23 or 81 trams. Once there, the sights are all within walking distance of each other.

The **Stade Roi Baudouin** (*see p203*) was previously the Heysel Stadium, where 39 people died in 1985 before the Liverpool vs Juventus European Cup Final, when terrace violence led to the collapse of a wall. Its cool Bob van Reeth redesign kept the original neo-classical entrance by Joseph van Neck from 1929. Next door is the immense **Parc des Expositions**. Eleven palaces were built here, the first in 1935, to mark a century of Belgian independence. The largest, the Grand Palais built by van Neck, is a classic art deco triangular composition with ever-decreasing pavilions flanking the imposing, four-columned centre building. The halls now house a constant stream of major trade fairs, detailed at www.bruexpo.be.

Directly down the boulevard du Centenaire is the iconic **Atomium** (*see below*). At 102 metres (335 feet) tall it never fails to impress by its sheer scale and size, a crystal molecule of metal magnified 165 billion times. Built for the 1958 World Fair – and certainly not meant to last 50 years – its tatty state is being addressed with a year-long overhaul from September 2004.

Close to the silver balls is the entrance to the **Bruparck** (*see p173*), an off-beat conurbation of family amusements. The complex includes **Kinopolis** (*see p178*), the original multiplex cinema with nearly 30 screens and a capacity of 7,500. There's also **Océade** (*see p173*), a water park with a tropical theme, but the most kitsch, yet irresistible, attraction is **Mini-Europe**. Here exact copies of famous landmarks are laid out in a park to a scale of 1:25. So expect the Houses of Parliament, the Acropolis, the Eiffel Tower and a rather good mock-up of the Grand' Place. Kids seem to like launching an Ariane rocket, watching a TGV train fly into a tunnel

or seeing Vesuvius bubble over. Around it all is the Village, an uninspiring name for an uninspiring set of kit-built gable houses with the usual fast food restaurants and shops.

For something more subtle, more peaceful, more entrenched in real history, walk south to the lovely **Parc du Laeken**. Its centrepiece is the **Château Royal**, the residence of the Belgian royal family. Built in 1782-84 for the Austrian governor-general, it was originally called Schoonberg, but after the arrival of the French in 1794, it lost its name and family. It lay abandoned until Napoleon decided he'd like it; it was here that he planned the catastrophic invasion of Russia. Eventually, he did a deal with Josephine and swapped Laeken for the Elysée Palace in Paris. Now it is very much a private residence, and unlike the **Palais Royal** in town (*see p76*), this palace is not open to the public. However the magnificent **Serres Royales** – the Royal Greenhouses – do open at certain times each year (*see p168*). Try to visit at night when they are lit up by spotlights. The the **TIB** tourist office (*see p301*) has details.

Also in the park are a couple of royal follies, whims of King Léopold II after he visited the 1900 Paris Exhibition and saw two oriental buildings he'd like in his own back garden. The **Tour Japonaise** (*see p97*) is a five-level red tower which holds temporary exhibitions, but is interesting enough at any time. Across avenue Jules van Praet, the **Pavillon Chinois** (*see p97*) is another curiosity with oriental ceramics.

Ten minutes' walk from the Château Royal is **Notre Dame de Laeken** (*see p97*), the burial place of Belgium's royals. Viewing is restricted.

Atomium

Boulevard du Centenaire (02 475 47 77/www. atomium.be). Métro Heysel/tram 23, 81. **Open** *Apr-Aug* 9am-7pm daily. *Sept-Mar* 10am-5.30pm daily. **Closed** Sept 2004-Sept 2005. **Admission** €6; €3 concessions. Combined ticket to Bruparck, see website. **Credit** AmEx, DC, MC, V. **Map** p326 B2.
Designed by André Waterkeyn for the 1958 World Fair, this iconic structure has a classic Flash Gordon look about it, giving it a retro appeal for modern times. Sadly, its interior has been decaying for decades, with tired exhibits and an abandoned 1950s café with an out-of-season seaside feel. This is about to change. Dynamic new curator Diane Hennebert – responsible for recent shows of 1950s memorabilia here – has negotiated a €24 million

Extravagant Léopoldine folly at the **Tour Japonaise**.

renovation between the state, Brussels City and the owners to do up the old molecule. Closed from September 2004 to September 2005, the new Atomium will have interactive exhibitions, a visitors' centre and a complete inside-out spruce-up – plus a trendy restaurant at the top.

Notre Dame de Laeken

Parvis Notre Dame (02 478 20 95). Métro Bockstael/ tram 81, 94/bus 53. **Open** 2-5pm Tue-Sun. **Admission** free. **Map** p326 E3.

Although opening times are restricted, the huge, neo-Gothic exterior, designed by Poelaert in 1851, is worth a wander. Look out for the 13th-century Madonna on the altar. In the cemetery are tombs of important Belgians – including Poelaert himself – and a cast of Rodin's sculpture *The Thinker*. There is also a mosque and an Egyptian temple.

Pavillon Chinois

44 avenue Jules van Praet (02 268 16 08/www. kmkg-mrah.be). Tram 23, 52. **Open** 9.30am-5pm Tue-Fri; 10am-5pm Sat, Sun. **Admission** €2; €3 combined tour with Tour Japonaise. **No credit cards. Map** p326 D1.

Built as a restaurant for Léopold II, then left to its own devices for years, the Chinese Pavilion is now home to a collection of fine Chinese porcelain.

Serres Royales

61 avenue du Parc Royal (02 513 89 40). Métro Heysel. **Open** May. **Admission** €2; free under-18s. **No credit cards. Map** p326 D1.

This sequence of 11 linked greenhouses was built on the orders of Léopold II by Balat and the young Victor Horta in the 1870s. They are soaring edifices of the time, all iron and glass, a cathedral to botany. Léopold moved into one on his deathbed, and other royals have set up writing desks and seating areas. They are usually open to the public in May – contact the tourist office (*see p301*).

Tour Japonaise

44 avenue Jules van Praet (02 268 16 08/www. kmkg-mrah.be). Tram 23, 52. **Open** 9.30am-5pm Tue-Fri; 10am-5pm Sat, Sun. **Admission** €2; €3 combined tour with Pavillon Chinois. **No credit cards. Map** p326 D1.

This mock pagoda, set around Japanese gardens, houses temporary Japanese exhibitions.

Schaerbeek & St-Josse

Peeling grandeur and ethnic charm.

The **Halles de Schaerbeek**.
See p99.

The huge grey expanse of **Schaerbeek** stretches across northern Brussels, its southern edge bordering the tiny *commune* of **St-Josse**, which hugs the north-east portion of the Petit Ring. Apart from a few sights, neither are on the tourist trail, but each has its own attractions.

Schaerbeek

Before the construction of the Gare du Nord in 1841, Schaerbeek was a bucolic idyll of cherry orchards, family-run bakeries and breweries. The commune grew with the new Belgian state. At independence in 1830 there were 1,600 people living here; by 1900 there were 65,000, travelling to work in trams rattling down busy boulevards, past grand houses, many built in art nouveau style for the new bourgeoisie. Such grandeur had faded by the time the prodigal son of Schaerbeek, *chanteur* **Jacques Brel** (*see p100* **Brel's Brussels**) grew up here.

Modern times left Schaerbeek behind. In the area to the west of rue Royale, around the Gare du Nord, drab sex shops are being replaced by Moroccan stores selling halal meat, miniature indoor waterfalls and suitcases. Chaussée de

Haecht is the place to find Turkish bakeries, Muslim butchers and cafés filled with Turkish football flags. Without a metro station, Schaerbeek is a visibly poor commune – bad street lighting, erratic refuse collection and no glamorous shops – but don't let that put you off. Renowned cartoonist François Schuiten, who has lived in Schaerbeek all his life and used its peeling grandeur as inspiration for epic urban comic tales such as his seminal *Brüsel* (*see p36* **Brave new world**), has been occupied with renovating the commune's most treasured art nouveau legacy: the **Maison Autrique** (266 chaussée de Haecht), Victor Horta's first design commission. Persuading the local authorities to buy this 1893 gem, and collaborating with his co-author Benoît Peeters, he intends to turn it into an imaginative exploration of the city's past. It's a typical three-storey Brussels townhouse, known as an *enfilade*: tall, narrow and four rooms deep. Behind a white stone façade, its sober domesticity is enlivened by characteristic details like the carved wooden staircase and the swirling mosaics on the ground floor. The Schuiten and Peeters revamp,

Sightseeing

due to open in summer 2004 and known as the **Maison Imaginaire**, is half-museum and half-theatrical *mise-en-scène*. Visitors will walk through nine rooms, from the laundry to the attic, experiencing local life the way it was a hundred years ago.

The street itself is the spine of Schaerbeek, all built on a rather grandiose scale, with long avenues sweeping down to monumental buildings and churches overlooking the city. Branching off from the rue Royale, the royal route leading past the palaces of the Upper Town down to the jaws of the Palais de Justice, chaussée de Haecht links the local landmarks of the churches of **Ste-Marie** and **St-Servais**, the **Halles de Schaerbeek** and the **Hôtel Communal** in place Colignon.

Place Colignon was constructed around the Hôtel, its houses equally grand with gables, turrets and flagpoles. The Hôtel itself was inaugurated in 1887 by Léopold II. Damaged by fire at the beginning of the century, the Flemish renaissance-style building is constructed from red brick, with numerous towers and windows. Down rue Royale Ste-Marie from the square is the large, beautiful and decaying church of **St-Servais**. It holds services in Spanish and Italian, and has a commanding view over avenue Louis Bertrand. This formerly grand boulevard leads east to pretty Parc Josaphat. Here you'll find ponds, an animal reserve, a sculpture museum, various sporting facilities and free concerts on summer Sundays.

Near St-Servais stand the **Halles de Schaerbeek**. (*See also p193 and p214*.) A rare example of 19th-century industrial architecture, the Halles (there is a Grande and Petite Halle) are another recent example of a Brussels renovation success story. Millions were spent on converting this former market into a fully functioning theatre and concert hall. Opened in 1865, burned down in 1898, they were rebuilt according to the original design – 2004 marks the 30th anniversary of their reconstruction and a handful of modest events are planned.

Beside the Halles, dominating the northern end of the rue Royale, the church of **Ste-Marie** is a neo-Byzantine mosque-like building, arched and curvaceous, with an octagonal dome. It marks the border with the commune of St-Josse.

St-Josse

Almost completely North African and Turkish in character, St-Josse is full of fruit shops and tiny ethnic eateries. Situated near the Petit Ring, its main attractions are an easy hop from the city centre: the art nouveau restaurant **De Ultieme Hallucinatie** (*see p124*) and further down rue Royale, the **Botanique** (*see p167 and p192*), an inspired mixture of neo-classicism, glass and iron, built in 1826. Formerly the city's greenhouse, it is now the cultural centre for the francophone community – with a cinema, theatre and exhibition halls – which maintains a hothouse atmosphere.

Hidden Brussels Edith Cavell

It was one of World War I's most heroic episodes, but far away from the trenches of Flanders. In Brussels, British nurse Edith Cavell organised the escape of over 100 British soldiers, and young Belgians and French – and paid for it with her life.

Born in Norfolk in 1865, Cavell went to Brussels, where she was appointed matron of the Berkendael Surgical Institute training school for nurses. At the outbreak of war in 1914 it became a Red Cross hospital. Cavell tended both German and Allied wounded, and refused to leave the city when Brussels fell, preferring to remain at her post.

Having joined the underground, she used the institute as a shelter for allied troops before smuggling them to neutral safety in the Netherlands.

Cavell's escape network continued through to the summer of 1915, even though by then she knew the Germans were on to her. She

tried to send a message back to England through a Belgian aristocrat, the Count de Borchgrave, but it was too late. She was arrested that August. She was condemned for passing soldiers to the enemy and shot on 12 October at the military firing range in Schaerbeek, despite appeals from the Vatican. Her execution site, the Enclos des Fusillés, is reached along a narrow lane from rue Colonel Bourg. Her grave, and those of other executed patriots, are here too, behind a hedge. Cavell's is No.4.

News of her death brought worldwide outrage and she became a martyr: recruitment into the British army doubled. She is fondly remembered in Brussels: her nursing school in Uccle is now the Institut Edith Cavell. A nearby memorial, erected in 1920, stands at the junction of rues Edith Cavell and Marie Depage, another war victim and co-founder of the hospital.

Brel's Brussels

For a man who's been dead since 1978, Jacques Brel has been extremely busy. After a decade of neglect in his home town, the most accomplished and successful singer/songwriter in Belgian pop history – if not European history – has at last been fêted in his own land.

The singer of such classics as *Ne Me Quitte Pas*, *Amsterdam* and *Jacky* – all international hits and covered by the likes of David Bowie, Scott Walker and Marc Almond – Brel has been given a new lease of afterlife thanks to a series of events around Brussels to mark the 25th anniversary of his passing. Nearly a quarter of a million people have seen the 90-minute multi-media exhibition *Brel, Le Droit de Rêver* (50 rue de l'Ecuyer; 070 22 30 13) and the screening of his ferociously intense official farewell concert at the Paris Olympia, shown at his own **Fondation Internationale Jacques Brel**. Set to run throughout 2003, both have been extended into May 2004 and maybe longer. For more information, check www.jacquesbrel.be.

In his day, Brel was as big as Gainsbourg. He sang of life's little ties and miseries, set against the backdrop of grey everyday life, the grey everyday life he grew up with in Brussels.

He was born to Flemish-speaking parents in 1929 in Schaerbeek, 138 avenue du Diamant, where a plaque now stands. '*Il a chanté le plat pays...*' it begins, recounting Brel's bitter-sweet homage to his flat homeland of Belgium. His father, Romain, had made his money in the Belgian Congo, and Jacques' brother Pierre remembers a flat full of African artefacts. Brel senior moved his wife Lisette and their children a short distance to a luxury flat at 55 avenue des Cerisiers, in Woluwe-St-Lambert, but rapid economic hardship saw him move back into town, to 66 boulevard d'Ypres. Romain Brel went into cardboard and there he stayed until retirement, at a factory in Molenbeek, described by Brel in his song *Il Pleut*.

Another bitter-sweet Brel work, *Les Vieux*, relates parental lives and sacrifices. His father gradually climbed the factory ladder and managed to move the family to nicer digs at 26 boulevard Belgica in Jette (equipped with a radio and piano), before finally settling at 7 rue Jacques Manne in Anderlecht. By then Jacques was married and had been found a day job at his father's factory.

But Jacques had begun to write songs – poignant ones, angry ones, tender ones – trying them out before modest audiences. In Brussels he received polite applause;in Flanders they pelted him with tomatoes. He kept to Brussels, at the long-defunct Coup de Lune in the Marolles and at the Rose Noire cabaret, then adjacent to the restaurant **Aux Armes de Bruxelles** (*see p109*) in 1952. This was his big local break.

A year later he left for Paris, planning to make it as a songwriter. But his own performances caught the French public's imagination, and within a couple of years he was a star. Brel's lyrics painted vivid pictures of working-class life – and the country he had left behind. He sang of Brussels, of its sorrow and its dignity, and in his proud Bruxellois accent he lambasted the bourgeoisie. France made him. He then toured the world, giving an emotional show at Brussels' **Ancienne Belgique** (*see p191*) once a year.

In 1966 he quit touring. A farewell gala before bourgeois couples in pearls and penguin suits at Brussels' Palais des Beaux-Arts, then that heart-stopping last gig at the Paris Olympia in front of hip young beatniks and short-skirted beatnikettes, and he left Europe, via a last engagement in Quebec.

He took his boat, Askoy, across the seven seas and settled by Gauguin's bordello, the House of Orgasm, on Hiva Oa island in the middle of the Pacific. There you'll find a museum, and his grave.

In Brussels, until fairly recently, little marked Brel's passing. Ironically, the metro stop between his parents' last house and his father's former factory of Vanneste & Brel Cardboard, near the Anderlecht abattoir, was renamed Jacques Brel.

After years of inertia, his daughter France set up the Jacques Brel International Foundation, without sufficient funds to turn it into a major attraction. The 2003 festivities have seen it spruced up, its shop well stocked with his CDs and books – and queues all day for Brel's farewell concert film.

Fondation Internationale Jacques Brel

11 place de la Vieille Halle aux Blés, Lower Town (02 511 10 20/www.jacquesbrel.be). Métro Gare Centrale/bus 34, 48, 95, 96. **Open** 11am-6pm Tue-Sat. **Admission** €5. **Credit** MC, V. **Map** p315 C4.

Green Brussels

Chill out in the green belt.

Beyond Ixelles and St-Gilles spreads a vast swathe of greenery. Not too long ago it was all the **Forêt de Soignes**, the hunting ground of the Dukes of Brabant. In the mid 18th century the Austrians replanted much of the original oak forest with beech trees, some 12,000 hectares (29,650 acres). Today it's a quarter of that.

Nearer to town, the forest is divided between the leafy southern and eastern *communes*. In **Forest** and **Uccle**, green patches such as the once-elegant Parc de Forest and Parc Duden, both rather ramshackle, were captured for urban use in the 19th century. At the same time, immediately south of Ixelles, the forest's northern tip was landscaped as a leisure park and christened **Bois de la Cambre**. This is the closest Brussels gets to having its own Central Park. Closed to cars on Sundays, it's the haunt of joggers, cyclists and rollerbladers.

To the south-east are villages that make for fine afternoons out, either by virtue of their bucolic setting (such as **Watermael-Boitsfort** or **Genval**) or because of a major cultural attraction – such as the **Musée Royal de l'Afrique Centrale** in **Tervuren**.

Forest & Uccle

The Parc de Forest and the Parc Duden lead you from the southern edge of St-Gilles into Forest, where the houses are less elegant and the shops cheaper. Further south stretch the sedate, suburban streets of Brussels' largest commune, Uccle, a quaint area filling with nouveau riches eager for green surroundings close to town. Cutting through Uccle, the lengthy chaussée d'Alsemberg houses classic taverns like **Au Vieux Spytigen Duivel** (*see p142*); nearby, chic terrace bars such as **Ici le Bô-Bar** (*see p142*) attract the in-crowd.

In among it all, unexpectedly, stands one of the most remarkable museums in Brussels. The house at 41 avenue Léo Errera was built in 1928 for David Van Buuren, a wealthy Dutch banker who became enamoured of the art deco style. Opened in 1973 as the **Musée David et Alice Van Buuren** (*see below*), it combines art, architecture and landscaping.

Beyond the museum extends plenty of greenery, perhaps the most charming space being the Parc de Wolvendael, owned by successive royals through the centuries.

Musée David et Alice Van Buuren

41 avenue Léo Errera (02 343 48 51/www. museumvanbuuren.com). Tram 23, 90/bus 38, 60. **Open** *Museum* 1-6pm Mon, Sun; 2-6pm Wed. *Garden* 2-6pm daily. **Admission** *Museum* €10; €5-€8 concessions. *Garden* €5. **No credit cards.**
Every object here – even the custom-made piano – conforms to the polished lines of the art deco movement favoured by its pre-war owner, David Van Buuren. His art collection, spanning five centuries, is remarkable; there is a version of Bruegel's *Landscape with the Fall of Icarus*, as well as works by Ensor, Wouters and Gustave van de Woestyne (a friend of the Van Buurens), plus a Braque, and a Van Gogh charcoal and watercolour sketch of the *Potato Eaters*. A framed letter from David Ben Gurion shows the Van Buurens' dedication to the Zionist cause. Outside, the garden is laid out in a maze by Belgian landscape architect René Péchère.

Watermael-Boitsfort

South-east of Ixelles, Boitsfort – or Watermael-Boitsfort (www.watermael-boitsfort.be), to give it its official title – makes a fine half-day detour if you fancy leaving the centre for a while. With 24,000 inhabitants, W-B hits the spot between city and country, a bustling suburb of Brussels half-covered by the Forêt de Soignes. Expats love the village feel, large houses and the huge International School here. Watermael and Boitsfort were separate entities until Napoleon combined them by imperial decree in 1811. They still have separate railway stations, though, Watermael's a pretty little design from 1844 – but Boitsfort's has attractions beyond.

Its three main squares are Bischofsheim, Gilson and place Wiener, the terminus of the No.94 tram from town. Wiener's Sunday morning market provides the focus for village life, with spice stalls, authentic Spanish food, Thai goodies and a farm dairy selling lumps of cheese and fresh milk and cream. Bar-hopping around the market is a must: Au Poilu buzzes with market traders; the refurbished Café du Tram throngs with shoppers. Nearby on place Bischofsheim is the Michelin-starred Au Vieux Boitsfort (No.9, 02 672 23 32).

Boitsfort is known for its pretty ponds and sculpture gardens. Two residential areas were earmarked in 1922 to become showcases of floral urban living. Le Logis, centred around the Trois Tilleuls area with streets named after

birds, is laid out in the English style. Cottages have green doors and shutters, with hedges and cherry trees in their gardens. Le Floréal is on the other side of the forest, and therefore a taxi away, but is another charming example of model city living. The streets around here are named after flowers and the similarly styled houses have a dominant yellow theme. Other buildings of architectural note are the Maison Haute and the Maison Communale, both on place Gilson, the administrative offices for the commune. The striking church of St-Hubert (Jagersveld 6, 02 672 23 95) has a cathedral-like spire and nave, which dominate the surrounding landscape.

Up in Watermael, the pretty little church of St-Clément (rue du Loutrier 50, 02 672 52 29) has a tower dating from the tenth century. From here it's only a short walk to café-lined place Keym, the renovated central square.

Avenue de Tervueren

Tervuren is an old Flemish dwelling bordering Boitsfort deep in the Forêt de Soignes, whose link with Brussels was established by Léopold II. Having found a suitable venue to show off his ill-gotten gains in the Congo – on the site of Charles of Lorraine's old palace in Tervuren – Léopold II had built a ten-kilometre (six-mile) avenue from his grand monuments in the Parc du Cinquantenaire to what is now the **Musée Royal de l'Afrique Centrale** (*see p103*).

Today tram No.44 from runs the length of avenue de Tervueren, from the métro station at Montgomery, past embassies and grand apartment blocks, through the Forêt de Soignes to its terminus by the Central African Museum.

Little Geneva

As you come to the end of the 20-minute train ride from Brussels, you'll already have a feeling for **Genval** (www.genval.com). After passing through the beech trees of the Forêt de Soignes, the Geneva-like water spout on Lake Genval marks your arrival. A picturesque little station, all 19th century, red brick and gabled, gives access in one direction to the lake, and in the other to the high street, complete with hairdresser, florist and dusty electrical shop. Genval is a blip on the political and linguistic map. No bilingualism here: it's outside of the Brussels region and, deep in the Flemish belt, it remains buckled up and sturdily francophone.

Genval is perfect for getting out of the city on a hot day. The lake is a natural magnet for those who want to sit on a café terrace by the water, hire a rowing boat or bike, or stroll round the wooded edges. Until the turn of the century the lake was a series of ponds and springs until the local Meer family turned it into the lake that sparkles now. As part of that development, the **Château du Lac** manor house was built, originally as a spa for the gentry to take the waters, but then as home to the Schweppes family for 50 years. Now it's a five-star hotel and conference centre (Hotel Château du Lac, 87 avenue du Lac, 02 655 73 73/www.chateaudulac-belgium.com). You can get a top-notch lunch at its **Genval Les Bains** lakeside terrace restaurant. Another option is quirky **Le Grilloir** (301 avenue Albert 1er, 02 652 01 31), by the station. With specialities of oysters, lobster, fondue and grilled meats, it offers bargain lunchtime menus and evening meals.

Genval has a museum, too, the **Musée de l'Eau et de la Fontaine** (63 avenue Hoover, 02 654 19 23/www.pixelsbw.com/musee-eau-fontaine), showing the history of water distribution. It's not quite as dull as it sounds: the pumps and fountains give a decent social history, and kids will love the working models. All in all Genval makes an easy half-day trip from town (with trains every 30 minutes), or even a relaxing weekend break.

(Note that you require a separate ticket for the whole journey, as you are leaving the boundary of Brussels.) From Montgomery you'll pass the Palais Stoclet at 281 avenue de Tervueren, a stark anti-art nouveau statement built between 1906 and 1911 by Joseph Hoffmann, not open to the public. Further, the Parc du Woluwe, is a beautifully unstructured space; opposite is the **Musée du Transport Urbain Bruxellois** (*see below*), with its bygone trams and buses.

The tram trundles on through the thick Forêt de Soignes, in which the tram stops are like country halts. As it circles into the Tervuren terminus, whole families of rabbits sit staring defiantly before darting away for safety.

Diagonally opposite the tram terminus stands Brussels' most controversial museum, housing the world's largest collection of African ethnography: the Central African Museum. The building itself – built between 1904 and 1910 – was inspired by Versailles and the Petit Palais in Paris. Surrounding it are the grounds of a previous royal palace, which still contain the remains of 18th-century stables and the Renaissance Chapelle St-Hubert. Beyond is the rambling Parc de Tervuren, full of pretty canals, woodlands and a lake, ideal for picnics and much less formal than the inner-city parks.

Musée Royal de l'Afrique centrale

13 chaussée de Louvain, Tervuren (02 769 5211/ www.africamuseum.be). Tram 44. **Open** 10am-5pm Tue-Fri; 10am-6pm Sat, Sun. **Admission** €4; €1.50-€3 concessions. Free after 1pm 1st Wed of mth. **No credit cards**.
Until now this museum was a lazy, uninspiring display of arrogance and ignorance, something long accepted by pundits and the authorities alike. As well as major ethnological and zoological collections,

the museum is home to the archives of Henry Morton Stanley, the explorer who was commissioned by Léopold II to help found his despotic empire in the Congo. Some 95% of the museum's collection remains stored away from public gaze. This sorry state of affairs is loaded with historical baggage, and something museum director Guido Gryseels is committed to putting right. Successive governments and funding cuts have meant that the museum has hardly changed since the current permanent exhibition was established in the 1960s, a time when the European 'look what we got' view of the colonies was rather different from today's. Bringing the museum's message and image up to date with its current outlook and involvement with Africa is the aim of a major overhaul to be completed in time for the museum's centenary celebration in 2010. The famous crocodile gallery, the only exhibit that remains in its original 1910 form, will be preserved. The rest is destined to go the way of colonialism, replaced by a fully interactive, scientific and visitor-friendly archive. In the meantime, from 27 January to 2 October 2005, 'Congo, the Colonial Era: More than Just One Story' is the working title of an enormous exhibition tracing Belgium's African experience from Stanley's (in)famous explorations to the post-colonial present.

Musée du Transport Urbain Bruxellois

364 avenue de Tervueren, Woluwe-St-Pierre (02 515 31 08/www.mtub.be). Tram 39, 44/bus 36, 42. **Open** *Apr-Oct* 1.30-7pm Sat, Sun, public holidays. **Admission** €1.50. **No credit cards**.
The Brussels Transport Museum houses a collection of beautifully restored old trams and trolleybuses dating as far back as 1869. A vintage tram makes a regular journey from the Parc du Cinquantenaire to Tervuren; tickets cost €4, which includes entrance to the museum.

Eat and drink your way around the world

Eat, Drink, Shop

Restaurants

Reach for the (Michelin) stars.

L'Elément Terre. *See p123.*

One memory the visitor is guaranteed to take away from Brussels is the amazing number and variety of restaurants, from tiny café-cum-snack bars to Michelin star winners. It seems that everywhere you turn there is a restaurant beckoning. Brussels has 2,000 restaurants for a population of one million. Trying to get a booking at the more popular places only confirms the maths, especially at weekends, when it is commonplace for the 'house full' sign to go up. In fact, it is claimed that Belgians eat out more per capita than any other nation on earth, and whether or not this is true, eating out is without doubt a national pastime. Every Belgian will have a favourite restaurant, everyone will be able to offer a recommendation – and opinion – on the finer details of a menu, or a particular chef's way with rabbit.

The consistently best restaurants are those with little fuss or complicated design. Look for wood-panelled walls, tiled floors, bright white lighting and an open kitchen. Here you will find wholesome Belgian food cooked simply but perfectly and in gigantic portions. Moving up the scale, art nouveau or art deco influences may creep in, giving more sophistication and,

often, higher prices – waiters in white jackets and gold epaulettes provide a classic clue. You may well find that service in general can be verging on brusque; rest assured that this is par for the course and not personal. Eating out is a great social leveller, everyone is there for the food (staff included), and they would prefer to deliver your plate at its peak rather than waste time being too deferential.

In keeping with its international flavour, Brussels has restaurants from around the globe and choice can be bewildering. Belgian restaurants can be found throughout the city, with a particularly good spread around the Grand' Place. It's worth taking a walk along rue des Bouchers and its Petite sister. Here you will find rows of brash restaurants and neon lights, vast seafood stands and attractive displays of fish – a real sight and full of atmosphere, especially in summer. But you'll feel battered by the barkers on the street trying to entice you in, and the dining experience can be disappointing, despite the glitzy promise. You won't find locals eating here; if they want fish they go to Ste-Catherine. Bear in mind that the majority of restaurants – especially those described in this guide – have been around for years. If a new one arrives and doesn't come up to scratch, it simply has to close. Brussels diners are not prepared to compromise on their expectations.

PRACTICALITIES

Brussels is not particularly cheap for eating out, nor is there a law (as in France) that restaurants must offer a set menu. This remains at the discretion of the *patron*. The best bargains can be found at lunchtime (*midi*) when there is a *plat du jour* on offer, often with a glass of wine or coffee thrown in. The price of spirits and wine is more reasonable than other cities and can help balance out a bill; house wines are usually of a high standard.

The restaurants below are ordered in area and then by cuisine style. We've listed the average price of main courses and, where applicable, the cost of a set menu. Almost all restaurants now accept credit cards, though there are still traditional stalwarts who cannot resist the rustle of cash in their tills. Bills come with service included, so there is no obligation to tip; most diners leave a little extra to round off the evening; in top-quality restaurants, a healthier treat is expected.

The website www.resto.be is the most wide-reaching resource and also includes visitors' reviews. The search engine works in French, Dutch and English, though is hyper-sensitive and not smart enough to find a restaurant if you mistype the name or try for a near match.

Grand' Place & around

The tiny streets around the Grand' Place are alive with restaurants and bars. Surprisingly, their location in the centre of the tourist area doesn't necessarily mean that they're either of poor quality or overpriced. Many are used by locals and have a true Belgian feel about them. Restaurants in the area are busy year-round and it's always best to book ahead if possible.

Belgian & French

Belga Queen

32 rue du Fossé aux Loups (02 217 2187/ www.resto.be/belgaqueen). Métro/pré-métro De Brouckère. **Open** noon-2.30pm, 7pm-midnight daily. **Main courses** €14-€43. **Set menu** €30-€44. **Credit** AmEx, DC, MC, V. **Map** p315 C2.
Everything about this glitzy place is unashamedly Belgian. The design, the menu, the produce, even the wine is sourced from Belgian producers abroad. The restaurant sits in a vast bank building with original pillars and a massive stained-glass skylight, giving an air of loftiness and space. Yet once at the table, it can feel surprisingly intimate (though couples alone are rare – this seems to be a place to go with a

crowd). A nice touch is the wall of honour, where the names of famous Belgians are listed. The BQ is renowned for its oyster bar, where heaving seafood platters are composed. The hot food is inventive and thoroughly modern; the famous farm bird, Coucou de Malines, is sat on gingerbread with a hot pear sauce, though more traditional methods are used, such as slow braising in beer. The unisex toilet doors are transparent, and it's up to you to work them out. Don't expect us to give the game away.

Chez Léon

18 rue des Bouchers (02 511 14 15/www.chezleon. be). Métro Gare Centrale/pré-métro Bourse. **Open** noon-11pm Mon-Thur, Sun; noon-11.30pm Fri, Sat. **Main courses** €10-€24.50. **Credit** AmEx, DC, MC, V. **Map** p315 C3.

The best Restaurants

Best dressed
Belga Queen (*see left*) has a beautiful stained-glass skylight, classical columns and marble floors.

Best for kids
Not a takeaway, **Chez Léon** (*see above*) is a family-friendly place with well-priced local dishes and kids' menus.

Best Italian
Sleek and minimalist **Divino** (*see p116*) has the freshest pastas and most well-endowed pizzas.

Best cheap eats
Tacky **Thiên-Long** (*see p118*) has fab steaming plates of Vietnamese food at unreal prices. Lunch for €6!

Best Belgian
Unequivocally good, the **Roue d'Or** (*see p108*) is as Belgian as can be.

Best French
Saint Boniface's (*see p121*) duck and goose fat are straight from the Dordogne.

Best museum piece
The authentic decor at **De Ultieme Hallucinatie** (*see p124*) are of another era.

Best atmosphere
The Friday night cabaret at **Le Pré Salé** (*see p113*) is a local institution – book early.

Best of the best
Comme chez Soi (*see p108*). This classic three-star is worth every cushioned cent.

Belgian dining at **La Roue d'Or**.

Léon Vanlancker first opened a tavern in 1893, and ten years later unveiled a *frites* shop on the site of the current restaurant. How times have changed: Chez Léon weaves through nine interconnecting houses and can seat 400 people. Its fast-food feel and atmosphere keeps the nose-in-air locals away – or maybe it's the paper napkins and menu with photographed dishes. Whatever, there's no denying that this is a temple to mussels and other Belgian classics, such as rabbit in sour cherry beer. Léon is good for families; kids under 12 get a free set menu as long as there are two paying adults. You may not be treated like a king here, but you'll certainly eat like one.

Comme chez Soi

23 place Rouppe (02 512 29 21/www.commechezsoi. be). Pré-métro Anneessens. **Open** noon-2.15pm, 7-11pm Tue-Sat; last orders set menu 1.15pm, 9.15pm; last orders à la carte 1.30pm, 9.30pm. Closed July. **Main courses** €32-€95. **Set menu** €64-€152. **Credit** AmEx, DC, MC, V. **Map** p318 B4.

Eating out doesn't get much better than this. The art nouveau interior, the immaculate – nay, exquisite – food, and the master, Pierre Wynants, Belgian hero and one of Europe's top chefs. Oh, and let's not forget the three Michelin stars. Comme chez Soi is a family concern, with wife Marie-Thérèse seating you *à table* and son-in-law Lionel Rigolet second-in-command in the kitchen. Think of scallops stuffed with spinach, saddle of hare with foie gras and wild mushrooms, and sole infused with langoustine and

white truffle, and you get the picture. Yet old habits die hard: after a beautifully sculpted course arrives at your table, waiters return with an unassuming bowl of second helpings, proving that small artistic portions are never enough in Belgium. The set menus make the bill a little more bearable. Be sure to book far in advance.

La Maison du Cygne

9 Grand' Place, entrance at 2 rue Charles Buyl (02 511 82 44/www.lamaisonducygne.be). Pré-métro Bourse. **Open** 12.15-2pm, 7.15-10pm Mon-Fri; 7.15-10pm Sat. **Main courses** €30-€48. **Set menu** €90. **Credit** AmEx, DC, MC, V. **Map** p315 C3.

There can surely be no grander building or location in which to eat. Sitting right on the Grand' Place, the building has associations with Karl Marx but now displays an authoritative, distinctly capitalist air. The Cygne showcases Belgian grandeur at its stuffy best, but it's not without substance: chef Jean-Philippe Bruneau was named Chef of the Year in 2003 and the Maison's cellars hold more than 35,000 bottles of outlandishly expensive wine. Expect classic French cuisine using the likes of turbot, pheasant and rack of lamb, but be warned – there's no mention of a vegetarian option anywhere. A slightly cheaper (and supposedly more informal) place, Ommegang, has opened downstairs (same phone number); here you can pick up a lunch for €15. But if you're on expenses, as most of the diners seem to be, you'll know where to go – and how to dress.

L'Ogenblik

1 galerie des Princes (02 511 61 51/www.ogenblik. be). Métro Gare Centrale. **Open** noon-2.30pm, 7pm-midnight Mon-Sat. **Main courses** €22-€28. **Set menu** €51-€58. **Credit** AmEx, DC, MC, V. **Map** p315 C3.

Set on the edge of the glamorous covered galleries, this place is a must for flash-the-cash professionals. The eclectic interior is sort of old-railway-station-meets-Conran, with a sprinkle of salt on the floor to give it that old soak feel. But the food is of gastronomic quality: try the millefeuille of lobster and salmon with a coulis of langoustines. Watch the prices, though, as the bill adds up in an *ogenblik* (blink of an eye). Also look out for Madame, who takes the bookings and prepares the bills; she sits at an ancient shop till with a little wooden foot stall, dancing pumps, half-moon glasses and a mess-with-me-and-you're-dead look. Classic.

La Roue d'Or

26 rue des Chapeliers (02 514 25 54). Pré-métro Bourse. **Open** noon-midnight daily. **Main courses** €12.50-€22. **Credit** AmEx, DC, MC, V. **Map** p315 C3.

The Golden Wheel takes its name from the gold motif at the heart of a stained-glass window above the open kitchen. Through the window you can watch the team of chefs toiling away at what can be described as grandma's cooking. The fine spread of good old Belgian grub includes mussels, oysters, lamb's tongue, pig's trotter, brawn, rabbit, slabs of beef; not surprisingly, vegetarians will feel rather left out. And while the ingredients are no-nonsense, presentation and flavours are as fine as can be, ensuring that the restaurant remains a favourite with locals, who adore the wholesomeness of the place. So you're sure you know what you're letting yourself in for, the menu is also offered in English.

Fish & seafood

Aux Armes de Bruxelles

13 rue des Bouchers (02 511 21 18/www.armebrux. be). Métro Gare Centrale. **Open** noon-11.15pm Tue-Sun. **Main courses** €18-€39. **Set menu** €29-€45. **Credit** AmEx, DC, MC, V. **Map** p315 C3.
Sitting rather grandly like a grounded galleon in the gaudy sea of fish restaurants near the Grand' Place, Aux Armes is a classically mullioned institution

beloved by business folk and middle-aged, middle-class Belgians since 1921. The deco interior is as classy as the waiters, who slide around with the utmost professionalism, delivering piled plates of mussels, turbot and the occasional steak. It's seafood that folk come for, the perfect *moules-frites* and creamy fish *waterzooi*. You'll pay a little more for this true brasserie experience, but you're getting top quality and a slice of the good life. Booking a must.

Restaurant Vincent

8-10 rue des Dominicains (02 511 26 07/ www.restaurantvincent.com). Métro/pré-métro De Brouckère. **Open** noon-2.45pm, 6.30-11.30pm Mon-Sat; noon-3pm, 6.30-10.30pm Sun. **Main courses** €11-€23. **Credit** AmEx, DC, MC, V. **Map** p315 C3.
Up a little side street from the main glare of rue des Bouchers is the unassuming frontage of Vincent. Newcomers hesitate to enter because there seems to

Belgian cuisine

For such a small country, Belgium has a big reputation for its approach to cooking and the all-important ingredients that go into the pot. Belgian food – and its beer – have become an international brand. Yet *moules-frites* are only one part of the overall picture.

The Romans tucked into mussels and oysters, but it was later invaders who gave Belgium its cuisine. Dutch, French, Spanish and Austrian rulers brought different cooking styles, and we can see from Breugel's vivid paintings of village revelry and the banqueting scenes in old Flemish tapestries that eating has always been a celebratory national pastime. This was the centre of the European spice trade, with goody bags from the Far East unloaded at Antwerp and Rotterdam. Brewers used coriander, ginger and nutmeg to flavour beer, and beer was used to flavour food, in the same way as it is today.

Belgium's green pastures are ideal for growing the potatoes, root vegetables, chicory and asparagus so important to its cooking. They support the famous Blanc-Bleu Belge cattle for the generic *steak-frites*. The forests and rugged landscape of the Ardennes give a home to the venison, boar and wild hare that appear on menus in hunting season between October and December. Then there is the coast and the cold North Sea, giving bountiful quantities of tiny shrimps (*crevettes grises*), sole, crab and, of course, the mussels and oysters from Zeeland.

Any titillation of local cuisine is perfectly acceptable and finer French designs are welcomed, nay encouraged, in the best

restaurants. Even here, though, they never stint on portions – fancy, frilly servings are frowned upon. You can see this in the gutsy, resolutely Belgian dishes, where presentation remains secondary. Take **Anguilles au vert**, a thick soupy affair in which suck-size chunks of eel lie suspended in a startling sauce made of sorrel, parsley and other greenery – powerful and filling, it offers little that is pleasing to the eye. Neither does **Andouillette**, a massive banger filled with a coagulation of innards. Spiced and seasoned, these hefties are A-graded according to roughness. Their softer cousin is the **Boudin** from Liège, in a black (blood) or white form.

Filet Américain is raw, minced and spiced up with onion, paprika and the like. Order this and you'll have a vast pink mound on your plate, looking a little like cat food, though surprisingly tasty; of course, the finer the restaurant, the finer the mix. A much safer bet is **Waterzooi**, found on every traditional Belgian menu. Made with chicken or fish, this thinnish stew from Ghent is enriched with egg yolk and cream.

As starters, you'll see two types of deep-fried croquettes which are uniformly best. The **Fondues au Fromage** are filled with a thick cheese sauce, whilst the **Croquettes aux Crevettes Grises** drip with taste-explosive shrimps. For dessert, there's **Dame Blanche**, a tower of vanilla ice-cream served with a side pot of gluggy hot chocolate sauce – it can end the dinner or finish the diner, but is typical of the no-nonsense approach to eating in Belgium, where standards must never slip.

Eat, Drink, Shop

be only a kitchen entrance. Correct. Be brave and walk past the steaming chefs, and the dry maître d' will meet you at the other side. Vincent's fame comes from its tiled dining room (*salle carellée*), with a mural depicting old-time fishing and wild seas, which dates from 1905. Some of the tables are shaped like fishing smacks, just in case you miss the theme. Ask for this when booking or you could end up in the unexceptional dining room next door. Not surprisingly, fish and seafood are the main draws, cooked to perfection in a basic, homely way. This is one of those places where the final touches are rustled up at table by the epauletted waiters who love nothing better than to show off their flambé skills in the old style. Brussels at its crackling best.

Sea Grill

Radisson SAS Hotel, 47 rue du Fossé aux Loups (02 227 31 20). Métro/pré-métro De Brouckère. **Open** noon-2pm, 7-10pm Mon-Fri. **Main courses** €40-€55. **Set menu** €49-€210. **Credit** AmEx, DC, MC, V. **Map** p315 C2.

The Sea Grill – regarded by many as Belgium's top seafood restaurant – is buried deep inside the five-star Radisson SAS (*see p41*), so while the entrance is rather corporate, once inside you sit in pure cushioned luxury, surrounded by etched-glass panels of Norwegian fjords. Chef Yves Mattagne seems to win every award going for his supreme blend of traditional French techniques with international modern strokes, red mullet with truffle risotto and roast tuna with sautéed goose liver being specialities. But be aware that a starter here could set you back more than an entire meal elsewhere.

International

Rugantino

184 boulevard Anspach (02 511 21 95). Pré-métro Anneessens. **Open** noon-3pm, 6.30pm-midnight Mon-Fri; 6.30pm-midnight Sat. **Main courses** €9-€17. **Credit** MC, V. **Map** p315 B3.

From the outside it looks more like an art deco hat shop than a family-run restaurant, yet Rugantino is decidedly authentic in terms of food and atmosphere, its interior like a faded dance-hall, with ironwork and potted palms. The usual run of pastas and wood-fired pizzas (a little on the small side) is jazzed up with a raft of specials chalked on the walls, such as kidneys in chilli sauce, rabbit in wild mushrooms and peas with ham (don't knock it till you've tried it). An ultra-friendly multicultural staff whisk away your coats on arrival and line up to wave goodbye as you leave, so the personal touch is there. In the early evening, Rugantino fills with folk meeting up for a night out down the Marché au Charbon, but there's always a whispering couple tucked into some quiet corner or other.

Samourai

28 rue du Fossé aux Loups (02 217 56 39). Métro/pré-métro De Brouckère. **Open** noon-2pm, 7-9pm Mon, Wed-Sat; 7-9pm Sun. **Main courses** €22-€35. **Credit** AmEx, DC, MC, V. **Map** p315 C2.

Seek and ye shall find. The entrance to Samourai is tucked away in a little arcade off the main drag. The first room is like a walk-in wardrobe, with a bar jammed into it, Sardi's-style caricatures and travel posters on the wall. Winding stairs lead up through

Breaking bread

Like all good ideas, the concept behind **Le Pain Quotidien** (16 rue Antoine Dansaert, 02 502 23 61, www.painquotidien.com; nine branches in Brussels, two in Antwerp, one each in Bruges, Leuven, Liège and Namur) is simple. For one, the food is uncomplicated and tasty: highlighted by the titular *pain*, a naturally fermented wholewheat sourdough variety, and supported by croissants, cakes and other lunchy, brunchy items.

In addition, the decor is plain and attractive: antique country furniture, wooden dressers, thick floorboards and marble counter tops. Friendly, young staff too.

However, the masterstroke behind Le Pain Quotidien, the reason for its success, sits in the middle of the room. It doesn't look like much, just a vast, scrubbed pine kitchen table. But it turns Le Pain Quotidien from a café into something more, and has transformed the operation, founded by

renowned Belgian baker Alain Coumont, from a Brussels experiment into a major international brand with branches all over France, and in places as far away as Rome, Geneva, New York and Los Angeles.

Reserved Brits may blanche at the idea of brunching with complete strangers, but the Belgians have taken to it like fish to water. The table gives each branch a community feel. Regulars come and go, popping by for a cuppa and croissant or something more substantial; a tasty roast beef and caper mayonnaise sandwich, say. Some natter the morning away, while others read in silence. Whatever: it's up to you. It's meant to be relaxed and relaxing, so relax.

Le Pain Quotidien's takeaway bakeries serve breads, pastries, fruit tarts and *bombe au chocolat*, a rich chocolate-mousse cake. But really, it's the table that makes the place. So pull up a chair, and enjoy.

Restaurant Vincent. *See p109.*

The mussels
from Brussels

a labyrinth of minimalist rooms, stacked together. For lovers of Japanese food, there is no better. This is serious stuff, with tempura and sushi bars, tables or floor-cushioned dining and a brigade of highly trained chefs. So renowned is Samourai that Japanese tourists come here by the busload – it's included on many tour itineraries – so booking is advisable. The wine list is vast, but gaspingly expensive (Romanée-Conti, €2,000). For the sake of your wallet, stick to the saké.

Tai Hon

35 rue du Marché aux Fromages (02 514 50 58). Métro Gare Centrale. **Open** noon-3pm, 6-11pm Mon-Sat. **Main courses** €7-€14. **Credit** AmEx, MC, DC, V. **Map** p315 C3.

Sitting on the corner of a street full of neon and kebabs, this quietly minimalist restaurant is a gem. Subtle tones of terracotta and black draw you in through the old shop windows, while the menus are written on blackboards outside in the street. This is no ordinary chow mein place, but more like Taiwanese with Japanese influences, resulting in a menu that's exciting and modern. Take crispy duck with scampi and oyster sauce, for instance, or seared beef fillet with black bean sauce. The Japanese twist comes with the use of pickled vegetables, not just raw, but added to the cooking pot for flavour and texture. Service is exceedingly friendly, as is the price of the set menus.

Ste-Catherine & St-Géry

Ste-Catherine was originally filled with canals, on which fishing boats trawled for goodies. The canals have long since been covered over, but they still lend a special atmosphere to what is now the main dining area in Brussels for lovers of fish and seafood. It's lovely in summer, when many restaurants set up canopied terraces.

Once a run-down part of town, St-Géry is now a thriving and upmarket area with a mass of bars and lively restaurants in among its tangle of small streets. For oriental food, amble along the modest Chinatown on and off rue Jules van Praet; for trendy spots, look around place St-Géry and rue Antoine Dansaert.

Belgian & French

In 't Spinnekopke

1 place du Jardin aux Fleurs (02 511 86 95). Prémétro Bourse. **Open** noon-3pm, 6-11pm Mon-Thur; noon-3pm, 6pm-midnight Fri; 6pm-midnight Sat. **Main courses** €9-€16. **Credit** AmEx, DC, MC, V. **Map** p316 B3.

The Spider's Head is a gem of a 17th-century cottage, which would look more at home in a country lane than in the centre of a bustling city. The square at the front has recently been refurbished, giving the restaurant the opportunity to put up a grand outdoor terrace boxed in with geraniums (which makes

a strong contrast to the dark brown, low-ceilinged interior). The food is fish – especially cod – and heavy Belgian beer-cooked meats, which are a little over-sweet for some tastes. Also, service can verge on the brusque. But for all its irritating little failings, this place remains a favourite, no doubt because of its history. If you want to dip a toe, there's a bar on the right-hand side, where you can sip a beer and make a decision.

Le Pré Salé

20 rue de Flandre (02 513 65 45). Métro Ste-Catherine. **Open** noon-2.30pm, 6.30-10.30pm Wed-Sun. **Main courses** €12-€24. **Credit** AmEx, MC, V. **Map** p316 B2.

What an institution this is. A white tiled dining room leads through to an open kitchen at the back, where you can see madame chef slave away with her little helpers, cooking everything to order. When she's done, she comes out for a drink and a chat with friends. Friday night is cabaret night, a decades-old tradition, with *bruxellois* jokes, bawdy humour and a bit of a knees-up; it's near impossible to get a table for this, so book at least three weeks in advance. Food comprises hefty meat and fish dishes, with excellent cod, salmon and mussels and a huge beef rib for two people. There's absolutely no subtlety at the Pre-Salé – it's all bright lights, big noise and vast plates of food, which is why we love it.

Fish & seafood

Bij den Boer

60 quai aux Briques (02 512 61 22/www.bijdenboer. com). Métro Ste-Catherine. **Open** noon-2.30pm, 6-10.30pm Mon-Sat. **Main courses** €15-€25. **Set menu** €25. **Credit** AmEx, DC, MC, V. **Map** p316 B2.

The Farmer's looks a bit like a transport caff and can seem a little intimidating from the outside as it's always packed with local customers – you always get the feeling you're gatecrashing someone's private do. Once inside, the decor is un-awe-inspiring but is made up for by a noisy, chattering atmosphere. The restaurant is famous for its mussels and bouillabaisse, and prices are rather good for the area, in particular the four-course menu. On the other hand, the service is infuriatingly slow. The staff are friendly enough, and dash around at a rate, but never, it seems, towards your table. But persevere and you will leave feeling mightily satisfied. This is Belgium at its shoulder-shrugging best.

Jacques

44 quai au Briques (02 513 27 62). Métro Ste-Catherine. **Open** noon-2pm, 6.30-10pm Mon-Sat. **Main courses** €25-€45. **Credit** AmEx, DC, MC, V. **Map** p316 B2.

A real favourite with locals, Jacques oozes traditional Belgian charm, especially in summer when the huge windows are open and the restaurant meets the street. An old-fashioned, wood-panelled interior, tiled floors and globe lamps give the place its atmosphere, although the newly added back room is lack-

Deciphering the menu

Virtually all menus in Brussels are written in French, though most restaurants in the centre also have versions in Dutch and English.

Meat (viande)

agneau lamb; **andouillette** chitterling sausage of offal; **biche** venison (doe); **bœuf** beef; **boudin noir/boudin blanc** black or white pudding; **caille** quail; **canard** duck; **confit de canard** preserved duck leg; **magret de canard** duck breast; **caneton** duckling; **cerf** venison (stag); **cervelle** brain; **cheval** horse; **chevreuil** venison; **dinde** turkey; **escargot** snail; **faisan** pheasant; **foie** liver; **gésier** gizzard; **gibier** game; **(cuisses de) grenouille** frog's legs; **jambon** ham; **jambonneau** ham (normally knuckle) on the bone; **langue** tongue; **lapin** rabbit; **lard** bacon; **lardon** small cube of bacon; **lièvre** hare; **oie** goose; **perdreau** young partridge; **perdrix** partridge; **pied** foot/trotter; **pintade/pintadeau** guinea fowl; **porc** pork; **poulet** chicken; **ris** sweetbreads; **rognon** kidney; **sanglier** boar; **saucisse** sausage; **tripes** tripe; **veau** veal; **volaille** poultry/chicken; **suprême de volaille** chicken breast. *Meat cooking terms* **bleu** all but raw; **saignant** rare (**rosé** pink, for lamb, duck, liver and kidneys); **à point** medium rare, **bien cuit** well done.

Fish & seafood (poisson & fruits de mer)

crustacé shellfish; **anguille** eel; **bar** similar to sea bass; **barbue** brill; **brochet** pike; **cabillaud** cod; **carrelet** plaice; **coquille Saint Jacques** scallop; **colin** hake; **crevette** shrimp; **crevettes grises** tiny sweet shrimps; **daurade** sea bream; **écrevisse** crayfish (freshwater); **eglefin** haddock; **espadon** swordfish; **flétan** halibut; **hareng** herring; **homard** lobster; **huître** oyster; **langoustine** Dublin Bay prawn/scampi; **limande** lemon sole; **lotte** monkfish; **loup de mer** similar to sea bass; **maquereau** mackerel; **merlin** whiting; **merlu** hake; **morue** dried salt cod; **moule** mussel; **palourde** clam; **plie** plaice; **poulpe** octopus; **raie** skate; **rouget** red mullet; **roussette** rock salmon/dogfish; **St Pierre** John Dory; **sandre** pike-perch; **saumon** salmon; **scampi** prawn; **seïche** squid; **thon** tuna; **truite** trout.

Vegetables (légumes)

ail garlic; **artichaut** artichoke; **asperge** asparagus; **aubergine** aubergine/eggplant; **betterave** beetroot; **céleri** celery; **céleri rave** celeriac; **cèpe** cep mushroom; **champignon** mushroom; **chicon** chicory/Belgian endive; **chou** cabbage; **choucroute** sauerkraut; **chou-fleur** cauliflower; **cresson** watercress; **échalote** shallot; **épinards** spinach; **fève** broad bean/fava bean; **frisée** curly endive; **girolle** pale wild mushroom; **haricot** bean; **haricot vert** French bean; **morille** morel mushroom; **navet** turnip; **oignon** onion; **pleurotte** oyster mushroom; **poireau** leek; **poivron vert/rouge** green/red pepper/bell pepper; **pomme de terre** potato; **truffe** truffle.

Fruit (fruits)

ananas pineapple; **banane** banana; **cassis** blackcurrant; **cerise** cherry; **citron** lemon; **citron vert** lime; **fraise** strawberry; **framboise** raspberry; **griotte** morello cherry; **groseille** redcurrant; **groseille à maquereau** gooseberry; **marron** chestnut; **mûre** blackberry; **myrtille** blueberry/bilberry; **pamplemousse** grapefruit; **pêche** peach; **poire** pear; **pomme** apple; **prune** plum; **pruneau** prune; **raisin** grape.

Desserts (desserts)

crème anglaise custard; **crème chantilly** whipped cream; **Dame Blanche** vanilla ice-cream with hot chocolate sauce; **feuilleté** layers of puff pastry; **gâteau** cake; **glace** ice-cream; **glacé** frozen or iced; **île flottante** soft meringue floating on custard sauce; **macédoine de fruits** fruit salad; **massepain** marzipan; **mignardises** small biscuits or cakes to accompany coffee; **soufflé glacé** iced soufflé; **tarte tatin** caramelsed upside-down apple cake.

Herbs & spices (herbes & épices)

aneth dill; **basilic** basil; **cannelle** cinnamon; **cerfeuil** chervil; **ciboulette** chive; **citronelle** lemongrass; **estragon** tarragon; **fenouil** fennel; **muscade** nutmeg; **persil** parsley; **romarin** rosemary; **sauge** sage; **thym** thyme.

General

amande almond; **beignet** fritter or doughnut; **beurre** butter; **chaud** warm/hot; **chèvre** goat's cheese; **cru** raw; **farci** stuffed; **frites** chips; **froid** cold; **fromage** cheese; **fumé** smoked; **gaufre** waffle; **gelée** aspic; **haché** minced; **lentille** lentil; **miel** honey; **moutarde** mustard; **noisette** hazelnut; **noix** walnut; **nouilles** noodles; **oeuf** egg; **pain** bread; **pâtes** pasta; **poivre** pepper; **potage** soup; **riz** rice; **sel** salt; **sec/sèche** dry; **sucre** sugar; **thé** tea; **végétarien(ne)** vegetarian.

In 't Spinnekopke: 17th-century country cottage in the heart of downtown. *See p113.*

lustre and merely acts as a sounding board for the kitchen. Service is efficient but abrupt. Jacques is famous for its turbot with sauce mousseline, sublimely light and buttery, but the *moules-frites* make an excellent and well-priced alternative. Wines can be expensive, but the house white is perfectly decent. Booking is essential, especially for the front room.

Vismet
23 place Ste-Catherine (02 218 85 45). Métro Ste-Catherine. **Open** noon-2.30pm, 7-11pm Tue-Sat. **Main courses** €15-€25. **Credit** AmEx, MC, V. **Map** p315 B1.
Sitting apart from its more traditional neighbours, Vismet brings a young, modern approach to the fish market area. For a start, the design is bleached woods and downlighters, which sits rather well in the red-brick 17th-century gabled house. Then there's the chef, Tom Decroos, who received his training under Yves Mattagne at the award-winning Sea Grill (*see p110*). An open kitchen allows you to see the work at hand; what comes out of it is modern, fresh fish prepared stylishly: tandoori roast salmon, Victoria sea bass with fried chicory and capers. Informal yet professionally smart.

Le Vistro
16 quai aux Briques (02 512 41 81). Métro Ste-Catherine. **Open** noon-2.30pm, 7-10.30pm Mon-Fri; 6.30-10.30pm Sat. **Main courses** €20-€40. **Set menu** €20. **Credit** AmEx, DC, MC, V. **Map** p316 B2.
The narrowest house of a terrace of fish restaurants, this is a compact and welcoming bistro. No pink tablecloths and silk flower arrangements here, but brick and natural wood. The fish is on the traditional

French side – think buttery sauces – but what makes Vistro special is its heaving platters of fresh seafood. They groan with oysters, mussels, clams, winkles, whelks, and are crowned with a choice of crab or lobster. No starter is needed, but as it's all opened fresh you should be prepared to wait. Across the way in the summer, a canopied terrace awaits, where waiters have to dodge the traffic to get to your table.

International

Les Ateliers de la Grande Ile
33 rue de la Grande Ile (02 512 81 90). Pré-métro Bourse. **Open** 8pm-1am Tue-Sun. **Main courses** €10-€15. **Credit** AmEx, MC, V. **Map** p316 B3.
This quirky Russian restaurant is in a 19th-century foundry near place St-Géry. Peer through the front window and it could be someone's living room, with its Victorian-looking piano. But beyond is a rambling covered courtyard with further rooms, a little shabby, but perfect for the atmosphere of the place – raucous and full of screeching violin music. The menu is what you'd expect: blinis, chicken shashlik and borscht, plus specials such as salmon pasta with rice and mushrooms. There's a scary list of vodkas and you can order little saucers of salami or cheese to help it down. Unsuitable for a quiet night out.

Bonsoir Clara
22-26 rue Antoine Dansaert (02 502 09 90). Pré-métro Bourse. **Open** noon-2.30pm, 7-11.30pm Mon-Thur; noon-2.30pm, 7pm-midnight Fri; 7pm-midnight Sat; 7-11.30pm Sun. **Main courses** €17-€24. **Credit** AmEx, MC, V. **Map** p316 B3.

Kasbah: Middle Eastern restaurant with attitude.

Bonsoir Clara is the restaurant that started it all off for rue Antoine Dansaert, a beacon of trend in an area waiting to become something. A decade on, it still pulls in the crowds, with its understated sophistication and brilliantly eclectic food. To say it's modern French is too simplistic – the menu borrows from around the world and incorporates Asian spices, Italian delicacies and Californian reductions. Seared tuna, carpaccio of duck, and a pair of quails stuffed with dried fruit and ginger gives you an idea of the range. The look is clean and streamlined, with white tablecloths and white lilies, while a vast panels of back-lit coloured glass adds a bit of flair. Wear something from the designer shops along the road and your social status is assured.

Comocomo

19 rue Antoine Dansaert (02 503 0330/www. comocomo.com). Pré-metro Bourse. **Open** noon-3pm, 7-11pm daily. **Set menu** €7-€24. **Credit** AmEx, DC, MC, V. **Map** p316 B3.
The latest sensation to hit the Brussels food scene couldn't be in a better part of Happening Street, amid the designer shops and trendy eateries. The success comes from both the food and the concept, a Basque *pintxo* (tapas) bar in the style of sushi conveyor-belt factory. Clean and modern, with great splashes of coloured light, the restaurant is inviting and up-to-the-minute, with a wi-fi connection for those who can't bear to be offline. The *pintxos* wend their way around the snaking belt in colour codes, depending on theme: purple for pork, blue for fish, green for veggie (natch) and so on in seven different categories. Try fried quails' legs, boar carpaccio, octo-

pus or black olive and mushroom. You get charged for however many empty plates you end up with. Comocomo has succinctly hit the trendy g-spot; it must be the start of something big.

Divino

56 rue des Chartreux (02 503 39 09). Pré-métro Bourse. **Open** noon-2.30pm, 6.30-11.30pm Mon-Fri; 6.30-11.30pm Sat. **Main courses** €8-€10. **Credit** AmEx, MC, V. **Map** p316 B3.
The influence of the St-Géry area slowly spreads along this charismatic street, with its idiosyncratic shops and eateries. Divino is a splash of inspiration in a row of old houses still waiting to find its identity. Owner Moses Guez has managed to create a retro-minimalist dining space that buzzes as diners attack gigantic pizzas topped with goat's cheese and Parma ham or carpaccio of beef. The pasta dishes are subtle and make liberal use of seafood and fresh vegetables. A lovely old brick-walled terrace in summer means the front of house is empty, but don't think it's fallen out of favour – on the contrary, folk keep coming back for more.

Kasbah

20 rue Antoine Dansaert (02 502 40 26). Pré-métro Bourse. **Open** noon-3pm, 6.30pm-midnight Mon-Fri; 6.30pm-midnight Sat, Sun. **Main courses** €10-€25. **Credit** AmEx, MC, V. **Map** p316 B3.
Out of the stable of local entrepreneur Fred Nicolay (*see p139* **Right said Fred**) comes this Middle Eastern restaurant with attitude, much beloved by the chattering classes of the fashion district. You really can't miss it: a window filled with oranges gives way to lanterns over low-lit tables, resulting

in a romantic, almost fairy tale-like feel. The sharp service delivers plentiful mixed mezze, tagines, skewered lamb and couscous, along with a careful selection of Moroccan wine. It works for loved-up couples as well as groups on a night out and can also please the most dedicated vegetarian.

Le Pataya

49 rue Antoine Dansaert (02 513 3057). Pré-métro Bourse. **Open** noon-3pm, 6-11.30pm Mon-Fri; 6-11.30pm Sat, Sun. **Main courses** €7.30-€13. **Credit** AmEx, DC, MC, V. **Map** p316 B3.

A totally unremarkable interior belies the quality and richness of the Thai food here. Ignore the bizarre bamboo paint splashes, the pine tables and lonely Buddha. Concentrate instead on the piquant soups, the curries in red, yellow and green and the ample use of basil and coriander: Thai food as it should be. It's always, always busy, so booking a table is advised, though turnaround is quite fast. Everything is put in the middle of the table, perfect for sharing. The best news of all is that a decent slap-up meal here does not break the bank. All in all, a rather satisfying experience.

Sakura

1 rue du Pont de la Carpe (02 502 4365). Pré-métro Bourse. **Open** noon-2.30pm, 6-11pm Mon-Sat; 6-11pm Sun. **Main courses** €11-€27. **Set menu** €11-€25. **Credit** DC, MC, V. **Map** p316 B3.

The Sakura brand is known for its informal approach to Japanese dining. The food is neatly packaged up into menus, cutting out the hard work for the uninitiated. Having said that, the little wood-grilled kebabs are easy enough to sort out – duck, prawn, beef and a range of charred vegetables – and all well-known bases are covered, from sushi to sashimi to tempura. Yet there's no conveyor-belt mentality here: while the room is fairly unimaginative red and black, the service is charming, and you're treated like a guest of honour.

Shamrock

27 rue Jules van Praet (02 511 49 89). Pré-métro Bourse. **Open** 7pm-midnight Tue-Sun. **Main courses** €7-€12. **No credit cards**. **Map** p315 B3.

Only in Brussels could you find a truly authentic Indian restaurant with a truly authentic Irish name. Its dingy exterior looks like a pub, with its mullioned

On the move

Under the bright blue awning of the Mer du Nord fish shop on the corner of place Sainte-Catherine, well-dressed, sensible people stand chatting, shopping bags in hand. Wafting through them, a fishy head of steam from an enamel cooking pot on a flame; as well as buying their turbot and mussels, they are tucking into a bowl of escargots – not the snails we know from France, but rubbery whelks from the North Sea. On the square itself, a quieter group stand at the oyster stall, taking a dozen *fines claires* with a glass of Chardonnay. This is fast food, Brussels-style, where eating on the street doesn't always mean greasy paper napkins and mayonnaise moustaches.

Of course, this is the more genteel take of eating on the move, but it neatly sums up the democracy of enjoying food in Belgium. Across from the Bourse is the van-on-wheels of Chez Jef & Fils, a far more working-class establishment, serving escargots to regulars and passers-by for more than a couple of generations. No Chardonnay here, just a serving of good old gossip.

Street snacks cut across age and class as long as unspoken – but well understood – rules are observed. People will not blink at you eating a sandwich on the métro, but try a burger and chips and you'll know about it. Look around for fast-food detritus – it's not

there in quantity as it is in other cities. Sure, downtown around the bars has kebab shops and snack bars, not least along gaudy rue du Marché aux Fromages, but that's exactly what it is, an area. It's localised.

In burger chains, people prefer to sit in and eat. The Belgian Quick dominates the market, and with it comes a set of Belgian values. The golden arches of McDonalds are severely restricted, with one flagship restaurant opposite the Bourse. This is not just to do with home-grown loyalties, it's also to do with the home-grown *frite* and the fact that *MacDo* simply don't do them right. The best frites in town come from the little stalls dotted around the city (the best being Maison Antoine on place Jourdan). They are double-fried in beef dripping and served with a whole range of sauces in a cone with a plastic fork, acceptable street food for anyone.

Then there's the famous waffle, or *gaufre chaud*. The plain *gaufre de Liège*, sugary sweet but smaller, is popular, while the Brussels version is a more full on, with toppings such as cream and strawberries. For a sugar boost without the mattress, stop at any Leonidas (or even upmarket Wittamer; *see p158* **Sweet success**) and ask for one praline of your choice. They sell by weight and are more than happy to pop a single one in a bag for you. Now that's democratic.

Eat, Drink, Shop

windows and boozer signage, and when you walk in, you could be forgiven for thinking that the bar should have beer pumps lined along it. That's because this was an Irish pub that now has a restaurant in it. There's nothing flashy here, with the food a no-nonsense preparation of North Indian and Pakistani cuisines. Every dish can be ordered according to a three-chilli quotient. It's cheap, it's cheerful, the family banter with each other and the kids roll their toys around until they're packed off to bed. Marvellous.

Strofilia

11-13 rue du Marché aux Porcs (02 512 32 93). Métro Ste-Catherine. **Open** noon-2pm Mon-Fri; 7pm-midnight Mon-Sat. **Main courses** €15-€20. **Credit** AmEx, MC, V. **Map** p316 B2.

Now let's be clear from the start: this is not your package holiday type of place, where you down your ouzo and smash some plates. No, this is Greek chic, fine and sophisticated and attracting a fitting type of clientele, from young EU types to the Greek embassy set. It's set in a former pig market, and has a New York loft feel, but pass downstairs to the cellar – designed as an after-hours piano bar – and you are in dark, atmospheric underground Brussels. It is in the shadows of this vaulted cave that the fine Greek wines are kept under lock and key. All of them hand-picked by Stefanos Svanias, who had already built his local reputation with the L'Ouzerie (235 chaussée d'Ixelles, 02 646 44 49). The menu is big on fine meze, the service big on detail.

Thiên-Long

12 rue van Artevelde (02 511 34 80). Pré-Metro Bourse. **Open** noon-3pm, 6-11pm Mon, Tue, Thur-Sun. **Main courses** €7.50-€13. **No credit cards.** **Map** p316 B3.

First impressions of this Vietnamese restaurant is that it's a wooden-tabled caff incongruously set in a jungle of kitsch artefacts from the Far East, including the obligatory fluoro waterfall and red-tasselled lanterns. Despite this outlandish decoration, it is too self-effacing for its own good. It calls itself a *snack-resto*, but it's so much more than that. Great steaming bowls of hot chilli soup, lacquered duck, beef with bamboo and crunchy stir-fried vegetables sum up one of the longest menus this side of Hanoi. The food is sublime, the portions huge, and they're all concocted by the smallest chef you've ever seen. At lunchtime you can get a *plat du jour* for €6. Really.

The Marolles

This resolutely working-class area doesn't blow its own trumpet when it comes to restaurants, yet there are gems tucked away in the tiny streets that criss-cross rues Blaes and Haute. Old Marollien culture can still be found in the numerous cafés around place du Jeu de Balle, worth a visit for a raucous sandwich and an accordion tune on Sunday mornings.

Belgian & French

La Grande Porte

9 rue Notre-Seigneur (02 512 89 98). Bus 27, 48, 95, 96. **Open** noon-3pm, 6pm-2am Mon-Sat. **Main courses** €13-€17. **Credit** MC, V. **Map** 318 B4.

You realise why this restaurant is named La Grande Porte the minute you arrive and walk through a huge studded wooden door. Inside is a cosy room with an old bar running along one wall. But turn the corner and you could be in a different world. It seems as if this restaurant has been stitched together from two different patterns, the modern addition quite soulless compared to the buzz of the main room. Wherever you sit, though, this place is great for late-night Belgian classics: mussels, steaks with sauce, *stoemp, waterzooi*, served with deep bowls of fresh *frites*. Expect to find artists, actors, musicians and groups of chums who just don't want to go home.

L'Idiot du Village

19 rue Notre-Seigneur (02 502 55 82). Bus 27, 48, 95, 96. **Open** noon-2pm, 7.30-11pm Mon-Fri. **Main courses** €17-€25. **Credit** AmEx, DC, MC, V. **Map** p318 B4.

This small bistro, beloved by celebs, is hidden away in a side street off the antiques hub of rue Blaes. The chairs and tables are of the type you'd hope to find in the nearby flea market, the walls midnight blue and deep carmine, the flowers dried, the chandeliers camp. It sounds clichéd, but it works perfectly, as does the eclectic food by chef Alain Gascoin – down to earth but well executed, the succulent rabbit and leek stew full of wine and herbs. The overall feel is of being a guest in a private home. Booking a must.

Les Petits Oignons

13 rue Notre-Seigneur (02 512 47 38/www.petits-oignons.be). Bus 27, 48, 95, 96. **Meals served** noon-2.30pm, 7-11pm Mon-Sat. **Main courses** €15-€29. **Set menu** €44-€90. **Credit** AmEx, DC, MC, V. **Map** 318 B4.

From the outside this fine old vine-covered house from the 1600s looks as if it could be straight out of a Breugel painting. Walking in, you feel warm and welcomed, though there is a strange 1970s air about it. In winter there's a blazing log fire, in summer a green and lantern-lit terrace at the back. The food is unfussy French/Belgian, but cooked with finesse, arriving at the table in invigorating portions. A veal cutlet looks like the side of a horse, the fillet of dorade is thick and fleshy. Depending on the menu, they sometimes ask you to order desserts at the beginning of the meal, which might be difficult for purists to grasp, but it only goes to show that this is a restaurant that likes to get things right. This is one of those places that suits any reason to eat out, from laziness to major celebration.

Au Stekerlaplatte

4 rue des Prêtres (02 512 86 81). Métro Hôtel des Monnaies. **Open** 7pm-1am Tue-Sun. **Main courses** €13.25-€16.75. **Credit** MC, V. **Map** p318 B5.

Antique chic – **L'Idiot du Village**. *See p118.*

A late-night restaurant for traditional no-nonsense food at no-nonsense prices. At first glance you may think it full and turn to leave, but it is a warren of rooms and corridors and it's worth walking deeply into the maze in the knowledge that there is bound to be a table somewhere. It's a friendly place, despite its darkness and offbeat location, becoming more desirable as the area improves. Prepared in the time-honoured way, there are steaks and sauces with great fat fries, grilled pig's trotter, spare ribs and black pudding (vegetarians beware). Whatever you go for, you'll be among a growing number of people who crowd in here after the cinema or theatre.

International

Les Larmes du Tigre

21 rue Wynants (02 512 18 77). Métro Hôtel des Monnaies. **Meals served** noon-2.30pm, 7-10.30pm Mon, Wed, Thur; noon-2.30pm, 7-11pm Fri; 7-11pm Sat; noon-2pm, 7-9.30pm Sun. **Main courses** €12-€16. **Credit** AmEx, DC, MC, V. **Map** p318 B5.
Run by Marc Breukers and sister Muriel, this is one of the best Thai restaurants in town. Situated in the shadow of the vast Palais de Justice, the interior is a riot of clean colour, white walls with a swathe of multicoloured parasols hanging from the ceiling. A neat little walled terrace and conservatory does very nicely in the summer months. The menu is upmarket, fine and considered: curried fish and seafood soufflé in a banana leaf is a typical example. Service is quietly efficient, if a little off-hand, but it doesn't stop the professional crowd flocking to it.

Upper Town

Most dining in the Upper Town is centred around Sablon and its main square, one of the most upmarket areas in Brussels. Prices tend to be steeper, and design and fanciful presentation are to the fore. The choice ranges from old-style café or brasserie to pricey designer restaurants for the wealthy set. In summer, trendy young types pour on to the terraces by the square. The museum cafés provide a great place for lunch.

Belgian & French

Le Cap Sablon

75 rue Lebeau (02 512 01 70). Métro Gare Centrale/tram 92, 93, 94. **Open** noon-11.30pm Mon-Wed; noon-midnight Thur-Sun. **Main courses** €11.70-€19.50. **Credit** MC, V. **Map** p315 C4.
Among all the upmarket glitz of the Sablon, this understated little brasserie continues to shine through. Its simple, understated art deco interior gives a homely, comforting feel, which is reflected in the menu. Basic but succulent roasts and grills, fish livened up by oriental spices and wicked desserts all make for a satisfying, reasonably priced meal. The chattering Sablon set know about this place, but the Cap has resisted any pressure to trendify. There's a small terrace for outdoor dining, but make sure you specify it when booking.

Chez Marius en Provence

1 place du Petit Sablon (02 511 1208/www.chez-marius.be). Tram 92, 93, 94. **Open** noon-2.30pm, 7-10.30pm Mon-Fri. **Main courses** €24-€49. **Set menu** €38-€56. **Credit** AmEx, DC, MC, V. **Map** p319 C5.
Set in an 18th century house at the posh end of the Sablon, Marius is everything you'd expect from a soft-carpeted, chandeliered restaurant where the napkins are like floral displays. It's all here – the goose liver, the snails, the venison and Bresse chicken. But it's the bouillabaisse that keeps people coming back, a truly exquisite Provençale version, also available as part of a three-course menu. It is dear, though the interesting set menus make for a softer bill, and what you're paying for is the classic French dining experience in the old style.

Lola

33 place du Grand Sablon (02 514 24 60). Tram 92, 93, 94. **Open** noon-3pm, 6.30-11.30pm daily. **Main courses** €15-€30. **Credit** AmEx, MC, V. **Map** p315 C4.
Lola is one of those institutions loved by urban professionals and consistently recommended in guidebooks. It has the name, it has the location, it has the right clientele. It also has a sort of 'emperor's new clothes' ring about it, where everybody says it's fabulous, therefore it must be. The food is absolutely fine, in a modern brasserie way: rabbit with almonds and orange blossom or, for vegetarians, risotto and parmesan chips. This is not a place to whisper sweet

Eat, Drink, Shop

nothings – it's loud and gregarious and has everything the young set needs. Go for the buzz, but, as with so many places of this genre, you may leave wondering if anyone ever noticed you were there.

Maison du Boeuf

Hilton Hotel, 38 boulevard de Waterloo (02 504 13 34). Métro Louise/tram 91, 92, 93, 94. **Open** noon-2.30pm, 7-10.30pm daily. **Main courses** €35-€50. **Credit** AmEx, DC, MC, V. **Map** p319 C5.

Looking at the bland 1960s tower-block Hilton (*see p46*) by avenue Louise, it is hard to imagine that it could house one of Brussels' finest restaurants. It does, and it succeeds exceedingly well. The room is genteel and stylish and, of course, has astounding views. But it's the Michelin-star cooking of chef Michel Thuerel that makes it what it is. Fine French dining it most certainly is, but as the name suggests it's the beef that does it for most diners, the signature dish being a US rib of beef roasted in a salt crust. It's not just hotel guests and expense accounts; the locals love it too, though by its nature it is extremely well heeled and well dressed.

Le Poulbot de Bruxelles

29 rue de la Croix de Fer (02 513 38 61). Métro Parc. **Open** noon-2pm, 7-10pm Mon, Wed-Fri; noon-2pm Tue; 7-10pm Sat. **Main courses** €17-€25. **Credit** AmEx, DC, MC, V. **Map** p317 D3.

A *poulbot* is a street urchin, but there's nothing scaggy about this chic little find at the back of the Belgian Parliament. You could be mistaken for believing it was Japanese, what with the grey and white minimalism, accented with red splashes. Far from it: this is classic French cooking assembled with the greatest care and dignity by young chef Simon Saïdi. A starter of tiny potatoes stuffed with truffles and Jura sausage makes you pay attention, as does the startling vertical presentation of baby rabbit with wild mushrooms and goose liver. The service is impeccable, but the real achievement is in creating fine dining in an informal atmosphere – jeans and relaxation are the order of the day.

EU Quarter

Here rues Archimède and Franklin house global restaurants and Irish pubs, place du Luxembourg is lined with bars and restaurants, and place Jourdan has a local flavour, the *frites* stand of Maison Antoine in the middle of it. Lunchtimes are ever busy. The evenings are quiet, and many venues close at weekends.

Belgian & French

L'Atelier Européen

28 rue Franklin (02 734 91 40/www.atelier-euro.be). Métro Schuman. **Open** noon-2.30pm, 7-10pm Mon-Fri. **Main courses** €13-€21. **Set menu** €22-€27.50. **Buffet** €9.50 starter; €16.20 main meal. **Credit** AmEx, DC, MC, V. **Map** p321 G3.

Here you walk into a courtyard through a lovely set of coach doors. Long ago the coach would have pulled in to set its passengers down, then continued to the stables at the back. The space was converted into a studio and then a restaurant, though the studio feel is still here – light, airy, beamed roof and whitewashed walls. Food is a mix of Belgian and French, particularly fish, though the buffet is a good alternative. Prices are reasonable for the area, which makes the place lively, especially in summer when the courtyard and its climbing plants come into their own. Popular with large groups out for the night.

L'Esprit de Sel Brasserie

52-54 place Jourdan (02 230 60 40/www.espritdesel. be). Métro Schuman. **Open** noon-midnight daily. **Main courses** €11-€22. **Set menu** €24. **Credit** AmEx, DC, MC, V. **Map** p322 F5.

What used to be two restaurants are now co-joined with a door between the two. The menu is the same, but the looks are different: one slightly more trad, with an amazing Murano glass chandelier, the other all wood, marble and copper. But it matters not a jot when you get round to tucking into the best of Belgian, from a simple chicken and chips to rabbit in sour beer and beef tournedos with port. Busy and buzzy all year round, this is a meeting place for artistes, free thinkers and the occasional celebrity.

International

Kafeneio

134 rue Stevin (02 231 55 55). Métro Schuman. **Open** 9am-1am Mon-Sat; 10am-1am Sun. **Main courses** €9-€20. *Meze* €4-€7. **Credit** MC, V. **Map** p320 F4.

The new kid on the block is doing very well for itself, adaptable for breakfast, lunch and dinner, or just coffee and cake or a swift beer. But it's at lunchtime that it swings into action, with every table taken and a queue forming at the door. The reason is the buffet meze bar, where – accompanied by a waiter – you pick from 50 hot and cold dishes, sit down with a drink and await delivery. A welcome change of style for the area that has clearly hit the mark.

Le Rocher Fleuri

19 rue Franklin (02 735 00 21). Métro Schuman. **Open** noon-3pm, 6-10pm Mon-Fri. **Main courses** €12-€16. **Buffet** €12.95. **Credit** AmEx, DC, MC, V. **Map** p321 G3.

A sign outside shouts: 'Chicken and Eggs from EC!' No risk of bird flu here, then. This attention to detail makes this place stand out, though the real star is the owner: Madame Lâm Thi Thiêu Quang, former tight-rope walker and magician, now chef extraordinaire. She stands at the hub of her kitsch empire, purveying all that goes before her. But then she gets down to cooking… and what cooking it is! Fish curries, black ducks, roaringly hot chilli soups, stir-fries and steam-ups. It's a massive menu and it's all quite brilliant. The buffet option is only available at lunchtimes and Friday evenings.

Ixelles

This vast commune is a blend of downright earthy and damn expensive. From the little local restaurants of the Matongé and chaussée d'Ixelles to the glamour of avenue Louise, there is something to match all pockets and tastes. For that young, urban feel, head for the busy St-Boniface area, or the more upmarket Châtelain, where sophistication sits gladly with hedonism.

Belgian & French

Chez Marie

40 rue Alphonse de Witte (02 644 30 31). Tram 81, 82/bus 71. **Open** noon-2.15pm, 7.30-10.30pm Tue-Fri; 7.30-10.30pm Sat. **Main courses** €22-€28. **Credit** AmEx, MC, V. **Map** p325 E7.

Marie's has become a little star in the restaurant scene, especially after super-chef Lilian Devaux won herself a Michelin sparkler for her efforts. Sitting by the ponds, the small (40-cover) restaurant smacks of country living, with rustic touches: wood panelling, an old bar, open kitchen, checks and homely curtains. The contrast comes in the modern take on French cooking, which banishes heavy cream-laden sauces for fresh reductions and concentrated flavours. Seafood brought in from Brittany, pigeon and duck from the south-west of France give an idea of the attention to detail and the quality of the produce. Not surprisingly, booking is essential.

Le Fils de Jules

35 rue du Page (02 534 00 57/www.filsdejules.be). Tram 81, 82, 91, 92. **Open** noon-2.30pm, 7-11pm Mon-Thur; noon-2.30pm, 7pm-midnight Fri; 7pm-midnight Sat; 7-11.30pm Sun. **Main courses** €9.95-€18.50. **Sun set menu** €25. **Credit** AmEx, DC, MC, V. **Map** p324 D7.

Jules is integral to Châtelain, drawing classy urbanites after the authentic French foodie experience. The difference here is that the menu is firmly based in the Landais and Basque region, with dripping duck products, chunks of fish, thick lentils and Salardais potatoes drenched in garlic. The wine list is a discovery too, with its illegible local-language labels. Set Sunday menus assure a packed house. The decor is a blend of New York art deco and '70s copper, but the punters add the real colour.

Le Garde-Manger

151 rue Washington (02 346 68 29). Tram 93, 94. **Open** noon-3pm, 6-11pm Mon, Wed-Fri; 6-11pm Sat. **Main courses** €12-€16. **Credit** AmEx, DC, MC, V. **Map** p324 D8.

Le Garde-Manger is a true corner bar and restaurant. Locals drop by for a drink in the front room, with plenty of hand shaking and laughter, while further back, the theatrical dining room, with its taupe and aubergine walls, flickering candles, heavy drapes, and bohemian lighting, gives a softly camp, intimate feel. Irish Brian out front and chef Belgian Claude are welcoming hosts. The food is homely but delicate, with such delights as softly scrambled eggs and duck breast in lavender sauce. A busy, buzzy summer terrace will keep you chatting until dark.

La Quincaillerie

45 rue du Page (02 538 25 53/www.quincaillerie.be). Tram 81, 82, 91, 92. **Open** noon-2.30pm, 7pm-midnight Mon-Fri; 7pm-midnight Sat, Sun. **Main courses** €15-€45. **Credit** AmEx, DC, MC, V. **Map** p324 D7.

The name means ironmonger, but don't think this is any theme restaurant. The fine interior is largely untouched, its tables set with the original wooden drawers for holding nails, screws and widgets. A cast-iron gallery circles the ensemble, overlooked by a giant clock. The seafood bar, piled with crustaceans, is thought one of the best and the restaurant attracts a wealthy set, so it's a puzzling that the service is often abrupt, even rude. It doesn't seem to scare anyone off – book for any night of the week.

Saint Boniface

9 rue St-Boniface (02 511 53 66). Métro Porte de Namur/bus 71. **Open** noon-2.30pm, 7-10pm Mon-Fri. **Main courses** €15-€20. **Credit** AmEx, MC, V. **Map** p319 D5.

Little Italy

If you stand on the corner of rue Archimède and look up rue Franklin you will see six Italian pasta and pizza parlours, all nudging up to each other. Each has its merits, each is good at what it does and – especially in the summer, when the tables spill on to the street – it's often a case of taking the one that has space. **A La Brace** at 1 rue Franklin (02 736 57 73) differs in that it specialises in wood-fired pizza and grilled meats. On the opposite side at No.18 is **Pappa e Citti** (02 732 61 10), a more upmarket affair, quick to proclaim its Sardinian origins. At 43 rue Archimède is **Rosticceria Fiorentina** (02 734 92 36), resolutely traditional with not a hint of pizza, but the most fantastic osso buco and veal escalopes. Into rue Stevin is **Napoli** at No.76 (02 733 91 31), friendly and relaxed, with cottage-style decor. At No.180 is a newcomer, **Senso** (02 732 09 94), more minimalist, more stylish, more expensive. And finally, the oddly named **Le Lovely** is at No.206 (02 734 64 38). The name has nothing to do with the café interior, with its bizarre murals, but the splendid walled garden for summer eating (booking is essential). In its cooking, Le Lovely spills out of the standard Italian and into a wider Mediterranean approach.

Eat, Drink, Shop

Although only opened in 1987, the Boniface looks like it has stood on its little plot forever, beamed up from a distant Dordogne village. It cares not a jot for its trendier neighbours, its red and white checked cottage-feel throwing out a warm, traditional light. Old posters and oil lamps stand guard over a menu of rich and hearty Périgordine classics: duck, Puy lentils, foie gras, lamb studded with garlic and sliced potatoes soaked in goose fat. Notices pinned to the wall warn that mobile phones are not welcome. All well and good – you shouldn't be distracted from the authentic eating in this geographical time warp.

De la Vigne à l'Assiette

51 rue de la Longue Haie (02 647 68 03). Métro Louise/tram 93, 94. **Open** noon-2pm, 7-10pm Tue-Fri; 7-10pm Sat. **Main courses** €12-€20. **Credit** AmEx, MC, V. **Map** p319 D5.

Eddy Dandimont, joint owner of this tiny brasserie, is an award-winning sommelier. Now his stunning and reasonably priced wine list complements the eclectic world kitchen perfectly, which serves up dishes that are French based but feature quirky use of spices, herbs and subtle infusions. Much care is taken with the vegetables and salads, and nothing screams for lack of attention. The room is rustic in feel, with globe lamps and scrubbed walls and tables, and a youngish Ixelles clientele adds to the atmosphere. A wonderfully modest little place, which many would prefer to keep secret.

Fish & seafood

La Table d'Abbaye

62 rue du Belle-Vue (02 646 33 95/www.la-table-abbaye.be). Tram 93, 94. **Open** noon-3pm, 6-10pm Mon-Fri; 6-10pm Sat. **Main courses** €20-€48. **Set menu** €15 lunch; €45-€48 dinner. **Credit** AmEx, DC, MC, V. **Map** p325 E8.

Just off avenue Louise, this precise yet romantic restaurant, all soft yellows and blues, has immaculately laid tables and linen cloths. The back garden of the grand old townhouse is one of the city's best, the tables tented in creamy gauze with statuary and flaming torches adding to the atmosphere. It's not cheap, but then you are getting classic fish dishes in classic French sauces, fine wines and impeccable service. The set menu makes the bill more bearable, but the booze costs can creep up on you unawares.

International

Anarkali

33 rue Longue Vie (02 513 02 05/www.anarkali.be). Métro Porte de Namur/bus 54, 71. **Open** noon-2.30pm, 6pm-midnight daily. **Buffet set menu** €12-€14.50. **Credit** AmEx, DC, M, V. **Map** p319 D5.

This was a fairly average Indian restaurant looking for ideas to increase turnover. Inspiration hit when the owners introduced a buffet-style concept, with diners able to help themselves to as much as they wanted, all for one price. Now crowds constantly stand waiting for a table – the set menu includes everything from popadoms to that final coffee. The buffet is restricted to small-choice fresh items, with nothing allowed to curl at the edges. Great all round, then, provided you can get a table.

Cose Cosi

16 chaussée de Wavre (02 512 11 71). Métro Porte de Namur. **Open** noon-3pm, 6-11pm Mon-Thur, Sun; noon-3pm, 6pm-midnight Fri, Sat. **Main courses** €13-€25. **Credit** AmEx, MC, V. **Map** p319 D5.

From the outside, Cosi looks just a bit smarter than your average Italiano. The first surprise is the size of the place and how many it manages to pack in. Then you notice the antelope heads, animal skins, Zulu spears, faux shuttered windows, tropical plants and you could be in a safari lodge – except there's a baby grand piano where staff step up for a quick song. As bizarre as it may sound, it hangs together surprisingly well, tied by atmosphere and great big plates of finely prepared Italian staples and grilled meats and fish. The staff are exceedingly friendly and efficient, the wine flows, the chatter is loud. All in all, a fine night out.

La Crèche des Artistes

21 rue de la Crèche (02 511 22 56). Métro Porte de Namur/bus 54, 71. **Open** noon-3pm, 7-11pm Mon-Fri; 7pm-midnight Sat. **Main courses** €12-€25. **Credit** (only taken at weekday lunchtimes) AmEx, MC, V. **Map** p319 E6.

Don't be put off by the location of this restaurant, opposite one of the very few public-housing high rises in the centre of Brussels. This delightful candelit cellar place is run by the Vincenzo family from Naples, who have been serving up top-notch Italian cuisine since 1992. Buzz to be let in and by the time one of the brothers has taken your coat and led you to your table, another one will be serving you a welcoming glass of Prosecco. Five starters and nine mains, scribbled on a blackboard, use the freshest ingredients available. The portions can be delicate or substantial, depending on the dish, and the wines are all Italian. Booking is recommended, and cash is preferred (and obligatory in the evenings).

Les Perles de Pluie

25 rue du Châtelain (02 649 67 23/www.lesperlesdepluie.be). Tram 93, 94. **Open** noon-3pm, 7-11pm Tue-Fri, Sun; 7-11pm Sat. **Main courses** €13-€25. **Set menu** €39-€49. **Lunch buffet** €15.50. **Sun buffet** €30. **Credit** MC, V. **Map** p324 D7.

Being in the golden square of trendy Châtelain, this Thai restaurant tries to be smart and rather more upmarket than it needs to be. It's heavily decorated and rather chi-chi, a Buddha and lotus blossom dominating the richly decked room. But it's not the decor that people come for, but the Sunday buffet. And rightly so. It's spread along huge tables and includes most of the dishes from the main menu. Only small portions are brought out at a time, which ensures freshness. On the downside, the service sometimes falters, especially as the place hots up.

Not just any old iron at **La Quincaillerie**. *See p121.*

La Porte des Indes

455 avenue Louise (02 647 86 51/www. *laportedesindes.com). Tram 93, 94.* **Open** noon-2.30pm, 7-10.30pm Mon-Thur; noon-2.30pm, 7-11pm Fri, Sat, 7-10.30pm Sun. **Main courses** €16.50-€22. **Set menu** €37.50-€48. **Credit** AmEx, DC, MC, V. **Map** p325 E9.

Not for the curry-and-pint-of-Kingfisher crowd, this. La Porte is refined and expensive, hushed and cushioned, decorated in Maharaja baroque, with vast palms and over-the-top lighting and artefacts. It all hangs together in a rich and warming way, creating the perfect atmosphere for the top-notch southern Indian food (with nods to the north). A dish from the royal court of Hyderabad – lamb cutlets soaked in garam masala, ginger and lemon – is an example of the finesse and careful balance achieved in the kitchen. Dress well and expect to spend well.

Vie Sauvage

12 rue de Naples (02 513 68 85). Métro Porte de Namur. **Open** noon-2pm, 7-11pm Tue-Sun. **Main courses** €12.50-€20. **Credit** AmEx, DC, MC, V. **Map** p319 D5.

Tucked away down a quiet residential street is one of the more authentic Moroccan restaurants in town (ring the bell for entry). The management has made an effort to transport you to the heat and dustiness of North Africa, with hanging pots and earthen walls, but it's the food that impresses. A full menu of specialities includes tagines and couscous, plus plentiful salads. Service can sometimes be erratic and laid back, so don't go there in a hurry, just take in the mellow atmosphere – even peruse a lengthy and unlikely list of Scots whiskies.

Vegetarian

L'Elément Terre

465 chaussée de Waterloo (02 649 37 27). Tram 91, 92. **Open** noon-2.30pm, 7-10.30pm Tue-Fri; 7-10.30pm Sat. **Main courses** €15. **Credit** DC, MC, V. **Map** p324 C8.

The 'Elementary' is small, with an almost restrictive atmosphere that suggests that all vegetarians are deadly serious people. The excellent food seems to arrive wearing slippers, and voices are rarely raised, maybe in reverence for the fine organic char-grilled, caramelised vegetables, and the clever combinations of pulses and grains. The 'discovery plate' is a good way into the menu, offering a taste of this and that. Tasty, perhaps, but not the most riotous night out.

St-Gilles

Overshadowed by its blousy Ixelles neighbour, St-Gilles is residential, full of local restaurants. Outsiders go to the chaussée de Charleroi for its lounge-bar restaurants and hip brasseries. Over in Parvis de St-Gilles are Moroccan restaurants and tiny family-run places in back streets.

Belgian & French

Ma Folle de Soeur

53 chaussée de Charleroi (02 538 22 39). Métro Louise/tram 91, 92. **Open** noon-2.30pm, 6-10.30pm, Mon-Fri. **Main courses** €8-€15. **Credit** MC, V. **Map** p319 C6.

Run by two sisters, the small restaurant has a huge picture window facing on to the street and a door that opens directly into the understated and mellow dining room, its wooden bar and tables softened by yellow walls and soft candlelight in the evening. The menu has flair and a touch of adventure – it's Belgian in nature, with French bistro influences. Meat (duck, steak, even horse) is to the fore, and dressed with imaginative sauces, and fish always featured too. The suits give way to young lovers and groups of friends in the evening. A back garden, too.

Salons de l'Atalaïde
89 chaussée de Charleroi (02 537 2154/www. lessalonsatalaide.be). Tram 91, 92. **Open** noon-3pm, 7-11.30pm Mon-Thur; noon-3pm, 7pm-midnight Fri-Sun. **Main courses** €12.50-€21. **Credit** AmEx, DC, MC, V. **Map** p319 C6.
This former auctioning house is now an off-the-wall, eclectic, over-the-top restaurant that preens itself in its own baroque mirrors. Ornate chandeliers, over-sized paintings, gothic candles and ostentatious palms combine to give this place an unreal, surreal edge. The menu is as mixed as the decor, with fair-ly standard fare, such as steak and chips, and cod with olive oil mash. Vegetarians only get a couple of choices, but a startling range of Japanese spe-cialities has recently appeared, taking up almost half of the menu, and at a very reasonable price. So the Atalaïde continues to surprise – make sure to book.

International

Aux Mille et Une Nuits
7 rue de Moscou (02 537 41 27/www.aux-mille-et-une-nuits.be). Pré-métro Parvis de St-Gilles. **Open** noon-3pm, 6-11.30pm Mon-Sat. **Main courses** €10.50-€15.50. **Credit** AmEx, DC, MC, V. **Map** p318 B6.
You may think twice before walking into this pink-painted Tunisian restaurant, but its full-on lighting and kitsch decor gives it an edge in an area packed with North African restaurants. It resembles a mod-ern Bedouin tent, with oriental rugs hanging from the walls and thousands of tiny lights sparkling brightly above like stars. And the food? Out of this world. For starters, try the harira chickpea soup or honey-soaked chicken in crispy pastry. Then there's the eternal dilemma of tagine or couscous, although you can't go far wrong with the caramelised lamb couscous or chicken tagine with grapes and honey. The service is impeccable.

Further afield

Belgian & French

Restaurant Bruneau
75 avenue Broustin, Koekelberg (02 427 69 78/ www.bruneau.be). Métro Simonis. **Open** noon-2pm, 7-10pm Mon, Thur-Sun. **Main courses** €38-€104. **Set menu** €65-€175. **Credit** AmEx, DC, MC, V.

Jean-Pierre Bruneau, one of the city's finest and most innovative chefs, delivers the top-notch goods in his sleek, modern restaurant near the Basilica. Although one of Brussels' top restaurants, Bruneau dropped one of its three Michelin stars in 2003, sending the whole restaurant scene into a tizzy. Of course, this remains seriously high cuisine, with such surpris-ing delights as scallops stuffed with minced pig trot-ter, and fillet of sea bass smothered with Oscietra caviar. Naturally it's pricey, but if you're going to push the boat out you may as well do it here.

Les Brasseries Georges
259 avenue Winston Churchill, Uccle (02 347 21 00/ www.brasseriesgeorges.be). Tram 23, 90. **Open** 11.30am-12.30am Mon-Thur; 11.30am-1am Fri, Sat. **Main courses** €10-€28. **Credit** AmEx, DC, MC, V.
The feel of a fin-de-siècle Parisian brasserie is gen-erated by the twisting copper and brass, the vast stained-glass windows, potted palms and statuettes of classical muses, all opened up by the obligatory red curtain as you walk through the doors. The spe-cialities are the crustacea: oysters, whelks and the like, all brought together either as a starter or a great dripping *plateau de fruits de mer*. Perfection.

De Ultieme Hallucinatie
316 rue Royale, Schaerbeek (02 217 06 14/www. ultiemehallucinatie.be). Métro Botanique/tram 92, 93, 94. **Open** noon-2.30pm, 7-10.30pm Mon-Fri; 7-10.30pm Sat. **Main courses** €25-€30. **Credit** AmEx, DC, MC, V. **Map** p320 E1.
The name comes from a little hobby that famed architect Victor Horta used to practise: growing mushrooms in his cellar. You may well think you're hallucinating as you enter this perfectly preserved Arts and Crafts house. Every detail, down to the piano, benches, skirting boards and window frames, are in this late 19th-century style, with a real sense of stepping back in time. The darkly brooding but stylish restaurant at the front, with its Tiffany-style chandeliers and lamps, serves classic French food with classic service and classic prices – though you may be put in the cheaper, blander café extension at the back. Visit even for a look and a quick sandwich.

International

Senza Nome
22 rue Royale Ste-Marie, Schaerbeek (02 223 16 17). Tram 92, 93, 94. **Open** noon-2.30pm, 7-10.30pm Mon-Fri; 7-10.30pm Sat. **Main courses** €18-€25. Credit MC, V. **Map** p320 E1
This means 'without a name', perhaps because it wants to escape the usual Italian restaurant syn-drome. Senza specialises in Sicilian dishes, which have more earthy flavours and strong infusions of chilli. In-yer-face ingredients such as *sèche* (whole baby squid, guts included) and black-inked pastas vie with *branzino* (sea bass) full of citrus and sun-ripe tomatoes. Do book, especially if you're eating late; once the nearby Halles de Schaerbeek (*see p99*) empties its audience, the place fills quickly.

Bars

More bars than stars in heaven.

Casual, social or deathwish, drinking here is invariably a pleasure. The range of bars, the range of beers and the rage of thirst they inspire combine to produce a drinking culture unmatched this side of Berlin. And culture it is, as ritualised as wine-tasting in Burgundy and as traditional as tea-drinking in England.

At the centre of this culture is beer. Not just any old beer, but some 600 varieties in almost as many colours and flavours, brewed by everyone from Trappist monks to major multinational concerns (*see p128* **The beers of Belgium**). Most bars serve around 20 types; some stock 200. They'll be served, with a '*s'il vous plaît*' from the waiter or barman, in a specially shaped and logoed glass, plonked on to a logoed beermat. Yet despite such ceremony, few bars are pretentious enough to warrant a reciprocal nose-in-the-glass and nod of approval. Sip it, sup it, neck it; simply down the beer as you would anywhere else, before going on to think about the next one.

Ask for '*une bière*' and you'll get a standard glass of standard draught lager, invariably Maes, Stella or Jupiler, costing €1.50-€2. French speakers note that asking for a '*demi*', as you would do for a standard small glass in France, will get you a half-litre and nods from fellow drinkers. '*Une blanche*' will get you a €2 glass of draught wheat beer. For a bottle of one of the more interesting brews, choose by name from a lengthy drinks menu. To up the ante, chase beers with genever, a grain spirit native to Flanders (*see p134* **Going against the grain**).

Then look around you. Dutch bars are dreary; German ones plain beery; provincial French ones drab. Mostly, they are average. Rare is that twinkle of irony that keeps many coming back to Brussels. There may also be touches of the art nouveau, surrealism and art deco that influenced decor at key points of the last century. Unwitting retro also abounds: pinball machines from the 1950s; gaudy neon; and period publicity posters. Behind the counter, boxes of Royco cup-a-soups. Pub grub of *stoemp*, sausages and stews may also be available throughout the day; if not, Belgian tapas of salami nibbles and cheese on sticks.

Opening hours are gloriously lax. Drinking until midnight almost anywhere in town is easy; past 1am, you'll need to be in the centre, where dawn is not an uncommon closing time.

Tradition rules at **A La Bécasse**. *See p126.*

Downtown drinking begins, inevitably, with the Grand' Place , lined with imposing, terraced guildhouse pubs, where aproned waiters serve hulking portions of food. Prices are higher, but not budget-bustingly so. Around it fans a network of bar-starred streets. South-west snakes rue du Marché au Charbon, the spine of the gay quarter, Brussels' best bar-hop. Across boulevard Anspach, St-Géry is home to style cafés (instigated by bar guru Fred Nicolay; *see p139* **Right said Fred**), perhaps not for the discerning, but responsible for a convivially continental terrace atmosphere in summer.

Elsewhere, bars tend to reflect the area they serve. Sablon's are as glitzy as the neighbouring Marolles' are scuzzy. Ixelles' are a mixture of African (rue Longue Vie), trendy (around place St-Boniface), student-oriented (near Ixelles cemetery) and snobbish (avenue Louise). Those in St-Gilles have a boho, villagey feel, while the pubs of the EU Quarter provide expats with a drinking and networking facility.

A La Bécasse

11 rue de Tabora (02 511 00 06). Pré-métro Bourse.
Open 10am-1am Mon-Thur; 10am-1am Fri, Sat;
11am-midnight Sun. **Credit** MC, V. **Map** p315 C3.
This bar comes as a total surprise. From the street,
all that marks its presence is a red neon light, hint-
ing there's something tacky involved. Not at all.
Look down at your feet and see the stone and brass
welcome mat fixed to the pavement. Follow the alley
through the houses and you see the Dickensian-style
bottle windows. Behind is an ancient tavern where
customers sit at long tables and have their beer,
including draught Lambic, poured from jugs by
aproned waiters. It's of the same genre and ownership as L'Imaige de Nostre-Dame (8 rue du Marché
aux Herbes, 02 219 42 49) nearby.

Cirio

*18-20 rue de la Bourse (02 512 13 95). Pré-métro
Bourse.* **Open** 10am-1am daily. **No credit cards.**
Map p315 B3.
Le Cirio is named after the Italian grocer, today
remembered on a million sauce cans, who shipped
wagons of goodies over the Alps from Turin to his

ornate delicatessen here by the stock exchange.
Both the Bourse and deli have since folded, but the
ornamentation remains – beautiful fittings and
Vermouth promotions, cash registers and century-
old gastronomy awards – along with the eternally
popular *half-en-half* wine (half sparkling, half still,
wholly Italian). Grandes dames and their lookalike
poodles sip away the afternoon, the former from a
stemmed glass, the latter from a bowl of tap water.
Pre-war toilets complete the experience.

Café Dada

*29 rue du Fossé aux Loups (02 218 13 54). Métro/
pré-métro De Brouckère.* **Open** noon-late Mon-Fri;
4pm-late Sat, Sun. **No credit cards. Map** p315 C2.
Venerable downtown bar with a wooden interior
and a timeless feel, traditionally frequented by middle-aged men escaping dismal marriages or middle-
aged couples rekindling old romance. Its appeal has
been broadened by the recent arrival of Brussels'
Flemish bohemia, bar staff, music and all. This
means: (a) unfeasibly late and tantalisingly indefi-
nite closing times; (b) a cool clientele happy for you
to join them round the bar; and (c) perhaps the best
music policy in town. Much here is pot luck – you
could be a table next to thrice-marrieds or Franz

Eat, Drink, Shop

The best Bars

For tropical cocktails a go-go
Cane those cane spirits at **Ma Cabane
Bambou** (*see p138*), strong Antillean punch
a house speciality.

For picking up racing tips
L'Ecuyer (*see p127*) has all the form –
punters, jockeys and a four-legged renegade
from a vintage roundabout.

For philosophical debate
Intellectuals gather every Wednesday night at
the **Kafé Kan'h** (*see p128*) to discuss the
meaning of life and slam back bloody strong
dark-rum cocktails.

For artistic heritage
Khnopff (*see p141*) is set in a house where
the artist of the same name had a studio in
the 1880s. Forty years later, **La Fleur en
Papier Doré** (*see p127*) was a meeting place
for the surrealists.

For variety of beers
Chez Moeder Lambic (*see p141*) has scores
of 'em, albeit in dusty surroundings; **Le Bier
Circus** (*see p136*) is somewhat cheerier,
while **A La Bécasse** (*see p126*) serves rare
draught Lambic by the jug.

For outdoor drinking
Le Terrasse (*see p138*) is the perfect spot on
a summer's eve; the **Brasserie Verscheuren**
(*see p142*) gives out on to a paved main
square, while the front terrace of **Ici le Bô-Bar**
(*see p142*) is located in leafy Uccle.

For original fittings
The classic **Cirio** (*see above*) features the
same ornamentation as the fin-de-siècle
Italian delicatessen once housed there; on
the other side of the Bourse, **Le Falstaff**
(*see p127*) has a period art nouveau interior,
as does the lesser-known **Le Perroquet**
(*see p136*) near the Sablon.

For French pop from Aznavour
to yé-yé
Goupil le Fol (*see p127*) has 3,000 choice
slices of crackly vinyl to suit every mood.

For late-night drinking
The **Café Dada** (*see above*), **Kafé Kan'h** (*see
p128*) and **L'Archiduc** (*see p134*) all like to
keep things open-ended, which is how we like
to keep things.

Simply the best
L'Archiduc (*see p134*) rules.

Make yourself at home at **Cirio**. *See p126.*

Probably the most famous bar in Brussels, and certainly the most evergreen. An awning on one side of the Bourse barely prepares the first-time visitor for the eye candy of the art nouveau interior, which has been attracting Bruxellois of every stripe for the better part of a century. It's a restaurant, too, but the reasonably priced mains are but a side dish to the range of beers and generous hours. A mere step from the main square, this is more than most European capitals can dream about.

La Fleur en Papier Doré

55 rue des Alexiens (02 511 16 59). Pré-métro Anneessens. **Open** 11am-midnight Mon-Thur, Sun; 11am-2am Fri, Sat. **No credit cards. Map** p315 B4.
As the haunt of the surrealists, this quirky venue would make a mint from the tourist trail were it not stuck on an obscure, steep, grey street whose only function is to connect the Lower and Upper Towns. It's not that Le Fleur is far from the action: it's just that it's the wrong side of a pleasant stroll. It attracts the more unusual tourist, happy to gawp at the doodles and sketches and stagger around in Magritte's wonky footsteps. An artistically active bunch of regulars, albeit a modest one, alleviate their solitude.

Fontainas

91 rue du Marché au Charbon (02 503 31 12). Pré-métro Anneessens or Bourse. **Open** 10.30am-1am Mon-Thur, Sun; 10.30am-2am Fri, Sat. **No credit cards. Map** p315 B3.
Possibly – no, probably – the best bar on Brussels' best stretch of bar crawl, the Fontainas is so wonderfully understated. Opposite the equally recommended Au Soleil (*see p131*), the Fontainas is full of lovely little retro touches – beaded curtains, formica chairs with chrome legs, vintage advertising – which would do justice to a 1950s milk bar. Yet the place is as determinedly 21st century as the gay/straight mixed clientele: reliably excellent sounds from fiery DJs; strong cocktails; rare Orval and Maredsous brews. Throw in a few terrace tables when the sun's out, and you have somewhere head and shoulders above anything going on in St-Géry.

Ferdinand fans – but fall in here after midnight and you should be thoroughly entertained.

L'Ecuyer

3 rue de l'Ecuyer (02 219 65 19). Métro/pré-métro De Brouckère. **Open** 9am-3am daily. **No credit cards. Map** p315 C2.
Fabulously quirky downtown bar by the Opera, the Horseman, its interior and its clientele, are linked to the local racing fraternity. Within a sober, wooden-panelled main room, a large carousel horse guards the stairs to the bar staff's quarters. You may spot a few jockeys around the bar counter talking shop. In the daytime, it's used as any other city centre bar, for quiet drinks, light lunches and polite chat, but come nightfall, something conspiratorial takes hold, and regulars begin to whisper and make frantic calculations. Later on, once outsiders take the hint, they may even lock the door and natter on about the nags until the cows come home.

Le Falstaff

19-25 rue Henri Maus (02 511 87 89). Pré-métro Bourse. **Open** 10am-2am daily. **Credit** AmEx, DC, MC, V. **Map** p315 B3.

Goupil le Fol

22 rue de la Violette (02 511 13 96). Métro Gare Centrale. **Open** 7.30pm-5am daily. **No credit cards. Map** p315 C3.
Now in all the guidebooks, Goupil – the stocky, grey-haired gent handing out sweets at the narrow squeeze by the front door by the end of the night – can but cash in. He has his staff force his questionable house fruit wines upon too many a tourist, while only providing standard Jupiler (at €2.50 a glass!) by means of any beer alternative. In Brussels, mind. So, what is there to recommend about it? Well, Goupil is a kooky labyrinthine junk-shop of a bar, where all trace of time can be lost thanks to a jukebox of 3,000 choice slices of vinyl. Intimacy is all. It's eccentric, velvety and nostalgic; check the beads and commie kitsch. On the right night – in a group, or better yet, *à deux* – it is perfect. Pass the fruit wine.

Kafé Kan'h

30 place de la Vieille Halle aux Blés (02 502 00 07/ www.kanh.be). Métro Gare Centrale. **Open** 4pm-late Mon-Fri; 11am-late Sat, Sun. **No credit cards**. **Map** p315 C4.

Opened in 2001, the Kan'h is firmly on the scene thanks to its fresh agenda of entertainment. As its menu says: 'Kan'h is more than just a *kafé*, it's a place of discovery and expression'. Quite. Midweek debates and improv music precede weekend DJs and jazz (*see p196*), for which a cover charge is levied. If this puts you off, Kan'h is a fine bar, of classy decor – penny-chew-coloured bar-stools against sombre wood – and classy cocktails: a Kan'h, of dark rum, fresh orange and lemon, and grenadine makes a change after a weekend on the beer. There's food, too. In warm weather, terrace tables face the Brel Foundation across a quaint square. Recommended.

Beers of Belgium

Beer is Belgium's national treasure. Crafted with love and precision over the centuries, the nation's 600-strong range of brews represents a tradition beyond compare.

Variety is the key here. Offering everything from bog-standard lagers mass-produced by multinationals to finely honed ales brewed by monks to medieval recipes, Belgium is a beer-lover's paradise. Like fine wines, the brewing process can take years. And, as with fine wines, there are strict controls on how any company can describe its brew.

Every bar will stock at least one draught lager, generally Stella, Maes or Jupiler, along with a wheat beer, '*une blanche*', or a '*witte*' – usually Hoegaarden but occasionally Brugs or Limburgse. The taste for this cloudy tipple died out after the war, but was revived in the 1990s. Served in tumblers, it's the classic summer drink, thirst-quenchingly quaffable.

A fair number of bars provide a few more adventurous ales on draught (*au fût/van 't vat*), while a select clique offers an almost encyclopaedic range, on tap and from the bottle. Of Brussels' bars, **L'Atelier** (*see p138*), **A La Bécasse** (*see p126*), **Le Bier Circus** (*see p136*) and **Chez Moeder Lambic** (*see p141*) offer the most choice. The latter runs the gamut from abbey beers to Westvleteren, the most obscure of the five breweries officially designated as Trappist.

Many Belgian brews hint at monastic origins, and many were popularised during times of plague. However, only the famous five of Chimay, Orval, Rochefort, Westmalle and Westvleteren have truly been touched by the hand of God. Aside from the dark, unclassifiable Orval, the tricky exception, all are deep brown and creamy; for deep brown and creamy with a kick, select the *dubbel* or *trippel* versions, which deliver the wallop of up to nine per cent ABV.

Each Trappist brewery is a working monastery, but few welcome personal visits and sales are strictly controlled. Near each monastery, however (check www.belgium-tourism.net or www.visitflanders.com for directions and details), will be at least one bar and shop happy to flog the stuff. The next ecclesiastical step down are abbey beers such as Leffe and Grimbergen, both frequently spotted on tap due to national distribution deals.

The most unusual family of beers are the Lambics, particular to the Brussels area. Lambics are naturally fermented with no added yeast, a process that takes at least

La Lunette

*3 place de la Monnaie (02 218 03 78). Métro/
pré-métro De Brouckère*. **Open** 9am-1am Mon-Thur;
9am-2am Fri, Sat; 10am-1am Sun. **No credit cards**.
Map p315 C3.

This has become a bit of an institution, partly
because of its location near the commercial zone, and
partly because of its beer list, with eight welcome
on-tap varieties. Measures here come in a standard
glass or a Lunette, which is like a magnum champagne glass. That's a polite way of putting it; ask
for a Lunette and you get a bucket. A sleek two-floor-
interior of curved green banquettes would be
remarked upon in somewhere like Amsterdam – in
Brussels it's pretty much par for the course. The
atmosphere is exactly what you would expect from
a continental café full of shoppers, drifters and folk
waiting for a film to start.

a couple of years. A young Lambic is called a
Faro, and quite rare. Indeed, straight Lambic
is hard to find; it provides the base for two of
Belgium's most popular and idiosyncratic
beer types, Gueuze and fruit Lambic. A
sometimes painfully acquired taste, Gueuze
is the delicate mix of young and old Lambic –
as manufactured at the brewery of the same
name in Anderlecht (*see p94*). Lambic's very
tart taste – tinned cider is one approximation
– also makes it the perfect base in which to
mix small, dark cherries (*kriek*) and
raspberries (*framboise* or *frambozen*).

Finally come the hundreds of ales of
all colours and for all seasons. Some –
particularly brown ales from Oudenaarde, red
beers from Rodenbach, strong golden ales
such as Duvel and amber De Koninck from

Antwerp – are produced by successful
provincial breweries. Others – banana beer,
anyone? – are obscure almost for the sake
of it. Think of a colour, or a fruit, and it will
have been bottled and labelled.

Almost all varieties of beer will be served to
you in itsown shaped glass, with its own logo
and beermat. Here there's no social stigma
attached to any selection you choose; you
won't be singled out as a bearded obsessive
if you happen to order the most obscure one
on the menu (and most places will have a
drinks menu, an extensive one at that). Beer,
remember, is a matter of national pride and
drinks are drunk by all: male, female, young
and old alike. There are even *bières de table*
for weaning children. Only in Belgium could
beer match mother's milk.

A place of discovery and expression – **Kafé Kan'h**. See p128.

Café Métropole

31 place de Brouckère (02 219 23 84/www.metropole hotel.be). Métro/pré-métro De Brouckère. **Open** 9am-1am daily. **No credit cards. Map** p315 C2.

For a little fin-de-siècle finesse, pop into the café of the grand Hotel Métropole. This place is of a different age: over-burdened chandeliers, mirrored walls, ornate ironwork and a hush that hasn't changed for a century. Sarah Bernhardt stayed here and she is reincarnated in the ladies with hairdos who sit on the terrace in sunglasses and fur coats all year round. Aperitifs dominate the drinks menu, plus champagnes by the bottle, half-bottle and quarter-bottle, delivered by bow-tied waiters. It's not all glamour, though – note the Heinz ketchup on each table, and a pillar of autographed guests features Emerson Fittipaldi and Vera Lynn. Ah, Brussels.

Mokafé

9 galerie du Roi (02 511 78 70). Métro Gare Centrale. **Open** 7am-midnight Mon-Sat; 8am-midnight Sun. **Credit** AmEx, DC, MC, V. **Map** p315 C3.

Near the opera and opposite Brussels' best classical music shop, the Mokafé attracts a terrace full of arty types all year round, protected from rain and scorn by covered galleries. It's good for lunch, with reasonably priced Belgian café food and pasta. On Sunday mornings, locals bring their newspapers and sit for hours with coffee, croissant and a West Highland terrier. Everyone pretends to be in their own little world, but just watch eyes dart and ears prick when a newcomer takes a table; knowing nods to regulars and faux lack of interest at strangers.

A La Mort Subite

7 rue des Montagnes aux Herbes Potagères (02 513 13 18/www.alamortsubite.be). Métro Gare Centrale. **Open** 11am-12.30am Mon-Sat; 1pm-12.30am Sun. **Credit** MC, V. **Map** p315 C3.

Named after a card game and a variety of fruit beer whose hangovers easily assume the mantle of sudden death, the popularity of this classically dissolute café soon saw the name pass into legend. Earning such post-booze pain is a real pleasure in this narrow, wood-and-mirror haven of ensozzlement, ever thick with tobacco smoke and rife with bar tales. You could write your lifework novel before any of the waiters deign to serve you – in fact, attempting to do so would fail to raise many eyebrows – but it's all part of the character. Be warned though: this is one of the few venues in town to serve the local Gueuze, to be handled with care.

Le Petit Finistère

3 rue aux Choux (02 218 14 86). Métro/pré-métro De Brouckère or Rogier. **Open** 9am-9pm Mon-Sat. **No credit cards. Map** p317 C2.

Authentic locals' bar just off the main shopping drag of rue Neuve, where champagne is cracked open and decks of cards snapped together as soon as the rattle of shopfronts signals a new day. A tangle of fern and tinsel (any particular Christmas?) provides a cosy welcome, although sadly the jukebox is long gone. From May onwards, a modest terrace beckons, although the view would be improved by someone bulldozing the improbably grim City 2 shopping centre. Oh yes, and at €1.20, the beer is surely the cheapest anywhere in the town centre.

Plattesteen

*41 rue du Marché au Charbon (02 512 82 03/
www.plattesteen.be). Pré-métro Anneessens.* **Open**
11am-midnight daily. **Credit** AmEx, DC, MC, V.
Map p315 B3.

This traditional Belgian bar-café is truly multi-
functional. It acts as a neighbourhood bar, as an
inexpensive restaurant and as a place for ladies with
poodles, ladies with men and men with men. It's a
great melting pot on the corner of the street, joining
shopping Brussels to gay Brussels and the rue du
Marché au Charbon. Thus it is a great meeting place,
especially in summer when you can sit on the terrace and watch the world cruise by arm-in-arm. It's
one of the great Brussels contradictions; homely and
unexceptional decor slap in the middle of the new
trendsville. 'Established 1968' if you please.

Le Roi d'Espagne

*1 Grand' Place (02 513 08 07/www.roidespagne.be).
Pré-métro Bourse.* **Open** 10am-1am daily. **Credit**
AmEx, DC, MC, V. **Map** p315 C3.

The king of the guildhouses on the gilded square
(it was the HQ of the bakers' guild), Le Roi is a
classic spot in a prime location, taking full
advantage of the tourist trade by filling its
warren of dark rooms and corners with dangling
marionettes, old prints and pigs' bladders. Don't
pity the poor pigs: it's the waiters in monk
outfits for whom you should be feeling sorry, as
they struggle to keep tabs on busy tables while
tourists scrap it out for one with that view over
the Grand' Place. Many a diplomatic incident has
been caused in grabbing one.

Au Soleil

*86 rue du Marché au Charbon (02 513 34 30). Pré-
métro Anneessens or Bourse.* **Open** 10am-1am Mon-
Thur, Sun; 10.30am-2am Fri, Sat. **No credit cards**.
Map p315 B3.

Set in an extravagant old tailor's, Au Soleil is filled
with a constant buzz from early doors, so much so
that passing by without popping in can be difficult.
Everyone seems to be talking on top of one another,
that is when they're not looking impossibly interesting amid the fug of fumes. It's all a pose, of course,
but it's quite fun for all that, and it lures punters to
tumble down Charbon like lemmings. Inside, once
the smoke clears, it has a somewhat stern interior,
plenty of marble and weighty metal, backdropped
by picture windows and passers-by out on the town.

Toone

*21 petite rue des Bouchers (02 513 54 86).
Pré-métro Bourse.* **Open** noon-midnight Tue-Sun.
No credit cards. **Map** p315 C3.

This might be a well-known spot on the tourist trail,
but to call it a trap would be doing the Toone family a great injustice. Eight generations have worked
the puppet theatre here, cynical in six tongues (*see
p63* **Talk of the Toone**). This cosy two-room
dark-wood establishment is the theatre bar, a familiar stop for many Brussophiles as it's quirky enough

to show off to first-time visitors (dangling marionettes and the like), quiet enough to enjoy in whis-
pered intimacy, and not too quaint to put you off
coming again. It's signposted from alongside the
Musée de la Ville de Bruxelles on the Grand' Place.

Un Lombard

*1 rue du Lombard (02 514 33 40/www.unlombard.
com). Pré-métro Anneessens.* **Open** 9am-1am Mon-
Thur; 9am-2am Fri, Sat; 10am-1am Sun. **No credit
cards**. **Map** p315 B3.

New venue on the Charbon scene – it stands on a
prominent corner where this street of bars cuts
through the intersection of Plattesteen, rue des
Teinturiers and Lombard – One Lombard has the
gravitas its name suggests. A simple, effective interior fronts an efficient café-restaurant operation
busy from breakfast through until pre-club drinks.
The kitchen stays open pretty much throughout,
watch out for €8-€10 three-course daily specials –
the main courses are well priced, too. A mixed clientele, as varied in terms of age and sexuality as that
of the Plattesteen (*see above*) opposite, makes for an
interesting vibe almost round the clock.

The classy **Café Métropole**. *See p130.*

The king of the guildhouses – the **Roi d'Espagne**. *See p131.*

Ste-Catherine & around

Le Daringman
37 rue de Flandre (02 512 43 23). Métro Ste-Catherine. **Open** noon-1am Tue-Thur; noon-2am Fri; 4pm-2am Sat. **No credit cards. Map** p316 B2.
Also known as Chez Haesendonck or Chez Martine, this entertainingly retro bar hidden between the fashion quarter and the canal attracts a Flemish clientele of watchable variety. Theatre-going older couples share tobacco smoke and squeezed-in tables with folk of a younger, more boho bent. Surrounding them, jumble-sale shots of Elvis, Ella and others contrast with the wood panelling and an iconic Stella sign from the 1950s. House plants, too. It's bookended by a modest bar counter and regularly topped up with flyers and listings leaflets covering every art form, over- and underground.

Kafka
6 rue de la Vierge Noire (02 513 54 89). Pré-métro Bourse or métro/pré-métro De Brouckère. **Open** 4pm-2am Mon-Thur, Sun; 4pm-2am Fri, Sat. **No credit cards. Map** p315 B3.
If it's late and you're lashing back the vodkas, chances are you're in the Kafka. Not that you'll necessarily remember this the next day, but the Kafka boasts a directory of vodkas, genevers and other assorted white spirits, plus all the usual beers to chase the chasers with. You may remember the clientele – downtown flotsam and jetsam, eccentric chess-playing intellectuals – but probably not the decor: brown and bare tiles. Deliberately dressed down, and open until way past your bedtime, the Kafka is not the pretentious poserie you were afraid it might have been.

De Markten
5 rue Vieux Marché aux Grains (02 512 34 25). Métro Ste-Catherine/pré-métro Bourse. **Open** 9am-5pm Fri. **No credit cards. Map** p316 B3.

Before you step into this ground-floor café, take a step back and look at the magnificent building. The café is part of a cultural centre, and as such attracts young arty types from the Flemish school of thought. The style is postmodernist industrial chic. OK – it looks like a school canteen, but its minimalism is just what these possessions-are-capitalist folk want. A terrace, filled with tables in summer, looks on to the square. All very continental.

Monk
42 rue Ste-Catherine (02 503 08 80). Métro Ste-Catherine. **Open** 4pm-2am Mon-Fri, Sun; 4pm-3am Fri, Sat. **No credit cards. Map** p315 B3.
Although the nearby quay area of Ste-Catherine is crowded with little local bars, few warrant particular attention. Monk is unusual in that someone – Yves de Vresse, in fact, who used to run Kafka (*see above*) – has taken the trouble and considerable expense to create a kind of JD Wetherspoon *à la belge* out of what was for many years another bog-standard local, Het Zinneke. Set in a 17th-century gabled house close to the main square, it's set apart by its big picture window and contemporary logo, a lettered square logo used on its sign and stickers. The interior comprises a long, dark wood bar, soft-lit by railway carriage wall lights above a row of mirrored panels. Jazz sounds go with the territory – Monk as in Thelonious Monk – and the crowd are somewhat on the stylish side.

La Tentation
28 rue de Laeken (02 223 22 75/www.latentation. org). Métro/pré-métro De Brouckère or métro Ste-Catherine. **Open** 9am-4am Mon-Fri; 5pm-4am Sat, Sun. **Credit** V. **Map** p316 B/C2.
An urban-chic converted drapery warehouse with huge windows, brick walls and effective low lighting, with a stylish and civilised vibe – a good spot to start the evening or for a quiet drink. It's run by

Going against the grain

Genever is Belgium's national spirit, as clear as its history is colourful. Its origins date back to the pre-Plague days when medieval alchemists brewed DIY digestives from boiled rainwater and juniper berries. When the Black Death struck the Low Countries in the 14th century distilled water replaced the rainwater. The distillation then became alcohol, in varying forms and tastes. The most palatable and popular was grain brandy, occasionally flavoured with juniper berries: genever (*genièvre* in French, *jenever* in Flemish).

Even today, juniper is not essential to genever. The Dutch were keen to experiment with various fruit flavours. Frequent local bans didn't halt production. Instead profitable brewers upped stills and moved operations to northern France and western Germany. When it was legal to produce the drink, there was still no law to control the strength of its ingredients. Its fortifying qualities became popular with

British soldiers fighting in Flanders fields in the 1500s. 'Dutch courage' was taken across the Channel and adapted as plain old gin.

With the industrialisation of Belgium in the 19th century, the maverick approach to gin production became a huge social problem.

Brussels' Galician community, but this is only really apparent in the menu (Spanish liqueurs, tapas, cheese and cold meats), the (re)lax(ed) staff, and the odd folk music night (*see p196*). It cannot always be banked on to be doing business as usual. When it does, it's a hit with all age groups and types, and suits tête-à-têtes and large gatherings.

De Walvis

209 rue Antoine Dansaert (02 219 95 32). Métro Ste-Catherine. **Open** 11am-late 2am Mon-Thur, Sun; 11am-4am Fri-Sat. **No credit cards. Map** p316 A2.
Deep at the dark, canal end of Antoine Dansaert, the Whale is beached between night shops, kebab joints and shabby phone centres – but this bar is no small fry. It's another brash venture from the Nicolay team, responsible for revamping St-Géry at the more fashionable end of this same street (*see p139* **Right said Fred**). This venue has been given more gaudy retro touches than most of the others in the empire. Traffic-light red is the *couleur du choix*, in an otherwise bare interior offset by a quite bizarre ceiling. You'll find Chinese Tsing-Tao beer among the usual Belgian favourites, a modest menu of tasty snacks and sandwiches, and an up-for-it clientele. Occasional jazz and regular DJs on Saturday nights bring crowds from across Brussels. Counter service.

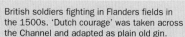

St-Géry

L'Archiduc

6 rue Antoine Dansaert (02 512 06 52/www. archiduc.be). Pré-métro Bourse. **Open** 4pm-dawn daily. **Credit** AmEx, MC, V. **Map** p316 B3.
The duke of all dives, the baron of all bars, the art deco L'Archiduc was reopened by Jean-Louis and Nathalie Hernant in 1985 in time to be part of the cultural wave that swept down rue Antoine Dansaert and washed over the rest of Brussels (*see p67* **Fashionably late**). Its predecessor dated back to 1937 and boasted an impeccable jazz pedigree. Charlie Parker played here, Nat King Cole too. Class will out. L'Archiduc proved the perfect vehicle for fashionistas and their chic cohorts; that vehicle was an ocean liner, its two-floor interior resembling the smooth curves of a ballroom drifting across the Atlantic. The ambience is flung further forwards by the early-evening tinklings of a jazz pianist (*see p195*) and the skill of a staff adept at waltzing through the mingle of waifs, strays and long-term strayed with trays of cocktail glasses rattling at shoulder level. It's a fine line here of decadence and decorum. Doorbell entry, pre-dawn drinking and demi-monde regulars dot the 'i' of the illusion.

Cheap, industrial alcohol – using such raw materials as sugar beet and molasses – was befuddling and endangering the working population. In the port cities of Brussels, Antwerp and London, gin was the opiate of the masses. Sailors, dockers and dizzy damsels merrily drank for a franc and death-wish drank for two. Locals were downing the stuff not because of its taste – the grainy flavour had all but disappeared – but to stupefy themselves at either end of the grim working day.

Invading German troops confiscated all copper stills in 1914. A year later, the Vandervelde law banned or severely limited sales of strong spirits. In any case, the drink had earned itself a scuzzy reputation. By the time it became available on the black market, genever had fallen out of fashion. In any case, by 1919, it was completely prohibited.

As customs – and Customs and Excise – relaxed in the 1970s, genever sales slowly picked up. But it wasn't until 1984 that the prohibition law of 1919 was repealed.

Almost at once, as if asserting national pride (and catching up with the Dutch, whose own tasting houses, *proeflokalen*, dot the dark alleyways of Amsterdam) genever bottles again lined the shelves of Belgium's bars. Immediately after legalisation, one bar in Antwerp, **De Vagant** (*see p233*), collated a stock of some 200 varieties. Fruit genevers began to be produced in bulk and, lower in alcohol, are now the most popular type.

With the fashionable bars of Brussels (in particular **Kafka**, *see p133*) promoting its virtues, genever gradually lost its old soak image and began to be appreciated across the board. Chefs prepared fine meals with it and arguments raged over its origins and qualities. Unsurprisingly, the Dutch and Belgians both claimed historic ownership. Antwerp is considered one source, though Hasselt in East Flanders boasts both the National Genever Museum (Witte Nonnenstraat 19; 011 24 11 44, www.jenevermuseum.be) and Belgium's biggest distillery, Smeets.

Responsible for the famous brand Extra Smeets, the company is one of only nine producers who distil what is considered authentic Belgian genever. Bruggeman's Hertekamp and Peterman, and Filliers' Oude Graanjenever are other leading brands to lure the initiated and the curious. For those yet to try it, genever is sipped and not slammed.

Bar à Tapas

11 rue Borgval (02 502 66 02/www.baratapas.be). Pré-métro Bourse. **Open** noon-1am Mon-Sat; 5pm-1am Sun. **Credit** MC, V. **Map** p316 B3.
Right in the heart of St-Géry, on a busy corner, this tapas bar stands out thanks to its role as a major meeting point. Just as they do in Spain, folks snack, chat and enjoy a couple of aperitifs before moving on elsewhere – and with no mock Mexicana or microwaved *merluza* in sight. The chalked-up lunch specials drag in an ever-changing mix of tourists and office workers; the mood changes in the evening when the lights flicker in the twisted lampshades and the intimate interior fills with expectant punters. There's a lengthy selection of tapas too. Altogether, it's the perfect venue for a bunch of weekenders on a communal jolly. The new branch in Ixelles, already nicknamed BAT2, where the chaussée de Waterloo meets avenue Brugmann, makes for a roomier, more relaxing experience.
Other location: 412A chaussée de Waterloo, Ixelles (02 538 03 01).

Gecko

16 place St-Géry (02 502 29 99). Pré-métro Bourse. **Open** 8am-2am Mon-Thur; 8am-3am Fri; 10am-3am Sat; 10am-2am Sun. **No credit cards. Map** p316 B3.

A welcome non-branded bar that has come on in leaps and bounds since its opening in late 2002. This once in-the-know splinter of St-Géry, narrow of interior and clientele, is now a full blown bar-resto attracting an across-the-board clientele with cut-price lunches (compared with other prices around the square), zingy cocktails and the cosy alcoves and casual furnishings of its welcome expansion. Above a bar counter of colourful mosaic, a friendly face beckons. Come in. Pull up a wooden fold-up chair or push up a dinky cushion. It's characterful, it's individual, and it's right on Happening Square.

Le Greenwich

7 rue des Chartreux (02 511 41 67). Pré-métro Bourse. **Open** 10.30am-1am Mon-Thur; 10.30am-2am Fri, Sat. **No credit cards. Map** p315 B3.
Past the slow creak of the wooden door, the other side of the ornate partition separating window seats from sedate interior, a library hush signals a sense of decorum to be assumed upon entering. Clack! A chess piece moves. Tock! An oval clock ticks over the elaborate bar counter. Tack! Another tupperware box of chess pieces is taken from the middle pillar and placed on one of four rows of marble tables as a board is unfolded. Amid the concentrated rolling of tobacco, an eyebrow is raised, then

straightened once more. Magritte hustled pictures and Bobby Fischer hustled chess here, but please don't shout about it. Don't shout about anything, in fact. Order up a drink, open up a book and observe.

Le Java
31 rue St-Géry (02 512 37 16). Pré-métro Bourse or Anneessens. **Open** 5pm-2am daily. **No credit cards. Map** p316 B3.
An imposingly cool bar composing the bow of St-Géry as it meets rue de la Grande Ile, Le Java makes the best of its three-sided space. Flemish in origin, international in clientele, it's great when all you want is a quiet drink amid attractive decor and among attractive company. The interior is dominated by a heavy round bar counter, footrailed by twisted metal and offset by half a tree and half a globe. Daily specials complement Bel pils and Steendonk beers on draught, all served with the same smile that welcomed you in. Cocktails are available too.

The Marolles

A la Clef d'Or
1 place du Jeu de Balle (02 511 97 62). Métro/pré-métro Porte de Hal/bus 27, 48. **Open** 5am-5pm Tue-Sun. **No credit cards. Map** p318 B5.
This large loud caff is a fave with locals, so it can be a squeeze for the casual visitor. Sunday mornings are the best and busiest, partly because of the earnest accordionist and party atmosphere. Unintentionally retro, it sports vinyl chairs and pink neon advertising signs. The food is of the *croque monsieur* and fried-egg variety. Madame skates around in her mules and black leggings, while monsieur stands at the coffee-machine barking orders to the overworked staff. Oh, he's also in charge of the *soupe du jour* pot, which means he lifts the occasional ladle.

Chez Marcel
20 place du Jeu de Balle (02 511 13 75). Métro/pré-métro Porte de Hal/bus 27, 48. **Open** 7.30am-5pm daily. **No credit cards. Map** p318 B5.
Other bars may be more comfortable, but of all the venues in this downbeat flea market square, this one is the most true to local life. As tatty as the traders it serves, Marcel's stocks Cantillon Gueuze, a local rarity from the Anderlecht brewery of the same name, cheaper more standard beers, toasted sandwiches and heavy local lunches. A Manneken-Pis in Union football colours and prints of the market from a similar bygone era complete the authenticity. Plonk your market purchase on the modest terrace, call up a beer and keep an ear out for local banter.

Le Renard
233 rue Haute (02 512 36 02). Métro/pré-métro Porte de Hal/bus 27, 48. **Open** 9.30am-10pm Mon-Fri; 10am-10pm Sat, Sun. **No credit cards. Map** p318 B5.
The Fox offers the little touches that typify the Marolles without ever needing to stoop to the extremes of sorrow and kitsch seen in similar dives

nearby. (Le Petit Lion opposite, for example, specialises in framed pictures of pets long gone and frequently reminisced over, a strange honour given their lifetime of bored servitude imprisoned under a bar stool while master drank away entire winters.) Here, in a classic wood-and-mirror interior, proudly stand a Wurlitzer jukebox, a Belgian pinball machine and, occasionally, members of the local pub first XI pictured on the main wall. Confusing combinations of tombola, cards and lottery, and derivatives thereof, abound. The room is dominated by the circular bar counter in the middle and the constant patter of neighbourhood gossip.

Upper Town

Le Bier Circus
89 rue de l'Enseignement (02 218 00 34/www. biercircus.com). Tram 92, 93, 94. **Open** noon-2.30pm, 6pm-midnight Mon-Fri. **No credit cards. Map** p317 D3.
This somewhat bland brick bar would not merit mention but for its quite astonishing range of beers, some 200 of them, filling 17 pages of a menu directory handed to you by a well-informed, well-intentioned barman. Vintage beers – Belle-Vue New Gueuze €24 a bottle, Hanssons Olde Gueuze €14 – warrant four pages. It's then that you notice the mounted beermats and a blackboard of seasonal beers breaking the monotony of brick. Delve a little deeper, and you'll find an intimate side room and a back room decked out in cartoon characters, but the regulars – no few rotund bods from the nearby EU Quarter – prefer the sanctity of the bland brick.

Le Grain de Sable
15 place du Grand Sablon (02 514 05 83). Tram 92, 93, 94. **Open** 8am-late daily. **Credit** AmEx, MC, V. **Map** p315 C4.
An at-first-glance understated bar on one of Brussels' poshest squares. Although surrounded by the big and blousy, there is no fear of le Grain suffering from an inferiority complex. For a start, the pavement terrace snakes its way around a corner, and in the warm weather becomes a right-angle of bright buzz and respectable rendezvous. Inside, funky Latin-jazz plays in the tiny ground-floor bar, while the flickering candles seem to find their own bossa rhythm. The customers tend towards the vodka-Schweppes rather than the beer bottle. There are no startling effects here, just a modest room filled with beautiful people and the friendliest of muscular staff. It's as if this tiny 17th-century house never closes. Doesn't it do well considering its age?

Le Perroquet
31 rue Watteau (02 512 99 22). Tram 92, 93, 94. **Open** 10am-1am daily. **No credit cards. Map** p315 C4.
Authentic art nouveau bar that features mirrors aplenty plus stained glass, a striking black and white tiled floor and a summer terrace. A popular haunt of well-to-do young things in summer,

This year's model – **Khnopff**. *See p141.*

before it's reclaimed by the autumnal flock of EU *stagiaires*, it's a stylish complement to the bland upmarket terrace bars of place du Grand Sablon a two-minute walk away. It's quite dinky inside, so expect a scramble for a table after office hours on a Friday. But once you've settled in, a mighty range of beers and more modest selection of salads and sandwiches can be ordered – eventually – from the waiting staff.

EU Quarter & Etterbeek

Chez Bernard
47 place Jourdan (02 230 22 38). Métro Trône then bus 34, 80. **Open** 7am-2am daily. **No credit cards. Map** p323 F5.
Sitting unfazed amid the mock-nouveau wine bars and brasseries on this busiest of squares, Bernard's Place remains rock-solid traditional. A long mirrored room leads to an unlikely glass conservatory at the back, giving the impression that a tea room has been stuck on the back of a beer hall. Madame spots you at table, takes a drag on the fag that could be her last, clacks over to take your order, greeting you with the friendliest of *s'il vous plaîts* you could hope to hear. It greets in equal measure Eurocrats feeling good about mixing with locals, locals feeling indifferent about mixing with Eurocrats, Sunday

morning shoppers and diners from Maison Antoine, the famous *frites* stall opposite. (*See p117* **On the move.**) Yep, you can buy your chips, bring them here and they'll offer you a napkin and a beer list.

Fat Boy's
5 place du Luxembourg (02 511 32 66/www.fat-boys.com). Métro Trône. **Open** 11am-late daily. **Credit** V. **Map** p322 E5.
Fat Boy's is Brussels' main expatriate sports bar, conveniently set in the considerable shadow of the European Parliament. Although it's American in style, Brits flock here in droves to spend beery Sunday afternoons gawping at any of nine screens showing Premiership action and scoffing their way through the meaty menu of ribs and burgers. Fat Boy's improves when the post-work crowd fills its long interior, spilling on to the terrace in summer. By dusk on a Friday, most have had the sense to escape, thus avoiding the woeful live R&B and Celtic drivel somehow conceived as a regular attraction.

The Open
17 boulevard St-Michel, Etterbeek (02 735 49 89). Métro Montgomery. **Open** 11am-2am daily. **Credit** MC, V.
A large well-to-do brasserie/restaurant near the main roundabout of Montgomery, just east of the Parc du Cinquantenaire. By day a business clientele,

and by night the bright young things of Woluwe flock here in droves, to an attractive terrace and neat interior whose mounted violins, flying pigs and piano fail to alleviate a palpable sense of decorum. If this sounds like one of Dante's warmer loops of hell, so be it, but there is a strange, gilded underbelly to Brussels, and places such as this, with no paid entrance or dress code, allow open season on its observation. From time to time, someone will loosen their collar and entertain with a tune or two. The range of beers and food – and quality of service – is in accordance with the environs.

Schievelavabo

52 rue du College St-Michel, Etterbeek (02 779 87 07). Métro Montgomery. **Open** 11am-2.30pm, 7pm-midnight Mon-Fri; 7pm-midnight Sat, Sun. **Credit** AmEx, DC, MC, V.

Capitalising on the success of the original branch, located in a traditional old house in Uccle, the Schievelavabo ('Wonky Washbasin', or – if you prefer – 'Skew-whiff Sink') brings a little bonhomie and retro conviviality to this grey residential patch stuck between the EU Quarter and Woluwe Park. Although somewhat smaller than its sister, the formula is the same: solid wooden furniture; hefty portions of classic Belgian fare; enticing options of fine local beers; dependable staff; a young, professional clientele. It would be excruciating if it were transposed to a London setting – Wimbledon, say. Here, it's a perfectly pleasant stop-off.

Other location: 20 rue Egide van Ophem, Uccle (02 332 20 91).

Le Terrasse

1 avenue des Celtes (02 732 28 51). Métro Mérode. **Open** 11am-1am daily. **Credit** AmEx, DC, MC, V. **Map** p323 H5.

The other side of the Parc de Cinquantenaire from the EU institutions, this is an ideal meeting spot thanks to its proximity to Mérode metro and the sun-dappled terrace of its name. Set back enough from the traffic of avenue de Tervueren to give the illusion of rustic supping, Le Terrasse is not just a summer retreat; in autumn, while the kitchen is cooking up mussels in eight varieties, the respectable clientele moves inside to a chatty, old-style brasserie of wooden furnishings beneath globe light fittings.

Ixelles

L'Atelier

77 rue Elise (02 649 19 53). Métro Louise then tram 93, 94/bus 71. **Open** 6pm-3am daily. **No credit cards. Map** p325 G9.

Tucked away amid drab streets 'twixt Ixelles lakes and cemetery, L'Atelier is a little gem, and a recently polished one, too. The renovation has done nothing to change the character of this cosy, wood-and-brick candlelit scout hut of a bar, with a counter separating a conspiratorial back room from the front of house. Behind the dividing line is a vast fridge of bottled beers, meticulously labelled.

Draught options – Kriek, Barbar, Chouffe, Pecheresse among them – are chalked up, as are local genevers and wines. Also displayed is a league table in honour of the diversity of Belgium's ales, many examples of which are happily available. Beer buffs mingle with the intellectual end of the student fraternity from the nearby university.

Ma Cabane Bambou

11 rue du Prince Royal (02 512 26 86). Métro Louise then tram 91, 92, 93, 94. **Open** 6pm-late Mon-Sat. **No credit cards. Map** p319 D6.

For 20 years this was Le Requin Chagrin restaurant, where Marlène Dépêche offered the exotic cuisine of the Reunion Island, running a little rum as a side attraction. In the summer of 2003, Marlène transformed the Despondent Shark into a merry rum bar of broader provenance, with cane spirits from Reunion and other former French territories, including those in the Caribbean. They are put to good use in a bright cocktail selection, which includes an 'Aphrodisiaque' with fresh ginger, and a variation of a strong Antillean punch known to Marlène as 'Le P'tit Pépé Loulou'.

Café Belga

18 place Flagey (02 640 35 08). Bus 71. **Open** 9.30am-2am Mon-Thur, Sun; 9.30am-3am Fri-Sat. **No credit cards. Map** p322 D7.

The shop window of the prestigious Flagey arts complex (*see p88* **All aboard!**), the Café Belga spreads itself over the ground floor of this former broadcasting house, where its zinc-and-chrome 1950s look another attractive design by leisure guru Fred Nicolay and his team of bar-fitters. (*See p139* **Right said Fred.**) It's sleek, certainly, and spacious, definitely, but not without charm, and always, always busy. Unless you're having food – soups, salads and sandwiches – brought to the table, it's counter service only, and not cheap, either, but that hasn't stopped a constant flow of young arty types through its rather grandiose doors. The outdoor terrace will come into its own once the roadworks on the square outside have finished – fingers crossed and ears plugged until deep into 2004.

Couleur Pourpre

463 avenue de la Couronne (02 649 87 00/www. couleur-pourpre.be). Bus 95, 96. **Open** 10am-2pm daily. **Credit** MC, V.

New and stylish haunt in the busy student quarter in the far south of Ixelles, by the cemetery, the Colour Purple is a seductive bar-restaurant whose vast interior is personalised by oriental furnishings and walls of purple. Communal ingestion of coffee, croissants and light lunches give the daytimes here an academic feel, but come dusk, the mortarboards are cast aside with gusto. Strong cocktails, as long a selection of whiskies as you'll find anywhere in town and caipirinhas are devoured amid filtered disco lighting, while an acceptable DJ beat taps away. Havana cigars, too. What kind of student loan system do they have in this town – and where can you apply?

L'Horloge du Sud

141 rue du Trône (02 512 18 64/www.horloge dusud.be). Métro Trône/bus 95, 96. **Open** 11am-1am Mon-Fri; 5pm-1am Sat, Sun. **Credit** AmEx, MC, V. **Map** p322 E5.

Adjacent to the heart of Brussels' African quarter of the Matongé (*see also p87* **African Brussels**), L'Horloge du Sud is a far cry from the tacky, lurid, crowded bars of nearby rue de Longue Vie. Spacious and comfortable, L'Horloge comprises a loose collection of old tables and chairs, plants, warrior statues, musical instruments and a massive mirror, all of which merge woozily as the drum rhythms and plentiful selection of Caribbean rums and cocktails kick in. There's African and Belgian cuisine, occasional live music, more frequently DJs at weekends, and the reliably constant vibe of a totally mixed clientele having fun. Praiseworthy.

Bar Parallèle

27 place Fernand Cocq (02 512 30 41). Métro Porte de Namur/bus 54, 71. **Open** 10am-1am Mon-Sat; 5pm-1am Sun. **No credit cards. Map** p322 D6.

One of a smattering of tidy outlets whose terraces embellish this lively, uneven square, the Parallel Bar draws a younger, less fashion-conscious crowd than the lovelies who flock to L'Amour Fou diagonally opposite. A large, plain interior (this used to be a traditional beer hall) fills with intellectual chatter from early evening, before a post-dinner influx keeps the place nicely ticking over until past midnight at weekends. A modest selection of meals and appetisers is served by a gratifyingly attentive staff.

People.

11 avenue de la Toison d'Or (02 511 64 05). Métro Porte de Namur. **Open** 11am-midnight Mon-Thur; 11am-2am Fri-Sat. **Credit** MC, V. **Map** p319 C5.

Right said Fred

After 15 years of setting up an equal number of establishments across Brussels – transforming the city's once staid bar scene as he did so – leisure entrepreneur Fred Nicolay has turned from firebrand mover and shaker to humble and well-paid consultant. Tired of the pressures of day-to-day management, Nicolay is happy to lend his voice of experience to ongoing projects across Brussels. Hidden corners of this once moribund, grey city – the Ixelles ponds, St-Gilles, the western canal zone – are constantly being brightened by brash new bars in the spirit, or at least the style, of those opened by Nicolay himself in the St-Géry quarter in the early part of the 1990s.

Now in his late 30s, Nicolay began his career as a catering graduate from Namur, taking off to work in the kitchens of London and New York. Back in Brussels, Nicolay worked with Alain Coumont before he launched the Pain Quotidien chain (*see p110* **Breaking bread**), and ran a couple of restaurants on a sixpence. He finally decided to swap the frying pan for the cocktail shaker in St-Géry. The fashion quarter of rue Antoine Dansaert was about to burgeon on his doorstep. Nicolay's timing couldn't have been better. 'The area had been left to rot,' he recalls. 'Right in the centre of Brussels, too. It seemed ripe for opportunity.'

Nicolay seized it. **Mappa Mundo** (2-6 rue du Pont de la Carpe; 02 514 35 55), **Zebra** (33 place du St-Géry; 02 511 09 01) and **Le Roi des Belges** (35 rue Jules van Praet; 02 503 43 00) were all brash, high-concept style

bars, each themed up to a point, but all very much of a type. They worked. 'The whole town followed us, place to place, reviving urban space,' says Nicolay. 'We boomed.'

St-Géry became the place to be. Almost overnight, Brussels had a nightlife hub. Having established his brand, Nicolay expanded it. His instinct didn't fail him. A modern European restaurant (**Bonsoir Clara**; *see p115*), an urban bare-brick bar-resto in the student quarter (**Le Tavernier**; *see p141*) and a retro café near the canal quarter (**De Walvis**; *see p134*) were all heavily expensive investments for the Duvel Moortgat brewery, which was backing his hunches – and all hugely successful. Most prestigiously, Nicolay and his team were behind the conversion of the ground floor of the old national broadcasting house into a classy bar for what is now the Flagey arts complex: the **Café Belga** (*see p138*). In each of these operations, no detail was left to chance, no touch of decor too slight to worry about. The most recent projects touched by the hand of Fred include a '50s-style steakhouse near Flagey (**Le Variétés**, 4 place Ste-Croix; 02 647 04 36), round the corner from a wine bar of similar Nicolay-esque finishing (**Le Delecta**, 2 rue Lannoy; 02 644 19 49).

But try as he might to escape, Nicolay is forever drawn to the centre of things. He and his partners are rumoured to have been acquiring properties on rue Antoine Dansaert, and Brussels' street of chic may once again undergo radical transformation – 20 years after Nicolay capitalised on the first one.

Eat, Drink, Shop

Music where Baudelaire mused – **Au Vieux Spytigen Duivel**. *See p142.*

In the fashionable quarter of town where avenue Louise meets the Petit Ring, People. is the most liberal – and liberating – of the glitzy club bars that epitomise the nightlife scene in this rarified enclave. By day a diner of affordable quality, by night People. kicks back its classy slingbacks and, with some decorum, rocks. Downstairs, the lounge bar is invariably loud and busy, thanks to quality cocktails and acceptable DJing, while the upstairs dining area is forever a-chatter over the woosh of boulevard traffic beneath. Immediately below is the rather brash Americana of Conway's (10 avenue de la Toison d'Or, 02 511 26 68), destination of choice should you require coverage of the Superbowl or NBA play-offs.

Rick's Bar

344 avenue Louise (02 647 75 30). Métro Louise then tram 93, 94. **Open** 11am-midnight Mon-Sat; 10am-4pm Sun. **Credit** AmEx, DC, MC, V. **Map** p324 E8.
Rick's is by far and away the best-known American bar in Brussels, almost as well known in these parts as the *Casablanca* bar that spawned its concept. Housed in a magnificent three-storey townhouse on avenue Louise, it's swish, chic and, yes, expensive – but serves arguably the best bar brunch in town. There are full meals, too – T-bone steaks, Rick's ribs and the like – but it's mainly used as a networking bar. Frequented by suits, it's a busy after-office haunt, and the rear terrace is glorious in summer.

Roxi

82 rue du Bailli (02 646 17 92/www.roxi.be). Métro Louise then tram 93, 94. **Open** 8am-1am Mon-Thur, Sun; 8am-2am Fri, Sat. **Credit** MC, V. **Map** p319 D7.

Trendy new bar set in an old corner pub attracting chic urbanites of the Châtelain quarter with its three floors of stark decor, all-day cuisine and unfussy background sounds. Metal staircases link the floors, from the ground-floor bar with its wide windows to the dinky red stools of the tea room, and on up to the modest balcony and its welcome panorama. Immediately opposite, at No.79, stands the Bank, one of the more acceptable of the two dozen Brit/Irish pubs in Brussels, heaving on major football nights.

En Stoemelings

7 place de Londres (02 512 43 74). Métro Trône. **Open** 11am-2am Mon-Fri; 5pm-2am Sat, Sun. **No credit cards.** **Map** p322 E5.
Lived-in neighbourhood local overlooking a quiet square set between the Royal Palace, the European Parliament and the African quarter. Its name is the Flemish rendition of 'on the quiet', and the regulars in this cosy, cubby-hole of a bar certainly like to keep themselves to themselves, musing over a sneaky Kriek or two. Cheap, filling bowls of hot bar food draw a studenty element later on, when admirably late hours are kept despite a deep silence in the immediate vicinity. Two prime spots by the window lend themselves perfectly for a winter's eve *à deux*.

Le Tavernier

445 chaussée de Boondael (02 640 71 91/www.le-tavernier.be). Bus 71, 95, 96. **Open** 11am-3am Mon-Thur, Sun; 11am-4am Fri, Sat. **No credit cards.** **Map** p325 G9.
Slap in the student quarter of south Ixelles, St-Géry mover and shaker Fred Nicolay (*see p139* **Right said Fred**) has plonked this tidy hunk of Hoxtonia,

an industrial bar-resto of exposed brick and loungey brown furniture. Consisting of one main room with a long bar counter, a separate side bar with a DJ deck in the corner, and two courtyards, a leafy outer one and a heated inner one, Le Tavernier is busy all day round, all year round. You'll find the usual beers – although Guinness is a rarity for a Belgian bar – and snacks, with unusually good music most of the time. Occasional films shown, too.

St-Gilles

Khnopff
*1 rue St-Bernard (02 534 20 04/www.khnopff.com).
Tram 91, 92.* **Open** 11.30am-2am Mon-Sat. **Credit** AmEx, DC, MC, V. **Map** p319 C6.

As 2004 is the year of Khnopff – with a major retrospective of this symbolist painter's work at the Bozar all spring – it seems apt that Brussels' most talked-about new venue should be set in one of his old studios. Khnopff, Fernand, dandy and anglophile, had an installation on the first floor of 1 rue St-Bernard in 1888; Khnopff, lounge bar/resto, was actually opened at the end of 2002, when the artist being celebrated was Miguel Cancio Martin. Best known for the Buddha Bar in Paris and Johnny Depp's Man Ray bar/restos in Paris and the US, Cancio Martins studied at the nearby St-Luc. Using purples and reds offset by vast pillars around a long counter, he has brought a brash, cosmopolitan vibe to this sleepy residential area just off the chaussée de Charleroi. Khnopff is a destination bar in its own right – although there is a full-blown restaurant under the same roof. For all its artistic heritage, it earns its plaudits because of the expertly mixed music and cocktails, as fine as any in Brussels.

Chez Moeder Lambic
68 rue de Savoie (02 539 14 19). Pré-métro Horta or Albert/tram 81, 82. **Open** 4pm-3am daily. **No credit cards**.

Happy to collect dust in its own little corner, the collectors' cavern of Chez Moeder Lambic hides from the soaring St-Gilles town hall behind beer-labelled windows. Inside it's a dark hive, three long shelves of obscure bottles framing the bar counter and wooden tables. It would take a lifetime to sample every cobwebbed variety here – some of shabby Pink Floyd ilk are still trying – but to pass the time, racks of comic books line one wall. Outsiders can only guestimate the number of brews, daring to stab at 300. Insiders? If they know, they're not letting on, but they've probably recorded it by quill in a weighty tome under the counter, another collector's item collecting dust while the outside world and his wife guzzle mass-produced lagers in brighter bars.

La Porteuse d'Eau
48 avenue Jean Volders (02 537 66 46/www.laporteusedeau.be). Métro/pré-métro Porte de Hal. **Open** 10am-10pm Mon, Sun; 10am-midnight Tue-Sat. **No credit cards**. **Map** p318 B6.

The **Brasserie Verscheuren**. *See p142.*

Once upon a time, this was Le Lion de Waterloo, whose name is still evoked by crinkly locals. As if in keeping with the fancy architectural style of the houses along rue Vanderschrick, which it abuts, La Porteuse d'Eau was converted into a beautiful and nouveau café, all dinky and curlicued, the perfect spot to launch an illicit affair. Horta wouldn't have given it house room, of course, but that's not the point. Its grand entrance is guarded by a pair of vast, green curtains that usher you into an extravagant, interior. A swirl of bar counter is offset by bundles of green plants and a spiral staircase leading to an atrium themed with friezes of water women. Toast, sandwiches and, incongruously, tagliatelle, make up a food menu available till 11pm. Tea is as widely sipped as wine or beer, but far from compulsory.

Brasserie de l'Union

55 parvis de St-Gilles (02 538 15 79). Pré-métro Parvis de St-Gilles. **Open** 7.30am-1am daily. **No credit cards. Map** p318 B6.

A tatty-round-the-edges bohemian bar happy to serve the local community at large – some befriended solely by spaniels, deep in one-way conversations – the Union comprises one large, busy room propping up a corner of the focal parvis de St-Gilles. Its picture windows giving out on to the paved square were fringed with the blue and yellow of the local team (*Allez l'Union!*) until a recent change of management saw such football paraphernalia replaced by bijou images of Jimmy Cagney, and Union's support use a different bar to run its coaches from. A mounted and scowling Screamin' Jay Hawkins remains, though, as does the boho chain-smoking gang of Bukowksi-esque thirst who turn this local into a den of joyous iniquity. A Sunday morning's market browsing here is accompanied by an accordionist squeezing out tunes incapable of drowning out the din of children running amok. After they depart, along with the spaniels, the squeezeboxer and the senile, the night is retaken by characters from the covers of pulp fiction.

Brasserie Verscheuren

11-13 parvis de St-Gilles (02 539 40 68). Pré-métro Parvis de St-Gilles. **Open** 8am-2am daily. **No credit cards. Map** p318 B7.

The classier of the corner bars serving the parvis, the Verscheuren twinkles with art deco touches. Three rows of tables and banquettes are waited on by an erratic staff safe in the knowledge that few of the boho-intellectual regulars pay much attention as to why they came here in the first place; the Verscheuren is simply their natural habitat, drink or no drink. If they cared to look up, they'd find a more than adequate selection of beers – including bottled rarities such as Pecheresse – complemented by a hearty lunch menu. Rather incongruous alongside the classic station clock and delicate window panelling, a vast league ladder of football club names from the lower local divisions occupies the back wall, each team name delineated in bright Subbuteo colours. This place is suitable any time, busy at lunchtimes – but perfect when the outdoor tables catch the last rays of a summer's evening.

Uccle

Ici le Bô-Bar

22 parvis St-Pierre (02 343 43 03/www.icelebobar. be). Tram 55, 91, 92. **Open** noon-1am Mon-Fri; 2pm-2am Sat. **No credit cards.**

This new-style designer bar attracts the bright young things of Uccle with its showy interior, giant screen of pop videos and classy, if standard, cocktails. A bay window gives out on to a front terrace filled with well-to-do young adults, not quite rich enough to pass up the chance of the unusual happy hour of two for the price of one after ten of a Saturday night, discouraging them from taking daddy's T-bird into town. There's nothing the Bô-Bar likes more than putting on an event, a masked ball or screening a major football match.

Imprimerie

666 chaussée de St-Job (02 372 93 25). Train St-Job/ tram 92/bus 60. **Open** 6pm-1am Tue-Sat. **Credit** AmEx, DC, MC, V.

Unusual loft bar set in green suburbia just south of the Royal Observatory, where owner Guy-Philippe de Ribaucourt offers rare beers alongside an evening menu of quality main dishes. A printer by trade, and a member of the Vandenheuvel dynasty of master brewers, de Ribaucourt's Printer's is, indeed, right behind a printing works and somewhat industrial in feel. Huge vats line up behind the bar counter, although beers here can be tasted in delicate 15cl measures. In fact, Guy-Philippe insists. The main draughts – lager, pils, stout and wheat – are brewed according to traditional recipes once used by Ekla, a popular beer company before the war. There are plenty of botted options, too.

Au Vieux Spytigen Duivel

621 chaussée d'Alsemberg (02 344 34 55). Tram 55. **Open** noon-midnight Mon-Fri; 4.30-11pm Sat. **No credit cards.**

Famous old bar by the Bens tramstop on the No.55 route, with a charming interior that has changed little since Baudelaire sat here and dashed off his vitriolic elegies to Belgium. (*See p69* **Baudelaire's Brussels**.) Actually, that's not quite true: there is a jukebox, its mounted speaker and a telephone cabin, all from the mid 20th century, when renowned Flemish poet Jan van Nijlen spent most of his working life here. If scribbling's your game, the Spytigen's got the literary pedigree. Three long rows of heavy wooden tables fill the large bar-room, its walls covered in a century of local history: Union team line-ups from the championship-winning days between the wars, a *Paris-Match* feature from 1967 relating Baudelaire's patronage, plus enough old prints to inspire you out of your seat for a wander while the barman slowly pours you another draught Leffe or, rarer still, Westmalle.

Shops & Services

Find a new line in local fashion, rare vinyl or exotic bric-a-brac.

Chine Collection. See p151.

Most visitors don't come to Brussels for its shopping. It could never hope to rival Paris or London, but it does have interesting pockets well worth exploring. Particular fortes include antiques, bric-a-brac, and, of course, chocolate and beer, *see p158* **Sweet success** and *p128* **Beers of Belgium**.

If you're here for more than a weekend, it's worth considering a trip to Antwerp, just half an hour away by train. It's trendier and livelier than Brussels; not surprisingly, many big names – in particular, designers – have chosen to open there rather than the capital. For shopping in **Antwerp**, *see pp235-8*.

LOWER AND UPPER TOWNS

Around the Grand' Place, and particularly near the Manneken-Pis, are the tourist-dependent chocolate, lace and EU merchandise shops. Thankfully, you don't have to go very far from here to get away from the tourist traps and find good stuff. To the south-east of the Grand' Place, **rue des Eperonniers** has quirky old-fashioned gift shops; south-west, **rue du Midi** is lined with stamp, camera and art shops. Parallel **boulevard Anspach/Maurice Lemmonier** has comic shops, second-hand

book and record stores and an assortment of dusty but quirky little businesses. (*See p147* **Rare junk**.) In between, **rue des Pierres** and **rue du Marché au Charbon** are home to a mix of vintage clothes shops and streetwear boutiques.

North-east of the square are the stunning Galeries St-Hubert, the most famous of the city's *galeries*, or shopping arcades, opened in 1847. Divided into the galerie du Roi, de la Reine and du Prince, they house expensive, old-fashioned boutiques selling lace, gloves, hats and bags.

Pedestrianised **rue Neuve**, Brussels' main shopping drag, is a nightmare, especially on a Saturday. Think Croydon at its busiest. It's home to high-street names Benetton, Esprit, H&M, Morgan and Zara, alongside lesser-known but similar brands such as Vero Moda and Bershka. At its northern end are the landmark department store **Inno** and the horrendous **City 2** shopping centre, the highlight of which is the comprehensive bookstore **Fnac** (*see p145*). South of the place de la Monnaie are **rue des Fripiers** and **rue du Marché aux Herbes**, both offering high-street shops and independent boutiques.

Eat, Drink, Shop

Brüsel – a different kind of strip joint altogether. *See p145.*

Ste-Catherine, known for its seafood restaurants, is also home to some excellent food shops. Adjoining **St-Géry**, and, in particular, **rue Antoine Dansaert**, are the places to go for trendy streetwear, cool gift shops, modern furniture stores and boutiques of established and up-and-coming Belgian designers. *See p150* **Brussels back in fashion** *and p67* **Fashionably late.**

If antiques are your thing, then the Sablon is the place to head. Expensive boutiques are to be found along **rue Lebeau, rue des Minimes** and **place du Grand Sablon**, where an antiques market is held every weekend. More downmarket – and more exotic – antiques shops can be found down below in the adjoining neighbourhood of the Marolles, on **rues Blaes** and **Haute**. In the centre is **place du Jeu de Balle**, site of the daily flea market. *See p153* **Good housekeeping**.

AVENUE LOUISE AND IXELLES

Avenue Louise and **boulevard de Waterloo** are the closest Brussels gets to glitz. This is where foreign money and Belgian inheritances are spent in the boutiques of MaxMara, Chanel, Gucci, Cacharel and Bulgari – just a sprinkling of the big names dotted along these two wide, tree-lined streets.

Avenue de la Toison d'Or (the name given to the southern side of boulevard de Waterloo) is a little more mid-range, with international clothing shops such as Women'Secret, Massimo Dutti and Petit Bateau. The three galeries that run off avenue de la Toison d'Or (de la Toison d'Or, Porte Louise and Espace Louise) are all linked to each other and play host to a mix of shops selling high-street and designer labels. Shoe shops are especially well represented.

About halfway along avenue Louise, running west, is **rue du Bailli**. Here, and radiating out to the surrounding streets, are a selection of gift shops and clothing boutiques, interspersed with chic cafés and restaurants, which converge around place du Châtelain. Bailli itself is blessed with a fair number of shoe shops.

Running almost parallel with avenue Louise, **chaussée d'Ixelles** has some of the chains, and **chaussée de Wavre** is home to ethnic shops. In between the two, rue St-Boniface is dotted with unusual boutiques.

TAX-FREE SHOPPING

Prices include sales tax of up to 21 per cent (rates vary depending on the item). In many shops (and particularly perfume stores and chocolate shops), non-EU residents can request a Tax-Free Cheque on purchases of more than €145, which can be cashed at customs when leaving the EU to reclaim VAT. Savings Shops in the scheme have a 'Tax-Free Shopping' sticker on their door, but it's not always obvious, so do check.

SALES AND OPENING TIMES

Historically, sales have been strictly regulated in Belgium – which isn't such a bad thing as it means that they're that much more genuine. For the first few weeks in January and July stores slash prices across the board. Of course, resourceful shopkeepers always manage to work their way round the law, offering a few specific discounts and promotional prices throughout the year and particularly around special events, such as Valentine's Day.

Most shops in Brussels are closed on Sundays. Many smaller shops also close on Mondays, while the larger ones sometimes have more restrictive hours.

Bookshops & newsagents

L'Ame des Rues – Librairie de Cinéma

49 boulevard Anspach, Lower Town (02 217 59 47/ www.belgianmovieposters.be). Métro/pré-métro De Brouckère. **Open** noon-6pm Mon-Sat. **Credit** AmEx, DC, MC, V. **Map** p315 B3.

This shop is a real mecca for film buffs, packed as it is with film stills, posters and postcards, plus television- and film-related books and memorabilia.

Anticyclone des Açores

34 rue du Fossé aux Loups, Lower Town (02 217 52 46/www.anticyclonedesacores.com). Métro/pré-métro De Brouckère. **Open** 10.30am-6.30pm Mon-Sat. **Credit** AmEx, MC, V. **Map** p315 C2.

This welcoming travel bookshop is stocked with maps, guidebooks, reference books and attractive coffee table material on Brussels and the rest of Europe and beyond, in French, Flemish and English. The collection of globes is especially impressive.

Fnac

City 2, rue Neuve, Lower Town (02 275 11 11/ www.fnac.be). Métro/pré-métro Rogier. **Open** 10am-7pm Mon-Thur, Sat; 10am-8pm Fri. **Credit** AmEx, DC, MC, V. **Map** p317 C2.

Head to the top of the City 2 shopping centre to find this ever-dependable mammoth store that sells all kind of media. The book stock is excellent in all disciplines and languages (the French section is particularly strong), and the prices aren't bad. There are also CDs, videos, DVDs, computer games and assorted audio-visual and computer equipment. By the door is a ticket office for concerts around town.

Sterling

38 rue du Fossé aux Loups, Lower Town (02 223 62 23/www.sterling-books.be). Métro/pré-métro De Brouckère. **Open** 10am-7pm Mon-Sat; noon-6.30pm Sun. **Credit** AmEx, MC, V. **Map** p315 C2.

The ground floor of this bookshop has an excellent range of contemporary fiction, children's books, magazines and newspapers in English, while the first floor stocks classic fiction, plus non-fiction (such as computer and travel books). There's also a comprehensive section of books on Brussels.

Waterstone's

71-75 boulevard Adolphe Max, Lower Town (02 219 27 08/www.waterstones.co.uk). Métro/pré-métro Rogier. **Open** 9am-7pm Mon-Sat; 11.30am-6pm Sun. **Credit** AmEx, MC, V. **Map** p317 C2.

Just like its UK counterparts, the local Waterstone's has a good collection of English-language reading material (books, mags, papers) on its two floors. Prices are higher, though.

Comics

For a detailed history of the comic-strip genre, *see pp32-36* **Cartoon Brussels**.

La Boutique Tintin

13 rue de la Colline, Lower Town (02 514 51 52/ www.tintin.com). Métro Gare Centrale. **Open** 10am-6pm Mon-Sat; 11am-5pm Sun. **Credit** AmEx, DC, MC, V. **Map** p315 C3.

If you're a Tintin fan, then it's hard to walk into this shop and not buy something, even though prices are high. The range includes clothes, stationery and soft toys, as well as the comic strip books themselves. If you're a serious collector, there are also some limited edition miniatures (and not so miniatures).

Brüsel

100 boulevard Anspach, Lower Town (02 511 08 09/ www.brusel.com). Pré-métro Bourse. **Open** 10.30am-6.30pm Mon-Sat; noon-6.30pm Sun. **Credit** AmEx, DC, MC, V. **Map** p315 B3.

One of the best shops in its genre, with a huge choice of local favourites, as well as popular European and American comic strips such as Peanuts and Calvin & Hobbes, both in English and the Belgian languages. Aside from books, the shop stocks plastic and resin miniatures, posters and lithographs.

Le Dépôt

108 rue du Midi, Lower Town (02 513 04 84/ www.depotbd.com). Pré-métro Anneessens. **Open** 10am-6.30pm Mon-Sat. **Credit** MC, V. **Map** p315 B4.

This store buys and sells all types of new and old comic strips, as well as figurines, cards, posters, limited edition lithographs and DVDs.

Other locations: 142 chaussée d'Ixelles, Ixelles (02 513 46 22).

Super Dragon Toys

6 rue Ste-Catherine, Lower Town (02 511 56 25). Métro/pré-métro De Brouckère. **Open** 11am-6.30pm Mon-Sat. **No credit cards**. **Map** p315 B3.

This shop sells everything a manga fan could need, from DVDs to figurines, video games and music. A huge range of manga comics is available in French, English and Flemish, and if you're still not satisfied you can have them ordered.

Utopia

39 rue du Midi, Lower Town (02 514 08 26). Pré-métro Bourse. **Open** 11am-6.30pm Mon-Fri; 11am-7pm Sat. **Credit** MC, V. **Map** p315 B3.

This shop specialises in American comic strips, plus TV and film merchandise, with a good collection of Batman and The Simpsons gear.

Second-hand

See also p147 **Rare junk**.

Nijinski

15-17 rue du Page, Ixelles (02 539 20 28). Tram 81, 82, 93, 94/bus 54. **Open** 11am-7pm Mon-Sat. **No credit cards**. **Map** p324 C8.

This large second-hand store sells books in many languages, with an impressive English room. A play area has toys and kids' books in English too. Staff are relaxed and friendly, and prices are reasonable.

Eat, Drink, Shop

Pêle-Mêle

55 boulevard Maurice Lemonnier, Lower Town (02 548 78 00/www.occases.com). Pré-métro Anneessens. **Open** 10am-6.30pm Mon-Sat. **No credit cards.** **Map** p316 B4.

The best of the second-hand stores along this stretch, Pêle-Mêle is stuffed with books, comics, magazines, CDs, records, videos, DVDs and computer games, which it buys and sells. There is a decent English section too. Patient delving usually proves rewarding, and prices are more than fair.

Cameras & electronics

Ali Photo Video

150 rue du Midi, Lower Town (02 511 71 65). Pré-métro Anneessens. **Open** 9am-6pm Mon-Fri; 10am-6pm Sat. **Credit** AmEx, DC, MC, V. **Map** p315 B4.

One of several photo-video shops on rue du Midi, Ali Photo Video sells new still and video cameras of all makes, as well as buying, selling and exchanging second-hand ones. Staff develop photos, slides and black-and-whites, and look after your digital needs.

Michel Campion

13 & 15 rue St-Boniface, Ixelles (02 512 17 21). Métro Porte de Namur/bus 54, 71. **Open** No.13 9am-6pm Mon-Sat; 10am-6pm Sun. *No.15* 10am-1pm, 2-6.30pm Wed-Sat. **Credit** AmEx, DC, MC, V. **Map** p319 D5.

Michel Campion has two shops on opposite sides of the street. No.15 only sells new cameras and accessories, while No.13 stocks a pretty large selection of second-hand photographic equipment.

Technoland

22-24 rue Haute, Lower Town (02 511 51 04). Bus 20, 48. **Open** noon-7pm Tue-Sat. **Credit** MC, V. **Map** p318 C4.

Come here for second-hand, high-end audio-visual equipment and computers, usually in good condition and at fair prices.

Department stores

Hema

117 rue Neuve, Lower Town (02 227 52 11/www.hema.be). Métro/pré-métro Rogier. **Open** 9.30am-6.30pm Mon-Sat. **Credit** MC, V. **Map** p317 C2.

Hema is hardly a department store – it's more like a Flemish Woolies. Its two floors are filled with basics, such as candles, underwear, chinaware, kitchenware, stationery and other random goods, of varying quality but often at ludicrously cheap prices. Don't go with high expectations, have a good rummage around and you may just leave triumphant. **Other locations:** throughout the city.

Inno

111 rue Neuve, Lower Town (02 211 21 11/ www.inno.be). Métro/pré-métro Rogier. **Open** 9.30am-7pm Mon-Thur, Sat; 9.30am-8pm Fri. **Credit** AmEx, DC, MC, V. **Map** p317 C2.

Inno is Brussels' main department store. Established in 1897, it has 15 shops in Belgium, four in Brussels. This is the largest of them, with five floors of all the usual departments, such as mens-, womens- and childrenswear, shoes, home furnishings and so on. Within each are small franchise outlets such as Sisley and Betty Barclay. Notable are the handbag, jewellery and lingerie departments. **Other locations:** 12 avenue Louise, Ixelles (02 513 84 94); 699 chaussée de Waterloo, Uccle (02 345 38 90); 150 avenue Paul Hymans, Woluwe-St-Lambert (02 771 20 50).

Dry-cleaning

De Geest

41 rue de l'Hôpital, Lower Town (02 512 59 78). Métro Gare Centrale. **Open** 8am-7pm Mon-Fri; 8am-6.30pm Sat. **No credit cards.** **Map** p315 C4.

This dry cleaner will launder virtually anything, including leather and suede items and upholstery.

Fashion

For more on local fashion, *see p150* **Brussels back in fashion**.

Boutiques

Autour du Monde (Bensimon Collection)

70 rue de Namur, Upper Town (02 503 55 92/ www.bensimon.be). Métro Porte de Namur. **Open** 10am-6.30pm Mon-Sat. **Credit** AmEx, MC, V. **Map** p319 D5.

This is the Brussels branch of a Parisian lifestyle boutique, which sells a co-ordinated mix of clothes, bags, toiletries, home furnishings, stationery and accessories in various colours and prints, teamed with classic designs. Fortes include leather jackets and coats, simple tops and jumpers.

Ethnic Wear

25 rue des Chartreux, Lower Town (02 514 78 08). Pré-métro Bourse. **Open** 11am-7pm Mon-Sat. **Credit** V. **Map** p316 B3.

Ethnic Wear opened in autumn 2003 in the beautiful building that once housed the quirky Album Museum. It sells ecologically sound (and generally brightly coloured) clothes, shoes and accessories designed and made on site by Marie Cabanac, as well as a few pieces made on a fair-trade basis. Men, women and children are all catered for.

Icon

11 rue des Teinturiers, Lower Town (02 502 71 51). Pré-métro Bourse. **Open** 1-6.30pm Mon; 11am-6.30pm Tue-Sat. **No credit cards.** **Map** p315 B3.

This small boutique sells a mix of casual and elegant items aimed at young, urban women. Pieces by Diesel, Replay, Cacharel and Twin Set all feature, with shoes by Isabelle Marant and Prairies de Paris.

Rare junk

Belgians are great recyclers. Instead of chucking out books, records and CDs they don't want any more, they take them to the nearest second-hand store, sell them for a pittance – and then buy a stack of books from the same place to replace them. This means that Brussels is a treasure trove for collectors; you can pick up that rarely seen paperback or unusual back catalogue LP for a fraction of the price you would find it in London or on E-bay. Unlike London, first editions and rarities are few and far between (in English, that is – there are plenty in French). But they do exist, and unlike London, are likely to be massively undervalued, because the store's owners are taking them on as stock-fillers and are not experts in that market. Nor do they have tourists from around the world trudging through their shop, tempting them to inflate prices. So hunt treasure and you may just get lucky – and you'll have fun browsing. All the key venues are all within a short walking distance of the Grand' Place.

Pêle-Mêle (*pictured; see also p146*) is an institution. On Saturdays the selling queue and the buying queue snake around the shop floor, almost colliding into each other. As well as books, CDs, records and magazines, it also stocks videos and DVDs, comic books and graphic novels, board games, cameras and even computers. It's dusty, grimy and packed on Saturdays – but it's the perfect place to while away a Monday afternoon.

Many of its books are in English. This is a result of Brussels' international community having itchy feet: the average expat stays less than three years, and when they go, they too queue up at Pêle-Mêle – but manage to avoid joining the other queue before they reach the door. Admittedly, many of the books are spy novels or corporate thrillers, but there are also classics and works of non-fiction hidden among the Robert Ludlums.

Nearby are **Bibliopolis** (30 boulevard Maurice Lemonnier, 02 512 02 32) and two branches of **Evasions** (rue du Midi No.89, 02 502 49 56, and No.147 02 513 63 84).

At the next junction up from Pêle-Mêle is **Découvertes** (2 place Anneessens, 02 502 44 25) – same idea, less crowded. Head to the basement and you're confronted with an entire wall of second-hand English books. If you can't see a certain Agatha Christie there, ask for it and they'll send up another box.

For second-hand music, Brussels can provide equal riches. Approaching Pêle-Mêle from the Bourse, you pass a dozen second-hand record stores. **Jukebox** (165 boulevard Anspach, 02 511 67 51) is unmissable – there's usually a large shaggy dog asleep outside. It stocks every conceivable genre of music, but specialises in rock 'n' roll. There are 50,000 LPs and 150,000 singles in stock – LPs start from €2.50. Next door is **Mob Records** (also known as B-Sides; No.167, 02 502 10 83), which sells new and second-hand vinyl and CDs – it often has LPs of '60s Italian spy flick soundtracks in its window. If neither of those contain the gem you're looking for, **Arlequin** (*see p162*), a short walk away, is good for punk and jazz rarities.

Eat, Drink, Shop

Isabelle Baines

48 rue du Pépin, Upper Town (02 502 13 73). Métro Porte de Namur. **Open** 2-6pm Mon; 10.30am-6pm Tue-Sat. **Credit** MC, V. **Map** p319 D5.
Local designer Baines opened her first boutique in Brussels in 1986, selling her machine-knitted but hand-finished jumpers, cardigans and gilets. The winter collection is made from wool and cashmere, while the summer clothes are cotton. Top-quality, long-lasting classic pieces with a modern twist.

Kaat Tilley

4 galerie du Roi, Lower Town (02 514 07 63/ www.kaattilley.com). Métro Gare Centrale. **Open** 10am-6.30pm Mon-Sat. **Credit** AmEx, DC, MC, V. **Map** p315 C3.
Kaat Tilley opened her shop in the Galeries St-Hubert after studying fashion in Brussels and Antwerp. Her designs are ingeniously constructed out of delicate materials, sown together in layers. The different lines are bridal and eveningwear, prêt-à-porter, knitwear, casualwear and womenswear.

Lodge

42 rue Antoine Dansaert (02 503 36 76). Pré-métro Bourse. **Open** 2-6.30pm Mon; 10.30am-6.30pm Tue-Fri; 10am-6pm Sat. **Credit** AmEx, MC, V. **Map** p316 B3.
Where once there was Via della Spiga selling top-of-the-range designer brands, now there is Lodge, which is pitching itself at the 25- to 50-year-old age group and selling smart casualwear, such as Armani Jeans, Sportmax and Strenesse.

Maison Degand

415 avenue Louise, Ixelles (02 649 00 73). Métro Louise then tram 93, 94. **Open** 10am-7pm Mon-Sat. **Credit** AmEx, DC, MC, V. **Map** p324 E9.
Maison Degand, housed in a grand fin-de-siècle mansion with most of the original interior preserved, sells luxury clothes for men and women, including made-to-measure suits and cashmere sweaters. It also stocks accessories, such as cufflinks, ties, cravats, cigar cutters and hip flasks. The annex to the store sells more casual weekend wear.

Ming Tsy

24 rue du Page, Ixelles (02 424 29 68). Tram 81, 82, 93, 94. **Open** 10am-6pm Tue-Sat. **No credit cards. Map** p324 C8.
Taiwanese designer Ming Tsy uses oriental fabrics to create stunning clothes, scarves and bags; she will make to measure providing you give her input in the design. She has also launched a line of lovely understated wedding dresses and stationery sets. Clothes start at €200, not bad for such exquisite items.

Nina Meert

1 rue St-Boniface, Ixelles (02 514 22 63). Métro Porte de Namur. **Open** 1.30-6.30pm Mon; 10.30am-6.30pm Tue-Sat. **Credit** MC, V. **Map** p319 D5.
Nina Meert was born into a family of painters and worked at Pucci in Florence and Cacharel in Paris before opening her own shop in 1979. Isabelle Adjani

Francis Ferent, label heaven. *See p149.*

and Meryl Streep are just two examples of famous names who have worn her creations, which are simple, comfortable and made from natural fibres like wool and silk. Her top-notch knitwear collection has been very successful recently, but if you want something a bit more special Meert can make to measure.

Ramona

21 rue de la Grande Ile, Lower Town (02 503 47 44). Pré-métro Bourse. **Open** noon-6.30pm Tue-Sat. **Credit** AmEx, MC, V. **Map** p316 B3.
Enter this boudoir and you're likely to find Chilean Ramona Hernández Collao lying on a chaise longue, knitting her latest creation. She will turn her hand to any kind of clothing, including jumpers, trousers, coats, dresses and tops. Each piece is unique, being a different colour, texture (ranging from chunky to slinky) and design (ranging from plain to patterned, embroidered and/or sequinned). Made to measure is also available, with jumpers from around €175.

Stijl

74 rue Antoine Dansaert, Lower Town (02 512 03 13). Pré-métro Bourse. **Open** 10.30am-6.30pm Mon-Sat. **Credit** AmEx, DC, MC, V. **Map** p316 B3.
If you dare enter the stark interior of Stijl, with its condescending assistants, you'll find a boutique packed with some of the most cutting-edge design that Belgium has to offer – at a price. Owner Sonia

Noël has a knack for spotting home-grown talent, having signed up first-time collections several decades ago from Ann Demeulemeester, Dries van Noten and Martin Margiela, three of the Antwerp Six, and, more recently, Olivier Theyskens and Xavier Delcour. (*See also p67* **Fashionably late** *and p237* **Antwerp: Fashion capital**.)

Children

Baby 2000

35F Weiveldlaan, Zaventem-Zuid (02 725 20 13/ www.baby2000.be). Bus 351, 358. **Open** 10am-7pm Mon-Fri; 10am-6pm Sat. **Credit** MC, V.
This vast store is near the airport, so it is a pain to get to, but for those in search of a wide selection of clothes, toys, pushchairs, car seats, high chairs and bath paraphernalia from major European manufacturers, this is the place to come.

Histoire de pieds

54 rue de Namur, Upper Town (02 502 15 50). Métro Porte de Namur. **Open** 10am-6pm Mon-Sat. **Credit** AmEx, DC, MC, V. **Map** p319 D5.
A wide selection of good-quality kids' shoes, with styles ranging from conservative to fashionable.

Kat en Muis

33 rue Antoine Dansaert, Lower Town (02 514 32 34). Pré-métro Bourse. **Open** 10.30am-6.30pm Mon-Sat. **Credit** AmEx, DC, MC, V. **Map** p316 B3.
This is the kids' version of the cutting-edge fashion store Stijl further along the street (*see p148*). In other words, expect designer clothes at high prices.

Designers

Annemie Verbeke

64 rue Antoine Dansaert, Lower Town (02 511 21 71). Pré-métro Bourse. **Open** 11am-6pm Mon, Wed-Sat. **Credit** AmEx, DC, MC, V. **Map** p316 B3.
Fashionistas flock to Annemie Verbeke's shop, in a beautiful old building, for her classic clothes, in particular, her knitwear, which is simple but often features subtle detailing around the sleeves and neckline.

Francis Ferent

60 avenue Louise, Ixelles (02 545 7830/www.ferent. be). Métro Louise/tram 93, 94. **Open** 10am-6.30pm Mon-Sat. **Credit** AmEx, DC, MC, V. **Map** p319 D5.
This is the flagship store of a small empire of boutiques stocking international labels for men, women and children. Brands include DKNY, Dolce & Gabbana, Sonia Rykiel, Miu Miu, Marc Jacobs, Helmut Lang and Prada. You might get an icy reception – the assistants seem to think they own the place. **Other locations**: throughout the city.

Greta Marta

58 rue de l'Aqueduc, Ixelles (02 534 8824/ www.gretamarta.com). Tram 81, 82. **Open** noon-6.30pm Mon; 10am-6.30pm Tue-Sat. **Credit** AmEx, DC, MC, V. **Map** p324 C7.

The shop may bear the owner's name, but 80% of the stock bears the label of Diane von Furstenberg, the Belgian designer who made her name in the '70s with her classic wrap dress and is now experiencing a renaissance. The boutique aims to sell unique pieces within Belgium, stocking just one size of each design. Naturally, such exclusivity comes at a price.

Kwasi

18 place St-Géry, Lower Town (02 511 85 89). Pré-métro Bourse. **Open** 11am-6.30pm Mon-Sat. **Credit** AmEx, DC, MC, V. **Map** p316 B3.
You shouldn't have any problems making yourself understood in this shop: it's run by a Belgo-Scot who was one of the first to open a boutique selling international men's labels more than 15 years ago. Clothes, shoes and accessories are by Olivier Strelli and Kenzo, among others.

Lena Lena

60 rue Antoine Dansaert, Lower Town (02 502 22 33). Pré-métro Bourse. **Open** 12.30-6.30pm Mon; 10.30am-6.30pm Tue-Sat. **No credit cards**. **Map** p316 B3.
This Flemish designer sells funky and stylish clothes for sizes 38-52. Beautiful, original materials and designs to suit the curvaceous woman.

Martin Margiela

114 rue de Flandre, Lower Town (02 223 75 20). Métro Ste-Catherine or Comte de Flandre/tram 18. **Open** 11am-7pm Mon-Sat. **Credit** AmEx, DC, MC, V. **Map** p316 B2.
Keep an eye on the street numbers, as Martin Margiela's store, like his men's and women's clothes and accessories, is unlabelled. The Paris-based Flemish designer opened this shop (the first branch in Europe) in 2002. Run by Sonia Noël, owner of the Stijl designer emporium (*see p148*) and renowned fashion connoisseur, it's an all-white space housing black clothes and accessories, with just the odd splash of colour for good measure.

Nicolas Woit

80 rue Antoine Dansaert, Lower Town (02 503 48 32). Pré-métro Bourse. **Open** 10.30am-1pm, 2-6pm Tue-Fri; 10.30am-6.30pm Sat. **Credit** AmEx, MC, V. **Map** p316 B3.
Woit studied fashion in Paris before opening this store in 1998. Taking inspiration from period fabrics as well as Asian influences, he creates garments from luxuriant materials that have a bold, girlie and light-heartedly glamorous feel. Accessories such as hats, scarves, bags and jewellery made from semi-precious stones are integral to the outfit.

Nicole Cadine

28 rue Antoine Dansaert, Lower Town (02 503 48 26/www.nicolecadine.com). Pré-métro Bourse. **Open** 10am-6.30pm Mon-Sat. **Credit** AmEx, DC, MC, V. **Map** p316 B3.
French-born, Antwerp-based designer Nicole Cadine creates dramatic women's clothes in rich colours and fabrics, with prices that are not at all unreasonable

Eat, Drink, Shop

Brussels back in fashion

Antwerp has always been the Belgian hotspot for cool fashion (*see p237* **Antwerp: fashion capital**), but these days all the talk is of a renaissance in Brussels itself.

In the last ten years, the capital's fashion school **La Cambre** has produced some great designers. Laetitia Crahay collaborates with Karl Lagerfeld at Chanel; Jose Enrique Ona Selfa works for Loewe; and the star name, **Olivier Theyskens**, designs the couture collection for Rochas.

As a 20-year-old, Theyskens was rocketed into the limelight when Madonna chose to wear one of his creations to the 1998 Academy Awards. Overnight, the previously unknown Theyskens became a fashion superstar, responsible for dressing the pop icon through her Gothic stage and making the hook and eye the ultimate clothes fastener. Other devotees include Nicole Kidman, Gwyneth Paltrow and Queen Rania of Jordan. While his own label waits to be revived, Theyskens is focusing purely on Rochas.

Another young designer responsible for putting Brussels firmly back on the fashion map – and another former La Cambre student – is 24-year-old **Xavier Delcour**, born in Tournai, who has resisted the temptation of working for an established designer and has his own name label (*pictured*). For the first few years, he only designed menswear – although that didn't stop Madonna wearing them – but in 2004 he launched his first women's range. Although he doesn't have his own shop yet, surely it's just a matter of time – Delcour's clothes can be found in Brussels at **Stijl** (*see p148*).

One designer who has just opened her first store in the Belgian capital is **Marina Yee**, one of the famous Antwerp Six, emphasising that Brussels is equally important in fashion terms. Not surprisingly, it's located in the area synonymous with Belgian fashion: rue

Antoine Dansaert and its environs. (*See also p67* **Fashionably late**). A small and simple shop (MY Workshop, 3 rue du Marché aux Porcs, 0496 335 870, open 11am-7pm Fri, Sat) with fluorescent yellow-green walls, it sells her very limited and numbered editions to aficionados.

Die-hard fashionistas interested in learning more about Belgian designers and their work should check out the website for Modo Bruxellae (www.modobruxellae.be), effectively ambassador for the entire Belgian fashion industry. It organises a Fashion Designers' Trail every other year (2004, 2006, etc) in the last weekend of October, during which various Belgian designers choose a special location – from cafés and galleries to shops and apartments – in which to display their clothes.

considering that they are 'designer'. Although the emphasis is on beautiful eveningwear and bridal dresses, knitwear and accessories are also stocked.

Olivier Strelli

72 avenue Louise, Ixelles (02 512 56 07/www.strelli. be). Métro Louise/tram 93, 94. **Open** 10am-6.30pm Mon-Sat. **Credit** AmEx, DC, MC, V. **Map** p319 C6.
Born of Italian parents in the former Belgian Congo, Olivier Strelli focuses on creating contemporary classics – simple designs that he brings to life with the vibrant colours of his birthplace, plus various hues

of black and grey. He designs own labels for both sexes, plus a women's casualwear range, 22 October. **Other locations**: 44 rue Antoine Dansaert, Lower Town (02 512 09 42).

Smadja Men

21 avenue Lepoutre, Ixelles (02 346 50 13). Tram 91, 92/bus 60. **Open** 11am-6.30pm Mon-Sat. **Credit** AmEx, DC, MC, V. **Map** p324 C8.
Jacques Smadja, a tailor by trade, was one of the first Belgian boutique owners to stock Paul Smith. He still does, as well as choice items by other famous names.

High-street chain stores

Chine Collection

82-84 avenue Louise, Ixelles (02 512 45 52). Métro Louise then tram 93, 94. **Open** 10am-6.30pm Mon-Sat. **Credit** AmEx, DC, MC, V. **Map** p319 D7.
Designer Guillaume Thys launched this upmarket Belgian chain in 1991, with a prêt-à-porter range for women that aims to produce feminine clothes that are also functional, versatile, ultra-light and easy to wear. Printed and plain silks sourced from the Far East are a mainstay, although fur, leather, denim, wool and cashmere also feature. A range for girls, Mimi Chine was recently introduced.
Other locations: 2 rue van Artevelde, Lower Town (02 503 14 99).

Massimo Dutti

47 avenue de la Toison d'Or, Ixelles (02 289 10 50/ www.massimodutti.com). Métro Porte de Namur or Louise. **Open** 10am-6.30pm Mon-Sat. **Credit** AmEx, DC, MC, V. **Map** p319 D5.
Another successful Spanish export, Massimo Dutti serves up smart, classic clothes for men, women and children. The elegant, practical attire is of dependable quality, if not always breathtakingly exciting.
Other locations: Woluwe Shopping Center, rue St-Lambert, Woluwe-St-Lambert (02 779 81 88).

Rue Blanche

35-39 rue Antoine Dansaert, Lower Town (02 512 03 14/www.rueblanche.com). Pré-métro Bourse. **Open** 11am-6.30pm Mon-Sat. **Credit** AmEx, DC, MC, V. **Map** p316 B3.
Two Belgian designers, Marie Chantal Regout and Patrick Van Heurck, launched Rue Blanche back in 1987, with just seven different styles of cotton knitted jersey. Now their business has expanded to include more than 100 timeless items of clothes in gorgeous fabrics, as well as beautiful accessories such as evening bags, scarves and shoes. Household items, such as candles, vases and glossy books, complete the stock.
Other locations: throughout the city.

Lingerie

Underwear

47 rue Antoine Dansaert, Lower Town (02 514 27 31). Pré-métro Bourse. **Open** 10.30am-6.30pm Mon-Sat. **Credit** AmEx, DC, MC, V. **Map** p316 B3.
Men's and women's undies, homewear, nightwear and beachwear by Hanro, Eres and Oxo.

Women'Secret

2 rue Neuve, Lower Town (02 217 10 28/www. womensecret.com). Métro/pré-métro De Brouckère. **Open** 10am-6.30pm Mon-Sat. **Credit** AmEx, DC, MC, V. **Map** p315 C2.
Women'Secret stocks an excellent selection of fun, reasonably priced lingerie, nightwear, beachwear, some maternitywear and a range of comfortable clothes for lounging around the home.

Other locations: 43 avenue de la Toison d'Or, Ixelles (02 503 58 16); Woluwe Shopping Centre, rue St-Lambert, Woluwe-St-Lambert (02 772 20 04).

Second-hand & vintage

Bernard Gavilan

27 rue des Pierres, Lower Town (02 502 01 28/ www.bernardgavilan.com). Pré-métro Bourse. **Open** 2-7pm Mon; noon-7pm Tue-Sat. **No credit cards.** **Map** p315 B3.
You can't miss this store: it always has one of the most flamboyantly stylish window displays in town. Owner and shopkeeper Bernard sells a mix of second-hand and customised vintage clothes, including old trainers, sports bags and a huge selection of belts. In addition to fashion, he has started selling on furniture from the 1950s, '60s and '70s.

Dod

16 chaussée de Louvain, St-Josse (02 218 04 54/ www.dod.be). Métro Madou. **Open** 10am-6.30pm Mon-Sat. **Credit** AmEx, DC, MC, V. **Map** p320 E3.
Dod, which takes a warehouse approach to selling designer fashion at discount prices, has now been in business for over 20 years. There are various shops, each specialising in either menswear, womenswear, childrenswear or, more recently, shoes. Along with this menswear branch, there's a women's one at No.44 (02 219 80 42), a children's one at No.41 (02 217 52 08), and branches in Ixelles listed below.

Bernard Gavilan.

Other locations: *Children's* 8 rue du Bailli (02 640 64 83); 179 avenue Louise (02 640 60 40). *Men's* 89 rue du Bailli (02 538 02 47). *Women's* 64 rue du Bailli (02 640 38 98).

Les Enfants d'Edouard

175-177 avenue Louise, Ixelles (02 640 42 45). Métro Louise then tram 93, 94. **Open** 10am-6.30pm Mon-Sat. **Credit** AmEx, MC, V. **Map** p319 D6.

This store sells second-hand designer labels and end-of-line stock. All of it is in excellent condition, and as a result prices can lean towards the expensive. Brands include Guess, Balmain, Charles Jourdan and Ferragamo. Womenswear is at 175 avenue Louise, menswear next door.

Gabriele

14 rue des Chartreux, Lower Town (02 512 67 43). Pré-métro Bourse. **Open** noon-6pm Tue-Fri; 1-7pm Sat. **Credit** AmEx, DC, MC, V. **Map** p315 B3.

Gabriele Wolf, who owns vintage clothing boutique, started collecting period hats when she worked in the theatre. In addition to hats, her shop sells clothes such as elegant evening dresses, coats and shoes, all dating from the '20s onwards.

Idiz Bogam

76 rue Antoine Dansaert, Lower Town (02 512 10 32). Pré-métro Bourse. **Open** 11am-7pm Mon-Sat. **Credit** AmEx, DC, MC, V. **Map** p316 B3.

This quirky boutique sells second-hand and vintage clothing for both men and women from London, New York and Paris, much of it customised with sequins, ruffs and so on. There are also some wacky wedding dresses, as well as a good assortment of old and new shoes, hats and retro furniture.

Look 50

10 rue de la Paix, Ixelles (02 512 24 18). Métro Porte de Namur/bus 54, 71. **Open** 10am-6.30pm Mon-Sat. **No credit cards. Map** p319 D5.

This second-hand shop is vintage at its rawest. No glam, no horrifying price tags, no pretence. Here, customers dig through the tightly packed mess of clothes to find the item that suits them best. The dominating era is the '70s, with leather jackets, old polyester dresses, funky vibrant shirts and fun hats.

Modes

164 rue Blaes, Lower Town (02 512 49 07). Métro/pré-métro Porte de Hal/bus 27, 48. **Open** 10am-2.30pm Tue-Fri; 10am-3.30pm Sat, Sun. **Credit** AmEx, MC, V. **Map** p318 B5.

This shop specialises in vintage clothing made prior to 1950. Most pieces are for women, but there is a small children's section and a room at the back for men. Among the amazing pieces are furs, coats, dresses, shirts, skirts and hats, plus glasses, gloves, hat pins, purses and boas. There's also a limited range of linens, laces, ribbon and fabric.

Ramon & Valy

19 rue des Teinturiers, Lower Town (02 511 05 10). Pré-métro Bourse. **Open** 11am-7pm Mon-Sat. **Credit** AmEx, DC, MC, V. **Map** p315 B3.

This elegant corner shop stocks only the best vintage clothes from French designers such as Yves Saint Laurent, Dior, Givenchy and Christian Lacroix, as well as Italian labels like Gucci and Roberto Cavalli. Vintage shoes and accessories are also on the menu, which is aimed primarily at women, but also has a few offerings for men and children.

Streetwear

Hype

4 rue des Riches Claires, Lower Town (02 502 88 70/www.hypeshop.com). Pré-métro Bourse. **Open** 10.30am-7pm Mon-Sat. **Credit** AmEx, DC, MC, V. **Map** p316 B3.

Hype was one of the first streetwear shops in Brussels and it continues to be a stylish purveyor of modern skate fashion and trainers for men. Sister shop, Zoe, recently opened at 8 rue des Riches Claires, stocking female skate fashion and trainers. Both stores sell a wide range of labels, including Diesel, Kulte, Sealkay and Carhartt.

Privejoke

76-78 rue du Marché aux Charbon, Lower Town (02 502 63 67). Pré-métro Bourse. **Open** 11am-7pm Mon-Sat. **Credit** AmEx, V. **Map** p316 B3.

Privejoke, another of Brussels' original streetwear boutiques, is a funky choice. At least it is if you make your way to the back of the shop, where the men's clothes are to be found in a dark room. The women's section at the front is far more bright and girlie, dotted with chandeliers. Brands stocked include Kangol, Pringle, Seven Jeans and Puma, as well as lingerie by Belgian label La Fille d'O.

Under Elvis

29 rue des Pierres, Lower Town (02 502 47 87). Pré-métro Bourse. **Open** 10.30am-6pm Mon-Sat. **No credit cards. Map** p315 B3.

Set in a massive industrial space, this temple of street style features a myriad of sought-after urban brands such as Carhartt, G-Sus, Religion, Aem-Kei, Playboy and Boxfresh. A range of skater shoe brands like Vans, Etnies and Emerica is also available. Check out the graffiti mural by Zenith, as well as the regular art exhibits and musical events.

Fashion accessories

Annick Tapernoux

28 rue du Vieux Marché aux Grains, Lower Town (02 512 43 79). Pré-métro Bourse. **Open** 1-6pm Fri; 11am-6pm Sat; also by appointment. **Credit** MC, V. **Map** p316 B3.

Annick Tapernoux studied in Antwerp and then London's Royal College of Art, prior to setting up her eponymous shop, which displays both her silver jewellery (inspired by the elegance of the 1920s and '30s) and her silver homewares, such as bowls and vases. She also works to commission, either adapting existing designs or creating new pieces.

Good housekeeping

Nothing typifies more the difference between upmarket Sablon and its scruffier neighbour Marolles than its shops. Upper Town Sablon interests the serious collector with the rarest of antiques; browse around the Marolles for an hour, and you can fill your flat ten times over with second-hand furniture and obscure bric-a-brac. Yet with more and more exotic home furnishing boutiques creeping into the low-rent Marolles, the area is slowly losing its cheap-and-cheerful tag.

Not entirely, though. At its epicentre is place du Jeu de Balle, where a compact **flea market** (www.marcheauxpuces.org) has been held since 1873, and on a daily basis since 1919. Today many traders still lay their wares on the cobblestones, specialising in a particular item: chandeliers, cutlery, glass statues, for example. Other 'stalls' are nothing more than a clutch of cardboard boxes filled to the gills with what appears to be complete junk – one shoe, scratched vinyls, broken crockery – and placed on the ground. But if you're prepared to take time and sift through the toot, there are definitely items worth buying. Original Bakelite phones, antique linens, decent wooden furniture and fur coats are just some of the things that spring to mind: be prepared to bargain hard. Some say the prices are lower during the week, but there are more traders at weekends.

At the other end of the price scale, nearby boutiques have begun to specialise in rustic minimalism. These include **Big Nose** (55 and 134 rue Blaes, 02 503 37 65), **Atchoum** (253 rue Haute, 02 514 38 11) and **Momentum** (57-59 rue Haute, 02 514 07 87). The latter is the largest, and also has an Oriental flavour. Prices here are relatively steep: a beautiful caramel-coloured four-seater leather sofa will be more than €2,000, a striking teak and bamboo wardrobe €750 (admittedly half its usual price). Even if you don't actually buy anything, it's a great store to walk through – check out the beautiful old doors inside.

Sturdy teak seems to be something of a fixture along rue Haute: check out **Wood Factory** (No.67, 02 513 06 01) and **TCH** (No.97, 02 503 41 27), a couple of doors down from neighbourhood standby **New De Wolf** (*see p162*). Tiny TCH stocks tables and chairs at very attractive prices. For a little extra, the shop will treat table and chairs so that they match and are protected from stains.

Not all the shops in the Marolles sell contemporary wooden furniture, however. More unusual items can be found at both branches of **Rambagh** (*see p162*) – including extravagant imports from India and elsewhere, often at very good prices. Owner Sylvie Carpentier is to give both stores a facelift, and will introduce textiles and gift ideas. There's a small but seductive selection of table lamps at **Abal'jour** (122 rue Blaes, no phone), where you can mix and match shades.

The area has several shops specialising in modern antiques from the 1930s through to the '70s. One of the better ones is the teeny store **Ygrek** (105 rue Blaes, 0479 732 086), which offers a sparkling selection of 1950s furniture, jewellery and objects.

Passage 125 (*see p162*) is more than just your average antiques store – 25 dealers show their wares over 900 square metres (9,677 square feet). Walking through it is a heady experience: one moment you feel like you're in a Scottish castle, the next as though you're back in the nearby flea market. All life is here, from a '50s fire hydrant to art deco clocks, wooden trunks, doors and even a massive 18th-century French crucifix. If you're refurnishing an embassy or a country estate, this is the place to come: a Chesterfield armchair will set you back €700, and you can buy statues, chandeliers and antique radiators to complete the look.

Eat, Drink, Shop

Arcane

54 rue du Midi, Lower Town (02 511 91 42).
Pré-métro Bourse. **Open** 11am-6.30pm Mon-Sat.
Credit AmEx, DC, MC, V. **Map** p315 B3.
This shop has a wide range of affordable jewellery
in all shapes and sizes. Many pieces are made from
silver; some are classic, simple designs, while others are more exotic, from India, Mexico, Thailand
and Israel. Some also incorporate leather, satin ribbons, semi-precious stones and beads.

Christa Reniers

29 rue Antoine Dansaert, Lower Town (02 510
06 60/www.christareniers.com). Pré-métro Bourse.
Open 10.30am-1pm, 2-6.30pm Mon-Sat. **Credit**
AmEx, DC, MC, V. **Map** p316 B3.
Since she sold her first piece of jewellery in the early
1990s, Christa Reniers has become Belgium's most
famous jewellery designer. Self-taught, she creates
several new pieces each season, adding to the
already exquisite collection. Each piece is hand-cast
and -finished in the workshop located above this
flagship store. Prices start at €110 for earrings.

Delvaux

27 boulevard de Waterloo, Upper Town (02 513
05 02/www.delvaux.com). Métro Louise or Porte
de Namur. **Open** 10am-6.30pm Mon-Sat. **Credit**
AmEx, DC, MC, V. **Map** p319 C5.
Delvaux is something of an institution in Belgium,
creating top-quality leather products since 1829. On
the whole its products are conservative. Expect to
find handbags, wallets, belts, a small range of hand
luggage, silk scarves and ties, and desk accessories.
Other locations: 31 galerie de la Reine, Lower
Town (02 512 71 98).

Marianne Timperman

50 rue Antoine Dansaert, Lower Town (02 675 53
82). Pré-métro Bourse. **Open** 11am-6.30pm Mon-Sat.
Credit MC, V. **Map** p316 B3.
Marianne makes the majority of the handmade jewellery on display in this shop, but there are a few
pieces by an Italian designer Tiziana Redavid.
Marianne's speciality is silver; some items are oxidised so that they appear black, while others are
made from granulated silver, resulting in a bobbly
effect. She also incorporates semi-precious stones
and pearls into various designs, and sells gold work
too. Prices are reasonable.

Les Précieuses

83 rue Antoine Dansaert, Lower Town (02 503 28
98/www.lesprecieuses.com). Pré-métro Bourse.
Open 11am-6.30pm Mon, Wed-Sat. **Credit** MC, V.
Map p316 B3.
Pili Collado (Belgian of Portuguese descent) designs
beautiful pieces of jewellery, using velvet ribbons,
fine strands and clusters of polished chunky semi-
precious stones and pearls. She sells them alongside
Jamin Puech's sequinned and embroidered evening
bags and flamenco-inspired shawls, Diptyque
candles and perfume, and scarves and tops by a
Japanese label called Antipast.

Tarlatane

22 rue Ernest Solvay, Ixelles (02 502 79 29). Métro
Porte de Namur/bus 54, 71. **Open** 11am-6.30pm
Tue-Sat. **Credit** MC, V. **Map** p319 D5.
Valérie Janssens makes a range of accessories with
a very girlie feel. Among the goodies are hats (particularly cloches and berets), bags (recycled wool
day bags, silk evening bags), jewellery (made from
sparkly cut-glass and buttons) and scarves.

Milliners

Christopher Coppens

2 rue Léon Lepage, Lower Town (02 512 77 97).
Métro Ste-Catherine. **Open** 11am-6pm Tue-Sat.
Credit MC, V. **Map** p316 B2.
Flemish Christopher Coppens' hats are mainly for
women, but in 2005 he is due to create a full men's
collection. Coppens uses all kinds of materials to create the hats, which range in price from around €100
to sky's-the-limit (for made to order). Scarves, gloves
and brooches are also for sale.

Gillis

17 rue du Lombard, Lower Town (02 512 09 26).
Pré-métro Bourse or Anneessens. **Open** 10am-6pm
Mon-Sat. **Credit** AmEx, DC, MC, V. **Map** p315 B3.
Gillis is something of a Brussels institution, dating
from 1910. There's a small range of ready-made
hats, which are mostly for women, but in winter a
few men's hats are also available. However, the real
speciality is made-to-measure hats (from €130),
which are created on the premises.

Shoes

Hatshoe

89 rue Antoine Dansaert, Lower Town (02 512 41
52). Pré-métro Bourse. **Open** 12.30am-6.30pm Mon;
10.30am-6.30pm Tue-Sat. **Credit** AmEx, DC, MC, V.
Map p316 B3.
Designer footwear for both men and women by
Patrick Cox, Costume National and Belgian designers Dries van Noten and Veronique Braquinho. Hats
and scarves are by designer Cécile Bertrand.

People Shoes Design

14-18 rue du Lombard, Lower Town (02 502 17 64).
Pré-métro Bourse or Anneessens. **Open** 11am-7pm
Mon-Fri; 10.30am-7pm Sat; 1.30-6.30pm Sun. **Credit**
DC, MC, V. **Map** p315 B3.
The focus of this shop (which used to house the shop
of mad hatter Elvis Pompilio) has changed, so that
it now sells as much street fashion for men and
women as it does designer-trendy urban footwear.
Kids, however, still only get shoes. Brands stocked
include Diesel, Puma, Dirk Bikkembergs and G-Star.

Sacha Shoe Design

27 rue des Fripiers, Lower Town (02 218 79 65).
Métro/pré-métro De Brouckère or pré-métro Bourse.
Open 10am-6.30pm Mon-Sat. **No credit cards.**
Map p315 C3.

AM Sweet for my sweet.

This funky Dutch-owned shoe mecca sells everything from eccentric clubbing heels and boots to conventional office shoes for boys and girls. All the latest trends and top brands are covered, including Le Coq Sportif, Converse, Diesel and Dr Martens.

Y-Enzo

Galerie Espace Louise, 47 avenue de la Toison d'Or, Ixelles (02 514 65 68). Métro Louise. **Open** 10am-6.30pm Mon-Sat. **Credit** AmEx, DC, MC, V. **Map** p319 C5.

This ultra-upmarket footwear shop stocks shoes by Yves Saint Laurent, Gucci, Stephane Kélian and Dirk Bikkembergs, among others, plus a limited number of designer bags and clothes.

Flowers

Bo Flower Bar

49 place du Chatelain, Ixelles (02 646 66 96/www.boflowerbar.com). Tram 93, 94. **Open** 2-8pm Mon; 9am-8pm Tue-Thur, Sat; 9am-9pm Fri; 9am-2pm Sun. **Credit** MC, V. **Map** p324 D7.

The first Bo Flower Bar opened in 2000, and already another four shops have sprung up, two others in Brussels. No wonder – they're open late and produce beautiful flower arrangements at reasonable prices. **Other locations**: 378 avenue Rogier, Schaerbeek (02 726 28 20); 107 avenue du Panthéon (02 428 78 68).

Fleurop-Interflora

0800 99669/02 242 29 64/www.interflora.com. **Open** 24hrs daily. **Credit** AmEx, DC, MC, V.

For those who want to say it with flowers, at any time of the day or night.

Het Witte Gras

7 rue Plétinckx, Lower Town (02 502 05 29). Pré-métro Bourse. **Open** 9am-6pm Mon-Sat. **Credit** AmEx, DC, MC, V. **Map** p316 B3.

Het Witte Gras is a pretty corner shop out of which house plants and flowers spill on to the pavement. Inside is an abundance of attractive vases and pots, plus plenty of expert advice.

Food & drink

Bakeries & patisseries

AM Sweet

4 rue des Chartreux, Lower Town (02 513 51 31). Pré-métro Bourse. **Open** 9am-6.30pm Tue-Sat. **No credit cards**. **Map** p316 B3.

This lovely old-fashioned tea house and sweet shop sells biscuits, chocolate, cakes, sweets, teas and coffees, some of which are made in house and some of which are imported. The foodstuffs range from traditional recipes (such as *pain d'épices* and baked marzipan) to the latest innovative concoctions, such as the French crystallised flowers, made from real rose, lavender, violet and mint leaves.

Dandoy

31 rue au Beurre, Lower Town (02 511 03 26). Pré-métro Bourse. **Open** 8.30am-6.30pm Mon-Sat; 10.30am-6.30pm Sun. **Credit** MC, V. **Map** p315 C3.

The oldest cookie shop in town sells the best melt-in-your-mouth *speculoos* (traditional Belgian ginger biscuits), *pains d'amande* (wafer-thin biscuits), *pain d'épices* and *pain à la grecque*.

Le Pain Quotidien

16 rue Antoine Dansaert, Lower Town (02 502 23 61/www.painquotidien.com). Pré-métro Bourse. **Open** 7am-7pm daily. **Credit** MC, V. **Map** p316 B3.
This successful chain of café/bakeries has branches from Brussels to California. This one's the most central but the one on avenue Louise is a favourite, with its conservatory. Shoppers can pick up something as simple as a croissant or delicacies such as raspberry clafoutis, tarte au citron, and the legendary chocolate bomb cake. (*See p110* **Breaking bread**.)
Other locations: throughout the city.

Chocolate

See also p158 **Sweet success**.

Corné Port-Royal

9 rue de la Madeleine, Lower Town (02 512 43 14). Métro Gare Centrale. **Open** 10am-8pm daily. **Credit** AmEx, DC, MC, V. **Map** p315 C3.
A good-quality chocolatier (similar to Neuhaus and Godiva), with franchises around town (though this is the only one in the centre).

Mary's

73 rue Royale, Upper Town (02 217 45 00/www. marychoc.com). Métro Botanique/tram 92, 93, 94. **Open** 9.30am-6pm Mon-Sat. **Credit** MC, V. **Map** p317 D2.
For years after it opened in 1919 Mary was the top chocolate-maker in Brussels – until the arrival of Pierre Marcolini and others. Their prices remain high, however. Not only does the shop stock delectable pralines, it also sells jellies and bonbons.

Pierre Marcolini

39 place du Grand Sablon, Upper Town (02 514 12 06/www.marcolini.be). Tram 92, 93, 94. **Open** 10am-7pm Mon-Thur; 10am-8pm Fri; 9am-8pm Sat; 9am-7pm Sun. **Credit** AmEx, DC, MC, V. **Map** p317 C4.
Brussels' latest international name in chocolate. *See also p158* **Sweet success**.
Other locations: 75 avenue Louise, Ixelles (02 538 42 24); 1302 chaussée de Waterloo, Uccle (02 372 15 11); 14 avenue de Hinnisdael, Woluwe-St-Pierre (02 771 27 20).

Planète Chocolat

24 rue du Lombard, Lower Town (02 511 07 55/ www.planetechocolat.be). Pré-métro Bourse or Anneessens. **Open** 11am-6.30pm Tue-Sun. **Credit** MC, V. **Map** p315 B3.
As well as being a chocolate shop and a tea house, where gay-friendly dances are held every Sunday afternoon, Planète Chocolat offers (bookable) group demonstrations of chocolate-making. The chocolate itself is among the funkiest in town: chocolate lips and bouquets of chocolate 'flowers' are specialities.

Wittamer

6 place du Grand Sablon (02 512 37 42/www. wittamer.com). Tram 92, 93, 94. **Open** 9am-6pm Mon; 7am-7pm Tue-Sat; 7am-6pm Sun. **Credit** AmEx, DC, MC, V. **Map** p317 C4.

Renowned local chocolate dynasty with a glitzy store and café on the Sablon. *See also p158* **Sweet success**.

Delis & health food

Au Suisse

73-75 boulevard Anspach, Lower Town (02 512 95 89/www.ausuisse.be). Pré-métro Bourse. **Open** 10am-8pm Mon, Wed-Fri; 10am-7.30pm Tue; 10am-9pm Sat; 5-9pm Sun. **No credit cards**. **Map** p315 B3.
Despite the name and flags, there's nothing Swiss about this place. It's been a quintessential Brussels café and deli since 1876, and is the place to nip into for real Belgian fare, to take out or eat in. Salads, cheeses, cold meats, *maatjes* (herring) are up for grabs, along with drinks, milkshakes and ice-cream. The deli next door serves pretty much the same, plus international specialities such as Madeiran wine.

Claire Fontaine

3 rue Ernest Allard, Upper Town (02 512 24 10). Tram 92, 93, 94. **Open** 10am-6.30pm Tue-Sat. **No credit cards**. **Map** p319 C4.
This little shop just off the Sablon always appears so inviting. As well as sandwiches, soups and pastries to take away, there's a host of international gastronomical delights such as foie gras, lobster soup, olives, dry goods, teas and tisanes, absinthe and Belgian fruit wines.

Le Tartisan

27 rue de la Paix, Ixelles (02 503 36 00/www. tartisan.be). Métro Porte de Namur/bus 54, 71. **Open** 10am-9pm Mon-Sat. **Credit** AmEx, DC, MC, V. **Map** p319 D5.
Le Tartisan deli was so popular that it moved around the corner from its old location and added a restaurant section. The speciality of the house is, not surprisingly, tarts – savoury and sweet, all made on site according to traditional recipes. They're astonishingly light, and come in both veggie and carnivore options, with lemon, walnut and chocolate or frangipane for sweet-toothed customers.

Drink

Beer Mania

174-178 chaussée de Wavre, Ixelles (02 512 17 88/ www.beermania.be). Métro Porte de Namur. **Open** *Jan-Nov* 11am-9pm Mon-Sat. *Dec* open 11am-9pm daily. **Credit** MC, V. **Map** p322 E5.
Beer Mania has been open for more than 20 years and now boasts a range of more than 400 beers, along with matching glasses, gift packages, accessories and books. There's even a bar, so that you can sit and sample beers in comfort.

De Boe

36 rue de Flandre, Lower Town (02 511 13 73). Métro Ste-Catherine. **Open** 9am-6pm Tue-Fri; 9am-5pm Sat. **Credit** AmEx, DC, MC, V. **Map** p316 B2.

This family-run shop, which opened way back in 1896, is known for its high-quality coffees: the family chooses the best beans to ensure great taste and aroma each year and then creates six blends, all freshly roasted on the premises. The range of teas is selected just as discerningly, as are the fine wines and liqueurs, dried and candied fruits, chocolates and other deli delights.

Délices et Caprices

51 rue des Pierres, Lower Town (02 512 14 51/ 02 512 18 83). Pré-métro Bourse. **Open** *Winter* 2-7pm Mon, Wed-Sun. *Summer* 2-10pm Mon, Wed-Sun. **Credit** AmEx, MC, V. **Map** p315 B3.
This place is run by a Swiss, Pierre Zuber, who's been in Belgium for 20 years and knows his beers. In addition to ale, beer glasses and other paraphernalia are sold, plus a few quality products such as wines and genevers. Tastings are held on site.

Mig's World Wines

43 chaussée de Charleroi, St-Gilles (02 534 77 03/ www.migsworldwines.be). Métro Louise then tram 91, 92. **Open** 11am-7pm Mon-Sat. **Credit** AmEx, DC, MC, V. **Map** p319 C6.
This store may be best known for its Australian wines (the owner Miguel Saelens stocks around 100 varieties), but it also sells wines from almost 30 other regions and countries, including Belgium and Eastern Europe, plus fruit wines, grappa and whisky. Mig is usually in the store and is always happy to offer advice. Go on a Saturday and you'll be invited to join the weekly wine tasting.

Le Palais des Thés

45 place de la Vieille Halle aux Blés, Lower Town (02 502 45 59/www.palaisdesthes.com). Métro Gare Centrale. **Open** 11am-7pm daily. **Credit** AmEx, DC, MC, V. **Map** p315 C4.

Sweet success

Belgian chocolate is renowned throughout the world for its excellence. But not all Belgian chocolate is great. Head for one of the tourist traps around the Grand' Place in Brussels and you'll end up with a tasty box of chocolates to write home about.

If you find yourself in the Sablon, however, you're guaranteed to find some truly great chocolate. It may cost you an arm and a leg, but you can rest assured it will be sublime. That's because place du Grand Sablon is home to two of the best chocolate-makers in Brussels. No, in Belgium. No, make that the world.

Wittamer (*see p157*), easily recognisable thanks to its bright pink canopies, is the grand old dame of the two. Opened in 1910 by Henri Wittamer, it is still a family-run business, with two grandchildren overseeing the entire operation (a chocolate shop at No.6, a patisserie at No.12 and next door at No.13 an upmarket tea-room, run by a great-grandchild).

The chocolate shop always smells divine – not surprisingly, since the chocolates are made at the back of the store – and has the most amazing window displays, which change every three months. Imagine one side of the Grand' Place, a life-size model

of Diane von Furstenberg or a desk with functioning table lamp all carved out of solid chocolate.

Almost exactly opposite the square stands **Pierre Marcolini** (*see p157*), the eponymous shop and pretender to the Wittamer crown. Having won many accolades, Marcolini is expanding fast, with branches all over the world, including London, Tokyo and Paris.

The shop in the Sablon, however, was one of the first and remains a real temple to his craft. Not only does it stock his chocolates – with their innovative flavours, such as ganache with jasmine tea and fondant bar with thyme and orange peel – but it also sells his chocolate cakes, which sit in the window and are edible works of art.

Beer Mania – lager than life. *See p157.*

The interior of this shop is very stylish, with around 250 varieties of tea from 30 countries, including Georgia and Turkey. Free tastings are offered, while gift ideas include beautiful teapots and scented teas.

International

Gallaecia

6 rue Charles Martel, EU Quarter (02 230 33 56). Métro Maelbeek. **Open** 11am-7pm Mon-Fri; 11am-3.30pm Sat. **No credit cards**. **Map** p320 F3.
If you can't live without Spanish produce, then this is the place to come. It sells *empanadas*, as well as olive oil, Manchego cheese, Serrano ham, tinned fish and preserves. Sweet treats such as *turrones* and *polvorones* are popular, as are the wines and cava.

MNS

25-27 boulevard d'Ypres, Lower Town (02 217 71 49). Métro Yser. **Open** 7am-6.30pm Mon-Thur, Sat, Sun. **No credit cards**. **Map** p316 B1.
A small warehouse – one of many in the area – packed to the rafters with industrial-sized pots of olives, olive oil, herbs, spices and cheap juice drinks.

Tagawa Superstore

119 chaussée de Vleurgat, Ixelles (02 648 59 11). Tram 81, 82, 93, 94/bus 38, 60. **Open** 10am-7pm Mon-Sat. **No credit cards**. **Map** p324 E7.
Fresh and frozen Japanese specialities and dishes, plus wasabi – and newspapers.

Thai Supermarket

3-9 rue Ste-Catherine, Lower Town (02 502 40 32). Pré-métro Bourse or métro Ste-Catherine. **Open** 9.30am-6.30pm Mon-Sat; 10am-3pm Sun. **No credit cards**. **Map** p315 B3.
Next door to the vast Chinese supermarket is this more manageable Thai Supermarket. Expect to find exotic fresh, dry and tinned produce as well as Thai homewares. The staff are helpful and speak English.

Markets

Brussels has a number of food markets easily accessible from the city centre. The largest and most colourful is around the **Gare du Midi**, on Sundays from 6am, with a Mediterranean and North African flavour. The other *communes'* markets are more akin to farmers' markets, with cured meats, fine cheeses, and so on. The most popular is at **place du Châtelain** in Ixelles on Wednesdays from 2-7pm, although the one at **parvis de St-Gilles** on Sunday mornings offers excellent local produce.

Gifts & stationery

Bali-Africa

154-156 rue Blaes, Lower Town (02 514 47 92). Métro/pré-métro Porte de Hal/bus 27, 48. **Open** 10am-6pm Tue-Sat; 10am-4pm Sun. **Credit** AmEx, DC, MC, V. **Map** p318 B5.
It's easy to get lost in this giant maze of a shop, though luckily the owners have signposted the rooms and provided a painted yellow line on the floor and stairs to help you find your way around. Wares include statuettes, masks, bongos and furniture from across the globe, from Indonesia to Zimbabwe, via Latin America.

Dukah

8 rue des Chartreux, Lower Town (02 502 69 30/ www.dukah.com). Pré-métro Bourse. **Open** 11.30am-6.30pm Tue-Sat. **Credit** AmEx, DC, MC, V. **Map** p316 B3.
Originally this simple shop sold mostly handmade wooden items designed by the owners and produced in Kenya, but now it's diversifying to include pieces made from other natural fibres, such as banana leaf and raffia, and recycled rubber. The emphasis is on fair-trade and environmentally friendly sources.

Eat, Drink, Shop

Stylish stationery store **Plaizier**.

La Maison du Miel

121 rue du Midi, Lower Town (02 512 32 50).
Pré-métro Anneessens. **Open** 10.30am-6.30pm Mon-
Fri, Sun; 10.30am-7pm Sat. **Credit** AmEx, MC, V.
Map p315 B4.
Make a beeline for this shop, which was founded in
1887 and sells all things honey-themed, scented and
flavoured, from edible goodies to toiletries.
Other locations: 13 rue Marché aux Herbes, Lower
Town (02 513 57 50).

Ma Maison de Papier

6 galerie de Ruysbroeck, Upper Town (02 512 22 49).
Métro Gare Centrale/bus 34, 48, 95, 96. **Open** 1-7pm
Wed-Fri; 3-7pm Sat. **No credit cards. Map** p315 C4.
A store of treasures, with its drawers of prints,
plaques and posters of art exhibits and adverts from
the late 1800s to the present.

Maison d'Art G Arekens

*15 rue du Midi, Lower Town (02 511 48 08). Pré-
métro Bourse.* **Open** 10.30am-1pm, 2-6pm Mon-Sat.
Credit V. **Map** p315 B3.
You'd think this place was simply a picture-framing
gallery, but pop inside and you'll find a variety of
religious icons such as crucifixes and triptychs.
There are also small plaster-cast reproductions of
non-religious statues, but the real highlight is the
55,000 postcards and reproduction etchings.

Plaizier

*50 rue des Eperonniers, Lower Town (02 513 47 30/
www.plaizier.be). Métro Gare Centrale.* **Open**
11am-6pm Mon-Sat. **Credit** AmEx, DC, MC, V.
Map p315 C3.

Most people come here for the excellent postcards,
generally original and artistic, but there's also a well-
chosen selection of books, posters and diaries.

Rosalie Pompon

*1 rue de l'Hôpital, Lower Town (02 512 35 93/
www.rosaliepompon.com). Métro Gare Centrale.*
Open noon-6.30pm Mon; 10.30am-6.30pm Tue-Sun.
Credit AmEx, DC, MC, V. **Map** p315 C4.
A cross between a gift shop and toy shop, attracting both the young at heart and the young in age.
Papier-mâché giraffes and elephants jostle for space
with flower-adorned wellies, colourful fairy lights,
wacky lamps and clocks and old-fashioned puppets.

Rose

*56-58 rue de l'Aqueduc, Ixelles (02 534 9808). Tram
91, 92.* **Open** 10.30am-6.20pm Tue-Sat. **Credit** MC,
V. **Map** p324 C7.
Rose was established in December 2003 by Elodie
Gleis, who gave up a job in advertising to open this
temple to all things girlie. She sells a mix of decorative objects for the home, fashion accessories and
small gifts, which she sources from different parts
of Europe (including Cath Kidston from the UK).

Yannart-Remacle

*11 rue du Marché au Charbon, Lower Town
(02 512 12 26). Pré-métro Bourse or Anneessens.*
Open 8.30am-6pm Mon-Fri; 8.30am-2.30pm Sat.
No credit cards. Map p315 B3.
This old-fashioned shop sells everything that a
jeweller could need to perfect his or her art, including crystals and semi-precious stones. Staff also do
engravings and settings.

Z'art

223 chaussée d'Ixelles, Ixelles (02 649 06 53). Bus 54, 71. **Open** 11am-7pm Tue-Sat. **Credit** AmEx, DC, MC, V. **Map** p322 D6.

Z'Art is the perfect place to browse for a gift, because it specialises in novelty items with a function: think octopus salt shakers, snail-shaped Sellotape dispensers and cow-adorned toilet roll holders.
Other locations: 40 rue des Pierres, Lower Town (02 502 61 21).

Health & beauty

Cosmetics & perfume

Ici Paris XL

37 rue Neuve, Lower Town (02 219 22 07). Métro/pré-métro De Brouckère or Rogier. **Open** 9am-6.30pm Mon-Sat. **Credit** AmEx, DC, MC, V. **Map** p315 C2.

Founded in Belgium in the late 1970s, this is the largest chain of perfumeries in the country: with more than 150 outlets in total. Each shop is stylish, while the range of luxury fragrances in most stores includes all the top brands.
Other locations: throughout the city.

Planet Parfum (Cloquet)

56-62 rue Neuve, Lower Town (02 219 38 28). Métro/pré-métro De Brouckère or Rogier. **Open** 10am-6.45pm Mon-Sat. **Credit** AmEx, DC, MC, V **Map** p315 C2.

Ubiquitous fragrance store selling a wide selection of perfumes and some cosmetics.
Other locations: throughout the city.

Make-Up Forever

62 rue du Midi, Lower Town (02 512 10 80/www.makeupforever.com). Pré-métro Bourse. **Open** 10am-6.30pm Mon-Sat. **Credit** AmEx, DC, MC, V. **Map** p315 B3.

As well as selling its own-brand cosmetics, this French chain offers facials, massages, manicures and pedicures, as well as giving lessons on their application. Booking is essential.

Hairdressers

Anthony-And

165 rue de Linthout, EU Quarter (02 736 45 35). Métro Mérode. **Open** 9am-7pm Mon-Sat. **No credit cards. Map** p321 H3.

Trendy yet unpretentious, this salon has quality hairdressers and great prices. Drop in and get a cut and style for €41 (€29 for students) or colour from €24.

Burlesque

64 rue du Midi, Lower Town (02 513 01 22). Pré-métro Bourse. **Open** 10.30am-6.30pm Tue-Sat. **No credit cards. Map** p315 B3.

For more than a decade Scottish-American hairdresser Laurence B has been wielding a pair of scissors and a bottle of hair dye dextrously, producing trendy cuts and great colouring for a loyal clientele.

Nicole Jocelyn

37 chaussée de Wavre, Ixelles (02 511 28 74). Métro Porte de Namur. **Open** 9.30am-7pm Mon-Sat. **No credit cards. Map** p319 D5.

One of the largest and most popular hairdressers in the area, specialising in Afro hair. Men, women and children are all catered for.

Hobbies, arts & crafts

De Banier

85 rue du Marché au Charbon, Lower Town (02 511 44 31/www.debanier.be). Pré-métro Bourse or Anneessens. **Open** 10am-1pm, 2-6pm Mon-Fri; 10am-1pm, 2-5pm Sat. **No credit cards. Map** p315 B3.

This quiet little shop is packed with an extensive selection of arts and crafts supplies, including wood, paints, dyes, felt and beads. There are also 'how to' books and magazines, mainly in Dutch and French.

Le Chien du Chien Vert

50 quai des Charbonnages, Molenbeek (02 414 84 00/www.chienvert.com). Métro Comte de Flandre. **Open** 10am-6pm Mon-Sat. **Credit** AmEx, DC, MC, V. **Map** p316 A2.

There are really three parts to this textile store: Le Chien du Chien Vert, the more specialised outlet with smarter furnishing fabrics, silks and leathers, which includes the second section, Les Puces du Chien, a bargain area of remnants. The third section along the road, Les Tissus du Chien Vert (2 rue du Chien Vert, 02 411 54 39), is more of a general cloth store. The ranges and colours are amazing in themselves, but almost more so is the interior decor: Le Chien du Chien Vert has been built out of several canal-side buildings and filled with boats (the owner is a keen sailor), as well as a car, a rickshaw and a number of water features. Les Tissus, meanwhile, is home to a light aircraft. A quirky and refreshing shopping experience.

Schleiper

149 chaussée de Charleroi, St-Gilles (02 538 60 50). Tram 91, 92. **Open** 9.30am-6.30pm Mon-Sat. **Credit** AmEx, DC, MC, V. **Map** p319 C6.

An excellent choice of all types of art supplies, as well as an efficient framing service, framed art for sale and some office supplies.

Home furnishings

The best place for a browse is the Marolles, and the two main streets of rues Blaes and Haute leading to the daily flea market on place du Jeu de Balle. *See p153* **Good housekeeping**.

Art & Influences

221 avenue Louise, Ixelles (02 643 2843). Métro Louise then tram 93, 94. **Open** 10am-7pm Tue-Sat. **Credit** MC, V. **Map** p321 D7.

This huge store stocks an amazing range of household items, from delicate little vases to large sofas, in a wide range of colours and styles, including modern, African and Asian. There's also a café on site.

Cap Orient

123 & 133 rue Haute, Lower Town (No.123 02 513 13 02/No.133 02 513 13 05/www.caporient.com). Métro/pré-métro Porte de Hal/bus 27, 48. **Open** noon-6.30pm Mon-Thur; 10am-6.30pm Fri-Sun. **Credit** AmEx, DC, MC, V. **Map** p318 B5.

Of the two branches on rue Haute, the homestyle shop at No.123 specialises in Chinese antiques and repro furniture, while the sister shop at No.133 sells Indian antiques, antique-style pieces and artefacts.

Dille & Kamille

16 rue Jean Stas, St-Gilles (02 538 81 25/www.dille-kamille.be). Métro Louise/tram 91, 92, 93, 94. **Open** 9.30am-6.30pm Mon-Sat. **Credit** MC, V. **Map** p319 C6.

Recently expanded, Dille & Kamille is a chi-chi garden and home store. Plants and decorative baskets are at the front, while foodstuffs (olive oils, mustards, herbs, teas) are towards the back. The middle section features lots of household basics, kitchen gadgets, cookbooks and traditional wooden toys. Great for browsing.

Espace Bizarre

17-19 rue des Chartreux, Lower Town (02 514 52 56/www.espacebizarre.be). Pré-métro Bourse. **Open** 10am-7pm Mon-Sat. **Credit** AmEx, DC, MC, V. **Map** p316 B3.

Espace Bizarre sells modern furniture, half of it influenced by the clean lines and simplicity of Japanese design. At No.19, therefore, you will find futons and tatami mats, along with low tables and chairs, bowls and chopsticks, slippers and kimonos, as well as a few colourful key pieces. The more recent opening, No.17, offers high-end modern pieces by international designers such as Mobileffe, Edra and Desalto.

Max

90-101 rue Antoine Dansaert, Lower Town (02 514 23 27). Pré-métro Bourse/métro Ste-Catherine. **Open** 11am-1pm, 2.30-6.30pm Tue-Fri; 11am-6pm Sat. **Credit** MC, V. **Map** p316 B2.

The designer furniture on show here tends be somewhat minimalist in look, using plenty of leather and chrome, and predominantly dark in colour. However, the odd splash of colour is provided by curvy armchairs and wacky, cartoon-like sofas and bright papier-mâché sculptures. Prices are pretty steep.

Les Memoires de Jacqmotte

92-96 rue Blaes, Lower Town (02 502 5083/www.lesmemoiresdejacqmotte.be). Métro/pré-métro Porte de Hal/bus 27, 48. **Open** 10am-6pm Mon, Tue, Thur-Sat; 10am-4pm Sun. **Credit** MC, V. **Map** p318 B5.

About ten years ago the warehouse of the Jacqmotte coffee emporium was converted into this space, where dealers can buy floor space and display their goods. Expect to find art deco antiques, including furniture, porcelain and jewellery, plus earlier pieces.

New De Wolf

91 rue Haute/40 rue Blaes, Lower Town (02 511 10 18). Bus 27, 48. **Open** 10am-6.30pm Mon-Sat; 10am-4pm Sun. **Credit** AmEx, MC, V. **Map** p318 B5.

This shop offers eclectic and inexpensive home furnishings and homewares, from the tacky to the tasteful. Opposite the entrance on rue Haute there's an extension selling kitchen items.

100% Design

30 boulevard Anspach, Lower Town (02 219 61 98). Métro/pré-métro De Brouckère. **Open** noon-6.30pm Mon; 10am-6.30pm Tue-Sat. **Credit** AmEx, DC, MC, V. **Map** p315 B3.

This is a fantastic place to come if you are in search of a present: it's a bright, cheerful gift shop packed with all kinds of bits and bobs, including Cow Parade statues, household items in lurid hues, fluffy cushions, Alessi pieces and more. Its sister shop (02 223 40 62) on the opposite side of the mall entrance is slightly more sophisticated and focuses on elegant vases and sculptural flower arrangements.

Passage 125 Blaes

125 rue Blaes, Lower Town (02 503 10 27/www.passage125.be). Bus 27, 48. **Open** 10am-5pm Mon, Wed, Fri; 10am-6pm Tue, Thur, Sat; 10am-5.30pm Sun. **Credit** AmEx, DC, MC, V. **Map** p318 B5.

Passage 125 Blaes used to be a Protestant church, before being converted into a wallpaper shop and finally a temple to all things old. A real treasure trove, it is home to 30 dealers spread over four floors, who display a full range of wares, from antique jewellery to bric-a-brac to serious antiques and architectural salvage. Great for a browse.

Philippe Lange

2A place de la Justice, Upper Town (02 503 46 18). Métro Gare Centrale/bus 34, 48, 95, 96. **Open** 11am-1pm, 2-6pm Tue-Sat; Sun by appointment only. **Credit** AmEx, DC, MC, V. **Map** p315 C4.

This is the place to come if you're looking to buy 20th-century antiques and classic pieces. Art deco, art nouveau and new design are specialities, with Panton chairs and Knoll furniture from the 1950s and '60s. There's also the odd bit of African art.

Rambagh

64-70 rue Haute, Lower Town (02 502 25 20/www.lamaisoncoloniale.com). Bus 27, 48. **Open** 10am-7.30pm daily. **Credit** AmEx, DC, MC, V. **Map** p318 B5.

It's possible to walk along rues Haute and Blaes and furnish your house out in whatever style takes your fancy. If the colonial look – large rattan sofas and teak – are your thing, head for Rambagh.

Music & video

Fnac (*see p145*) also sells music. For more on second-hand records, CDs and DVDs, *see p147* **Rare junk**.

Arlequin

7 rue du Chêne, Lower Town (02 514 54 28/www.arlequin.net). Pré-métro Anneessens or Métro Gare Centrale. **Open** 11am-7pm Mon-Sat; 2-7pm Sun. **Credit** MC, V. **Map** p315 B4.

Eat, Drink, Shop

This shop has all kinds of second-hand music, but focuses on rock, punk, import and jazz; the other two stores specialise in soul, funk, jazz, rap, reggae, classical and world music. Quality is high, and staff are friendly. Only this branch opens on Sundays. **Other locations**: 7 & 8 rue de l'Athenée, Ixelles (02 512 15 86/02 514 30 64).

BCM

6 Plattesteen, Lower Town (02 502 09 72). Prémétro Bourse. **Open** 11am-6.30pm Tue-Sat. **No credit cards**. **Map** p315 B3.
This is the best place in Brussels to find dance music on vinyl: techno, house, speed garage and drum 'n' bass. The staff are more than helpful, and it's a good source of information for prospective clubbers.

Le Bonheur, Epicerie Audiovisuelle

53 rue des Eperonniers, Lower Town (02 511 64 14/ www.lebonheur.net). Métro Gare Centrale. **Open** 11am-7pm Mon-Sat; 2-7pm Sun. **Credit** AmEx, DC, MC, V. **Map** p315 C3.
For such a small space, this store offers a wide range of (mostly experimental) music, videos and DVDs. There are facilities for listening and a modest but judicious selection of art-house movies.

Caroline Music

20 passage St-Honoré, Lower Town (02 217 07 31). Métro/pré-métro De Brouckère or pré-métro Bourse. **Open** 10am-6pm Mon; 10am-6.30pm Tue-Sat. **Credit** MC, V. **Map** p315 C3.
Caroline Music stocks a varied and extensive range of CDs, with huge sections devoted to indie and French music. It's also a good source of gig tickets.

Free Record Shop

Anspach Centre, off boulevard Anspach, Lower Town (02 219 90 04/www.freerecordshop.be). Métro/pré-métro De Brouckère. **Open** 10am-7pm Mon-Sat; 1-6pm Sun. **Credit** AmEx, DC, MC, V. **Map** p315 C3.
Aside from the more wide-ranging Fnac (*see p145*), FRS is the biggest music store in town. As well as CDs, it stocks videos, DVDs and computer games. There's also a ticket booth for gigs and official raves. **Other locations**: throughout the city.

Music Mania

4 rue de la Fourche, Lower Town (02 217 53 69/ www.musicmaniarecords.com). Métro/pré-métro De Brouckère or pré-métro Bourse. **Open** 11am-6pm Mon-Sat. **Credit** MC, V. **Map** p315 C3.
One of the best independent music shops in town, selling vinyl and CDs to DJs as well as regular punters. Staff are friendly and knowledgeable.

Musical instruments & equipment

Azzato

42 rue de la Violette, Lower Town (02 512 37 52/ www.azzato-music.com). Métro Gare Centrale. **Open** 9.30am-6pm Mon-Sat. **Credit** AmEx, DC, MC, V. **Map** p315 C3.

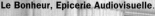
Le Bonheur, Epicerie Audiovisuelle.

Azzato sells a fantastic range of guitars, string and wind instruments, plus exotic and ethnic instruments from around the world.

Hill's Music
37-39 rue du Marché au Charbon, Lower Town (02 512 77 71/www.hillsmusic.be). Pré-métro Bourse or Anneessens. **Open** 9.30am-12.30pm, 1.30-5.45pm Tue-Sat. **Credit** AmEx, MC, V. **Map** p315 B3.
This beautiful shop specialises in quality acoustic string instruments, from guitars to harps.

The Music Office
156 rue du Midi, Lower Town (02 502 38 70). Pré-métro Anneessens. **Open** 10.30am-6.30pm Mon-Sat. **Credit** AmEx, DC, MC, V. **Map** p316 B4.
The place to go for musical instruments and recording equipment.

Opticians

Theo (Depot)
81 rue Antoine Dansaert, Lower Town (02 511 04 47/www.hoet.be). Pré-métro Bourse or métro Ste-Catherine. **Open** 10.30am-6.30pm Mon, Wed-Sat. **Credit** AmEx, DC, MC, V. **Map** p316 B3.
Theo's trendy specs and sunglasses have a very distinctive look, with thick, brightly coloured frames. Not for the faint-hearted.

Sport

Entre Terre et Ciel
20 place Stéphanie, Ixelles (02 502 42 41). Métro Louise/tram 91, 92, 93, 94. **Open** 10.30am-6.30pm Mon-Sat. **Credit** MC, V. **Map** p319 C6.
This is a luxury megastore for outdoor pursuits, selling an extensive range of kit for skiing, snowboarding, sailing, camping and mountaineering, plus scouting accessories.

Lillywhites
City 2, 16 rue des Cendres, Lower Town (02 217 46 23/www.lillywhites.com). Métro/pré-métro Rogier. **Open** 10am-7pm Mon-Thur, Sat; 10am-7.30pm Fri. **Credit** AmEx, MC, V. **Map** p317 C2.
Brussels' branch of the famous store in Piccadilly, and the largest sports goods store in town. Punchbags, golf clubs and hiking equipment are among the many items here. There is also a service for bike repairs, and restringing tennis rackets.

Montagne & Randonnée
27 rue des Vergnies, Ixelles (02 640 58 20). Tram 81, 82/bus 38, 60, 71. **Open** 10am-1pm, 2-6.30pm Mon-Fri; 10am-6pm Sat. **Credit** AmEx, V. **Map** p322 E7.
A specialist store for climbing and camping, staffed by experts in the field. Detailed local maps too.

Ride All Day
39 rue St-Jean, Lower Town (02 512 89 22). Métro Gare Centrale. **Open** noon-6.30pm Mon-Sat. **No credit cards. Map** p315 C4.

This shop sells boards, shoes and clothing to rats, who congregate around the skating hotspot of the neighbouring Mont des Arts. The staff (all of whom are die-hard skaters) are happy to provide plenty of tips and advice.

Velodroom
41 rue van Artevelde, Lower Town (02 513 81 99/www.velodroom.net). Pré-métro Bourse. **Open** 10am-6.30pm Mon, Tue, Thur-Sat. **Credit** MC, V. **Map** p316 B3.
Velodroom is run by a non-profit organisation that promotes cycling in Brussels as an environmentally-friendly alternative to cars. As well as selling all kinds of bikes and accessories, it also does repairs.

Toys & magic

A&T Lewis Magic Circus Shop
45 rue van Artevelde, Lower Town (02 511 24 07/www.atmagicshop.be.tf). Pré-métro Bourse. **Open** 10am-6.30pm Mon-Fri; 10.30am-6.30pm Sat. **Credit** V. **Map** p316 B3.
A full-on magic store – with a cordoned-off section that is out of bounds to non-magicians – as well as some costumes and masks.

The Grasshopper
39 rue du Marché aux Herbes, Lower Town (02 511 96 22/www.egmonttoys.com). Métro/pré-métro De Brouckère or métro Gare Centrale. **Open** 10am-7pm daily. **Credit** AmEx, DC, MC, V. **Map** p315 C3.
This fantastic toy store, with eye-catching window displays, has expanded next door. The ground floor of the original store is chock full of trinkets and small playthings, timeless classics (yoyos, kaleidoscopes), novelty lamps and lots more. Upstairs there are puzzles, educational and craft-based games, and larger items such as rocking horses. The new store has plenty of great ideas for decorating kids' rooms, as well as clothes, costumes and shoes.

Serneels
69 avenue Louise, Ixelles (02 538 30 66/www.serneels.be). Métro Louise then tram 93, 94. **Open** 9.30am-6.30pm Mon-Sat. **Credit** AmEx, DC, MC, V. **Map** p319 C6.
Deluxe toy store with high-flying prices that stocks just about everything a little heart could desire. There are modern electronic favourites, as well as beautiful-looking traditional puppets, rocking horses, doll's houses and enormous cuddly toys. A whole section is devoted to board games and puzzles.

Travel agents

For cheap flights, try **Airstop** (28 rue du Fossé aux Loups, Lower Town, 070 233 188/www.airstop.be) or **Connections** (19-21 rue du Midi, Lower Town (070 233 313/02 550 01 00/www.connections.be). Otherwise, log on to **SN Brussels Airlines** (www.flySN.com) or **Virgin Express** (www.virginexpress.com).

Arts & Entertainment

Festivals & Events

Parades, pageants and a panoply of culture.

Ommegang – Brussels' equine three-day event. *See p168.*

Because of its northern European climate, most of Brussels' seasonal activities – certainly the outdoor ones – bloom in spring and summer. Even without guaranteed sun, locals live it up without allowing the weather to put a dampener on things. In winter, it is perfectly reasonable to wrap up warm for the Christmas markets and ice-skating (*see p169* **Christmas on ice**), or head for the provinces at carnival time, the most famous being in **Binche** (*see p280*). Belgians take a huge and uncynical delight in tradition and folklore, and it is not unusual to come across an unexplained procession of giant mannequins or a marching band as you walk around Brussels at the weekend. Old habits die hard, and rituals are played out as they have been for centuries.

For details on seasonal events and festivals, the Brussels Tourist Information Board (02 513 89 40, www.brusselsinternational.be) is the best source. For events held further afield, contact the Belgian Tourist Information Office (02 504 03 90, www.visitbelgium.com).

Spring

Brussels International Festival of Fantastic Film

Nova *3 rue d'Arenberg, Lower Town. Métro Gare Centrale.* **Map** p315 C3.
Passage 44 *44 boulevard du Jardin Botanique, Lower Town. Métro Botanique.* **Map** p317 D2.

Both *02 201 17 13/tickets 02 218 27 35/ www.bifff.org.* **Tickets** available by phone, from FNAC or the website. **Date** 2wks in Mar.
This horror/sci-fi festival continues to pack in the gore-loving punters. With more than 150 films from all over the world (40% of them Belgian), lovers of the genre have plenty to feast on. In addition, there are fantastic sidelines: body-painting competitions, weird and wacky fashion shows and amazing art and installations. At the end, the fabled Vampire's Ball – entrance in costume only. *See also p176.*

Ars Musica

Various venues (02 542 11 22/www.arsmusica.be). **Tickets** available by phone or from the Bozar box office (23 rue Ravenstein, Lower Town; 02 507 82 00). **Date** mid Mar-early Apr.
This festival of contemporary classical music sets the scene for the upcoming season and has become one of Brussels' best-loved music festivals. It's an event of discovery and education, where risks are taken and new composers given a chance to show their work. Work with young people is given particular emphasis. *See also p187* **The Best Fests**.

Brussels International Film Festival

Various cinemas in Brussels (02 533 34 20/ www.fffb.be). **Admission** varies. **Date** Apr.
This festival, now mainly based at Flagey, usually features various themes, with Belgian films running alongside shorts and other European/US mainstream and art house pictures. There is also a European

Arts & Entertainment

competition for features, and a Belgian one for shorts and documentaries. Note that the festival will move to July after 2005. *See also p176.*

Printemps Baroque du Sablon

Streets around the place du Grand Sablon, Upper Town (tickets & information from the Bozar, 02 507 82 00/www.pbl-festival.be). Tram 92, 93, 94/bus 27, 95, 96. **Map** p315 C4. **Date** mid-late Apr.
An annual festival in the upmarket antiques district. Based around the main square, the streets are set up with small stages where lunchtime and afternoon concerts give way to evening chamber orchestras – all very baroque. Top chamber ensembles perform and young up-and-coming outfits are given a chance to blow their bassoons.

Kunsten Festival des Arts

Various venues (information 02 219 07 07/tickets 070 222 199/www.kunstenfestivaldesarts.be). **Open** *Box office* Mar, Apr 11am-6pm Mon-Wed, Fri; 11am-8pm Thur. *During festival* 11am-8pm daily. **Admission** €12.50; €10 concessions. **Credit** MC, V. **Date** 3wks in May.
What makes this major arts festival so different is that it appeals to all the languages in Belgium, refusing to identify itself solely with French or Flemish. Established in 1994 by Brussels arts supremo Frie Leysen, the festival is a true across-the-board arts fest, attracting important and often controversial international names. *See also p212* **Summer fests**.

Jazz Marathon

Venues throughout Brussels & nearby towns (02 456 0486/www.brusselsjazzmarathon.be). **Admission** free. **Date** weekend in May.
For three days (virtually non-stop), jazz-lovers can see live music in bars, clubs and restaurants all over Brussels. In 2003 it attracted 250,000 fans to the city to see 400 musicians play. In 2004 all events are free, but it was unclear if this would be the case in future. A free shuttle bus runs between venues.

Dring Dring Bike Festival

Parc du Cinquantenaire, EU Quarter (02 502 73 55/www.provelo.org). Métro Mérode or Schuman/ tram 27, 80, 81, 82.. **Admission** free. **Map** p323 H5. **Date** Sun in early May.
A popular bike festival centred in the Parc du Cinquantenaire, with bikes for hire, guided bike tours around Brussels and its outskirts, and bike-riding and maintenance classes. Pro-Vélo *(see p206)*, which organises the event, rents out bikes during the event and throughout July and August.

Les Nuits Botanique

Le Botanique, 236 rue Royale, St-Josse (02 218 37 32/www.botanique.be). Métro Botanique. **Tickets** phone for details. **Map** p317 D2. **Date** mid May.
This major music festival has been moved to May. For a fortnight, bands play in the various rooms, marquees and gardens at the Botanique cultural centre. Groups are of the indie variety, many from the UK, appearing in the size of venue they would have

played before they became famous. All the atmosphere of a festival without the mud and the portable loos. *See also p187* **The Best Fests**.

Brussels 20km

Race begins & ends in Parc du Cinquantenaire (02 511 90 00/www.20kmdebruxelles.be/20km). **Admission** €12 participants; free spectators. **Date** last Sun in May.
This event starts and finishes in the Parc du Cinquantenaire, passing through the Bois de la Cambre and the avenue Louise. First held 25 years ago, it is now an established part of the Brussels calendar, attracting about 20,000 runners, mainly amateurs. Witness as the city comes to a standstill.

Concours Musical International Reine Elisabeth de Belgique

Bozar, 23 rue Ravenstein, Upper Town (information 02 213 40 50/box office 02 507 82 00/www. concours-reine-elisabeth.be). Métro Gare Centrale or Parc/tram 92, 93, 94. **Open** *Phoneline* 9am-7pm Mon-Sat. *Box office (23 rue Ravenstein)* 11am-7pm Mon-Sat. **Tickets** €5-€85. **Date** May-mid June.
Regarded as one of the world's most important music competitions, this was founded over 40 years ago by Belgium's former Queen Elisabeth, a keen violin player. Aimed at young professional musicians and singers, it alternates between three categories – singing, violin and piano – with the final featuring 12 competitors. The final concert is at the Bozar; others are held at the Conservatoire Royal de Musique *(see p188). See also p187.*

Summer

Battle of Waterloo

Waterloo Visitors' Centre, 254 route du Lion, Braine l'Alleud (02 385 19 12/www.waterloo1815.be). **Open** Nov-Mar 10am-5pm daily. Apr-Oct 9.30am-6.30pm daily. **Date** every 5yrs in mid June.
A large-scale re-enactment of the 1815 Battle of Waterloo takes place every five years in the Brussels suburb (the next one is in 2005). It's a spectacular event: about 2,000 men don period uniforms, wield vintage guns and play war – some under Wellington and Blücher, others Napoleon. For more details, *see p17* **Where Napoleon met his demise.**

Festival of Wallonia

Various venues in Brussels & Wallonia (081 73 37 81/www.festivaldewallonie.be). **Admission** varies. **Date** June-Sept.
Belgian and international orchestras play in a vast programme all over francophone Belgium, though the major events are in Brussels. From churches to the main concert halls, the festival's reach is truly impressive. *See also p187* **The Best Fests**.

Festival of Flanders

Various venues in Flanders (070 77 00 00/www. festival.be). **Admission** varies. **Date** June-Oct.
One of the two giants of classical musical festivals, this one is in fact eight separate fests, with different

themes playing in all the major Flemish cities. One to watch out for is KlaraFestival (www.klarafestival.be), featuring everything from classical to jazz to roots. *See also p187* **The Best Fests**.

Drive-in movies

Esplanade du Cinquantenaire, EU Quarter (www.dedi.be). **Tickets** €15 per car; €10 concessions. **Map** p323 H5. **Date** July, Aug.

At 10.30pm on Friday and Saturday evenings in July and 10pm in August, the Parc du Cinquantenaire turns into a drive-in cinema. Films are current and mainstream, and the sound system is excellent.

Ommegang

Grand' Place, Lower Town (02 512 19 61/www.ommegang-brussels.be). Pré-métro Bourse or métro Gare Centrale. **Admission** *Grand' Place performance* €40-€62. **Map** p315 C3. **Date** 1st Thur in July.

This three-day event is marked by a spectacular parade of people dressed as nobles, guildsmen, jesters and peasants marching from the Sablon to the Grand' Place, some on horseback, others on foot, commemorating the glorious entry into Brussels of Charles V, the new emperor of the Spanish Netherlands, 500 years ago. It ends up with a horse parade, stilt-fighting and a jousting tournament in the Grand' Place. You can buy seats for the grandstand in the Grand' Place (book by May), sit at a bar in the place du Grand Sablon and watch the start or catch the parade along its route.

Brosella Jazz & Folk Festival

Théâtre de Verdure, Parc d'Osseghem, Laeken (02 270 98 56/www.brosella.be). Métro Heysel. **Admission** free. **Map** p326 B1. **Date** 2nd weekend in July.

An annual outdoor festival of folk and jazz in the shadow of the Atomium. Brosella attracts a cross-section of music-lovers, including families who take a picnic for the Sunday afternoon. The line-up is international, and includes some 30 acts.

Foire du Midi

Boulevard du Midi, Lower Town (TIB 02 513 89 40). Métro/pré-métro Gare du Midi. **Map** p318 A5. **Date** mid July-mid Aug.

Each year the largest travelling funfair in Europe arrives in Brussels and sets itself up along a one-kilometre stretch of the inner ring road near the Gare du Midi. There has been a fair on this site since the Middle Ages, but today's hyper-electric affair bears no resemblance whatsoever to the spit-roasted-suckling-pig event of yesteryear. Families turn up after midday and enjoy the rides and games until early evening, when a more adult crowd emerges.

National Day

Parc de Bruxelles, rue Royale, place des Palais, Upper Town. Métro Gare Centrale, Parc or Trône. **Map** p317/319 D4. **Date** 21 July.

National Day is taken seriously in Belgium, and the festivities naturally focus on Brussels. The royals

are out in force and there's a large military parade – tanks, artillery, the lot. The rest of the day settles down into more lighthearted fairs, neighbourhood celebrations and fireworks late into the night.

Meyboom (Planting of the Maytree)

Rue des Sables & rue du Marais, Lower Town (http://users.skynet.be/calomme/meyboom). Métro/pré-métro De Brouckère. **Map** p317 C/D2. **Date** 9 Aug.

This ancient and unusual ceremonies dates to 1308, when the first tree planting took place. It's all to do with fighting off rebels from Louvain and the ensuing thanksgiving to the patron St Laurent, whose symbol is the fabled tree. It's just an excuse to dress up, parade around the city with the tree, plant it before 5pm by the Centre Belge de la Bande Dessinée (*see p34* **Brussels walks**) and party into the night.

Tapis des Fleurs

Grand' Place, Lower Town (TIB 02 513 89 40/www.dreamit.be/flowercarpet). Pré-métro Bourse or métro Gare Centrale. **Map** p315 C3. **Date** mid Aug.

Every other year, for three days, the Grand' Place is the scene of a spectacular floral carpet (*tapis*) made of up a million cut begonia heads. The flowers are supplied and designed by growers from Ghent, and laid painstakingly on the ground in a different design each year. The balcony of the Hôtel de Ville is open for an aerial view of the result (admission €3). The next *tapis* begins on 12 August 2005.

Autumn

Journées du Patrimoine

Brussels (02 204 24 49/www.monument.irisnet. be). **Admission** free. **Date** 3rd weekend Sept (Brussels).

A once-a-year chance to peek inside hundreds of buildings around Belgium usually closed to the general public. After Flanders (03 212 29 55, www.monument. vlaanderen.be) and Wallonia (081 332 384, www. skene.be), it is Brussels' turn to fling open doors of homes and businesses for a glimpse of local hidden history. The choice of buildings opened changes every year, and the theme for 2004 is art deco and modernism. The royals also open their greenhouses, the Serres Royales (*see p97*), to the public in May, and the Palais Royal (*see p76*) from late July through to September, after National Day (*see above*). Contact the TIB tourist office (02 513 89 40) for more information.

Circuses

TIB 02 513 89 40. **Date** Oct, Nov.

A number of circuses visit Brussels every year – usually in October and November, and sometimes until Christmas and the New Year. Regular ones include the Bouglione circus in place Flagey and the Florilegio at the Hippodrome de Boitsfort. Some shows can be traditional and, for many, objectionable: there are performing tigers and elephants, as well as dogs and even, on occasion, ducks and geese. For dates, call the tourist information number above, or look out for posters around town.

Christmas on ice

Christmas festivities in Brussels used to be centred on the Grand' Place, the perfect backdrop for a life-size Nativity, towering tree and bedecked market stalls. And when Christmas was done, the ice-skating rink took over and happy New Year revellers went a-gliding. Yet the reality of this idyllic scene was that it was all getting too big for its own good – far too many crowds, with not enough time to browse at the stalls.

In 2001 it was decided to break with tradition, move Christmas and extend it from the square – but not so far that you'd need worry. It still houses the Nativity, a full-size affair with proper roof and a cast of characters as if in a department store window. The massive tree is still there, with hundreds of white lights, surrounded by Day-glo animals in paddocks and a puppet theatre. In 2003 the Town Hall tower was lit with thousands of shooting coloured lights. A scaffolding gateway leads you from the square to the market proper, which begins at the back of the Bourse and follows a festively lit trail across boulevard Anspach and onward to Ste-Catherine. Each market stall is a little wooden-roofed hut (some with an illuminated sheep). There are expected to be 220 stalls in 2004 – selling mainly arts and crafts or food and drink, all of them having a pan-European flavour, tying Brussels in neatly with the Utopian single-market dream. By the time you reach place Ste-Catherine and the quays beyond, not only are you decently warmed up, but you're at the heart of the festivities. The stalls continue, punctuated by Heath Robinson-like merry-go-rounds, a cycling course, the biggest travelling big-wheel in Europe and, of course, the skating rink. Set up for the whole month, it's overlooked by a Liberace-style mirror ball, throwing pinpoints on the old gabled houses. It's here that the crowds gather and settle; in the beer tents, at the food stands, in the surrounding

restaurants and bars. The atmosphere is thick and warm, as are the plastic cups of mulled wine, helping keep out the cold air.

The extended Christmas works, both conceptually and commercially. In 2003 a million people trod the enlightened path. Now imagine that lot squeezing in a cobbled square no bigger than a football pitch.

Ice-skating

Place du Marché-aux-Poissons, Lower Town (TIB 02 513 89 40/www.plaisirsdhiver.be). Métro Ste-Catherine. **Admission** *€5.* **Map** *p316 B2.* **Date** *1st weekend in Dec-1st weekend in Jan 11am-10pm daily. Christmas Day & New Year's Day 2-10pm.*

Le Marché de Noël

Grand' Place to place Ste-Catherine (TIB 02 513 89 40/www.plaisirsdhiver.be). Pré-métro Bourse or métro Gare Centrale. **Admission** *free.* **Map** *p315 C3/B2.* **Date** *mid Dec.*

Zany Zinneke

Brussels loves nothing better than a street knees-up with noise, colour and painted faces, gigantic figures, stilt walkers, flags and fireworks. Deep inside that studied reserve is a carnival just waiting to burst out, a deep-rooted chaos that has been implanted there since medieval times. What a magical concept, then, is Zinneke, a biennial parade and festival. At its heart lies tradition and a uniquely Bruxellois way of celebrating, but it's a thoroughly modern, urban phenomenon aimed at galvanising the spirit of this multicultural city.

Zinneke was born in 2000 when Brussels was a European City of Culture, from which came a deluge of social and urban renewal projects. The idea was to develop creative workshops throughout the city, particularly in *communes* where life was tough. The aim? To bring together whole communities, regardless of age, race, culture and gender, in an extravaganza of artistic endeavour. So professionals work with amateurs in art, music, theatre, circus, in schools, youth centres, cultural spaces, folkloric associations and all the groups and gangs that make up a living community. Language takes on new meaning – this is a movement that celebrates linguistic diversity and promotes a tongue of its own. Zinneke is for locals, or *Zinnekes*, who work in the *Zinnôpoles* (five regions) at the *Zinnodes* (local workshops). Together, they aim to make one big melting pot of the capital of Europe, the capital of Belgium, the city of *Bruzzel*. The parade, of course, is only the

tip of it all: the workshops are ongoing throughout the year, where work and skills are developed and shared, and the Zinnodes perform in local and major events. But when Z-Day arrives, the Zinnekes leave their *communes* and retake the city in a spirit of sovereignty. The parade is awe-inspiring in its size and energy, it takes hours to pass by, and fills the streets of downtown Bruzzel. Simply put, Zinneke is unlike anything you'll have ever zeen before.

Zinneke

02 214 20 07/www.zinneke.org. **Date** May every 2yrs (next one 2006).

Independent Film Festival

Centre Culturel Jacques Franck, 94 chaussée de Waterloo, St-Gilles (02 649 33 40/www.centre multimedia.org). Métro/pré-métro Porte de Hal. **Tickets** €3 per screening; €15 for 6 days. **Map** p318 B6. **Date** 1st wk in Nov.

This festival began in 1974, when Super8 reigned supreme. Now incorporating a mix of media, the philosophy remains the same: to allow young directors to find a springboard for their work. In 2003, over 100 films from 60 countries were shown, many of them for the first time. *See also p176.*

Winter

St Nicholas

Streets around Grand' Place. Pré-métro Bourse. **Parade** 5pm. **Map** p315 C3. **Date** 6 Dec.

Belgian children receive their main presents on the feast of St Nicholas, rather than at Christmas, so shops are geared up for the earlier date. St Nicholas distributes gifts and *speculoos* (a ginger biscuit, which is a Belgian speciality), accompanied by Zwarte Piet – or Black Peter, the bogeyman.

New Year's Eve

Grand' Place & around. Pré-métro Bourse. **Map** p315 C3. **Date** 31 Dec.

Masses pour into Grand' Place on 31 December. The atmosphere is good, the crowds friendly and high-spirited, but it's certainly not for the faint-hearted. The jollity extends to the streets around the square, as you're more likely to find a comfortable niche there. Wait a while as the square thins out, then music is played over the speakers and folk start dancing – it all becomes magical from that moment on. There's also a firework display from the Parc de Bruxelles.

Children

Big fun for little people.

Musée des Enfants. *See p172.*

Families are well catered for in Brussels. Not only are there two children's museums, a hands-on science museum, several big parks with adventure playgrounds, natural woodlands, dedicated skateboard zones and bowling alleys, but it's also easy to find restaurants (even smart ones) that welcome kids, and cafés where they can slurp down a hot chocolate (*cécémel chaud*). As if that wasn't enough, within easy reach of the city are theme parks, wildlife centres and a sandy coastline.

If your trip coincides with Belgium's month-long carnival season (which starts on Mardi Gras/Shrove Tuesday) or at puppet show time (October to May), then you're in for a good time. And if you're here in the run-up to Christmas, you're in luck (or maybe not, depending on your view) – this is when the circus comes to town.

On the downside, pushchair access is poor, pavements are badly maintained and parking is difficult – which means that carrying tiny tots is the most sensible option.

For children's clothes and toys, games and magic shops, *see pp143-164.*

Babysitting

In addition to these following official groups, a handful of Brussels' upmarket hotels offer a babysitting service. *See pp38-52.*

La Ligue des Familles
127 rue du Trône, Ixelles (02 508 76 10/ www.liguedesfamilles.be). **Phone enquiries** Mon, Wed, Thur 10am-4pm. **Rates** €5/hr.
The leading French-language resource for families in Belgium runs a babysitting service. They might ask you to take out an annual membership.

Office de la Naissance et de l'Enfance (ONE)
95 chaussée de Charleroi, St-Gilles (02 511 47 51/ www.one.be). **Phone enquiries** 9am-5pm Mon-Fri.
For longer-term childcare arrangements, the ONE can send you a list of state and private nurseries, crèches and registered childminders around town.

Service des Etudiants de l'ULB
02 650 21 71. **Phone enquiries** 10am-noon Mon-Fri. **Rates** €3.50-€7.50/hr.

A babysitting service run by students at the city university. Ring a day in advance for a sitter.

Museums

Several of Brussels' museums are likely to appeal to kids. Almost every child is fascinated by the huge iguanadon dinosaur skeletons displayed in the **Institut Royal des Sciences Naturelles** (*see p81*), though small kids are sometimes terrified by the life-size automated models. The **Musée des Instruments de Musique** (*see p74*) is another attraction likely to appeal to kids, mainly because they can put on headphones to listen to the musical instruments. For cartoon fans, there's the **Centre Belge de la Bande Dessinée** (*see p34* **Brussels walks**), where they can find out how animated films work, and step inside full-size replicas of comic book scenes (though it's not a place where they can run wild). Or head out of town to the **Africa Museum** in Tervuren (*see p103*) to look at dioramas of stuffed animals in African landscapes.

Many museums in Brussels run workshops for children, usually on Wednesday afternoons, weekends and during school holidays.

Ice-cream

Ice-cream vans park close to schools and playgrounds, but the best ice-cream comes from salons dotted around the suburbs. It's difficult to resist the Italian gelateria **Il Gelato** at 168 rue Vanderkindere (02 344 34 95) or, almost opposite, **Zizi** (57 rue de la Mutualité, 02 344 70 81). Other favourite addresses include **Capoue**, with branches at 36 avenue des Celtes, Etterbeek (02 733 38 33) and 395 Chaussée de Boondael, Ixelles (02 647 07 98), and **Mont Blanc** at 3 Markt in Tervuren (02 767 43 64).

Circuses

Several circuses put up tents in Brussels around the Christmas period. The more traditional circuses are criticised by animal rights activists, but **Florilegio** (www.florilegio.com), which makes an annual visit to the Hippodrome de Boitsfort (51-53 chaussée de la Hulpe, Uccle, 02 533 10 80, www.florilegio.com), is acclaimed for its showmanship and acrobatics.

Kids under two

Parks

The cobbled streets of Brussels are not made for pushchairs, so you may find yourself spending a lot of time in the city parks. Most

have playgrounds that have been recently re-equipped with safe equipment and soft ground. Close to the centre, the **Parc de Bruxelles** (*see p70*) has a good playground and a café selling ice-cream. The **Bois de la Cambre** at the end of avenue Louise (entrances on chaussée de Waterloo and avenues Louise and Roosevelt) is a large landscaped park with a lake, lawns, horse-riding trails and woodland rambles. There are two cafés, one with a playground and the other facing a roller-skating rink. Several main roads through the park are closed to traffic at weekends, creating a huge loop that is popular with cyclists, rollerbladers and kids learning to ride bikes. The small **Parc Tenbosch** (entrances on chaussée de Vleurgat and place Tenbosch) in Ixelles has a safe playground with well-maintained wooden equipment, a sandpit, football pitch and pond with lazy terrapins.

Some wilder retreats are found in Uccle, the city's leafy southern commune, including the **Sauvagère** nature reserve in Uccle (entrance on avenue de la Chenaie), which has an outdoor playground ideal for young children, a picnic area, basketball court, duck pond and farm animals in enclosures. Also in Uccle, the lovely **Parc de Wolvendael** (entrances on avenues de Fré and Paul Stroobant) has an outdoor café, mini golf and a playground. It is located on a sloping hill that makes a perfect place to ski or sledge in winter. The **Parc de Woluwe** (entrance on avenue de Tervuren) is another popular spot for sledging. The **Rouge Cloître** park on the edge of the Forêt de Soignes has two newly built playgrounds with excellent climbing equipment. Further out of town, the **Park van Tervuren** (entrance on Leuvensesteenweg) has woodland rambles and cycle trails. Take tram 44 through the forest.

Kids from two to eight

Musée des Enfants

15 rue du Bourgmestre, Ixelles (02 640 01 07/ www.museedesenfants.be). Tram 23, 90/bus 71. **Open** 2-5.30pm Wed, Sat, Sun, school holidays. **Admission** €6.70. **No credit cards. Map** p325 F8.
A rambling townhouse in Ixelles has been turned into a superb children's museum, with rooms for theatre, dressing up, giant interactive puzzles, educational games, painting and clay modelling. There's a kitchen where kids are taught baking, a domestic animal enclosure and an adventure playground. Not surprisingly, it gets mobbed on wet Sundays.

Théâtre du Ratinet

44 avenue de Fré, Uccle (02 375 15 63). Bus 38, 41. **Shows** Oct-May Wed, Sat, Sun afternoons. **Tickets** €5.50. **No credit cards.**
Several small puppet theatres have survived in the city, putting on shows for small children. The

Skateboarding around the Upper Town.

productions are usually in French, but the atmosphere is infectious even if your kids don't quite grasp the plot. The Théâtre du Toone (*see p63* **Talk of the Toone**) puts on puppet versions of classical plays, but more with an adult audience in mind.

Musée du Jouet

24 rue de l'Association, Upper Town (02 219 61 68/ www.museedujouet.be). Métro Botanique or Madou. **Open** 10am-noon, 2-6pm daily. **Admission** €3.50; €2.50 children. **No credit cards. Map** p317 D2.
This cluttered private museum is run by an enthusiastic toy collector. Recently reopened after renovations, it displays a vast collection of clockwork toys, puzzles, games, train sets and dolls' houses.

Kids from eight to 12

Bruparck

1 avenue du Football, Heysel (Mini-Europe 02 478 05 50/Océade 02 478 43 20/Atomium 02 475 47 77/www.bruparck.com/www.oceade.be/www.minieuro pe.com). Métro Heysel. **Open** *Mini-Europe* mid Mar-June, 9.30am-5pm daily; July, Aug, 9.30am-7pm; Sept 9.30am-5pm; Oct-early Jan 10am-5pm daily. *Océade* Apr-June 10am-6pm Tue-Fri; 10am-10pm Sat, Sun; July, Aug, school holidays 10am-10pm daily; Sept-Mar 10am-6pm Wed-Fri; 10am-10pm Sat, Sun. **Admission** *Mini-Europe* €11.70; €8.70 under-12s. *Océade* €13.50; €11 children up to 1m 30cm. **Credit** AmEx, DC, MC, V. **Map** p326 A/B2.
An attraction park at the foot of the Atomium (*see p96*) with a fairground carousel, the multiscreen Kinepolis cinema complex (*see p178*), fast-food restaurants and cafés. The main attraction is Mini-Europe, a theme park with miniature replicas of famous European buildings such as the Eiffel Tower and Big Ben. The Océade pool has slides and chutes. Ask about special deals and family tickets.

Scientastic Museum

Underground level 1, Bourse, boulevard Anspach, Lower Town (02 732 13 36/www.scientastic.com). Pré-métro Bourse. **Open** 2-5.30pm Sat, Sun, school holidays. **Admission** €5; €4 under-26s; free under-4s. **Credit** MC, V. **Map** p315 B3.
A private museum in a dingy underground concourse above Bourse station. Inside it's a magical place, crammed with interactive experiments aimed at kids. There are factsheets in English and workshops in French and Dutch. The museum sometimes opens for additional hours (check the website) and can be opened by appointment too.

Teenagers

Older kids with energy to burn off are spoilt for choice in Brussels, with various venues for all kinds of sports and activities, from bowling to skateboarding. For further details, *see pp203-208.*

Out of town

It's fairly easy to get out of Brussels for a day at the beach or a canoe trip in the Ardennes. The country has a dense network of motorways, but there's also a good, cheap train service that runs to most places of interest. Belgian Railways (www.sncb.be) publishes a free brochure listing special excursions, many of them suited to kids.

Day trips

Kayak Ansiaux

Kayak Ansiaux, 15 Rue du Vélodrome, Anseremme (082 21 35 35/www.ansiaux.be). Train to Anseremme. **Open** Apr-Oct daily. **Price** €10-€18. **Credit** MC, V.

The biggest of the many kayak centres in the Ardennes (see p282) is based at Anseremme on the River Lesse, near Dinant. From the station, a minibus takes you to the starting point a few kilometres upstream, lined with kayaks.

Parc d'Aventures Scientifiques (Pass)

3 rue de Mons, Frameries (070 22 22 52/ www.pass.be). Bus 1, 2 from Mons station. **Open** *Sept-June* 9am-5pm Tue-Sun; 10am-6pm Sat, Sun, school holidays. *July, Aug* 10am-6pm daily. Closed 2wks Sept, 2wks Jan. **Admission** €12.50; €7.50 6-14s. **Credit** MC, V.

Belgium's interactive science centre is located in a former coal mine near Mons. The site was restyled by French architect Jean Nouvel, adding a sloping entry ramp and other modern touches. Regularly changing, innovative, hands-on exhibitions keep the crowds coming back.

Parc Paradisio

Domaine de Cambron, Cambron-Casteau (068 45 46 53/www.paradisio.be). Train to Cambron-Casteau. **Open** *Easter-June, Sept-early Nov* 10am-6pm daily. *July, Aug* 10am-7pm daily. **Admission** €18.40; €13.40 3-11s. **Credit** MC, V.

The grounds of an old abbey near Ath have been turned into an exotic bird sanctuary. The ruins form the backdrop for shows involving birds of prey. The estate also has a river, several lakes, water gardens and flower beds. The main attractions for kids are the giant walk-through aviary for birds of paradise, a giant tortoise, and an Antarctic section. There's also an adventure playground with slides and rope bridges, a petting farm and a restaurant.

Planckendael

582 Leuvensesteenweg, Muizen, near Mechelen (015 41 49 21/www.planckendael.be). Bus 284, 285 from Mechelen station or canal boat from station in summer. **Open** *Jan, Feb, Nov, Dec* 10am-4.45pm daily; *Mar, Apr, Oct* 10am-5.30pm daily; *May, June, Sept* 10am-6pm daily; *July, Aug* 10am-7pm daily. **Admission** €14; €9.50 3-11s, concessions. **Credit** AmEx, MC, V.

The wide open spaces of Planckendael wildlife park provide an ideal habitat for rhinos, deer, antelope, wolves, birds and cranes. Founded by Antwerp zoo as a breeding park, the estate has a restaurant, adventure playgrounds and rope bridges.

Six Flags Belgium & Aqualibi

9 rue Joseph Deschamps, Wavre (Six Flags 010 42 15 00/Aqualibi 010 42 16 00/www.sixflags europe.com). Six Flags-Bierges station. **Open** *Six Flags* Apr-Oct 10am-6/8/11pm daily. *Aqualibi* Jan-Mar, Nov, Dec 2-10pmWed, Fri; 10am-10pm Sat, Sun; Apr, May-mid-June 1-10pm Wed-Sun; mid-June-mid-July 2-10pm daily; mid-July, Aug 6-11pm daily; Sept, Oct Wed, 2-10pm Fri-Sun. **Admission** *Six Flags & Aqualibi* €28.50; €23.50 3-11s. *Aqualibi* €13.50; €10 6-11s; free under-6s. **Credit** AmEx, MC, V.

The biggest and oldest theme park in Belgium was taken over by the US leisure giant Six Flags, but most Belgians still insist on calling it Walibi. The new owners have beefed up the rides and added a rollercoaster, bringing the total to seven. The park also has several merciless water rides, and a few relics, including a boat ride past a collection of somewhat dilapidated *Tintin* characters. Aqualibi is a big water park with chutes, wave machines and several pools and is linked to the complex.

Technopolis

Technologielaan, Mechelen (015 34 20 00/ www.technopolis.be). Train to Mechelen then bus 282, 283. **Open** 9.30am-5pm daily; closed 1st wk Sept. **Admission** €8.50; €6 3-11s, concessions. **Credit** AmEx, DC, MC, V.

One of the best science museums in Europe. Kids can ride a bike along a high wire, try out a flight simulator, lie on a bed of nails or star in their own pop video. The staff are friendly and only too pleased to explain Newton's Third Law in English.

The Belgian coast

The 14 resorts along the 65-kilometre (40-mile) Belgian coastline boast wide sandy beaches and a solid infrastructure of swimming pools, bowling alleys, mini golf courses, cinemas, ice-cream shops and decent restaurants. They also lay on busy summer programmes featuring kite-flying festivals, Flemish pop idol contests and beach races. Kids will also insist that you rent one of the little go-carts that are found in every resort. They come in every imaginable design, including some that allow up to 12 people to take to the Belgian roads without so much as a single seat belt between them.

Ostend (see p273), the biggest resort, may be the best fun for adults but it's the least suited to children. The busy resort of **Blankenberge** has more for children to do, with a modern Sea Life Centre (116 Koning Albert I Laan, 8370 Blankenberge, 050 42 43 00, www.sealifeeurope.com, open 10am-6pm daily, tickets €11-€12.50) allowing intimate contact with sharks. **Knokke-Heist** is more elegant, and has a butterfly park and bird sanctuary. Elsewhere, there are fishing boats to watch in **Nieuwpoort**, shrimp fishermen on horseback at **Oostduinkerke** and a former Russian submarine moored in **Zeebrugge**'s Seafront centre (www.seafront.be). But young kids might be just as happy muddling around with Belgian families in one of the quieter resorts, like **Oostduinkerke**, which has a fishing museum, or **De Haan**, which has, well, nothing much except for picturesque fin-de-siècle architecture. All of the resorts are linked by a coast tram that runs from **De Panne** to Knokke-Heist. The Belgian Tourist Information Office at rue du Marché aux Herbes (see p301) can provide further practical information.

Film

Summer drive-ins, art deco cinemas and plenty to see in English.

Nova. *See p178.*

According to a recent calculation, 450 cinemas opened in Brussels in the last century. Of those, only 13 currently remain. But don't let that put you off – the choice of films on show here is way beyond that in other cities of comparable size. If you want to catch a major new release at the weekend, you'll have to book in advance.

2003 saw major changes at the consumer end of the industry. Typically, local screens are of two types: the **UGC** and **Kinepolis** circuit, which mainly show blockbusters and take the lion's share of the audience; and an art house circuit, showing repertory films, as well as Belgian and world cinema. When these latter cinemas started to feel the pinch, the various councils dug deep and came up with extra grants for almost all of the local screens, and offered money for these cinemas to form a network sharing ticketing, a logo and perhaps even a publication. The results of that should be apparent later on into 2004 – if the cinemas can agree on the details.

Meanwhile the multiplexes march on. The UGC network surprised its competitors with UGC Unlimited, a ticket system whereby a monthly fee gives unlimited access to the company's 56 screens in Belgium; Kinepolis quietly fitted out its Brussels complex with the country's only digital projection equipment, preparing themselves for the end of celluloid.

TIMINGS AND TICKETS

Film programmes change on Wednesdays. Listings can be found in most daily newspapers (look out for the supplements in *La Libre Belgique* and *Le Soir* on Wednesday) and in the English-language weekly, *The Bulletin*. The Belgian cinema website www.cinebel.be has the times of showing at major cinemas all over the country, and tickets can be booked from the site. Films are screened on average four times a day, with evening showings at 7-8pm and 9-10.15pm. Features start 20 minutes after the advertised time. Average ticket prices are in the region of €6-€7.5. Outside the UGC and Kinepolis circuit, tipping attendants is expected: you will be rewarded with a gossip magazine with news of upcoming releases.

Belgium, unusually, has only two film classifications: **ENA/KNT**, meaning over-16s only, and **EA/KT**, meaning entrance is for all. Films categorised as **VO** are in their original language, invariably English, and **st. ang** are films with English subtitles. Dubbing is rare.

UGC De Brouckère. *See p178.*

SPECIAL EVENTS

It's worth looking out for various mini seasons and special events. The **Musée du Cinéma** (*see also p73*) regularly has guest directors visiting to present their work (such as Martin Scorsese and Nanni Moretti in 2003). **Lanterne magique** is a cinema club for youngsters at the **Palais des Beaux-Arts** (*see p72* **A new broom at the Bozar**), presenting everything from Murnau's *Nosferatu* to *Singin' in the Rain*; screenings are preceded by a playlet introducing the themes of the films in Flemish and French. **Flagey** runs a similar season each year, *Une Séance pour Tous* (A Screening for All), where a popular or forgotten classic is preceded by Sunday brunch.

On Fridays and Saturdays in August and September, the **Nova** cinema goes walkabout, providing free open-air screenings at sundown of offbeat movies like King Vidor's vintage *The Fountainhead* in unlikely settings. The carnival atmosphere is supplemented by free concerts and finger food.

On Friday and Saturday nights in July and August, the **Cinquantenaire** park hosts drive-in movies (www.dedi.be; *see also p168*). Most of the films are reprises of the year's blockbusters, and the screen is huge. Cars require an FM radio to pick up the soundtrack.

Many Brussels cinemas offer pre-release screenings: look out for *avant-premières* (sneak previews) in magazine listings.

FESTIVALS

After disappearing for a year, the Brussels Film Festival has reinvented itself, moving to Flagey and giving attention to European filmmakers who are just starting out in their careers. Held in April (*see p166*), the festival guarantees fresh talent and new names; this, along with parallel sessions by better-known European names, mean that few viewers should be disappointed. The festival bar is also good value, and usually staffed by a director or a well-known actor. Recent hits have included Penny Woolcock's film opera *The Death of Klinghoffer*. For more details, contact 02 533 34 20 or www.fffb.be.

If horror is more your thing, you won't want to miss the **Brussels International Festival of Fantastic Film**, at the Nova and the Passage 44 in March (www.bifff.org, 02 201 17 13; *see also p166*). Now in its 22nd year, it also takes in a vampires' ball, a body-painting contest, and late-night screenings of some seriously weird cinema. Recent guests included Ken Russell and Christopher Lee.

Anima, the Brussels animation festival, now boasts an international competition, and offers around 100 films over a two-week period in February. There are fewer Belgian films than a decade ago, but 30,000 annual viewers still enjoy it. It's often an opportunity to get a sneak preview of upcoming US blockbusters, as well as more controversial fare from the likes of Bill Plympton or Marc Caro. For further details, see www.awn.com/folioscope or call 02 534 41 25.

Summer for many film buffs means a season ticket for **Ecran Total** at the **Arenberg Galeries** (July to September), which offers a wide range of retrospectives and new cinema from around the globe.

November in St-Gilles sees the **Independent Film Festival** at the Centre Culturel Jacques Franck (www.centremultimedia.org; *see also p170*), which has eclectic programming from around the world. It runs around the same time as the **Festival of Mediterranean Film** (www.cinemamed.com, 02 800 83 54), held mostly at the **Vendôme**.

Many new Belgian and French films are featured at the **Francophone Film Festival** in Namur at the end of September (www.fiff.be), and Flemish ones at the **Flanders Film Festival**, held in Ghent in mid October (www.filmfestival.be, 09 242 80 60), a bash renowned for its soundtrack awards. Bruges showcases world cinema at the **Novo** festival in March (www.cinemanovo.be, 050 33 54 86); almost all the films have English subtitles.

Arts & Entertainment

Cinemas

Actors Studio

16 petite rue des Bouchers (2nd entrance rue de la Fourche), Lower Town (02 512 1696/information 0900 27854). Métro/pré-métro De Brouckère. **No credit cards. Map** p315 C3.

It might take a bit of finding the first time – tucked into a hotel basement among the busy restaurants near the Grand' Place – but this two-screen studio is one of Brussels' little gems. If your taste leans towards Korean horror rather than the Hollywood variety, or you want Finnish films by the Kaurismaki brothers in VO, the Actors is for you. Great coffee in the bar too.

Arenberg Galeries

26 galerie de la Reine, Lower Town (02 512 80 63/ www.arenberg.be). Métro Gare Centrale. **No credit cards. Map** p315 C3.

Back in 1895 the magnificent Arenberg Galeries hosted Belgium's first film show. Today these two art house screens are still Brussels' poshest cinematic address by a mile. Programming is eclectic, mixing good-looking world cinema with the French avant-garde; Ecran Total, the annual summer bash, blends recent hits with cycles devoted to big name art house directors or nostalgia from yesteryear.

Aventure

57 galerie du Centre, Lower Town (02 219 17 48). Métro/pre-métro De Brouckère or pre-métro Bourse. **No credit cards. Map** p315 C3.

If you miss a big film on its first run, your best chance of catching it in Brussels (if you don't have a DVD player) is to head for this rather run-down picture house in a shopping mall. Sound and picture quality on these two screens isn't great, but you can't fault the number of films on offer – it squeezes in more titles than anyone else, week after week.

Almost famous

For a country of ten million people split into three language groups, Belgium punches way above its cinematic weight. It can't compete with the costly productions turned out by the French cinema industry, but it can use French distribution to ensure a larger audience than a small country normally allows. Key Belgian directors are on the cusp of global fame.

Bigger grants – and the French market – mean that francophone films now enjoy a high profile on the European mainland. Luscious period pieces aimed at the mass market have become something of a specialty for **Gérard Corbiau**, whose renowned *Farinelli* was followed by the equally ambitious *Le Roi Danse* in 2000, but the most notable success has been **Frédéric Fonteyne**'s *Une Liaison Pornographique*, a study in contemporary sexual mores that quickly became the most widely distributed European film of 2002. The follow-up, *La Femme de Gilles*, due out in 2004, is eagerly awaited.

Dutch-language filmmaking is generally a smaller concern, but still leapfrogs over the bigger-grossing francophones on occasion. *Iedereen beroemd!* (Everybody's Famous), a gameshow satire by **Dominique Deruddere**, got an Oscar nomination in 2000 and **Stijn Coninx** deserved a second Belgian nomination in 2004 with *Further than the Moon*, a winsome tale about religion, alcoholism and an Apollo moonshot in deepest Flanders.

But the biggest names of all are **Luc** and **Jean-Pierre Dardenne**, two Liège-based filmmakers whose taut social realism has won them honours at Cannes. In dramas like *Rosetta*, *La Promesse* and most recently *Le Fils*, the brothers (a literature teacher and a philosophy graduate) have made stars of newcomers like Emilie Dequenne, Jérémie Regnier and **Olivier Gourmet**. This moon-cheeked marvel has played in all of their features to date, and, following a best actor award in Cannes for *Le Fils*, is now one of the most sought-after actors in France.

In the acting world, comedian **Benoît Poelvoorde** is a law unto himself. When his sparkling debut as the unrepentant assassin in *Rémy Belvaux*'s *Man Bites Dog* was released on an unsuspecting world in the early '90s, Europe woke up to a great new talent. Later roles as everything from a journeyman cyclist in the Tour de France to an impersonator of French pop idol Claude François have confirmed that Belgians do sophisticated humour far better than their neighbours to the south.

Few neighbouring countries can boast art house successes as diverse as **Boris Lehman**, whose ongoing autobiographical investigations were fêted in a season at the Pompidou centre in Paris in 2003, or **Jan Bucquoy**, whose multifarious projects have taken in everything from a banned Tintin pastiche to an underwear museum. His five-volume cinematic essay, the idiosyncratic *Sexual Life of the Belgians*, recently culminated with *Friday Fish Day*, the story of an ill-fated affair with a mermaid.

Flagey

Place Ste-Croix, (next to place Flagey), Ixelles (02 641 10 20/www.flagey.be). Tram 81, 82/bus 38, 60, 71. **Credit** AmEx, DC, MC, V. **Map** p322 D7.

Brussels' newest cinema, at the new arts centre, seats little more than 100 people, but the comfort is second to none. Programming is done jointly with the Musée du Cinéma (*see p178*), and blends popular classics like *Cat on a Hot Tin Roof* with more adventurous modern fare – first year hits included *Abouna* from Chad and *Extraño* from Argentina. After the screenings you can repair to the Café Belga, open until 2am and popular with the arty crowd. *See p138, p189* and *p88* **All aboard!**

Kinepolis

Bruparck, avenue du Centenaire, Laeken (bookings 02 474 26 00/information 0900 00 555/www. kinepolis.com). Métro Heysel. **No credit cards.** **Map** p326 A/B2.

Don't be fooled by the run-down look, or the location, for that matter – Kinepolis is state of the art. With its giant screens (24 in total) and scary sound systems, this is total cinema, Flemish-style. Cutting-edge technology also includes one of the few servers powerful enough to download a whole movie by satellite for the big screen. The choice is sometimes rather limited – mainly US and European blockbusters – but for the full multiplex experience, Kinepolis is hard to beat.

Movy Club

21 rue des Moines, Forest (02 537 69 54). Tram 52/bus 49, 50. **No credit cards.**

This cavernous, out-of-the-way art deco jewel is like a relic from a bygone age – it's one of the city's last neighbourhood cinemas. The films on offer are all deeply moral, but it's a unique experience, popular with students and locals too tired to make the trek to the centre. Warm clothing is advisable in winter – the heating isn't always 100% reliable.

Musée du Cinema

Palais des Beaux-Arts, 9 rue Baron Horta, Upper Town (02 507 83 70/www.cinematheque.be). Métro Gare Centrale or Parc/tram 92, 93, 94/bus 38, 60, 71. **No credit cards.** **Map** p317 D4.

With programming that draws on the 50,000 features sitting in its vaults, and live piano accompaniment to silent films every night of the year, the Film Museum is the closest you'll get to cinema heaven. Each month three or four movie cycles focus on a director or a theme – anything from ethnographic shorts from the silent era to Dirty Harry-period Clint Eastwood. Tickets are cheap, but the silent cinema is tiny, so book ahead for classics like Wiene's *Caligari* or Medvedkin's *Happiness*. The site also houses a selection of early cinema equipment, and a wide range of film magazines.

Nova

3 rue d'Arenberg, Lower Town (02 511 24 77/ www.nova-cinema.com). Métro Gare Centrale. **No credit cards.** **Map** p315 C3.

Creaky seats, trash-aesthetic decor and the most adventurous programming in the capital ensure that the Nova regularly features on lists of best alternative cinemas in the world. A local collective that has miraculously survived on almost invisible means for eight years now, it shows anything from Czech animation by Jan Svankmajer to midnight screenings of *Flesh Gordon,* with a bias towards socially committed art of any description. The monthly Open Screens, when budding debutant filmmakers showcase their wares, are well-attended, raucous affairs.

Styx

72 rue de l'Arbre Bénit, Ixelles (02 512 21 02/ information 0900 27854). Métro Porte de Namur/ bus 54, 71. **No credit cards.** **Map** p319 D6.

The Styx is Brussels' most perfect fleapit. The sound quality is less than perfect, but the programming is irresistible – from Truffaut retrospectives and *Amores Perros* to modern Belgian classics in the making. It marks its 35th anniversary in 2004, but may not see a 40th – this is the sort of place that has suffered since the advent of the DVD. Notable for late-night screenings.

UGC De Brouckère

38 place de Brouckère, Lower Town (French 0900 10 440/Flemish 0900 10 450/www.ugc.be). Métro/pre-métro De Brouckère. **Credit** MC, V. **Map** p315 C2.

A mid-town mecca for multiplex fans. It's not all popcorn and blockbusters, though: you can order beer in the bar, sink back into the bucket-sized armchairs and marvel at the gold-leaf surroundings in one of the city's biggest auditoriums. Look out for American Movie Day on 4 July, with fireworks in the streets and up to a dozen pre-release films from the US that take over the whole complex. Luckily, it's done with style.

UGC Toison d'Or

8 avenue de la Toison d'Or, Ixelles (French 0900 10 440/Flemish 0900 10 450/www.ugc.be). Métro Porte de Namur. **Credit** MC, V. **Map** p319 D5.

With its 15 screens (confusingly, on two not-quite-adjacent locations), the UGC Toison d'Or is the only serious competition to Kinepolis – and its more adventurous programming often carries the day. First-class sound and fabulous picture quality make this the best address to randomly turn up at, not knowing what you want to see. UGC tickets on the whole aren't cheap, but the lunchtime shows are.

Vendôme

18 chaussée de Wavre, Ixelles (02 502 37 00). Métro Porte de Namur. **No credit cards.** **Map** p319 D5.

Round the corner from the Toison d'Or, this five-screen independent is a gem, and as it has just received its first-ever government grant, things should get better still. The films are mainly European and US art house, but the cinema is also a regular on the local festival circuit, and home to O ce court!, an annual short film festival. Where else are you going to catch Icelandic marvels like Baltasar Kormakur's *The Sea*?

Galleries

All dressed up and nowhere to go.

Brussels Art Fair.

Belgium's savvy top private collectors of contemporary art, admired for their deep pockets and exemplary discretion, tend to shop abroad, filling the coffers of galleries in Cologne, London and New York. The downside to this, of course, is that the country's own commercial galleries are often circumvented. While the situation is changing with the coming of age of a new generation, most established contemporary art gallerists struggle to survive.

New galleries appear and disappear almost overnight. A flurry of excitement in the mid '90s saw the formation of an art hub on the canal's edge, where a dozen or so galleries set up shop in two huge, dilapidated but luminous and once-elegant buildings. Both have emptied out: one totally; the other, **Kanal 20**, significantly. The exodus is attributed to an increase in rent and poor maintenance rather than low sales figures. Many of the former gallery residents are now re-established elsewhere in the city, but the hoped-for centralised 'scene' has evaporated. Unless you're in town during the annual **Brussels Art Fair** in spring (www.artexis.com/artbrussels), getting a first-hand impression of the wide scope and variety of contemporary art in Brussels entails schlepping far and wide.

The limited gallery scene and relatively large artists' population are two sides of the same coin. Brussels' geographic centrality, affordable rents and laid-back professional climate attract young artists from all over the world who can't pay the high living costs and don't desire the pressure-cooker atmospheres of many art 'capitals'. In Brussels, artists are considered local if they happen to be based here, not because they're natives.

Despite decent living standards and creative freedom, there is a shortage of venues for public presentations of artworks and ideas. Successful solutions to the problem have been found by artists joining together to create their own showcases or impress their needs upon public art institutions and government agencies. The immense Horta Hall at the **Palais des Beaux-Arts** (*see p72*) has become (for a year, and possibly longer) a stage for solo exhibitions selected by the country's most prominent artists' association, **NICC** (Nieuw Internationaal Cultureel Centrum). In other instances, city property has been made available for artists' use: **Le Comptoir du Nylon** (13 rue Ste-Catherine, Lower Town), an abandoned shopfront still bearing its

Usage Externe. *See p181.*

commercial name, serves as a vitrine for single-artist projects; the **Chapelle des Brigittines** (Petite rue des Brigittines, Marolles, 02 506 43 00, www.brigittines.be), a deconsecrated baroque chapel, and **Recyclart** (*see p200*) also sporadically function as exhibition spaces.

GOING PUBLIC

The major art galleries and museums are covered in the Sightseeing section of this guide. Of these, the **Palais des Beaux-Arts** (*see p72*), reinventing itself as the more populist 'Bozar', is a showcase for a wide variety of exhibitions produced in house or in co-operation with other institutions; the **Musée Communal d'Ixelles** (*see p89*) runs a programme of small monographic shows by emerging Belgian artists and regularly mounts major historical exhibitions; more erratic in scheduling and quality, the **Botanique** (*see p192*) maintains a contemporary focus; the **Hôtel de Ville**'s (*see p59*) offerings are hit or miss, with promising titles too often belying disappointing fare.

INFORMATION

To find out what's on and where while you're staying in town, consult English-language weekly *The Bulletin*, *Park Mail* distributed in cinemas, and the cultural supplement *MAD* in the Wednesday edition of the French-language daily *Le Soir*.

Argos

13 rue du Chantier (02 229 00 03/www.argos arts.org). Métro Yser. **Open** 2-7pm Wed-Sat. **Map** p316 B1.

Argos is a non-profit centre for the exhibition, production and preservation of art in new media. Its critical approach and generous programming have made it a mecca for video, film and digital artists and their audiences. Among its attractions are a stimulating exhibition programme; a major annual international festival held in multiple venues across the city; a film and video conservation project; editing facilities that are made available to artists and non-profit organisations; and a media library (open to the public by appointment) containing some 3,000 audio-visual productions and 2,500 printed volumes.

Art en Marge

312 rue Haute (02 511 04 11/www.artenmarge.be). Métro/pré-métro Porte de Hal/bus 20, 48. **Open** noon-6pm Wed-Fri; 11am-4pm Sat. **Map** p318 B5.

In the heart of the Marolles, this non-profit gallery is devoted to exhibiting 'outsider' art, also known as *art brut*: works created by artists relegated to society's margins by mental illness and other causes. The excellent programme is divided evenly between national and international production.

Bastien

61 rue de la Madeleine (02 513 25 63). Métro Gare Centrale. **Open** 11am-6.30pm Tue-Sat; 11am-1pm Sun. **Map** p315 C3.

If you're spending any length of time in town, you're bound to pass Ms Bastien's beautiful gallery, which is located a few steps down from the Gare Centrale and Albertine Library. As with most of the galleries along this stretch, Bastien is hardly revolutionary, but displays relatively modern works of a certain value. Among the artists here are Serge Vandercam, Pierre Alechinsky, Bernard Buffet and Zao Wou Ki.

Drantmann

13 rue du Chantier (02 223 57 07/www.drantmann. be). Métro Yser. **Open** 2.30-7pm Wed-Sat. **Map** p316 B1.

This upbeat ground-floor gallery benefits from the traffic of its upstairs neighbour, Argos (*see above*), and rightly so. Christian Drantmann follows his passions, which are well informed and unerringly up to date, as testified by his promotion of works by Gillian Wearing, Dawn Mellor and Elke Krystufek.

Etablissement d'en Face Projects

161 rue Antoine Dansaert, (02 219 44 51/www. etablissementdenfaceprojects.org). Métro Comte de Flandre or Ste-Catherine. **Open** 2-6pm Wed-Sat. **Map** p316 B2.

Among many other activities, this artist-run association stages exhibitions in this unreconstituted store-front gallery. Works are by members and non-members alike. Unclassifiable, and never, ever dull.

Les Filles du Calvaire
20 boulevard Barthélémy (02 511 63 20/www. fillesducalvaire.com). Métro Comte de Flandre. **Open** 2-6pm Wed-Sat. **Map** p316 A2.
The Belgian outpost of the Parisian gallery of the same name, featuring predominantly young French and American artists (Steven Parrino, Barbara Gallucci, James Hyde), who produce work of high quality. It occupies two floors in the building known as Kanal 20 (*see p179*), and one of the few remaining tenants in this erstwhile warren of galleries.

Jan Mot
190 rue Antoine Dansaert (02 514 10 10/www. galeriejanmot.com). Métro Comte de Flandre. **Open** 2-6.30pm Thur-Sat. **Map** p316 A2.
If proof were needed that good things come in small packages, this is it. Opened in 1996 in a virtual cubby hole, the gallery later moved along the street to well-designed (by architect Christian Kieckens), appreciably larger (although still tiny) premises. Mot has a sixth sense for the durable cutting edge as well as how to show it. His stable includes Douglas Gordon, Tinho Sehgal and Pierre Bismuth.

Meert Rihoux
13 rue du Canal (02 219 14 22). Métro Yser. **Open** 2-6pm Tue-Sat. **Map** p316 B2.
Class act on the third floor of a converted turn-of-the century industrial building in the heart of downtown. Featured artists include blue-chip American minimalists and conceptualists Donald Judd, Robert Mangold, Richard Tuttle and also Robert Barry; Vancouver school exponents Jeff Wall, Ian Wallace and Ken Lum; Italian abstractionists Carla Accardi and Enrico Castellani and their younger peers Liliana Moro, Grazia Toderi, Eva Marisaldi and Mario Airo; and locals Jef Geys and Sylvie Eyberg.

Usage Externe
46 rue du Vieux Marché aux Grains (02 502 68 09). Métro Ste-Catherine. **Open** 10am-6pm Tue-Sat. **Map** p316 B3.
While the Flemish community subsidises multi-media centre Argos (*see p180*) and its activities, the French-speaking community funds this fledgling non-profit art venture, opened in 2001 with the aim of presenting creations by francophone residents under 35. Design, fashion and comic strips are here with the oils and acrylics, sculpture and ephemeral installations one might expect. Wearables and collectibles by Usage Externe's exhibiting artists are sold for a song in the boutique.

Ixelles & St-Gilles

Aeroplastics Contemporary
32 rue Blanche, Ixelles (02 537 22 02/www.aero plastics.net). Métro Louise then tram 91, 92, 93, 94. **Open** 2-7pm Wed-Sat. **Map** p319 C6.
Aeroplastics occupies a huge space in a stunning house on the Ixelles/St-Gilles border. The choice of art is somewhat incongruous with the grand setting – contemporary trends are the keynote to the energetic collection, with featured artists John Isaacs, John Waters, Anton Corbijn and Daniele Buetti.

aliceday
62 rue de l'Aurore, Ixelles (02 646 31 53/ www.aliceday.be). Métro Louise then tram 93, 94. **Open** 1-7pm Wed-Sat. **Map** p325 E8.
A new gallery formed by the merging of Damasquine and Art and Com, aliceday has an eclectic roster of superior international talents, Belgians included. Among the latter are poet/painter Walter Swennen and the ironic, self-mocking Jacques Lizène, ever the conceptual cut-up. Formal and cultural diversity, not to mention compelling interest, are high on the agenda, as indicated by solo shows of Kinshasa's pre-eminent popular painter Cheri Samba, furry-toy fabulist Charlemagne Palestine, Nobuyoshi Araki, Danwen Xing and Dolorès Marat.

Baronian_Francey
2 rue Isidore Verheyden, Ixelles (02 512 92 95/ www.baronianfrancey.com). Métro Louise/tram 93, 94. **Open** noon-6pm Tue-Sat. **Map** p319 D6.
A recently created partnership and move to handsome new quarters situated between avenue Louise and chaussée d'Ixelles have heightened this gallery's profile and reinforced its reputation as Brussels' longest-running commercial showcase for contemporary art. Established by Albert Baronian in the 1970s, it continues to exhibit eclectic fare: modern masters to emerging younger artists, from minimalism and Arte Povera to experimental new media.

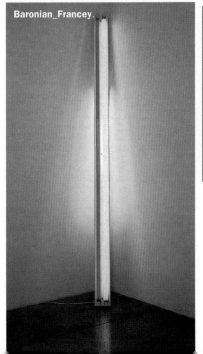
Baronian_Francey.

Camouflage

*37 rue du Prince Royal, Ixelles (02 502 01 17/www.
camouflage-world.com). Métro Porte de Namur/
bus 54, 71.* **Open** 2-7pm Wed-Sat. **Map** p319 D5.

This is the HQ for a non-profit, artist-run organisation that promotes contemporary African art by curating shows, advising collectors and setting up institutions in Europe and Africa. The gallery sets up and hosts provocative theme and solo exhibitions by African artists from all over the world, but not of the traditional carving variety. To enter, tap 45C into a code box by the letterboxes and ring the bell.

Espace Photographique Contretype

*1 avenue de la Jonction, St-Gilles (02 538 42 20/
www.contretype.org). Tram 81, 91, 92/bus 54.* **Open** 11am-6pm Wed-Fri; 1-6pm Sat, Sun. **Admission** €2.50. **No credit cards.**

Set in the art nouveau splendour of the Hôtel Hannon (*see p91*), this non-profit photo gallery (*contretype* meaning contact print) has a lively programme of exhibitions, lectures and discussions. Shows tend to be monographic, and composed of images made in Brussels – often in the gallery's very premises – by photographers invited for long-term residencies.

Rodolphe Janssen

*35 rue de Livourne, Ixelles (02 538 08 18). Métro
Louise then tram 93, 94.* **Open** 2-7pm Tue-Sat.
Map p319 C6.

Founded in 1991, Janssen was the first gallery to make a major commitment to contemporary photography. It still excels in the field, while gaining notice for its shows of works in other mediums by international artists such as Anya Gallaccio, Hiroshi Sugimoto, Bernard Voita, Gregory Crewdson, Matthew McCaslin and Pia Fries.

Le Salon d'Art et de Coiffure

*81 rue de l'Hôtel des Monnaies, St-Gilles (02 537 65
40). Pré-métro Parvis de St-Gilles.* **Open** 2-6.30pm Tue, Fri; 9.30am-noon, 2-6.30pm Wed, Thur, Sat.
Map p318 B6.

A unique place, this, consisting of a barber shop, art gallery and antiquarian bookshop rolled into one. Jean Marchetti began his business as a hairdresser, then discovered art along the way. So in 1976 he turned his salon into a smart, whitewashed gallery, bringing in a daring choice of writers and artists, as well as the likes of Jean-Pierre Maury, Stéphane Mandelbaum and Alechinsky. Marchetti brings out limited editions under three publishing imprints: La Pierre d'Alun, La Petite Pierre and La Haute Pierre, pairing writers with artists, producing works that are pieces of art as pieces of text. Great haircuts too.

Taché-Lévy

*74 rue de Tenbosch, Ixelles (02 344 23 68/
www.tache-levy.com). Métro Louise then tram 93, 94/
bus 60.* **Open** 11am-6.30pm Tue-Fri; noon-6pm Sat.
Map p324 D8.

The list of artists built up by this impressive gallery in just five years eloquently speaks for itself. Confirmed, heterogeneous, hip and with a refreshing complement of women, Taché-Lévy's stable is right out of the art mags: Maria Marshall, Dietmar Lutz, Merlin Carpenter, Vanessa Beecroft and so on.

Xavier Hufkens

*8 rue St-Georges, Ixelles (02 639 67 30/www.
xavierhufkens.com). Métro Louise then tram 93, 94.*
Open noon-6pm Tue-Sat. **Map** p324 E9.

Occupying an elegant townhouse converted to its present purpose by the Dutch architectural team of Robbrecht & Daem, Hufkens is Brussels' most prominent player on the international scene. With the spacious ground-floor galleries reserved for monographic exhibitions of blue-chip art and the upper level for presentations by younger artists, all that's missing is a place to sit down. This is the only gallery in town for solo shows by the likes of Louise Bourgeois, Robert Mapplethorpe, Jan Vercruysse, Malcolm Morley and iconic precursor Joseph Albers.

Further afield

Atelier 340

*340 drève De Rivieren, Jette (02 424 24 12/
www.atelier340muzeum.be). Métro Simonis then bus
13/tram 18, 19, 81, 94.* **Open** 2-7pm Thur-Sun for exhibitions. **Admission** €5. **No credit cards.**

Atelier 340 provides the sole window on art for this northern commune and its environs. Started singlehandedly as a sculpture centre, the place has changed the face and outlook of the neighbourhood by means of its gradual physical expansion, ambitious exhibitions and their attendant publications. Run on a shoestring by a dedicated, resourceful and very small staff, it has managed not only to survive but to preserve its autonomy for some 25 years.

Centre d'art contemporain

*63 avenue des Nerviens, Etterbeek (02 735 05 31).
Métro Mérode or Schuman.* **Open** 9am-1pm, 2-5pm Mon-Fri. **Map** p323 G5.

The French-speaking community's contemporary art outlet deserves praise for keeping a broad view despite its cramped quarters. African and Eastern-European art have figured prominently on its exhibition calendar, giving much-needed local exposure to the cultural production of these regions. Francophone Belgian artists are also showcased.

Marijke Schreurs House

*475 avenue Van Volxem, Forest (02 534 18 69/
www.marijkeschreurshouse.com). Tram 52/bus 49,
50.* **Open** 2-7pm Sat, Sun.

This unique gallery is situated in the home of its eponymous proprietor, who gives invited artists almost carte blanche to show or create works on all four levels of her charming 19th-century house. Theme and solo exhibitions feature site-specific installations, video, performance, photography, painting and sculpture. Hospitality is extended equally to visitors, who are welcome to attend lectures and participate in dinners and conversations organised around the art on view.

Gay & Lesbian

Same-sex marriages and an easy-going scene make for a warm welcome.

L'Homo Erectus. *See p184*.

With the gay capitals of Amsterdam, Cologne and Paris no distance away, Brussels tends to get bypassed on the gay and lesbian tourist map. But for locals, Belgium's liberalism and moral freedom ensure that living here is easy. The scene is relaxed and cosy, smaller local bars and clubs being the order of the day – though regular mega-bashes add a luxuriant layer. This laissez-faire attitude, from outside and within the gay community, is also reflected politically. From 2003, same-sex partners can marry and enjoy the same partnership rights as heterosexual couples. While the legislation only works for couples whose native country recognises such things (ie Dutch and Belgians), most believe this is just the beginning, with a bill for adoption rights being drafted in 2004.

The gay quarter is concentrated in the area surrounding the Bourse. Such a tight-knit city centre and rare entrance fees make bar hopping an essential pastime. There is something for everyone, although the commercial scene, as elsewhere, is dominated by clubs for the boys. But this is laid-back Belgium and there is no feeling of ghettoisation: most bars extend a friendly embrace to women. From the renowned leather bars in Antwerp (*see p233*) to the drag bars in Brussels, gay men, women and their friends enjoy a happy, non-threatening milieu in which to party. Add to that a cosmopolitan mix, and all the ingredients are there for a relaxed scene that doesn't take itself too seriously.

Culturally, the gay scene has integrated well into the Brussels calendar, particularly with the annual **Lesbian & Gay Pride** in May (*see p185* **Pink Saturdays**). Another annual bash with international clout is the **Gay & Lesbian Film Festival** (www.fglb.org) in January. This is not just a loose collection of themed films but a full-on event with live acts and special nights. **Brussels Gay Sports** (www.bgs.org) has also become an institution, with regular parties and charity fundraising events, winning support from across the sexuality divide.

For a small city, Brussels is big on politics, with a whole raft of associations based here, including the headquarters of **ILGA**, the International Gay & Lesbian Association.

Le Belgica or bust.

AIDS remains high on the political agenda, and numerous Brussels-based associations throw their efforts into support, advice, lobbying and radical action.

Bars

Le Belgica

32 rue du Marché au Charbon, Lower Town (no phone/www.lebelgica.be). Pré-métro Bourse. **Open** 10pm-3am Thur-Sun. **No credit cards.** **Map** p315 B3.

This is a must-visit bar, filled with gay men and their friends of both sexes at the start of an evening. But that's not early – it doesn't get buzzing until 11pm. And then it buzzes some. Hefty house music plays to the shoulder-to-shoulder crowd against the famed Belgica backdrop of distressed chic. Looking over it all is a bust of Léopold II, who is clearly not amused.

Chez Maman

7 rue des Grandes Carmes, Lower Town (no phone/ www.chezmaman.be). Pré-métro Bourse. **Open** midnight-dawn Fri, Sat. **No credit cards.** **Map** p315 B3.

Tiny bar, big reputation, the in-your-face queer CM becomes a sweat-box as the crowds pile in to see Maman strut her stuff on the bar in her size 11 stilet-tos. The drag is '70s in style and all mimed, but the guys and gals just love their bouffant doyenne. Outside, the doormen will make you wait if it's too busy, on a one-out-one-in basis.

Le Comptoir

26 place de la Vieille Halle aux Blés, Lower Town (02 514 05 00/www.comptoirv2.be). Métro Gare Centrale. **Open** 7pm-3am daily. *Restaurant* 7pm-midnight Mon-Thur; 7pm-1am Fri-Sun. **Main courses** €12-€18. **Credit** MC, V. **Map** p315 C4.

Set in a stunning 17th-century building, Le Comptoir is popular with a well-heeled and slightly holier-than-thou crowd, who adore its brick minimalism. It's a good place to meet as it's one of the few bars to open in the early evening. The restaurant used to have a poor reputation, but great efforts have been made to transform it and it's now seen as a decent place to eat before hitting the town – despite its shocking blue tablecloths.

Le Duquesnoy

12 rue Duquesnoy, Lower Town (02 502 38 83/ www.duquesnoy.com). Métro Gare Centrale. **Open** 9pm-3am Mon-Thur; 9pm-5am Fri, Sat; 3pm-3am Sun. **No credit cards.** **Map** p315 C4.

Probably the sleaziest doorbell in Brussels, the Duq is dark and cruisy with kinky porn on the TV and a range of owner Gérard's favourite tracks on the sound system. Leather men, denim and wannabe skinheads all jostle for pole position, especially in the labyrinth of dark rooms in the basement and upper floors. But be warned – the stairs in this old Brussels house are not for the unfit. Occasional theme nights on Saturdays and regular Sunday afternoon parties give the place its fetish edge. And if none of this interests you, the good old Duq is also great for a beer and can be as friendly as anything.

Le Gemeau

12 rue de Laeken, Lower Town (02 219 23 36). Métro/pré-métro De Brouckère. **Open** 10pm-dawn Fri, Sat. **No credit cards.** **Map** p315 B2.

This bar/disco is so ingrained on the Brussels gay scene it seems to have been around for ever. Its orange walls, fish tanks and top-hat light shades speak of an earlier era but the crowd is a total mix of all ages and all styles, all out for a good night of dancing to 1970s and '80s classics. With down-to-earth bar prices and a mirror ball, it's perfect for a seriously good time. The door policy can be sniffy, particularly with large, mixed-sex groups.

L'Homo Erectus

57 rue des Pierres, Lower Town (02 514 74 93/ www.lhomoerectus.com). Pré-métro Bourse. **Open** noon-late daily. **No credit cards.** **Map** p315 B3.

The name really only works in French, but you get the intended pun. Thirty seconds from the Grand' Place, you can't miss this tiny bar with its Darwin-like window of apes slowly evolving into macho man. It's already a victim of its own success – you need to evolve into a snake to be able to squeeze through to the bar. But L'Homo is brilliant fun, especially when the chaps start jumping on the bar for a song. If it gets too much, pop along to the Smart at No.28 for a blast of house music.

La Reserve

2A petite rue au Beurre, Lower Town (02 511 66 06). Pré-metro Bourse. **Open** 11am-2am Mon, Thur, Fri; 4pm-1am Wed; 3pm-2am Sat, Sun. **No credit cards. Map** p315 C3.

Jimmy and Marcel run this bar in a newly scrubbed-up old house near the Grand' Place. The decor is English country pub, the atmosphere reminiscent of a gay bar in the old style, with a mixed clientele who come here to chat with the regulars. The younger boys around town smirk at its kitsch charm, but everyone goes there at some point, if only because of its user-friendly opening hours and unlikely potential as a pick-up joint.

The Slave

7 Plattesteen, Lower Town (02 513 47 46). Pré-métro Bourse. **Open** 10pm-4am Mon-Thur, Sun; 10pm-6am Fri, Sat. **No credit cards. Map** p315 B3.

Despite its name, this popular bar is not a chains and whips place. Having said that, it does veer on the sleazier end of the market with its corrugated iron walls and ultra-dark basement. But hey, this is Brussels, and in the middle of all that macho metal is a roaring open fire to keep the boys warm. Porn plays on one video, cartoons on the other. The good-looking staff are lovely, and smile through to the early hours – unlike some of the customers.

La Démence

208 rue Blaes, Lower Town (02 511 9789/www.la demence.com). Métro/pré-métro Porte de Hal. **Open** 10pm-noon monthly. **Admission** €7 before 11pm; €15 after 11pm. **No credit cards. Map** p318 B4.

They literally bus the boys in from Lille, Paris and Amsterdam for this, Belgium's biggest gay party, with sounds – and muscles – pumping out on two floors. From house to techno, the beats keep a micro-cosm of the gay world, from moustached clones to fluoro queens, on the move. And when it's all too much there's a chill-out area and a room with no lights. Pure unadulterated Eurotrash. Check the websites for exact dates.

Mega-Bitches

Le Palace, 85 boulevard Anspach, Lower Town (no phone/www.mega-top-biches.org). Pré-métro Bourse. **Open** 10pm-late 3rd Fri of mth. **Map** p315 B3.

A new concept for lesbian partying in Brussels, with hard-hitting sounds and hard-hitting messages of being out and proud of it. Outside of music, Bitches is a collective, bringing in literature, art and personal stories to raise the dyke profile and temperature.

Next

La Raffinerie, 21 rue de Manchester, Molenbeek (no phone/www.next-party.be). Bus 63. **Open** 11pm-6am 1st Sat of mth. **Admission** €8; €5 before 11pm. **No credit cards**.

Pink Saturdays

The story of the Belgian Lesbian & Gay Pride is a recent one. After a false start between 1979 and 1981 – when only small demonstrations took place – the first *Roze Zaterdag* proper was held in Antwerp on 5 May 1990. Numbers were swelled by Dutch supporters who travelled down to make sure the first Belgian Pride made its mark. It worked: the movement was galvanised into action and the organisers decided to stage an event every two years. Then, in 1996, Pink Saturday was shifted to Brussels, not only as a way of attracting more participants, but also to centre the movement's equality demands on the capital, where all political decisions are made. So successful was this parade that it soon became an annual event on the first Saturday of May, though at this time it remained more of a protest than a celebration.

In subsequent years, numbers have grown dramatically, with more floats, more colour and noise and a huge public following packing the downtown streets along the parade route.

But for all the camp, riotous fun, there is still a serious message of reform, AIDS issues and equal rights for all.

Since 2000, the parade (09 223 69 29, www.blgp.be) has gathered in Ste-Catherine and moved along boulevard Anspach, passing by the major shopping centres and the busy area around the Bourse. At the head of it, a vast rainbow flag carries a sense of unity. The festivities then move back to the fish market, where crowds pack into the old quays and where beer tents, food stands and sound stages with live performances keep the atmosphere heightened until 7pm. After that, the city's bars and clubs keep going deep into the night, along with a couple of official events for good measure. Throughout, the atmosphere is electric, everyone is out for a good time, drag queens mix freely with disco bunnies, hand-holding same-sex couples meander among families with kids and groups of tracksuited teens here for the music or just to see what all the fuss is about.

The brain child of DJs Luuuk and Piiit, Next has become an important night for gays and lesbians to play together in a real queer atmosphere. Now in a great new venue, just out of town, it attracts a young, right-on crowd who love the eclectic music and non-commercial feel. There's a free bus every half-hour from 11 rue du Lombard, bringing you back into the centre again until 6am. Now that's service for you.

Salvation
Mirano Continental, 38 chaussée de Louvain, St-Josse (no phone/www.salvation-brussels.be). Métro Madou. **Open** 11pm-late. **Map** p320 E3.
The international gay club brand has hit Brussels and plays occasional one-off nights to an ecstatic crowd. Because Salvation is on a never-ending world tour, dates are rare, and it has become a highly desirable collectable. Keep your eye on the website.

Strong
Résidence Palace, 155 rue de la Loi, EU Quarter (no phone/www.strong.be). Métro Schuman. **Open** 10pm-6.30am monthly. **Admission** free before 11pm; €12 after 11pm. **No credit cards. Map** p322 F4.
Strong Cabaret *Galerie Louise basement, avenue Louise, Ixelles (no phone/www.strong.be). Métro Louise.* **Open** 11pm-6am Sun; days before holidays 10pm-9am. **Admission** free before midnight; €12 after midnight. **No credit cards. Map** p319 C5.
Strong has become a huge club name in Brussels, whether it's at the once-a-month club night on a Saturday or its outrageous Sunday cabarets, with live acts and serious house music. The image is important, avoiding gay clichés, striving for new sounds and appealing to an undeniable hedonism in its punters. Wild stuff.

Hairdressers

Man to Man
11 rue des Riches Claires, Lower Town (02 514 02 96). Pré-métro Bourse. **Open** 10am-6.30pm Tue-Sat. **No credit cards. Map** p316 B3.
The window of this hair salon has become iconic. Not only does it appear in worldwide personal photo albums, but it pops up in guidebooks as an essentially quirky Brussels phenomenon. Hanging from an iron grid are leather undies, handcuffs and other fetish bits and pieces that belie its true intent as a men's hairdresser's. Inside it's much softer and friendlier than the exterior suggests.

Saunas & gyms

Macho II
106 rue du Marché au Charbon, Lower Town (02 513 56 67/www.machosauna.com). Pré-métro Anneessens. **Open** noon-midnight daily. **Admission** €15; €10 concessions; €10 Thur. **No credit cards. Map** p316 B3.
The Macho is well known for its serious saunas and decently equipped fitness room. It's a big, well-kept

establishment and the staff are warm and attentive. Expect a youngish crowd, particularly later at night. A ticket allows repeat access on the same day.

Oasis
10 rue van Orley, Upper Town (02 218 08 00/ www.oasis-sauna.be). Métro Madou. **Open** noon-1am daily. *Sun brunch* 11am-3pm. **Admission** €15; €10 Tue. **Credit** AmEx, DC, MC, V. **Map** p317 D2.
This is set in a vast townhouse and the bar area is still very much a *grande salle*, with marble fireplace and corniched ceilings. Some parts are seedier, but they're meant to be. It's clean, it's popular and it has all the facilities, including a stylish whirlpool area. The stairs, especially the old servants' ones at the back, challenge even the most nimble-footed.

Spades4our
23-25 rue Bodeghem, Lower Town (02 502 07 72/ www.saunaspades4.be). Pré-métro Anneessens. **Open** noon-midnight daily. **Admission** €15; €10 Wed; €7.50-€10 concessions. **Credit** AmEx, DC, MC, V. **Map** p316 A4.
Brussels' biggest and most exclusive sauna is spread over 1,400sq m (15,054sq ft) on six floors. It's tastefully designed, has an excellent bar and good food, and the staff are friendly and helpful. Facilities include legitimate massage, an SM labyrinth and a cinema, as well as masses of private rooms. There is also a well-equipped fitness room and a roof terrace.

Sex shops

Erot'X Stars
28 rue Malines, Lower Town (02 217 77 37). Métro/ pré-métro Rogier. **Open** 11am-8pm Mon-Sat; noon-6pm Sun. **Credit** MC, V. **Map** p317 C2.
OK, this isn't the most glamorous of places, but it does have a huge range of men-to-men videos to buy or rent, which can be sampled in private cabins.

Orly Centre
9 boulevard Jamar, Lower Town (02 522 10 50). Métro/pré-métro Gare du Midi or pré-métro Lemonnier. **Open** 10am-midnight Mon-Fri; noon-midnight Sat, Sun. **Credit** AmEx, MC, V. **Map** p318 A5.
The shop, selling mainly videos, is also a window for a three-screen cinema complex and a seedy sauna called Club 3000. It's close to Midi station, so is an (extremely) alternative waiting room for your train. Don't take your bags – it's dark and labyrinthine.

Where to stay

Les Ecrins
15 rue du Rouleau, Lower Town (02 219 36 57/ www.lesecrins.com). Métro Ste-Catherine. **Rates** €45-€70 single; €55-€80 double. **Credit** AmEx, MC, V. **Map** p316 B2.
A neat, gay-run but mixed hotel in the centre of town. Set in an old house with original features, its rooms are ample size. A friendly welcome too.

Music

Plenty of funding, plenty of fun.

Classical & Opera

'Music is an expensive noise', King Léopold II is supposed to have said. Not an encouraging attitude from a head of state, one might think. Yet music has always had an important place in Brussels' cultural scene. An opera performance at the **Théâtre de la Monnaie** in 1830 precipitated events that led to Belgium's creation as an independent state. The first performances of some major symphonic works by Bartók and Stravinsky took place in Brussels, and students come from all over the world to study at the **Conservatoire**.

While not all of this heritage survived cuts in public funding – the French radio orchestra folded in 1991, while the Flemish one moved to Leuven – in 2003 the splendid former broadcast hall of the combined National Radio Orchestra on place **Flagey**, the Institut National de Radiodiffusion, reopened for concerts and other events (*see p88* **All aboard!**).

The last few years have seen some other notable revivals. The Monnaie's new conductor, Kazushi Ono, has proven a solid successor to the Covent Garden-bound Antonio Pappano. Heading the National Orchestra, the young Finnish conductor Mikko Franck continues to introduce new works at the revamped **Palais des Beaux-Arts** (*see also p72* **A new broom at the Bozar**). Several new venues have also sprung up, with an endless stream of new performers eager to give concerts in them.

This apparently paradoxical growth, despite reduced subsidies, is due to increasing audience interest. Belgian concert-goers are often keen amateur musicians. Besides six conservatories, Belgium has a large network of preparatory academies where anyone can learn an instrument for a modest fee. Graduates unable to find professional work often end up in the many amateur orchestras and choirs. There is even a network (www.icambristi.be) for players to get together for chamber music sessions.

All this may help to explain the excitement every May for the world-class **Concours Musical International Reine Elisabeth de Belgique** (Queen Elisabeth International Music Competition), which changes focus each year between violin, piano and voice. Founded by the renowned Belgian violinist Eugène Ysaÿe and the then Queen Elisabeth of Belgium (herself a violinist), the first winner was David Oistrakh in 1937. The level of virtuosity has remained high. The final-round gala concerts are always sold out and shown live on Belgian TV.

The splendid **Musée des Instruments de Musique** (*see p74*), housed in the superb art nouveau Old England building since 2000, is as popular for its occasional concerts on period instruments as for its well-presented collection. Many of the instruments exhibited can be heard on earphones, recorded by local specialists.

Brussels is also a centre of excellence for early music and original-instrument ensembles. The more notable are the pioneering **La Petite**

The best Fests

Ars Musica
Started in 1989, Ars (www.arsmusica.be; March) is an exciting and innovative contemporary classical music fest.

Brussels Jazz Marathon
A weekend bash (www.brusselsjazz marathon.be; May) featuring 400 jazz events across the city.

Les Nuits Botanique
Ten days of indie and alternative music (www.botanique.be; May), much of it UK-based.

Couleur Café
One of Europe's biggest world music festivals (www.couleurcafe.org; June).

Rock Werchter
This award-winning old-style rock festival (www.rockwerchter.be; June) takes place outside of Leuven.

Festival Midi-Minimes
Lunchtime season of classical concerts (www.midis-minimes.be; July/August).

Audi Jazz Festival
Staged across Belgium (www.audijazz.be; October/November), with 50 concerts in Brussels alone.

Bande; **Philippe Herreweghe**, his orchestra **Chapelle Royale** and chorus **Collegium Vocal**; **Il Fondamento**; and **Anima Eterna**. Their concerts take place in the city's smaller venues or outlying *communes*.

Contemporary music fans should check out the annual **Ars Musica** festival (*see p166*), which stages events throughout Brussels. Local groups specialising in new music include **Ictus Ensemble**, **Oxalys** and **Musique Nouvelle**. Specialising in accompaniment, the variable-sized **Ensemble Orchestral de Bruxelles** offers young soloists a chance to play and record concertos with a symphony orchestra.

INFORMATION AND TICKETS

Details on all concerts can be found every Thursday in *The Bulletin*. The Philharmonic Society (02 507 84 30), which organises the bulk of big-name concerts in Brussels, issues a brochure of its events, including many foreign orchestras, soloists and chamber groups, plus the equally glossy bi-monthly *Bozar Magazine*; call 02 511 34 33 for a copy.

Ticket prices vary from one event to another, even for the same venue. Philharmonic Society events are about €9 to €60, with gala concerts such as the Queen Elisabeth finals costing up to double the usual price. At Théâtre de la Monnaie expect to pay at least €10, and up to €50, for orchestra seats. Prices at other venues range from €4 to €40, but there are no strict guidelines. The **TIB** tourist office (*see p301*) has details for most events and sells tickets to many concerts. You can also buy tickets to events in Brussels and Antwerp at **Fnac** (*see p145*).

Venues

Conservatoire Royal de Musique

30 rue de la Régence, Upper Town (box office 02 507 82 00/24hr info in French & Flemish 02 507 84 44). Métro Porte de Namur/tram 92, 93, 94. **Open** *Box office* 1hr before performance or 10 days in advance from the Palais des Beaux-Arts. **Tickets** varies. **No credit cards. Map** p319 C5.

The Conservatory's fine hall is a little too narrow for full-size symphonic orchestras but perfect for chamber formations and solo recitals. Ignore the peeling paint, the acoustics are excellent in a hall partially designed by French organ-builder Cavaillé-Coll. It is here that the preliminary rounds of the Queen Elisabeth competition are held – and the most interesting part, according to contest connoisseurs.

Palais des Beaux-Arts (Bozar)

23 rue Ravenstein, Upper Town (box office 02 507 82 00/24hr info in French & Flemish 02 507 84 44/ www.bozar.be). Métro Gare Centrale or Parc/tram 92, 93, 94. **Open** *Box office* 11am-6pm Mon-Sat. **Tickets** €10-€62; 25% discount concessions. **Credit** AmEx, MC, V. **Map** p317 D4.

Home of the National Orchestra and seat of the Philharmonic Society, the Palais is Brussels' most prestigious venue, well suited to host the finals of the Concours Musical International Reine Elisabeth de Belgique. Acoustics in the splendid Salle Henri LeBoeuf were greatly improved for both musicians and the public by major renovation a few years ago. The smaller 400-seat chamber music hall is excellent, though concerts here are rarer. *See also p72* **A new broom at the Bozar.**

Churches

Cathédrale de Sts Michel et Gudule

Place Ste-Gudule, Upper Town (02 217 83 45/ 02 343 70 40/www.cathedralestmichel.be). Métro Gare Centrale or Parc. **Open** varies. **Tickets** varies. **No credit cards. Map** p315 C3/p317 D3.

Brussels' most grandiose church is too large, alas, for music more complicated than Gregorian chant. Nevertheless it's the venue for quite a few major events, especially organ concerts on the excellent instrument high above the audience. The interior is just as grand as the exterior; both have recently undergone expensive refurbishments. Audiences of a thousand or so help absorb some of the ten-second echo. Sunday 12.30pm mass (10am in summer) features special concerts during much of the year; evening concerts are rarer. *See also p73.*

Chapelle Royale

Eglise Protestante, 2 rue du Musée, Upper Town (02 213 49 40). Métro Gare Centrale. **Open** varies. **Tickets** varies. **No credit cards. Map** p315 C4.

A pleasure both acoustically and architecturally for musicians and audience. Too small for anything larger than a baroque chamber orchestra, it's ideal for period instruments. As maximum audience size is 150, early booking is advised. It's well heated, a plus as most concerts are held in the evening; the 11am church services also feature fine musicians.

L'Eglise de St Jean et St Etienne aux Minimes

62 rue des Minimes, Upper Town (02 511 93 84). Bus 27, 48. **Open** varies. **Tickets** varies. **No credit cards. Map** p319 C5.

This high-baroque church, between the Sablon and the Marolles, has average acoustics but hosts a huge number of concerts. The Philharmonic Society produces some of its early music recitals here. The imaginative Midi-Minimes summer festival (www.midis-minimes.be) attracts tourists and locals here at lunchtime. One Sunday morning a month during the rest of the year, a mixed amateur/professional ensemble La Chapelle des Minimes (www.minimes.be) presents fine performances of Bach cantatas, as it has done for the past two decades. The admission fee is voluntary, so try to arrive half an hour before the 10.30am starting time for these often standing-room-only events.

Théâtre du Vaudeville. *See p190.*

Occasional venues

Several highly original new smaller venues have appeared on private initiatives. Concerts of surprisingly good quality can happen in the most unexpected places. One example is **Libretto** (52 rue du Bailli, Ixelles, 02 646 97 35, tickets €10), a small hall behind an Ixelles townhouse. The **Music Village** (*see p196*) puts on quality dinner concerts. More unusually, **Skenegraphia** (02 375 51 47, tickets €20) is organised by music-loving architects who produce concerts in different large homes of special architectural interest. Each concert's repertoire is deliberately matched to the style and epoch of its particular venue, making for events with lots of ambience.

Other interesting places in and around the capital – museums, chateaux or large townhouses – hold concerts sporadically. The Château de la Hulpe (15 kilometres/ten miles south-east of Brussels), the setting for the film *The Music Teacher*, puts on summer opera. Many outlying communes have cultural centres with halls used for concerts.

Flagey

Place Ste-Croix (next to place Flagey), Ixelles (02 641 10 20/www.flagey.be). Tram 81, 82/bus 38, 60, 71. **Tickets** varies. **Open** *Box office* 11.30am-6.30pm Mon-Sat & 1hr before event. **Credit** AmEx, DC, MC, V. **Map** p322 D7.

Reopened after lengthy and expensive renovation work, Flagey, former home of the National Radio Orchestra, folded during the 1990s. In its heyday, the main studio was acoustically one of Europe's finest and hosted some memorable world premières. It now has a couple of new balconies, but the sound is still great. Programming is slanted towards the new and adventurous, but there's still something for everyone. *See p88* **All aboard!**

Hotel Astoria

103 rue Royale, Upper Town (0900 28 877 for automated reservations in French or Flemish). Métro Parc or Botanique/tram 92, 93, 94. **Open** *Concerts* 11am Sun (except July, Aug, hols). **Tickets** €10; €5 concessions. **No credit cards**. **Map** p317 D3.

Enjoy magnificent turn-of-the-20th century elegance in a working hotel that hosts concerts for Sunday brunch. The small, opulent hall is ideal for chamber music – ambience guaranteed. *See also p45.*

Kaaitheater

20 square Sainctelette, Lower Town (02 201 59 59/ www.kaaitheater.be). Métro Yser. **Open** *Box office* 11am-6pm Tue-Fri. **Tickets** €12.50; €10 concessions. **Credit** MC, V. **Map** p316 B1.

Used mostly for Flemish-speaking theatre productions, this medium-sized hall occasionally features opera and contemporary music; Ictus is the resident ensemble. There's also a smaller studio at 81 rue Notre Dame du Sommeil. *See also p210.*

Théâtre St-Michel

2 rue Père Devroye, Etterbeek (02 736 76 56). Métro Montgomery/pré-métro Boileau. **Open** *Box office* 10am-1pm Mon-Fri. **Tickets** varies. **Credit** AmEx, MC, V.

This fairly large hall, attached to one of the major preparatory schools, has acoustics that are more suitable for theatre, but audiences and players appreciate its shape and generous volume.

Théâtre de la Monnaie – the stuff of revolution.

Théâtre du Vaudeville

13-15 galérie de la Reine, Lower Town (02 512 57 45). Métro Gare Centrale. **Open** varies. **Tickets** varies. **No credit cards. Map** p315 C3.

Originally built in 1846 as a flower market, then transformed into a casino and dance hall, the Vaudeville became a popular cabaret theatre at the turn of the 19th century. Renovated after 20 years of neglect, this splendidly ornate 280-seat theatre in the heart of central Brussels is now used for all sorts of events: concerts, cabaret dinners, dancing or shows. The acoustics are surprisingly good.

Opera

Théâtre de la Monnaie

Place de la Monnaie, 4 rue Léopold, Lower Town (02 229 12 11/www.lamonnaie.be). Métro/pré-métro De Brouckère. **Open** *Box office* 11am-6pm Tue-Sat & 1hr before event. **Tickets** €7.50-€94; 25%-50% discount concessions. **Credit** AmEx, DC, MC, V. **Map** p315 C3.

The national opera house soaks up the lion's share of arts subsidies, hardly surprising as it's the jewel in Brussels' cultural crown, reflected in its opulent interior. Its repertoire strives for a balance between contemporary works and innovative productions of the classics, with performers not yet famous enough for prices to be out of reach. Director and organist Bernard Foccroulle has had success with baroque works played by period instrument ensembles. The results are consistently first-class and tickets for many productions are scarce. Last-minute ones exist, but there are always more people than seats.

Rock, World & Jazz

Brussels' reputation as a centre for live music cannot compare to London or Paris, and you won't get a choice of dozens of gigs every night. But for a town with a population of one million, it's ace. Ticket prices are reasonable, thanks partly to the rivalry between the culture ministries of each linguistic faction trying to outdo each other by running or subsidising venues. Many independent places, too, are non profit-making ventures, which engender an eclectic and inventive local music scene.

At the top end, big international artists have a range of venues to choose from: Eminem and Tom Jones have played the city's biggest (too big?) indoor venue, the **Forest National**. Blur and Iggy Pop favoured the more intimate setting of the **Ancienne Belgique**, a renovated theatre a stroll away from the Grand' Place. The other medium-sized venue, **Le Botanique**, is unique and marvellous. This large, beautiful greenhouse has three superb concert spaces.

If a sweaty moshpit is your natural habitat, then check out the **VK Club** or **Magasin 4**, both of which attract an array of ear-splitting leftfield bands and the occasional cult legend.

LOCAL BANDS

The domestic music scene is pretty lively for such a small country. Unlike in France, radio stations are not obliged by law to playlist home-grown records – local acts have to vie for airplay with foreign ones. A thriving local music scene encompasses all styles: even the smallest Flemish village has a couple of young bands doing the odd night in the local bar. Many artists regularly appearing in Brussels' bars might have a good chance of success if they sought it – and didn't come from Belgium. *See p192* **Local heroes**.

One highly original example on the Brussels small venue circuit is Brian is Back, who mix Joy Division (Portuguese singer Franklin does a passable impersonation of Ian Curtis's dancing style) and Captain Beefheart influences with classical-style double bass. Another regular from the opposite end of the musical spectrum is **Enzo Piccinato**, a studiedly ironic and very cool performer who deadpans wry lyrics over minimalist electronic backing, enlivened by glammed-up female backing singers.

Belgian audiences have one major weakness: an inexplicable fondness for oldish blokes impersonating bluesmen. This explains why on a recent Botanique night there were people clamouring for spare tickets for the pedestrian but popular **Fred and the Healers**, while Franz Ferdinand were playing relatively unnoticed in the venue's smaller space.

INFORMATION, TIPS AND TICKETS

For concert information, check *The Bulletin*, the French-language monthly *Kiosque* or the *MAD* supplement with *Le Soir* on Wednesdays.

Live music in small or occasional venues doesn't always make it into the listings, so look out for flyers in bars like **Le Tavernier** (*see p140*) and **Au Soleil** (*see p131*), and the café of the **Beursschouwburg** in the city centre. Don't be afraid to give the smaller places a try – chances are the bands will be interesting and, even if they aren't, the audiences are usually determined to enjoy themselves without the world-weary attitude found in bigger cities.

For name acts, venues apart from the cavernous Forest National tend to be small, which means you can usually get a great view of your pop idol. But it also means gigs can sell out fast. Plan ahead to avoid disappointment – tickets can be booked at www.inthepocket.be or through the sites of individual venues. Get there at the time stated on the tickets. If you stay for a drink in the bar next door, you'll arrive in time for the encore. Most concerts in Brussels are over by 10.30pm so there's plenty of time for a drink afterwards.

At many venues, including the Ancienne Belgique and Cirque Royal, queue up to pay for drinks tokens first, then swap them over at the bar counter. You have to queue twice, but

it's much quicker. There's also a discount for returning empties, so you'll see spiky types wandering around with teetering piles of glasses. Also, unlike many UK venues, the beer is worth the wait. No watered-down lager here.

Rock venues

Ancienne Belgique

110 boulevard Anspach, Lower Town (02 548 24 24/www.abconcerts.be). Pré-métro Bourse. **Open** *Box office* 11am-6pm Mon-Fri. **Tickets** €10-€30. **Credit** AmEx, MC, V. **Map** p315 B3.

This place used to be old, down-at-heel and great. Jacques Brel put in many an electrifying performance on its stage. Now it's new, shiny – and still great, a rare example of a successful renovation which transforms a venue without losing any of its spirit. It has recently attracted Blur, Iggy Pop, David Byrne, Goldfrapp and the Darkness. Its main hall can hold 2,000, mostly standing, with an adjacent side bar poignantly decked out in posters for shows by performers no longer with us: Joe Strummer, Johnny Thunders and so on. Downstairs are handy lockers and pay toilets. Upstairs features local bands, entry €10. Despite its French name, AB is partly funded by the Flemish Cultural Community, which provides friendly staff. Ask for '*een pintje*' rather than '*une bière*' when you hand over your beer token at the bar. All in all, the perfect example of how a rock venue should be run.

Beursschouwburg

20-28 rue Auguste Orts, Lower Town (02 550 03 50/www.beursschouwburg.be). Pré-métro Bourse. **Open** *Box office* 10am-6pm Mon-Fri. *Café* 8.30pm-3am Thur-Sat. *Theatre* varies. **Tickets** €10; €8.50 concessions. **No credit cards**. **Map** p315 B3.

After two years of renovations, one of the gems of central Brussels is at last back in business. A 19th-century theatre, the Beursschouwburg is funded by the Flemish Cultural Community and hosts a colourful and diverse range of events with an often eccentric vibe: concerts, club nights and jam sessions are held in either the theatre or the brilliant café, worth a visit even when nothing special is on. They also organise outdoor events, concerts and street parties in July in the place de la Monnaie. *See also p210.*

Botanique

236 rue Royale, St-Josse (02 226 12 11/reservations 02 218 37 32/www.botanique.be). Métro Botanique/ tram 92, 93, 94. **Open** 10am-6pm daily. **Tickets** €10-€18. **Credit** AmEx, MC, V. **Map** p317 D2.

The unmissable 'Le Bota' is managed by the French-speaking Cultural Community. The main corridor is lined with luxuriant foliage and ponds, a reminder of when the building was the centre of a vast botanical garden before the war. Acts here revel in indie rock – Franz Ferdinand, Yeah Yeah Yeahs, the Bell Rays and Stereolab were all booked recently. The best of the three separate venues in Le Botanique is the mid-sized La Rotonde (capacity 350), where the audience stands on steep steps and everyone gets a great view of the band – and of the glass cupola high overhead. Le Botanique plays host to Les Nuits Botanique rock festival (*see p167*) – moved to May from 2004 – for which they erect an enormous marquee to accommodate the biggest acts. No tickets needed for the excellent Botanique bar, where you'll find bands before and after their set. There's also a terrace perfect for summer nights.

Café Central

14 rue de Borgval, Lower Town (0486 72 26 24/ www.lecafecentral.com). Pré-métro Bourse. **Tickets** free. **Map** p315 B3.

Since it took over the premises used by legendarily sleazy haunt Acrobate, Café Central has become one of the capital's trendiest venues in the heart of trendydom. It has kept the Acrobate's dancefloor and cleaned off the sticky bits. Concerts are staged

Local heroes

Nearly all the Belgian acts who have notched up sales outside their own country come from a Dutch-speaking background – even those who ply their trade *en français*, like flame-headed **Axelle Red**, who fills stadiums in France.

Belgium's best-known band abroad, Antwerp post-grunge outfit **dEUS**, are back recording together again after a period of solo projects. For lead singer Tom Barman, that included making a fairly well-received feature film *Anyway the Wind Blows*, set in his home town. Former bass player Stef Kamil Carlens left permanently for **Zita Swoon**, whose *Life = A Sexy Sanctuary* put the band into the mainstream market in and beyond Belgium. A new album is due out in 2004 and remixes of the Tom Tom Club, CJ Bolland and Praga Khan have re-established credibility.

Veterans **De Mens** (Mankind), a powerful yet melodic punky three-piece, have a following among ex-rebellious teenagers who now have kids themselves. By singing only in Dutch, their vocalist and leader, spectacularly bald former rock journalist Frank Van der Linden, has little chance of success outside Flanders or Holland.

Equally bald Fleming **Flip Kowlier** is now a solo singer/guitarist. He's adopted a more melodic pop style after making records as a rapper with the cult hip hop combo 't Hof van Commerce. He too sings in his native language, a West Flanders dialect that's incomprehensible even to other Dutch speakers. But that doesn't stop him selling out the Ancienne Belgique or seeing his album hit the top of the Dutch charts. **Hooverphonic**, trip hop from Sint-Niklaas, have no such linguistic puritanism, and continue to sell records by the truckload all over Europe.

After big success with **Soulwax**, Ghent siblings and walking pop encyclopaedias Stephen and David Dewaele – whose dad was a 1960s radio DJ – reinvented

themselves in 2001-2 as **2ManyDJ's** (*pictured*). A compilation of the same name featured 46 short mixes of popular classics by everyone from Dolly Parton to the Velvet Underground, with vocals from one track over the music from another. This 'bootlegging' style was fresh and sealed their reputation as Belgium's coolest-ever pop exports. More material is available on the internet and on unofficial CDs – and they still appear in Ghent, where it will cost a good deal less to see them than at one of their many London shows. Catch them if you can.

Also from Ghent are four-piece **Das Pop**. Two albums and singles, including the polished *Wonderwall*-esque hit *Telephone Love*, have established them as a Belgian radio favourite.

Antwerp's **Traktor** use accordion, clarinet, saxes, charango and a euphonium, as well as improvised instruments, to loud and joyful effect and claim all sorts of musical influences from French trad and folk to techno. Don't let their striptease stage act put you off – their music is original and it's good. Brussels' own **Jaune Toujours** lay claim to a similar mantle – between Les Négresses Vertes and Balkan band music.

twice a month, usually on Thursday at 10pm, ranging from experimental music played with building materials to bossa nova.

Cirque Royale

81 rue de l'Enseignement, Upper Town (02 218 20 15/www.cirque-royal.org). Métro Madou. **Open** *Box office* 9am-6pm Mon-Fri; 10.30am-6pm Sat. **Tickets** varies. **Credit** MC, V. **Map** p317 D3.

This is the nearest thing Brussels has to the Albert Hall. It's plush and it's spherical, with great acoustics, and it tends to draw the grand old men of rock. And they don't seem to want to leave – Elvis Costello played about ten encores at a recent appearance. Even top grouch Lou Reed was spotted smiling when he played here. There's no dancing, though – in keeping with its other role as a classical venue, it insists you sit down and look enraptured. Even talking to your neighbour can draw disapproving glances. *See also p214.*

Forest National

208 avenue Victor Rousseau, Forest (02 340 22 11/ www.forestnational.be; tickets 0900 00991/ www.sherpa.be). Tram 18, 52/bus 48, 54. **Open** *Box office* 8am-10pm daily. **Tickets** €40-€60. **Credit** MC, V.

It might be called Forest, but unlike Le Botanique there are no trees in sight. The biggest indoor venue in Brussels, this huge concrete and metal shed can accommodate 11,000. But you have to really like an act to want to see it here. It feels a bit like an aircraft hangar and, unless you're near the stage your idols will look the same size as they do on the telly. It gets top names: Bob Dylan, Eminem, Robbie Williams and so on. As long as Brussels doesn't have a regular venue between the size of Ancienne Belgique and this, they and their fans will have no choice but to trek out to the southern edge of the city for the Forest National experience. Allow plenty of time to get there, the traffic is awful and the buses and trams full on gig nights.

Grain d'Orge

142 chaussée de Wavre, Ixelles (02 511 26 47). Métro Porte de Namur. **Open** 11am-3am Fri (concerts 9pm). **Tickets** free. **Credit** MC, V. **Map** p322 E5.

If you sport a flared denim suit with beer towels sewn in, you'll love it here. Brussels' ultimate spit-and-sawdust bar, the Grain d'Orge hosts gigs every Friday night. Most of the acts tend to favour American-style rock, blues or country – one regular local band is Fried Flying Chicken Wings. Everyone has a good time and this being Belgium, a certain knowing sense of irony is not entirely absent.

Halles de Schaerbeek

22 rue Royale Ste-Marie, Schaerbeek (02 218 21 07/www.halles.be/tickets at www.sherpa.be). Tram 90, 92, 93, 94/bus 65, 66. **Open** *Box office* 2-6pm Mon-Fri. **Tickets** €20. **Credit** MC, V. **Map** p320 E1.

The Halles began life as a covered market in 1865 and is a multi-use French cultural centre with a mis-

Ancienne Belgique. *See p191.*

sion to promote both avant-garde and mainstream, whether rock, folk, theatre or dance. The Victorian architecture gives this spot a sense of grandeur. Smaller concerts take place in the downstairs club but bigger acts – recent visitors include PJ Harvey and Beck – appear in the main hall. It's gorgeous and you can get a great view from the impressive balcony, but it wasn't really designed for loud music and the sound can be a bit muddy. *See also p99.*

Kultuurkaffee

Vrije Universiteit Brussel (Flemish University), boulevard de la Plaine 2, Ixelles (02 629 23 25/ www.vub.ac.be/cultuur). Métro Montgomery then tram 23, 90. **Open** *Concerts* 10pm Thur. **Tickets** free. **No credit cards.**

A good place to sample the rather hidden but often quite adventurous culture of Brussels' minority Flemish student community, akin to their British counterparts when it comes to late nights and a good drink. The Kultuurkaffee, with support from radio station Studio Brussel, puts on a mixture of rock acts, including the occasional semi-well-known group like Traktor, world music and sometimes Flemish wannabes impersonating what they see as more exotic cultures.

Magasin 4

4 rue de Magasin, Lower Town (02 223 34 74/ www.magasin4.be). Métro Yser/tram 18/bus 47. **Open** usually 8pm on gig nights. **Tickets** €5-€8. **No credit cards. Map** p316 B1.

Punk's not dead at **Magasin 4**. *See p193.*

Punk's not dead while Magasin 4 is still going. It's basic, it's dilapidated, it's sweaty – and it's wonderful. Run by an association with charity status, Magasin 4 resembles an outsized New York subway train before Mayor Giuliani jailed all the graffiti artists. Spray-painted murals are its only nod towards decoration. Marky Ramone, Thee Headcoats and the Legendary Pink Dots are just three of the acts that have made a recent appearance here.

Recyclart

Gare de Bruxelles-Chapelle, 25 rue des Ursulines, Lower Town (02 502 57 34/www.recyclart.be). Métro Gare Centrale/pré-métro Anneessens/bus 95, 96. **Open** *Concerts around 10pm Fri, Sat, last Sun of mth.* **Tickets** free-€7. **No credit cards. Map** p315 B5.
This very alternative venue, in several wonderful spaces in a now little-used train station, is well worth a visit for the concerts, club nights and other events, from kids' puppet shows to philosophical debates. It might look like it has been squatted by anarchists, but in fact the non-profit association that runs it has the full backing of the city and regional authorities and the place was set up with a grant from the European Commission. Specialises in post-rock electronica – sometimes including stars from the US and UK underground scene like Califone – but also showcases other more traditional styles. *See also p200.*

VK Club

76 rue de l'Ecole, Molenbeek (02 414 29 07/ www.vaartkapoen.be; tickets can be reserved by email at vkconcerts@skynet.be). Métro Comte de Flandre/ bus 89. **Open** *Box office 9am-6pm. Concerts 7.30pm.* **Tickets** €10-€17. **No credit cards. Map** p316 A2.

Just as the nominally Francophone Botanique has its Flemish counterpart in the Ancienne Belgique, Magasin 4 (*see p193*) has a Flemish twin in the Vaartkapoen or VK. It is managed by civil servants from the Flemish Cultural Community and is used by day for literacy courses for the unemployed, an adult education centre with a huge glitterball on the ceiling. It's also one of the few places where bad-tempered Mancunian sage Mark E Smith seems to enjoy himself – he is a regular visitor with The Fall. It is also popular with ageing reggae greats – Desmond Dekker, Sugar Minott and Freddie McGregor all played here recently. The place itself is great, but beware that the area can be rough. The venue run buses from the Gare Centrale – phone for details.

Jazz, folk & world venues

Brussels has a venerable jazz tradition. Belgians **Django Reinhardt**, **Bobby Jaspar** and especially **Toots** (*Midnight Cowboy*) **Thielemans** made global reputations after the war. Reinhardt and Jaspar died young but Thielemans is very much alive, kicking and blowing his harmonica well into his 80s. He is sometimes partnered on stage by another Belgian jazz great, guitarist **Philip Catherine**, who recorded with Chet Baker in the 1980s and also accompanied Charlie Mingus. Other star contemporary names are pianist **Nathalie Lorier**, guitarist and composer **Maxime Blésin** and the **Houben family**, sax player father **Steven** and trumpeter son **Gregory**.

Arts & Entertainment

The number of traditional jazz clubs may have fallen, but this is symptomatic of the economics of running small venues, not of any end to Brussels' love affair with jazz. Newer venues include the **Music Village** and **L'Arts-O-Base**, and the number of jazz acts appearing at the bigger rock and pop venues are testimony to the continuing enthusiasm. A new venue entirely devoted to the genre, the **Jazz Station** is due to open in early 2005 in an old railway station at 193 chaussée de Louvain in St-Josse. It's being set up by the musicians' association **Les Lundis d'Hortense**, presided over by leading sax player Manuel Hermia. The association also provides listings and contacts at www.jazzinbelgium.org.

The annual **Jazz Marathon Festival**, though aimed more at pub crawlers than musical purists, attracts visitors from around Europe for hundreds of gigs in May.

Brussels also stages some of the best world music around, much of it home-grown: award-winning a cappella outfit **Zap Mama** grew out of an African vocal workshop in Brussels. For visits from some of Africa's biggest stars, keep an eye out for fly posters around Matongé, the African quarter in Ixelles (*see also p87* **African Brussels**). The main world music event is the **Couleur Café** festival in June at the **Tour et Taxis** (*see also p94* **On the Waterfront**).

Beware that jazz venues also host exponents of *chanson française*, romantic balladeers with occasional Belgian humour. The big names – Frenchman **Alain Bashung** or Brussels' own **Maurane** (Claudine Luypaerts) – can sell out faster than most rock acts.

L'Archiduc
6 rue Antoine Dansaert, Lower Town (02 512 06 52/www.archiduc.be). Pré-métro Bourse. **Open** 4pm-dawn daily. **Tickets** free-€10. **Credit** AmEx, DC, MC, V. **Map** p316 B3.
Built in the 1930s, this little art deco jewel used to be an after-hours club for jazz fans. Nat King Cole used to drop by for an après-gig drink and to tinkle the ivories. Brel was also a regular. Bands at the Ancienne Belgique tend to finish the night here. Free Saturday gigs (Jazz Après Shopping) feature local musicians; Sunday concerts (€10) bring in artists from further afield. Both begin around 5pm. Ring the doorbell to enter. *See also p134.*

L'Arts-O-Base
43 rue Ulens, Molenbeek (0477 46 48 06/www.jazzvalley.com/venue/arts-o-base). Métro Yser. **Open** 7.30pm-late Tue-Sat. *Concerts* 9.30pm. **Tickets** €6-€10; free Tue. **No credit cards.**
This atmospheric jazz club across the canal from the city centre presents music ranging from the tradi-tional to the challenging and guarantees a good night out into the bargain. Wednesday nights, when bands are booked in for a four-week stint, provide

an opportunity for them to try out new things – and customers to enjoy a decent three-course meal with the €21 entrance fee. Friday tends to attract some slightly better-known artists, Saturday brings world music and Tuesday's jam sessions are free.

Athanor Studio
Arlequin Hotel, 17-19 rue de la Fourche, Lower Town (02 514 16 15/www.studio-athanor.be). Métro/pré-métro De Brouckère. **Open** 9pm-late Tue-Sat. **Tickets** free-€10. **Credit** MC, V. **Map** p315 C3.
Although part of a bland city centre hotel – you have to go through the foyer to get in – there's a real night-club ambience to the Athanor, with a long bar down one side and plenty of intimate corners. No night is the same as the next: its regular programme includes everything from hip hop DJs (*see p199*) to self-styled purveyors of 'ethno-Coltranian rock' Slang, with local jazz luminary Manuel Hermia. Budding musi-cians can work join the Wednesday music school (8-10pm, book ahead), followed by a jam session.

Le Backstage
36 rue du Fossé aux Loups, Lower Town (02 223 04 34). Métro/pré-métro De Brouckère. **Open** 7.30pm-late Wed-Sat. *Concerts* 10pm. **Tickets** free; €5 Fri. **No credit cards. Map** p315 C2.
This bright new venue in the city centre concen-trates on showcasing up-and-coming young talents in jazz, blues and *chanson française*. On Wednesday nights anyone can turn up and perform. Friday is party night with resident all-female vocal quartet Singing Coyote Team performing their swooping harmonies over backing tracks. Saturdays tend to feature more relaxed acts.

Candelaershuys
433 avenue Brugmann, Uccle (02 343 46 58/www.candelaershuys.be). Tram 91, 92. **Open** varies. **Tickets** €8-€12. **No credit cards.**
Like VK (*see p194*) this is part of the local network of state-supported Flemish cultural centres. Unlike VK, it's in a beautiful old house in a well-heeled (though not very Flemish) part of town. Just about everything goes on here, from theatre groups through poetry readings to concerts a couple of times a month by prestigious jazz, rock and world acts. These have recently included Toots Thielemans, Flip Kowlier and an eight-piece from Romania called the Virtuozzii Transilvaniei.

Espace Senghor
366 chaussée de Wavre, EU Quarter (02 230 31 40/www.senghor.be). Métro Maelbeek/bus 59. **Open** varies. **Tickets** €5-€15. **No credit cards. Map** p322 F5.
The French-speaking community restored and now runs this venue adjacent to the ghastly concrete and cultural desert that is the EU district of Brussels. It has an imaginative and popular programme of jazz and world music concerts, usually three or four times a month. It's not the place for a riotous night out and there's unlikely to be any dancing in the aisles, but the choice of music is usually excellent.

Arts & Entertainment

Flagey

Place Sainte-Croix (next to place Flagey), Ixelles (02 641 10 20/www.flagey.be). Tram 81, 82/bus 38, 60, 71. **Open** varies. **Tickets** €10-€25. **Credit** AmEx, DC, MC, V. **Map** p322 D7.

This new arts complex in the gorgeous art deco building that formerly housed Belgium's state TV and radio stations has an eclectic mix of live music with jazz the first Thursday of every month and sometimes other nights too. There's also a varied programme of world music featuring major artists. *See also p88* **All aboard!**

Kafé Kan'h

30 place de la Vieille Halle aux Blés, Lower Town (02 502 00 07/www.kanh.be). Métro Gare Centrale. **Open** 4pm-late Mon-Fri; 11am-late Sat, Sun. *Concerts* 9pm. **Tickets** free-€7. **No credit cards. Map** p315 C4.

Although it styles itself as a 'cultural meeting place' and hosting philosophical debates and yoga classes, the Kan'h is unpretentious, relaxed and fun. There's live African or Caribbean music on Wednesdays (free) and improvised jazz on Thursdays (free), plus everything from DJs to nude contemporary dance on Fridays and jazz, world or *chanson française* on Saturdays (€5-€7). It also organises 'Lazy Sundays' from 5pm, with board games and music. The food is good, and cheap too. Highly recommended for an intriguing night out. *See also p128.*

Music Village

50 rue des Pierres, Lower Town (02 513 13 45/ www.themusicvillage.com). Pré-métro Bourse. **Open** 7pm-late Wed-Sat. *Concerts* 9pm. **Tickets** €10-€18; €9 concessions; *membership* €7-€10/year, €2/day. **Credit** MC, V. **Map** p315 B3.

Opened in 2000, the Music Village is a members-only club (but you can join for the night) occupying two 17th-century buildings near the Grand' Place. The Village provides a home for more traditional jazz styles, as well as the occasional more avant-garde act (booking advisable). Every other Wednesday is new talent night, and on the first Thursday of every month there is a jam session led by a professional but open to all. Weekdays attract a lot of business visitors but Fridays and Saturdays are reserved for performers sufficiently well known to fill the place with local jazz aficionados.

Sounds Jazz Club

28 rue de la Tulipe, Ixelles (02 512 92 50/www. jazzvalley.com/sounds). Métro Porte de Namur/bus 54, 71. **Open** 8pm-4am Mon-Sat;. *Concerts* 10pm. **Tickets** free-€15. **No credit cards. Map** p319 D6.

For nearly 20 years, Sounds has been a compulsory port of call for the local jazz nomenclature. Far enough out of town – though only 15 minutes by bus – to discourage tourists, Sounds attracts a fair measure of expats and Eurocrats who've swapped their grey suits for glad rags. One Saturday a month it's the Brussels Rhythm and Blues Club, which interprets its remit loosely enough to welcome rock and soul artists. The rest of the time, Sounds favours modern-ish jazz, but there is also the odd big band night and Wednesday is usually Latino. It also stays open very late for that authentic next-day pallor.

La Soupape

26A rue Alphonse de Witte, Ixelles (02 649 58 88/ www.lasoupape.be.tf). Tram 81, 82/bus 38, 60, 71. **Open** *Concerts* 9pm Fri, Sat. **Tickets** €8. **No credit cards. Map** p325 E7.

Intimate, fun venue in a side street in the ever more lively area near place Flagey and the Ixelles lakes. Specialises in *chanson française* – it holds heats for its national bi-annual competition. La Soupape hosts many acts destined to be seen later by far more than the 50 people squeezed around its rickety tables.

La Tentation

28 rue de Laeken, Lower Town (02 223 22 75/ www.latentation.org). Métro/pré-métro De Brouckère. **Open** 7pm-1am Fri, Sat, event nights. **Tickets** €5-€10. **Credit** AmEx, DC, MC, V. **Map** p315 B2.

This fine building with its Horta staircase was saved by the Centro Gallego, run by Brussels' Galician community. It has a commendably eclectic approach in its world music concerts, held twice monthly. As well as traditional Galician music, it puts on flamenco, salsa and even Flemish folk (flamenco, the Spanish for 'Flemish', was originally a perjorative catch-all for all undesirables, not least Gypsies and Flemish representatives at the Spanish court). The centre also runs courses in belly dancing and the Galician bagpipes. *See also p133.*

Théâtre Marni

23-25 rue de Vergnies, Ixelles (02 639 09 80/ www.marni.org). Tram 81, 82/bus 71. **Open** 8pm-2am Tue-Sat. *Concerts* 8.30pm. **Tickets** €5-€15. **No credit cards. Map** p322 E7.

This renovated theatre, a former bowling alley near place Flagey, has a varied and frequent agenda of high-quality jazz and world music from Belgium and beyond. Gigs take place in the large and comfortable main theatre or in the entrance hall. The organisers of the late and much lamented Travers jazz club, whose own venue closed in 2000, continue to host innovative new performers here, mainly during two seasons in May and September. Like many venues, the Marni also has a splendid bar – no need to go home once the gig has finished.

Tours et Taxis

3 rue Picard, Molenbeek (02 420 60 69/www.tour taxis.be). Métro Ribaucourt or Belgica/bus 14. **Open** *Concerts* varies. *Festival* last weekend in June. **Tickets** *Festival* €21/day; €50/3 days. **No credit cards.**

During its slow renovation this vast former customs warehouse provides the four stages for one of the biggest world music festivals in Europe, Couleur Café (www.couleurcafe.org). There's space for a crafts village, workshops and 50 food stalls. The festival is yet to find a permanent home; while it does, the Tours is establishing itself as a venue in its own right. *See also p94* **On the waterfront.**

Nightlife

An easy scene in Brussels and beyond.

The Fuse. *See p199.*

In this small country, club culture spreads nationwide rather than being dependant on Brussels to provide focused inspiration. The serious clubber can be in Ghent or Antwerp in a shorter time than it takes to cross London, and with trains starting early in the morning, the trip home is guaranteed too. This doesn't mean that Brussels is bereft of decent places to party, far from it, but it does tend to be safer in its mix, appealing to a more mainstream dance crowd, while the provinces delve deeper into the underground. For events in **Antwerp**, **Bruges**, **Ghent**, **Leuven** and **Liège**, *see pp217-283*.

Belgium takes its clubbing very seriously, arguing that it was the birthplace of European techno. This techno-babble is largely down to one man, the legendary DJ Pierre who placed Brussels' most enduring club, the **Fuse**, firmly on the dance map. This is a venue that any DJ wants to work and it oversees the most renowned spinners – Sven Väth included – as they pump up the volume.

But it's not just about techno. Belgium is the land of experimental electronica, breakbeats, deep house, drum 'n' bass and a full-on psychedelic trance scene. The latter is a classic example of the regions coming up trumps, with Brussels largely left out of the fluoro-party scene, and places like Ghent, Antwerp and even the

pastoral Lier drawing the more alternative crowd. The best place to find out about trance parties is www.goatrance.de, an international database with detailed listings (you can even organise car lifts for remote places). For the whole gamut of party genres in Brussels and beyond, www.noctis.com is the most informative and up-to-date site. Also, http://boups.be has full listings, albeit in a more restrained way.

Back in Brussels, the scene divides itself into the permanent branded club, running its own agenda, or the one-offs held at different venues around the city (some are in the darker recesses, so be prepared to cab it). Apart from the Fuse, there is the distinctive **Recyclart** whose mission is to give new talent a kick-start. Once their reputation is assured, they have to move on – giving the venue a cutting-edge, risky feel. **Ric's Boat** remains an institution, a barge on the canal that keeps the punters afloat with a range of sounds from garage to techno. The **Mirano Continental** has worked its way into the night-psyche with its weekly **Dirty Dancing**. On top of this, Brussels has a reputation for what are known as 'night bars', places to dance without having to wear the mantle of a club. Examples include the effervescent **Pablo Discobar**, the iconic **Dali's Bar** and steamy **Havana**, one of many Latin-inspired places in town.

A recent development is the opening of Thursday after-work clubs, aimed at single people. The one at the Mirano, **@Seven**, attracts a well-dressed professional crowd who exchange business cards as they dance. Havana on Wednesday nights even offers free tapas.

Admission prices to clubs are reasonable, often with reductions for early entry; drinks bills are bearable. Credit cards are rarely accepted. Some clubs still have the bouncer on the door who shoves their hand out as you leave – give them a euro, it finishes the evening

Brussels by night Cosy Mozzy

Local talent DJ Cosy Mozzy, aka Renaud Déru, and his crew Dirty Dancing have taken Brussels nightlife by storm. To say that a new soirée in the capital was needed is an understatement: young night owls were flying off to booming Ghent or proudly established Antwerp. Luckily, Cosy Mozzy signed a contract in 2003 as artistic director of the **Mirano Continental** (*see p197 and p201*), firing up both his career and the local scene. Renaud, who started mixing rock and new wave at the age of 12, is no newcomer to the scene, previously acknowledged for his house nights in Brussels spanning a decade. Now he holds residencies all over town, and pops

up at festivals and one-nighters all over the country, including **Ten Days Off** (*see p262* **The best fest in Belgium**) and the **Culture Club** (*see p264*), both in Ghent. His eclectic style and music tastes – house, electro, nu-jazz, new wave and pop – ensures he remains adaptable not just to the style of the set, but to the needs of the crowd. Despite all this, it's **Dirty Dancing** (*see p201*) that has grabbed the attention of the city's movers. 'I wanted to start a night that merged class, a cosmopolitan crowd, gay and straight, and innovative tunes into a space where people can meet every Saturday night,' says Renaud. Ambitious, maybe. Successful, definitely.

nicely. A last practical point: be sure of the dress code for your party. Those that attract a professional thirtysomething crowd may not be too enamoured with trainers, while the underground mob will sneer at Gucci loafers.

Clubs

Athanor Studio

17-19 rue de la Fourche, Lower Town (02 514 16 15/www.studio-athanor.be). Métro/pré-métro De Brouckère or métro Gare Centrale. **Open** 9pm-late Tue-Sat. **Admission** free-€10. **Credit** MC, V. **Map** p315 C3.

To find this tucked-away music club, you need to walk into the gallery at the front of the Hotel Arlequin (*see p41*); there's little sign of it from the street. The Athanor has a reputation as a jazz venue (*see p195*) and very good it is too, but it regularly throws its doors open to strictly clubby nights, with an emphasis on solid black roots music. Serious funk, reggae and ragga, plus the monthly old-school funk and soul night Strictly Niceness with DJ Kwak from the African music bar Kafé Kan'h (*see p196 and p128*). In terms of overall feel, it's a loungey and sophisticated sort of place with its crimson plush sofas and seats, it develops decently into a red-tinged night of thickly atmospheric rhythms.

Beursschouwburg Café

20-28 rue Auguste Orts, Lower Town (02 550 03 50/www.beursschouwburg.be). Pré-métro Bourse. **Open** 7.30pm-late Thur-Sat (DJs from 10pm). **Admission** free. **Map** p315 B3.

The theatre and bar are back with a bang after a couple of years' overhaul (*see p210*) and the gap that was left in this busy part of town has been refilled. Bar is something of a misnomer for this cavernous space, raw brick and red, with young trendy Flemings dancing to hard house and new-wave electronica. The joy of the Beurs is that you can come and go as you please; as the evening deepens, so does the atmosphere. The tables laid out for earlier evening conversation stay in place, but not the punters who make use of any space available to lose themselves awhile. Also, as part of the new programming policy, more right-on club nights are planned including the regular Fotones 5.0, an electronic experiments night in collaboration with a Brussels-based record label.

Le Coaster

28 rue des Riches Claires, Lower Town (no phone). Pré-métro Bourse. **Open** 8pm-5am Mon-Thur; 8pm-7am Fri, Sat. **Admission** free. **No credit cards**. **Map** p316 B3.

Not a club per se, the Coaster is a wild blip in the regularised St-Géry bar scene. Two rooms crammed into a 17th-century house fill up with young guys and gals out for a night of danceable music without the rigmarole of a nightclub. There's even table football. Reasonable drinks prices (with intelligent happy hours up to 11pm), an easy-going crowd out for a laugh and dancing on the tables when there's no more space makes Le C soar like a rocket. A doorman will keep you outside if it's dangerously packed to its old rafters.

Dali's Bar

35 petite rue des Bouchers, Lower Town (no phone). Métro/pré-métro De Brouckère or métro Gare Centrale. **Open** 10pm-5am Tue-Sat. **Admission** free. **No credit cards. Map** p315 C3.

This petite club – it holds around 120 – has become a byword for nightly partying on a human scale. Trip hop, house, chill and even didgeridoo competitions give the place an edge. Well-known DJs such as Cosy Mozzy (*see p198* **Brussels by night**) and Svenus are happy to play here and the 1970s disco nights some Thursdays are exactly what you'd expect. But retro it ain't and Dali's keeps smack up to date with cutting-edge nights like the FWF crew (www.futureworldfunk.be). Dali's isn't deep and meaningful, but it's a firmly fixed fun spot on the Brussels scene.

The Fuse

208 rue Blaes, Lower Town (02 511 97 89/www.fuse.be). Métro/pré-métro Porte de Hal/bus 27, 48. **Open** 10pm-5am Thur; 10pm-7am Fri, Sat. **Admission** 10-11pm €3; after 11pm €8. **Credit** V. **Map** p318 B4.

The Fuse celebrates its tenth birthday in 2004, and over the last decade has seen the world's best DJs at its decks. Fuse is the only club in Brussels with a truly international reputation and the current residents – Pierre, Deg, T-Quest and Psychogene – draw crowds from all over Benelux, France and Germany. On the first floor, Motion is a differently styled dancefloor filled with uplifting UK house and deep house mixed by resident St Dic and more experimental jocks. The Fuse also hosts La Démence (*see p185*), the biggest and brightest gay night in Belgium. Don't come expecting a sleek futuristic superclub: the Fuse is more like a disused Spanish hacienda turned into a crazy music box of two floors of 2,000 people cranked up to the max.

Havana

4 rue de l'Epée, Lower Town (02 502 12 24/www.havana-brussels.com). Tram 92, 93, 94. **Open** 7pm-3am Wed; 7pm-4am Thur; 7pm-7am Fri, Sat. **Admission** free. **Credit** MC, V. **Map** p318 B5.

In the shadow of the Palais de Justice, Havana is a classy joint carved out of an old Marollien house, attracting an international, professional crowd. You can eat, drink (three bars) or just dance to Latin-based live acts, degenerating into a popular, wild free-for-all as the evening moves into the wee hours.

Lounge Club

25 rue Henri Maus, Lower Town (02 510 05 52). Pré-métro Bourse. **Open** midnight-8am Fri, Sat. **Admission** free-€12. **Credit** AmEx, DC, MC, V. **Map** p315 B3.

It couldn't be more different from its neighbour, the art nouveau café Falstaff (*see p127*), but the Lounge has made its mark on downtown Brussels in just the same way. A deep, dark spot with a soaring sound and light combo and an atmosphere of faded glory, Lounge draws on a young repeat crowd of up to 800. Primarily a weekend club, its fame rests on its embedded Friday drum 'n' bass/hip hop night, Caramel, and its Saturday deep house parties. Web presence is low, so you'll have to check out www.noctis.com (*see also p197*) or just turn up for a deeply wild weekend blow-out.

MP3 Café

17-19 rue du Pont de la Carpe, Lower Town (no phone). Pré-métro Bourse. **Open** 5pm-late Mon-Sat. **No credit cards**. **Map** p316 B3.
Busy late-night DJ bar in the heart of St-Géry, with a stylish interior of a curving bar counter, a row of brown stools and a bar length of mirror. Facing this across a narrow space is a stretch of banquette leading to a modest raised dance area, two semi-circles of seats and a disco ball. All of this is mere decoration – a hindrance, even – to the buzz of activity by the decks at the far end of the bar counter, and the confined vibrant dancing post-midnight. The DJs could do with a little polishing, but that's Brussels for you – hey, there might just be some work in this town for you. A nearby larger version of same might empty the place, but not just yet.

Pablo Discobar

60 rue du Marché aux Charbon, Lower Town (02 514 51 49/www.pablodiscobar.com). Pré-métro Bourse. **Open** 9pm-3am Wed-Sat. **Admission** free. **No credit cards**. **Map** p315 B3.
This old stalwart, in the heart of bar-crawl land, has been pulling in the cocktail-sipping set since 1996. More a bar than a club, it draws top name acts (Felix Da Housecat, Eva Gotan Project, to drop but two) who play solid, funky house and garage to a crowd that loves the thick and cosy atmosphere. Perfect for those in a crowd or on the pull.

Recyclart

Gare de Bruxelles-Chapelle, 25 rue des Ursulines, Lower Town (02 502 57 34/www.recyclart.be). Métro Gare Centrale/pré-métro Anneessens/bus 95, 96. **Open** varies. **Admission** free-€7. **No credit cards**. **Map** p315 B4.
Part of an urban regeneration project under the old Chapelle railway station, Recyclart is a hotbed of discovery. A full agenda of new electronic sounds gives the young crowd something to funk about, as new talent gets a chance to showcase its spin-doctoring. Varied, inventive and always throbbing, this place is a must-be for anyone who wants to be in the know – tomorrow's big names start here. Occasional exhibitions are also held here (*see p180*).

Ric's Boat

44B quai des Peniches, Lower Town (02 203 67 28/ http://users.skynet.be/rics-art-boat). Métro Yser. **Open** & **admission** varies. **No credit cards**. **Map** p316 B1.
It's an unlikely setting, but this floater, moored up on the Brussels canal, is one of the city's most sought-after venues. It hosts a whole range of hard-core nights, from garage through drum 'n' bass to deeply hypnotic trance and techno, though its most valued event has to be the monthly NEMO party (www.undergroundadventures.be), a deeply underground adventure that kicks hard.

Festivals

Pay & Go Groove City

www.paygogroovecity.be.
A classic case of the men in suits – in this instance the Belgacom mobile provider – deciding a groovy name on behalf of a young audience. Despite that, this annual (November) electronic dance bash in Brussels is huge and draws an eclectic crowd to its techno, drum 'n' bass, house and chill rooms. Check the website for further details.

Brussels by night Olivier Gosseries

Olivier Gosseries has been an essential and influential mover on the Belgian nightscape since 1986, when he started out with his mentor, Poltergeist, in the now defunct Brussels club, Imagin'Air. House was the name of the game, straight in from America, and OG soon developed his own house style of mainstream disco and funk, interspersed with the latest US sound. Showing no fear of the purely danceable, he featured at the **Mirano Continental** (*see p197 and p201*) and Antwerp's **Café d'Anvers** (*see p234* **Antwerp: Clubbing capital**), which sent his career into an upward spiral. The famed Who's Who Land took him on as resident DJ, his

blend of funk, R&B and happy house sending him on to Paris (Queen's and Palace), Pacha of Ibiza and, nearer home, the **Fuse** (*see p197 and p199*) and **La Rocca** in Lier (*see p201*).

In 2001, he started an eponymous record label, and his own radio show, *Noise in Fun* on Fun every Saturday (104.7 FM, 10pm-midnight). His most recent residency was at the gay **Strong** club and cabaret (*see p186*), where he kicked up a storm with his happy house for happy boys. Now permanently on tour, OG remains Belgium's top house DJ and producer; locals are proud of their home-grown boy – wherever he appears, they're sure to follow.

One-nighters

@Seven

Mirano Continental, 38 chaussée de Louvain, St-Josse (02 227 39 56/www.at7.be). Métro Madou. **Open** 7pm-1am Thur. **Admission** €75 annual membership; €5 pass for 1st visit. **No credit cards. Map** p320 E3.
Started by German Patrick Strum, this is a meet-and-greet concept borrowed from New York. Deliberately international and multilingual, it reaches deep into those expat parts that other clubs can't reach. Dressy in a casual way, the after-workers come here to dance and network – there are even conversation tables to break the ice for those difficult moments. The concept is spreading through Belgium and looks set to break a mould in early evening clubbing.

Club Les Minimes

57 rue des Minimes, Lower Town (no phone/ www.bncevents.be). Tram 92, 93, 94/bus 20, 48. **Open** 11pm-5am Sat. **Admission** €5. **No credit cards. Map** p318 C5.
A rotation of progressive house nights gets this cosy place full and hot. Residents Chris Dee and Sebu keep it moving, with occasional drop-ins from the Progressivity outfit (house, trance and a bit of retro). Minimes is popular with the Sablon set and entrenched bar-hoppers from the dens of the Marolles, making it a safely steamy after-hours place to be.

Dirty Dancing

Mirano Continental, 38 chaussée de Louvain, St-Josse (02 227 39 48/www.dirtydancing.be). Métro Madou. **Open** 10.30pm-6am Sat. **Admission** before midnight €5; midnight-4am €10. **No credit cards. Map** p320 E3.
Dirty has clambered its way to the top of the pile, from being a risky newcomer to full-on acceptance with the picky club crowd. Three concepts take centre stage on a rotating basis: house night Everybody Hates House Music with guests such as UK DJ Justin; electro night Rockneedselectrofreaks with internationally acclaimed guests such as DJ Hell and resident Cosy Mozzy (*see p198* **Brussels by night**); and Future Pop, a night blending all styles from 1980s hits to Kylie. Future Pop always features a midnight rock concert, taking advantage of the large stage. There's also a rotating dancefloor, interactive concerts and live acts, a 1930s themed chill-out lounge upstairs, plus breakfast at 4am. You need to look good to get in here, so dress sharp.

Essential

Various venues (no phone/www.submedia.com).
Essential started up at Recyclart (*see p200*) and established itself as a premier breaks 'n' beats combo, serving up a slice of freshly elegant electronica with eerie vocals and freeform samples to give it edge. Since then it hasn't settled into any one venue on a regular basis, but when it does, the young alternative crowd are there for the spiky sounds and deep underground feel. Keep an eye on the website for party dates – you won't be disappointed.

Mirano, home to @Seven and Dirty Dancing.

Further afield

La Bush

180 chaussée de Tournai, Esquelmes (06 955 61 17/ www.labush.com). **Open** 11pm-8am Sat, Sun, nights before holidays. **Admission** €10. **Credit** AmEx, DC, MC, V.
One of the biggest and most popular trance clubs in Belgium, with a capacity of 2,100.

Cherry Moon

144 Gentsesteenweg, Lokeren (09 349 01 38/www. cherrymoon.com). **Open** 10pm-7am Fri, Sat, nights before holidays. **Admission** €8. **No credit cards.**
One of Belgium's biggest (room for 2,000 people) and longest-serving clubs – playing hard trance and techno since 1991.

Club Mystique

10 Hoeven, Vosselaar (01 442 37 25/www.club mystique.be). **Open** 11pm-8am Fri, Sat, nights before holidays. **Admission** €10. **No credit cards.**
Saturdays and every second and third Friday on two levels: hard trance on the upper deck, club and disco on the lower. A hefty party spot.

La Rocca

384 Antwerpsesteenweg, Lier (03 489 17 67/ www.larocca.be). **Open** 11pm-7.30am Fri-Sun. **Admission** €5-€10. **No credit cards.**
Between Antwerp and Mechelen, Rocca is part of Belgium's clubbing history, all-hallowed and treated with the greatest respect. No trackies or trainers.

The Zoo

106 Kempischesteenweg, Hasselt (0477 29 88 01/ www.thezoo.be). **Open** 9pm-late Fri, Sat. **Admission** free-€5. **No credit cards.**
Described as the ultimate electronic dance café (it actually holds around 400 people), Zoo is democratic partying at its best. Drum 'n' bass, techno, breaks and psytrance make up the mix.

Arts & Entertainment

Sport & Fitness

Let's get physical.

Sport in Belgium isn't about glamour. The more obscure the sporting pastime, the better. Finch-singing contests (www.avibo.be) are a feature of spring Sundays around Flanders. Pigeon racing, French boules and, above all, cycling, are national obsessions. Grocer's son Eddy Merckx won the Tour de France five times, but it's the sport's amateur status and muddy grind that have engrained it into the psyche in both Flanders and Wallonia. Each community has its own sports organisation: French-speaking **ADEPS** (02 413 23 11, www.adeps.be) and Flemish **BLOSO** (02 209 45 11, www.bloso.be).

Belgium's cultural and linguistic fracture is embodied in the only figures to qualify as true sporting heroes, tennis aces Justine Henin-Hardenne and Kim Clijsters. Fleming Clijsters, daughter of international footballer Leo, has met Walloon Henin for all-Belgian Grand Slam finals in Australia, France and America. Their

success is not matched in other sporting disciplines – Belgium's football team failed to qualify for the European Championships of 2004.

Belgium has only once played host to the Olympics, in Antwerp in 1920. With Jacques Rogge president of the International Olympic Committee, Belgium may bid for the Games of 2016; if 2012 goes to Paris, Belgium's chances are nil. But one local annual event, borrowed from Paris, has brightened up the sporting horizon: August's city beach (www.brucity.be) at canalside quai des Péniches boasts volleyball and sunbathing.

Spectator sports

With only a limited number of suitable venues, Brussels is hardly a world stage for spectator sports. The national stadium, **Stade Roi Baudouin**, hosts most major events, such as international athletics, cycling races and home games of the national football team. News on all spectator sports can be found at www.sport.be.

Stade Roi Baudouin

Avenue du Marathon, Laeken (02 474 39 40). Métro Heysel or Roi Baudouin. **Map** p326 A2.

Formerly the Heysel, Belgium's national stadium was a crumbling ruin when it closed after the tragedy of 1985, when 39 fans died at a European Cup Final. Ten years later it re-opened as the Roi Baudouin, a 50,000-capacity all-seater with its own metro stop and sports bar, Extra-Time. The four stands are colour-coded: *tribune* 1 (red) houses the most expensive seats, 2 (yellow) and 4 (blue) are behind the goals and 3 (green) is along avenue des Athlètes by the Heysel métro stop.

Athletics

The prestigious Ivo Van Damme Memorial (www.sport.be/memorialvandamme), held at Roi Baudouin in September, draws top stars.

Cycling

The main event on the pro circuit is the Tour of Flanders (www.rvv.be) on the first Sunday in April, a day-long race in which riders tackle the steep cobbled hills of the Ardennes. The Grand Prix Eddy Merckx is the main speed trial, at the Roi Baudouin in August.

Football

Belgium began an eternal rivalry with France and the Netherlands in the early 1900s, and made the World Cup semi-finals in 1986. The current side lack experience and face a tough time against Spain and Serbia to qualify for the 2006 World Cup finals in Germany.

A league of four divisions is dominated by **Anderlecht**, Brussels' major club and the most recognisable name in Belgian football. To watch a First Division match you need to buy a Fan Card for €12.50, obtained from any club's ticket office. For Anderlecht, arrange one before match day. The Belgian FA runs an extensive website at www.footbel.com. The daily sports supplement in French-language *La Dernière Heure* has full coverage of the local scene.

RSC Anderlecht

Stade Constant Vanden Stock, 2 avenue Théo Verbeeck, Anderlecht (02 522 15 39/tickets 02 529 40 67/www.rsca.be). Métro St-Guidon. **Admission** €11-€32. **No credit cards**.

Anderlecht are still the biggest club in the land, the club's regular appearances in the Champions League harking back to European triumphs 25 years ago. On match days the bars along avenue Théo Verbeeck by the impressive stadium are packed

with fans. (If you've failed to organise the necessary club card, one bar offers a service of borrowing one in order to nip to the stadium and buy a ticket.) The home end, stand 4, is raucous, and heavy if Bruges are in town. *See p205* **Purple reign**.

FC Brussels

Stade Edmond Machtens, 61 rue Charles Malis, Molenbeek (02 411 69 86/www.fcmbs.be). Métro Gare de l'Ouest then tram 82, 83. **Admission** €10-€30. **No credit cards**.

FC Brussels was created in 2003 with the fusion of RWD Molenbeek and KFC Strombeek. Currently bidding for promotion to the top flight, FCB have a small following of fans and a lively brass band who liven up home games amid the gloom of Molenbeek.

Royale Union St-Gilloise

Stade Joseph Mariën, 223 chaussée de Bruxelles, St-Gilles (02 344 16 56/www.rusg.be). Tram 18, 52/bus 48, 54. **Admission** €7.50 standing; €12.50-€25 sitting. **No credit cards**.

Champions before the war, and Brussels' flagship team before the arrival of Anderlecht, Union exist on past glories. Their pitch hewn out of the Duden forest, Union are a football romantic's dream, the communal atmosphere in the clubhouse on Sunday afternoons a treat in these cold, commercial times.

Motor sport

The Spa-Francorchamps track, two and a half hours from Brussels is a tricky course built into dense Ardennes forest. It hosts motorbike races, a 24-hour event and the Belgian Grand Prix in late August (070 23 23 10, www.belgium-grandprix.be). Buses 4 and 4A run the eight kilometres (five miles) from Spa station to the track. Many Belgians prefer the motorcross equivalent, the Namur Grand Prix, also in August (www.gpnamur.com).

Tennis

For ten days in February top players compete for a thousand-diamond studded tennis racket in the Proximus Diamond Games, held at Antwerp's Sportpaleis (www.sport.be/proximusdiamondgames). Any player who wins three years in a row gets to keep the prize.

Participation sports

With its large expat contingent, Brussels is full of sports clubs in almost every discipline. Most gyms, courts and clubs listed do not need long-term contracts or memberships. Contact www.expatsinbrussels.be, www.xpats.com, and the **American Women's Club of Brussels** (02 358 47 53, www.awcb.org). For youngsters, the **Brussels Sports Association** (02 354 11 14, www.bsasports.org) runs sports for the expat and local communities; the **British School** sports centre (19 Leuvensesteenweg, Tervuren, www.britishschool.be) for Brits. Municipal sports centres are spread over the city. Bounded by forests and parkland, Brussels also offers ample opportunity for jogging and cycling, easily accessible by public transport. Sports federations can be found at www.sport.be.

Badminton

The Brussels International Badminton Club (www.brusselsbadminton.com) reserves courts in Wezembeek Oppem, Woluwe-St-Lambert and Waterloo up to four times a week for matches, coaching and casual play for its members. The Irish International Badminton Club plays Tuesday nights from September to June at the British School (*see above*). Many fitness centres (*see p206*) hire out courts, and Move Zone (12 Général Thys, Ixelles, 02 644 55 44) has five to rent at €14 per hour. The sports centre at VUB university (*see p206*) also hires to non-members.

Billiards, snooker & pool

Cercle Royal de Billard Leopold

Palais du Midi, 3 rue Roger Van der Weyden, Lower Town (02 511 10 08/http://users.skynet.be/leoserie). Pré-métro Anneessens. **Open** 2pm-midnight Mon, Tue, Thur, Fri; 2-6pm Wed; 2-8pm Sat. **No credit cards. Map** p318 B4.
Members can enjoy a quiet hour at the baize for €3.50 on the third floor of this sports complex. Membership is available for €30-€60 per year.

Sharkey's

32 rue Marché aux Poulets, Lower Town (02 219 49 01). Métro/pré-métro De Brouckère or pré-métro Bourse. **Open** 11am-2am Mon-Thur, Sun; 11am-4am Fri, Sat. **Admission** €8.15 per hr. **No credit cards. Map** p315 B3.
A big and smoky games den, with rows of pool and snooker tables around a central bar.

Bowling

Brussels has a handful of bowling alleys; two of the biggest are listed below. For details of other alleys and bowling clubs, refer to the Belgian Bowling Federation (www.bowling.be).

Crosly Super Bowling

36 boulevard de l'Empereur, Lower Town (02 512 08 74/www.crosly.be). Métro Gare Centrale. **Open** 2pm-1am Mon-Thur; 2pm-2am Fri, Sat; 10am-midnight Sun. **Admission** €2.30-€4.50 per game. **Credit** MC, V. **Map** p315 C4.
Twenty bowling lanes and a late bar, plus Q-Zar laser games for €5.
Other locations: 43 quai au Foin, Lower Town (02 217 28 01).

Climbing

The Belgian Climbing Network (www.belclimb. net) organises expeditions, and its website has a database of climbing routes. The Rochers de Freyr, near Dinant in the Ardennes, is the most important climbing area in Belgium, with seven main crags and over 600 routes. There are a number of man-made walls for all skill levels in outer Brussels. Recommended climbing spots include:

New Rock

136 chaussée de Watermael, Auderghem (02 675 17 60/www.newtoprock.com). Métro Demey/bus 72, 96. **Open** noon-midnight Mon-Fri, Sun; noon-8pm Sat. **Admission** €7.50. **No credit cards.**
This large indoor climbing centre boasts a 7m (23ft) wall for the less experienced, and an 18m (59ft) wall with 21 ropes for the more adventurous. Climbing must be done in pairs. Harnesses and shoes can be hired for €2.50. Courses are available for all levels.

Stone Age

Centre Sportif de la Woluwe, 87 avenue Mounier, Woluwe-St-Lambert (02 777 13 05/www.stone-age.be). Métro Stockel. **Open** 4-11pm Mon, Tue, Thur, Fri; 1-11pm Wed; 1-9.30pm Sat; 11am-9.30pm Sun. **Admission** €7.10. **No credit cards.**
A new climbing centre in a sports complex and a top spot. Individual and group courses for all ages.

Cricket

The Royal Brussels Cricket Club (www.rbcc.be) are the oldest club in Belgium and today play at a top-notch ground in Ohain. The 12 Stars Club (www.12stars.cricket.org) are an international group who play at the British School (*see above*) and run a Junior Cricket programme. See www.cricket-belgium.com for more details.

Cycling

Tramlines, cobbled streets and unfriendly drivers are just a few of the obstacles here. To compensate, some of the wealthier and greener communes have tried to create a network of cycle lanes, but some end abruptly at the next *commune*. Cycle tracks can be found at the Bois de la Cambre and the Forêt de Soignes. Watch for the **Dring Dring Bike Festival** in May (*see p167*), organised by **Pro Vélo**. To do some cycling out of town, use the cheap and easy bike hire scheme run by Belgian railways (02 555 25 55, www.b-rail.be) from April to September. Buy a 'Train-Plus-Vélo' ticket to 23 stations in Belgium and your bicycle will be reserved for you when you arrive. For mountain biking, check out the English-speaking club at www.bigm.be. See www.visitbelgium.com/bike.htm

Purple reign

'Iedereen is bang van Anderlecht, Iedereen is bang van Anderlecht!' *'Est-ce que j'ai pas raison? Oui, tu as raison! Anderlecht, Anderlecht, Anderlecht – champion!'*

Football fans, same the world over, eh? Perhaps not in Brussels. A largely francophone island in a Flemish-speaking region, the city has two communities with different languages, cultures and traditions. Yet the complex politics are transcended by the city's flagship football team, Anderlecht. The club span the linguistic divide in a way politicians could only dream of.

So Anderlecht's fans (www. anderlecht-online.be) sing different songs in two different languages, they hate different teams from their respective (though not respected) communities and they root for different players in the same mauve-and-white shirts. They cry different things at crucial points of the game, a stray ball hitting an opponent's arm causing shouts of 'Main!' from 14,000 spectators or 'Hands!' from the other 14,000 crammed into the intimidating 28,000-capacity Parc Astrid.

The mauve-et-blanc/ paars-witte are based on the industrial western side of Brussels, rarely visited by tourists or, indeed, most residents: neutral ground. Anderlecht can claim nationwide support, with 38 supporters' clubs scattered over Belgium. The players and staff are divided equally among French and Flemish speakers, and switch effortlessly from one language to another mid-sentence. On the pitch English is gradually taking over, the squad numbering up to 15 different nationalities and no one wanting to make an error of judgement due to a misheard call in the fatal rectangle.

Traditionally, Anderlecht were francophone, but in the last 25 years Flemings have flocked to the club from the suburbs and any region not within the Bruges catchment area. As the song says, *'En we breken met z'n allen Brugge af, clap! clap!'* The Walloons, however, are reading from a different hymn sheet: *'Et le Standard, et le Standard, et le Standard! C'est du caca lalala!'*. Standard Liège are the hate figures in half the ground. As for favourites, Pal Zetterberg is a star for Walloon fans (even though he's Swedish), gritty Flemish defender Olivier Deschacht the one whom Flemings sing for.

Stade Roi Baudouin. *See p203.*

for cycling tours organised by the tourist office and www.gamber.net/cyclebel for cycling routes running along Belgium's waterways.

Pro Vélo

15 rue de Londres, Ixelles (02 502 73 55/ www.provelo.org). Métro Trône. **Open** *Nov-Mar* 10am-6pm Mon-Fri. *Apr-Oct* 10am-6pm Mon-Fri, 1-6pm Sat, Sun. **No credit cards. Map** p319 E5.
The unofficial centre of cycling in Brussels is an umbrella organisation working to make the city cycle-friendly. Pro Vélo runs tours and hires out bikes at €12 per day, €20 per weekend. During the summer, it rents out from the Bois de la Cambre, Parc Roi Baudoin in Jette and the Woluwe Park in Woluwe-St-Pierre.

Fitness centres

Many of the private sports centres in town also specialise in certain disciplines, such as martial arts, boxing, squash or swimming. **ADEPS** (*see p202*) runs a number of multi-functional centres. The two in the Brussels area are located in the Forêt de Soignes (02 672 22 60, www.csfds.be) and Woluwé-St-Lambert (02 762 85 22, www.centresportifdelawoluwe.be).

Courts and pitches for many sports can be reserved in advance. Sportcity Woluwe-St-Pierre (02 773 18 20, www.sportcity-woluwe.be) has a similar set-up.

Aspria

View Building, 26-38 rue de l'Industrie, EU Quarter (02 508 0800/www.aspria.be). Métro Arts-Loi. **Open** 6.30am-11pm Mon-Fri; 9am-7pm Sat, Sun. **Admission** €690 per 6mths. **Credit** AmEx, DC, MC, V. **Map** p322 E4.
Aspria has a 21m swimming pool, gym, sauna and crèche. Oasis next door offers beauty treatments and massage therapies. You can book in for a day if accompanied by a member.

Champneys

71B avenue Louise, Ixelles (02 542 46 66/ www.champneys.be). Métro Louise. **Open** 6.30am-10pm Mon-Fri; 8am-8pm Sat, Sun. **Admission** €105-€300 per day; €1,950 plus €300 fee per yr. **Credit** AmEx, DC, MC, V. **Map** p319 C5.
For the ultimate in luxury fitness and spa facilities, Champneys in the Conrad (*see p49*) has a pool, sauna, spa treatments and superior pampering.

Florida Gym

90 avenue des Saisons, Ixelles (02 649 59 39/ www.florida-gym.be). Tram 93, 94/bus 71. **Open** 10am-10pm Mon-Fri; noon-6pm Sat, Sun. **Admission** €7.50 per day; €25 per mth; €275 per yr. **No credit cards. Map** p325 G8.
For a gym without the extras, Florida is a handy and well-priced set-up for weights and cardio machines.

Golden Club

33 place du Châtelain, Ixelles (02 538 19 06/ www.goldenclub.be). Métro Louise then tram 93, 94. **Open** noon-10pm Mon-Fri; 10am-4pm Sat, Sun. **Admission** €25 per day; €200 per mth; €665 per yr. **Credit** AmEx, DC, MC, V. **Map** p324 D7.
Jean-Claude van Damme started building his fit physique here and his former coach is still the manager – not surprisingly, the Golden Club is big on pumping iron and martial arts. A hammam, sunbed and single-sex saunas put glowing skin over that toned physique. *See p91* **Van Damme's Brussels**.

VUB Sportdienst

2 boulevard de la Plaine, Ixelles (02 629 23 11/ www.vub.ac.be/sport). Métro Delta/tram 23, 90/bus 34, 71. **Open** *to public* noon-2pm, 5-10pm Mon-Fri. **Admission** €7.70 per day; €32.50 per mth; €264.40 per yr. **Credit** MC, V.
The sports complex at the university is open to non-students for reasonable rates. As well as a gym, there's a pool, sauna, squash, tennis, badminton, a climbing wall and classes in many activities.

Winner's

13 rue Bonneels, St-Josse (02 280 02 70/ www.winnersclub.be). Métro Madou. **Open** 8am-10pm Mon-Fri; 8am-7pm Sat, Sun. **Admission** €10 per day; €50per mth; €380 per yr. **Credit** DC, MC, V. **Map** p320 F3.

A popular and functional multi-sports centre with climbing, squash courts, gym and saunas. Aerobics classes cost €8 (no membership required).

Football

The three biggest expat teams are British United (www.bufc.org), FC Irlande (www.fcirlande.be) and Royal Brussels British (www.rbbfc.org). These teams all play in the ABSSA league (www.abssa.be). British United are based in Tervuren, where senior, veteran and ladies' teams train. FC Irlande – with five teams including veterans – train in Woluwe-St-Etienne. Royal Brussels British have six sides, including two veterans' teams, also based in Tervuren.

Go-karting

City Kart

5A square Emile des Grées du Loû, Forest (02 332 36 96/www.citykart.com). Train Forest/ tram 18, 52/bus 50, 54. **Open** noon-11pm Mon-Fri; 9.30am-11pm Sat, Sun (children only until 2pm weekends). **Admission** €10-€14 per 15mins. **Credit** MC, V.
A kilometre of indoor karting track located near to Forest railway station provides plenty of late-evening, juvenile fun.

Golf

The leafy outskirts are littered with courses, with the Royal Golf Club of Belgium (02 767 58 01, www.ravenstein.be) in Tervuren the top spot. The chateau clubhouse was a gift from Leopold II. The Brabantse Golf Club (02 751 82 05) near Zaventem, the first Flemish golf club in Brussels, is cheap and pleasant. The Brussels Golf Club Academy and Training Centre (02 672 22 22, www.brusselsgolfclub.com), a public course in parkland by the Forêt de Soignes, is best for beginners. For a multi-pass package with hotels, contact 02 352 18 19, www.passbw.com. All details can be found at www.golf.be.

Horse riding

The Forêt de Soignes and the Bois de la Cambre are the best options. The Belgian Equestrian Federation (02 478 50 56, www.equibel.be) has details of competitions and riding clubs.

Royal Etrier Belge

19 champ du Vert Chasseur, Uccle (02 374 38 70/ www.royaletrierbelge.be). Bus 41. **Open** 8am-9pm daily. **Admission** €19 per lesson. **No credit cards.**
Lessons are given on a long-term basis, but one-time treks can be arranged around the Bois de la Cambre.

Ice skating

An traditional open-air rink is set up at Ste-Catherine at Yuletide (www.plaisirsdhiver.be; *see also p169* **Christmas on ice**), for €5 including skate hire. Permanent rinks include:

Patinoire de Forest

36 avenue du Globe, Forest (02 345 16 11). Tram 18, 52/bus 48, 54. **Open** *early Sept-1 May* 8.30am-4.30pm Mon-Thur; 8am-11pm Fri; 10am-6pm Sat, Sun. **Admission** €5; €2.50 skate hire. **No credit cards**.
This large outdoor rink, home to the Brussels Ice Hockey Club, is at the Forest National entertainment complex. Private lessons, ice-hockey coaching and an artistic skating school are also on site.

Patinoire Poséidon

4 avenue des Vaillants, Woluwe-St-Lambert (02 762 16 33). Métro Tomberg. **Open** *Sept-Apr* noon-10pm Mon; 10am-10pm Tue, Wed, Sat; 10am-9pm Thur; 10am-6pm Sun. **Admission** €4.50; €3.50 concessions; €3 skate hire. **No credit cards**.
A semi-covered, Olympic-sized rink in a sports centre that also houses a gym and swimming pool.

Rollerblading & skateboarding

Brussels' rainy cobbled streets hardly provide the ideal conditions for skating – although there are plenty of rats boarding down the Mont des Arts. A skateboard park has been created on a square outside the old Chapelle train station.

On summer Fridays 30,000 bladers wend their way through the Bois de la Cambre and the city centre; they meet at 8pm at the Attelages crossroads in the Bois de la Cambre. See www.belgiumrollers.com. The Bois de la Cambre also has an outdoor skating rink at 1 Chemin du Gymnase (02 649 70 02, open when dry, inline skates can be hired). On most Sundays the paths of the Bois de la Cambre are closed to cars and left to rollerbladers and cyclists to run rampant.

Roller Park

300 quai de Biestebroeck, Anderlecht (02 522 59 15). Métro Bizet. **Open** 10am-10pm Mon-Sat; 10am-7pm Sun. **Admission** €5; €2.50 skate hire; €5 skateboard hire. **No credit cards**.
Offers rollerblading and skateboarding, with rails and ramps to challenge the most avid dudes.

Rugby

The Brussels Barbarians are the biggest expat club (www.brusselsbarbarians.com), with two men's and one ladies' team, who train at the British School (*see p204*) on Tuesdays and Thursdays. The Belgian Rugby Federation (www.rugby.be) has all the details.

Skiing & snowboarding

In winter downhill and cross-country skiers flock to the Ardennes and its 70 small ski stations. Contact Ardennes Tourism (084 41 19 81, www.catpw.be) for details. In town, try:

Yeti Ski & Snowboarding

Drève Olympique 11, Anderlecht (02 520 77 57/ www.yetiski.be). Métro Eddy Merckx. **Open** *Sept-May* 1-11pm Mon, Wed, Fri; 6-11pm Tue, Thur; 10am-8pm Sat, Sun. **Admission** €10 per hr. **No credit cards.**
This slope in the Parc de Neerpede sports complex is covered with plastic carpet for the feel of snow.

Squash

Some fitness centres (*see p206*) and tennis clubs (*see below*) also have squash courts.

Belgica Squash Centre

120 avenue Jean Dubrucq, Molenbeek (02 425 30 42/ www.belgicasquash.be). Métro Belgica. **Admission** €15 per hr. **Open** 10am-1am Mon-Sat. **Credit** MC, V.
Eight squash courts and occasional tournaments.

Liberty's Squash Club

1068 chaussée de Wavre, Auderghem (02 734 64 93/www.stadium.be). Métro Hankar. **Open** 9am-midnight Mon-Fri; 9am-10pm Sat, Sun. **Admission** €8 per 30mins. **Credit** MC, V.
A large squash centre with 16 courts. Membership needed for phone bookings.
Other locations: Stadium, 1 avenue du Sippelberg, Molenbeek (02 414 40 41).

Swimming

Proper trunks and swimming hats are required at Belgian pools.

Sportcity Woluwe-St-Pierre

2 avenue Salomé, Woluwe-St-Pierre (02 773 18 20/ www.sportcity-woluwe.be). Tram 39/bus 36. **Open** 8am-7pm Mon-Thur, Sat, Sun; 8am-8pm Fri. **Admission** €3. **No credit cards.**
This big leisure centre has an Olympic-sized pool, warm tubs and waterslide, plus tennis, squash, basketball, a solarium and steam baths.

Victor Boin

38 rue de la Perche, St-Gilles (02 539 06 15). Prémétro Horta/tram 18, 81. **Open** 8am-7.30pm Mon-Fri; 9am-7.30pm Sat. **Admission** €2 pool; €18 all facilities. **No credit cards. Map** p318 A7.
Beautiful art deco pool with hydrotherapy and a Turkish bath, reserved for women on Tuesdays and Fridays, men the rest of the week.

Tennis

Many fitness centres (*see p206*) rent courts to non-members by the hour. Members-only clubs include the Castle in Wezembeek-Oppem (02

731 68 20, www.sports-valley.be). The Tennis Federation (02 513 29 20, www.aftnet.be) has details of all clubs and courts.

Tennis Club de Belgique

26 rue du Beau-Site, Ixelles (02 648 80 35/ www.tennisclubdebelgique.be). Métro Louise then tram 93, 94/bus 54. **Open** *To non-members* mid Apr-mid July 7am-10pm Mon-Fri. **Admission** €12.50-€18.50 per hr. **Membership** €75.
No credit cards. Map p319 D7.
A well-heeled club with three indoor courts hired out on summer weekdays to non-members. Evening slots are scarce. Coaching is available.

Uccle Sport

18 chaussée de Ruisbroeck, Uccle (02 376 3779/ www.ucclesport.be). Tram 18, 52/bus 50. **Open** 8am-11pm daily. **Admission** €16 8am-5pm; €22 5-11pm. **No credit cards.**
Open to non-members, but a €25 membership fee saves €5 on rental. Twelve clay courts and a school.

Walking & running

Weekend runs for expats are organised by the Brussels Hash House Harriers (http://users. skynet.be/bruh3) on Saturday afternoons, the Brussels Manneke Piss Hash House Harriers (www.bmph3.com) on Sundays, and walks by the Irish Club (www.irishclub.be) on Sundays.
The biggest running event (www.sport.be/ running) is the **Brussels 20km** (02 511 90 00, www.20kmdebruxelles.be/20km) on the last Sunday in May, when 20,000 head from the Bois de la Cambre to the Parc du Cinquantenaire. Entrance fee is €12; sign up early. In 2004 the Brussels Marathon (www. ingrunningtour.be) was revived with a new route.

Yoga

Many fitness centres (*see p206*) offer yoga classes. The Belgian Association of Yoga Teachers & Practitioners (01 969 99 71, www. yoga-abepy.be) has details of all yoga centres.

Ashtanga Yoga Institutes

610 chaussée d'Alsemberg, Uccle (02 340 67 81/ www.yoga-ashtanga.net). Tram 55. **Admission** €15 per lesson; €95 10 lessons. **No credit cards.**
Jean Claude Garnier is renowned as a teacher of ashtanga – an energetic form of yoga practised by various celebrities, including Madonna. All levels are catered for, mainly in French, but English classes are available on request.

Yoga Traditionnel

111 rue de Livourne, Ixelles (02 648 14 07/www.okc-net.org). Tram 93, 94. **Admission** €8.50 per lesson; €80 11 lessons. **No credit cards.**
Classes in hatha yoga by an experienced instructor; they're usually in French, or in English on request.

Theatre & Dance

Trilingual theatre and dynamic dance.

Theatre

Going to the theatre in Brussels is a generally laid-back affair and, the classical theatres apart, attracts a young, enthusiastic and mostly loyal audience. Brussels' official bilingual status means that spoken-word theatre is organised along strict language lines, particularly so in the large subsidised production houses, which rely on money from their regional governments. French remains the dominant language in the experimental spaces and smaller receiving theatres, the café theatres and vaudeville houses; Flemish is prominent in larger, more solid organisations such as the **Kaiitheater**.

Two of Belgium's largest arts subsidies go to the **Royal Flemish Theatre** (KVS) and the **Théâtre National**. Both are resolutely representative of their language communities and there is little crossover between the two. The KVS has been in a temporary home (a converted bottle plant in a run-down part of town) since 1999, while its old base in rue de Laeken is given a much-needed rebuild. The project has seen delay after delay and the administration has only just moved into its new offices. As for the theatre space and new studio, it seems the KVS is pinning its hopes on starting the 2004-2005 season there, but no one is holding their breath. Similar uncertainty reigns at the National, now playing rather successfully in a downtown converted cinema complex. The National is promised a brand new building on boulevard Emile Jacqmain. At the time of writing an impressive glass façade was in place, but it seems unlikely that the move-in date will be before 2005. On top of this, Philippe Van Kessel, artistic director since 1990, is leaving to be replaced by Louis Colinet from the Théâtre de la Place in Liège. All this is balanced by the welcome return of the **Beursschouwburg** to its renovated home opposite the Bourse. It's firmly in the trendy Flemish quarter, but this is one space that opens its doors to all, regardless of language affiliation, while maintaining a high-level programme of international theatre, dance, music and visual arts. The Beurs belongs to the biggest sector of theatre in Brussels, that of receiving house, where touring productions make up most of the programme. These mixed programmes present work from all over the world, so while Flemish and French don't necessarily mix, any other language does.

AMATEUR THEATRE IN ENGLISH

There are numerous English-language theatre groups in Brussels, organised along national lines. These include the **American Theatre Company** (www.atc-brussels.org), **English Theatre Brussels** (the theatrical arm of the English Comedy Club; www.angelfire.com/nb/eccbrussels), **Brussels Light Opera Company** (www.brulightopera.be), **Brussels Shakespeare Society** (www.geocities.com/theatrebe/Shakespeare.html) and the **Irish Theatre Group** (www.irishtheatre-group.be). Between them, they produce copious amounts of theatre, from café entertainment through studio to main-stage productions (check out the websites or *The Bulletin* for further details). The results are varied, especially in the main-stage productions. But three of the theatre groups – the Irish, English and American – clubbed together to buy their own premises and now have a base known as the **Warehouse Studio** (73 rue Waelhem, Schaerbeek, no phone), which has a small 60-seater studio space. It is here that the best work takes place, with new writing by locals and more controversial productions such as the recent *Trainspotting*.

Also of interest is **FEATS** (Festival of European Anglophone Theatrical Societies; www.feats.org) which stages a theatre competition in Brussels every year.

TICKETS AND INFORMATION

Ticket prices are cheap and most venues offer concessions to students, the unemployed, the over-60s and groups. It's usually best to call in advance, although there is a culture of turning up on the night. Central reservations and online bookings are becoming more popular, but you pay booking fees for these. The smaller theatres may also charge commission for credit card bookings. The main central booking agencies are limited by whether the venues choose to place tickets with them. The websites list a full agenda of events for which they hold tickets: **Fnac** (premium rate 0900 00600, www.fnac. be); **In the Pocket** (www.inthepocket.be) and **TicketClic** (www.ticketclic.be).

The best listings are found in *The Bulletin* on Thursday and in *Le Soir* on Wednesday. The

season runs from September to June and venues are mostly closed in summer, though this is when the performing arts festivals take over. *See p212* **Summer fests**.

Venues

Beursschouwburg

20-28 rue Auguste Orts, Lower Town (02 550 03 50/www.beursschouwburg.be). Pré-métro Bourse. **Open** *Box office* 10am-6pm Mon-Sat. **Tickets** €10; €8.50 concessions. **No credit cards. Map** p315 B3.
After a grand re-opening in February 2004, the Beurs is back on track as a centre of excellence for modern cross-form art and performance. Its new look is industrial and minimalist, giving a cool backdrop to its innovative, international programme. The bar – more like a nightclub – opens at weekends for the arty party crowd late into the night. *See p199.*

Kaaitheater

20 square Sainctelette, Lower Town (02 201 59 59/ www.kaaitheater.be). Métro Yser. **Open** *Box office* 11am-6pm Tue-Fri. **Tickets** €12.50; €10 concessions (occasional performances €20-€25). **Credit** MC, V. **Map** p316 B1.
The art deco Kaai is one of Brussels' most invigorating performance spaces, and stands truly at the forefront of the avant-garde. It has a solid stable of visiting theatre and dance companies, including Forced Entertainment (UK), the Wooster Group (USA) and Toneelgroep (NL), and key local troupes Jan Decorte and Josse de Pauw. (*See also p189.*)

Koninklijke Vlaamse Schouwburg

58 rue Delaunoy, Molenbeek (02 412 70 40/www. kvs.be). Métro Etangs Noirs. **Open** *Box office* noon-6pm Tue-Sat. **Tickets** €12.50; €7.50 concessions. **Credit** AmEx, MC, V.

Known as the KVS, the Royal Flemish Theatre is one of the big subsidised houses providing serious theatre in Dutch. Productions range from weirdly modern to the firmly classical, with a sprinkling of guest productions from Belgium and Europe. Once it's finally back in its new home on rue de Laeken, there's rumour that visiting English-language productions will start appearing again.

Théâtre des Martyrs

22 place des Martyrs, Lower Town (02 223 32 08/ www.europictures.com/martyrs). Metro/pré-métro De Brouckère or Rogier. **Open** *Box office* 11am-6pm Tue-Fri; 2-6pm Sat. **Tickets** €12-€14; €7.50-€11.50 concessions. **Credit** DC, MC, V. **Map** p315 C2.
The fabulously modern interior in a classic townhouse is representative of the Martyrs, one of the city's most exciting theatre spaces, run by artistic director Daniel Scahaise. The production style is modern and resolutely French, with an emphasis on new takes on classic plays: Shakespeare, Beckett, Molière and Duras. Visiting companies add texture to the solid honesty of Scahaise's work.

Théâtre National

85 boulevard Anspach, Lower Town (02 203 53 03/www.theatrenational.be). Pré-métro Bourse. **Open** *Box office* 10am-6pm Mon-Fri. **Tickets** €15; €7.50-€10 concessions. **Credit** MC, V. **Map** p315 B3.
The National has had its ups and downs recently, but it sails through it all with confidence and savoir faire. Remember, this isn't truly a national theatre, as it serves only the French-speaking community, but nonetheless it is one of Belgium's most important producing houses and one of its most heavily subsidised. The National has found great success in its temporary home with a solid mix of classical, modern, satirical and youth theatre, though none of its work could be called cutting edge.

The **Rosas** dance company. *See p212.*

Théâtre 140

140 avenue Eugéne Plasky, Schaerbeek (02 733 97 08/www.theatre140.be). Pré-métro Diamant/bus 29, 63. **Open** *Box office* noon-6pm Mon-Fri, performances Sat. **Tickets** €13; €7.50 concessions. **Credit** MC, V. **Map** p321 H2.

Evergreen Jo Dekmine runs the 140 as he has done for decades. He was mates with Gainsbourg and Brel and gave chances to Pink Floyd in the early days. Forever looking for the new and exciting, his programme includes physical and innovative theatre from home and abroad. The 140 has benefited from new seats, making it an altogether more comfortable venue, and the after-show bar is worth a visit itself.

Théâtre de Poche

1A chemin de Gymnase, Ixelles (02 649 17 27/www. poche.be). Tram 23, 90, 93, 94. **Open** *Box office* 10am-5.30pm Mon-Sat. **Tickets** €14; €9-€11 concessions. **Map** p324 E10.

The little Pocket Theatre was founded by Roger Domani in 1951, and originally opened its doors on the chaussée d'Ixelles until being demolished to make way for a shopping gallery. Since then it has sat in a small building in the Bois de la Cambre, which has been the making of it. Audiences seem to love going there and feeling part of a real theatrical experience. The work is demanding and hard-hitting and always pushes limits, taking world politics as it starting point. Look out for the posters around town, recognisable works of art in their own right.

Théâtre du Rideau de Bruxelles

Palais des Beaux-Arts, 23 rue Ravenstein, Upper Town (02 507 83 61/www.rideaudebruxelles.be). Métro Gare Centrale or Parc. **Open** *Box office* 11am-7pm Mon-Sat. *Phone bookings* 9am-7pm Mon-Sat. **Tickets** €16-€18; €8-€13 concessions. **Credit** AmEx, DC, MC, V. **Map** p317 D4.

The Rideau has been resident at the Palais since 1943 and is a key part of the French-language theatre scene. It appeals to the middle-class, middle-brow set, with modern classics and safe costume dramas, but every now and then surprises with an eyebrow-lifting biographical piece (*Rimbaud*, for example). A good place to go if you want to try some French theatre – the actors speak very clearly.

Théâtre Royal des Galeries

32 galerie de la Roi, Lower Town (02 512 04 07/ www.theatredesgaleries.be). Métro Gare Centrale. **Open** *Box office* 11am-6pm Tue-Sat. **Tickets** €9-€22; €8-€15 concessions. **Credit** AmEx, DC, MC, V. **Map** p315 C3.

A theatre was first built here in 1847 as part of the glass-covered Galeries St-Hubert, but was pulled down (in true Brussels style) and rebuilt in the 1950s. This little gem's claim to fame is that Magritte painted a fresco on the ceiling, though the powers-that-be couldn't cope with his strange spherical bells flying through the clouds, so they placed a vast glass-balled chandelier there instead. Today it is best known for its New Year revue, and also for old staples such as *Cyrano* and the odd Agatha Christie.

Théâtre Royal du Parc

3 rue de la Loi, Upper Town (02 505 30 30/www. theatreduparc.be). Métro Arts-Loi or Parc. **Open** *Box office* 11am-6pm Mon-Fri; 11am-1pm, 2-6pm Sat, Sun. **Tickets** €5.20-€23.50; €9 concessions. **Credit** MC, V. **Map** p317 D3.

This stunner was built as a playhouse for the rich in 1782 and since then has managed to hang on to its genteel audience. Most of what is performed here falls into the category of comedy, French comedy being something different to the English variety. Even Eugene O'Neill's Long Day's Journey Into Night is described here as a '*comédie dramatique*'.

Théâtre de la Toison d'Or

396 galeries de la Toison d'Or, Ixelles (02 510 05 10/www.theatredelatoisondor.be). Métro Porte de Namur. **Open** *Box office* 10am-4pm Mon; 10am-6pm Tue-Fri; 2-6pm Sat. **Tickets** €19; €10-€16 concessions. **Credit** AmEx, MC, V. **Map** p319 D5.

A magnet for camp, madcap comedy and revue: off-beat takes on Eurovision; piss-takes of the sci-fi genre; stand-up comedy, and café-theatre summarises the wacky Belgian fare here. Or, as another bit of blurb puts it: you can't make tortillas without cracking eggs. Exactly.

Théâtre du Toone

21 petite rue des Bouchers, Lower Town (02 217 27 53/www.toone.be). Métro/pré-métro De Brouckère. **Open** *Box office* noon-midnight Tue-Sun. **Tickets** €10; €7 concessions (Fri, Sat). **No credit cards**. **Map** p315 C3.

This tiny place has been going for generations. It is a world-famous, world-class marionette theatre with productions in Bruxellois dialect. The atmosphere and visuals balance out any incomprehension, though you may be lucky enough to catch *Hamlet* in Brussels English. *See p63* **Talk of the Toone**.

Théâtre Varia

78 rue du Sceptre, Ixelles (02 640 82 58/www.varia. be). Bus 38, 60, 95, 96. **Open** *Box office* 1-7pm Tue-Fri. *Performances* 2.30-7pm Sat. **Tickets** €14-€17; €7.50-€11 concessions. **Credit** MC, V. **Map** p322 F6.

Firmly French in nature, the Varia mixes new writing (Belgian and Moroccan) with new takes on Shakespeare in translation – recently *Richard III* and *Hamlet*. It's a space that makes an effort to welcome everyone – it even has a babysitting service.

Théâtre de la Vie

45 rue Traversière, St-Josse (02 219 60 06/www. theatredelavie.be). Métro Botanique/tram 92, 93, 94. **Open** *Box office* 1-4pm Mon-Fri. **Tickets** varies; usually €12.50; €7.50 concessions. **No credit cards**. **Map** p320 E2.

The de la Vie is where the controversial can – and does – happen. The work tends to be new, reflecting world politics, but also impacting on the communities it serves (mostly Turkish and north African). It is often text heavy, and as such only really suitable for those with a deep understanding of French.

Dance

The independence of dance from the spoken word may account for the diversity and high standards of the Belgian variety. Many theatres include dance in their programme and most of the big annual festivals – such as the **Kunsten Festival des Arts** (*see left, below* **Summer fests**) – feature a mix of performing art forms.

The only truly classical company is the **Royal Ballet of Flanders** (www.koninklijk balletvanvlaanderen.be) which produces ballet and musical theatre of outstanding quality. Surprisingly, there is no ballet in Brussels – the city prefers to welcome visiting companies, both national and from abroad.

The influence of modern dance makers on the international stage is astounding for such a small country. The undisputed dancing queen is **Anne Teresa de Keersmaeker**, director of the Rosas company (www.rosas.be/rosas) and resident at the Brussels opera. Definitive dance works – such as the ever-touring *Rain* – have placed her firmly at the pinnacle of the genre. De Keersmaeker's sphere of influence is based on three pillars: to intensify the link between dance and music, to build a repertory, and to launch a dance school (**PARTS**; *see p214*). Not only has she succeeded in all three, but she has received top awards in Belgium and internationally. Proud locals pack out every performance. De Keersmaeker is also renowned for her collaborations with Brussels-based **Michèle Anne de Mey**, another firebrand.

Equally regaled is the company Charleroi Danses/Plan K (www.charleroi-danses.be), led by the legendary **Frédéric Flamand**. This company is now among the top three subsidised arts companies in Wallonia, which only goes to prove the high esteem in which dance is held. **Michèle Noiret**, resident choreographer at **Les Tanneurs**, worked for years with

---

Summer fests

The performing arts blossom in summer, when a host of events take place across Brussels, from one-day specials to season-long superfests. Check with the festivals section of www.idearts.com/agenda/index.htm for details.

The biggest two festivals are the **Kunsten Festival des Arts** (www.kfda.be) in May and the **Festival Bellone-Brigittines** (www.bellone.be), held in August and September. The KFA is one of Brussels' most prominent arts festivals, thanks to the tenacity of impresario Frie Liesen. Its premise is to unite the arts regardless of language, with around 140 cutting edge drama and dance productions from Belgium and around the world. Its base is now the reopened **Beursschouwburg** (*see p210*). For strikingly new and in-yer-face work from across Europe, the Bellone-Brigittines draws an arty crowd, particularly to the magical **Chapelle des Brigittines** (*see p214*). A central theme draws each annual programme together – 2003 was 'What Today Promises'.

Royal Ballet of Flanders. *See p212.*

Stockhausen, who used her to develop a new codified body language. While his influence remains, they were tortuous times and she has broken from his straitjacket by developing a freer, looser style, with her dancers often moving in silence.

Wim Vandekeybus and his company Ultima Vez (www.ultimavez.com) is renowned for harsh, startling imagery with no room for compromise. His latest show *Blush* is a co-production with the KVS and is confrontational and very physical, seemingly a trademark of the Wim style. Making a splash on to the global scene is **Alain Platel**'s celebrated company Les Ballets C de la B (www.lesballetscdelab.be). The work is urban, often bleak, with touches

of humour and pathos; this is young dance for young people using startling imagery and popular music thrown together with hardcore classical. Another name to look for is **Sidi Larbi Cherakou**, an extraordinary young Belgian choreographer of Moroccan descent, who has directed some stunning work for C de la B.

Belgian dance is keeping ahead of the field with its willingness to push limits and to embrace other art forms as a legitimate part of its development. Opera and jazz singers on stage, actors reading ancient texts, modern music ensembles and the use of video and film are all being introduced as integral parts of the dance evolution. Belgian choreographers – and dancers – are not afraid to take risks.

Venues

Chapelle des Brigittines

1 petite rue des Brigittines, Lower Town (02 506 43 00/www.brigittines.be). Bus 27, 48. **Open** *Box office* 10am-6pm Mon-Fri. **Tickets** €8; €5 concessions. **No credit cards. Map** p315 B4.

The Chapelle des Brigittines by the abandoned railway station of Bruxelles-Chapelle is an extraordinary multimedia space; a decommissioned church taken back to its bare arches and pillars. Known primarily as a dance venue and as the centre of a summer dance festival (*see p212* **Summer fests**), it is also used for theatre and installation art projects.

Cirque Royal

81 rue de l'Enseignement, Upper Town (02 218 20 15/www.cirque-royal.org). Métro Madou. **Open** *Box office* 9am-6pm Mon-Fri; 10.30am-6pm Sat. **Tickets** vary. **Credit** MC, V. **Map** p317 D3.

A vast theatre space hosting the big international tours. Come here if you want to see the St Petersburg Ballet or the Chippendales. It's also used by the Béjart company as it is one of the few venues to offer a large stage and auditorium, making it a popular place on the rock music circuit (*see p193*).

Halles de Schaerbeek

22B rue Royale Ste-Marie, Schaerbeek (02 218 21 07/www.halles.be). Tram 90, 92, 93, 94/bus 58, 65, 66. **Open** *Box office* 2-6pm Mon-Fri. **Tickets** vary. **Credit** MC, V. **Map** p320 E1.

This magnificent ex-agricultural hall has become a key venue for art forms across the board. The wide open space underneath a glass-and-steel roof is flexible. Cross art-form companies love it for the ease with which they can erect giant video screens and multiple stages, and experiment with the artist-audience relationship. An important cultural centre for the Schaerbeek communities, it's a major venue for rock concerts too. (*See also p99 and p193.*)

Kaaitheaterstudio's

81 rue du Notre-Dame du Sommeil, Lower Town (02 201 59 59/www.kaaitheater.be). Métro Ste-Catherine. **Open** *Box office* 11am-8pm Mon-Fri. **Tickets** €12.50; €10 concessions. **Credit** MC, V. **Map** p316 A2.

The renowned studio complex of its bigger sister, the Kaaitheater (*see p210*), Kaaitheaterstudio's stages smaller theatre productions, as well as the more esoteric of dance companies, in an intimate setting. Two Belgian companies are based here: Meg Stuart's Damaged Goods and Thomas Hauert's Cie Zoo; both are at the forefront of avant-garde work, both with an international reputation.

Théâtre de la Monnaie

Place de la Monnaie, Lower Town (070 23 39 39/www.lamonnaie.be). Métro/pré-métro De Brouckère. **Open** *Box office* 11am-6pm Tue-Sat. **Tickets** €15-€148; 25-50% concessions; €8 all unsold seats 5mins before performance. **Credit** AmEx, DC, MC, V. **Map** p315 C3.

As a federal theatre with no resident classical ballet, the Monnaie mainly concentrates on opera (*see p190*). The key exception to this policy is that the theatre is home to Anne Teresa de Keersmaeker, Belgian dance supremo and artistic director of the world famous company, Rosas. The majority of de Keersmaeker's premières are staged here.

Théâtre les Tanneurs

75 rue des Tanneurs, Lower Town (02 512 17 84/www.lestanneurs.be). Métro/pré-métro Porte de Hal or Gare du Midi/bus 20, 48. **Open** *Box office* 1hr before performance. **Tickets** €7.50. **No credit cards. Map** p318 B5.

Situated in the heart of the Marolles, Les Tanneurs has won the approval of a loyal local crowd. This is mainly because of the theatre's radical approach to theatre and dance, and its uncompromising belief in its role in the immediate community. Add to that Belgian dance goddess Michèle Noiret as resident choreographer and the little theatre's appeal starts to make a lot of sense.

Classes & institutes

Centre de Danse Choreart

985 chaussée d'Alsemberg, Uccle (02 332 13 59/www.choreart.be). Tram 55/bus 38, 41, 43.

The biggest dance school in Brussels caters for tots in tutus right up to chaps in trainers. Ballet, jazz, tap, Latin, it's all here. Annual membership is €7; a week of classes costs €96-€144.

Maison du Spectacle – La Bellone

46 rue de Flandre, Lower Town (02 513 33 33/www.bellone.be). Métro Ste-Catherine. **Open** *Library* noon-6pm Tue-Thur. **Map** p316 B2.

This essential reference point for theatre and dance, includes an archive and library and hosts many government-supported arts organisations. It's worth walking in just to see the magnificent 18th-century house in the glass-covered courtyard.

PARTS

164 avenue Van Volxem, Forest (02 344 55 98/www.rosas.be/Parts/index.html). Tram 52/bus 49, 50.

The Performing Arts Research and Training Studios (PARTS) is a joint initiative of the dance company Rosas and La Monnaie. Its director, Anne Teresa de Keersmaeker, designed the artistic and pedagogical curriculum. The school offers a full-time training in contemporary dance and the working language is English.

Vlaams Theater Instituut

19 place Sainctelette, Lower Town (02 201 09 60/www.vti.be). Métro Yser. **Open** *Library* 2-6pm Mon-Fri. **Map** p316 B1.

The Flemish Theatre Institute is the resource centre for Flemish theatre in Belgium. An archive, library, study centre and a centre of research, the institute is regarded as the pulse of the Flemish theatre arts, including dance. It also publishes books and articles.

Trips Out of Town

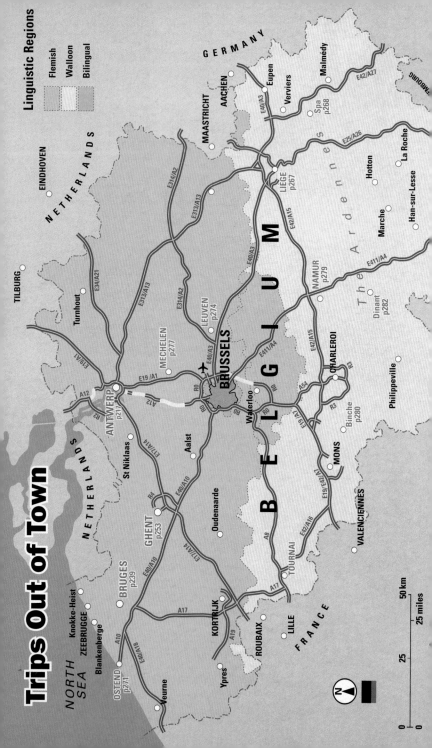

Antwerp

Diamonds, design and delicious style.

The locals call Antwerp 'the Metropolis'. Not known for their modesty, Antwerpenaars have a fierce pride in their city and have played an integral part in its radical transformation. From a dour bomb-damaged port town after World War II, a phoenix has risen and Antwerp is now one of the hottest cities on the European style and culture map.

The town developed as a significant trading port in the 12th century. As the rival port of Bruges silted up and the Flemish textile industry flourished, so Antwerp boomed. By the mid-16th century, it was the leading trading centre in Europe, with a population of 100,000. A diamond industry set up by Jews escaping Portugal brought magnificent wealth. It was a time of great cultural prestige, the architecture reflecting the city's status. A raft of artists chose it as their home, Peter Paul Rubens (*see p221* **Home is where the art is**) and Anthony van Dyck among them.

This era of prosperity came to a savage end with the Reformation and subsequent religious riots and repression. By 1589 the population had shrunk to 42,000. The death blow was dealt by the Treaty of Münster in 1648, closing off the River Scheldt to shipping. The Industrial Revolution saw Antwerp again prosper, to

the extent that it ranked as the world's third largest port by the end of the 19th century. The hosting of the World Fairs in 1885, 1894 and 1930, and the Olympic Games in 1920, confirmed the city's global status. Although Antwerp suffered badly during the two world wars and the interim slump, it recovered again in the 1990s.

Today is Antwerp's second golden age. It's famous for fashion, particularly after the impressive Mode2001 concept exhibition which engulfed the city. There's still a huge diamond business; Antwerp is the world's hub for the uncut diamond industry. And, of course, its rich artistic and cultural heritage is evident in the historic centre and numerous museums. The long-neglected southern side, 't Zuid, around the Fine Arts and Contemporary Art Museums (for both, *see p223*), is scattered with galleries and new nightclubs, restaurants and bars. To the north, the old Bonaparte dock area has an urban, bohemian air to it, as bars vie for space with lofts, especially in the much-anticipated renovation of the 't Eilandje quarter. The most ambitious project is Extra City (Kattendijkdok), an exhibition and concert space slated to open in the summer of 2004. Spoken-word events here link to the city's stint as World Book

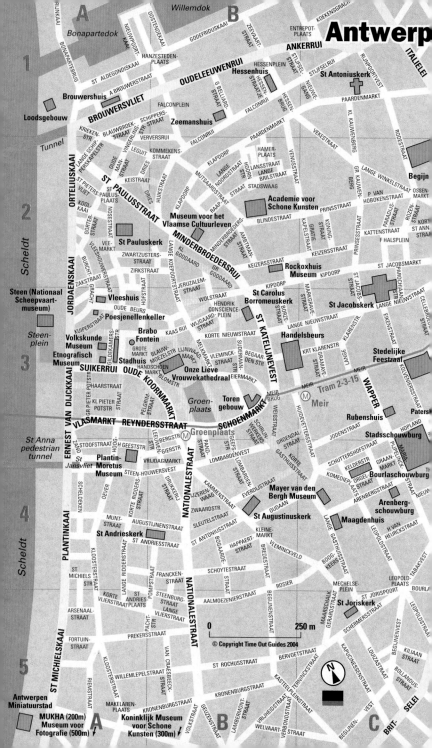

Capital until 2005. Above it, a 50-metre (164-foot) tower is being built, with a hotel room right at the top.

Grand civil projects are the theme of the day, with the major ring roads in the city centre being completely rebuilt (drivers beware; parking's a nightmare) and the new law courts (Justitiepaleis), designed by Richard Rogers, due for completion in 2004. In the grand old railway station, a Eurostar and TGV terminus will be ready by the end of 2005.

Then there's Antwerp's timelessness. This is a city made for walking – no hills, streetloads of pedestrianised areas, the gentle tring of a bicycle. At night Antwerp comes into its own, and in summer every terrace is abuzz with chatter and music. Its nightlife is among the best in northern Europe and attracts clubbers from afar. (*See p234* **Antwerp: Clubbing capital**). More come for the summer arts festival, Zomer van Antwerpen (June-Aug, www.zva.be), when outdoors is full of music, theatre and circus. Another impressive sight is when the Cutty Sark Tall Ships Race (www.tallshipsraces.com) calls in and the river is lined with magnificent cutters. Cosmopolitan and stylish, in harmony with its past and constantly designing its future, Antwerp is the thriving metropolis of local legend.

GETTING THERE

Four trains an hour shuttle between Brussels and Antwerp, a journey of 40 minutes.

Sightseeing

Note that all museums are closed on Mondays – and many have free admission on Fridays.

The Grote Markt & the cathedral

Antwerp's historical centre clusters around the lovely **Grote Markt**, with its ornate guildhouses and 16th-century **Stadhuis** (Town Hall). In the centre of the market square is a 19th-century statue of **Brabo**, symbol of the city. According to legend, a giant called Druon Antigon cut off the hand of any sailor who could not pay the toll to sail on the River Scheldt. The giant carried on chopping off hands and terrifying sailors until he was defeated by a Roman, Silvius Brabo, who then became Duke of Brabant. The legend curiously fits the name of the city: with slight alteration, Antwerp translates as 'hand throwing' in Dutch.

The **Onze Lieve Vrouwekathedraal** (Our Lady's Cathedral), the largest Gothic church in Belgium, is just off the square. Although a chapel was built here in the 13th century (there is evidence that there may have been an earlier church on the site), work on the cathedral itself began in the 14th century, before Antwerp's Golden Age. With trade and wealth steadily increasing over the succeeding centuries, ambitions for the cathedral grew and grandiose plans were drawn up to make it one of the most gigantic in Europe. The resulting construction

Onze Lieve Vrouwekathedraal, aka the **Cathedral**, restored to its former glory.

was interrupted several times by fires and the city's changing fortunes; these same fires, iconoclastic fury and damage caused at the time of the French Revolution also resulted in the destruction of many of the cathedral's original features. A 25-year renovation has restored much of the building's original splendour, and the white, light-filled interior now gleams.

The interior is adorned with a rich collection of paintings and sculpture, the most celebrated of which are by Rubens (*see p221* **Home is where the art is**). Many of his works in Antwerp are inspired by religion rather than Greek mythology, so those who are not great fans of the ample, sensuous ladies for which Rubens is renowned may find themselves drawn to his work in his home town. The cathedral houses four of his works: *The Raising of the Cross*; *The Descent from the Cross*; *The Resurrection* and *The Assumption*. The latter is located directly over the altar and can only be seen from a distance. Its dynamism and dazzling colours are self-evident, but it is difficult to appreciate the detail. The other paintings are more dramatic. *The Raising of the Cross* is a rich, emotional work. The masterpiece, though, is *The Descent from the Cross*.

Glimpses of the earlier church can be seen beneath the choir, where parts of a Romanesque choir and some brick tombs are visible. Outside, the sole tower/spire rises 123 metres (404 feet) and would have been flanked by its twin had funds not dried up.

Onze Lieve Vrouwekathedraal

Handschoenmarkt (03 213 99 40/www.dekathedraal. be). **Open** 10am-5pm Mon-Fri; 10am-3pm Sat; 1-4pm Sun. **Admission** €2; €1.50 concessions; free under-13s. **No credit cards. Map** p218 B3.

West of the Grote Markt

To the north-west of the Grote Markt, along Vleeshouwersstraat, is the **Vleeshuis** (Butcher's Hall), built as a guildhouse and meat market by the Butchers' Guild in 1503. It's a puzzling construction, in late Gothic style, with little turrets and walls which alternate red brick and white stone. Today the hall is used as a museum for archaeological finds, applied art and objects pertaining to local history, but is being developed into a museum of musical instruments. It also holds early music concerts. Much of the area in the immediate vicinity has been renovated, but the style of the new houses is insipid. The intention must have been to build in a manner that would not be at odds with the medieval and Renaissance architecture nearby. The policy is sound, but the end result makes you wish the city fathers had had the nerve for something more daring.

South of here, behind the Stadhuis, are two museums: the small **Volkskunde Museum** (Folk Museum), and the **Etnografisch Museum** (Ethnography Museum), which has an excellent reputation. It is arranged on several floors (which would benefit from better lighting), each representing a different part of the world. The top floor is generally reserved for temporary exhibitions.

A minute's walk west brings you to the Scheldt and the **Steen**. This bulky castle once guarded the river and houses the **Nationaal Scheepvaartmuseum** (National Maritime Museum). The Steen is almost as old as Antwerp itself and has become a symbol of the city. Built in 1200, it was part of the fortifications. Later it served as a prison, where inmates had to pay the guards for their stay. This meant that the wealthier prisoners lived in better conditions than the poorer ones, regardless of their crimes. For a while it served as a sawmill before being turned into a museum. Today you'll find an endearingly old-fashioned collection of maps, maritime objects and countless models of ships. Of more general interest are the old photos of Antwerp dock life. There is labelling in English. Real ships can be found in the outdoor section.

Spacious terraces by the castle allow for a quiet drink and pleasant stroll by the Scheldt.

Etnografisch Museum

19 Suikerrui (03 220 86 00/http://museum. antwerpen.be/etnografisch_museum). **Open** 10am-5pm Tue-Sun. **Admission** €4; €2 concessions; free under-12s. **Credit** MC, V. **Map** p218 A3.

Steen (Nationaal Scheepvaartmuseum)

1 Steenplein (03 232 08 50/http://museum. antwerpen.be/scheepvaartmuseum). **Open** 10am-5pm Tue-Sun. **Admission** €4; €2 concessions; free under-12s. **No credit cards. Map** p218 A3.

Vleeshuis

38-40 Vleeshouwersstraat (03 233 64 04/ http://museum.antwerpen.be/vleeshuis). **Open** 10am-5pm Tue-Sun. **Admission** €2.50; €1.25 concessions; free under-12s & Fri. **No credit cards. Map** p218 A3.

Volkskunde Museum

2-6 Gildekamerstraat (03 220 86 66/http://museum. antwerpen.be/volkskunde). **Open** 10am-5pm Tue-Sun. **Admission** €2.50; €1.25 concessions; free under-18s. **No credit cards. Map** p218 A3.

North of the Grote Markt

Between the Vleeshuis and the Napoleon Docks, near Verversrui, is what remains of the red-light district. Perhaps because it is so close to the historic centre, many of the prostitutes are being persuaded to move elsewhere. This seems

Home is where the art is

As Da Vinci is to Florence and Warhol is to New York, so Rubens is to Antwerp. The baroque master not only made it his home, he made it his studio and gallery, creating his major works in the city and hanging them in churches and private homes. He was a celebrity of his time; an artist, writer and diplomat who was commissioned by royals and 17th-century fat-cats. The relationship between city and man was symbiotic, an interdependence that continues to this day.

Having decided to organise a major Rubens retrospective in 2005, Antwerp discovered the intentions of Lille, as Cultural Capital of Europe 2004, to mount one too – tying the artist into his own history with that city. To avoid arty tantrums, a deal was struck that the two shows should run together, and **Rubens2004** was born (www.rubens2004.be/ 070 233 799), with two cities linked by a common artist and a 75-minute train journey.

Lille may have an impressive collection of paintings, but Antwerp has the edge; works in the Fine Arts Museum are one thing, but there are also paintings in the very churches for which they were commissioned, in the same place Rubens envisaged for them, their scale and subject matter made to measure for the space. There's the **Rubenshuis** (see p223; pictured above The Annunciation), a living memorial to the man and his life, and as if to put an exclamation mark on the proceedings, there's his tomb in **St Jacobskerk** (see p222), overlooked by his modestly sized Mary Surrounded by Saints.

Most of the major Antwerp shows took place in the first half of 2004, but the **Fine Arts Museum** (see p223) is running **The Invention of Landscape** until 1 August, and **Copyright Rubens (Rubens and Graphic Art)** until 12 September. Also until that date

the **Rockoxhuis Museum** (see p223) has an exhibition of graphics reproduced from Rubens' work from 1650-1800 in **Rubens in Black and White**. Ongoing from 12 June is **Rubens and Book Illustration** at the **Museum Plantin-Moretus** (see p225). This shows the partnership between publisher and artist and Rubens as art director; the richly illustrated books on show were to set a publishing and style precedent across Europe.

However, the most enduring legacy from Rubens2004 – apart from the ongoing solidity of the Rubenshuis – is the creation of three Rubens walks around the city. **Rubens Open Door** allows you to discover the 17th-century Antwerp that Rubens knew, the shops, friends' houses, taverns and places of business he frequented. **Rubens in Higher Spheres** has a more spiritual edge and aims to discover the religious and scientific inspirations that informed his work, looking at how contemporary thought was represented in biblical and mythological themes. Finally, **Looking at Rubens** takes you to the Rubens room at the Fine Arts Museum and gives an in-depth look at 20 major works. The walks can be done either as a guided group or individually and vary in length from 90 minutes to three hours. Full details and the walks guide (€4) can all be found at the tourist office (see p226).

While Rubens has become an international commodity (at the beginning of 2004 there were major shows at London's National Gallery and Somerset House), Antwerp can rest assured that the great artist will never truly leave home; the city drips with his jewels and it can proudly continue to wear the crown of his lasting legacy – Antwerp, city of Rubens – way beyond 2004.

Trips Out of Town

a little harsh, especially since many women working in the red-light district helped save a slew of Old Masters when fire broke out in 1968 in **St Pauluskerk** (03 232 32 67; May-Sept 2-5pm daily; free). St Paulus' 16th-century exterior is in flamboyant Gothic style and is crowned with a late 17th-century baroque bell tower. The baroque interior contains some stunning Flemish masters (including Rubens, Jacob Jordaens and van Dyck) and wonderfully carved wood panelling; there's also a treasure room. The church stands on a lively square – not as neat, perhaps, as others in the centre, but somehow more integrated into city life.

North of here are the docks, built by Napoleon in the early 19th century but now becoming an upmarket area with new bars, restaurants and inner-city loft living. You will still be able to get a fair picture of what the port must have been like in the 19th century, or you can take a boat around the port proper, further north – ask at the tourist office. The **Hessenhuis**, a 16th-century storehouse, is a complex devoted to social history, design and architecture. In typical Antwerp style, it also has a gay café and nightclub (*see p233*).

Hessenhuis

53 Falconrui (03 206 0350/http://museum. antwerpen.be/hessenhuis/eng). **Open** varies. **Admission** varies. **No credit cards**. **Map** p218 B1.

East of the Grote Markt

The narrow, tortuous streets behind the cathedral emerge at the baroque church of **St Carolus Borromeuskerk** (03 231 37 51; see schedule by door for opening times) on Hendrik Conscienceplein. On one side of this square – one of the prettiest in the city – stands the church, and opposite is the old city library. Built for the Jesuits in the early 17th century, St Carolus is an exuberant, frothy monument to baroque excess. The façade is elaborate and ornate, with columns and statues. Rubens produced 39 widely praised ceiling paintings and three altarpieces for the church, only for the lot to go up in smoke during a fire in 1718. Close by is the lovely **Rockoxhuis Museum**. Mayor Nicolaas Rockox was a friend of Rubens and his 17th-century town house is filled with period furnishings. It's more gallery than re-created home, though, and the main attraction is the small but perfectly formed art collection, which includes works by Matsys, van Dyck and local boys Joachim Beuckelaer and Frans Snyders (who lived next door). To the north is the **Koninklijke Academie voor Schone Kunsten** (Royal Academy of Fine Arts). It was the fashion department here that was the

driving force behind the original Antwerp Six, who took London Fashion Week by storm in 1987. *See p237* **Antwerp: Fashion capital**. While it's very much a place of learning, the classical building is worth a visit as is its extensive library.

East of here on Lange Nieuwstraat is the fine **St Jacobskerk**. As you walk towards it from a distance, this church looks impressive, but the closer you get the more it seems to diminish. Little houses completely surround it, barely making space for the main and side entrances. The interior is decorated in heavy baroque style, reflecting the fact that this was a wealthy district of Antwerp and the parishioners made sure the church reflected their status. It is as Rubens' burial place that St Jacob's is best known. The artist painted the work that hangs over his tomb, *Our Lady Surrounded by Saints*, specifically for this purpose. St George is believed to be a self-portrait, while the Virgin is a portrait of Isabella Brant, Rubens' first wife. Mary Magdalene is a portrait of Hélène Fourment, his second wife.

Not far south of the church is one of the city's major tourist draws, the **Rubenshuis**, home to the artist for most of his life. He bought it in 1611, after his return from Italy, and soon after being appointed city painter by Archduke Albrecht and Isabella. It's wise to come early if you want to avoid the tour parties. Speed through the ugly modern ticket office outside the house and plunge into the wonderful interior. This is one of the major baroque buildings in Antwerp, which in Rubens' time, much to his regret, was mainly Gothic. The house passed through several owners before the city of Antwerp bought it. It has been fully renovated and the garden entirely reconstructed. Much of the furniture dates from the 17th century but was not originally in the house. Highlights include the semi-circular gallery (based on the Pantheon in Rome) where Rubens displayed his collection of classical sculpture, and his spacious studio, overlooked by a mezzanine, where his work could be admired by potential buyers. Rubens was an exceptionally prolific painter (knocking out around 2,500 works), chiefly because he didn't do all the painting himself. Canvases were mass-produced by staff in his workshop; he would direct proceedings and add the necessary key brushstrokes. With pupils such as Jordaens and van Dyck, he could afford to limit the extent of his contribution to attentive supervision. The only disappointment in the house is that there aren't more of Rubens' paintings on display. Look out, though, for an endearing self-portrait (c1630) and a later, more anxious-looking one in the studio.

Koninklijke Academie voor Schone Kunsten

*31 Mutsaardstraat (03 213 71 00/http://
academieantwerpen.ha.be).* **Open** *Library* 8.30am-
5pm Mon-Wed, Fri; 8.30am-7pm Thur. **Map** p218 B2.

Rockoxhuis Museum

12 Keizerstraat (03 201 92 50). **Open** 10am-5pm
Tue-Sun. **Admission** €2.50; €1.25 concessions; free
under-12s & Fri. **No credit cards**. **Map** p218 B2.

Rubenshuis

*9-11 Wapper (03 201 15 55/http://museum.
antwerpen.be/rubenshuis).* **Open** 10am-5pm Tue-Sun.
Admission €5; €2.50 concessions; free under-18s.
No credit cards. **Map** p218 C3.

St Jakobskerk

*Lange Nieuwstraat (03 232 10 32/www.topa.be/
sint-jacobskerk).* **Open** *Apr-Oct* 2-5pm Mon-Sat.
Nov-Mar 9am-noon Mon-Sat. **Admission** €2; €1.50
concessions. **No credit cards**. **Map** p218 C2/3.

South of the Grote Markt

The south side of Antwerp is home to the city's
older residential districts and contains many
of its best museums. A few minutes' walk south
of the Grote Markt is the Vrijdagmarkt; each
Friday bailiffs come here to auction off debtors'
seized goods. That aside, the square is lined
with idiosyncratic cafés as well as the **Museum
Plantin-Moretus**, home of printing pioneer
Christophe Plantin. Legend has it that French-
born bookbinder Plantin was injured in a brawl
in 1555 and, with the hush money he was paid,
bought a printing press. The business he was
to build in this immense 16th-century house
became the largest printing and publishing
concern in the Low Countries (with 22 presses),
and became a magnet for intellectuals. Plantin
printed many of the greatest works of his day,
including an eight-volume polyglot Bible. Here
you can discover all the intricacies of printing,
and examine the huge presses, a beautiful
proofreading room and a foundry. There are
maps by Mercator (the famous cartographer,
a contemporary of Plantin's, was born in nearby
Rupelmonde), Plantin's Biblia Regia, one of
the rare Gutenberg Bibles and other invaluable
manuscripts. When Plantin died in 1579 the
business was taken over by his son-in-law Jan
Moretus and run by his family until 1865, when
the city authorities bought the ailing company.
In 1877 they converted it into a museum.

Equally enjoyable is the idiosyncratic **Mayer
van den Bergh Museum**. A worthwhile five
or so minutes' walk south-east from the centre,
this thoroughly engaging display of the private
collection of Fritz Mayer van den Bergh is
housed in a re-created 16th-century town
house. Purpose-built in 1904 by Mayer van den

Bergh's mother after the early death of her son
aged 33, this immensely charming place boasts
as its prize exhibit Pieter Bruegel the Elder's
astonishing *Dulle Griet* ('Mad Meg'), a Bosch-
like allegory of a world turned upside down.
Look out also for a powerful crucifixion triptych
by Quentin Matsys, works by Bouts, van Orley,
Cranach and Mostaert and some beautiful 15th-
century carved wooden angels.

On the same street is the **Maagdenhuis**, a
one-time foundling hospital that now contains
a small art collection and a largest display of
medieval porridge bowls.

The city's major museums are a short walk
further south (or tram No.8 from Groenplaats).
It's a journey that lovers of art should make,
especially to the **Koninklijk Museum voor
Schone Kunsten** (Royal Museum of Fine
Arts), the focal point of southern Antwerp.
This outstanding museum, covering Flemish
painting from 1350 to the present day, is best
known for its collection of Flemish Primitives
and works from Antwerp's Golden Age. The
Primitives include Rogier van der Weyden,
Hans Memling and Jan van Eyck, whose
significant improvements to oil painting
techniques can be seen with his unfinished
picture of St Barbara. The most stunning section
is the one devoted to the 17th century, with
paintings by Rubens, Jordaens and van Dyck.
The Rubens works are mostly religious, with
Venus Frigida a notable exception; Jordaens'
compositions are less dramatic but his range
of subjects more varied, such as his famous *As
the Old Sang, the Young Play Pipes*; van Dyck's
work is less flamboyant than either, as seen in
Portrait of the Painter Marten Pepyn. The
museum has a large collection of works by James
Ensor, the surrealists and the CoBrA artists.

Antwerp has a brash, optimistic attitude
towards encouraging new artistic talent.
The high-profile contemporary art museum
MUHKA (Museum voor Hedendaagse Kunst
van Antwerpen) displays works from the '70s
onwards. The focus is on temporary exhibitions,
and the strength of the museum lies in the way
in which space is used in the light-flooded,
mostly white-painted rooms. The result is a
relaxed atmosphere, ideal for contemplating
works that are not always effortlessly accessible.

Meanwhile, fashion followers will adore
MoMu (ModeMuseum; www.momu.be), the
new museum devoted to design, located in the
beautiful late 19th-century ModeNatie complex
(www.modenatie.com). The building is home to
the Flanders Fashion Institute and the fashion
department of the Royal Academy of Fine
Arts, as well as a trendy café-restaurant, library
and workshops. But the big draw for visitors is
MoMu. Contemporary fashion and a historic

Trips Out of Town

These books are made for walking

costume and lace collection are highlights, while the overall aim is to make the museum a living and evolutionary space, where processes are as important as the finished product, and where fashion and design are put into a social context. Currently the collection is being catalogued and photographed, making it available as a public archive in the impressive museum library. Keep an eye out for major exhibitions: Goddess (8 May-22 August 2004) looks at how costume worn by the ancient Greeks influences design in the 21st century; Malign Muses (18 September 2004-30 January 2005) deciphers how to curate dress by looking at the contrast between object and space.

Photography buffs should head to the **Museum voor Fotografie**. A new wing designed by architect Georges Baines contains large exhibition halls and houses the Antwerp Film Museum. The museum's photography collection is one of Europe's most important, for equipment and images. It takes an interactive approach with workshops, temporary exhibitions, film performances and lectures – and there's a great café.

Koninklijk Museum voor Schone Kunsten

1-9 Leopold de Waelplaats (03 238 78 09/ http://museum.antwerpen.be/kmska). **Open** 10am-5pm Tue-Sun. **Admission** €5; €4 concessions; free under-18s & Fri. **No credit cards**.

Maagdenhuis

33 Lange Gasthuisstraat (03 223 53 20). **Open** 10am-5pm Mon, Wed-Fri; 1-5pm Sat, Sun. **Admission** €2.50; free Fri. **No credit cards**. **Map** p218 C4.

Mayer van den Bergh Museum

19 Lange Gasthuisstraat (03 232 42 37/http:// museum.antwerpen.be/mayervandenbergh). **Open** 10am-5pm Tue-Sun. **Admission** €4; €2 concessions; free under-18s. **Credit** MC, V. **Map** p218 C4.

MoMu

28 Nationalestraat (03 470 27 70/www.momu.be). **Open** 10am-5pm Tue-Sun; 10am-9pm 1st & 3rd Thur of the mth. **Admission** €6; €3.50-€4 concessions. **No credit cards**. **Map** p218 B4.

MUHKA

16-30 Leuvenstraat (03 260 99 99/www.muhka.be). **Open** 10am-5pm Tue-Sun. **Admission** €5; €3 concessions. **Credit** V.

Museum voor Fotografie

47 Waalsekaai (03 242 93 00/www.fotomuseum.be). **Open** 10am-5pm Tue-Sun. **Admission** free.

Museum Plantin-Moretus

22 Vrijdagmarkt (03 221 14 50/03 221 14 51/http:// museum.antwerpen.be/plantin_moretus). **Open** 10am-5pm Tue-Sun. **Admission** €4; €2 concessions; free under-12s & Fri. **No credit cards**. **Map** p218 A4.

The left bank

South of the Steen, in St Jansvliet, is the entrance to the 600-metre (1,969-foot) **St Anna pedestrian tunnel**, which connects the right and left banks. Wooden escalators take you underground from the art deco bulkhead, then it's a ten-minute walk to the other side of the river and a view of the Antwerp skyline. Antwerp was built mainly on the right bank of the Scheldt and consequently the left bank is not particularly lively. The architect Le Corbusier had an ambitious plan to move all the administrative buildings to the left bank, thinking that this was the only way in which it might have a chance to develop. The project was turned down and the left bank never did pick up. Nevertheless, the left bank can claim the only beach in Antwerp, the **St Anna Strand**. It gets crowded in fine weather, but despite the reappearance of fish in the river, it is still considered unsafe to swim in the Scheldt. The beach is a good 15 minutes' walk north once you reach the west bank.

Centraal Station, the diamond district & the Meir

Antwerp's striking **Centraal Station** is east of the centre. Built in 1905 by Louis Delacenserie in iron and glass, with an impressive dome, majestic stairs and lashings of lavish gold decoration, it's a surprising and splendidly ostentatious construction. Major works to accommodate TGV and Eurostar trains are scheduled to finish at the end of 2005, linking the city to London and the rest of Europe. Next to the station is Antwerp's extensive **Zoo**. It's the biggest in Belgium, and one of Europe's oldest (opened in 1843). The original architecture is more impressive than the animals' living quarters; check out the giraffe house.

West of the station is the **diamond district**, a predominantly Jewish area. The Diamantsbeurs in Pelikaanstraat is heavily guarded. The **Provinciaal Diamantmuseum**, on an impressive square facing Centraal Station, has three floors of treasures. Visitors are taken on an interactive tour showing how rough diamonds become polished and end up as gorgeous jewellery. The surrounding area itself glitters rather less than the stones in which it trades, and has a highly visible police presence.

The **Meir**, Antwerp's main shopping street, takes you from the station to the historic centre. Don't let the window displays cause you to miss some remarkable 19th-century buildings, such as the art deco **Boerentoren**, the first skyscraper in Europe. Just off the Meir, the

MoMu. *See p223.*

Handelsbeurs (Stock Exchange) is on the site of one of the oldest stock exchanges in Europe. The original building was replaced in the 16th century; the current structure dates from 1872.

Further afield, it's well worth getting out to the splendid **Openlucht Museum voor Beeldhouwkunst Middelheim**. This open-air sculpture museum has works from Rodin to the present day, including Belgian artists Panamarenko and Vermeiren. It's about five kilometres (three miles) from the city centre. City trams Nos.7 and 15 stop a 15-minute walk short of it; buses Nos.18 and 32 go closer, or it may be easier to take a taxi. The biennial summer exhibition of international sculpture here should not be missed.

In the same direction, you'll find an old power station housing the huge works of eccentric local artist Panamarenko. Obsessed with space, energy and the force of gravity, Panamarenko (short for Pan American Airlines Company) is famed for his bizarre flying creations. In summer his studio, the **Antwerp Airship Building**, is open to the public. Take trams Nos.10 or 24 towards Bergerhout.

Antwerp Airship Building

2 Karolgeertstraat (03 216 30 47/www.panamarenko. net). **Open** *June-Aug* 10am-6pm Mon, Wed-Sun. **Admission** free.

Antwerp Zoo

26 Koningin Astridplein (03 202 45 40/ www.zooantwerpen.be). **Open** *Sept-June* 10am-6pm daily. *July, Aug* 10am-7pm daily. **Admission** €14; €9.50 concessions; free under-3s. **Credit** AmEx, DC, MC, V.

Openlucht Museum voor Beeldhouwkunst Middelheim

61 Middelheimlaan (03 828 13 50/http://museum. antwerpen.be/middelheimopenluchtmuseum). **Open** *Oct-Mar* 10am-5pm Tue-Sun. *Apr, Sept* 10am-7pm Tue-Sun. *May, Aug* 10am-8pm Tue-Sun. *June, July* 10am-9pm Tue-Sun. **Admission** free.

Provinciaal Diamantmuseum

19-23 Koningin Astridplein (03 202 48 90/ www.diamantmuseum.be). **Open** *Nov-Apr* 10am-7pm daily. *May-Oct* 10am-6pm daily. **Admission** €6; €4 concessions; free under-12s & Fri. **Credit** MC, V.

Tourist information

For information on Antwerp's many churches, visit www.topa.be.

Toerisme Antwerpen

13 Grote Markt (03 232 01 03/fax 03 220 82 96/ www.visitantwerpen.be). **Open** 9am-6pm Mon-Sat; 9am-5pm Sun. **Map** p218 A3.
For information about Antwerp province, try the tourist office at 16 Koningin Elisabethlei (03 240 63 73, fax 03 240 63 83, www.tpa.be).

Accommodation

Hotels are plentiful, although it can be busy in summer so booking is advisable. The tourist office can book for you, often at cheaper rates.

Astrid Park Plaza

7 Koningin Astridplein, 2018 Antwerp (03 203 12 73/fax 03 203 12 75/www.parkplaza.com). **Rates** single €125; double €150. **Credit** AmEx, DC, MC, V.

Trips Out of Town

Situated on the square outside Centraal Station, the exterior of the Astrid Park Plaza looks like it has been made out of Lego. Fortunately the inside is much easier on the eye, and the view of the city from the Astrid Lounge is certainly impressive. Among the hotel's long list of facilities are a pool, sauna and fitness room, bar, café and restaurant, as well as a Nintendo in every room.

Diamond Princess

2 St Laureiskaai (Bonapartedok), 2000 Antwerp (03 227 08 15/fax 03 227 16 77). **Rates** single €65; double €85-€125; suite €139. **Credit** AmEx, DC, MC, V. **Map** p218 A1.
This five-deck 'boatel' has 57 luxuriously furnished en-suite rooms. There's a restaurant (La Combuse), a 'beach deck' (terrace), bar, library and disco.

Hotel Florida

59 De Keyserlei (03 232 14 43/www.hotelflorida.be). **Rates** single €60-€69; double €80-€90. **Credit** MC, V.
Opposite the station, the Florida can be an impersonal space, but offers good-value, high-standard rooms. You can choose from the renovated part of the hotel or the newly built extension. A good breakfast buffet is offered in the price.

Greta Stevens – Miller's Dream

35 Molenstraat, 2018 Antwerp (03 259 15 90/ http://users.pandora.be/molenaarsdroom). **Rates** single €40-€60; double €50-€65. **No credit cards.**
Greta Stevens' beautiful colonial-style house is near the town park, just to the south of Britselei. The three spacious en-suite B&B rooms are decorated with modern art, two looking out on to an interior courtyard, the third with a balcony overlooking the street. No smoking.

Hilton

Groenplaats, 2000 Antwerp (03 204 12 12/ www.hilton.com). **Rates** single/double €270-€380. **Credit** AmEx, DC, MC, V. **Map** p218 B3.
The Antwerp Hilton takes up nearly an entire side of this pleasant, busy square near the Grote Markt. The hotel offers all the facilities and services associated with the chain (including a Nintendo in each room), but with more charm than you might expect.

Hotel Prinse

63 Keizerstraat, 2000 Antwerp (03 226 40 50/ www.hotelprinse.be). **Rates** single €102; double €120; suite €137. **Credit** AmEx, DC, MC, V. **Map** p218 C2.
The historic exterior of this 16th-century private house hides a striking modern interior and a lovely courtyard. Not far from the main shopping and sightseeing areas, the four-star hotel has 35 rooms (all en-suite). Breakfast is included in the price.

New International Youth Hostel

256 Provinciestraat, 2018 Antwerp (03 230 05 22/ www.niyh.be). **Rates** dorm €14; single €29; double €44-€55; quad €74-€86. **No credit cards.**
A ten-minute walk south of the station, this hostel has only 30 rooms so booking is essential. Rooms are for one, two, four or eight people; six have their own bathroom. There's also a TV room, bar and restaurant. Price includes breakfast.

'T Sandt

17 Zand, 2000 Antwerp (03 232 93 90/ www.hotel-sandt.be). **Rates** *Mon-Thur* single €160; double €175; *Fri-Sun* single €130; double €145. **Credit** AmEx, DC, MC, V. **Map** p218 A4.
A one-time customs house, soap factory and fruit importing company office, now converted into a very classy hotel. All rooms in this neo-rococo

19th-century building by the Scheldt are suites (some are duplexes) and very spacious; each is decorated in a different style. An Italianate garden and rooftop terrace bar are further attractions.

Vandepitte B&B

49 Britselei bte 6, 2000 Antwerp (03 288 66 95). **Rates** double €55-€62; penthouse €100. **No credit cards. Map** p218 C5.

It may be located at the top of an unprepossessing modern block on the busy inner ring road, a good ten- to 15-minute walk from the centre, but it has one of the most elegant and stylish B&B rooms you'll ever stay in. Two of the three rooms are relatively small (although one does have a bathroom to die for), but it's the penthouse that steals the show: black stone floors, views over Antwerp, a flash stereo, ethnic art and bags of space. Breakfast is equally impressive.

Hotel Villa Mozart

3 Handschoenmarkt, 2000 Antwerp (03 231 30 31/ fax 03 231 56 85). **Rates** *Mon-Thur* single €132; double €170; suite €236-€268. *Fri-Sun* single €92; double €96; suite €199-€210. **Credit** AmEx, DC, MC, V. **Map** p218 A/B3.

The 25 luxury rooms and suites here, in the centre of the old town, are decorated in Laura Ashley style. Hotel services include a sauna and babysitting.

De Witte Lelie

16-18 Keizerstraat, 2000 Antwerp (03 226 19 66/ www.dewittelelie.be). **Rates** single €180-€250; double €240-€320. **Credit** AmEx, DC, MC, V. **Map** p218 C2.

An absolute stunner. The building may be 17th century, but the interior is utterly contemporary. Expect good-sized rooms, oceans of white, lashings of low-key luxury and a generous inclusive breakfast. Ideally located for exploring the trendy part of town.

Gay accommodation

Bed & Breakfast 2000 Guesthouse

8 Van Boendalestraat, 2000 Antwerp (03 234 12 10/http://guestrooms.happygays.be). **Rates** €35 single; €50 double. **No credit cards.**

Friendly B&B in an old terraced house with good-sized, comfortable rooms and shared lounge areas.

G8 Gay Guesthouse

8 Geulincxstraat, 2060 Antwerp (0477 62 62 81/ www.g8.be). **Rates** vary. **No credit cards.**

A no-nonsense bed-and-breakfast place catering more for the fetish-type crowd.

Eating & drinking

Restaurants

Absoluut Zweeds

12 Wijngaardstraat (03 237 28 43/www.absoluut zweeds.be). **Open** noon-2pm, 6-10.30pm daily. **Main courses** €25. **Set menus** €39, €49. **Credit** MC, V. **Map** p218 B3.

Absoluut Zweeds (Absolutely Swedish) is absolute class. Not just the starkly minimalist interior punctuated with black tables and Arne Jacobsen chairs, but also in the design of the stylish menu. Absolute clarity reigns supreme here, with a Swedish paella as star of the show. Head chef and owner Christer Elfving sticks by his slogan 'Swedish Roots, Future Food' by introducing delicate sashimi and tempura into solid Scandinavian stock. And if you're not sure what to order, the taster menu does the work for you.

Amadeus

20 Sint-Paulusstraat (03 232 25 87). **Open** 6-10.30pm Mon-Thur; 6-11.30pm Fri, Sat; 5-10.30pm Sun. **Main courses** €15. **Credit** AmEx, DC, MC, V. **Map** p218 A2.

Long rows of wooden tables in an old art nouveau glass factory give this spare-rib restaurant a unique edge. A litre of house red sits unceremoniously on the table at arrival – drink as much or as little as you like, you're charged only for the amount you quaff. Then there are the ribs, as many as you can eat with the accompaniment of your choice. No knives and forks necessary, just get those fingers working. A great buzz at a great price.

Broers van Julienne

45-47 Kasteelpleinstraat (03 232 02 03). **Open** noon-10.30pm Mon-Sat; 6-10.30pm Sun. **Main courses** €20. **Credit** MC, V. **Map** p218 C5.

There's a certain hush about this non-meat restaurant. It's all to do with the decor and reading-room atmosphere created in a calming colonial style, with a pretty garden under shady trees in summer. The food is prepared using natural and biologically sane ingredients. North African influences creep in with Moroccan salads and tagines. A shop and bakery at the front are equally classy.

Chez Fl'Eau

1 Tavernierkaai (03 225 36 37/www.chezfleau.be). **Open** noon-10.30pm Mon-Thur; noon-11pm Fri; 6-11pm Sat; noon-10pm Sun. **Main courses** €20. **Set menu** €35. **Credit** AmEx, MC, V.

This old harbour-master's house in the dock area was built to last and it's not taking second place to any sissy redevelopment or modern notions. Inside is resolutely loft-inspired, the rows of iron pillars holding up the great roof. Wooden tables and yellow and blue tones finish the overall look of this stylish brasserie. The food is as you'd expect, world influences combined with classic favourites such as swordfish sizzled in a wok with soy and chilli or duck breast with confit of fig. Book ahead.

Ciro's

6 Amerikalei (03 238 11 47). **Open** 11am-11pm daily. **Main courses** €12. **Credit** MC, V.

Ciro's was last decorated in 1962 and, in the way of the design world, has gone full circle in its own retro way. The clientele comes for the steak and chips, regarded as the best in Antwerp. Waitresses schlep around delivering the no-nonsense food unceremoniously to the table, the diners talk loudly and get stuck in. Don't feel that as a visitor you will be out of place; there is a welcome for everyone and a well-meaning tour of the menu for hapless foreigners.

Désiré de Lille

14-18 Schrijnwerkerstraat (03 232 62 26/ www.desiredelille.be). **Open** 9am-10pm daily. **Main courses** €12. **No credit cards**. **Map** p218 B3.

Desiré started off as a funfair stand, selling freshly made waffles, fruit-filled doughnuts and *laquemants*, a kind of baked pancake. It celebrated its centenary in 2003 and continues to trade in its genteel 1930s restaurant, its big windows opening up to the street, its interior filled with banquettes and railway carriage lights. A glass pergola at the back gives a conservatory feel and leads out into a magnificent garden. It's a great blend of the old style and the new wave, as typified by the broad mix of people who come here.

Farine's Food & Future

40 Vlaamsekaai (03 238 37 76). **Open** 7-11pm Mon, Wed-Sun. **Main courses** €12. **Credit** AmEx, DC, MC, V.

A long scrubbed pine table seating around 20 is the centrepiece of this small cantina. At one end is what looks like grandma's kitchen, complete with tea

Industrial chic at **Het Pomphuis**. *See p230*.

towels hanging to dry. The homeliness theme continues with great yellow jugs of milk and sugar bowls left along the length of the table. But that's where familiarity ends, for painted on the wall is a mural from a psychedelic world, full of fairies and frogs and other magic things. This is an in-the-know place for cool customers who sit and philosophise as funky music thumps quietly in the background. Choose from curries, doorstep sarnies or an all-day fry-up; vegetarians are well catered for too.

Het Nieuwe Palinghuis

14 Sint-Jansvliet (03 231 74 45/www.hetnieuwe palinghuis.be). **Open** noon-3pm, 6-10pm Wed-Sun. **Main courses** €25. **Credit** AmEx, DC, MC, V. **Map** p218 A4.

A very fishy restaurant indeed, serving the freshest fish prepared by patron Erik Haentjens, who's had the place for 20 years and keeps it all shipshape. The look is olde worlde with pink cloths and boating collectibles, the walls hung with sepia prints of 19th-century Antwerpenaars fishing their cotton smocks off. Even the loo seats have shells embedded in them, so there's a bit of a theme going on. Fish is the order of the day – eel, bouillabaisse, scallops with truffles and naughty-but-nice pot mussels in cream with garlic. A bit pricey, but you won't be disappointed.

Hippodroom

10 Leopold de Waelplaats (03 248 52 52). **Open** noon-2.30pm, 6.30-11pm Mon-Fri; 6.30-11pm Sat, Sun. **Main courses** €25. **Credit** AmEx, MC, V.

Hippodroom's long, slender dining room contrasts perfectly with its turn-of-the-century exterior, a 1904 house facing the Fine Arts Museum. Massive works of art and photographs mounted on coolly coloured walls look over a slim line of minimally set tables perched on wooden floors. It's chic, and its confident aesthetic extends to the menu: Iranian caviar, sushi, French-inspired fillet of lamb with truffle risotto, and vegetarian options. A garden gives an alluring glow to the overall sensual ambience.

De Kleine Zavel

2 Stoofstraat (03 231 96 91). **Open** noon-2.30pm, 6-10.30pm Mon-Thur; noon-2pm, 6.30-11pm Fri; 6.30-11.30pm Sat; noon-2pm, 6-10.30pm Sun. **Main courses** €23. **Credit** AmEx, DC, MC, V. **Map** p218 A4.

In a long room among old beer and wine crates and distressed furniture, once the breakfast room of an old hotel, unclothed tables lend a bistro air. The menu surpasses that idea by leaps. The KZ is one of Antwerp's dining hotspots, with chef-owner Carlo Didden serving up imaginative French-inspired food in no mean portions to a discerning yet unpretentious crowd. Rare meats, foie gras and wild mushrooms all find a harmonious place with flair and style. Service is multilingual perfect. Don't miss it.

Lucy Chang

16-17 Marnixplaats (03 248 95 60/www.lucychang. be). **Open** noon-midnight daily. **Main courses** €11. **No credit cards**.

If it's Tuesday it must be **Soep & Soup**.

The first thing you see here is an oriental market stall, to the right of which is a long, low bar. This is designed for those who want to pop in and take a small plate of dim sum or a bowl of noodle soup. Tables are set simply with paper napkins and chopsticks. But this is no oriental theme-park, it is slick and modern with just the right amount of tradition to nudge you east. The food is from Laos, Vietnam, Thailand, Malaysia and China, and is designed as one-dish meals, where everything comes at once and can be shared. Authentic cooking at great prices.

Maritime
4 Suikerrui (03 233 07 58/www.maritime.be).
Open noon-2.30pm, 6-9.30pm Mon, Tue, Fri-Sun.
Main courses €24. **Credit** AmEx, DC, MC, V.
Map p218 A3.
Between the Grote Markt and the river, there is a run of seafood restaurants catering largely to the tourist trade. Tucked in among them, though, is one worthy of a visit, a true petunia in an onion patch that has been around for 50 years. Maritime is classical Belgian in its look with its wooden beams, chi-chi chairs and red tablecloths. The food is equally classic with a heavy leaning to eels and mussels. And not just eels in green sauce – try them in cream or fried in butter, or have a go at mussels in a Madras curry sauce. Maritime likes its lobster too. All in all, perfect if you're after a treat.

Het Pomphuis
Droogdok, 7 Siberiastraat (03 770 86 25). **Open** 11am-2.30pm; 6-11pm Mon-Fri; 11am-11pm Sat, Sun.
Main courses €20-€30. **Credit** AmEx, DC, MC, V.

This magnificent old building, the pumphouse for the dry dock, was converted in 2003 into an equally magnificent restaurant. Massive arched windows and lofty ceilings of the industrial age now surround crisply laid tables of the new one. The menu is unusual for Antwerp: Pacific Rim with Asian influences. A goat's cheese salad comes with dates, apples and beetroot syrup. More familiar fare is available too. If this place is anything to go by, Antwerp's docklands have a bright future.

Soep & Soup
89 Kammenstraat (03 707 28 05). **Open** 11am-7pm Mon-Sat. **Main courses** €10-€15. **Credit** AmEx, DC, MC, V. **Map** p218 B4.
Scrawled along the wall of this utterly happening soup bar is the classic legend: 'In this bowl you may know heaven'. A bold statement from Molière, a bolder one from the kitchen – but absolutely true. Each day brings a choice of five soups in various sizes for eating in or taking out; imagine a meal-size Italian minestrone with mushroom ravioli, chicken and parmesan croutons, all served with hunks of wholemeal bread. Soep & Soup is in the heart of the trendy fashion district, so its minimalist, modernist outlook hits the mark splendidly.

Sombat Thai Cuisine
1 Vleeshuisstraat (03 226 61 90). **Open** noon-2.30pm, 6-10.30pm Tue-Fri; 6-11pm Sat, Sun. **Main courses** €20. **Credit** AmEx, MC, V. **Map** p218 A3.
Owner Sombat opened Les Larmes du Tigre in Brussels (*see p119*) before moving to Antwerp and setting up this big restaurant in the shadow of the

Gothic Butcher's Hall. This is Thai cooking at its best – a world away from run-of-the-mill westernised Thai menus. Mixed dishes are popular here: so spring rolls turn up with minced pork in a banana leaf, crispy noodles and dipping sauces. Regarded by locals as Antwerp's finest, this Thai has a genteel, studied feel, making it a bit of a class act.

De Varkenspoot

3 Graanmarkt (03 232 63 63/www.varkenspoot.be). **Open** noon-2.30pm, 6-10pm Mon-Thur; noon-2.30pm, 6-11pm Fri, Sat. **Main courses** €19. **Set menus** €22-€34.50. **Credit** AmEx, MC, V. **Map** p218 C4.
De Varkenspoot (the Pig's Foot) isn't a particularly glamorous name for a restaurant, but Guido van Landeghem's restaurant has been trotting along nicely for 16 years. Sitting in a handsome house on a quiet square behind the Bourla theatre makes for artistic eating and a decent summer terrace. The small menu is big on fish and meat and seasonal specials give it an edge; asparagus in spring, game in autumn. Beware, the pig's trotter does make an appearance as a starter. A bit of an institution – and modestly sized – so you should book.

Bars

Bar Tabac

43 Waalsekaai (03 238 19 37). **Open** *Oct-May* 8pm-late Tue-Sat; 9pm-late Sun. *June-Sept* 7pm-late Mon-Thur; 4pm-late Fri; 1pm-late Sat, Sun. **No credit cards**.
BT doesn't really start to shake its tail feather until gone midnight, when a superb soundtrack (from Madonna to Serge Gainsbourg, via most points in between) complements an atmosphere rarely more than a couple of notches from cool. If you've had an evening of standard drinking in designer bars indistinct from any others and were wondering exactly why Antwerp is hyped to the nines, breeze into the Bar Tabac, particularly on a Sunday night, and all will become clear.

Café Beveren

2 Vlasmarkt (03 231 22 25). **Open** 12.30pm-late Mon, Thur-Sat; 1pm-late Sun. **No credit cards**. **Map** p218 A3.
This is your actual dockside Antwerp, the kind of spot you might find in Rotterdam or Hamburg, except here the good-time Johnnies and steamboat Willies have mellowed with age, fumbling with their reading glasses before another round of cards. These days the Beveren is a lovely old corner bar, of the type you'd be pushed to find around trendy 't Zuid. The red-lined banquettes encase the café in a lost era – note also the fully working De Cap fairground organ and old Rowe Ami jukebox – and watch out for spontaneous outbreaks of old-time dancing.

Cappuccino Club

13 Sint-Laureiskaai (no phone). **Open** *May-Aug* noon-4am daily. *Sept-Apr* 6pm-4am Tue-Sat. **No credit cards**. **Map** p218 A1.

Key venue in the uncharted territory of the old docks and warehouses of 't Eilandje in the north of the city. Few places are better positioned, overlooking the steady lap of the Bonaparte Dock, than the Cappuccino Club. Tatty out and in, the CC is saved by clever touches of design – an Italian menu running over wall and ceiling, a mirror ball throwing candlelight in patterns over the well-stocked bar – making it worth the modest trek.

Den Engel

5 Grote Markt (03 233 12 52). **Open** 9am-late daily. **No credit cards**. **Map** p218 A3.
Antwerp's bar of all bars. It isn't fab or fashionable, and whatever edges it once cut blunted long ago; it is simply an institution, ramshackle relief from the official goings-on next door at the Town Hall. Councillors clink glasses with nervous fiancés, journalists accept drinks and gossip from politicians, while locals of all ages provide a cheery backdrop. Next door's Den Bengel (the Miscreant) copes with the overflow from Den Engel (the Angel).

Entrepôt du Congo

42 Vlaamsekaai (03 257 16 48). **Open** 8am-3am Mon-Fri; 8am-4am Sat, Sun. **No credit cards**.
This pioneering enterprise began the regeneration of the southern quaysides into the trendy quarter of galleries and designer bars it is today. A century ago, Congo boats would dock here, unloading crates of colonial plunder into this grand corner edifice. Now a classy, bare wood-and-floortile interior displays only one deference to decoration: a framed portrait of King Baudouin in postage-stamp humour over the bar. The place is still justifiably popular, despite a plethora of competition a mere anchor's toss away – the excellent bar food might well have something to do with it.

Kleine Bourla

3 Kelderstraat (03 232 16 32). **Open** 11am-late Mon-Sat. **Credit** AmEx, DC, MC, V. **Map** p218 C4.
Built by Pierre Bruno Bourla at the time of Belgian independence, the splendidly restored Bourla Theatre is served by two fancy cafés: the ornate De Foyer on the first floor and the Kleine Bourla next door. Both do justice to the artistic surroundings and operate as entities separate from the theatre. The Kleine Bourla bistro boasts a tasteful interior, with a life-size harlequin set against a background of stunning red. A popular spot in which the literary and theatre sets gather for power elevenses and afternoon teas, it also serves main meals best enjoyed on its terrace in summer.

'T Oerwoud

2 Suikerrui (03 233 14 12). **Open** noon-late daily. **Credit** AmEx, MC, V. **Map** p218 A3.
A step back from the quayside, two steps from the brazen tourism of the town centre and opposite the medieval fortress of the Steen, 'T Oerwoud (the Jungle) is a relaxing lunch spot – salads, soups and pastas, with many dishes served until late – but

Trips Out of Town

mostly serves as a busy pre-club livener. Spotlights blaze over the curved bar, speakers boom with popular dance sounds, and the nachos machine and upholstered leather seating of the chill-and-chat back area soon become buried in a fog of Bastos.

De Pelikaan

14 Melkmarkt (03 227 23 51). **Open** 9am-late daily. **No credit cards. Map** p218 B3.

The downtown, downbeat Pelican has been dragging writers, designers and musicians through its doors and keeping them glued to its bar counter for longer than most care to remember – 50 years in fact. Located in the shadow of the cathedral, it makes no effort to appeal to curious passers-by, leaving all the dressing-up to tackier establishments nearby. For that matter, it isn't even dressed down: it's just got out of bed and put on whatever it could find on the bedroom floor, invariably the same as what it found there yesterday. Enter, drink, swap stories, get drunk, go home. Perfect.

De Scène

2 Graaf van Hoornestraat (03 238 64 42). **Open** 4pm-3am Mon-Wed, Sun; 4pm-5am Thur-Sat. **No credit cards.**

De Scène is a happening bar near the Fine Arts Museum, where studiously hip trendies gather and gesth beneath a strange, sunbeam-surfaced globe. Musicians and DJs flock here in their dozens to hear weekend spinners such as DJ Joe Tattoo, a heavy name to drop in these parts. The drinks fall into the usual range, but are served with swift aplomb by the kind of bar staff who practise and preach the religion of hair gel.

De Vagant

25 Reyndersstraat (03 233 15 38). **Open** 11am-late Mon-Sat; noon-late Sun. **No credit cards. Map** p218 A/B3.

Genever was to Antwerp what gin was to London, the opiate of historic port cities drowned in a sea of cheap alcohol (*see p134* **Going against the grain**). Prohibition arrived in 1919 and wasn't repealed until 1984. This innocuous bar opened a year later, with 200 types of once-forbidden genever in myriad strengths and flavours, accompanied by small chunks of cheese and deft slices of meat. Sipped and not slammed (spot the foreigner!), genever's potted history embellishes De Vagant's drinks menu and exquisite interior of old flagons and pre-prohibition posters. Upstairs, a restaurant serves dishes concocted from the stuff. Downstairs, a genial barman dispenses little else, apart from De Koninck and chaseable lagers.

Het Zand

9 Sint-Jansvliet (03 232 56 67). **Open** 11am-late daily. **No credit cards. Map** p218 A2.

Located by the grand entrance of the St Anna foot tunnel, Het Zand displays the calculating hand of the Celtic fraternity. Yet, despite the fading promise of a peeling Guinness Gift Shop sign, this is essentially a boozy hostelry in the classic Antwerp tradition. Het Zand is as close as you're ever likely to get to sitting in a pre-war Antwerp living room – with a bar attached. Wooden tables heave under heavy lunches, old geezers prop up the tall brick bar, while the unusual local tradition of displaying death masks of former regulars is upheld overhead.

Cafe Beveren. *See p231.*

Zuiderterras

37 Ernest van Dijckkaai (03 234 12 75). **Open** 9am-
midnight daily. **Credit** AmEx, MC, V. **Map** p218 A3.
Straddling the promenade that lines the Scheldt just
before it heads for the North Sea, Zuiderterras is a
ship-shaped, sheeny-interiored BoB van Reeth
creation. The sleek two-floor operation centres on a
circular bar counter serviced by a smart wait staff,
whose abrupt efficiency doesn't begin to dent the
romantic mood of the twinkling Scheldt at sundown.
It's pricey, sure, but potentially a weekend highlight.

Gay & lesbian bars & clubs

Antwerp is a gay mecca, and its nightlife scene
is livelier than anything in Brussels. Unless
stated, the venues below have no entry fee. *See
also p234* **Antwerp: Clubbing capital**.

Atthis

27 Geuzenstraat (03 216 37 37). **Open** 8.30pm-2am
Fri, Sat. **No credit cards. Map** p218 B5.
A women-only private club that's a little more
refined than most in Belgium. There's a video
library and a lesbian centre under the same name.

Boots

22 Van Aerdstraat (03 233 21 36/www.the-boots.com).
Open 10.30pm-5am Fri, Sat. **No credit cards.**
The grandaddy of Belgium's dark and cruisy bars
and probably the sleaziest. Stairs lead up and up
through a dark bar area into an even darker play
area where anything that can happen is likely to
happen. There is a strict dress code, but you can
change on the premises. You'll also need ID to get a
temporary membership. Sunday afternoons see the
Kink Link themed parties – doors are open until
4pm; after that they're locked.

Hessenhuis

53 Falconrui (03 231 13 56/www.hessenhuis.com).
Open 10am-late daily. **No credit cards. Map**
p218 B1.
By day, Hessenhuis serves as a museum and gallery
(*see p222*), but at night it becomes a popular pre-club
venue, attracting townie gays and their girlfriends.
The interior is a combination of modern and rustic,
though the clientele is full-on millennium chic, ready
to party and enjoy the live entertainment or theme
nights. Breakfast is served on Sunday mornings.

The Kinky's

*10 Lange Beeldekensstraat (03 295 06 40/
www.kinkys.be).* **Open** 9pm-late daily. **Admission**
€2.50; €10 special nights. **No credit cards.**
Located near the train station, Kinky's is a newish
kid on the block catering for a fetish crowd. Special
themed parties mean special dress codes, so check
the agenda before you go.

Popi

22 Riemstraat (03 238 15 30/www.popi.be). **Open**
Winter 6pm-late Tue-Sat; 4pm-late Sun. *Summer*
5pm-late Tue-Sat; 4pm-late Sun. **No credit cards.**

Brash, cheeky (its name refers to the Russian for
backside) and impossibly pink, Popi doesn't take
itself in the least bit seriously. Abba, Eurotrash and
drag sum up the free-fall entertainment. Popi is five
years old in 2004, but it still doesn't know – or care
– what it wants to be when it grows up.

Red & Blue

*11-13 Lange Schipperskapelstraat (03 213 05 55/
www.redandblue.be).* **Open** 11pm-late Fri; 11pm-
7am Sat. **Admission** varies. **No credit cards.**
Map p218 A2.
The name comes from the club's location in
the old red-light district. The girls may have moved
on, but the boys have arrived and plan to stay.
Saturday night's men-only night is regarded, along
with Brussels' La Démence (*see p185*), as Belgium's
best, with Dutch dance-divas pouring across the border (Fridays are mixed). More than a disco, R&B is
an event, especially with its occasional Studio 54
nights – Grace Jones once drove through the sweaty
dancers in a stretched limo. Serious party time.

Rubbzz

28 Guelinckxstraat (03 232 78 14/www.rubbzz.org).
Open 11pm-4am Tue-Thur, Sun; 11pm-6am Fri, Sat.
Admission varies. **No credit cards.**
An industrial warehouse look is the Rubbzz brand,
a friendly place with live DJs at weekends. At the
darker, cruisier end of the scale, its regulars love the
sleazy atmosphere and the funky house music.

Shakespeare

24 Oude Koornmarkt (03 231 50 58). **Open** 10pm-
late Fri, Sat. **No credit cards. Map** p218 B3.
Catering to a largely butch crowd, this small, dark
pub is the oldest survivor on the Antwerp lesbian
landscape. Music is a mix of rock, soul, house and
disco; men are welcome if accompanied by a woman.

Shopping

Antwerp's role as one of the world's most
celebrated fashion hubs (*see p237* **Antwerp:
Fashion capital**) has made it a shopper's
paradise. Designer-led stores with a hip
reputation to maintain open their pilot stores
in Antwerp rather than Brussels. It is cooler,
cleaner and has that buzz that other Belgian
cities strive for but just don't pull off. The main
shopping drag with all the international chains
is the **Meir**, the traffic-free stretch between the
station and the city centre. **Huidevetterstraat**
to the south is more upbeat with some one-off
boutiques, and things start to get interesting
around **Schutterhofstraat**, where there are
hip bathroom shops, contemporary jewellers
and understated designer clothing stores. The
avant-garde core is the warren of streets closed
to traffic and known as 'De Wilde Zee'. It
includes **Kammenstraat**, the place to go for
young, upbeat streetwear stores and retro

Trips Out of Town

Antwerp: Clubbing capital

The reputation of Antwerp's nightlife comes from its status as a fashion capital, a gay centre and a city that is at ease with itself. Youth culture rules on the streets and in the bars and clubs, with swathes of preppy Prada preenies and Drunknmunky alternatives moving from one place to another, deciding what's hot and what's not. As sure as the seasons change, so do the attitudes of the clubbing classes as they're always on the lookout for the new, the exciting, the different.

First, though, a quick word about clothing in this stylish fashion mecca. You may think those newly sprung, air-bubbled skater shoes are the best thing ever, but Belgian bouncers won't give them legroom. Only the whispered-about underground clubs will welcome trainers and your baggy-hip camos; in the mainstream, it's always best to dress to impress.

Otherwise, the visitor needs a go-with-the-flow approach and a bit of research. Check the agenda on **www.noctis.com** to tap into one-off parties or festivals or drop into urban shops like **Fish & Chips** (*see p235*) to pick up flyers. A good starting place is the legendary **Café d'Anvers** (15 Verversrui, 03 226 38 70, www.cafe-d-anvers.com; *pictured*). The red-brick Anvers was a church and cinema before its transformation to a kicking deep house club in 1991. Expect uplifting house from Thursday to Saturday, with resident DJs Smos, Baby B, Isabel, Prinz, Kenneth, Filliz and Bartholomeo. A new club-in-club concept is **Club Mississipi**, an urban night on the first Sunday of the month (0486 89 41 88, www.mississipi.be). The brick and iron, tanned wood, thick curtains and elegant armchairs will be forever d'Anvers.

Once the Friday night **Fill Collins Club** (11-13 Lange Schipperskapelstraat, 03 213 05 55, www.fillcollinsclub.com) was filled to the rafters with funky housers, but after a closure it now returns only occasionally. It's a packed treat when it does happen. Today the men-only **Red & Blue** happens there on Saturday nights (*see p233*), while Friday nights have a gay edge but are mixed. **Industria** is one of Antwerp's sparkling places (10 Indiestraat,

03 234 09 92, www.clubindustria.be). This is a big and beautiful old factory space with echoing UK and NYC club house, and funky soul played by residents Bill and Hetrix. For something a little more underground, try **Club Dust** (29 Frankrijklei, no phone) where DJ Peran (www.djperan.com) organises weekend progressive trance and techno parties.

Soul and house reign supreme here and **Club Geluk** (6 Luikstraat, 03 294 44 32, www.clubgeluk.be) hits the spot. The right people in the right place funk away on Thursdays (6pm-2am), Fridays and Saturdays (11pm-7am). The more alternative crowd like the hefty drum 'n' bass and scratchy electronica of the weird and offbeat **Kaaiman** (57 Napelstraat, 0486 47 70 33, www.kaaiman.be), set in an atmospheric cellar in the dock area. For one-off parties, it's also worth clicking on to **www.5voor12.com**, a production company that stages major club nights throughout the country, but hosts irregular nights at **De Cinema** (12 Lang Brilstraat, 03 226 49 63, www.decinema.be). This venue is also home to **Couleur d'Anvers**, a Saturday night of African and black music.

Twice a year, the city comes alive with **Antwerp Is Burning** (www.antwerpisburning.be), a one-night seven-club extravaganza, one entrance ticket allowing access to a free shuttle between venues. The next one is due to take place on 4 September 2004.

Nearby Linkeroever hosts **Clubland**, an enormous event bringing together a batch of Europe's biggest clubs in a field. This year's takes place on 8 August.

shops; **St Antoniusstraat**, where Walter van Beirendonck hangs out; and **Nationalestraat**, home to Dries van Noten's temple of fashion. Antwerp also has a well-deserved reputation for its fine antiques and bric-a-brac shops, most of which can be found in the district known as St Andries: **Lombardenvest**, **Steenhouwersvest** and **Kloosterstraat** (a short walk south of Groenplaats). All the shops listed below are closed on Sundays unless otherwise stated.

Fashion & accessories

Ann Demeulemeester
38 Verlatstraat (03 213 01 33). **Open** 11am-7pm Mon-Sat. **Credit** AmEx, DC, MC, V.
Demeulemeester, star member of the Antwerp Six, designs clothes that are slick yet sensual, soft with big attitude, but all seemingly right for the times. Her minimalist shop is in a different part of Antwerp from that of her contemporaries, opposite the Fine Arts Museum in the south of the city. *See also p237* **Antwerp: Fashion capital**.

Christa Reniers
8 Vrijdagsmarkt (03 233 26 02/www.christareniers. com). **Open** noon-6.30pm Tue-Thur; 10.30am-1pm, 2-6.30pm Fri, Sat. **Credit** AmEx, MC, V. **Map** p218 A4.
Brussels-based Reniers is considered Belgium's top jewellery designer, creating naturally inspired rings, chokers and bracelets in silver and gold.

Closing Date
15 Korte Gasthuisstraat (03 232 87 22). **Open** 11am-6.30pm Mon-Sat. **Credit** AmEx, DC, MC, V. **Map** p218 B4.
Clubbers with cash and eccentrics with panache gather here to pore over racks of clothes by the likes of Owen Gaster, Dsquared2 and Amaya Arzuaga. Even Vivienne Westwood gets a look in.

Coccodrillo
9A/B Schuttershofstraat (03 233 20 93). **Open** 10am-6pm Mon-Sat. **Credit** AmEx, DC, MC, V. **Map** p218 C4.
Prada, Patrick Cox, Jil Sander, Ann Demeulemeester, Dries van Noten and Helmut Lang are among those represented at this full-on fashion footwear mecca.

Erotische Verbeelding
10-12 Ijzerenwaag (03 226 89 50/www.erotische verbeelding.com). **Open** 11am-6pm. **Credit** AmEx, MC, V. **Map** p218 B4.
This women-only store – aimed at pleasuring women – stocks sex aids, tasteful-looking dildos, a smattering of S&M and slinky lingerie in a safe and sophisticated environment.

Fish & Chips
36-38 Kammenstraat (03 227 08 24/ www.fishandchips.be). **Open** 10am-6.30pm Mon-Sat. **Credit** AmEx, MC, V. **Map** p218 B4.

A bright, brash, chaotic store and legendary supplier to Antwerp's youth culture. On Saturdays, DJs spin party music in a booth overhanging the ground floor, which is racked up with skater gear, urban grunge and raver retro labels. There's a fruit and veg juice counter and lounge area upstairs.

Huis Boon
4 Lombardenvest (03 232 33 87). **Open** *Mar-Aug* 11am-6pm Mon-Sat. *Sept-Feb* 10am-6pm Mon-Sat. **Credit** AmEx, DC, MC, V. **Map** p218 B4.
A wonderfully evocative time capsule of a glove shop, with hundreds of different pairs for men and women, displayed on dark wooden shelves and in little drawers. Staff soften leather gloves by putting them on wooden hand models before you try them on. Such service, such style.

Louis
2 Lombardenstraat (03 232 98 72). **Open** 10am-6pm Mon-Sat. **Credit** AmEx, MC, V. **Map** p218 B4.
This small boutique was one of the very first to champion Belgian fashion, and is now a shrine for the fashion-conscious. Martin Margiela, Veronique Branquinho and Olivier Theyskens are the staple labels. The management has recently changed, so here's hoping the stock doesn't.

Het Modepaleis
16 Nationalestraat (03 470 25 10). **Open** 10am-6.30pm Mon-Sat. **Credit** AmEx, DC, MC, V. **Map** p218 B4.
Internationally renowned Dries van Noten sells his own collections in this landmark building dating from 1881. Both the men's and women's floors are decorated with late 19th-century furniture, complemented by contemporary lighting and furnishings. This is top-level shopping with class, flair and style. *See also p237* **Antwerp: Fashion capital**.

Nadine Wijnants
26 Kloosterstraat (03 226 45 69/www.nadine wijnants.be). **Open** 11am-6pm Tue-Sat. **Credit** MC, V. **Map** p218 B3.
One of the top youngish jewellery designers in Belgium, Wijnants creates charming pieces with semi-precious stones and oxidised or sterling silver, bronze and gold plate. Incorporating influences that run from India to street-style, Wijnants always aims to make her collections affordable.
Other locations: 14 Nationalestraat (03 231 75 15).

Naughty I
65-67 Kammenstraat (03 213 35 90). **Open** 11am-6.30pm Mon-Fri; 11am-7pm Sat. **Credit** AmEx, MC, V. **Map** p218 B4.
Outrageously camp and trashy, this second-hand shop is the perfect place to find platform shoes, bell-bottoms, pointy-collar shirts and fluorescent boob-tubes. Brilliant for a kitsch rummage and reminisce.

Nitya
9D Schuttershofstraat (03 213 07 37). **Open** 10am-6pm Mon-Sat. **Credit** AmEx, MC, V. **Map** p218 C4.

extraordinary and rather ambiguous space, which comes over as a gallery as much as a shop. Wendy houses, white boxes and even a massive recumbent teddy bear conceal a choice selection of designer labels and van B's collections Wild & Lethal Trash and Aesthetic Terrorists.

XSO

13-17 Eiermarkt (03 231 87 49). **Open** 10am-12.30pm, 1-6pm Mon-Sat. **Credit** AmEx, DC, MC, V. **Map** p218 B3.
Wrapping around a quiet courtyard in the centre of town, this shop has stunning decor, mixing Japanese purity (white walls, slate floors) with Italian flourishes. Appropriately enough, it stocks clothes by Issey Miyake, Kenzo and Giorgio Armani.

Food & confectionery

Goossens

31 Korte Gasthuisstraat (03 226 07 91). **Open** 7am-7pm Tue-Sat. **No credit cards. Map** p218 B4.
Founded in 1884, this small and popular traditional bakery offers a good choice of pastries and cakes, all displayed on metal racks.

Kashandel Vervloet

28 Wiegstraat (03 233 37 29). **Open** 8am-6pm Mon-Sat. **No credit cards. Map** p218 B3.
Run by master cheese-buyer Luc Wouters, who specialises in cheeses from Belgium, including his own, a hard goat's cheese.

Philip's Biscuits

11 Korte Gasthuisstraat (03 231 26 60). **Open** 10am-6pm Mon-Sat. **No credit cards. Map** p218 B4.
If you can get past the glorious window display, Philip's is the place for macaroons, *speculoos* (ginger biscuits) and the traditional hand-shaped butter biscuits so loved by Antwerpenaars.

Gay & lesbian shops

Toys 4 Boys

6 Nosestraat (03 232 08 27/www.toys4boysleather. com). **Open** 11am-8pm Thur-Sat; 2-7pm Sun. **Credit** AmEx, MC, V. **Map** p218 A2.
A darkly atmospheric shop – especially in the cellar – selling a whole range of fetish gear, as well as made-to-measure leather and rubber clothes. Dutch couple Marcel and Cor give the place a calm and relaxed air – something you'll need if you take them up on their piercing service.

'T Verschil

42 Minderbroedersrui (03 226 08 04/ www.verschil.be). **Open** noon-6pm Wed-Sun. **Credit** MC, V. **Map** p218 B2.
Looking more like a traditional bookseller in its old glass-fronted house, Verschil sells a vast range of books, magazines, DVDs and videos for gays and lesbians. In the cellar, there's a lovely old vaulted café to help with the browsing.

Wakko – the clue's in the name. *See p237.*

A luxury Indian label for women designed by a team of international designers. The result is a superb collection with an Asian twist: separates, suits and shawls. The cotton and silk fabrics are from China, suit cloths from France and the embroidery and other hand finishings are done in India.

SN3

46-48 Frankrijklei (03 231 08 20/www.sn3.be). **Open** noon-6.30pm Mon; 10am-6.30pm Tue-Sat. **Credit** AmEx, DC, MC, V.
Housed in a former cinema, this designer boutique carries principal collections by the likes of DKNY, Gaultier, Dior, Galliano and Prada. The idea is that each name has a shop within the shop, a sort of designer mall, though, as you might expect, it comes with a good dose of snob value.

Verso

11 Lange Gasthuisstraat (03 226 92 92). **Open** 11am-6.30pm Mon; 11am-6.30pm Tue-Sun. **Credit** AmEx, DC, MC, V. **Map** p218 C4.
Set in an old bank building, Verso is a temple to cutting-edge design, fashion and its own architecture. Here the fashionistas glide around the glass cabinets and wooden counter-tops, fingering a whole range of style from the likes of Helmut Lang, Miu Miu, YSL, Armani and Versace. It's so exclusive it hurts.

Walter

10 St Antoniusstraat (03 213 26 44/www.walt.de). **Open** 1-6pm Mon; 11am-6.30pm Tue-Sat. **Credit** AmEx, DC, MC, V. **Map** p218 B4.
This creation by two of the original Antwerp Six (Walter van Beirendonck and Dirk van Saene) is an

Health & beauty

Soap

13 Plantinkaai (03 232 73 72). **Open** 9am-6.30pm Mon-Thur; 9am-8pm Fri; 9am-6pm Sat. **Credit** MC, V. **Map** p218 A4.

The salon in Belgium where the ultra-stylish get their hair dyed, fried or laid to the side. The interior features large paintings of Japanese manga art and milky fluorescent colours, and it has been the backdrop for a fair few fashion shoots. English spoken. **Other locations**: 2 Korte Schipperskapelstraat (03 213 10 13).

Wakko

3 St Rochusstraat (03 233 46 04/www.wakko.be). **Open** varies. **Map** p218 B5.

Wakko is one of the wackiest hairdressers you could hope to visit, a kitsch temple to hair, colour and extensions. The friendly staff cut on dry hair and can give you anything from classic to hyper-cyber.

Home furnishings

Avant-Scène

3-5 Hopland (03 231 88 26). **Open** 11am-6pm Tue-Sat. **Credit** MC, V. **Map** p218 C3.

Antwerp: Fashion capital

In the late 1980s, fashion pundit Helena Ravijst declared: 'Fashion was, is and will remain Belgian'. As a native of Antwerp, Ravijst tapped into the psyche of the city's folklore and the mantra has stuck. The truth is that Belgium – and Antwerp in particular – took the catwalks by storm in 1987 when six graduates from the Royal Academy of Fine Arts showed their collections at London Fashion Week.

As Dries van Noten put it: 'We never thought anyone would take designers with such unpronounceable names seriously'. Himself, Ann Demeulemeester, Walter van Beirendonck, Dirk Bikkembergs, Dirk van Saene and Marina Yee became known as the Antwerp Six, hitting the headlines and challenging perceptions. From that point on, Belgian fashion never looked back.

The most commercial of them all is **van Noten**, his soft, layered look appealing to world-wide fashionistas. The 1989 opening of his Antwerp shop, **Het Modepaleis** (*see p235*) marked a turning point in the designer's career, followed in 1991 by his first men's prêt-à-porter collection in Paris. Now he has showrooms in Paris, Milan, Tokyo and Hong Kong, but devotees flock to Antwerp, ready to buy the ready-to-wear amid antique furniture and crystal chandeliers. It's an important fact that he and four of the Six – **Bikkembergs** excepted – still live and work in Antwerp. The high water-level came in 2001, when the year-long fashion exhibition 'Mode2001 Landed-Gelanded', organised by van Beirendonck, took over the city as one big canvas for fashion design. The landmark punctuation mark was a massive capital letter 'A' on top of the Boerentoren; even the repainted trams became a fashion statement. The exhibition put Antwerp firmly

on the design map and the fashion industry firmly in the hearts of the locals. Now a more permanent feature, the city's fashion museum **MoMu**, in the ModeNatie complex, drives the point firmly home (*see p223*), with textile and costume collections dating from the 16th century to the present day.

Van Beirendonck was an obvious choice to head up 'Mode2001'. He is regarded as the *enfant terrible* of the Six, designing clothes inspired by nature and technology, urban themes and science fiction. He now teaches at the Royal Academy, designs for theatre, images pop groups and curates shows; his own collections have recently downscaled to two themes: 'Wild & Lethal Trash' (pronounced 'Walt'); and 'Aesthetic Terrorists'. A visit to his self-named shop (*see p236*) is a wild experience.

Ann Demeulemeester continues to be a cult figure among the cognoscenti. Her shop near the Fine Arts Museum (*see p235*) is minimalist and clean, allowing her modern, romantic, unashamedly sensuous designs to speak for themselves. While the Six led – and still mostly lead – the way, a second wave has appeared in recent times. **Martin Margiela** graduated only a year after the others and could almost be called the seventh; he's media-shy but outspoken in his avant-garde creations which shun branding (even the labels are plain white). Among the younger set, **Veronique Branquinho** and Brussels-born **Olivier Theyskens** stand out on the international circuit, with Branquinho opening her own Antwerp flagship store in 2003 (73 Nationalestraat, 03 233 66 16). The Antwerp fashion set does not rest on its laurels. Who will be the first to head up a major fashion house is still unknown, but one thing's for sure: it's bound to happen.

Belgian design talent doesn't halt at fashion. A crop of furniture designers are making a name for themselves on the international scene. You'll find pieces here by the van Severen brothers, Maarten and Fabiaan, and by rising star Xavier Lust.

'T Koetshuis (Chelsea)

62 Kloosterstraat (03 248 33 42). **Open** noon-6pm Tue-Sun. **No credit cards**. **Map** p218 A4.
This store's official name is Chelsea, but 't Koetshuis (coach-house) is what you'll find written over the front door. The art deco and art nouveau furnishings – large and small – are chosen and displayed with care, so don't expect any bargains. On the first floor there is a cosy, rustic café-bar.

Scapa World

26-30 Hopland Complex, Hopland (03 226 79 93). **Open** 10am-6.30pm Mon-Sat. **Credit** AmEx, DC, MC, V. **Map** p218 C3.
Ralph Lauren is the name that springs immediately to mind upon entering this gleaming homestore: Turkish, Irish and Austrian are a few of the many cultures influencing the clothes and home furnishings on display. Great household linen too.

Music & books

Mekanik Strip

73 St Jacobsmarkt (03 234 23 47/www.mekanik strip.be). **Open** 10am-6.30pm Mon-Fri; 10am-6pm Sat. **Credit** AmEx, DC, MC, V. **Map** p218 C2.
Mekanik Strip has more than 15 years of experience in comics. It has a huge selection of English, French and Dutch comics, plus magazines, books, videos, posters, Tintin collectibles – and its own gallery.

Metrophone

47 Kammenstraat (03 231 18 65). **Open** 10am-6pm Mon-Fri; 10am-6.30pm Sat. **Credit** AmEx, DC, MC, V. **Map** p218 B4.
Packed to the rafters with new and used vinyl and CDs, Metrophone is a place to dive in for rock, indie, techno, house – anything really.

Theatre, film & art

Kladaradatsch! Cartoon's (4-6 Kaasstraat; 03 232 96 32), in the historical city centre opposite the Steen, is an attractive café and excellent alternative cinema.

Commercial galleries

Antwerp's thriving contemporary art scene is conveniently centralised near the Waalsekaai, between the **Royal Museum of Fine Arts** and the **MUHKA** (for both, *see p223*). While the galleries below should not be missed, many others of interest are clustered nearby. Their details are given on the exhibition calendars available free at the establishments listed.

Micheline Szwajcer

14 Verlatstraat (03 237 11 27/www.gms.be). **Open** 10am-6pm Tue-Fri; noon-6pm Sat.
Szwajcer is Lohaus' older-generation counterpart. Still committed to many of the early conceptual artists she started out with in 1980 (Lawrence Weiner, On Kawara, Niele Toroni, Mark Luyten), she has kept a keen eye out for fresh talent and ideas. She represents some of Belgium's finest artists, from Guy Mees and Marthe Wery to the younger generation of Ann Daems and David Claerbout.

Stella Lohaus

47 Vlaamsekaai (03 248 08 71/www.stellalohaus gallery.com). **Open** 4-6pm Wed-Sat.
Eight years young, this gallery has stood by and grown up with the top-flight concept artists that it began with. Most of them are Belgian and Dutch and now in their 30s and 40s. If Joelle Tuerlinckx, Sven't Jolle, Angel Vergara, Job Koelewijn, Erik van Lieshout and Elske Neus can be said to share anything, it would be high seriousness coupled with ebullience. Other Europeans with similar predilections have been added gradually.

Zeno X

16 Leopold de Waelplaats (03 216 16 26/www.zeno-x.com). **Open** 2-6pm Wed-Sat.
Two of Belgium's star painters – Raoul De Keyser and Luc Tuymans – show here, along with a disparate cast of other nationally and internationally acclaimed artists. The gallery has recently opened a second venue, Zeno X Storage (Appelstraat 37) on the southeastern outskirts near Panamarenko's Antwerp Airship Building (*see p226*).

Venues for performing arts

DeSingel

25 Desguinlei (03 248 28 28/www.desingel.be). **Open** *Box office* 10am-7pm Mon-Fri; 4-7pm Sat. **Tickets** €10-€40. **Credit** MC, V.
One of the country's top arts complexes, DeSingel is Antwerp's modern equivalent to Brussels' Bozar, with cutting-edge dance and theatre in a massive concrete setting, and a consistently intelligent programme of events. The huge Blue Hall can accommodate major philharmonic orchestras, while the Red Hall is ideal for smaller groups. The acoustics in both are excellent.

Vlaamse Opera

8 Van Ertbornstraat (03 202 10 11/www.vlaamse opera.be). *Box office: 3 Frankrijklei (070 22 02 02)*. **Open** *Box office* 11am-5.45pm Tue-Sat. **Tickets** €4-€70. **Credit** AmEx, DC, MC, V.
The Flemish Opera productions are divided between the opera house in Ghent and the old but acoustically splendid Antwerp Hall. The emphasis is on quality rather than big names, but productions are thoroughly rehearsed. The management encourages players from the renowned orchestra to participate in weekday lunchtime concerts in the foyer.

Bruges

Mobbed with tourists, but still one of Europe's gems.

Bruges is a wonderful, misty, ancient, romantic town of canals and cobbled lanes, old churches and almshouses, steeples and bells. It is also, for much of the year, a nightmare. This modest town of 116,000 people is mobbed by about three million tourists every year, many of them from Britain, making it the most popular destination for visitors to Belgium.

The British have always been seduced by Bruges. One of the earliest English settlers was Gunhilde, sister of King Harold, who settled in Bruges after the Battle of Hastings in 1066. By the Middle Ages, the city was full of English wool merchants, including William Caxton who picked up the art of printing in Flanders. Charles II spent several years in exile in Bruges and English Catholic nuns founded a convent within the city walls.

The city enjoyed a golden age in the 15th century when it was a flourishing port and trading city. Merchants came here from all over Europe to trade in wool, lace and diamonds, constructing impressive Gothic brick houses and banks along the canals and narrow lanes in the northern quarter. This glorious period is also reflected in the rich collections of art in the museums and churches.

It all came to an end when the Zwin estuary began to silt up, cutting the city off from the sea. Trade moved to Antwerp. Bruges went into hibernation for 300 years, missing out on the Industrial Revolution and the prosperity of the rest of the country. In the early part of the 19th century, British tourists passed through town on their way from the battlefield at Waterloo. Many were seduced by its sleepy charm and crumbling monuments untouched by industry. They urged the city fathers to preserve its character by constructing new buildings in a retro Bruges Gothic style. By the mid 19th century a thousand British had settled here, opening shops, hotels and tea rooms.

Bruges acquired a nickname, the Venice of the North, and was soon swamped by tourists. By the 1980s it was all getting too much for local residents, who put up posters in their front windows with the slogan 'SOS Brugge'. The city council was goaded into action. The city used its year as European City of Culture in 2002 to embark on major projects designed to change its image. Bruges finally abandoned its love affair with Gothic (real and fake) and the planning department approved the construction of the brutally modern, controversial red hulk of

the Concertgebouw (34 't Zand, 070 22 33 02, www.concertgebouw.be), a new concert hall seating 1,200. Two new bridges were built in the south of the city, including Jürg Conzett's sleek one spanning the Coupure canal, and a daring pavilion was added on the Burg by the Japanese architect Toyo Ito. Museums were also given a radical makeover: the **Memling Museum** (see p243) was redesigned and a spectacular Gothic loft opened to the public, while the Groeninge Museum (see p244 **Shock tactics**) was given a new look that downgrades the world-famous van Eycks from their star position. Was nothing sacred?

Bruges still has far too many chocolate shops and lace emporia, its boat trips are a let-down, and there are too few modern art galleries and new-style cafés. It is best approached *à deux* on a winter break. Wander by the canals, take in a couple of sights, enjoy a Flemish beer – and maybe then the city will begin to work its spell.

GETTING THERE & AROUND

From Brussels, there are two trains an hour (50 minutes). It's a 15-minute walk to the centre, or you can take a taxi or bus from outside the station. To call a cab, Taxi Snel (050 36 36 49/ 050 37 37 20) is as good as any.

Several shops rent out bikes by the hour, day or week; €5-€10 a day. Try 't Koffieboontje, 4 Hallestraat (050 33 80 27) or Eric Popelier, 14 Hallestraat (050 34 32 62). For details of guided bike tours contact Quasimodo (050 37 04 70).

MUSEUM PASS

With a dozen museums in town, there are too many to see in one visit. A Combiticket (€15), available from the **tourist office** (see p247) allows entry to five museums of your choice.

Sightseeing

The Markt & the Burg

The most enjoyable way to visit Bruges is on foot. It's compact, largely traffic-free and easy to get around – and anything must be better than one of those horse-drawn carriages.

The traditional starting point for any visit is the main square, the **Markt**. Its most striking monuments are the **Halle** (cloth hall) and **Belfort** (belfry). Both the belfry and market square are symbols of the civic pride and mercantile power of medieval Bruges; the view from the top of the 80-metre (263-foot) belfry makes the climb – all 366 steps – worth the effort. The city carilloneur climbs up every Sunday to play at 2.15pm, also giving ringings at 9pm on Mondays, Wednesdays and Saturdays in the summer.

Most buildings on the square are modern reconstructions, including **Craenenburg**, built on the site of the house where Emperor Maximilian was held prisoner by local citizens. The building contains a popular Bruges café with a typical Old Flemish interior (see p251).

The statues at the centre of the square are of Jan Breydel and Pieter de Coninck, who inspired locals to slaughter several thousand French citizens at the start of the 14th century, an early example of ethnic cleansing known as the 'Brugse Metten'. The statues were unveiled by King Léopold II, who is said to have spoken Dutch for the first time during the ceremony.

From here it's a very short walk to the **Burg**. This beautiful square was the site chosen by Baldwin I to build his castle in the ninth century. The site is now occupied by the **Stadhuis** (Town Hall), built in splendid Gothic style in the 14th century. The lavish Gothic Hall on the first floor has a spectacular vaulted ceiling, while the walls are painted with scenes relating the history of the city, often with more verve than accuracy. The paintings date from the early 20th century.

On one corner of the Burg stands the Old Recorders' House, the **Paleis van het Brugse Vrije**, built in the 16th century and renovated in the 18th. The façade overlooking the canal is all that remains of the original structure; the rest is neo-classical in style. Inside the palace there's only one room that can be visited, with an impressive baroque chimney piece (1528) of black marble and oak by Lancelot Blondeel, running almost the whole length of one wall.

The oldest building on the Burg, tucked away in a corner next to the Stadhuis, is the easily missed **Heiligbloed Basiliek** (Basilica of the Holy Blood). The bizarre interior is well worth a look. The Lower Chapel was built in the 12th century in honour of St Basil and is in a pure Romanesque style. Its refined sobriety is in surprising contrast to the generous interior of the Upper Chapel, which was built in the 12th century in Romanesque style, then rebuilt in Gothic style and finally heavily altered in the 19th century. The decorated wooden ceiling, many of the colourful frescoes, the marvellous stained-glass windows and globe-shaped pulpit all date from the last reconstruction.

It is in the Upper Chapel that the crystal phial containing two drops of holy blood, stored in a silver tabernacle, is exhibited every Friday. This is one of the holiest relics of medieval Europe. The phial is supposed to have been given to Thierry d'Alsace by the Patriarch of Jerusalem during the Second Crusade. Legend has it that the blood contained in the phial liquefied every Friday, but the miracle apparently stopped in the 15th century.

Trips Out of Town

Civic pride and mercantile power – the **Markt**. *See p241.*

The relic is carried through the streets every year on Ascension Day. The Procession of the Holy Blood, a major traditional event in Bruges, dates back to the early Middle Ages and involves thousands of participants dressed in rich costumes, musicians and even animals.

Belfort

Markt. **Open** 9.30am-5pm Tue-Sun. Last entry 4.15pm. **Admission** €5; €3 concessions; free under-13s. **No credit cards. Map** p240 B2.

Heiligbloed Basiliek

13 Burg. **Open** *Apr-Sept* 9am-noon, 2-6pm daily. *Oct-Mar* 10am-noon, 2-4pm Mon, Tue, Thur-Sun; 10am-noon Wed. **Admission** €1.25. **No credit cards. Map** p240 B2.

Paleis van het Brugse Vrije

11A Burg (050 44 82 60). **Open** 9.30am-12.30pm, 1.30-5pm Tue-Sun. **Admission** combined ticket with Stadhuis €2.50; €1.50 concessions; free under-13s. **No credit cards. Map** p240 B2.

Stadhuis

12 Burg (050 44 81 13). **Open** 9.30am-5pm Tue-Sun. **Admission** combined ticket with Paleis van het Brugse Vrije €2.50; €1.50 concessions; free under-13s. **No credit cards. Map** p240 B2.

Museums along the Dijver

From the Burg, head south to the **Vismarkt** (Fish Market), taking the narrow Blinde Ezelstraat (Blind Donkey Street). The fish

market still takes place every morning from Tuesday to Saturday. The walk east from here follows the **Groenerei** canal, one of the most attractive waterways in Bruges. The water, trees and gabled houses – especially the Pelican House at No.8 – make it a favourite romantic spot. It can be noisy during the day, so come back after dark, when most tourists have gone, to look at the beautiful floodlit bridges.

Just west of Vismarkt is Huidevettersplaats (Tanners' Square), which leads to the **Rozenhoedkaai**. The view of the canal, bordered by ancient buildings and trees, has captivated photographers since the mid 19th century, but it can get a bit too crowded. The quay leads to another picturesque canal, the **Dijver**. The main attraction here is the **Groeninge Museum** (*see p244* **Shock tactics**), famous for its collection of Flemish art, and the nearby **Brangwyn Museum-Arentshuis**. Set in the intimate Arentspark, this small museum is named after Bruges-born British painter and engraver Frank Brangwyn, whose works are shown inside. Next to the Brangwyn Museum, the **Gruuthuse Museum** occupies an extensive 15th-century mansion originally belonging to the powerful Gruuthuse family, who had a monopoly on *gruut*, a mixture of dried flowers and plants used in the brewing process before hops came into fashion. Lodewijk van Gruuthuse was a diplomat, patron of the arts, friend of Edward IV of England and Knight of the Golden Fleece; he

Trips Out of Town

also invented a rather nastier version of the cannonball. His motto, '*Plus est en vous*', is reproduced around the palace, which was bought by the city and opened as a museum.

The furniture in the reception hall dates from the 16th, 17th and 18th centuries, as do the silverware and ceramics. The bust of Charles V, showing a young and candid emperor, is one of the most important pieces in the collection. Many of the other exhibits are objects of daily life, including a beautiful collection of ancient musical instruments in the music cabinet and a large collection of lace. Lace-making is a Bruges tradition that dates back to the Middle Ages, when lace was made with imported linen, always by women and often in convents and *béguinages* (houses for lay sisters). In the 17th century, Bruges, Ghent, Brussels and Mechelen were unrivalled in the art.

A small stone bridge leads from Arentspark to the **Onze Lieve Vrouwkerk**, the Church of Our Lady. The bridge is constantly blocked as tourists take photographs, but few realise the bridge was built as recently as 1910. A cobbled lane leads to the church, an imposing brick structure with a massive tower, best seen from the garden. The church is famed for its works of art, which include Michelangelo's *Madonna and Child*. The modest sculpture was ordered by the Piccolomini family for Siena Cathedral, but a Bruges merchant bought it when the family failed to pay their debts. The sculpture is an early work by the artist and one of the few to have left Italy during his lifetime. It is delicate and tender, subtly moving rather than powerful. In the choir are the tombs of Charles the Bold and his daughter, Mary of Burgundy. Unlike her husband, Maximilian of Austria, Mary of Burgundy was loved by locals. Tragically, she died young after falling from a horse. Their joint mausoleum (overlooked by a giant altar painting of the crucifixion by Bernard van Orley) is both lavish and solemn. The golden brass glitters in the hazy light of the choir; a graceful brass sculpture of the princess lies over the heavily adorned base. The monument for Charles the Bold, made at a later date, is similar in style. There are also paintings here by Pieter Pourbus and Gerard David.

Directly opposite the church is the medieval **St Janshospitaal**, which was still in use as a hospital in the early 20th century. The street outside was raised in the 19th century, so that the entrance, like that of the Onze Lieve Vrouwkerk, now lies below ground level. The former hospital wards – with their vast oak ceilings – are occupied by an interesting museum of local history and medicine. The exhibits include old photographs, paintings and a grim collection of surgical instruments.

Within the hospital's old chapel is the renovated **Memling Museum**, dedicated to the 15th-century painter Hans Memling. This is a small, remarkable collection of the Frankfurt-born artist, who lived and studied in Bruges. Memling undertook commissions for the English aristocrat John Donne and the Italian banker Portinari. His talent as a portrait artist and his hunger for detail are quite astonishing. Like all the Flemish Primitives, Memling believed that the material world was a product of divine creation, and that it was necessary to reproduce God's work as faithfully as possible. His use of colours is brilliant and the scenes always carefully composed. He ended his days as a patient of the hospital and carried out several commissions for the institution.

The Mystical Marriage of St Catherine is one of several similar works by Memling (another is in New York's Metropolitan Museum). In the central panel, Jesus, sitting on Mary's lap, is sliding a ring on St Catherine's finger. Although Memling's paintings are often said to be rather devoid of feeling, here the colours are vivid and passionate. The *Sibylla Sambetha* is believed to be a portrait of Marie Moreel, whose father commissioned many works from Memling (one of them in the Groeninge Museum). Also on display is a shrine made by Memling in 1489, which contains the relic of St Ursula. The story of pagan martyr St Ursula and the 11,000 virgins was a popular legend; the shrine is shaped like a Gothic cathedral and decorated with scenes of the saint's life.

Brangwyn Museum-Arentshuis
16 Dijver (050 44 87 63). **Open** 9.30am-5pm Tue-Sun. **Admission** €2.50; €1.50 concessions; free under-13s. **Credit** AmEx, MC, V. **Map** p240 B3.

Gruuthuse Museum
17 Dijver (050 44 87 62). **Open** 9.30am-5pm Tue-Sun. **Admission** €8; €5 concessions; free under-13s. Ticket includes entry to Arentshuis. **Credit** AmEx, MC, V. **Map** p240 B3.

Memling Museum
38 Mariastraat (050 44 87 70). **Open** 9.30am-5pm Tue-Sun. **Admission** €8; €5 concessions; free under-13s. **Credit** AmEx, MC, V. **Map** p240 A3.

Onze Lieve Vrouwkerk
Mariastraat. **Open** 9.30am-12.30pm, 1.30-5pm Tue-Fri; 9.30am-12.30pm, 1.30-4pm Sat; 1.30-5pm Sun. **Admission** *Church* free. *Choir* €2.50; €1.50 concessions; free under-13s. **No credit cards**. **Map** p240 B3.

Begijnhof & Minnewater Park

Coming out of St Janshospitaal, turn right on Katelijnestraat and you find the **Begijnhof**, one of Bruges' most charming locations.

Shock tactics

Art lovers are still in shock following the radical makeover of the Groeninge Museum in 2002. While some praise the bare white walls and unconventional hanging, others complain that it has downgraded the medieval art. Before the recent changes, the Groeninge was known throughout the art world for its collection of works by the **Flemish Primitives**. Everything else in the large collection was considered secondary to the great paintings by **Jan van Eyck** and **Hans Memling**. The museum's 150,000 annual visitors had their expectations more than fulfilled by the glowing Flemish Primitive masterpieces displayed in rooms resembling Gothic chapels, starting with van Eyck's *Madonna with Canon George van der Paele (pictured)*.

This approach made sense. The booming commercial activity in 15th-century Bruges was paralleled by an unprecedented flourishing in the arts. Rich merchants and Italian bankers ordered a steady stream of altarpieces and portraits from local painters. While 15th-century Italian painting tended to glorify humanity, the Flemish masters remained more pious in their outlook, and medieval in their complexity and spirit. No master illustrates the concept of Flemish 15th-century painting better than Jan van Eyck, who achieved the illusion of texture and detail by inventing a technique of applying oil and varnish in painstaking layers. His influence in the technique of oil painting is visible to this day. The colours are not only longer lasting, but the malleability of the paints enabled him to achieve an unprecedented subtlety of clarity and hue. Van Eyck's technical virtuosity and strict attention to detail was so acclaimed that many artists, including Dürer, travelled to Flanders to learn his secrets.

Manfred Sellink, chief curator of the Groeninge Museum, decided it was time to reconsider the sober art deco museum building. He commissioned a redesign from a young trio of architects from Brussels named 51N4E after the geographical position of their firm. They came up with stark interiors of white tiled floors, white or black walls and blood red carpets.

The fresh vision has some disturbing features. Why close off the first gallery with long hanging strips of plastic, like a supermarket cold storage room? Why begin with a collection of 16th-century paintings of the Last Judgement, rather than van Eyck's *Madonna*? Yet there is no doubt that the new Groeninge forces visitors to ask questions about the role of art.

The most striking work in room 1 is **Hieronymus Bosch**'s *Final Judgement*, a relatively small but enticingly detailed vision of apocalyptic hell. The Flemish Primitives now occupy a single white-walled room (room 2). Here, the visitor can admire the two strands in van Eyck's work: religious painting and portraiture. *Madonna with Canon George van der Paele* is an extraordinary work, full of realism. The clothes are vivid, the carpet looks worn and the elderly Canon is clearly seriously ill. Van Eyck also painted the little *Portrait of Margareta van Eyck*, looking at his wife with his customary pitiless gaze, painting every little blemish in a way that no Italian artist would have dared. Despite the sharp realism, there is a sense of stillness that is quite mysterious.

The same room contains a good 15th-century *Portrait of Philip the Good*, copied from an original by **Rogier van der Weyden**, who combined the technique of van Eyck with his own emotional and dramatic vision. *The Death of Our Lady* is a mysterious work by **Hugo van der Goes**, a follower of van Eyck who invested objects with a strong religious symbolism. The Italian banker Portinari, who was resident in Bruges, ordered a triptych from van der Goes for a church in Florence. Now hanging in the Uffizzi, this composition impressed Italian Renaissance artists with its use of colours and minute reproduction of vases and flowers.

Two altarpieces stand on a white table in the middle of the room, as if they have just arrived from the artist's studios. The *Moreel Triptych*, by Hans Memling, was specially commissioned and named after a Bruges burgomaster. One of Memling's most impressive works, it includes portraits of Moreel and his five sons on the left panel, and his wife and numerous daughters appear on the right panel. The other altarpiece is by **Gerard David**, who became the official city painter after Memling's death. *The Baptism of Christ*, dating from the early 16th century, is one of David's best works, painted with a realism characteristic of all Flemish artists of the time. This unswerving realism becomes

difficult to handle in David's brutally lifelike diptych *Judgement of Cambyses*, which combines a legend from the Ancient World with an event in 15th-century Bruges. The work, which shows a corrupt judge being flayed alive, is considered to refer to the execution of the unfortunate city treasurer in 1488, who was beheaded for opposing the imprisonment of Maximilian.

Room 3 focuses on the Renaissance in Bruges, when the prolific **Pieter Pourbus** was the dominant artist. A great Italianate mannerist, Gouda-born Pourbus came to Bruges at an early age. His *Portrait of Jan van Eyewerve and Jacquemyne Buuck* shows a prosperous Bruges couple with city scenes in the background. The odd arrangement in room 4 – where 17th-century genre paintings are hung close together on one wall – is intended to evoke art rooms created by private collectors. A neo-classical section in Room 5 includes **Joseph Suvée**'s curious *Invention of the Art of Drawing*, which is said to illustrate an ancient legend.

Now comes the biggest shock. The museum has devoted a series of five rooms to temporary displays of works from its reserve collection. These are displayed on steel racks, or even occasionally hung from the ceiling. The fifth room contains a large collection of works by the Belgian surrealist **Marcel Broodthaers**, who once created a fake art museum in his Brussels living room.

The final rooms are devoted to 20th-century works, by Paul Delvaux, René Magritte and James Ensor. They end with a sample of Flemish Pop Art, with an installation by Roger Raveel, *Your world in my garden,* consisting of paintings, mirrors and a bird cage. The cage once contained two live canaries but the birds, like much of the Groeninge's collection, have since disappeared.

Groeninge Museum

12 Dijver (050 44 87 43). **Open** 9.30am-5pm Tue-Sun. **Admission** €8; €5 concessions; free under-13s. **Credit** AmEx, MC, V. **Map** p242 B3.

Rozenhoedkaai. *See p242.*

Walking back towards the Markt, you see the huge **St Salvator-kathedraal**, surrounded by old trees. Work on the cathedral began in the tenth century, but after four fires and the Iconoclastic Riots nothing of that period has survived except the base of the tower. This troubled history is also responsible for the varied and eclectic style of the interior. The choir dates from the 14th century, although part of an older 13th-century construction survives. The painted columns, similar to those in the Upper Chapel of the Heiligbloed Basiliek, are a relatively recent addition, as are the stained-glass windows. There are several paintings by Bernard van Orley in the right transept, but the lighting is bad and they are difficult to see. However, the treasury has recently been restored and relit, allowing visitors to admire a spectacular painting by Dirk Bouts known as the *Hippolytus Altarpiece*.

St Salvator-kathedraal

St Salvatorskerkhof. **Open** 2-5.45pm Mon; 8.30-11.45am, 2-5.45pm Tue-Fri; 8.30-11.45am, 2-3.30pm Sat; 9-10.15am, 3-5.45pm Sun. **Admission** *Church* free. *Treasury* €3. **Map** p240 A3.

St Anna quarter

The area of St Anna, north-east of the Burg, is a poorer and more populated area, and less visited by tourists. There are fewer shops and the bars are mostly frequented by locals, yet it's packed with charm. Follow Hoogstraat east of the Burg and turn left on Verversdijk canal, which is lined with impressive 18th-century houses. Down the little lane on the left, the Jesuit church of **St Walburga**, built between 1619 and 1641, is decorated with tall, solid, grey Tuscan-style columns. The style is baroque and the dominant colours gold and white, yet the interior is more harmonious than overbearing.

Back on the Verversdijk, cross the little bridge to reach the 17th-century **St Annakerk**, a rather austere building from the outside, but with a luxurious interior.

Immediately behind St Anna, on the corner of Peperstraat and Jeruzalemstraat, the curious **Jeruzalemkerk** was built by a wealthy family of Italian merchants, the church still belonging to its descendants. It's a curious, three-level building, supposedly constructed according to the model of the Holy Sepulchre in Jerusalem. Highlights within include a crucifix decorated with bones and skulls over the altar, a copy of the tomb of Christ in the crypt and some fine stained glass. Next door, the **Kantcentrum**, or Lace Museum, has women who are still able to demonstrate the intricate skills of lace-making. Walking north on Balstraat brings you to the **Engels Klooster**, an English convent and

Founded by Margaret of Constantinople in 1245, it features rows of modest whitewashed houses around an inner lawn, covered with daffodils in spring. The atmosphere is calm and serene, far removed from the crowded streets around. There are no longer any *béguines* (lay sisters) in Bruges; the last ones died in the 1930s. The women you see walking around the Begijnhof today are Benedictine nuns. It is possible to visit the church, and one of the houses is also open to visitors.

At the Begijnhof's southern entrance is the picturesque **Minnewater Park**, with swans, lawns and small houses. Before the Zwin silted up, barges and ships would penetrate this far into the city. The 16th-century lock-keeper's house is still standing on the north side of the lake, next to a 1398 guard tower. The lake is named after a woman called Minna who, legend has it, fell in love with a man of whom her father disapproved. She fled his house and hid in the woods by the lake. Unfortunately, her beloved was a little slow in finding her and Minna died in his arms. The heartbroken man still found enough strength in him to change the course of the water, bury Minna's body and let the waters flow over the grave again.

church on Carmersstraat. Ring the bell and a nun will appear to show you inside the church.

The houses in this part of town are far removed from the flamboyant style of the historical centre. This is no longer an open-air museum, but a living community where many elderly people live in tiny 19th-century houses. The numerous *godshuizen* (almshouses) are evidence of the rampant poverty that overtook the city after the 15th century. As the city's fortunes declined, people abandoned the city, leaving behind vast empty spaces. Richer citizens took it upon themselves to build almshouses to shelter the poor and elderly. There are about 30 of these *godshuizen* in Bruges, some still fulfilling their original role. The entrance is usually marked by a small statue of the Virgin. Within, you will often find a little courtyard surrounded by small almshouses, each with its individual character. The lawns are carefully tended and the gardens planted with flowers.

A ten-minute walk down the Potterierei brings you to the almost forgotten **Onze Lieve Vrouw ter Potterie Museum**, a former hospital dating back to the 13th century. You can wander through evocative rooms filled with baroque paintings, sculpture and furniture.

Jeruzalemkerk
3A Peperstraat (050 33 00 72). **Open** 10am-noon, 2-6pm Mon-Fri; 10am-noon, 2-5pm Sat. **Admission** combined ticket with Kantcentrum €1.50; €1 concessions. **No credit cards**. **Map** p240 C1.

Kantcentrum
3A Peperstraat (050 33 00 72). **Open** 10am-noon, 2-6pm Mon-Fri; 10am-noon, 2-5pm Sat. **Admission** combined ticket with Jeruzalemkerk €1.50; €1 concessions. **No credit cards**. **Map** p240 C1.

Onze Lieve Vrouw ter Potterie Museum
79 Potterierei. **Open** 9.30am-12.30pm, 1.30-5pm Tue-Sun. **Admission** €2; €1.50 concessions.

St Annakerk en Plein
J De Damhouderstraat. **Open** *Apr-Sept* 10am-noon, 2-4pm Mon-Fri; 10am-noon Sat. **Admission** free. **Map** p240 C1.

St Walburgakerk
Koningstraat & Hoornstraat. **Open** *June-Sept* 8-10pm daily. **Admission** free. **Map** p240 B1.

Tourist information

Toerisme Brugge
11 Burg (050 44 86 86/fax 050 44 86 00/ www.brugge.be). **Open** *Apr-Sept* 9.30am-6.30pm Mon-Fri; 10am-noon, 2-6.30pm Sat, Sun. *Oct-Mar* 9.30am-5pm Mon-Fri; 9.30am-1pm, 2-5.30pm Sat, Sun. **Map** p240 B2.

Accommodation

Bruges has more than 100 hotels, most of them conveniently located. The hotel sector is now being seriously challenged by a growing number of small B&Bs (*gastenkamers*), often located in lovingly restored houses in the old quarters. Many hotels close in January and early February. For details, check www.hotels-brugge.org. The tourist information office (*see above*) also manages a free accommodation booking service.

Hotels

Hotel Acacia
3A Korte Zilverstraat, 8000 Bruges (050 34 44 11/ fax 050 33 88 17/www.hotel-acacia.com). **Rates** single €98-€130; double €108-€238. **Credit** AmEx, DC, MC, V. **Map** p240 A2.
There has been a hotel on this spot since the 1430s. The original building was demolished in the 1960s; the current hotel was built 20 years later and is now part of the Best Western chain. Centrally located, it has 48 rooms (all en suite), plus an indoor swimming pool, sauna and jacuzzi.

Hotel Adornes
26 St Annarei, 8000 Bruges (050 34 13 36/ www.adornes.be). **Rates** single €90-€115; double €95-€120. **Credit** AmEx, MC, V. **Map** p240 C1.
A friendly family hotel in a ravishing canalside location near St Annakerk. Ideally located for exploring the historic centre and the quiet Guido Gezelle quarter to the east. Rooms are comfortable and stylish. The hotel also offers parking spaces and free bicycles to explore the town. Dogs welcome.

Hotel Aragon
22 Naaldenstraat, 8000 Bruges (050 33 35 33/ www.aragon.be). **Rates** single €97-€135; double €120-€172. **Credit** AmEx, DC, MC, V. **Map** p240 A2.
An appealing hotel in the heart of the historic merchant quarter, opposite a palace once owned by a Medici banker. The 42 rooms were recently renovated in a comfortable English style, the staff are friendly and the location is quiet.

Golden Tulip Hotel de' Medici
15 Potterierei, 8000 Bruges (050 33 98 33/fax 050 33 07 64/www.hoteldemedici.com). **Rates** single €144-€174; double €179-€209. **Credit** AmEx, DC, MC, V. **Map** p240 B1.
A modern hotel in a canalside location near the historic centre. The interior is clinically efficient, but rooms are spacious and comfortable. The hotel has a recreation centre with sauna, steam bath and gym.

Hotel De Orangerie
10 Kartuizerinnenstraat, 8000 Bruges (050 34 16 49/fax 050 33 30 16/www.hotelorangerie.com). **Rates** single €182-€310; double €256-€360. **Credit** AmEx, DC, MC, V. **Map** p240 B2/3.

Trips Out of Town

This central 15th-century convent, by a canal, has 20 rooms, all individually decorated by Antwerp interior designer Pieter Porters. He is also responsible for decor in De Tuilerieën (7 Dijver, 8000 Bruges; 050 34 36 91/www.hoteltuilerieen.com), a mansion from the same era under the same hotel ownership.

Hotel Die Swaene

1 Steenhouwersdijk, 8000 Bruges (050 34 27 98/fax 050 33 66 74/www.dieswaene-hotel.com). **Rates** single €160; double €185-€225. **Credit** AmEx, DC, MC, V. **Map** p240 B2.
Right in the centre of the city, this 15th-century mansion next to a canal is wonderfully romantic – real Venice of the North stuff. All 22 rooms are individually decorated; some have four-poster beds. Candlelit restaurant, pool and sauna, too.

Relais Oud-Huis Amsterdam

3 Spiegelrei, 8000 Bruges (050 34 18 10/fax 050 33 88 91/www.oha.be). **Rates** single €120-€368; double €140-€388. **Credit** AmEx, DC, MC, V. **Map** p240 B1.
A splendid hotel set in a beautifully renovated 17th-century house, overlooking one of the canals. With its carved wooden staircase, chandeliers, antique furniture and bare wooden beams, the opulent interior is quite staggering. Pretty interior courtyard.

Hotel Ter Reien

1 Langestraat, 8000 Bruges (050 34 91 00/fax 050 34 40 48/www.hotelterreien.be). **Rates** single €65-€70; double €75-€99. Closed early Jan-early Feb. **Credit** AmEx, MC, V. **Map** p240 C2.
A pleasant canalside hotel with a seductive inner courtyard, close to the centre. Rooms are bright and comfortable. The house was the birthplace of Fernand Khnopff, the symbolist artist who painted views of deserted Bruges quays.

Romantik Pandhotel

16 Pandreitje, 8000 Bruges (050 34 06 66/fax 050 34 05 56/www.pandhotel.com). **Rates** single €120; double €120-€320. **Credit** AmEx, DC, MC, V. **Map** p240 B3.
This charming 23-room hotel in a leafy corner of Bruges occupies an 18th-century carriage house. Expect a friendly welcome from Chris Vanhaecke, her family and staff.

B&Bs

Absoluut Verhulst

1 Verbrand Nieuwland, 8000 Bruges (050 33 45 15/ www.b-verhulst.com). **Rates** double €75-€93. **No credit cards. Map** p240 C2.
The Verhulsts run this B&B in a 17th-century house with creaking floorboards. There are three light, stylish rooms, including a duplex and a loft sleeping up to five people. Bikes rented out for the day.

Baert Gastenkamer

28 Westmeers, 8000 Bruges (050 33 05 30/ www.baert-gastenkamer.be). **Rates** double €70. **No credit cards. Map** p240 A3.

Huub Baert and Jeannine Robberecht run a stylish B&B in a restored stable building that belonged to a convent. They offer two bright rooms (pink or yellow), both with private canalside terraces that catch the sun. Born and bred in Bruges, Huub is an expert on local history. He offers a Bruges beer to guests on arrival, lets them park in his garage and sends them on their way with a little box of chocolates.

Dieltiens

40 Waalsestraat, 8000 Bruges (050 33 42 94/ http://users.skynet.be/dieltiens). **Rates** single €50-€60; double €55-€65. **No credit cards. Map** p240 B2.
A very stylish B&B run by Koen and Annemie Dieltiens in a beautiful 18th-century mansion in the heart of Bruges. There are only three rooms, so book well in advance. There is also a studio apartment to rent in a small renovated 17th-century house.

Gheeraert

9 Ridderstraat, 8000 Bruges (050 33 56 27/fax 050 34 52 01/http://users.skynet.be/brugge-gheeraert). **Rates** single €50; double €55. **No credit cards. Map** p240 B2.
This exquisitely decorated townhouse, just a couple of minutes from the Burg, has three second-floor guest rooms. Two have fine views out over St Walburga's church, and all are decorated in a classy, pared-down style and hung with prints by Flemish Masters. The breakfast is notable. The Gheeraerts also rent out self-catering holiday flats.

Van Nevel

13 Carmersstraat, 8000 Bruges (050 34 68 60/fax 050 34 76 16/www.brugesbb.com). **Rates** single €38-€53; double €45-€60. **Credit** MC, V. **Map** p240 C1.
Near the church of St Anna, ten minutes from the centre in a quiet area, the van Nevels rent out two well-equipped rooms in a 16th-century house.

Het Wit Beertje

4 Witte-Beerstraat, 8200 St Andries, Bruges (050 45 08 88/fax 050 45 08 80/www.hetwitbeertje.be). **Rates** single €35; double €45. **No credit cards.**
All rooms at Jean-Pierre Defour's friendly 'Little White Bear' guesthouse are en suite and come with a telephone and TV. Prices include breakfast. Located in the south-west suburb of St Andries, it's ten minutes to central Bruges or the train station.

Youth hostels

Bauhaus

135-137 Langestraat, 8000 Bruges (050 34 10 93/ fax 050 33 41 80/www.bauhaus.be). **Open** 7pm-midnight Mon, Tue, Thur-Sun; 7pm-1am Wed. **Rates** €14 per person. **Credit** AmEx, MC, V. **Map** p240 C2.
This is one of Bruges' largest youth hostels, with 80 rooms sleeping two, three, four or eight. The decor is an eclectic mix of oriental, colonial and religious, with lots of mirrors and a giant clock hanging on the wall. There's also bike rental, a cybercafé and a bar open to the public that attracts an international set.

Snuffel Sleep-In

47-49 Ezelstraat, 8000 Bruges (050 33 31 33/fax 050 33 32 50/www.snuffel.be). **Rates** €13 per person. **Credit** AmEx, MC, V. **Map** p240 A1.
For bargain hunters, the Snuffel offers hostel-like accommodation in rooms sleeping four, six, eight or 12 people. Breakfast costs extra.

Hotel Die Swaene. *See p248.*

Eating & drinking

It's not difficult to eat well in Bruges if you avoid the tourist traps on the Markt and by the Begijnhof. There are a wide range of places to eat, from Flemish taverns offering a honest fare for €15 to the sublime **Karmeliet**. Restaurants rely on tourism and some adapt their menus to offer delights such as English breakfast.

Restaurants

De Belegde Boterham

5 Kleine St Amandstraat (050 34 91 31). **Open** noon-6pm Mon-Sat. **Main courses** €5-€10. **No credit cards.** **Map** p240 A2.
De Belegde Boterham serves salads, sandwiches and other simple dishes. Friendly and trendy rustic decor, with plain wooden tables for sharing. It's very busy around lunchtime, mainly with local workers.

Bistro De Schaar

2 Hooistraat (050 33 59 79). **Open** noon-2.30pm, 6-11pm Mon-Wed, Fri-Sun. **Main courses** €15-€19. **Credit** AmEx, DC, MC, V.
A little way out of the tourist centre (just off Predikherenrei), this cracking little bistro offers a modern take on cosy rusticity and first-rate grills, as well as less traditional dishes of the day such as prawns in garlic and cheese-filled ravioli.

Chagall

40 St Amandstraat (050 33 61 12). **Open** 11am-12.30am daily. **Main courses** €11-€18. **Credit** AmEx, DC, MC, V. **Map** p240 A2.
This snug restaurant serves fine seafood in a relaxed environment. Specialities include scampi, eels, North Sea mussels and excellent shellfish.

Eetcafé de Vuyst

15 Simon Stevinplein (050 34 22 31). **Open** 10am-6pm Mon, Wed-Fri; 10am-9.30pm Sat, Sun. **Main courses** €12.90-€15.50. **Set menus** €12-€25. **Credit** AmEx, DC, MC, V. **Map** p240 A3.
A fun café-bar with newspapers on the walls and glass-topped tables containing original paintings. There are various *moules* options, as well as salads, crêpes and a good-value three-course lunch.

Karmeliet

19 Langestraat (050 33 82 59/www.resto.be/ karmeliet). **Open** 7-10pm Tue; noon-2pm, 7-10pm Wed-Sat; noon-2pm Sun. **Main courses** €40-€70. **Set menus** €50-€125. **Credit** AmEx, DC, MC, V. **Map** p240 C2.

Karmeliet is a wonderful restaurant with a three-star Michelin rating. Chef Geert van Hecke's staples include rabbit, special breeds of chicken, truffles and scallops. Special menus cover such themes as 'the flat country'. The decor is airy and modern and you can see Geert at work at the back of the dining room.

Parkrestaurant

1 Minderbroedersstraat (050 34 64 42/www. park-restaurant.be). **Open** Tue-Sun 11.30am-10pm. **Set menus** €25-€50. **Credit** AmEx, MC, V. **Map** p240 C2.

An elegant and friendly restaurant located in a patrician mansion facing the city's main park. The chefs produce wonderful dishes using Ardennes beef, fresh salmon, Ostend sole and Sisteron lamb. The garden is an idyllic spot for a summer meal.

De Stove

4 Kleine St Amandstraat (050 33 78 35/www. restaurantdestove.be). **Open** noon-1.45pm, 6.45-9.30pm Mon, Tue, Fri-Sun. **Main courses** €18-€28. **Set menus** €42-€55. **Credit** AmEx, MC, V. **Map** p240 A2.

A beguiling little restaurant, just off one of the main shopping streets, serving a variety of hearty meat and fish dishes. The interior is Old Flemish style with an ancient iron stove and chimney.

Tanuki

1 Oude Gentweg (050 34 75 12/www.tanuki.be). **Open** noon-2pm, 6.30-9.30pm Wed-Sun. **Main courses** €15.50-€60. **Set menus** €17-€60. **Credit** AmEx, MC, V. **Map** p240 B4.

Tanuki's oriental minimalism offers a contrast to the Flemish restaurants in the neighbourhood. Sushi and sashimi cost €16 to €24.50; noodle dishes €12.50.

In Den Wittekop

14 St Jacobstraat (050 33 20 59). **Open** noon-2pm, 6-10pm Tue-Sat. **Main courses** €15-€25. **Set menu** €28. **Credit** AmEx, MC, V. **Map** p240 A2.

Despite being close to the tourist centre, this brown café offers an authentic Bruges experience, complete with smoke-stained walls and old advertising signs. Solid Flemish food and excellent beers on offer.

Cafés & bars

Brugs Beertje

5 Kemelstraat (050 33 96 16/www.brugsbeertje.be). **Open** Tue, Thur-Sun 4pm-1am. **Main courses** €6.50-€8.50. **Map** p240 A3.

Drinkers rave about this dark brown pub which sells 300 beers. Set up by 'beer professor' Jan De Bruyne, it's now mainly run by his wife Daisy, who takes a more lenient line than Jan when asked for 'a lager'. Beers include Poperings Homelbier and Achouffe.

The Coffee Link

38 Mariastraat, in Oud Sint Janhospitaal (050 34 99 73/www.thecoffeelink.com). **Open** 11.30am-7pm Mon-Fri; 10am-8pm Sat; 11am-8pm Sun. **No credit cards.** **Map** p240 A3.

The historic **Craenenburg**.

A stylish coffee shop located in a former hospital building behind the Memling Museum. Internet facilities, sandwiches and apple cake all available.

Craenenburg

16 Markt (050 33 34 02). **Open** 7am-midnight daily. **Main courses** €5-€15. **No credit cards.** **Map** p242 A/B2.

Set on the site of the house where Maximilian of Austria was held captive, this is a typical Bruges tavern with yellowed walls, wooden tables and elaborate stained glass. *See also p241.*

Het Dagelijks Brood

21 Philipstockstraat (050 33 60 50). **Open** 8am-6pm Mon, Wed-Sun. **No credit cards.** **Map** p240 B2.

The Bruges branch of bakery chain Le Pain Quotidien: *see p110* **Breaking bread.** Decorated in rustic style, it's a good place for snacks, salads and sandwiches made with sourdough bread.

'T Estaminet

5 Park (050 33 09 16). **Open** 11.30am-late Fri-Sun. Credit V. **Map** p240 C2.

A old Bruges tavern facing Astrid Park in a quarter seldom reached by tourists. The owner has built up one of the best jazz collections in Bruges, attracting writers, politicians, and women with little dogs. Try the heavenly Poperings Hommelbier.

Est Wijnbar

34 Noordzandstraat (050 33 38 39/www.
estwijnbar.cjb.net). **Open** 5pm-late Mon, Thur, Sun;
3pm-late Fri, Sat. **Set menus** €7.50-€16. **No credit
cards. Map** p240 A2.
A wine bar with a garden at the back where you can
sample 90 different wines. Organises 'Lazy Sunday'
jazz concerts every Sunday from 8pm. Entry is free.

De Garre

1 De Garre (050 34 10 29). **Open** noon-midnight
Mon-Thur; noon-1am Fri; 11am-1am Sat; 11am-
midnight Sun. **No credit cards. Map** p240 B2.
At the end of the shortest blind alley in Bruges (off
Breidelstraat), this bar sells 130 different beers. It's
set in a 16th-century house with wooden beams,
brick walls and authentic Bruges atmosphere.

Joey's Café

16A Zuidzandstraat (050 34 12 64). **Open** 11.30am-
late Mon-Sat. **No credit cards. Map** p240 A3.
Located in the Zilversteeg shopping centre, Joey's is
a dark candlelit café run by a local musician. The
relaxed mood and good sounds draw a lively crowd,
with a summer terrace and live music once a month.

Mezzogiorno

25 Wollestraat (050 33 42 29/www.interiordufait.
be). **Open** noon-6.30pm Mon, Tue, Thur-Sat; 3-6pm
Sun. **Main courses** €8-€16. **Credit** AmEx, MC, V.
Map p240 B2.
Stylish Italian-style café above the design store B
(*see below*), whose decked terrace offers unexpected
views of the city spires. The little kitchen produces
excellent pasta, bruschetta and Illy coffee served
with a tiny glass of chocolate mousse.

Prestige

12-14 Vlamingstraat (050 34 31 67). **Open** 7.45am-
6pm Tue-Sun. **No credit cards. Map** p240 B2.
An elegant tea room near the Markt, perfect for
breakfast or a lunchtime bowl of home-made soup.
Anyone looking for an afternoon sugar rush should
try a coffee served with four miniature cakes (€5).

De Proeverij

6 Katelijnestraat (050 33 08 87). **Open** 9.30am-
6.30pm daily. **No credit cards. Map** p240 B4.
A stylish café with pale green walls in a busy street.
It can get crowded, but that is because the coffee is
served with a saucer of whipped cream and chocolates from Sukerbuyc (*see p252*) across the road. The
hot chocolate is served as a dish of pure melted
chocolate, which you add to a mug of steaming milk.

De Republiek

36 St Jacobsstraat (050 34 02 29). **Open** 11am-late
daily. **Main courses** €7-€13. **No credit cards.**
Map p240 A2.
This candlelit brown café attached to a cinema and
theatre complex is a good place to pick up word-of-
mouth tips on jazz, films and dance events. Here
you'll also find the late-night Cactus Club, the main
place in town for DJs and live music.

The Top

5 St Salvatorskerkhof (050 33 03 51). **Open** 6pm-
2am daily. **No credit cards. Map** p240 A3.
Lively bar in the shadow of the St Salvator
Cathedral. Attracts a mixed crowd, ranging from
young locals looking for a wild night out to tourists
hunting for decent dance sounds in the early hours.

De Versteende Nacht

11 Langestraat (050 34 32 93). **Open** 7pm-1am
Tue-Thur; 6pm-1am Fri, Sat. **Entry** €3. **Credit** MC,
V. **Map** p240 C2.
The manager of this jazz café is a fan of comic strips
and his bar is filled with comic books, its walls covered with cartoons. Weekly jazz sessions draw the
crowds on Wednesday nights. Simple food served.

Shopping

Dig a little deep, and you should find a lot more
than twee boutiques peddling chocolate and
lace. The main shopping street is **Steenstraat**,
which runs from the Markt to 't Zand and has
the usual international chains. **Geldmunt** and
Noordzandstraat have the high fashion
boutiques. **Wollestraat** has its share of lace
shops, but some small specialised ones, too.

Design

B

25 Wollestraat (050 49 09 32/www.b-online.be). **Open**
10am-1pm, 2-6pm Mon-Sat. **Credit** AmEx, DC, MC, V.
Map p240 B2.
A stunning contemporary design shop nestling
among the chocolate and lace shops. Founded by
Katrien van Hulle, B describes itself as 'Belgian
products with an A label'. Look out for the oversized
gadgets from Antwerp's wacky Extra Large.

Callebert

25 Wollestraat (050 33 50 61/www.callebert.be).
Open 2-6pm Mon; 10am-noon, 2-6pm Tue-Sat; 3-6pm
Sun. **Credit** AmEx, DC, MC, V. **Map** p240 B2.
International contemporary furniture and design in
a stylish shop next door to B. Check it out for ceramics by Pieter Stockman and architect Bob van Reeth,
or furniture by the van Severens brothers. Callebert
is also good for Scandinavian glassware and cool
cutlery. Stairs lead up to the Art-O-Nivo art gallery.

Fashion

L'Héroïne

32 Noordzandstraat (050 33 56 57). **Open** 10am-
6.30pm Mon-Sat. **Credit** AmEx, DC, MC, V. **Map**
p240 A2.
The upper floor of this gorgeous boutique has dresses by Belgian designers Mieke Cosyn, Kaat Tilley
and Ann Huybens. Downstairs are menswear by
Dries van Noten, womenswear by Martin Margiela
and jewellery by Antwerp duo Wouters & Hendrix.

Trips Out of Town

Joaquim Jofre

7 Vlaamingstraat (050 33 39 60). **Open** 9.30am-6.30pm Mon-Sat. **Credit** AmEx, DC, MC, V. **Map** p240 B2.

Worth going inside just to marvel at the art deco shop fittings imported from the owner's home country of Spain. The women's clothes are classic, well cut and beautifully finished and there is also a good line-up of accessories, including hats.

Mia Zia

17 Geldmuntstraat (050 61 65 69). **Open** 10.30am-6pm Mon-Wed; 10.30am-6.30pm Fri; 10am-6pm Sat; 1-6pm Sun. **Credit** AmEx, DC, MC, V. **Map** p240 A2.

Who says Bruges is frumpy? Mia Zia sells the latest bright fashions by the young French designer Valérie Barkowski. Her wonderful handmade clothes are inspired by traditional North African designs.

Olivier Strelli

3 Eiermarkt (050 34 38 37) & 19 Geldmuntstraat (050 33 26 75). **Open** 10am-6.30pm Mon-Sat. **Credit** AmEx, MC, V. **Map** p240 A2.

The Brussels designer has established a loyal following in West Flanders with his sober fashions for men and women, the men's at 19 Geldmuntstraat.

Rex Spirou

18 Geldmuntstraat (050 34 66 50). **Open** 9.30am-6.30pm Mon-Sat. **Credit** AmEx, DC, MC, V. **Map** p240 A2.

This wild store decorated by young graffiti artists sells streetware by name brands. The shop has managed to evade a local law banning neon signs.

Gifts

'T Apostelientje

11 Balstraat (050 33 78 60). **Open** 9.30am-6pm Mon-Sat; 10am-1pm Sun. **Credit** AmEx, DC, MC, V. **Map** p240 C1.

Be careful when you're buying lace; a lot of stuff around town is passed off as being authentic handmade Bruges handiwork when it's not. The genuine stuff is sold here by a mother (in the business for 20 years) and her daughter, who has written several books on the subject.

The Bottle Shop

13 Wollestraat (050 34 99 80). **Open** *Summer* 9am-11pm daily. *Winter* 9am-7pm daily. **Credit** MC, V. **Map** p240 B2.

From the outside, it's easy to dismiss this shop as a tourist trap. But that would be a big mistake: it stocks 850 types of Belgian beer: Trappist brews, hard-to-find Gueuzes, jars of genever and a quite astonishing selection of mineral waters.

Diksmuids Boterhuis

23 Geldmuntstraat (050 33 32 43). **Open** 9am-12.30pm, 1.30-6.30pm Mon-Sat. **No credit cards.** **Map** p240 A2.

A rustic, friendly shop selling butter, cheese and smoked ham fresh from the Flemish polders.

Dumon

6 Eiermarkt (050 34 62 82). **Open** 10am-6pm Mon, Tue, Thur-Sat; 10am-5pm Sun. **Credit** AmEx, DC, MC, V. **Map** p240 A2.

A tiny basement chocolate shop that may well prove difficult to pass by. Friendly staff and divine chocs.

De Patience

2 Spinolarei (050 34 21 89/www.bnart.be). **Open** 2-6pm Thur-Sat. **No credit cards.** **Map** p240 B1.

The US calligrapher Brody Neuenschwander (who worked on Peter Greenaway's *Prospero's Books* and *The Pillow Book*) has opened a small gallery and shop in Bruges. The exhibits include unusual art based on a mixture of calligraphy and collage. He also sells postcards that make unusual souvenirs.

The Soap Story

21 Wollestraat (050 61 52 71). **Open** 10am-6pm daily. **Credit** AmEx, DC, MC, V. **Map** p240 B2.

The Soap Story sells blocks of soap by weight in weird and wonderful scents and colours. Under the same ownership as The Bottle Shop (*see above*).

Sukerbuyc

5 Katelijnestraat (050 33 08 87/www.sukerbuyc.com). **Open** 8.30am-6.30pm daily. **No credit cards.** **Map** p240 A3.

A family-run chocolate shop that sells rich dark chocolates made with 100 per cent cocoa butter and sugar-coated sweets for Catholic christenings.

Tintin Shop

3 Steenstraat (050 33 42 92/www.tintinshopbrugge.be). **Open** 9.30am-6pm Mon-Sat; 11am-6pm Sun. **Credit** AmEx, MC, V. **Map** p240 A2.

Cartoon books, T-shirts and toys featuring the famous Belgian boy reporter.

Music & books

De Reyghere

12 Markt (050 33 34 03). **Open** 10am-12.30pm, 1.30-7pm Mon-Sat; 2-6pm Sun. **Credit** AmEx, DC, MC, V. **Map** p240 A/B2.

Established in 1888, De Reyghere specialises in international newspapers, books on Bruges and fiction, including a small section of English novels. Guide books are sold next door.

Rombaux

13 Mallebergplaats (050 33 25 75/www.rombaux.be). **Open** 9am-12.30pm, 2-6.30pm Mon-Fri; 9am-6pm Sat. **Credit** MC, V. **Map** p240 B2.

One of the most comprehensive classical music shops in Belgium, Rombaux has been run by the same family for three generations. They started out selling pianos (at 3 Kelkstraat round the corner) and later opened a music shop in a former private house. The shelves are filled with every imaginable CD recording, from classical composers to new wave Flemish folk, carefully catalogued by composer, country of concert or type. The back room has stacks of sheet music in alphabetical order.

Ghent

Historic, handsome and happening – without the tourist hordes.

St Michielsbrug. *See p255.*

Ghent has the pedigree of a wealthy city state. This history is also responsible for its somewhat undervalued brand as a tourist destination in the modern age. As a mid-point between Bruges and Antwerp, both of which aggressively market their historical virtues, Ghent and its burghers have always kept a low profile. They seem to like it that way, and the moment you arrive in Ghent it's easy to understand why. Here's a medieval city with a compact, traffic-free centre cut through with canals and little trip-trap bridges, an ancient castle slap in its middle, astonishing churches and a knock-out cathedral dripping with fine art. So while its history has made it what it is, Ghent doesn't go screaming it from the gabled rooftops. It wants visitors to want to go there, rather then feel they should, something totally in keeping with its modest character.

Ghent's history is rich and erratic, combining periods of great glory and wealth with suffering and persecution. In the Middle Ages, when it was the centre of the cloth and wool trade, it

was the largest town in western Europe and the university was considered one of the most scholarly. This wealthy, educated city later provided rich pickings for Luther and his followers, which led Ghent into a nightmare scenario of heretic bonfires and the infamous iconoclastic fury of 1566, when not a single church, monastery or convent remained undamaged. In 1540, Emperor Charles V – who was born in Ghent – returned to the city in a rage after its citizens refused to pay higher taxes. He had the rebellion's ringleaders executed and then forced 50 of the city's elders, dressed only in white shirts and with nooses around their necks, to beg for his mercy. Because of this, Ghent's residents are known as *stropdragers* (noose-wearers).

Gent to the Flemings and Gand to the Walloons, the capital of East Flanders and Belgium's second port – it's on the banks of two rivers, the Leie and the Ketel – is 56 kilometres (35 miles) north-west of Brussels. It could be another world. There's a sense of wealth in the

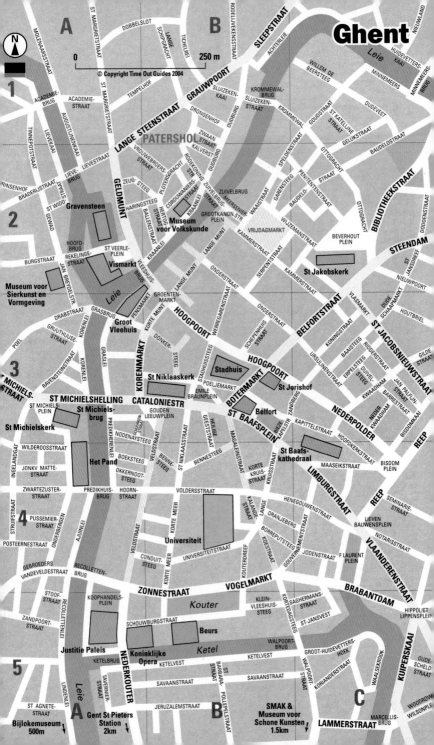

air, a sense of studied pride and, above all, organisation. Transport is a good case in point; escalators from the train station platform lead you directly down to the tram which then delivers you deftly into the centre of town. The good thing about Ghent is that it works. The streets are calm and uncluttered, yet the cafés and bars around the Korenmarkt are packed and energetic, giving Ghent a sophisticated atmosphere all of its own, a place where young and old have a feeling of belonging, and where visitors are welcomed – but left largely to their own devices.

GETTING THERE AND AROUND

Ghent is half an hour by train from Brussels. Four fast trains an hour shuttle between the two cities. From Gent St Pieters station take any one of five trams into town (Nos.1, 10, 21, 22 or 40; pay on board). If you arrive by car, follow the signs reading 'P-route'; this will take you through streets where you are allowed to park and, eventually, to a multi-storey car park.

Sightseeing

Ghent has the highest number of listed buildings in Belgium, but the must-see attractions are the towers of **St Niklaaskerk**, the **Belfort** and **St Baafskathedraal** (and the view of the three together); the van Eycks' *The Adoration of the Mystic Lamb* in St Baafskathedraal; and **Gravensteen castle.**

St Michielsbrug to St Baafskathedraal

St Michielsbrug is a good place to start a tour of the city. One of the best views of the cathedral is from this bridge over the Leie, which overlooks the **Graslei** (Herb Quay) and **Korenlei** (Corn Quay). Both are lined with beautiful houses, most built during the Flemish Renaissance but some dating back as far as 1000. Just south of the bridge, on the west side of the river, is **St Michielskerk**, standing alongside the former Dominican monastery Het Pand, now part of the University of Ghent – the public are free to wander around. On the other side of the bridge stands **St Niklaaskerk**. This outstanding piece of Scheldt Gothic architecture was built in the 13th century. Its interior is dominated by a fantastically over-the-top baroque altarpiece.

Next door stands the **Stadhuis** (Town Hall), designed to be the largest town hall in Europe. Building began in 1518 but had to be halted because of religious strife and diminishing funds (the bickering contributed to that tantrum of Charles V's). Work resumed at the end of

the 16th century, and the result of this staggered construction is clearly visible. One part, decorated with countless statues, is in an ornate Gothic style, while the more sober section of the façade reflects post-Reformation taste. Check with the **tourist office** (*see p257*) for information on guided tours.

Across the Botermarkt from the Stadhuis soars the **Belfort** (belfry), built in the 14th century (though later heavily restored). Its interior – containing a carillon and a bell museum – isn't exactly thrilling, but it's worth the entrance fee for the view over the city and the neighbouring cathedral.

Ghent's first cathedral was founded (as St Peter's) by the Brabant-born St Bavo in the seventh century. Built over six centuries, the current **St Baafskathedraal** is remarkable as much for its high and late Gothic style as for the works of art it contains. Laurent Delvaux's elaborate rococo pulpit, in oak and marble, is the first thing you see on entering, and Peter Paul Rubens' *Entry of St Bavo into the Monastery* is displayed in the north transept. But the cathedral's – and the city's – undisputed masterpiece is *The Adoration of the Mystic Lamb* by Hubert and Jan van Eyck. The painting is on show in the De Villa Chapel, which can become very crowded in high season. It's well worth the wait, though. The picture depicts a scene from the Apocalypse according to St John, but the colours are so bright and glistening that the painting seems to light up the whole chapel.

The 12th-century crypt is the oldest part of the cathedral. Although it contains tombs and the usual religious paraphernalia, it's more notable for its frescoes and for Justus van Gent's painting *The Calvary Scene.*

The area south and west of the cathedral contains Ghent's main shopping streets, including **Veldstraat** (running south from St Niklaaskerk), the most crowded but the least exciting, and the more interesting **Magaleinstraat** and **Koestraat**, which lie south of the Belfort.

Belfort

17A Botermarkt (tourist office 09 266 52 32). **Open** *Easter-Oct* 10am-1pm, 2-4pm daily. **Admission** €2.48; free under-7s. **No credit cards**. **Map** p254 B3. Free guided tours between 1 May and 9 September.

St Baafskathedraal

St-Baafsplein (09 225 49 85). **Open** *Nov-Mar* 8.30am-5pm Mon-Sat; 1-5pm Sun. **Admission** free. *The Adoration of the Mystic Lamb* **Open** *Nov-Mar* 10.30am-noon, 2.30-4pm Mon-Sat; 2-5pm Sun. *Apr-Oct* 9.30am-5pm Mon-Sat; 1-5pm Sun. **Admission** €2.48; €1.24 concessions; free under-6s. **No credit cards**. **Map** p254 C4.

Gravensteen castle & around

Surrounded by water on the north-west edge of the centre is **Gravensteen castle**. Built in 1180 by Philippe of Alsace, Count of Flanders, on the site of the first count's original stronghold, this is the only medieval fortress in Flanders. The arrestingly grim structure lost its military function centuries ago – it was subsequently used as a mint, a court of justice and even a cotton mill. It has a small collection of torture instruments, which young boys will love.

Next door to the castle, on St Veerleplein, a bas-relief Neptune towers over the entrance to the **Vismarkt** (fish market), while across the water stands the **Museum voor Sierkunst en Vormgeving** (Museum of Decorative Arts and Design). Located in an 18th-century house, this superb collection includes beautiful royal portraits set off by crystal chandeliers, silk wall coverings and tapestries. The furniture, mostly French, includes baroque, rococo and Louis XVI pieces. A modern extension houses temporary exhibitions. There is a stunning collection of modern design, including art nouveau pieces by Victor Horta, Paul Hankar and Henri van de Velde.

Just east of the castle on the Kraanlei is the quirky **Museum voor Volkskunde** (Folklore Museum, also called Het Huis van Alijn). Occupying 18 almshouses, with a garden and chapel, this museum is aimed primarily at children, but parents will also enjoy it. It aims to show life in Ghent in the 19th century: you can see candlestick-makers, cloth-makers, reconstructions of sweet shops, pubs and a chemist. The museum has been undergoing major refurbishment for the past two years.

Patershol, the atmospheric tangle of streets just north of here, is packed with excellent restaurants and bars, generally patronised by trendy young professionals rather than students. Market lovers should head back over the Leie to the **Vrijdagmarkt**, a vast square that used to be the focal point of political life and quarrels in the Middle Ages and is still used as a marketplace; restaurants and bars line its sides. There are market stalls on many squares and markets most days of the week. There's a fruit and vegetable market in **Groentenmarkt** every morning (except Sunday), and a bird market in Vrijdagmarkt on Sunday mornings. You'll come across several excellent traditional bakeries and cheese shops in the area, and plenty of cafés and tea rooms.

If you're a keen walker or are feeling energetic, you might want to venture outside the historical centre. The River Leie along **Lievekaai** and **St Antoniuskaai**, north of the castle, is a particularly charming walk.

Gravensteen
St-Veerleplein (09 225 93 06). **Open** *Oct-Mar* 9am-5pm daily. *Apr-Sept* 9am-6pm daily. **Admission** €4; free under-12s. **No credit cards**. **Map** p254 A2.

Museum voor Sierkunst en Vormgeving
5 Jan Breydelstraat (09 267 99 99/http://design. museum.gent.be). **Open** 10am-6pm Tue-Sun. **Admission** €2.50; €1.20 concessions; free under-12s. **Map** p254 A2.

Museum voor Volkskunde
65 Kraanlei (09 269 23 50/http://volkskunde. museum.gent.be/www.huisvanalijn.be). **Open** 11am-5pm Tue-Sun. **Admission** €2.50; €1.75 concessions; free under-12s. **No credit cards**. **Map** p254 B2.

South of St Pieters station

The area between St Pieters station and the city centre has three intriguing museums. Along the west side of the River Leie, the former Abdij (Abbey) van de Bijloke contains the **Bijlokemuseum**. The red-brick abbey was founded in the early 13th century and maintained its religious function until it was promptly closed down by the invading French revolutionaries in 1797. Today its interior provides a sympathetic surrounding to a varied collection of furniture, religious sculpture, paintings, guild banners and Chinese porcelain.

South of here, across the river (a five-minute walk from the train station; around 25 minutes from the centre) is the **Citadelpark**, laid out in the 1870s on the site of a Habsburg castle. Here you'll find the outstanding **SMAK** (Stedelijk Museum voor Actuele Kunst – Museum of Contemporary Art), which opened in 1999. Generally thought to be Flanders' finest collection of modern art, it boasts first-rate works by Francis Bacon, Joseph Beuys and David Hockney. There's also a good spread of minimal and conceptual art, with the 1960s particularly well represented with pieces by Christo, Warhol and Broodthaers.

Facing the SMAK is the **Museum voor Schone Kunsten** (Museum of Fine Arts, www.mskgent.be). Under renovation until 2006, the MSK its huge collection of paintings and sculptures from the 14th century to the early 20th at various museums around town.

Bijlokemuseum

2 Godshuizenlaan (09 225 11 06). **Open** 10am-6pm Thur; 2-6pm Sun. **Admission** €2.48; €1.24 concessions; free under-12s. **No credit cards**.

Museum voor Schone Kunsten

3 Nicolaas de Liemaerckereplein, Citadelpark (09 222 17 03/www.mskgent.be). **Open** 10am-6pm Tue-Sun. **Admission** €2.48; €1.24 concessions; free under-12s. **No credit cards**.
Closed for renovation until 2006.

SMAK (Stedelijk Museum voor Actuele Kunst)

Citadelpark (09 221 17 03/www.smak.be). **Open** 10am-6pm Tue-Sun. **Admission** €4.96; €3.71 concessions; free under-12s. **Credit** AmEx, DC, MC, V.

Tourist information

City of Ghent Tourist Office

Belfort, 17A Botermarkt (09 266 52 32/www. gent.be). **Open** *Nov-Mar* 9.30am-4.30pm daily. *Apr-Oct* 9.30am-6.30pm daily. **Map** p254 B3.
The useful and detailed website is also available in English and French.

Accommodation

Ghent can provide accommodation to suit all budgets – depending on the time of year. At Christmas, Easter and especially during the Gentse Feesten in mid-July (*see p262* **The best fest in Belgium**) you should book at least a month, in advance. To do this, call the tourist administration office (09 225 36 41, 8.30am-noon, 1-4.30pm Mon-Fri, www.gent.be). They will check availability within your price range, then reserve free of charge when you call them back 30 minutes later. Visitors to the office in town (*see above*) can have the English-speaking staff reserve rooms for a €5 deposit, deducted from the final bill.

Trips Out of Town

Maritime delights at the **Georges**. *See p259.*

The **Guild of Guesthouses in Ghent** (www.bedandbreakfast-gent.be) has 66 families who offer B&B accommodation, from a room in a cosy private home to a self-contained suite in a 17th-century cloister. Check the website for a list with descriptions; the tourist office also has an album of snapshots. Rates range from €20 for a room to €372 for a luxury suite. There is also a B&B bureau, the **Chambres d'Amis** (09 238 43 47, www.chambres@pandora.be), with a 24-hour reservation service. Doubles cost €45-€50 per room, including breakfast.

Hotel Adoma

19 St Denijslaan, 9000 Ghent (09 222 65 50/ fax 09 245 09 37/www.hotel-adoma.be). **Rates** single €50; double €58-€63; suite €75-€100. **Credit** AmEx, DC, MC, V.

A bargain – and it has the advantage of being a stone's throw from the station (a tram ride from the centre). The rooms are comfy and all have phones and TVs. There's also a car park.

Boatel

44 Voorhoutkaai, 9000 Ghent (09 267 10 30/fax 09 267 10 39/www.theboatel.com). **Rates** single €79-€94; double €105-€130. **Credit** AmEx, DC, MC, V.

Ghent's first floating hotel. This former transport boat near Dampoort train station, ten minutes' walk from town, has been converted into a seven-room hotel, complete with original woodwork and portholes. Good breakfast too.

Brooderie

8 Jan Breydelstraat, 9000 Ghent (09 225 06 23). **Rates** single €40; double €60-€65. **No credit cards**. **Map** p254 A2.

Charming three-room B&B in a gabled house overlooking the canal in the centre. The light-filled rooms are clean and fresh; toilets and shower are shared. Brooderie is also a bakery with a health-food café serving a hearty brunch (open 8am-6pm Tue-Sun).

Hotel Cour St Georges

2 Botermarkt, 9000 Ghent (09 224 24 24/fax 09 224 26 40/www.courstgeorges.be). **Rates** single €95; double €115; suite €160. **Credit** AmEx, DC, MC, V. **Map** p254 B3.

Facing the Stadhuis and by the Belfort, the Cour dates back to 1228 – Charles V and Napoleon were guests. The smallish rooms aren't as characterful as they might be but have all the mod cons.

De Draecke Youth Hostel

11 St Widostraat, 9000 Ghent (09 233 70 50/ www.vjh.be). **Rates** €15.74-€24 per person. **Credit** MC, V. **Map** p254 A2.

Set in a pretty part of the centre, De Draecke is ideal if you're on a tight budget. There are 106 beds in rooms sleeping two to six people, all en suite.

Erasmus

25 Poel, 9000 Ghent (09 224 21 95/09 225 75 91/ fax 09 233 42 41/hotel.erasmus@proximedia.be). **Rates** single €79-€99; double €99-€130; family room €130-€150. **Credit** AmEx, MC, V. **Map** p254 A3.

A cosy hotel only five minutes' walk from the medieval town centre. The owners have preserved the authentic character of the 16th-century building while providing the 11 well-furnished rooms with every desirable modern comfort. The hotel lounge is another plus point.

Hotel Gravensteen

35 Jan Breydelstraat, 9000 Ghent (09 225 11 50/ fax 09 225 18 50/www.gravensteen.be). **Rates** single €110-€140; double €148-€163. **Credit** AmEx, DC, MC, V. **Map** p254 A2.
A beautiful hotel in a 19th-century *hôtel particulier*. The Second Empire style is imposing and impeccable; the elegant rooms are all equipped with modern facilities. The hotel has a bar, sauna, conference room and private car park.

La Maison de Claudine

20 Pussemierstraat, 9000 Ghent (tel/fax 09 225 75 08/mobile 0495 443 130/maison.claudine@ newmail.net). **Rates** single €45-€65; double €70-€90. **No credit cards. Map** p254 A4.
For a classy B&B with a whiff of the bohemian about it, La Maison is hard to beat. Two luxury suites and one room (all non-smoking) are available. The largest suite is an enormous penthouse in the eaves, with a superbly comfortable bed and fine views over the towers of Ghent. The other suite is a self-contained former coach house, which looks out on to the walled garden. Every room has central heating, an en suite bathroom and TV. Breakfast is a communal affair in the owner's high-ceilinged living room.

PoortAckere Monasterium

50-58 Oude Houtlei, 9000 Ghent (09 269 22 10/fax 09 269 22 30/www.poortackere.com). **Rates** single €75-€100; double €125. **Credit** AmEx, DC, MC, V.
Not far from the centre, this renovated convent dates from 1278 and now houses a hotel, restaurant and concert venue, all arrayed around two lovely walled gardens. Some bedrooms are rather spartan, others are more luxurious, but all are fresh, clean and a welcome antidote to chain blandness.

Eating & drinking

Your impression of Ghent nightlife is likely to depend on the area of town you visit and the evening you happen to choose. The southern part of the city is certainly livelier and has the trendiest bars, largely because this is the student area and attracts a younger crowd. Most students, however, go home for the weekend and their big night out is usually Thursday. On Saturday the crowd is older and somewhat smarter. If it's quiet, don't worry – most locals don't think about going out until after ten.

Patershol, north of the historical centre, also has plenty of bars. With its canals and medieval streets free of traffic, it can be magical in the evening. Bars and restaurants here tend to be more elegant than in the student area.

Restaurants

Le Baan Thai

57 Corduwanierstraat (09 233 21 41). **Open** 6.30-10pm Tue-Sat; noon-2pm, 6.30-10pm Sun. **Main courses** €10-€15. **Set menu** €30. **Credit** AmEx, DC, MC, V. **Map** p254 B2.
This pretty restaurant, set back from the street and overlooking a courtyard, serves excellent Thai food to eat in or take away. Booking essential.

De Blauwe Zalm

2 Vrouwebroersstraat (09 224 08 52). **Open** noon-1.30pm Mon, Sat; noon-1.30pm, 7-9pm Tue-Fri. **Main courses** €28-€45. **Set menu** €28. **Credit** AmEx, DC, V.
The most talked-about restaurant in town, thanks to the expertise of chef Daniel de Cleyn and interior designer Hans Wyers, one responsible for exquisite fish dishes, the other for the striking piscine decor. Sure, it's as pricey as it gets in Ghent, but you're getting a standard of cooking, presentation and service that would put many restaurants in Antwerp to shame. Recommended.

Brasserie Keizershof

47 Vrijdagmarkt (09 223 44 46). **Open** noon-2.30pm, 5.30-11pm Tue-Sat. **Main courses** €14-€16. **Credit** MC, V. **Map** p254 B2.
A high-ceilinged, beautifully renovated restaurant in the centre of town. The wide-ranging menu has no shortage of traditional Ghent dishes, and also features fish, pastas, steaks and French standards. Prices are reasonable.

'T Buikske Vol

17 Kraanlei (09 225 18 80). **Open** 7-10pm Tue, Thur-Sun. **Main courses** €50-€70. **Credit** AmEx, DC, MC, V. **Map** p254 B2.
The upmarket Buikske Vol is well regarded. The open kitchen produces rather more daring dishes than you'll find in many local restaurants, such as wild rice risotto with prawns and shiitakes. Its speciality is fish *waterzooi* soup.

C-Jean

3 Cataloniëstraat (09 223 30 40). **Open** noon-2pm, 7-10.30pm Tue-Sun. **Main courses** €16-€25. **Credit** MC, V. **Map** p254 B3.
C-Jean, the former Chez Jean, enjoys a good reputation, and deservedly so. The food is first-rate and, for the quality, reasonably priced. Ghent specialities feature heavily, as do fish and shellfish dishes.

Georges

23-27 Donkersteeg (09 225 19 18). **Open** noon-2.30pm, 6.30-9.30pm Wed-Sun. **Main courses** €15-€20. **Credit** AmEx, DC, MC, V. **Map** p254 B3.
A father-and-son-run fish restaurant that has been in the same family since 1924. The prices are a tad steep – but the fish is ultra-fresh and expertly cooked. The scrupulously clean fishmonger's next door, with its tanks of lobsters, is under the same ownership and a good advert for the restaurant.

Trips Out of Town

De Hel

81 Kraanlei (09 224 32 40). **Open** noon-2pm,
6-10pm Mon, Fri, Sun; 6-10pm Thur, Sat. **Main
courses** €17-€20. **Set menu** €35. **Credit** AmEx,
DC, MC, V. **Map** p254 B2.

In years past De Hel (Hell) had a devilish decor to
match its name. Now the design of this cosy, wood-
beamed restaurant changes regularly – with the
exception of an old Chinese room that can be booked
for dinner. Flemish and French cuisine is served –
specialities include *waterzooi* and eel dishes –
although you might also find the likes of goat curry
on the menu.

'T Klokhuys

65 Corduwaniersstraat (09 223 42 41). **Open**
6-11pm Mon; noon-2.15pm, 6-11pm Tue-Sun.
Main courses €10-€20. **Set menu** €23.50. **Credit**
AmEx, DC, MC, V. **Map** p254 B2.

Green banquettes line the walls and dried hops
snake along the ceiling at rustic 't Klokhuys. Expect
a selection of local regional dishes – such as chicken
casserole or stewed eels in chervil sauce – with an
emphasis on seasonal produce.

De Kruik

5 Donkersteeg (09 225 71 01). **Open** 11.30am-
2.30pm, 6-11pm Mon-Wed, Fri, Sat; 11.30am-2.30pm
Sun. **Main courses** €15-€20. **Set menus** €20-€37.
Credit AmEx, DC, MC, V. **Map** p254 B3.

This fine, peachy-pastely restaurant, just off the
Korenmarkt, offers accomplished renditions of the
traditional Ghent dishes, as well as good fish and
first-rate French cuisine. There's also a menu of the
month (aperitif, three-course meal, wine, coffee).

Het Magazijn

24 Penitentenstraat (09 234 07 08/www.magazijn.be).
Open noon-2pm, 6pm-1am Mon-Thur; noon-2pm,
6pm-4am Fri; 6pm-4am Sat; 6pm-1am Sun. **Main
courses** €9-€10. **No credit cards**. **Map** p254 C2.

This café-restaurant is the flavour of the month,
partly because of its selection of vegetarian and
world dishes, but mainly because it's simply an ideal
place to eat with friends until the early hours. At
weekends, the dining invariably turns to dancing.

La Malcontenta

7-9 Haringsteeg (09 224 18 01). **Open** 6-11pm
Thur-Sun; reservations only Mon-Wed. **Main
courses** €15. **Set menu** €25. **Credit** AmEx,
DC, MC, V. **Map** p254 A2.

Don't be misled by the name of this restaurant: the
interior and staff may be a touch casual, but the
kitchen's keenly priced specialities from the Canary
Isles are a treat – try the seafood pancake or the
squid in spicy tomato sauce. Tapas available too.

Oranjerie

8 Corduwaniersstraat (09 224 10 08). **Open** noon-
2.30pm, 6.30-10pm Tue-Sat; noon-2.30pm Sun. **Main
courses** €16-€20. **Set menu** €9. **Credit** MC, V.

This newly renovated lounge restaurant is located in
the Patershol area. It's flashy, hip and cool, and not

yet as crowded as its more traditional neighbours.
Ghent and French specialities are on offer, and not
bad either – but most people are here for the vibe.

Pakhuis

41 Schuurkenstraat (09 223 55 55/www.pakhuis.be).
Open noon-2.30pm, 6.30pm-midnight Mon-Sat.
Main courses €14-€20. **Set menu** €22-€34.
Credit AmEx, DC, MC, V. **Map** p254 B2.

This large renovated storage depot is worth visiting
as much for its architecture as its French-Italian
food: the cast-iron pillars, wrought-iron balustrades,
parquet floor and impressive oak bar are the main
features of a classic interior. You can gawp at them
with just a drink if you don't fancy eating.

Tête à Tête

32-34 Jan Breydelstraat (09 233 95 00). **Open**
6.30-10pm Tue; noon-2.30pm, 6.30-10pm Wed-Sun.
Main courses €15-€20. **Set menu** €42. **Credit**
MC, V. **Map** p254 A2.

Successful and expensive, Tête à Tête serves light
and beautifully rendered French cuisine such as
magret de canard with green pepper sauce or a
hearty bouillabaisse. The decor is equally splendid,
with soft lighting, chrome and wood fittings, and a
pretty terrace overlooking the Gravensteen. Be
warned that booking is essential.

Vier Tafels

6 Plotersgracht (09 225 05 25). **Open** 6-10.30pm
Mon; noon-2pm, 6-10.30pm Tue-Sun. **Main
courses** €16-€30. **Credit** AmEx, DC, MC, V. **Map** p254 B2.

One of the most popular restaurants in Patershol.
It's not as expensive as other places nearby, but the
food is every bit as good with top-notch global
favourites and Ghent specialities. It also features a
holding bar, Virus, for those who want to sample the
excellent wine before their meal.

Wok Away

11 Korenmarkt (09 233 90 00). **Open** 11.30am-
10pm Mon-Sat. **Main courses** €7-€8.50. **Set
menus** €11-€12. **No credit cards**. **Map** p254 A3.

This new Asian fast-food restaurant is deservedly
popular with the young Ghent crowd, with speedy
service and great flavours. The restaurant turns into
a loungey cocktail bar in the evening.

Cafés & bars

Belga Queen

10 Graslei (09 280 01 00). **Open** noon-2.30pm, 7pm-
midnight daily. **Credit** AmEx, DC, MC, V. **Map** p254
A3.

This fancy, expensive cocktail lounge/restaurant, set
on the town's most beautiful quayside, attracts
hordes of nouveaux riches from Ghent's suburbs. As
if this wasn't enough to bring in the crowds – and
you really can't move here on a Friday night – the
Belga Queen boasts a wider range of beers than
most. Turn up on a weekday lunchtime – there isn't
a more pleasant bar in town for that quiet pint.

Limonada. *See p263.*

Charlatan

6 Vlasmarkt (09 224 24 57/www.charlatan.be).
Open 4pm-late Tue-Sun. **No credit cards.**
Map p254 C3.

Describing it as a music-café doesn't begin to tell the story – although there is live music, most evenings at 11pm, with a live radio link-up. The back room opens at weekends from 1am for urban house, disco and other danceable tunes. All sorts of performances take place, but Charlatan is simply a damn good hang-out, for musicians, night owls and locals who refuse to go home. It's at its best during the Gentse Feesten (*see p262* **The best fest in Belgium**), when this is *the* place to be at 8 in the morning.

Damberd Jazz Café

19 Korenmarkt (09 329 53 37/www.damberd.be).
Open 11am-late daily. **No credit cards.**
Map p254 A3.

An art nouveau jazz venue on two floors. The ambience is friendly and the crowd all ages. There's live jazz on Tuesdays (Mondays in winter), but the place is mainly used as a comfortable and convenient meeting place slap in the centre of town – some are happy just to delve into the music archives here too.

De Dulle Griet

50 Vrijdagsmarkt (09 224 24 55). **Open** noon-12.30am daily. **No credit cards. Map** p254 B2.

De Dulle Griet was the first pub in Belgium to specialise in local Flanders beers, so its dimly lit and curious interior has welcomed many a tourist by now. It's still fun though, mainly because locals love it as well – some indulge in the bizarre house custom of exchanging their shoe for a beer, and have the waiter winch it up in a basket. Go figure. It's Ghent.

Gainsbar

51 Oudburg (09 225 19 69). **Open** 7pm-late Tue-Sun. **No credit cards. Map** p254 B2.

A tiny new café near Patershol founded by the guy who started up the Pink Flamingo's (*see p263*). The decor here is less kitsch, with magazine posters of famous 1950s stars on the wall. Don't come here to drink beer (the owner doesn't serve any), as this is the place for champagne cocktails.

'T Galgenhuisje

5 Groentenmarkt (09 233 42 51). **Open** 11am-late daily. **No credit cards. Map** p254 B3.

A diminutive pub since the late 17th century, 't Galgenhuisje means 'the gallows', a reference to its medieval function. Downstairs in the 14th-century cellar, a restaurant serves fish and grilled meats.

Hotsy Totsy

1 Hoogstraat (09 224 20 12). **Open** 8pm-late Tue-Sun. **No credit cards.**

The Hotsy Totsy jazz bar is a Ghent institution. It pulls in a varied crowd who come to enjoy the strong drinks, jazz and eclectic stand-up performances – phone for details. Despite the heavy wooden door and curtains, it's open to all, a ten-minute walk from the centre across the Leie, over St Michael's Bridge.

Trips Out of Town

The best fest in Belgium

It's a big decision to make. Whether to see picturesque, medieval Ghent in all its calm glory, or to go there in the ten days over the third week of July when it's transformed into a party town and swelled by 1.5 million visitors. Each has its virtues, each has its own spirit.

De Gentse Feesten (www.genstefeesten. be) is a home-grown bash with centuries of history, aimed firmly at locals but attracting more visitors every year as news of its good-natured vibe spreads. Transform the city it most certainly does, not just in atmosphere but with portable loos, sound stages erected over the canals, makeshift drinking terraces on the pretty quays and a tidal wave of bright flags and balloons. The normally quiet cobbled streets resound with rock music, jazz bands and street theatre; the clean, ordered life of Ghent billows with excitement and an increase in discarded fast-food cartons.

Urban dross, some may think, but the truth is the Gentse Feesten is the happiest, most relaxed street party you could hope to see. Sure, it's one big piss-up (not just for the young), with folk staggering their way through the endless nights and knees-ups keeping the bars going till dawn, but there is never any trouble. Let's just say that again: there is never any trouble. Not a punch, not a brawl, nothing overturned, nothing trashed – except the good people of Ghent, who know how to behave even when beer-soaked.

The modern-day festival started in its current form in 1970 when local folk singer Walter De Buck wanted to get people on to the streets for a bit of popular culture – and give artists from all over the country the opportunity to promote themselves to a wider audience. He organised a ten-day programme of entertainment on the little square by St Jacob's church, and once the city council paid heed, sat up and got involved, it all started to snowball. Now the fest begins with a glitzy parade on the first Saturday, led by the town crier and followed by 40 outfits who can receive an €11,000 prize for being 'best in parade'. In 2003, the festival was based around four international sub-festivals: the **Blue Note** (jazz; www.bluenotefestival.com), **International Street Theatre** (www.istf.be), **International Puppet Buskers** and the highly infective and highly reputed **10 Days Off** techno festival (www.10daysoff.be). Yes, even the clubbing goes on for ten days – free

shuttle buses get you out to the Vooruit centre where the vast party thumps on.

These provide the frame on which hangs the rest; the open-air cinema at **Baudelo Park**, the alternative music acts at the **Trefpunt** (www.trefpuntvzw.be), free entrance to all the city's museums, and each square music-themed to help the ten days swing. The **Korenmarkt** is for pop acts; **Groentenmarkt** is country & western; **Beverout Plein** for a bit of rock 'n' roll and the free-for-all, freefall **Vlasmarkt** next door just goes for whatever it fancies. Local tradition continues to weave through; there is still the Stroppenommegang (Procession of the Noose-wearers) and the famous Kouter Ball which has been going strong in these parts since 1843 and gives citizens their best opportunity to turn out in their best. The Gentse Feesten is mad, wild, good-natured and friendly. It's a time when Ghent can celebrate in its own quite batty, bohemian way; a time when upright folk can stagger some, or simply dance in the squares. It's a class act.

Limonada

7 Heilige Geeststraat (09 224 40 95). **Open** 8pm-late Tue-Sat. **No credit cards**. **Map** p254 B3.
A laid-back bar with an atmosphere more appropriate to Antwerp than alternative Ghent. It's very popular these days and you need to grab any seat (or bag) you can find. Cocktails are the drink of choice.

Mosquito Coast Travel & Adventure Café

5 Serpentstraat (09 224 37 20). **Open** 3pm-late Tue-Sun. **No credit cards**. **Map** p254 B2.
An ideal place to meet like-minded adventurers. The cosy bar is littered with second-hand guidebooks, plus decent wines, snacks, cocktails and tapas.

Pink Flamingo's Lounge

55 Onderstraat (09 233 47 18). **Open** noon-midnight Mon-Wed; noon-3am Thur, Fri; 2pm-3am Sat; 2pm-midnight Sun. **No credit cards**. **Map** p254 B2.
This pub is well known for its collection of kitsch, which changes every three months. The place is packed with dolls, old records, cartoon books, religious figures and tat of every description. There's also a restaurant, open until 11pm.

Rococo

57 Corduwanierstraat (09 224 30 35). **Open** 9pm-late Tue-Sun. **No credit cards**. **Map** p254 B2.
Located in Patershol, Rococo is one of Ghent's moodier bars. Artists gather around candlelit tables and a piano sits in a corner, sometimes too tempting for the would-be *chanteur* who's had a few too many. There's also an outdoor café at the back.

Stereo

116 Sint Pietersnieuwstraat (0497 42 91 46). **Open** noon-late daily. **No credit cards**.
New venture of the successful Studio Brussel radio station (alma mater of pop phenomenon, local duo 2ManyDJ's), this small café is used for music launches, promotional bashes and so on. Slap next to the major concert venue in town, the Vooruit, and open to all, Stereo is understandably popular.

Den Turk

3 Botermarkt (09 233 01 97). **Open** 11am-late daily. **No credit cards**. **Map** p254 B3.
Dating all the way back to 1340, Den Turk is the oldest pub in Ghent, although you wouldn't know it from its distinctly ordinary decor. It hosts regular jazz (plus a dash of blues and flamenco) and you can munch on a sizeable choice of snacks.

'T Velootje

2-4 Kalversteeg (09 223 28 34). **Open** varies; phone for details. **No credit cards**. **Map** p254 B2.
One of the oldest brick houses in Ghent, partly built on the ruins of a Roman fortress, 't Velootje is crammed with religious objects and antique bicycles. Look for the blue-and-white 'Pater Lieven' sign on the apricot-painted house and the pile of junk outside – you'll never find it otherwise.

Pink Flamingo's Lounge.

electro and techno parties adding the necessary layers. Beyond the ring, and a five-kilometre (three-mile) taxi ride away, the **Mega-Temple** (5 Solariumdreeft, Destelbergen, www.mega-temple.be) is a legend, a national reputation earned as the famed Boccaccio, and still keeping a happy 1,500-strong crowd moving to usually commercial, uplifting sounds.

The main dance party is the **10 Days Off** festival, part of the **Gentse Feesten** (*see p262* **The best fest in Belgium**), ten nights of quality electro-dance featuring a range of top-class international DJs. Either side of it Ghent hosts the **City Parade** (www.cityparade.be) in June, which promises a wilder free street party than the one that started in Liège in 2001; and **I Love Techno** (www.ilovetechno.be), one of Europe's biggest festivals, at the end of summer. The venue for 2004 is slated to be the Flanders Expo centre on Ghent's Maaltekouter but this is likely to change for 2005.

Shopping

Ghent's central shopping district is compact, pedestrianised and generally free of crowds. **Veldstraat** is the main shopping drag, with the usual international chain stores and department giant Inno. **Bennesteeg** has Ghent's most upscale fashion boutiques, and streets **Volder**, **St Niklaas** and **Magelein** feature more quirky addresses. All the shops listed below are closed on Sundays. For a somewhat more bizarre shop in someone's living room, *see p265* **House music**.

Children's clothes & toys

Krokodil

5 Groot Kanonplein (09 233 22 76). **Open** 10am-6pm Mon-Sat. **Credit** AmEx, DC, MC, V. **Map** p254 B2.

Krokodil is a real winner: two floors of soft and wooden toys, puppets and board games. There are lots of beads, wooden ovens and doll's houses, and a large arts and crafts section with big pencils, paints and chunky chalks.

Puzzles

6 Bennesteeg (09 223 17 88). **Open** 10am-1pm, 2-6pm Mon-Fri; 10am-6pm Sat. **Credit** MC, V. **Map** p254 B4.

You can find clothes by Ghent designer Catharina Bossaert elsewhere – she supplies shops throughout Belgium – but this is her only dedicated store. The clothes, casual and practical, are for kids aged three to 14. Bossaert is an official licensee of comic-strip characters Quick & Flupke and Sachat, and many of the items are tastefully emblazoned with their iconic motifs.

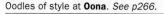
Oodles of style at **Oona**. *See p266.*

Het Waterhuis aan de Bierkant

9 Groentenmarkt (09 225 06 80/www.waterhuis aandebierkant.be). **Open** 11am-2am Mon-Fri; 11am-3am Sat, Sun. **Credit** AmEx, MC, V. **Map** p254 B3.

A good stop for beer lovers, with an excellent range of brews (including 14 on draught and all six Trappists), all described on the menu. Its riverside location makes it very popular, with terrace tables in summer.

Clubs & dance festivals

Cool and sophisticated Ghent goes for a subtle inner-city nightlife, with student bars, jazz cafés and all-hours lounge bars to keep night owls alert. Start at **Oude Beestenmarkt**, where there is a cluster of newbies, with folk hopping happily from one to the other; **Club 69** (No.5, 10pm-6am Thur-Sat) is a chart-topper at the moment, with its live DJ sets. For serious clubbing, Ghent's reputation rests on one venue: **Culture Club** (174 Afrikalaan, 09 267 64 42, www.cultureclub.be). Its classy design and bustin' light shows make it a must for those into house, R&B and hip hop, with special

Collectibles

The Fallen Angels

29-31 Jan Breydelstraat (09 223 94 15/www.the-fallen-angels.com). **Open** 1-6pm Mon, Wed-Sat. **Credit** MC, V. **Map** p254 A2.

A wonderful place to browse for an original souvenir from the many boxes of vintage postcards of Ghent. The shop also stocks a selection of antique toys. Next door the owner's daughter sells original posters and advertising signs.

Fashion & accessories

Ann Huybens

4 Trommelstraat, bottom of Kalversteeg (09 224 36 16). **Open** 1-6pm Tue-Sat. **Credit** V. **Map** p254 B2.

Huybens' ready-to-wear wild wedding dresses are sold in all the hippest bridal shops, but this is her own boutique. Get fitted out for a made-to-measure gown or choose from a limited selection.

Christa Reniers

1A Bennesteeg (09 224 33 52). **Open** 1-6pm Wed-Fri; 11am-6pm Sat. **Credit** AmEx, MC, V. **Map** p254 B4.

Reniers is Belgium's top avant-garde jewellery designer; her only other shop-cum-atelier is in her home city of Brussels. Reniers favours silver and platinum over gold, and most of her ring and necklace designs are inspired by plant and flower shapes.

Hot Couture

34 Gouvernementstraat (09 233 74 07/ www.hotcouture.be). **Open** 10am-6.30pm Mon-Sat. **Credit** AmEx, DC, MC, V. **Map** p254 B/C4.

The latest men's fashions and accessories by designers Dries van Noten, CP Company and Paul Smith. The shop, set out in several rooms, has velvety armchairs and charming staff.

Hydo

40 Mageleinstraat (09 233 06 37/www.hydo.be). **Open** 10am-6pm Mon-Sat. **Credit** AmEx, DC, MC, V. **Map** p254 B4.

Hydo sells designer handbags, wallets, briefcases, umbrellas and other accessories. The upmarket bags and belts include mostly Belgian labels by Scapa Interiors, Olivier Strelli, Emmy Wieleman, Xandres and Cat & Co.

Illmus

18 Jan Breydelstraat (09 233 40 90). **Open** 10am-1pm, 1.30-6pm Tue-Sat. **Credit** AmEx, MC, V. **Map** p254 A2.

Upscale fashion labels include Ghost, DKNY Jeans and Georges Rech for women, plus Paul Smith and Kenzo for men.

House music

If you had to describe *strodragers* – the inhabitants of Ghent – in one word, it would probably be 'relaxed'. Unlike the residents of Bruges, who are energetically selling lace and chocolates to Japanese tourists, or Antwerp, who are too busy checking out their reflections in shop windows, Ghent guys and girls seem to spend their days dawdling in cafés and record stores, chatting and chilling.

Marc van Peteghem is more laid-back than most. He's arranged life so that he has the shortest possible walk to work in the morning: his record store **Dune** (17 Geldmunt, 09 225 67 84) is in his apartment.

An optician by trade, van Petergham is also a passionate music fan, and found himself working in the city's massive Fnac record store. He found it all a bit stressful, so he decided to set up on his own. He began by selling copies of just one CD, the debut album by Oxford-based electric violinist Ed Alleyne-Johnson, which he had picked up at a record fair in the UK. Nowadays he stocks several hundred CDs – his only restriction is that he has to like it himself. He has eclectic tastes: obscure Irish folk, soundtracks from

forgotten films, Cuban jazz. The covers of his current favourites are pinned to the door with his hand-written notes providing background information and his descriptions of the music. 'I'll order stuff, too, of course,' he smiles. 'Pretty much anything you ask for, as long as it's not Celine Dion.'

The shop is laid out like a living room, with a small dining table and comfy chairs. Sit down, have a coffee and pick a booklet of covers to browse. When you find one you're interested in, let Marc know and he'll put it on the stereo. There's no hurry – most people stay for an hour or two. 'I don't like the idea of putting pressure on people,' he says. Part of the fun of the place is listening to Marc enthuse about the music.

If there are a lot of people in the shop (it can happen), or if you just fancy a rest, ask Marc if you can see his bedroom. It's tiny but cosy, with drapes, curtains, velvet pillows and a large painting reproducing a Magna Carta LP cover. There's a CD player in here, too, and Marc will leave you alone to listen to it in comfort, lying among the cushions. Just don't say it reminds you of Celine Dion.

Trips Out of Town

Lena Lena

*19 Bennesteeg (09 233 79 47/09 222 23 30/
www.lenalena.com).* **Open** 12.30-6.30pm Mon;
10.30am-6.30pm Tue-Sat. **Credit** AmEx, DC,
MC, V. **Map** p254 B4.

Miet Crabbé is the designer behind this label for
fashion-conscious voluptuous women. One half of
the shop has upscale decorative homeware by other
Belgians, including Christophe Coppens.

Movies

*5 St Pietersnieuwstraat (09 223 59 12/www.
movies.be).* **Open** 10am-6.30pm Mon-Thur; 10am-
7pm Fri, Sat. **Credit** AmEx, DC, MC, V.

Looking for a cool T-shirt, pullover, jeans or shoes?
Since 1984, Movies has been the fashion point in
Ghent. You'll find high-quality designer fashion in
a pleasant environment. Streetwear includes
Adidas, Fornari, G-Star, Schott and more.

Oona

12 Bennesteeg (09 224 21 13). **Open** 11am-1pm,
2-6pm Mon-Sat. **Credit** AmEx, DC, MC, V.
Map p254 B4.

The concrete walls and minimalist interior at
Oona's complements the designer women's clothes
by the likes of Barbara Bui, Costume National,
Joseph and Martine Sitbon.

Het Oorcussen

7 Vrijdagmarkt (09 233 07 65). **Open** 1.30-6pm
Mon; 10.30am-6pm Tue-Sat. **Credit** AmEx, MC, V.
Map p254 B2.

This stylish boutique in a 16th-century house offers
exclusively Belgian designers: Dries van Noten,
Dirk Bikkembergs, Ann Demeulemeester, AF
Vandevorst and Martin Margiela. There's also a
small collection of jewellery and accessories by
Wouters and Hendrix.

Orsacchino

7B Gouvernementstraat (09 223 08 47). **Open**
10.30am-6.30pm Mon, Wed-Sat. **Credit** MC, V.
Map p254 B/C4.

Sophisticated, daring lingerie and bathing costumes
for men and women. Men are restricted to D&G, but
women can also pick from Joop, André Sardá and
Pain de Sucre.

Food & confectionery

Temmerman

79 Kraanlei (09 224 00 41). **Open** 11am-6pm
Tue-Sat. **No credit cards**. **Map** p254 B2.

Temmerman is a confectioner of great charm, with
an absolutely fabulous assortment of chocolates,
biscuits, sweets, edible sugared flowers, honey and
teas. Every type of sweet has a history attached and
the staff are willing to tell you all about it.

Vishandel de Vis

48 Voldersstraat (09 224 32 28/www.devis.be).
Open 10am-6.30pm Mon; 9am-6.30pm Tue-Sat.
Credit MC, V. **Map** p254 B4.

A first-class food shop specialising in fish and all
kinds of seafood: the fresh variety on slabs, ready-
to-eat winkles and live oysters; freezer cabinets
stuffed with bags of shellfish and fish suppers; and
a *traiteur* with a wonderful selection of various
take-home-and-heat recipes.

Vve Tierenteijn-Verlent

3 Groentenmarkt (09 225 83 36). **Open** 8.30am-
6pm Mon-Fri; 8.30am-12.30pm, 1-6pm Sat.
No credit cards. **Map** p254 B3.

This shop, with the same original fittings as when
it first opened in 1858, specialises in mustard. A
huge vat prepared according to a family recipe of
1790 stands in one corner, and can be bought by the
gram and put in containers sold in the shop. Other
spices are sold, along with every type of mustard
seed imaginable.

Music, books & comics

De Kaft

*44 Kortrijksepoortstraat (09 329 64 38/
http://users.pandora.be/dekaft/home.html).*
Open 10am-6pm Mon-Sat. **No credit cards**.

This second-hand shop sells books, comics, vinyl,
CDs, posters, videos and computer software. It's
neat and tidy – not always the case with nearly-new
shops – so you should find what you're looking for.

Music Mania

*197 Bagattenstraat (09 225 68 15/www.music
maniarecords.com).* **Open** 11am-7pm Mon-Sat.
Credit MC, V.

Three floors of every type of music, although
drum 'n' bass, jungle, jazz and reggae are the specialities here. The shop used to be known for its
heavy metal selection, which is still very good.
Although no second-hand CDs are sold, you
should find some bargains on the third floor.
Check out the vinyl as well.

De Schaar

28 Serpentstraat (09 223 73 71). **Open** noon-
6.30pm Mon-Sat. **No credit cards**. **Map** p254 B2.

De Schaar has a vast collection of toys, comics and
film memorabilia. It's also *the* place in town to rent
alternative import videos from Japan.

Film

At the beginning of October, Ghent hosts the
annual **Flanders International Film
Festival** (www.filmfestival.be). Special
programmes are shown at the city's cinemas,
prizes are awarded and the odd celebrity pops
by. Among the local cinemas hosting the event,
and used throughout the year, are **Decascoop**
(12 Ter Platen, 09 265 06 00, www.kinepolis.be),
Sphinx (3 St Michielshelling, 09 225 60 86,
www.cinebel.com) and **Studio Skoop** (63 St
Annaplein, 09 225 08 45).

Day Trips

Carnival mayhem, white-water rafting and the tram-lined Belgian riviera – all on Brussels' doorstep.

Palais des Princes-Evêques, Liège. *See p268.*

Liège

If Bruges is the Venice of the North, Liège – great nightlife, superb restaurants, fashionable shops and an infectious, devil-may-care atmosphere – could stake a claim to being the Milan. The influence of the large number of Italian immigrants who came here after World War II to work in the coal mines is partly responsible for the city's fire and flair. Then again, a reputation for academic excellence in centuries past had some people calling it the Athens of the North. Identity crisis? Interesting personality would be closer to the mark.

Although 15 kilometres (10 miles) from the Dutch border, Liège – the de facto capital of the Ardennes and of its own province – is French-speaking. For centuries it was an independent power, governed by a succession of powerful prince-bishops between the tenth century and 1794, when French Revolutionary armies ousted the last of the ruling priests and destroyed a cathedral. Liège got back on its feet in the 1800s and enjoyed a period of prosperity as a coal and steel centre; then, in more recent times, the local heavy industry declined, which accounts for the grunginess of some of the city's neighbourhoods.

Today Liège is probably most famous for being the birthplace of Georges Simenon, the prolific, pipe-smoking author who wrote over 500 novels and, so the legend goes, slept with more than 10,000 women. He was born in 1903 at 24 rue Léopold, a stone's throw from the district of Outremeuse where he grew up: the building is now a discount junk shop. (Opposite is a nightlife must, the Maison du Pequet, pequet being a local type of gin with freshly squeezed fruit juices.) Simenon began his writing career as a cub reporter on the *Gazette de Liège*, wrote his first novel at the age of 17 and set many of his subsequent stories in Liège; indeed, he admitted in later life that almost all of his urban settings – even those in the US – were transpositions of his home town.

Today, amateur sleuths can pick up a few leads on the two-hour 'Sur les traces de Simenon' audio tour of the city (€6-€8, starting from the

Taking the waters

Given that it's more than a two-hour train ride from Brussels to Spa, it's probably best to plan an overnight break to this picturesque town in the heart of the Ardennes, especially if you're going to fully benefit from the town's excellent spa facilities.

Spa is the original spa, after which all other health resorts around the world are named. The Romans in the first century recognised the healing properties of its sulphur-laden waters – the word spa comes from the Latin *sparsa*, meaning 'gush forth'. However, it was only from the 16th century onwards that Spa really became established as a health destination, attracting royalty, statesmen and aristocrats from all over Europe. Regular visitors included Henry VIII, Peter the Great, Casanova, Victor Hugo and Charles II.

But by the 19th century, Spa's popularity was in decline. Although it retained its spa facilities, they always seemed rather quaint but out of touch with the modern preference for clinical white lines. Not any more. In the spring of 2004, an all-singing, all-dancing new spa was opened just above the town, with access via a funicular lift.

The new Thermes de Spa is an impressive site, with its large indoor and outdoor hydrotherapy pools – mineral-rich water from the Marie-Henriette spring is heated to 34°C and dispensed through an array of high-pressure jets and underwater massages to soothe city-break aches. There's also an up-to-date beauty centre, where you can muck in with body scrubs or a warm peat bath combining local Fagnes peat with carbonated water, plus special programmes such as a five-day mother and baby course designed to get new mums back into shape. Lastly, of course, there is an endless supply of Spa drinking water to cleanse the inside as well as the outside.

Spa Les Thermes is hoping to bring a whole new generation of spa enthusiasts – and there are plenty of them about these days – to the town. Prices range from €17 for a couple of hours in the pools to €595 for a full five-day mother-and-baby programme.

Those wanting to stay for the weekend – or even a week – should consider splashing out (so to speak) on the Radisson SAS Palace Hotel (39 place Royale, 087 27 97 00, www.radissonsas.com), which is located in the heart of Spa and has direct access to the new spa facility.

Thermes de Spa

Colline d'Annette et Lubin (087 77 25 60/ http://thermesdespa.phidji.com). **Open** 9am-8pm Mon-Thur, Sun; 9am-10pm Fri, Sat.

Maison du Tourisme, 35 place St-Lambert, 04 237 9292). The war memorial outside the Town Hall lists one Arnold Maigret, who furnished the writer with a surname for his famous detective, the star of 75 novels. The church of St-Pholien, in Outremeuse, is a grislier landmark: a young cocaine addict was found hanged from its door handle in 1922. The story inspired Simenon's 1931 thriller *Le Pendu de St-Pholien*.

The main railway station is two kilometres south of the centre on place Guillemins (there's a small information office here: 04 252 4419, 9.30am-12.30pm, 1-4pm Mon-Sat). It's a 25-minute walk to the historic heart of the city, the charmless place St-Lambert. Here you'll find the **Palais des Princes-Evêques**, the stately former home of the prince-bishops, dating from the 16th century but altered in subsequent centuries. The Palais now serves as the court for Liège Province, and usually only the outer courtyard is accessible to the public.

The older part of the city lies east of here, in the shadow of the steep Montagne de Bueren, atop which stand the remains of the ramparts of the **Citadelle**. It's a stiff climb, but rewarded with a fabulous panorama of the city. Parallel to the bottom of the hill runs Féronstrée, the backbone of this part of Liège. Many of Liège's museums are either on or just off Féronstrée.

The **Musée d'Art Religieux et d'Art Mosan** (rue Mère-Dieu, off rue Hors-Château, 04 221 4225, 11am-6pm Tue-Sat; 11am-4pm Sun, €2.50-€3.80) displays a fine selection of locally produced religious art. More things local are celebrated in the **Musée de l'Art Wallon** (86 Féronstrée, 04 221 9231, 1-6pm Tue-Sat, 11am-4.30pm Sun, €2.50-€3.80), which boasts more than 3,000 paintings and sculptures, giving a sample of the best of Brussels and Wallonia; it's a must for lovers of Magritte and Delvaux.

A little further along Féronstrée are the delightfully presented 18th-century furniture and furnishings of the **Musée d'Ansembourg** (114 Féronstrée, 04 221 9402, 1-6pm Tue-Sun, €2.50-€3.80). More impressive is the **Grand Curtius** (13 quai de Maestricht, 04 221 9404),

an ambitious expansion of the Musée Curtius that will result in a four-in-one museum complex. When the 17th-century Renaissance palace reopens in 2005, it will house the immense collection of arms and armour of the Musée d'Armes, the glass artefacts (some dating back to ancient Egypt) of the Musée du Verre, and the decorative and historic artefacts (many with religious significance and in precious metals and stones) of the Musée d'Archéologie and Musée d'Arts Décoratifs.

The area south and west of place St-Lambert may not be as old as around Féronstrée, but its pedestrianised streets and multitude of bars, restaurants and shops make it more appealing. There are also plenty of churches. The **Cathédrale St-Paul** on place Cathédrale (8am-noon, 2-5pm daily, €4) was begun in the 14th century but not finished until the 19th. It's not that interesting outside, but inside are some vibrant 16th-century ceiling paintings and stained glass. South of the cathedral, close to avenue Maurice Destenay, is the church of **St-Jacques** (9am-noon, 1.30-5pm Mon-Sat; 9-10am

Sun, free), founded in the 11th century. Only the western wing of the original church survives, with Gothic and Renaissance styles mingling in the rest of the church. The most notable feature of **St-Denis** (9am-noon, 1.30-5pm Mon-Sat; 9-10am Sun, free), between the cathedral and place Lambert, is its immense 16th-century retable. West of here, on place Xavier Neujean, stands **St-Jean** (June-Sept 10am-noon, 2-5pm Mon-Wed, Fri, Sat; 2-5pm Thur, Sun; Oct-May call 04 222 1441 for reservations; free). Dating from the tenth century, it was modelled on Charlemagne's church at Aachen, although only the tower remains of the original structure.

A key figure in Liègeois lore is Tchantchès, a legendary character with a huge nose and a passion for fighting and drinking. He's most often encountered today in puppet form, and is celebrated in the **Musée Tchantchès** at 56 rue Surlet (04 342 7575, 2-4pm Tue, Thur, €1). From October to Easter you should also be able to catch a puppet show here on Wednesdays at 2.30pm and Sundays at 10.30am; admission is €2.50 including the museum.

Coasting along

One of the glories of the Belgian coast is the Kusttram, the coastal tram, which runs along its length from De Panne to Knokke. It's not just a major civil engineering success story; it makes life easier for locals, allowing them to go about their seaside business, while for tourists, it makes a sightseeing trip in its own right. The tram – run by Flemish public transport company De Lijn – makes 70 stops along its way, calling in at all 16 coastal towns. It also ties in neatly with most major railway stations, making that final leg more bearable. Knokke station to Blankenberge seafront? Certainly.

In the summer, a tram goes by every ten minutes (20 minutes in off-season) and a daily pass means you can hop on and off whenever you like. For the hardy traveller who wants to do the whole journey in one hit, set aside around two hours and 20 minutes and make sure you bring something to cushion the bumps. Its real benefit lies in the flexibility it can offer; if you've had enough of sunbathing crowds, head off on the tram for some quiet dune walking. If the kids are screaming, pile aboard and go to a water park or funfair. If you want to sit lazing on the beach sipping Belgian beer all day, forget the car and take the tram to the sands. Perfect.

De Lijn
110 Nieuwpoortsesteenweg, 8400 Oostende (059 56 53 53/www.dekusttram.be). **Trams** around 5am-10.30pm daily. **Day ticket** €5.

The other main attraction on this side of the river Meuse is further south, at 3 parc de Boverie: the **Musée d'Art Moderne** (04 343 0403, 1-6pm Tue-Sat; 11am-4.30pm Sun, €2.50-€3.80). The museum holds a mixed bag of works by Chagall, Gauguin, Monet and Picasso.

Take a stroll around Le Carré (the Square), a pedestrianised area between the Théâtre Royal and the cathedral, whose narrow streets are packed with cafés, clubs, bars and shops.

Where to eat

Liège is a place to eat well. Diagonally opposite the end of the rue du Pot d'Or is **Le Bruit Qui Court** (142 boulevard de la Sauvenière, 04 232

1818), an elegant brasserie in a former bank serving modern French cuisine. **As Ouhès** (19-21 place du Marché, 04 223 3225) serves local specialities such as *boulettes* (Liège's traditional meatballs) and mashed potato mixed with black pudding. Nearby is the tiny **L'Erère** (9 place du Marché, 04 223 2813, closed Sun), which also serves classic Liègois dishes. It's often full. Just up the road is **Le Bistrot d'en Face** (8-10 rue de la Goffe, 04 223 1584), serving specialities for the braver gourmet: the menu includes pig's ears, herrings in oil and other hearty local fare.

Rue Tête de Boeuf is the best starting point for bars, although they are sprinkled around the city. If you've had a long night, you could have coffee and breakfast at **Café Lequet** (17 quai sur Meuse, 04 222 2134), an old haunt of the Simenon family, which opens at 6am on Sundays and serves a famous meatball and chips. It's the perfect spot to greet a new day in passionate, mysterious, hard-living Liège.

Getting there

From Brussels, there are four trains an hour to Liège. Journey takes 65 minutes.

Tourist information

City of Liège Tourist Office

92 Féronstrée, 4000 Liège (04 221 9221/fax 04 221 9222/www.liege.be). **Open** 9am-5pm Mon-Fri.

Ostend & the Coast

The Belgians are proud of their 67 kilometres (42 miles) of coastline. Not only does it provide a firm punctuation mark to their territory, but its sands are regarded as some of the finest in northern Europe. At low tide the soft beaches can stretch for 500 metres (1,626 feet), providing a safe kiddy environment and a paddler's paradise. And despite the cold, grey North Sea, which can whip up a fair wind all year round, the stalwart Belgians pour there in droves; in the summer it's shoulder-to-shoulder solid, while in the winter it's full of retired folk and city-types with second homes.

This tourist reclamation of the dunes has its downside; massive building projects along the coastline have left it overdeveloped in a mish-mash of styles, a sort of Benidorm *à la belge*, where apartment blocks, villas and commercial enterprises all vie for the perfect sea view. But all is not lost: the coast is redeemed by its broad promenades, which deftly separate sand from cement and provide a safe freeway for hired bikes, tandems and pedal cars, as well as long, lazy strolling.

Another charming feature uneclipsed by the building work is the humble beach hut. They remain in rows all along the Belgian coast as a testament to the 19th century when they were drawn by horse to the water's edge for modest mixed-sex bathing. ('Horror!' cried the English, though it didn't stop the young Victoria popping across for a go.) Today the huts are painted up a treat in ice-cream colours and can be hired or bought – though the waiting list is long, as families pass them down from generation to generation.

For those who prefer their coastline rugged and unspoilt, it's worth going to the area around **Zwin** where the dunes are rigorously protected in order to provide a sanctuary for indigenous birds and wildlife (Het Zwin Nature Reserve, 050 60 70 86, www.zwin.be). Zwin is at the northern end of the coastal run, close to the Dutch border, and is a natural extension to the posh resort of **Knokke-Heist**, with its designer shops, swanky restaurants and exclusive beach clubs, not to mention the very

Ostend.

Ostend, home of balls, brollies and bulls. *See p273.*

select **Royal Tennis Club du Zoute**
(7 Astridlaan, 050 60 28 60), and **Royal Zoute
Golf Club** (050 60 12 27). More downmarket
but no less a place to see and be seen is **Surfers
Paradise** (13 Acacialaan, 050 61 59 60, www.
surfersparadise.be), a semi-exclusive beach area
where you can hire boards and play cool. In the
evenings, smart dinners, smart discos and the
smartest casino are bound to inflict some
damage on your wallet. If seafood's your thing,
you could try **Aquilon** (6 Elizabethlaan, 050 60
12 74, closed Tue), famous for its lobster and
abundant use of truffles. **Ter Dijcken** (137
Kalvekeetdijk, 050 60 80 23, closed Mon & Tue)
is a classic French/Belgian restaurant both in
style and food. These two restaurants' main
courses average around €25. For a simpler
moules-frites, you can't go wrong at **'T
Kantientje** (103 Lippenslaan, 050 60 54 11).

The **Casino Knokke** (509 Zeedijk, 050 63
05 05, www.casinoknokke.be) is so much more
than a gaming house. Set in a beautiful 1920s
building, it has two nightclubs and a function
room that draws international stars. It is also
an art gallery of sorts, with frescoes by Keith
Haring and Paul Delvaux, and works by the
likes of Spilliaert. But it is the *Enchanted Fields*
murals in the dining room that attract most
attention as they're by Belgium's very own

René Magritte. Naturally, you need to be an
appropriately dressed paying punter to see all
this but, once inside, the atmosphere is fun and
relaxed (though you'll also need your passport).

If you want to stay the night, **La Réserve**
(160 Elizabethlaan, 050 61 06 06, €268-€518)
has all the five-star amenities, while a cheaper
option is the **Parkhotel**, close to the beach
and decorated in a clean, modern style (204
Elizabethlaan, 050 62 36 08, €84-€128).

A good way to pop into other resorts is to
take the coastal tram (*see p270* **Coasting
along**). De Haan (www.dehaan.be) has 11
kilometres (seven miles) of unspoilt beach and
is particularly geared up for kids' activities. It's
also proud of its pine-wooded dunes, which hug
the seashore and are laid out with ramblers'
walkways. This is one of the few spots where
belle époque architecture, harmonious pastel
façades and winding lanes have not given
way to the high-rises. **Blankenberge**
(www.blankenberge.be) also has its own
dunes, a 1930s pier, a harbour and a lengthy
promenade, with steep ladder-type steps down
to the bathing huts and beach. The town is
stuffed with attractions, including the **Sea Life
Centre** (116 Albert I Laan, 050 42 42 00) and
the **Serpentarium** (146 Zeedijk, 050 42 31 62),
a reptile park. Even **Zeebrugge**, known mostly

as a ferry port, is worth a look. It is now Belgium's main fishing port and the new fish market is a sight in itself. The old one has been converted into a major maritime theme park, **Seafront Zeebrugge** (Vismijnstraat 7, 050 55 14 15, www.seafront.be), where, among other things, you can clamber around a real Russian submarine and a lightship.

Ostend

Because of its royal connections, the Belgians call Ostend 'the Queen of Belgian Seaside Resorts'. Léopold I built a house here, but it was Léopold II, meisterbuilder of Belgium, who put up several villas and gave Ostend its royal character. Despite criticism that he was neglecting the capital, Léopold II spent far too much time here for his own good, partly because it provided the perfect hideaway for his numerous affairs. It was his association with the town that led to it becoming such a highly fashionable resort in the late 19th and early 20th centuries that it rivalled Monte Carlo for wealth, luxury, casinos and racecourses. World War II finally put paid to that and serious aerial bombardment destroyed much of the old fabric – including the original casino – resulting in the curious blend of grand imperialistic, '50s modern and '70s bland architecture that characterises the town today.

The atmosphere in Ostend is typically seaside, with the wide promenade and soft, flat sand giving it a calm air. A plethora of events takes place throughout the summer, from sporting (sailing, cycling, windsurfing) to artistic (a major theatre festival takes place in July and August; www.theateraanzee.be). One of the oddest is the shrimp-peeling competition in September in the **Visserskai**, the fishermen's harbour, which provides the wonderful sight of the daily catch coming in. Being a sea-transport hub, Ostend's harbours lend it much atmosphere, particularly the yacht harbour where the *Mercator*, an old Belgian navy training ship from the '30s, stands. The Souikom harbour is now used mainly for water sports. The wind can be cutting in winter, but hardy Belgians continue to use their holiday flats throughout the year, so it's never really empty. Over the Christmas and New Year period there is a skating rink and atmospheric Christmas market, beach fireworks on 31 December, and the strange communal ritual of burning Christmas trees on the beach after Twelfth Night.

Mercifully, there remain some architectural gems from old Ostend. **Fort Napoleon**, built in 1812, is the only intact Napoleonic fortress in Europe, while at the western end of the

promenade, there is Léopold II's 390-metre (1,280-feet) Galeries Royales, all Tuscan columns with a belle-époque pavilion as a finial. Léopold's former villa is now a luxurious hotel, the Thermae Palace (*see p274*). In the church of **St Peter and St Paul** is a darker relic, the marble mausoleum of the first Léopold's beloved wife, Louise-Marie, who died in Ostend in 1850. Inside the twin-towered church, the Belgian kings are depicted religiously in stained glass. But without doubt the crowning glory of the post-war period is the **Ostend Casino**, built in 1953 and the fourth casino to stand on the spot. The walls of the gaming room are decorated in frescoes by Paul Delvaux, though you have to take a place at the tables to see them. The casino is also used as a multi-purpose arts complex, particularly in summer. It has recently been undergoing radical refurbishment, returning the concert hall to its former glory and adding a roof patio, and is due to reopen in time for the 2004 season.

Ostend's links with art are legendary, especially those with James Ensor, who lived and worked here. There is an Ensor trail of 15 street panels, reproductions of his often macabre works, around the town and the **Ensorhuis**, his house and studio, is open to the public (27 Vlaanderenstraat, 059 50 53 35, www.artsite.be/musea/MSKOostende.htm, Easter & June-Sept 10am-noon, 2-5pm Mon, Wed-Sun, rest of the year 2-5pm Mon, Wed-Sun, admission €2). So small was its upstairs workshop that Ensor could never fully unfurl his ultimate masterpiece, *Christ's Entry into Brussels*. The house used to belong to his aunt, who sold seashells and other souvenirs, and the house shop continues in bizarre tradition.

The **Museum of Fine Arts** (Wapenplein, 059 80 53 35, www.artsite.be/musea/MSKOostende.htm, 10am-noon, 2-5pm, Mon, Wed-Sun, admission €2) lost about 400 paintings in the air raids, but has since been restocked with works by local Belgian artists, including Ensor and Spilliaert. The **Provincial Museum for Modern Art** (11 Romestraat, 059 50 81 18, www.pmmk.be, 10am-6pm Tue-Sun, admission €5) – known as the PMMK – exhibits local modern art from the expressionists to the present day and includes video art and installations by Panamarenko, the man with the flying machines.

Where to eat & stay

It's no surprise to learn that fish is the order of the day in Ostend. For a quick bite, go to the **Visserskai** where, throughout the day, small stands sell fishy finger food – prepared crab, mussels and young herring (*maatjesharing*), and, yes, you eat them raw. You shouldn't go wrong in any restaurant in Ostend, but among the pick of the bunch are **'T Vistrapje** (37 Visserskaai, 059 80 23 82) or at No.30 the **Thermidor** – guess what's on the menu there. For something a little ritzy try **Savarin** (75 Albert 1 Promenade, 059 51 31 71) and for something buzzier try **Art Café** (3 Romestraat, 059 80 56 86). The main nightlife and drinking haunts are around **Langestraat** and **Van Iseghemlaan**. Irish pubs abound, but one bizarre place is the **Cosy Corner Inn** (76A Langestraat, 70 92 61), full of atmosphere and good humour.

Hotels tend to be smarter than those at most seaside resorts. At the top end, Léopold's old villa, the **Thermae Palace Hotel** is one of Ostend's finest (7 Koningin Astridlaan, 059 80 52 74, €139). The modern **Hotel Europe** is only 50 metres from the promenade and is reasonably priced and comfortable (52 Kapucijnenstraat, 059 70 10 12, €68). A decent place near the railway station is the art-deco-styled **Hotel Louisa** (8B Louisastraat, 059 50 96 77, €55-€79). For a budget option try **Hotel Orbit** (46 Torhoutsesteenweg, 059 50 14 42, €38-€50). For more details, check the website www.hotels-belgium.com/oostende/hotels.htm.

Getting there

The motorways to the coast, particularly in the summer and at weekends throughout the year, can be a nightmare and parking comes with its own problems. By far the best way to get to Ostend is by the inter-city train from Brussels. Journey time is about 70 minutes.

Tourism information

Toerisme Oostende

2 Monacoplein, 8400 Ostend (059 70 11 99/ www.toerisme-oostende.be). **Open** 10am-6pm Mon-Sat; 10am-5pm Sun.

Leuven

The picturesque yet lively city of Leuven (Louvain in French), just east of Brussels, is Belgium's equivalent to Cambridge or Oxford, only with more beer. Lots more beer. It has its fair share of good restaurants, cool shops and riverside walks to enjoy. Bicycles rule around the city centre, with many streets closed to cars, and bike hire shops if you want to join in.

Most of all, though, Leuven is the beer capital of Belgium, no idle boast. The huge Interbrew conglomerate has its brewery here, not that the locals would touch it; Domus is the beer of

choice, although little could detract from the pleasure of sitting at a terrace on the bar-starred central Oude Markt in the early evening. (*See p276* **Only here for the beer**.)

A good place to start exploring is around the **university**, one of the world's oldest Catholic universities (founded 1425) and mercifully spared from two bouts of bombing during the world wars. It was also the scene of fierce linguistic battles in the mid 1960s. After four years of fighting, the university was split; the Flemings stayed and a new campus was built for francophones in Louvain-la-Neuve. It is hard to imagine the past as you stroll through its quiet, pleasant grounds and follow riverside walks or cool cycle paths.

The town centre (a five-minute walk from the train station along Bondgenotenlaan) is focused on **Grote Markt**. Here you'll find the city's architectural highlights. The impressive and elaborate **Stadhuis** (Town Hall), built between 1448 and 1469, is a masterpiece of Brabant late Gothic architecture. Its delicate pinnacles, towers and other intricate details have a fairy-tale harmony. It was supposed to outshine Brussels' town hall, back in the days when Leuven was prosperous from the cloth trade and was capital of Brabant. The original plan for statues in each of the 282 niches proved too ambitious, the money ran out and it wasn't until the mid 19th century that the majority of the niches were finally filled with non-medieval figures such as Napoleon and Belgian royalty.

The Town Hall faces Leuven's other major Gothic building, **St Pieterskerk** (016 22 69 06, 10am-5pm Mon-Sat; 2-5pm Sun; closed mid Dec-mid Jan; €5). The church has an unhappy past. Begun in the 1420s (on the site of a Romanesque basilica), it was intended to have three spires, the central one of which was to be a lofty 170 metres (558 feet) high, but the marshy subsoil proved unable to support such a structure. Work lasted 70 years and the prematurely capped current towers mark the builders' insurmountable problem. And then the exterior was badly battered during both world wars. Yet once you're inside, Gothic harmony is re-established in the vertiginous nave. In the ambulatory there's a worthwhile small museum – the **Treasury of St Peter**, which contains a copy of Roger van der Weyden's *Descent from the Cross* and two rare surviving triptychs from his apprentice Dirk Bouts, the city painter of Leuven.

Entrance to the museum costs €5, which also gets you into the **Museum Vander Kelen-Mertens** (6 Savoyestraat, 016 22 69 06, 10am-5pm Tue-Sat, 2-5pm Sun), near the **tourist office** (*see p276*). In mock-historical rooms, it contains an appealing miscellany of porcelain,

Leuven – stroll by day, sip by night. *See p274.*

ceramics, stained glass, sculpture (including pieces by Constantin Meunier) and paintings such as a *Holy Trinity* by van der Weyden.

Stroll south from St Pieterskerk along Naamsestraat to the superb baroque mid 17th-century **St Michielskerk**, then continue down to **Groot Begijnhof**, just off the street to the right. Founded around 1230, this gorgeous and extensive complex (with its 62 houses, ten convents, church and squares) was once home to lay sisterhoods (*béguines*), but is now mostly student accommodation.

If you want a change from culture, hot shops include **Profiel** (37 Mechelsestraat, 016 23 72 62) for cutting-edge womenswear by the likes of Ann Demeulemeester, Dries van Noten and Kaat Tilley, together with lesser-known and cheaper labels. Men have **Jonas** opposite (No.34, 016 23 41 04) for casual fashion by Antwerp Sixer Dirk Bikkembergs, and Paul Smith. For comic strip annuals, drop in at **Het Besloten Land** (16 Parijsstraat, 016 22 58 40) – the shop is piled high with titles in French, Dutch and English.

Time your visit for a Saturday morning and you'll catch the town's excellent **food market** on Brusselsestraat, where local farmers come to sell their produce. Cheese lovers should not miss **Elsen** (36 Mechelsestraat, 016 22 13 10), run by a professional cheese ripener who buys most of his specials from the food market outside Paris. It's a dream, and if you ask the owner nicely he'll show you the special ripening chambers.

Where to eat & stay

Make a beeline for the Oude Markt area, just south of the Grote Markt, and pick one of the many bars or cafés that line the square. (*See p276* **Only here for the beer.**) If you fancy making a real night of it, the **Silo** club (39 Vaartkom, 0496 23 72 52, www.silo.be) is one of Belgium's best clubs, set in an old warehouse. In August, the Oude Markt itself becomes the stage for the popular outdoor rock festival **Marktrock** (www.marktrock.be).

For eating, try Parijsstraat that runs parallel with the Oude Markt on the west side. There's a variety of restaurants here to suit most tastes and budgets. Top choices include the stylish **Kapsiki** at No.34 (016 20 45 87), which has

Only here for the beer

Millions of drinkers have probably clocked Leuven's name on the label of their **Stella Artois** without it even registering. But the Belgian HQ of the world's biggest beermaker is probably the least interesting sight in an otherwise lovely medieval university town, a classic case of brewer's droop in a place that prides itself as Belgium's beer capital.

Beermakers were around long before Sebastian Artois became a master brewer in 1708. A brewery was first mentioned under the name Den Horen (the Horn) in 1366, several decades before the founding of Belgium's oldest university in the town in 1425. Although one particular brewery took the Artois name from 1717 onwards, it wasn't until winter of 1926 that the company decided to create a bright, clear Christmas brew which they gave the Latin name for 'star' – Stella.

The present-day Stella brewery (*pictured*), a new creation to replace the old building that had been badly damaged during World War II, reveals little of the company's long history. A tour of the brewery on Vaartstraat (also the home of Leffe Blonde, not to be confused with the excellent Leffe Tripel brewed in nearby Hoegaarden) offers up big vats, big stats and a pint of the big-name brew, as well as the odd quirky fact. But while you might impress your friends by telling them how used Stella labels are recycled into toilet rolls, you

have to wonder why, when they've been brewing for over 600 years, they produce stuff discerning locals refer to as weak.

Fortunately, Leuven's mix of bonhomie and academia also includes a much better beermaker – **Domus** – which comes with a fine old bar attached to its brewery on Eikstraat, where you can knock back a *proefbedje* ('tasting rack') containing a trio of beers such as the red and deadly Engel. If you must drink Stella, the best place is **Jeeskesboom** on Diestestraat, rumoured to have direct piping from the brewery, if you believe what the regulars tell you.

After that, Leuven offers another 170 bars where you can put the world to rights. The boozy heart of the town is the **Oude Markt**, a short stagger from the central Grote Markt. This small cobbled square crams in 40 drinking holes, where you can find most of the 360 or so beers produced in Belgium.

They pretty much cater for all tastes in terms of ambience, too – pumping music joints like **Oase** and **Orient**, style spots like **Metropole**, dimly lit boho hangouts like **Eclips** and straightforward atmospheric drinking dens like **Plaza** and **Forum**. Many are open until 5am or later. The big night out is Thursday, before students take their washing home to mum for the weekend.

---

several vegetarian options and main courses at €15-€20; and upmarket restaurant-traiteur **Il Pastaio** (016 23 09 02; closed Sun; main courses €15) at No.33. The pasta is made in-house; try the sauce of scampi, tomatoes, basil and olive oil.

For quieter dining, consider **Ombre ou Soleil** (20 Muntstraat, 016 22 51 87, closed Sat lunch, Sun) where the menu features Med simplicity and the ambience is relaxed. On the same street, **Oesterbar** (No.23, 016 20 28 38) specialises in fish and oysters. Sit in front of an open log fire in winter. Or there's trendy **De Blauwe Zon** (28 Tiensestraat, 016 22 68 80, €22 per head) on five floors, with the kitchen serving modern fusion cuisine and wicked steaks. Finally, for a true gourmet experience and smart setting, go for **Belle Epoque** (94 Bondgenotenlaan, 016 22 33 89, closed mid July-mid Aug). House chef Ludo Tubée is one of Belgium's best chefs. In fair weather you can sit outside in the restaurant's pretty courtyard. Expect to pay from €50 per person, and book ahead at the weekend.

If you want to extend your stay, try **Jeff's Guesthouse** at 2 Kortestraat (016 23 87 80, €75-85). It's a hotel, a restaurant and a shop – all devoted to the Italian way of life. Some rooms overlook the square. The shop sells olives and their derivatives, including oils and beauty products. If you're willing to splash out, **Het Klooster** (22 Predikherenstraat, 016 213 141, www.hetklooster.com, from €200) has sleek, modern rooms in a 16th-century country house.

Getting there

From Brussels, there are five trains an hour to Leuven. Journey takes 35 minutes.

Tourist information

Leuven Tourist Office
Stadhuis, 9 Grote Markt, 3000 Leuven (016 21 15 39/fax 016 21 15 49/www.leuven.be). **Open** *Nov-Apr* 9am-5pm Mon-Fri; 10am-1pm, 1.30-5pm Sat. *Mar-Oct* 9am-5pm Mon-Fri; 10am-1pm, 1.30-5pm Sat, Sun.

Mechelen

At the rough halfway point between Brussels and Antwerp, Mechelen has almost all of the medieval majesty of Bruges, without the crowds of tourists.

Mechelen, Malines to the French, was one of the most powerful cities in Flanders. From 1473 it entered something of a golden age when the Burgundian prince Charles the Bold based his administration in the city. When the capital was moved to Brussels in 1530, Mechelen lost its political power and influence and became something of a backwater, but it is still the home of the Belgian Primate and therefore the country's ecclesiastical capital.

The city has a number of buildings dating from its golden era, including the **Stadhuis** (Town Hall), which was built at the start of the 16th century and stands proudly on the **Grote Markt**, almost as impressive as those in Brussels and Antwerp. Mechelen's main square

is also lined with impressive gabled structures, including the austere 14th-century **Lakenhalle** (Cloth Hall). Work began on a new wing of the hall in 1526, but it had to be abandoned in the 1530s due to financial difficulties. It wasn't until the late 19th century that the wing was completed, according to the original plans of 16th-century architect Rombout Keldermans. Close by stands a modern statue of the doll **Op Signoorke**, Mechelen's mascot, being tossed in a blanket. In the rich tradition of weird Belgian festivals, the townsfolk parade through the streets every September, flinging a dummy into the air from a bedsheet.

Just west of the Grote Markt is Mechelen's artistic showpiece, **St Romboutskathedraal** (015 27 19 90, 8.30am-5.30pm daily, free). It was started in the 13th century in early Gothic style, but finished, following a fire in 1342, in late Gothic. The west tower should have been the tallest in the world at the time (it was planned to be 167 metres/548 feet), but the general plummeting of Mechelen's fortunes after 1530 put a stop to such lofty ambitions – the unfortunate Keldermans was in charge of that project too. Still the 97-metre (318-foot) high tower dominates the Grote Markt, and was thought the eighth wonder of the world by Louis XIV's great military engineer Vauban. Both the Lakenhalle and St Rombout's feature on the UNESCO World Heritage List. The elegant interior soars upwards and is filled with light and Gothic purity (if you can ignore the later florid baroque additions). The painting to look out for is van Dyck's *Crucifixion*.

North of the cathedral is a clutch of intriguing religious buildings. Walking up Wollemarkt brings you to the gabled 16th-century **Abdij van St Truiden**. Almost opposite stands the Gothic **St Janskerk**, which contains a Rubens triptych of the *Adoration of the Magi*, but is, alas, rarely open. St Jansstraat runs along the side of the church and leads to the prestigious **Koninklijk Beiardschool** on the corner, one of the world's leading schools of carillon playing. Mechelen is an international centre for this particular art form, of playing bells sounded from a keyboard. The Russian word for carillon means 'the sound of Mechelen'.

Next door is the late Gothic, early 16th-century Museum Hof van Busleyden (015 20 20 04, 10am-5pm Tue-Sun, €2). Hieronymus van Busleyden was a lawyer and leading Flemish humanist who entertained the likes of Erasmus and Thomas More here. The latter was so impressed with the house he wrote three poems about it. It now contains a collection of paintings, bells and architectural bits and bobs.

If you head south-east from here, you come to Veemarkt, and the baroque **St Pieter en Pauluskerk** (Nov-Mar 1.30-4.30pm Tue-Sun; Apr-Oct 1.30-5.30pm Tue-Sun, free), next to the remains of the **Palace of Margaret of York**. The beautiful **Palace of Margaret of Austria** is also here.

From Veemarkt, Befferstraat leads back to the Grote Markt. Running south-west from here, past the Gothic Schepenhuis, is Ijzerenleen. Just before the street crosses the River Dijle, Nauwstraat leads off to the right, curving round via Draabstraat to an iron bridge leading to Haverwerf. Here are three superb façades, the most remarkable of which is the curious **Duivelhuis** (built in 1519) at No.23. Turn left here and walk along the river, looking out for **De Zalm**, a stunning Flemish Renaissance house with a gilded salmon over its entrance. Head down 't Plein on the right and finish up a the white sandstone church of **Onze-Lieve-Vrouw over de Dijle** (Nov-Mar 1.30-4.30pm Tue-Sun; Apr-Oct 1.30-5.30pm Tue-Sun, free). Started in the 15th century, it was not finished until the 17th, and the variety of styles in vogue

during these 200 years (from Gothic to baroque) is evident. Inside hangs Rubens' *Miraculous Draught of Fishes*.

One final tourist attraction that shouldn't be missed is the **De Wit Royal Tapestry Manufacturers** (Refuge of the Tongerlo Abbey, 7 Schoutetstraat, 015 20 29 05, www.dewit.be, guided tours 10.30am Sat, €6), where the age-old Flemish tradition of tapestry is maintained. With the largest private collection of tapestries in Belgium, you can see how new tapestries are made, learn how old ones are renovated, and discover the relevance of each masterpiece's subject matter.

Where to eat & stay

Foodies may want to splash out on Mechelen's two one-star Michelin restaurants. The more traditional and well established is **D'Hoogh** (19 Grote Markt, 015 21 75 53). More modern Mediterranean-influenced fare by chef Axel Colonna-Cesari at **Folliez** (19 Korenmarkt, 015 42 03 02), helped earn this new relative newcomer (opened in 1988) its Michelin star. The owner trained as a sommelier, so the wine list is always impressive. Booking is essential.

The local speciality is *Mechelse koekoek*, succulent Mechelen chicken, and the best place to try it is the traditional **Brasserie Royale** (29 Grote Markt, 015 20 68 81). Built in the 16th century, the building was a dancehall, then a German commander's lodgings in World War I and later a billiard hall owned by former world champion and local hero Raymond Ceulemans. The most recent restoration dates from two years ago, but the historic feel of the place remains intact, with 19th-century wood panelling. Of equally classic genre is the **Brasserie Den Beer** (32-33 Grote Markt, 015 20 97 06), adorned with black and white photographs of the town's cavalcade procession, which takes place every 25 years. The kitchen is imaginative, but you may just come here for a drink on the terrace.

Mechelen is fairly quiet as far as nightlife is concerned – most residents head to either Antwerp or Brussels for a real night out. There are plenty of nondescript bars on and just off the Grote Markt, but one with a little more (modern) charm is **Barramundo** (2 Steenweg, 015 27 64 65), which plays lounge music into the early hours. It's more of a bar for wine and cocktails than beer, and gets crowded with trendies at the weekend. Tucked away behind the cathedral is a great little bar – 20 people and it's packed – called **De Borrel-Babbel** (2 Nieuwwerk, 015 27 36 89). Make sure you get there early to bag one of the few bar stools. As well as beers, there's an excellent selection of local genevers.

For a drink with a view, **De Gouden Vis** (7 Nauwstraat, 015 20 72 06) is an art nouveau bar whose terrace overlooks the canal.

The recently opened **Novotel** (1 Van Beethovenstraat, 015 40 49 50, www.novotel. com) features spacious modern rooms and stylish public areas, plus a great location close to the old town. Good weekend deals in the €100 range too. For a little more Belgian character, try the three-star **Hotel den Wolsack** (16 Wollemarkt, 015 56 95 20, www.denwolsack.com, €110), housed in a beautifully renovated neo-classical building and well located close to the cathedral. Rates drop by nearly €20 at the weekend.

Getting there

From Brussels there are up to five trains an hour to Mechelen, with the journey taking about half an hour.

Tourist information

Dienst Toerisme Stad Mechelen

2 Hallestraat, 2800 Mechelen (015 29 76 55/ www.mechelen.be). **Open** 9.30am-4.30pm Mon-Fri; 10am-noon, 1-3pm Sat; 2-5pm Sun.

Namur

Lying some 60 kilometres (37 miles) south-east of Brussels is Namur, the capital of French-speaking Wallonia. It's a pretty cobbled little city located at the confluence of the rivers Sambre and Meuse. Once of strategic military importance, hence its hilltop citadel, the attraction of the town lies in its cosy squares and pedestrianised streets lined with grand old houses, chic shops, busy cafés and some excellent restaurants.

Namur was subjected to numerous invading forces, each struggling for control of what is one of the largest forts in Europe and now a major tourist draw, the mighty **Citadelle de Namur** (64 route Merveilleuse, 081 22 68 29, Apr-Nov 11am-6pm daily, last visit 5pm, €6). Although it has been fortified for 2,000 years, the citadel's current structure dates mainly from the period of Dutch rule between 1815 and 1830. Covering an area of around 80 hectares (200 acres), there are five self-guided walking tours and, from April to November, a tourist train and guides to take visitors through the atmospheric underground passages, where soldiers could live for up to a month without coming above ground. You'll also find exhibitions, an open-air theatre and various children's amuseuments. Also on the citadel

site is **Parfums Guy Delforge** (60 route Merveilleuse; 081 22 12 19, www.delforge. com), Belgium's only perfume manufacturer. At 3.30pm on Saturdays (and Tue-Sat in school holidays, €3), the company run guided tours to show the different stages of perfume making, from the raw materials kept cool deep inside the citadel to the composition and end product.

Down in the town, there are a number of museums worth checking out. The superb **Trésor du Prieuré d'Oignies** (17 rue Julie Billiart, 081 23 03 42, 10am-noon, 2-5pm Tue-Sat, 2-5pm Sun, €1.50) is a tiny but eminently worthwhile collection of exquisite early 13th-century gold and silver work by Brother Hugo d'Oignies. Considered one of Belgium's finest treasures, they were hidden away from French revolutionaries and Nazi soldiers during two of the more recent invasions of Namur. Just around the corner is the **Musée Archaeologique** (rue du Pont, 081 23 16 31, 10am-5pm Tue-Fri, 10.40am-5pm Sat, Sun, €1.50), which is where you'll find an old relief model of Namur. Prior to air reconnaissance and satellite imaging, European monarchs had scale models made of major towns so that they could plan their line of attack (or defence) should war break out. The relief model of Namur, a copy of the original made in the mid 18th century for Louis XV, provides an immaculate representation of how Namur once looked – the model-maker Larcher d'Aubancourt painstakingly walked around the town measuring every inch of ground.

Walk through the pedestrianised old town and you'll find the **Musée Félicien Rops** (12 rue Fumal, 081 22 01 10, www.ciger.be/ rops, 10am-6pm Tue-Sat & daily July, Aug, €3), located in an 18th-century manor house. Namur-born artist Rops was notorious during his lifetime for his epicurean appetites, his fascination with the occult and the erotic nature of his drawings. The museum has more than 1,000 works, plus an important collection of 2,000 engravings.

Close by, in another 18th-century manor house, is the **Musée de Groesbeeck de Croix** (3 rue Saintraint, 081 23 75 10, 10am-noon, 1.30-5pm Tue-Sat, €2), where the atmosphere of an aristocratic abode during the Enlightenment has been re-created. Highlights include the kitchen area and the French garden – a real oasis in the heart of the city.

Compared with the exquisite medieval gold and 19th-century symbolist pornography it offers, Namur's ecclesiastical sights are somewhat disappointing. The best of the bunch is the baroque **Église St-Loup** on rue du Collège, with a lovely interior built for the Jesuits in the early 17th century. It was here

Binche: Rio in the rustbelt

For most of the year Binche is a quiet little town in Belgium's industrial rustbelt, not far from Charleroi. There's not much for tourists to do, apart from looking at the ruins of a palace and wandering along a stretch of old city walls. But arrive on Shrove Tuesday (Mardi Gras) and you'll find yourself plunged into one of the most spectacular carnivals in the world.

Don't get the wrong idea. It's not like carnival in Cologne. You won't get kissed by a transvestite in an orange wig. Carnival in Binche is a serious celebration that involves months of preparation. There are strict rules and rituals covering every aspect of the festival, from the mysterious symbols stitched on to the costumes to the timing of the parades. The participants, known as Gilles, have to be male, Belgian and born in the town. The women's role is to make the costumes, which can only be worn in Binche.

No one is certain when it all began, but historians have found evidence dating back to the 14th century. The turning point came in 1549 when Mary of Hungary, governor of the Low Countries, put on a spectacular procession in honour of her brother, Charles V. At the same time, in another corner of his empire, explorers were discovering the civilisations of South America, and so the nobles in Binche decided to dress up as Incas.

The Binche Carnival season starts in early January with a crowded calendar of balls, processions and rehearsals. Eight days before Shrove Tuesday, thousands take to the streets wearing masks in a ceremony known as *Trouilles de Nouilles*. But the main events are packed into three strenuous days beginning on the Sunday before Shrove Tuesday. Starting at 3pm, the Gilles parade through the streets in their spectacular padded costumes, accompanied by brass bands, drummers and local revellers in fancy dress.

Shrove Monday is a more relaxed day, with a children's parade, barrel organ music and dancing in the street. The following morning, Shrove Tuesday, the Gilles are roused before dawn, helped into their costumes and given a glass of champagne. The streets are soon filled with groups of Gilles dancing to a hypnotic drum beat. They eventually arrive on the square in front of the town hall, where they put on wax masks decorated with glasses and a moustache. Then they begin a slow stamping clog dance on the cobbled square.

It goes quiet around lunchtime, when the Gilles retire to quaff oysters and champagne while everyone else tries to squeeze into a café. The revellers regroup at about 3.30pm for the main parade, when the Gilles wear huge head-dresses decorated with ostrich feathers. They then set off on a slow dance, accompanied by boys laden with baskets full of blood oranges. Now the rowdy part begins as the boys start hurling the oranges at the crowd. It's at this point you notice the shop windows are covered with chicken wire. The oranges are meant as gifts, and you must never throw one back.

---

that Baudelaire collapsed and was felled by a stroke in 1866. Just east of St-Loup, the rather prosaic 16th-century **Eglise St-Jean Baptiste** overlooks tranquil place du Marché-aux-Légumes; just west of St-Loup, past the former Jesuit college of the Palais Provincial, stands the **Cathédrale St-Aubain** on the square of the same name. A rather grand neo-classical pile, it was built in the mid 18th century on the site of two previous churches. Its treasures are contained in the **Musée Diocésian** (Easter-Oct 10am-noon, 2.30-6pm Tue-Sat, 2.30-6pm Sun, Nov-Easter 2.30-4pm Tue-Sun; €1.25). Its items have been gathered from diocesan churches from the region, and contain a golden crown reliquary from the 13th century, supposedly including two thorns from Jesus' Crown. There are a portable altar and ivory panels from a slightly earlier era.

For shopping, take a stroll down the traffic-free streets between the cathedral and the modern road of rue de l'Ange, which are packed with boutiques. Wine lovers will want to visit **Grafé Lecocq** (3 rue du Collège) for its fantastic selection: the cellars of this vintner are extensive, covering much of the subterranean level of the cathedral. For contemporary Belgian jewellery, it's worth checking out **Maya** (15 rue de la Halle), which stocks tempting pieces by Christa Reniers and Annick Tapernoux, among others.

Where to eat & stay

For refreshment, the area west of central place d'Armes is your best bet. The tiled **Tea Time Café** (35 rue Saint-Jean, 0496 52 44 22) is an ideal snack stop between sightseeing.

The people of Binche were enormously proud when an international committee voted in 2003 to include Binche Carnival on UNESCO's list of intangible world heritage. One of the delegates happened to suggest to the organisers that it might be a good idea to allow women a greater role. She was lucky that no one had any oranges to hurl.

The **Musée International du Carnaval et du Masque**, 10 Rue Saint Moustier (064 33 57 41), has a fascinating collection of masks and costumes from around the world. Note that, like everything in Binche, it is closed during carnival.

For more on Binche Carnival call 064 33 67 27 or go to www.carnavaldebinche.be.

For something more substantial, **Brasserie Henry** (3 place St Aubain, 081 22 02 04) serves up local specialities and international favourites in generous portions. At the family-run **La Bonne Fourchette** (112-116 rue Notre Dame, 081 23 15 36), located between the citadel and the Meuse, you'll find classic Wallonian cuisine. For gourmet fare, head for **La Petite Fugue** (5 place Chanoine Descamps, 081 23 13 20), which recently celebrated 15 years of outstanding cuisine, or **L'Olivier** (5 avenue Jean 1er, 0477 50 47 49), en route to the citadel, which is popular with families on Sundays.

If you're simply after a quiet drink, go to **Le Chapitre** (4 rue du Séminaire), with its extensive beer list. For something a little livelier, try either **Le Monde à l'Envers** (28 rue Lelièvre) or **L'Extérieure-Nuit** (6 place Chanoine Descamps), which have occasional live music. There are a few cafés lining place du Marché aux Légumes, including the **Piano Bar** (jazz and rock concerts most weekends).

The pick of the limited accommodation is **Hotel Les Tanneurs** (13 rue des Tanneries, 081 24 00 24, rooms €38-€210). Thirty very individual rooms have been created from an old tannery, each priced according to their size and facilities (some have their own jacuzzi and hammam). It has a rustic restaurant, too, and can provide half-board accommodation if required. More run-of-the-mill but affordable and central is the **Hotel Ibis** (10 rue du Premier Lanciers, 081 25 75 40, €61-€65).

Getting there

From Brussels there are up to five fast trains an hour making the 60-minute journey to Namur.

Information Kiosk Grognon

1 avenue Baron Louis Huart (081 22 34 24).
Open *Apr-Sept* 9.30am-6pm daily. Closed Oct-Mar.

Maison du Tourisme de Namur

*Square Léopold, 5000 Namur (081 24 64 49/
www.namur.be).* **Open** 9.30am-6pm daily.

The Ardennes

The Ardennes spreads over three provinces in
the south (Namur, Luxembourg, Liège) and the
region is as popular as the coast for a weekend
getaway. This is an area of enormous charm, of
gentle hills and valleys, rapid-flowing rivers and
dark forests, grottoes and megalithic sites. It's
touristy, but very relaxed, mercifully sparsely
populated and has kept a calm atmosphere.

Typical to the Ardennes are old stone
artisanal houses, beautiful abbeys and churches
and immensely pretty medieval villages,
dominated by imposing, crumbling castles.
The Ardennes is steeped in history. This was
the hunting grounds of some of Europe's most
famous rulers: Godfrey de Bouillon, Charles V
and Louis XIV. More recently, the Ardennes is
where Germany's final desperate advance of
World War II was stopped – memorials are
found at all the battle sites. Visit the **Musée
de la Bataille des Ardennes** in La Roche-
en-Ardenne (084 41 17 25, 10am-6pm daily,
€5.50) or the **American Historical Centre
& Memorial** in Bastogne (061 21 14 13,
Feb-Apr, Oct-Dec 10.30am-4.30pm daily; May,
June, Sept 9.30am-5pm daily; July, Aug 9.30am-
6pm daily; €7.50). This is where, on 22
December 1944, General McAuliffe famously
said 'Nuts!' to the Nazis' demand for surrender
(at least one café in the town is named Nuts).

Things to do

The Ardennes has something for everyone.
Typical activities include:

Eating: Even within a country as
gastronomically minded as Belgium, the
Ardennes is renowned for its food. It has great
local produce, including game, wild boar and
pike, and *jambon ardennois*, a smoked ham.

Architecture: Almost every village in the
Ardennes has a church or castle of note. The
churches (some dating from the 11th century)
are among the oldest in Belgium, while the
castles reinforce the feudal atmosphere. Of
particular note is Godfrey de Bouillon's 13th-
century castle at **Bouillon** (061 46 62 57, €4),
which is lit by torches at night in July and

August. During those months it's open 10am-
7pm Mon, Thur; 10am-10pm Tue, Wed, Fri-Sun;
phone for other times of the year.

Adventure sports: The Ardennes is
criss-crossed by rivers (Ourthe, Meuse, Semois),
hills, valleys and rocks. This makes it perfect
for all manner of sports including swimming,
kayaking, rafting, trekking, mountain biking,
rock climbing and skiing. For further details
about such activitites, contact **Durbuy
Adventure** (086 21 28 15, www.durbuy
adventure.be) or **Bouillon** (061 25 68 78).

Grottoes: The Ardennes' river valleys lend
themselves particularly well to the formation
of grottoes. Stunning examples are found at
Han-sur-Lesse (084 37 72 12, 10am-4pm/
5.30pm daily, with a break for lunch, €10.30)
and **Hotton**, where the 'Grotto of 1001 Nights'
was discovered in 1958. It is celebrated for
the variety in size and colour of its formations
(084 46 60 46, Apr-June, Sept, Oct 10am-5pm
daily, July, Aug 10am-6pm daily, Nov-Mar
call 083 68 83 65 for reservations, €7).

Parcs à Gibiers: Wooded nature reserves,
home to deer and wild boar, are found all over
the Ardennes. The park at **Han-sur-Lesse**
(084 37 72 12, €7.80) is the largest and has
rather more savage animals (lynx, bears,
wolves) than the others. It's open the same
hours as the grotto.

Festivals: The Ardennes has kept its
traditions, and festivals and processions
lend colour to villages throughout the year.

Dinant

Pretty Dinant is an easy getaway for the day.
There's enough here to occupy yourself for
a few hours or so – but probably not much
longer than that. Its principal attraction is the
Citadel (082 22 36 70, Nov-Mar 10am-4pm
daily, Apr-Oct 10am-6pm daily, €5.20) in the
main place Reine-Astrid. Included in the ticket
price is the cable-car journey; those of nervous
disposition can climb the 400 steps. The site of
many a fierce battle – including one in 1914,
after which occupying Germans set light to the
town and shot scores of locals – the Citadel has
been converted into a museum depicting the
conflict with the French, Dutch and Germans.

Another chairlift runs from rue en Rhée to the
Tour Mont Fat (082 22 27 83, Apr-Oct 10.30am-
7pm daily, €5), a park with panoramic views.
Dinant's other main attraction is the Gothic
Church of Notre-Dame (10.30am-6pm daily),
which has paintings by local artist Antoine
Wiertz. For a drink and a bite to eat, try **Le
Sax** (13 place Reine-Astrid). Musical inventor
Adolphe Sax came from Dinant; his home at
35 rue Adolphe Sax features a suitable mural.

The castle at **Bouillon** is lit by torches in summer. *See p282.*

St-Hubert

It's difficult to get round the Ardennes without a car – railway stations are few and buses are infrequent. St-Hubert has the great advantage of being near a train station. Once there, you are in the middle of the Ardennes forest and can trek or cycle to most places.

St-Hubert is the spiritual centre of the province of Luxembourg and one of the finest towns in the Ardennes. It is dominated by the imposing **Basilique St Pierre-St Paul-St Hubert**, which was founded in the 11th century, rebuilt in the Flemish Gothic style in the 16th, and given a classical façade in the 18th. The interior is full of magnificent late Renaissance sculptures, tombs and paintings.

The town is named after St-Hubert, the seventh-century patron saint of hunters and butchers, and is the European hunting capital. It is accordingly famous for its game restaurants. Though quiet and not renowned for its nightlife, it has its share of festivals throughout the year: the first Sunday of September is the Festival for Hunters; the last Sunday is the Festival of the Brotherhood of Butchers. Throughout July, there are classical music concerts every night. It is also a place of pilgrimage: on the Monday before Pentecost, the Landesdorf pilgrimage reaches the town, while Pentecost itself sees the Ardennes pilgrimage. On 3 November the Festival of St-Hubert provides folkloric processions, markets and solemn mass.

St-Hubert is surrounded by great natural beauty. Just a couple of kilometres outside the town is **Parc à Gibiers** (061 25 68 17, 9am-6pm daily) where deer, stags and wild boar roam at will. A little further along the same road is the **Fourneau St-Michel**: the iron forge that was

established by Dom Spirot, the last abbot of the Abbaye St-Hubert, in 1771. It still works. Here, also set in a valley, is a perfectly preserved pre-Industrial Revolution village of farms, small houses, granaries, printing house, church and schoolhouse. This is the **Musée de la Vie Rurale en Wallonie** (084 21 08 44, Mar-June, Sept-Nov 9am-5pm daily; July, Aug 9am-6pm daily; closed Dec-Feb, €2.50).

If you fancy overnighting it, try the **Hôtel Borquin** (6 place de l'Abbaye, 061 61 14 56, €45). Facing the basilica, this is a modest, comfy hotel with a highly recommended restaurant

To the west of St-Hubert is **Redu**, a village totally dedicated to books. Shops sell rare and precious books, while engravers, illustrators and binders have all set up shop here.

Getting there

From Brussels there is one train an hour to **Dinant**, journey time 90 minutes. To **Poix St-Hubert** (change at Jemelle), there is one train an hour from Gare Centrale; journey takes two hours 15 minutes. Then it's a six-kilometre (four-mile) bus journey to St-Hubert (12 buses a day; four a day at the weekend).

Tourist information

Dinant Tourist Office

8 avenue Cadoux, 5500 Dinant (082 22 28 70/ fax 082 22 77 88/www.dinant-tourisme.be). **Open** *June-Aug* 8am-6pm Mon-Fri; 9am-7pm Sat; 10am-6pm Sun. *Sept-May* 8.30am-6pm Mon-Fri; 9.30am-4pm Sat; 10.30am-2pm Sun.

St-Hubert Tourist Office

12 rue St-Gilles, 6870 St-Hubert (061 61 30 10/fax 061 61 54 44/www.sthubert.be). **Open** 9am-6pm daily.

TimeOut
Online

vw.timeout.cc

/er 50 of the world
greatest cities.
On one great site.

Directory

Features

Directory

Getting Around

Arriving in Brussels

By air

Brussels' international airport (www.brusselsairport.be, 0900 70000) at Zaventem, some 14 kilometres (nine miles) north-east of the capital, has good road and rail connections into the city centre. You'll find the information desk (7am-10pm daily) in the check-in area. Hotel information and a phone link for reservations are in the arrivals section. Hotel shuttle buses run from level 0.

A train service, **Airport City Express** (02 528 28 28, www.b-rail.be), runs to Gare du Midi, Gare Centrale and Gare du Nord. Tickets cost €2.60, first-class €3.90. There are four trains an hour from 6am to midnight; journey time 20 minutes. Women travelling alone at night are safer to disembark at Gare Centrale.

The **Airport Line** bus 12 (0900 10 310, www.stib.be), operated by Brussels transport authority STIB, leaves the airport about three times an hour between 8am and 7pm, less frequently 5-8am, 7-11pm and weekends. This service makes five stops in Brussels, with Schuman the most central, and costs €3. **De Lijn** (070 220 200, www.delijn. be), the Flemish transport service, also travels between Brussels and the airport; a single ticket to the Gare Centrale costs €1. The **SN Brussels Airlines Express** bus (052 33 40 00) runs hourly to Antwerp from 7am to 11pm and costs €8 for a single ticket.

Taxis wait by the arrivals building and should display a yellow-and-blue licence. The fare from Zaventem to central Brussels is around €30 – many accept credit cards. A rooftop indicator shows 1 or 2 for single or double tariff. Strictly speaking, the double tariff is only applicable outside the limits of the 19 *communes*. In practice, most drivers switch to double as soon as they're on a motorway. **Autolux** (02 411 41 42, www.autolux.be), with orange-and-white aeroplane stickers, offers a 20 per cent discount for a return journey taken within two months.

Car rental desks can be found in the arrivals hall and are open from 6.30am to 11pm. *See p289* **Car hire**.

Ryanair (www.ryanair.com) flies to what it calls Brussels South, a tiny airport 55 kilometres (34 miles) away in **Charleroi** (07 125 12 11, www.charleroi-airport.com). Bus No.68 connects with arrivals and runs the ten-minute journey to Charleroi train station, where a half-hourly train (€7.20) takes 50 minutes to reach Brussels. Ryanair runs a shuttle bus (€10 one-way) from Charleroi airport to the corner of rue de la France and rue de l'Instruction outside Gare du Midi. Journey time is about an hour. Buses leave Charleroi about 30 minutes after flights arrive and leave Gare du Midi two-and-a-half hours before flights take off. Taxis from Charleroi to central Brussels cost about €85. Note that future of the Ryanair service to Charleroi was in some doubt at the time of going to press.

By rail

There are nine Eurostar departures a day (seven on Saturday and Sunday) from Brussels Gare du Midi and London Waterloo, with a journey time of two hours 20 minutes. Check in at least 20 minutes before departure. Buy tickets online or from selected travel agents and rail stations.

Waterloo International

Call centre 01233 617575/local rate charges for callers within the UK 08705 186 186/www.eurostar.com. **Open** *Call centre* 8am-9pm Mon-Fri; 8am-8pm Sat; 9am-5pm Sun. *Travel centre at Waterloo International 7.45am-9pm daily.* **Credit** AmEx, DC, MC, V.
Prices from London to Brussels start at £59 for a 'Leisure Standard', a type of non-refundable and non-exchangeable return ticket that must be purchased 21 days in advance or include a Saturday-night stay. There are a number of cheap seats available on all trains, but when they are gone passengers are bumped up to the next price bracket. Reservations can be made 90 days in advance and early booking is recommended.

Gare du Midi

02 528 28 28/www.eurostar.com. **Open** 8am-8pm daily. **Credit** AmEx, MC, V. **Map** p318 A5.
Adult return prices from Brussels to London start at £85 (Leisure Saver). A business return ticket is €320. Book early (up to 90 days in advance) to get the cheapest fares.

By car

If you're driving to Brussels from the UK, Eurotunnel can transport you and your vehicle from the M20 near Folkestone to Coquelles near Calais in 35 minutes. There are good motorway connections to Brussels from there. It's a 24-hour service with up to three trains an hour 7am-midnight and one every two hours during the night. There are also facilities for the disabled. Tickets can be bought from a travel agent, Eurotunnel's website or call centre, or on arrival at the tolls (though tickets not reserved in advance are more expensive). Hertz and Eurotunnel have a Le Swap rental system so that you can drive a left-hand and right-hand-drive rental car in France and the UK respectively.

Eurotunnel

UK 08705 353535/ www.eurotunnel.com. **Open** 8am-7pm Mon-Fri; 8am-6pm Sat, Sun. **Credit** AmEx, DC, MC, V.
Ticket prices depend on time and length of travel, with cheaper fares available for advance booking. A short-stay return (2-5 days) starts at £103. Day return starts at £34. Discounts for online booking.

By coach

Eurolines (UK)

08705 808080/www.eurolines.co.uk. **Open** 8am-8pm daily. **Credit** AmEx, DC, MC, V.
A return fare from London Victoria to Brussels is £45 for adults, some discounts apply for children and seniors. A £29 return fare is available if booked 30 days in advance.

Eurolines (Brussels)

80 rue du Progrès, Schaerbeek (02 274 13 50/www.eurolines.com/ belgium). *Métro/pré-métro Gare du Nord.* **Open** 9am-11pm daily. **Credit** AmEx, DC, MC, V. **Map** p317 C1.
Eurolines buses depart from CCN Gare du Nord (80 rue du Progrès) and offer services to 500 destinations in 34 countries. A return ticket to London Victoria costs €73 (€49 if booked 14 days in advance) and the journey takes about seven hours. There is also an office for ticket sales at 50 place de Brouckère, Lower Town (02 217 00 25).

Public transport

Brussels' cheap, integrated public transport system is made up of metro, rail, buses and trams, with tickets allowing for up to an hour any changes en route. A map is invaluable, as stations are not well signposted.

Belgian railways

The SNCB runs an efficient, cheap national rail system. Most tourist spots are an hour or so from Brussels. Tickets, priced per kilometre, can be bought online (02 528 28 28, www.b-rail.be), in the station, or on board for a modest supplement of €2.40, provided you inform the conductor upon boarding the train.

Brussels has three mainline stations – **Gare Centrale** (1km from the Grand' Place), **Gare du Midi** (South Station) and **Gare du Nord** (North Station) – which are linked. All have baggage facilities. Midi's left luggage office is by the Eurostar terminal. *See p296* **Lost Property**.

Metro, trams & buses

The efficient public transport network in the capital is run by STIB/MIVB (Société des Transports Intercommunaux de Bruxelles). Maps and timetables are available from info centres at Gare du Midi, Porte de Namur and Rogier.

De Lijn

107 rue Bara, Anderlecht (070 220 200/www.delijn.be). Métro/pré-métro Gare du Midi. **Open** 7am-7pm Mon-Fri; 10am-8pm Sat, Sun.
Call for info on Flemish buses from Brussels and around Flanders.

STIB/MIVB

14 galerie de la Toison d'Or, Ixelles (02 515 20 00/www.stib.be). Métro Porte de Namur. **Open** 10am-6pm Mon-Sat. **Map** p319 D5.

TICKETS, LINES AND TRAVEL PASSES

Tickets are sold at metro and rail stations, on buses and trams, at STIB info centres and at newsagents. Points of sale for monthly passes are métro Porte de Namur, Gare du Midi, the SNCB stations and outlets. Tickets must be electronically stamped, or validated, by the machines at metro stations and on trams and buses at the start of the journey. Controllers run

checks and can fine you €55 for being without a validated ticket. The most economical way of travelling for a few days is to buy a batch of ten tickets (*une carte de dix voyages*) for €9.80. Five tickets cost €6.50, one costs €1.40 and a one-day travel pass is €3.80. Public transport operates from around 5.30am to midnight, depending on location.

Metro stations are indicated by a white letter 'M' on a blue background, while red-and-white signs mark tram and bus stops. Brussels is served by three metro lines and a pré-métro tram line running north-south through town, linking Gare du Nord and Midi. **Line 1** is divided into 1A and 1B. 1A runs from Roi Baudouin (close to the Atomium) to Hermann-Debroux; 1B goes from Erasme to Stockel. **Line 2** links Simonis to Clemenceau and mirrors the inner-city road ring above.

The **Brussels Card** for tourists offers unlimited public transport for three days, plus admission to 30 museums for €30. Children under six can travel free if accompanied by an adult with a valid ticket.

DISABLED TRAVEL

Public transport is not specially adapted for disabled passengers, but some trams have a low-level platform for access and some stations are equipped for wheelchairs (see www.stib.be). An STIB minibus service (02 515 23 65, www.stib.be), with vehicles equipped for wheelchairs, is available to transport disabled travellers door-to-door from 6.30am-11pm for the same price as a metro ticket. STIB has also installed facilities braille information panels, in several metro stations. (*See p289* **Two legs good, four wheels bad**.)

For those travelling outside Brussels by train or on certain bus services, the disabled passenger pays and any accompanying person travels free. Contact the train station in advance for travel with a wheelchair, which is carried free. There are also reductions for the blind (call SNCB for details; *see p287*).

Taxis

Brussels taxi drivers can be shifty – watch the meter. Ranks are found by mainline stations and at strategic points like Porte de Namur, place d'Espagne, the Bourse and De Brouckère. Taxis can take up to four people and the tip is included in the meter fare. If you have a complaint against a driver, or you've lost an item in a taxi, record the registration number of the vehicle and call the taxi service of the Ministry of Brussels Capital Region on 0800 147 95. The price per kilometre should be €1.14 if the journey is inside the 19 *communes*.

Autolux 02 411 41 42/
www.autolux.be
Taxi Bleues 02 268 00 00/
www.taxisbleus.be
Taxis Verts & Taxi Orange
02 349 49 49/www.taxisverts.be

Driving

It's not easy driving around Brussels. Unless you're leaving the city, you'd be better off to take public transport or walk. Although stiff penalties exist for drink-driving, the law is flouted (legal maximum blood alcohol level is 0.5g/l or one glass of wine). To say that bad driving was endemic would be an understatement.

Dents on the right side of many cars show the damage caused by the '*priorité à droite*' rule, the reason for so many accidents. Cars must give way to any vehicle from the right, even on a major road, unless marked otherwise. A white sign with a yellow diamond on your road means cars from the right must stop for you.

Another factor to contend with is the behaviour of local drivers, especially in rush hour and in tunnels. In contrast to motorways, roads in town are riddled with potholes and parking can be a nightmare. Remember also that trams have absolute right of way.

A comprehensive tunnel system links major points in the city, making it possible to traverse Brussels without seeing the light of day. The inner ring is a pentagon of boulevards (marked with signs showing a blue ring on which the yellow dot is your current location). The outer ring is a pear shape, divided into an east and west motorway ring.

The speed limit on motorways is 120kph (75mph), on main roads 90kph (56mph) and in built-up areas 50kph (31mph). There are no tolls on Belgian roads. The wearing of seat belts is compulsory in the front and rear of the car. A driving licence from your home country is acceptable if you are staying less than 90 days in Belgium. If your car is towed, go to the nearest police station to get a document releasing it. Police may give you the document free of charge or demand a nominal fee, depending on the area of town. They will then give the address of the garage holding your car. Present the police letter there and pay another fee – the sum can vary – to get your car back. On-the-spot fines are common for speeding.

It takes 40 minutes to Antwerp, 50 to Ghent, 90 to Liège and Bruges. Calais and Amsterdam are two-and-a-half hours away, Paris three hours. Names are signposted in two languages (except in Flanders); Antwerp is given as Anvers/Antwerpen, Ghent Gand/Gent and Bruges Bruges/Brugge.

For information on importing a car, registering a vehicle or getting a licence in Belgium, see http://vici.fgov.be/en.

Breakdown services

In the event of a breakdown, there are two national organisations to call:

Tourist Club Belgique (TCB)

24hr emergency service 070 344 777; enquiries (9am-5pm Mon-Fri) 02 233 22 11/www.touring.be.
Will assist non-members, but cheaper rates are available for members. Membership costs from €81.30 (for basic service) to €116.30 (including replacement car) annually.

Royal Automobile Club de Belgique

24hr emergency service 02 287 09 00; enquiries (8.30am-5pm Mon-Fri) 02 287 09 11/www.racb.com.
Membership is €80 per year for basic service, and a €110 package includes a replacement car. A non-member will be charged an extra €50 for breakdown assistance.

Car hire

To hire a car, you must have a full current driving licence (normally with a minimum of one year's experience) and carry a passport or identity card, as well as a credit card in your name. Many car hire companies also insist on a minimum age of 23. Car rental is expensive, with weekly rates around €260 with unlimited mileage. Day rates usually start at around €55, but it's worth shopping around.

Special all-inclusive weekend rates (Friday afternoon to Monday morning) are available from around €75. The major car hire companies can be found in the arrivals hall of Zaventem airport and at Gare du Midi. Offices are generally open from 6.30am to 11pm. Hire rates at the airport can be steeper than in town.

Avis

107 rue Colonel Bourg, Evere (02 720 09 44/www.avis.be). Métro Diamant. **Open** 8am-6pm Mon-Fri. *Airport* 8am-11.30pm daily. *Call centre* 8.30am-6.30pm Mon-Fri; 9am-5pm Sat. **Age requirement** over-25s only; driver's licence for one year. **Credit** AmEx, DC, MC, V.

Two legs good, four wheels bad

While Brussels has an exemplary public transport system in many ways – it's cheap, punctual and clean – it's very tricky to negotiate if you're in a wheelchair or pushing a pram. Of the city's 69 métro and pré-métro stations, only 11 have wheelchair access, with passengers able to enter via a lift or a ramp. And of those 11 stations, seven are at the ends of their lines. In the city centre, only De Brouckère, Gare Centrale and Maelbeek are accessible. Parents with prams will be able to enter most stations via their escalators, but the metro's only junction, Arts-Loi, doesn't have a lift and only has an escalator in one direction, so be prepared to carry your buggy down stairs.

To make life more difficult, train doors stay open for less than five seconds at each stop, and a pole in the middle of each compartment makes it tricky to get a pram on in time, let alone a wheelchair.

Only trams on the 94 and 91 lines have wheelchair access, though nearly 50 accessible new trams are scheduled to be in service by 2005. Older trams, such as the ones used on the pré-métro line, have doors with barriers in the middle, making it inaccessible for wheelchairs or prams.

It's a similarly gloomy story on the buses. Some serving the 28 and 36 routes are accessible, but not all. If you're waiting at the stop, there's no way of knowing when the next one with access will turn up. Prams can get on board, but it's not easy, and not advisable in rush hour.

Luckily, Brussels is a fairly small city, and it is possible to walk, or roll, to the majority of destinations – although you may have to contend with cobblestones. But when you do finally make it into town, you will find that many shops, bars, cafés and restaurants are very difficult to get into, as they have a few steps leading up to their entrances, or very small doorways. Under Belgian law, any building put up after 1975 must have wheelchair access. With older buildings, the law provides that owners must take 'reasonable measures' to provide access – a term that is almost always interpreted loosely.

About the only places you can be sure of getting into in a wheelchair are the major museums. As official public institutions, they have a legal obligation to offer access to the disabled. And if you have a pram, the best thing to do is follow all the signs for disabled access.

Budget

327B avenue Louise, Ixelles (02 646 51 30/airport 02 753 21 70/www. budget.be). Métro Louise/tram 93, 94. **Open** 8am-6pm Mon-Fri; 9am-noon Sat. *Airport* 7.30am-11pm Mon-Fri, Sun; 7.30am-3.30pm Sat. **Age requirement** over-21s only. **Credit** AmEx, DC, MC, V. **Map** p324 E8.

Hertz

8 boulevard Maurice Lemonnier, Lower Town (02 513 2886/airport 02 720 60 44/www.hertz.be). Pré-métro Anneessens. **Open** 7.30am-6pm Mon-Thur; 7.30am-7pm Fri; 8am-noon Sat; 8am-2pm Sun. *Airport* 6.30am-11.30pm daily. **Age requirement** over-25s only. **Credit** AmEx, DC, MC, V. **Map** p316 B4.

Repairs & services

The agents listed should be able to help or check 'Carrosseries (Reparations)/ Carrossierieherstellingen' in the *Yellow Pages*.

Autocenter East NV 'Toyota'

438 chaussée de Louvain, Zaventem (02 725 12 00). Bus 258. **Open** 9am-7pm Mon-Fri; 10am-5pm Sat. **Credit** MC, V. **Map** p321 H2.

BMW Brussels

22-38 rue du Magistrat, Ixelles (02 641 57 11). Métro Louise then tram 93, 94. **Open** 8.30am-12.30pm, 1-4.30pm Mon-Fri. **Credit** AmEx, DC, MC, V. **Map** p324 D7.

Rover Grand Garage St Michel

35-43 rue de l'Escadron, Etterbeek (02 732 46 00). Métro Thieffry. **Open** 8am-6pm Mon-Fri. **Credit** AmEx, DC, V.

Cycling

Cycling in central Brussels is a daunting prospect. However, cycling out of town is scenic and generally safe. Lanes are shown by two broken white lines and are less secure than the cycle tracks, which are separated from the traffic. A map of local lanes and tracks can be found at Pro-Velo:

Pro-Velo

15 rue de Londres, Ixelles (02 502 73 55/www.provelo.org). Métro Trône. **Open** *Nov-Mar* 10am-6pm Mon-Fri. *Apr-Oct* 10am-6pm Mon-Fri; 1-6pm Sat, Sun. **No credit cards**. **Map** p319 E5.
Bikes rented out by the hour and day, and tours organised. *See also p206.*

Walking

The centre of town, although uneven, is easy to navigate, with many traffic-free streets around the Grand' Place. The Institut Geographique National (www.ngi.be) has maps of trails outside the centre.

Resources A-Z

Addresses

When addressing an envelope, you should theoretically write the house number after the street name and place the postcode before the city, as:

Monsieur Ledoux
Avenue Louise, 100
1050 Bruxelles

Numbers may also be given before their street names, the style adhered to in this book. All the streets in Brussels have a French and Flemish version, and the confusing combination of the two is written out in full on all local maps and street signs. For brevity and clarity, in this book we have given the French versions only.

Age restrictions

In Belgium, you have to be 18 to drive, vote or marry, and 16 to drink and/or have sex. There are no age restrictions on smoking.

Business services

Chambers of commerce

American Chamber of Commerce (AmCham)

50 avenue des Arts, Box 5, EU Quarter (02 513 67 70/ www.amcham.be). Métro Trône. **Open** *Office by appointment. Phone enquiries 9am-5pm Mon-Fri.* **Map** p319 D4.

British Chamber of Commerce

15 rue d'Egmont, Ixelles (02 540 90 30/www.britcham.be). Métro Trône. **Open** 8am-5pm Mon-Fri. **Map** p319 D5.

Conferences

Espace Moselle

40 rue des Drapiers, Ixelles (02 504 97 00/fax 02 504 97 09/www.espace-moselle.be). Métro Louise. **Open** 8.30am-6pm Mon-Fri. **No credit cards. Map** p319 C5.

Conference and seminar rooms in an elegantly renovated 19th-century house, with translation service and audio-visual equipment. Food can be arranged for 250 people. Parking is available, and there's also a garden.

Management Centre Europe

118 rue de l'Aqueduc, Ixelles (02 543 21 00/fax 02 543 24 00/ www.mce.be). Métro Louise then tram 93, 94. **Open** 8.30am-6.30pm Mon-Thur; 8am-5.30pm Fri. **Credit** AmEx, DC, MC, V. **Map** p324 C7.
One of the top international business management and training organisations in Europe, hosting a variety of large seminars and conferences. It can also undertake organisation of conferences and training sessions.

Brussels International MICE

02 549 50 50/fax 02 549 5059/ www.bi-tc.irisnet.be. **Open** *phone enquiries 9am-5.45pm Mon-Thur; 9am-5pm Fri.*
An expert staff of meeting consultants will help you find a venue and put you in contact with everyone you need to plan a conference. This non-profit bureau is supported by the City of Brussels and its services are free of charge.

Couriers

New Poney Express

02 712 50 50/fax 02 712 50 89/ www.npe.be. **Open** 7am-7pm Mon-Fri. **No credit cards.**

Letters and packages can be picked up and delivered anywhere around Brussels. The cost for delivering a package immediately depends on distance. A delivery within 12 hours costs €15.50. Partner company World Courier are able to deliver to anywhere in the world.

DHL

19-21 rue Cornet de Grez, Schaerbeek (02 715 50 50/www. dhl. be). **Open** 8am-6.30pm Mon-Fri; phone enquiries 24hrs daily. **Credit** AmEx, DC, MC, V.
DHL can get a package across the city or across the world. The quicker it goes, the more you have to pay. Pick-ups also available.

Library

Royal Library

4 boulevard de l'Empereur, Upper Town (02 519 53 11/www.kbr.be). **Open** 9am-7.45pm Mon-Fri; 9am-4.45pm Sat. **Map** p315 C4.
Belgium's state library has a business section.

Office & equipment hire

New Telephone (Protel)

312 chaussée de Bruxelles, Ouderghem (02 354 60 98/fax 02 354 26 19). Bus W (Waterloo Centre stop). **Open** 9.30am-12.30pm, 2-6.30pm Mon-Sat. **Credit** AmEx, DC, MC, V.

Travel advice

For up-to-date information on travel to a specific country – including the latest news on safety and security, health issues, local laws and customs – contact your home country government's department of foreign affairs. These days most have websites packed with useful advice for would-be travellers:

Australia
www.dfat.gov.au/travel

Canada
www.voyage.gc.ca

New Zealand
www.mft.govt.nz/travel

Republic of Ireland
www.irlgov.ie/iveagh

UK
www.fco.gov.uk/travel

USA
http://www.state.gov/travel

Directory

New Telephone specialises in equipping offices with new telephone systems, answerphones, voicemail, faxes and mobile phones. It can also rent out photocopying machines.

Papeterie du Parc Léopold

177 rue Belliard, EU Quarter (02 230 69 12/www.parcleopold.com). Métro Schuman. **Open** 9am-6pm Mon-Fri. **Credit** AmEx, MC, V. **Map** p322 F4.
Often patronised by the local Eurocrats, this shop isn't cheap but it does stock an excellent selection of quality stationery.

Regus

6 rond point Schuman, box 5, EU Quarter (02 234 7711/www.regus.com). Métro Schuman. **Open** 9am-6pm Mon-Fri. **Map** p323 G4.
Reliable international company renting fully equipped offices with IT infrastructure and secretarial support across Belgium and worldwide.

Secretarial services

If you don't wish to use an employment agency, you can always place a classified ad in the weekly *Bulletin* (see p297).

Manpower

10 boulevard Anspach, Lower Town (02 512 38 23/fax 02 502 04 20/www.manpower.be). Métro/pré-métro De Brouckère. **Open** 8.30am-6pm Mon-Fri. **Map** p315 C3.
Can match up clients with secretaries who speak foreign languages. Rates vary according to requirements.

Vedior

Riverside Business Park, 55 boulevard International, Anderlecht (02 555 16 11/fax 02 555 16 16/www.vedior.be). Bus 78. **Open** 8am-6pm Mon-Fri.
One of Belgium's largest employment agencies, with a range of specialised staff. Call the corporate headquarters listed here to find the local office that can meet your requirements.

Translators

Also check the local *Yellow Pages* under *Traducteurs* to find real-time interpreters.

Abetras

11 rue de l'Ecole Moderne, Anderlecht (02 520 22 22/fax 02 520 15 84). Métro Clemenceau or métro/pré-métro Gare du Midi/tram 46, 56. **Open** *telephone enquiries* 24hrs daily.

As well as finding translators, this agency rents out microphones, receivers and booths. Provides interpreters for video conferences on an *à la carte* basis for €496 per day.

Dixit

55 avenue Stuart Merrill, Forest (02 340 90 20/fax 02 346 14 08/www.interpreters.be). Tram 55. **Open** 9am-6pm Mon-Fri.
Dixit has been offering interpreters in European languages for meetings and conferences for 15 years. One day's translation costs €470 and a half-day €370.

Consumer

To complain about shops that sell faulty merchandise or for general consumer protection issues, contact the Direction Générale Contrôle et Médiation at 02 208 3611 or click on to www.mineco.fgov.be.

If you are dissatisfied with the hygiene standards in a certain restaurant, café, food store or supermarket, contact the Agence Fédéale pour la Sécurité de la Chaîne Alimentaire on 02 208 33 01, www.afsca.be.

To complain about a taxi driver, call the taxi service of the Ministry of Brussels Capital Region at 0800 147 95. Operators can take your call in English; have the number of the taxi to lodge a complaint. *See also p288* **Taxis**.

Customs

The following customs allowances apply to those bringing duty-free goods into Belgium from outside the European Union:
● 200 cigarettes or 100 cigarillos or 50 cigars or 250g (8.82oz) smoking tobacco
● 2l litres of still table wine and either 1l litres of spirits/strong liqueurs (over 22% alcohol) or 2l litres of fortified wine (under 22% alcohol)/sparkling wine/other liqueurs
● 50g perfume
● 250ml toilet water
● 500g coffee or 200g coffee extracts/essences

● 100g tea or 40g tea extracts/essences
● other goods for non-commercial use up to a maximum value of €175.

If you are travelling from an EU member state, you are allowed to bring in as large a quantity of duty-paid goods as you can carry. But if you bring more than 110 litres of beer, 90 litres of wine, 10 litres of spirits and 800 cigarettes you could be asked to pay an additional tax. There's no limit to the amount of foreign currency that can be brought in or out of Belgium. For more information, call the Belgian Administration of Customs & Excise (02 210 38 15, open 9am-noon, 1-4pm Mon-Fri).

Disabled

New buildings in Brussels are required by law to be fully accessible to people who are not fully mobile and most of the big hotels are wheelchair-friendly. That said, the cobbled pavements are very uneven and there are steep hills. The many older buildings are often not equipped to handle disabled visitors. For disabled travel, *see p287* and *p289* **Two legs good, four wheels bad**. For a detailed guide to accessible shops, restaurants and sports facilities (in French) ask for the publication *Tourisme en Belgique Pour Personnes à Mobilité Réduite* (070 222 827, www.touringlanboo.be). Accessible City Breaks (www.accessiblecitybreaks.co.uk) has further information on accessibility of Brussels' hotels and tourist sites and can help you arrange a visit.

Electricity

The current used in Belgium is 220V AC. It works fine with British appliances (which run on 240V), but you'll need to buy an adaptor. Adaptors are

Directory

readily available at electrical goods shops, and airports. American appliances run on 110V. To use an American hairdryer in Belgium, you'll need to buy a converter, which can be pricey. Most good hotels should be equipped with hairdryers and provide adaptor plugs to fit appliances from most countries.

Embassies

It's advisable to phone to check opening hours of the embassies listed below. You may need to make an appointment to see someone and be aware that different departments usually keep different – and shorter – hours. In emergencies it's worth ringing after hours; there may be staff on hand to deal with crises. For embassies or consulates not listed, check the *Yellow Pages* or try www.embassyworld.com.

American Embassy
27 boulevard du Régent, Upper Town (02 508 21 11/www.usembassy.be). Métro Arts-Loi. **Open** 9am-6pm Mon-Fri. **Map** p320 E4.

Australian Embassy
6-8 rue Guimard, EU Quarter (02 286 05 00/www.austemb.be). Métro Arts-Loi. **Open** 8.30am-5pm Mon-Fri. **Map** p320 E4.

British Embassy
85 rue d'Arlon, EU Quarter (02 287 62 11/www.british-embassy.be). Métro Maelbeek. **Open** 9am-5.30pm Mon-Fri. **Map** p322 E4.

Canadian Embassy
2 avenue de Tervueren, Etterbeek (02 741 06 11/www.ambassade-canada.be). Métro Merode. **Open** 9am-12.30pm, 1.30-5pm Mon-Fri. **Map** p325 H5.

Irish Embassy
50 rue Wiertz, EU Quarter (02 235 66 71/www.irlgov.ie/iveagh). Métro Maelbeek/bus 21/train Luxembourg. **Open** 10am-1pm Mon-Fri. **Map** p322 E5.

New Zealand Embassy
Seventh floor, 1 square de Meeûs, EU Quarter (02 512 10 40/ www.nzembassy.com/belgium). Métro Trône. **Open** 9am-1pm, 2-5.30pm Mon-Fri. **Map** p322 E4.

South African Embassy
Mercator Building, 26 rue de la Loi, EU Quarter. Métro Arts-Loi (02 285 44 00/www.southafrica.be). **Open** 8.30am-5pm Mon-Fri. **Map** p320 E4.

Emergencies

The general standardised emergency number to call throughout Europe is **112**.

To ring the fire brigade or an ambulance, call **100**. For police, dial **101**. The Belgian Red Cross also offers a 24-hour ambulance service that can be reached at **105**.

For the Belgian Poison Control Centre dial 070 245 245 or see www.poisoncentre.be.

Gay & lesbian

Egalité
02 296 9329. **Open** *phone enquiries* 9am-noon, 1pm-6pm daily.
This organisation works to improve conditions for lesbians and gay men working in the EU institutions, with the ultimate aim of equality across the board in the workplace.

English-speaking Gay Group in Brussels
02 537 47 04/www.geocities.com/ eggbrussels.
Hosts informal parties every month for people of all nationalities to meet and greet. Get your name on the mailing list and you'll receive details of upcoming get-togethers.

Infor Homo
100 avenue de l'Opale, Schaerbeek 1030 (02 733 10 24/www.geocities. com/infor_homo). Métro Diamant. **Open** *Phone enquiries* 8-10pm Mon-Fri. **Map** p321 H3.
This francophone association offers advice and counselling and organises social events for men and women of all ages. Meetings take place in its café every Wed and Fri from 8pm to midnight). It also publishes *Regard*, a bi-monthly magazine.

International Lesbian & Gay Association
94 avenue de Tervueren, Etterbeek (02 732 54 88/www.ilga-europe.org). Métro Montgomery.
The International Lesbian & Gay Association is a network of international bodies that campaigns against discrimination. ILGA-Europe in Brussels receives funding from the European Commission and is an important lobbyist.

Rainbowhouse
42 rue du Marché au Charbon, Lower Town (02 503 59 90/ www.rainbowhouse.be) Pré-métro Bourse or Anneessens. **Open** 6-10pm Wed; 6pm-midnight Fri, Sat. **Map** p315 B3.
A meeting, information point, and café. Most local gay and lesbian organisations are members of Rainbow House and the website has details of events and activities.

Tel Quels
81 rue du Marché au Charbon, Lower Town (02 514 49 74/bar 02 512 32 34/www.telsquels.be). Pré-métro Bourse or Anneessens. **Open** 5pm-2am Mon-Thur, Sun; 5pm-4am Fri, Sat. **Map** p315 B3.
This collective organises events and activities for parents, students and singles among others, as well as a gay and lesbian film festival. The building also houses the Belgian and Lesbian Gay Pride association (09 223 69 29, www.blgp.be), which plans the giant Pride parade through central Brussels every May. (*See p185* **Pink Saturdays**.)

Health

Belgium enjoys an excellent healthcare system, with a doctor for every 278 people, and well-run hospitals. Many doctors are fluent in English. (*See also p293* **Doctor, doctor**.)

Accident & emergency

The following hospitals can provide 24-hour emergency assistance. For emergencies involving children, visit the Hôpital Universitaire des Enfants or the Hôpital St-Pierre. Call 105 for a 24-hour ambulance service.

Hôpital Brugmann
4 place van Gehuchten, Laeken (02 477 20 10/www.chu-brugmann.be). Métro Houba-Brugmann.

Hôpital Erasme
808 route de Lennik, Anderlecht (02 555 31 11/www.hopitalerasme.be). Métro Erasme.

Hôpital St-Pierre
322 rue Haute, Lower Town (02 535 31 11/www.stpierre-bru.be). Métro/pré-métro Porte de Hal/bus 27, 48. **Map** p318 B5/6.

Hôpital Universitaire des Enfants Reine Fabiola

Paediatric emergency room, 15 avenue Jean-Jacques Crocq, Laeken (02 477 31 00/www.huderf.be). Métro Houba-Brugmann.

Cliniques Universitaires St-Luc

10 avenue Hippocrate, Woluwe-St-Lambert (02 764 11 11/www. saintluc.be). Métro Alma.

Complementary & alternative medicine

A 1999 law gives recognition to acupuncture, homeopathy, osteopathy and chiropractic medicine, but alternative medicine in Belgium is still behind many other European countries and is not currently reimbursed under the *mutuelle* system (*see p295*) unless the practitioner is also a registered medical doctor. Refer to www.homeopathy.be for a list of doctors and dentists who subscribe to the principles of homeopathy and for more

information. There are also homeopathy sections in many pharmacies.

Contraception & abortion

Condoms are widely available and are sold at most supermarkets and pharmacies (although condom-vending machines are not widespread). Birth-control pills can be bought at pharmacies with a doctor's prescription.

Abortion has been legal in Belgium since 1990. A woman can have one up to the 12th week of pregnancy. After 12 weeks, in cases of foetal abnormality or of any health risks to the mother, the agreement of two independent doctors is required.

Dentists

Dental care in Belgium is of a high standard. The Health Unit at the American Embassy

(02 508 22 25) can provide a list of English-speaking dental practitioners, as can the Community Help Service helpline (02 648 40 14). Call 02 426 10 26 for a current list of dentists on duty in evenings and at weekends.

Doctors

The Health Unit of the American Embassy (02 508 22 25) will provide a list of English-speaking doctors with different specialties. Call 02 479 18 18 to find doctors, or click on www.mgbru.be. You are free to choose any doctor no matter where you live and without a referral. You may want to ask a local friend for a recommendation. (*See p293* **Doctor, doctor**.)

Unusually perhaps, most doctors with private practices don't employ receptionists, preferring to handle the administration of payments and appointments themselves. You can often walk in without an appointment during weekday office hours. If you are too sick to go in to the surgery, some doctors will make house calls. After hours, you can often reach your physician (or one on call) through an answering service. Even if you're insured, expect to pay for your visit on the spot, either in cash or with a cheque. The same goes for pharmacies. Hang on to all medical receipts to claim reimbursement from your insurance company.

Hospitals

Outpatient clinics at private or university hospitals have an excellent reputation worldwide for their state-of-the-art technology, but often suffer from overcrowded waiting rooms and bureaucracy. Despite the drawbacks, they have a convenient concentration of specialists in

Doctor, doctor

If you need to see a doctor in Belgium, the system is user-friendly and consumer-led. You simply find one (find your nearest surgery at www.mgbru.be), make an appointment and turn up – even if it's a specialist or consultant, there is no referral system here.

So if your back's gone, find a specialist at one of the numerous health clinics or any hospital out-patient department. All doctor appointments attract an on-the-spot fee, though these run to about €20-€40, depending on the type of specialisation. Tax-paying residents can use their *mutuelle* cards (*see p294*) to offset the bill, while

others will have to pay cash (hardly any doctors accept credit cards).

If you can show an E111 form, the fee should be reduced. If not, ask for a receipt so you can make a claim on your insurance. Any medicines you need will also have to be paid for at the pharmacy; these can be dear, particularly antibiotics.

If you need to go to hospital, they like proof that you can pay, though if it's an emergency you would get treated first before financial questions are asked. The E111 or proof of private cover are enough to make an administrator smile. Nearly all doctors in the bigger clinics speak English.

Directory

one place, as well as laboratory and X-ray facilities on hand. For details of emergency hospitals *see p292* or www. hospitals.be for a full list.

Opticians

There are numerous opticians around Brussels (*see p164*). The American Embassy (02 508 22 25) can provide a list of English-speaking ones.

Pharmacies

Pharmacies (*pharmacies/ apotheeks*) in Belgium are clearly marked with a green cross. Most are open 9am-6pm Mon-Fri. Some also open on Saturday mornings or afternoons. Phone 0900 10500 for the nearest on weekend or night duty, or enter your postcode at www.pharmacie.be to find the nearest one open.

HIV & AIDS

Act Up
145 rue van Artevelde, Lower Town (02 512 0202/www.actupb.org). **Open** *phone enquiries only* 2-5pm Tue, Sat.
Part of the international Act Up network, which campaigns aggressively for better research, recognition, and treatment for people living with AIDS.

Aide Info SIDA
45 rue Duquesnoy, Lower Town (02 511 45 29/free helpline 0800 20 120/www.aideinfosida.be). **Métro** *Gare Centrale.* **Open** *helpline* 6-9pm Mon-Fri.
An organisation offering support and care at home for people with AIDS, in hospital and in prison, with special emphasis on the needs of the young.

Women's clinics

See www.planningfamilial.net for clinics and locations.

La Famille Heureuse
4 place Quetelet, St-Josse (02 217 44 50). Métro Botanique or Madou/ Tram 94. **Open** 9am-8pm Mon; 9.30am-5pm Tue; 10am-5pm Wed; 9.30am-8pm Thur; 8.30am-4.30pm Fri. *Drop-in clinic* noon-3pm Wed. **Map** p317 E2.

One of Brussels' most comprehensive women's clinics. Services include contraceptive and psychological counselling, abortion, cervical smear tests, AIDS tests and referrals. A visit with a doctor will set you back about €18, and you can be reimbursed if you have insurance or a *mutuelle* (*see p295*).

Aimer à l'ULB
38 avenue Jeanne, Ixelles (02 650 31 31). Métro Louise then tram 93, 94/bus 71. **Open** 9am-6pm Mon-Fri; 9.30am-noon Sat. **Map** p325 F9.
Although located on the ULB university campus, this bright and cheery clinic is open to all. The cost of medical visits is based on income (most cost either €6 or €18 according to circumstance), so if you're on a tight budget this is the best place to come for a check-up, prescription or cervical smear.

Helplines

Brussels' large foreign community has established an extensive network of support groups. Unless indicated in the listings, the groups below are for English speakers. More organisations will be regularly listed in the weekly *Bulletin* (*see p297*) or on its website www.xpats.com. See the Clubs section for myriad help and advice groups.

Community Help Service (CHS) Helpline
02 648 40 14/www.chsbelgium.org. **Open** *Phone enquiries* 24hrs daily.
A group of trained English-speaking volunteers can handle problems ranging from the critical to the mundane. They will also be happy to refer you to other specialists. There is no charge for callers. To make an appointment for a private face-to-face counselling session with a professional counsellor, call the office at 02 647 67 80 during regular business hours. The consultancy rates are determined according to clients' means.

Alcoholism

Alcoholics Anonymous
29 avenue Jean Volders, St-Gilles (02 537 82 24/www.xpats.com/ Clubs/Id/AA.htm). Métro/pré-métro Porte de Hal. **Map** p318 B6.
This group holds two daily meetings in English and offers counselling by phone. Can link you with English-speaking AA groups in other areas.

Rape/battered women

Le Refuge (Collectif pour Femmes Battues)
29 rue Blanche, St-Gilles (02 647 00 12). Métro Louise, then tram 91, 92, 93, 94. **Open** 9am-5pm Mon-Fri. **Map** p319 C6.
There is one staff member at the Collective for Battered Women who speaks good English and others speak basic English. But it might be a good idea to try the CHS Helpline (*see above*) if you need more detailed help in English. Francophone Rape Crisis (SOS Viol) is at 24 rue Blanche, 02 534 36 36, 9.30am-5.30pm Mon-Fri.

ID

Belgium has an identity card system; citizens are expected to be able to show their card at any time. As a visitor, you are also expected to carry photographic ID, such as your passport, with you at all times.

Insurance

As members of the European Union, both the UK and Ireland have reciprocal health agreements with Belgium. You'll need to apply for the necessary E111 form at home first. British citizens can obtain this by simply filling in the application form in leaflet SA30, available in Department of Social Security offices or at post offices. Try to get the E111 at least two weeks before you travel. Make sure you read the small print on the back of the form so you know how to obtain medical or dental treatment at a reduced charge.

The E111 doesn't cover all medical costs – for example, dental treatment – so it's wise to take out private insurance. College students should check whether their university's medical plan already provides cover. A home-owner's policy may similarly cover holidays.

Non-EU citizens should take out full private insurance before travelling. Remember to keep all receipts for medicine or treatment. You'll need them to claim reimbursement from your insurance company once you're back home.

For long-term visitors, after six months of residence you are eligible for cover under Belgium's basic health insurance system, the *mutuelle*. It is part of the Belgian National Social Security system and entitles everyone to medical aid. It allows you to recover a large chunk of doctors' and dentists' bills, and other costs. Regular payments are automatically deducted from your salary. You are allowed to choose whichever *mutuelle* best meets your needs. For phone numbers consult the local *Yellow Pages* under '*Mutualités/Ziekenfondsen*'. Euromut (www.euromut.be) and Partena (www.parenamut.be) are two independent *mutuelles* with websites in English. (*See also p293* **Doctor, doctor.**)

Internet

Central Brussels has few cyber cafés; there's one underground at Bourse pré-métro station. A small patch of Ixelles, where rue de Dublin meets the chaussée de Wavre, has a few small offices; try **InterCall**. If you're staying for a while, one of the best bets for hooking up to the internet in Belgium is Skynet (0800 33 800, www.skynet.be). If you have cable or want to get a fast cable connection, try Brutélé (0800 800 25, www.brutele.be). Click on www.ispa.be for local internet service providers in Belgium. For websites, *see p306* **Further reference**.

Intercall Telecom
69 chaussée de Wavre, Ixelles (02 502 56 96). Métro Trône. **Open** 9am-midnight daily. **Map** p319 D5.

Left luggage

Main train stations have left-luggage offices, open 6am-midnight. Smaller stations have coin-operated lockers. *See p287* **Belgian railways**.

Libraries

Bibliothèque Royale de Belgique
4 boulevard de l'Empereur, Upper Town (02 519 53 11/www.kbr.be). Métro Gare Centrale/tram 92, 93, 94. **Open** 9am-7.45pm Mon-Fri; 9am-4.45pm Sat. **Map** p315 C4.
This is the state library, holding everything published in Belgium, as well as foreign publications. You need a membership card to consult the enormous collection of books here. Bring in a photograph, your identity card and €7.50 if you're a student (€15 non-students). Books must be read in the library and must be requested before 3.55pm. Details of library's vast catalogue is readily accessible at www.kbr.be.

ULB (Université Libre de Bruxelles)
50 avenue Franklin Roosevelt, Ixelles (02 650 47 00/www.bib.ulb.ac.be). Métro Louise then tram 93, 94/bus 71. **Open** 8am-10pm Mon-Fri; 10am-5pm Sat. *Hours when able to borrow books* 10am-4.30pm Mon-Wed, Fri; 10am-6pm Thur; 10am-1pm Sat. **Map** p325 10F.
Although the ULB library is intended for students at the university, it's also open to non-students for an annual fee (€12.50 for students with a student ID and €25 for non-students). It has a large collection of materials in English in various media, accessible on the website.

Lost property

Report lost belongings to the nearest police station or the police headquarters at 30 rue du Marché au Charbon, Lower Town (02 517 96 11); bear in mind you may have trouble finding an English-speaker. You must ask for a certificate of loss for insurance purposes. If you happen to lose your passport, contact your embassy or consulate (*see p292* **Embassies**). Note that staff may be present after office hours to cope with such an emergency.

Air

If you've lost luggage or left something on the plane on the way to Brussels, contact **Aviapartner** or **Belgian Ground Services**, the handling agents who represent most of the major airlines.

Aviapartner
02 723 07 07/www.aviapartner.aero. **Open** *Phone enquiries* 6am-11pm daily.
Aviapartner is the handling agent for British Airways, British Midlands and a number of other airlines who fly in to Brussels. To save time, you can fill out an online form on the Aviapartner website to initiate the tracing of your lost luggage.

So long, Séjour

EU nationals have the right to live and work in Belgium. What they do not have is the right to forego the tedious process of registration, one that involves queues and multiple visits to obtain a blue Carte de Séjour, or residence permit.

Now, an EU Directive agreed by all in March 2004 stipulates that EU citizens need no longer apply for residence in member states, giving true meaning to the word 'mobility'. EU countries have two years to get their administration in order, and Belgium's Foreigners' Office reckons the hallowed cards will be scrapped. But old habits die hard; and there is talk of a replacement, a piece of paper that you can wave when you hire a car or pick up a letter from the post office, perfect for a rubber-stamp culture. Still no mention of anything electronic, note.

Directory

Belgian Ground Services (BGS)

02 723 60 11/www.bgsfc.be. **Open** *Phone enquiries* 7am-11pm daily.
Aer Lingus and SN Airlines are two of the 15 airlines handled by BGS.

Airport

If you've misplaced something at Zaventem, head over to the airport's lost and found department.

Brussels International Airport Company

02 753 68 20. **Open** 8am-4.15pm Mon-Fri.
This office is in the public area of the new terminal, next to Arrivals.

Rail

For articles left on a train, enquire at the nearest railway station or check with the main rail lost property office at the Gare du Midi (02 24 88 62).

Metro, buses & trams

STIB/MIVB

Porte de Namur, Ixelles (02 515 23 94). **Open** 8.30am-4pm Mon-Fri. **Map** p319 D5.
The STIB/MIVB lost property office is at Porte de Namur métro station.

Taxis

If you have the number of the taxi cab where you left your item, or want to report an item you found in a taxi, call the taxi service of the Ministry of Brussels Capital Region on 0800 14795.

Media

Belgium has a decent-sized media sector of its own, but owing to the number of languages used in the country, its inhabitants are well attuned to competitors from neighbouring countries. Most newsagents and kiosks in Brussels stock the leading papers and magazines from Britain, France, Germany, the Netherlands and elsewhere (including the US). But the local press is still surprisingly broad, and runs the gamut from the conservative (*De Standaard*) to the more outrageous (*Humo, Ché*). Belgians are even more spoilt for choice when it comes to television. Cable TV has been widely available since the 1960s, and more than 90 per cent of households are hooked up to receive around 40 television channels, many of them from overseas.

Newspapers

La Dernière Heure

www.dhnet.be
Popular right-leaning French-speaking tabloid, with an emphasis on grisly crime and even grislier kiss 'n' tell stories. But its sports coverage is undeniably the best.

L'Echo

www.echonet.be
Pre-eminent French-speaking business paper in Belgium, crammed with pie charts, balance sheets, share tips and take-over rumours. Dry, but comprehensive.

European Voice

www.european-voice.com
This weekly English-language paper specialises in the workings of the European Union. Although published by *The Economist*, the *Voice* is much less acerbic, approaching the status of in-house paper for the EU – it has a special distribution agreement with the institutions. It carries some incisive political interviews and tries to remain lively. One of its main draws is the large number of high-profile, mostly EU-linked, job ads.

Het Laaste Nieuws

www.hln.be
Once renowned as the traditionally liberal Flemish daily, HLN allows itself to take an interest in the seamier side of life.

La Libre Belgique

www.lalibre.be
Very Catholic French-language daily with a serious tone and serious look. If you don't mind wading through moralising editorials about the papacy, it's a dependable read.

Metro

http://metro.rug.be/
This free newspaper is available at most metro stations in French (green) and Dutch (blue).

De Morgen

www.demorgen.be
Once the staple of socialist workers, De Morgen has evolved into a more general left-wing Flemish daily, covering the arts and human interest as well as national and international news. It has a reputation for investigative journalism and can be seen everywhere in the hands of commuters.

Le Soir

www.lesoir.be
The most widely read francophone daily, an independent-minded, quality broadsheet. Wednesday's issue contains *MAD*, an indispensible cultural supplement with the week's key listings, and Friday's includes *Victor*, a glossy lifestyle magazine.

De Standaard

www.standaard.be
The biggest Dutch-speaking daily takes few risks, opting for a conservative Catholic angle on most issues. But there are some decent arts pieces to be found among the slightly flat news coverage.

Vlan

www.vlan.be
Thousands of ads from property to cars to jobs to junk appear in this paper every Sunday. Along the lines of *Loot* in the UK.

Magazines

The Bulletin

www.ackroyd.be
Brussels' only English-language weekly has been around since the 1960s. It contains in-depth features on some very Belgian phenomena, often written by prominent Brussels-based journalists, as well as articles of interest to English-speaking expats. However, its text-heavy black-and-white layout is looking increasingly dated. It comes with a pull-out supplement of arts and entertainment listings (including TV schedules), and also runs job and accommodation ads. A must for any anglophone spending time in the city.

Ché

www.che.be
Flashy lad-mag bringing pictures of scantily clad young women and features on cars, gadgets and fashion to loaded young Flemings.

Dag Allemaal

www.dagallemaal.be
This Dutch-language TV and radio listings magazine also includes frothy celebrity interviews and glossy photo spreads.

Humo

www.humo.be
Originally a Flemish magazine with TV listings, Humo has become an irreverent, ironic and intellectual publication, in which politics and the arts all get a going-over.

Kiosque

Excellent pocket-sized, French-language monthly listings magazine.

La Libre Match

Joint venture between *Paris Match* and *La Libre Belgique*, with more of a focus on Belgium.

The Ticket

www.theticket.be
Pocket-sized arts and entertainment listings magazine in French and Dutch, available free from trendier shops, bars and clubs. Sometimes features bought-in interviews with celebrities and bands.

Le Vif-Express/Knack

These sister publications in French and Dutch are the country's only news magazines. Both come with upmarket supplementary magazines covering fashion, travel and lifestyle. Knack also includes *Focus*, a separate arts, entertainment and TV listings magazine.

Radio

To keep US and UK pop/rock music at bay, radio stations receiving subsidies must make at least 60 per cent of their music broadcasts in the language of the region from which the station is funded. Commercial stations are free to play as they choose, allowing for a diverse local music scene. Bear in mind that frequencies for the same station differ in other parts of the country.

Bel RTL

104 MHz
News, music and games on this French-speaking station, which began as a spin-off from the TV channel RTL-TVi (*see p298*).

Bruxelles-Capitale

99.3 MHz
News station, available only in Brussels, which makes the most of the intimacy of its listener-base.

Musique 3

91.2 MHz
French-owned classical music station.

La Première

92.5 MHz
The French-language state-owned station now has a distinctly old-fashioned air, but still schedules news programmes, political debates, game shows, sport and serials.

Radio Contact

102.2 MHz
The most visible radio station in Brussels. Its blue dolphin logo is on the back of every Renault Clio, its (never *quite* up-to-the-minute) pop output on the PA of every boutique.

Radio 21

93.2 MHz
Francophone pop-rock station that tends to play music that's neither new enough to be current nor old enough to be nostalgic.

Studio Brussel

100.6 MHz
As hip as Brussels gets: this Flemish station plays the latest singles by alternative rock and dance acts from both sides of the Atlantic, and occasionally dipping into 1980s and '90s indie obscurities. World music, reggae and jazz also get a spin.

VRT1

91.7 MHz
The most serious of the three Flemish state-owned radio stations, VRT1 features political discussions as well as classical music.

VRT2

93.7 MHz
The popular station in the Flemish state-owned VRT (formerly BRTN) triumvirate, generally concentrating on oldies and some Top 40 hits.

VRT3

89.5 MHz
High culture is this Flemish station's forte: you'll find profiles of composers, choral, chamber and classical concerts, and opera.

Television

Cable TV gives Belgians easy access to BBC1 and BBC2, CNN and MTV, as well as a host of channels from France and the Netherlands, and a smattering from Germany, Spain, Portugal and Italy. The selection varies slightly from region to region. Among the foreign channels, Canvas and Holland 1 often show popular British series. These are the main Belgian channels:

AB3

This privately owned French-speaking channel has a fast-moving schedule of cartoons, trashy thrillers and American soaps.

Kanaal 2

Sister station to VTM, showing mainly anglophone series and made-for-TV films. Broadcasts from 5pm to midnight. Excellent range of films, all in original language.

Ketnet/Canvas

Out of the VTR stable comes this populist channel with kids' programmes, English-language comedy and police dramas and the odd home-grown documentary. Also worth checking for films.

RTBF1 & 2

The state-run francophone station has retained respectability because of the lack of competition. It plays on two complementary channels. L'Une has a varied programme, including news, popular films and game shows; La Deux offers more cultural programming, with documentaries, cookery shows and undubbed films. Broadcasts from 6am to midnight.

RTL-TVi

The commercial French station is beginning to give state-owned TV a run for its money with its current affairs coverage. Otherwise, it's undemanding: soaps, sitcoms and talk shows. Its sister station, Club-RTL, shows cartoons and old movies. Both stations broadcast from noon till midnight.

Télé-Bruxelles/TV Brussel

Twin public-access French and Dutch stations covering local news with more streetwise flair than the state-owned and commercial stations. Done on a shoestring budget, which makes it more compelling. Their cameras are often seen on the streets interviewing everyday people. Broadcasts from 6pm to 2am.

VRT

The Flemish version of RTBF, this state-owned station (formerly BRTN) is fighting a prolonged ratings war with the commercial channels – hence the number of soap operas, serials and game shows. Even in its news and documentary coverage, VRT has lost its old dominance. Broadcasts from 6am to midnight.

VT4

This independently owned station started out as a cultural alternative to the populist VTM and stodgy VRT. Unfortunately, its experiments

Directory

with off-the-wall chat shows and would-be innovative series failed to attract sufficient ratings to justify costs, and it's since resorted to cheaper, largely American programming, with a plethora of soap operas. Broadcasts run from 7am to midnight.

VTM

This popular, privately owned station offers the best Flemish news coverage, as well as its own talk shows, soap operas and game shows. Broadcasts from 7am to midnight.

Money

The euro has erased all memory of old Belgian francs. There are euro banknotes for €5, €10, €20, €100, €200 and €500 and coins worth €1 and €2 plus 1, 2, 5, 10, 20 and 50 cents. Belgium is relatively inexpensive, especially when it comes to beer, buying food and public transport. Clothes and shoes are not particularly inexpensive, however, and hotels and restaurants around town can be pricey.

ATMs

ATMs are somewhat difficult to find in the city centre. As well as using a debit card to withdraw euros, you can also obtain a cash advance on most major credit cards from ATMs. Just keep in mind that cash advance fees can be steep. See www.mastercard.com/be or www.visaeu.com for a list of cashpoints.

Banks

Most banks open from 9am to between 3.30pm and 5pm, Monday to Friday. A few have half-days on Saturdays. Some also close for lunch. There will usually be staff members who speak English.

Bureaux de change

If for some reason you do need to change your currency into euros, banks are the best places to exchange. After

banking hours you can change money and travellers' cheques at bureaux de change around the centre of town (the money exchange at 88 rue Marché aux Herbes, just off the Grand' Place, is open 10am-7pm Mon-Sat and 11am-6pm Sun) or at offices in the Gare du Midi (7am-11pm daily) and Gare Centrale (8am-9pm daily). Several banks at the airport give cash advances on MasterCard or Visa, as well as convert currency. Most open early and close around 10pm.

Credit/debit cards

Most large shops, hotels and restaurants accept credit cards, including Visa, MasterCard and American Express. Many Belgians use debit cards, but don't expect anyone to accept one from a foreign bank.

Report thefts immediately to the police and to the 24-hour services listed below.

American Express
02 676 21 21/
www.americanexpress.com

Diners Club
02 206 99 00/www.dinersclub.be

MasterCard
toll free 0800 150 96/
www.mastercard.com/be

Visa International
toll free 0800 18397/
www.visaeu.com

Tax

Belgian VAT is 21 per cent, but if you're a non-EU resident, want to make a purchase of more than €145 and plan to take the purchase out of the country within three months, you can buy tax-free. Look for the 'Tax-Free Shopping' logo on shop windows. Bring your non-EU passport to make a purchase and you will be given a Tax-Free shopping cheque that can be stamped by customs officials in the airport and then cashed at the Europe

Tax-Free shopping desk. (Allow plenty of time in the airport for extra queues.) Shopping tax-free in shops without the Tax-Free logo is more complicated, but usually still possible. Request an itemised invoice at the shop and have it stamped by a customs agent when you leave Belgium. Then mail the invoice to the shop, which will send you the refund. This scheme works best if you happen to be flying out of Zaventem – customs officials at Charleroi airport are notoriously impossible to locate.

Natural hazards

The most common problem for the wide-eyed visitor might be simply walking the streets without having some sort of accident. There are many potential hazards to contend with when navigating Brussels streets, primarily ubiquitous dog leavings and uneven or missing cobbles that can leave puddles of water. Walking in heels can be a challenge.

Opening times

Many offices close for lunch or close early on Friday, although this is not official. Most shops open from 9am to 6pm, though certain groceries and supermarkets stay open till 9pm. Department stores open until 9pm on one day a week, usually Friday. For shops open late, look for a 'Night Shop' sign, or one of the (mostly) 24-hour grocer-tobacconists called White Night.

Most museums are open 9am to 5pm Tuesday to Saturday, and sometimes on Sunday. Nearly all close on Mondays. Several are only open from Easter Sunday to September. It's wise to call the museum before visiting. For banking hours, *see above* **Money**; *for post office hours, see p299* **Postal services**.

Police stations

For the police, call 101. The central police station in Brussels is at 30 rue du Marché au Charbon (02 279 79 79). For other emergency numbers, *see p292* **Emergencies**.

Postal services

Post offices are generally open 9am to 5pm Monday to Friday, but times can vary according to branch. The central office at **place de la Monnaie** is open until 7pm and the one by Gare du Midi (avenue Fonsny, St-Gilles, 02 524 43 08) is open from 7am to 11pm. Be advised that queues in post offices can be long and slow.

At the post office you will be asked if you want your letters to go '*prior*' or '*non-prior*', which basically means airmail priority or not. Letters mailed to the UK and other European countries *prior* usually take three days. *Prior* to the US takes about a week. A letter weighing up to 50g costs 59¢ *prior* or 52¢ *non-prior* to any country in Europe. A letter up to 50g to any country in the rest of the world costs 84¢ *prior* and 57¢ *non-prior*. Owing to the complexity of the post system, it's best to buy stamps at a post office rather than from a vending machine. Price is determined by the size of the envelope. Stick to using local Belgian envelopes, as non-standard sizes – even if different by only a fraction of an inch – can jack up the cost of postage. Staff will measure. Sending a postcard is the same price as a letter.

For a wealth of postal information and to find the nearest post office to you, refer to www.laposte.be.

Central Post Office

Centre Monnaie, place de la Monnaie, Lower Town (02 226 21 11). Métro/pré-métro De Brouckère. **Open** 8am-7pm Mon-Fri; 9.30am-3pm Sat. **Map** p315 C2.

Packages

Packages weighing more than 2kg (4.4lbs) are taken care of by Kilopost (07 815 5312), managed by La Poste/De Post. Just take any package weighing up to 30kg (66lbs) to the nearest post office. You can also use EMS Taxipost (www.emstaxipost.be), an express delivery service partnered with the postal system. Taxipost delivers same-day within Belgium and some nearby countries. It also delivers worldwide. It's cheaper but also can be a bit slower than other express delivery companies. *See also p290* **Couriers**.

A duty to eat

Belgium is a canny little country when it comes to taxation – especially where local restaurateurs and bar owners are concerned.

Landlords are one of the authorities' biggest headaches – the nature of their business means that they are difficult to keep tabs on. To try to solve this, a decade or so ago back the taxman introduced the controversial *souche TVA*, a little blue and white VAT slip that is supposed to be given to the paying customer at the end of every meal as proof that tax has been paid on it. Being busy people, waiters tend to forget this simple procedure, or customers leave them behind – that is unless they wanted to claim the meal on expenses (although this is still not allowed on Sundays, a decidedly non-business day for tax purposes).

Sometime in the mid 1990s, seeing that revenue from dining and drinking establishments was drying up, a wise tax mandarin decided it would be more efficient if burden of proof was passed on to customers – a somewhat silly move, even for for Belgium.

Bruxellois diners were outraged, especially as they could be stopped on the street by inspectors and fined if they couldn't produce the said ticket. (Surely only a country as madly bureacratic as Italy could organise such a body as the receipt police?!?) So the Souche TVA Law was quickly repealed and responsibility for providing a receipt was swiftly passed back to the restaurants. Now a paper receipt has to be given to every customer, busy waitstaff or not.

Unless, that is, if the establishment concerned only serves light meals such as sandwiches, a simple pasta or a cheese omelette. Which is why so many of Brussels' bars maintain small menus, and so many places advertise themselves as a Snack-Bar. You cannot walk a hundred metres around downtown Brussels without seeing one. In every other bar the sound of clinking glasses is accompanied by the ping! of the microwave.

At least as a customer the receipt is no longer your responsibility, so tuck in to your spag bol with impunity and let the patron decide what to do about the *souche*.

Poste restante

Poste restante is available at the central post office at De Brouckère (*see p299*). For information, call 02 226 39 30.

Religion

Many churches and synagogues hold services in English. For places away from the centre, it is advisable to call for directions. See the 'Religious Services' section at www.xpats.com for a list.

Anglican & Episcopalian

Holy Trinity Church

29 rue Capitaine Crespel, Ixelles (02 511 71 83/www.htbrussels.com). Métro Louise. **Map** *p319 C5.*
Holy Communion service in English is held on Sundays at 9am and 10.30am (with choir), and evening praise is at 7pm. An African-style afternoon praise session is at 2pm.

Jewish

Beth Hillel Reform Synagogue of Brussels

96 avenue de Kersbeek, Forest (02 332 25 28). Tram 18, 52 or bus 54. **Services** 8pm Fri; 10.30am Sat.
This liberal Jewish synagogue is now mostly francophone, but some Anglophones attend.

Muslim

Grande Mosquée de Bruxelles & Centre Islamique

14 Parc du Cinquantenaire, EU Quarter (02 735 21 73/www. centreislamique.be). Métro Schuman. **Map** *p323 G4.*
For a list of prayer times, see the website. Some conferences and events are held in English or French.

Protestant

International Protestant Church

International School of Brussels, 19 Kattenberg, Watermael-Boitsfort (02 673 05 81/www.ipc brussels.org). Bus 95. **English service & Sunday school** 10am Sun.

Roman Catholic

St Nicolas at St-Jacques-sur-Coudenberg

Place Royale, Upper Town (02 742 29 88). Métro Porte de Namur or Gare Central/tram 92, 93, 94. **Mass in English** 9.45am Sun. **Map** *p319 D4.*
The congregation meets here until its home church is renovated. (*See p61*.)

Our Lady of Mercy Parish

St Anne's, place de la Ste-Alliance, Uccle (02 354 53 43). Tram 43. **Mass in English** 5pm Sat; 10am Sun.

Quaker

Quaker House

50 square Ambiorix, EU Quarter (02 230 49 35/www.be-lux.quaker.org). Métro Schuman. **Meetings** 11am Sun. **Map** *p321 G3.*

Safety & security

Crime in Brussels is quite low compared with London or Paris, but be vigilant against petty theft. As Brussels becomes more cosmopolitan and the population grows, it is slowly starting to gain the less desirable attributes of a big city, including increasing levels of street violence. Pickpockets and bicycle thieves are part of the city's landscape, especially in crowded tourist areas during the day, and after dark in the grey streets downtown between the Grand' Place and the Gare du Midi. There have also been warnings about gangs of pickpockets working the major railway stations and incoming international trains. Use common sense and take the security precautions you would in any big city. (*See also p292* **Emergencies**.)

Smoking

Smoking in confined public places is banned by law. This amounts to no smoking in train stations (except on open-air platforms) and public buildings such as town halls and theatres. The law has had little effect on restaurants and few establishments feature non-smoking sections. Some of the city's better hotels have no-smoking rooms and floors.

Studying

Brussels is a major study centre. There are universities that teach in French, ones that teach in Dutch and many that offer courses in English.

Exchanges

Most universities have an office for exchange programmes, or at least their own branches of **Socrates** on campus. Listed below are the main offices. US students who wish to study in Brussels may contact the Council on International Education Exchange (www.ciee.org), based in the United States.

AIESEC

221 rue Royale, St-Josse (02 650 26 21/www.aiesec.be). Métro Botanique/tram 92, 93, 94. **Open** 10am-6pm Mon-Fri.
The International Association for Students in the Economic and Social Sciences assists students or recent graduates in finding traineeships or volunteer positions with non-profit organisations. There are AIESEC branches at universities in Belgium and worldwide.

Socrates, Leonardo & Youth TAO

59-61 rue de Trèves, EU Quarter (02 233 01 11/www.socrates-youth.be). Métro Maelbeek. **Map** *p322 E4.*
Socrates is Europe's education programme involving 30 countries. It offers people grants to study, teach, undertake a placement or follow a training course in another country. Included in Socrates are programmes for school education, language training, adult education and the popular Erasmus programme that organises university student exchanges. Leonardo is the EU's vocational training programme and the Youth programme promotes cooperation among youth in Europe and offers volunteer placements.

Tourist information

For tourist information tailored to the North American market, see www.visitbelgium.com. UK visitors can consult www.belgiumtheplaceto.be.

Brussels International Tourism & Congress

Hôtel de Ville, Grand'Place, Lower Town (02 513 89 40/www. bitc.be). Métro Gare Centrale or pré-métro Bourse. **Open** *Winter* 9am-6pm Mon-Sat. *Summer* 9am-6pm daily. **Map** p315 C3.
This small office, inside the grandest building on the Grand' Place, provides brochures and

information, including hotel and event details. It can also help businesses to arrange meetings and conferences in the city.

Office de Promotion du Tourisme Wallonie-Bruxelles

63 rue du Marché aux Herbes, Lower Town (02 504 03 90/www. belgium-tourism.net). Métro Gare Centrale or pré-métro Bourse. **Open** *Winter* 9am-6pm Mon-Fri; 9am-1pm, 2-6pm Sat; 9am-1am Sun. *Summer* 9am-6pm daily. **Map** p315 C3.
Brochures on all of Belgium. More spacious than its BIT counterpart round the corner, but it usually carries more info on arts events.

The school's fortés are architecture, graphic design and fashion. (*See p150* **Brussels back in fashion.**)

ICHEC

2 boulevard Brand Whitlock, Woluwe-St-Pierre (02 739 37 11/ www.ichec.be). Métro Montgomery/ tram 23, 44, 81, 90.
The Catholic Institute for Higher Commercial Studies has partnerships with universities around Europe and 25% of students are international. Courses are mostly taught in French, but a full semester in English is possible. Intensive language classes are also offered.

Open University

38 avenue Emile Duray, Ixelles (02 644 33 72/73/www.open.ac.uk). Tram 23, 90, 93, 94. **Map** p325 F9.
Study centre and office for the British Open University.

ULB (Université Libre de Bruxelles)

50 avenue Franklin Roosevelt, Ixelles (02 650 21 11/www.ulb.ac.be). Tram 93, 94/bus 71.
The largest university in Brussels, the French-speaking ULB has 18,000 students, of whom a third are foreign.

Vesalius College

2 boulevard de la Plaine, Ixelles (02 629 28 21/www.vesalius.edu). Métro Delta/tram 23, 90/bus 34, 71.
Vesalius is part of the VUB (*see below*) and linked with Boston University (*see above*). The language of instruction is English and the style of education is decidedly American – selective admission, small classes, close faculty-student relationships, and American-style fees. The student body is diverse, with over 50 nationalities represented.

VUB (Vrije Universiteit Brussel)

2 boulevard de la Plaine, Ixelles (02 629 21 11/www.vub.ac.be). Métro Delta/tram 23, 90/bus 34, 71.
The Dutch-speaking VUB has an enrolment of 9,000 students and two campuses. Although most courses are taught in Dutch, there are a number of English-language postgraduate degrees.

Language schools

The classified ads on www. xpatica.com and www.expatica. com are full of people willing to exchange conversation or teach one-to-one.

Alliance Française

26 rue de la Loi, EU Quarter (02 732 15 92/www.alliancefr.be). Métro Arts-Loi. **Open** 8.30am-6.30pm Mon-Thur; 8.30am-4.30pm Fri. **Map** p320 E3.
This bastion of French culture has group and private classes.

Amira Language School

283 avenue Louise, Ixelles (02 640 6850/www.amira.be). Métro Louise then tram 93, 94. **Open** 9am-7pm Mon-Fri. **Map** p324 E8.
One of the city's better schools.

Berlitz

306 avenue Louise, Ixelles (02 649 61 75/www.berlitz.be). Métro Louise then tram 93, 94. **Open** 7.30am-7.30pm Mon-Fri, 9am-noon Sat. **Map** p324 E8.
The most central of the four Berlitz centres in the Brussels area.

Language Studies International

50 rue du Taciturne, EU Quarter (02 217 23 73/www.lsi-be.net). Métro Schuman. **Open** 9am-8pm Mon-Fri; 9am-1pm Sat. **Map** p320 F4.
This well-reputed school teaches classes in myriad languages and is

extremely flexible about meeting the needs of its students.

Fondation 9

485 avenue Louise, Ixelles (02 627 52 52/www.fondation9.be). Métro Louise then tram 93, 94. **Open** 8am-7pm Mon-Thur; 8am-5pm Fri. **Map** p325 E9.
Sponsored by the ULB, the Chamber of Commerce and Brussels City, Fondation 9 offers group classes in all the EU languages and more.

Universities

Académie Royale des Beaux-Arts de Bruxelles

144 rue du Midi, Lower Town (02 511 04 91/www.aca-bxl.be). Pré-métro Anneessens. **Map** p315 B4.
Runs courses in illustration/comic strip art, advertising and design, but is best known for its painting and sculpture programmes.

Boston University Brussels

39 boulevard du Triomphe, Ixelles (02 640 74 74/www.bu.edu/brussels). Métro Petillon or Delta/tram 23, 90.

Ecole Nationale Supérieure des Arts Visuels de la Cambre

21 Abbaye de la Cambre, Ixelles (02 648 96 19/www.lacambre.be). Tram 23, 90, 93, 94/bus 71. **Map** p325 F9.
Part of the Erasmus programme, courses are given in French, in fine art, animation and industrial design.

After the privatisation of 2001, Belgacom is still Belgium's major operator, having improved its rates and service. For a longer stay here, sign up for one of Belgacom's special packages for cheaper calls to a

Directory

country of your choice (see www.belgacom.be/expats or call 0800 55800 for English customer service). Telenet (0800 66611, www.telenet.be) is Belgacom's main rival and also offers a range of services with competitive deals. You could also check out Toledo (0800 85000, www.toledo.be), Scarlet (0800 84000, www.scarlet.be) or Opticall (02 705 52 12, www.opticall.be). All you have to do is call and ask to be switched over (these carriers cannot hook you up; you must already have Belgacom service). Alternatively, you can use one of the services that lets you prefix a call with a number to use a different carrier, without ever switching from your primary provider. Try dialling 070 777 777, listen for a new dial tone, then dial your number for substantially reduced call tariffs to EU countries, Switzerland and North America (only works for land lines). Details of a similar service can be found on www.telonline.be.

For a short-term stay, a card is recommended, such as XL-Call (provided by Belgacom, information on 0800 22147), available in newsagents, post offices and supermarkets.

Dialling & codes

To make an international call from Belgium, dial 00, then the country code (Australia 61, Canada 1, France 33, Germany 49, Ireland 353, New Zealand 64, Netherlands 31, UK 44, USA 1), then the number. When in Belgium, dial the city code and number (Antwerp 03, Bruges 50, Brussels 02, Ghent 09, Liège 04), even when in the city itself. To call Belgium from abroad, first dial the international access code, then 32, then drop the 0 of each city code. 0800 numbers are free inland. See www.goldenpages.be or www.whitepages.be for telephone listings.

Public phones

Public telephone booths are more of a rarity since the mobile phone revolution, but look in stations, post offices and other usual locations. There are several close to the Grand' Place, around place de Brouckère and the Bourse. Booths sporting European flags can be used for direct-dial international calls. Many public phones accept only prepaid electronic telephone cards – coin phones are rare. You can buy phone cards at post offices, stations, newsstands and supermarkets. You could also try a 'telephone call centre' where you can make calls to all corners of the world at a reduced rate. There are many centres in Ixelles.

Operator services

Operator assistance
1324 French, 1224 Flemish
Directory enquiries
1405 (English enquiries for domestic and international numbers)
Telegrams
1325 French, 1225 Flemish
Time
1300 French 1200 Flemish
Wake-up service
0800 51248

Faxes

You can find a working phone, buy a telecard or send a fax, telex or telegram at TT (Telephone-Telegraphe/Telefoon-Telegraaf) centres. There are several telephone shops where you can also send faxes near place de Brouckère and another whole collection of them by the Matongé district of Ixelles, including Intercall Telecom (69 chaussée de Wavre, 02 502 56 96, open 9am-midnight daily).

Mobile phones

Belgium is part of the GSM mobile network. Phones on this system work in most of

western Europe and even beyond. You can rent GSM phones at the airport or from some car hire agencies. The rental fee is usually low but the cost per call is high. Network providers include Proximus (02 205 40 00, www.proximus.be), Mobistar (0495 95 95 00, www.mobistar. be) and Base (0486 19 19 99, www.base.be). Changing prices and packages mean that none can be particularly singled out as giving the best value. Each have their own shops, but most general outlets offer a range of networks and phones. For the best latest deals drop into a downtown store such as Phonehouse (98 rue Neuve, 02 227 53 83).

Time

Belgium is on Central European Time, one hour ahead of Greenwich Mean Time, six hours ahead of US Eastern Standard Time and nine hours ahead of US Pacific Standard Time. Clocks go back an hour in the autumn and forward an hour in the spring.

Tipping & VAT

Service and VAT are included in hotel and restaurant prices, though people often throw in a few extra euros if the service has been exceptional. At the lower-price restaurants, simply round up the bill by leaving a handful of loose change. There's no reason for you to feel embarrassed – Belgians will tell you that only tourists tip. At mid-priced restaurants customers often kick in up to five per cent extra. At first-class restaurants it's usual to add an extra ten per cent. Tips are also included in metered taxi fares, although taxi drivers expect extra tips from foreigners. At cinemas and theatres, tipping the attendant 20¢ to 50¢ for a programme is expected. For toilets, *see p303.*

Average monthly climate

Month	High temp (C°/F°)	Low temp (C°/F°)	Precipitation
Jan	6/42	1/34	81.3cm
Feb	6/42	1/33	50.8cm
March	10/49	3/38	81.3cm
April	13/55	5/40	53.3cm
May	17/63	8/47	73.7cm
June	20/67	11/52	73.7cm
July	22/72	13/56	58.4cm
Aug	22/72	13/55	43.2cm
Sept	19/66	11/52	68.6cm
Oct	15/58	8/46	83.8cm
Nov	9/48	4/39	61.0cm
Dec	7/44	2/36	68.6cm

Toilets

Toilets in Brussels are usually scrupulously clean. This is a direct result of the efforts of the attendant with the little white dish sitting at the entrance, a lady referred to by locals as Madame Pipi. Most restaurants and bars don't mind you using their loos – though you are expected to cough up anywhere between 10¢ and 50¢ for the white dish. Note that quite a few toilets in Belgian establishments are unisex, ie. the urinals are not closed off. Men can also use the occasional public outdoor urinals, or *pissoirs*, such as the ones against the walls of the Ste-Catherine church.

Visas & immigration

EU nationals and citizens of Iceland, Monaco, Norway, Liechtenstein and Switzerland can enter Belgium without a visa or a time limit. EU nationals only need to show a valid national ID card to enter. Citizens of Australia, Canada, New Zealand, Japan and the United States, among other countries, are permitted to enter Belgium for three months with a valid passport. No visa is needed. For longer stays,

they must apply for a Schengen type D visa from the Belgian consulate in their own country before entering Belgium. *See p304* **Working in Brussels** for more information on long stays. (*See also p295* **So long, Séjour**.)

When to go

Climate

Winters are cold, damp and windy, without much snow; summers are warm. Rain can fall all year round. The biggest drawback to winter in Brussels is the shortness of the days. The sky is dark until 9am and after 4pm in the shortest months. In April and May, average temperatures range between 5°C (40°F) and 17°C (63°F). The heat picks up in June and July, reaching the mid 20s°C (70s°F) and occasionally hitting the high 20s°C (80s°F). It's not uncommon to sit out on a café terrace at 10pm with the sky still light. September can be lovely and temperatures are usually around 8°C-15°C (46°F-58°F) during October.

Public holidays

Belgian public holidays are: New Year's Day (1 Jan); Easter Sunday; Easter Monday;

Labour Day (1 May); Ascension Day (6th Thur after Easter); Pentecostal Whit Monday (7th Mon after Easter); Belgian National Day (21 July); Assumption (15 Aug); All Saints' Day (1 Nov); Armistice Day (11 Nov); Christmas Day (25 Dec). Although it is not an official holiday, banks and government offices usually close on 15 November for King's Day. And as if the country didn't have enough holidays, the Belgians make a habit of tacking on more free days to make long weekends even longer. If a holiday falls on a Tuesday or Thursday, most offices, by tradition, will 'make the bridge' (*faire le pont/de brug maken*) and observe a four-day weekend. The longest of these 'bridges' is Easter, when many Belgians embark on short trips across Europe. The French and Flemish communities celebrate separate regional holidays. A day off on 11 July marks the anniversary of the Battle of the Golden Spurs in 1302 for the Flemish region of Flanders, while a holiday on 27 September commemorates the end of French-speaking Wallonia's revolution for independence from Holland in 1830. National Day, 21 July, is a rare joint celebration.

WHAT TO BRING

Bring clothes for varied weather: be ready for rain, sun or cold. Clothes that can be layered will prove especially useful, as will flat shoes for walking on Brussels' unevenly cobbled streets.

Women

Downtown Brussels in the daytime is open and female-friendly; women can enjoy a drink alone in a café with very little or no hassle. After dark, unaccompanied women should avoid the gloomier areas towards the Gare du Midi and Gare du Nord. *See p300* **Safety & security**.

The most comprehensive source of information on the activities of the myriad women's community groups can be found in the weekly *Bulletin* or its website www.xpats.com. A couple of the most popular women's groups for expatriates are the American Women's Club of Brussels (02 358 47 53) and the British & Commonwealth Women's Club of Brussels (02 772 53 13).

Amazone

10 rue du Méridien, St-Josse (02 229 38 00/www.amazone.be). Métro Botanique or Madou/tram 92, 93, 94. **Open** 9am-6pm Mon, Tue, Thur; 9am-5pm Wed, Fri. *Restaurant* noon-2pm Mon-Fri. **Map** p317 E2.
Provides comprehensive information on women's issues and is home to a number of women's organisations, as well as a library and archives that cover women's history. A conference centre and a restaurant open for lunch round off the centre. See the website for lists of women's organisations around Brussels.

Working in Brussels

EU nationals (apart from those from the ten countries that joined the EU in May 2004) and citizens of Iceland, Norway and Liechtenstein do not need a work permit.

However, you are required to register and get a residence permit, a process which will be transformed over the next two years (*see p295* **So long, Séjour**). For the time being, to register you must go to the town hall of the *commune* in which you are living. Take along three passport photos, pay a nominal fee, have your fingerprints taken (not all communes insist on this), and you should receive a three-month residence card. (Note that some communes require other paperwork such as proof of financial status or support; it is advisable to phone ahead and check.) The card is renewable for another three months, but some proof of employment – or otherwise self-employment – is generally required. You're then eligible to receive an ID card valid for five years, should you wish to stay. If you live or work in Belgium, you must carry your Belgian identity card (*carte d'identité/identiteitskaart*) with you at all times. If you don't have one, carry your passport. Not that they will, but Belgian police have the right to stop you at any time to see proof of identity. If you can't produce it, they can hold you at a police station until your identity is proven, even if you haven't committed a crime.

Before starting work EU nationals should apply for Council Regulations forms 1408/71 and 574/72, which concern social security payments for those moving within the EU. For non-EU citizens, the situation is a whole lot trickier. Due to high unemployment, it's becoming more difficult to get work permits (*permis de travail/ werkvergunning*). You are not allowed to enter the country to work without obtaining a type D Schengen visa from the Belgian consulate in your country of residence. The Belgian authorities grant these visas only for specific reasons. In order to get a work permit, your employer must apply for the permit on your behalf, after proving that no Belgian or other EU national can do the job. You will also need to provide three photos, a certificate of good health, proof of good conduct and a copy of your work contract. Processing can take anything up to 12 weeks. The type of permit you get depends on how long you are planning to stay in Belgium. Most people receive type B permits, which are valid for one year and then must be renewed; they are not transferable from one employer to another. After at least four years with a B permit (or an uninterrupted period of at least five years of legal residence in Belgium), you can apply for an A permit, which is valid indefinitely with any employer in any field. Working illegally is not recommended. Unlike France, seasonal cash-in-hand work is thin on the ground. The national governments of each of the Benelux countries have made concerted efforts to crack down on illegal employment. Those caught working illegally by the authorities can be fined, jailed or even deported.

Ministère Federal de l'Emploi et du Travail

51 rue Belliard, EU Quarter (02 233 41 11/www.meta.fgov.be). Métro Maelbeek. **Open** 9am-noon, 2-4pm Mon-Fri. **Map** p322 E4.
Contact for work permit information at the federal level or see the Metaguide on the website for detailed rules of employment.

Office Regional Bruxellois de l'Emploi

65 boulevard Anspach, Lower Town (02 505 16 96/www.orbem.be). Métro/pré-métro De Brouckère. **Open** 8.30am-11.30am Mon-Fri. **Map** p315 B3.
The Brussels office for work permits and employment information. Arrive early, take a number and be prepared to wait. For working in Wallonia see www.leforem.be; for Flanders, see www.vlaanderen.be/werk.

Languages

Although officially bilingual, Brussels is largely French-speaking. For this reason (and for simplicity's sake), we have usually referred to Brussels' streets, buildings and so on by their French name. In town, all street signs are given in both languages (as they are on our street maps, starting on p315).

French is also the language of Wallonia (the south), while Flemish, a dialect of Dutch, is the language of Flanders (the north). (The French, who consider the Belgians stupid, frown upon the easier Belgian numerical use of *septante*, *huitante* instead of the complicated French *soixante-dix* and *quatre-vingt*; the Flemings think that the Dutch spoken in Holland sounds like English.)

There is also a small German-speaking enclave in the east of the country. In the **Trips Out of Town** chapter (*see p215*) we use Dutch for place names in Flanders.

English is widely spoken in Brussels and Flanders, but attempts to speak French in Flanders will fall on deaf ears at best. At worst, it could earn you a punch on the nose. Simply put, the Flemings won't speak French and the French can't speak Dutch – but the issue is far more politically vexed than that. If you can't speak Dutch, use English if the following modest vocabulary doesn't stretch.

Words and phrases are listed below in **English**, then French, then *Dutch* – with pronunciation for the latter given afterwards in brackets.

Useful expressions

Good morning, hello bonjour *hallo* ('hullo'), *dag* ('daarg')
Good evening bonsoir *goedenavond* ('hoo-dun-aav-ond')

Good night bonne nuit *goedenacht* ('khoo-dun-acht')
Goodbye au revoir *tot ziens* ('tot zeens'), *dag* ('daarg')
How are you? comment allez-vous? *hoe maakt u het?* ('hoo markt oo hut')
How's it going? ça va? *hoe gaat het?* ('hoo hart hut')
OK d'accord *okay, in orde, goed* ('okay', 'in order', 'hoot')
Yes oui *ja* ('yah')
No non *nee* ('nay')
Please s'il vous plaît *alstublieft* ('als-too-bleeft')
Thank you/thanks merci *dank u* ('dank oo'), *bedankt* (bur-dankt')
Leave me alone laissez moi tranquille *laat me met rust* ('laat mu mat rust')
How much?/how many? combien? *hoeveel, wat kosthet?* ('hoofail' 'vot cost hut')
I would like... je voudrais... *ik wil graag...* ('ick will hraak')
My name is... je m'appelle... *mijn naam is...* ('mine narm iss')
Left/right gauche/droite *links/rechts* ('links'/'reckts')
Open/closed ouvert/fermé *open/gesloten* ('open'/'he-slo-tun')
Good/bad bon or bonne/mauvais or mauvaise *goed/slecht* ('hoot'/'sleckt')
Well/badly bien/mal *goed/slecht*
Stamp timbre *postzegel*
Toilet WC *toilet* ('twalet')
Do you know the way to... est-ce que vous savez où se trouve...*weet u de weg naar...*('vait oo de veg nar...')

Language expressions

Do you speak English? parlez-vous anglais? *spreekt u Engels?* ('spraykt oo engels?')
I don't speak French/Dutch je ne parle français/*ik spreek geen Nederlands* ('ick sprayk hain nay-der-lants')
Speak more slowly, please parlez plus lentement, s'il vous plaît *kunt u wat trager spreken, alstublieft?* ('kunt oo waht tra-her spray-cun, als-too-bleeft')
I don't understand je ne comprends pas *ik begrijp het niet* ('ick be-gripe hut neet')

Eating & drinking

I'd like to reserve a table... je voudrais réserver un table... *ik zou graag een tafel reserveren...*('ick zoo hraak an ta-full ray-sir-va-run')
...for two people/at eight o'clock ...pour deux personnes/

a vingt heures ...*voor twee personen/om acht uur* ('for tway per-sone-an/om acht oor')
Can I have the bill, please? l'addition, s'il vous plaît *mag ik de rekening, alstublieft?* ('mach ick de ray-cun-ing, als-too-bleeft')
Two beers, please, deux bières, s'il vous plaît *twee bieren/pilsjes/pintjes, alstublieft* ('tway beer-an/pils-yes/pint-yes, als-too-bleeft')

Accommodation

Do you have a room... avez-vous une chambre... *heeft u een kamer...* ('hay-ft oo an kam-er')
...for this evening/for two people? pour ce soir/pour deux personnes? *voor vanavond/voor twee personen?* ('vor vanarfond/vor tway per-sone-an')
Double bed un grand lit *een tweepersoonsbed* ('an tway per-sones-bed')
With bathroom/shower avec salle de bain/douche *met badkamer/douche* ('mat bat camer/doosh')
Expensive/cheap cher/pas cher *duur/goedkoop* ('doer/hoot-cope')

Numbers

zero zéro *nul;* **1** un/une *een;* **2** deux *twee;* **3** trois *drie;* **4** quatre *vier;* **5** cinq *vijf;* **6** six *zes;* **7** sept *zeven;* **8** huit *acht;* **9** neuf *negen;* **10** dix *tien;* **11** onze *elf;* **12** douze *twaalf;* **13** treize *dertien;* **14** quatorze *veertien;* **15** quinze *vijftien;* **16** seize *zestien;* **17** dix-sept *zeventien;* **18** dix-huit *achtien;* **19** dix-neuf *negentien;* **20** vingt *twintig;* **30** trente *dertig;* **40** quarante *veertig;* **50** cinquante *vijftig;* **60** soixante *zestig;* **70** septante *seventig;* **80** huitante *tachtig;* **90** nonante *negentig;* **100** cent *honderd;* **thousand** mille *duizend;* **million** million *miljoen.*

Days & months

Monday lundi *maandag;* **Tuesday** mardi *dinsdag;* **Wednesday** mercredi *woensdag;* **Thursday** jeudi *donderdag;* **Friday** vendredi *vrijdag;* **Saturday** samedi *zaterdag;* **Sunday** dimanche *zondag.* **January** janvier *januari;* **February** février, *februari;* **March** mars *maart;* **April** april *april;* **May** mai *mei;* **June** juin *juni;* **July** juillet *juli;* **August** août *augustus;* **September** septembre *september;* **October** octobre *oktober;* **November** novembre *november;* **December** décembre *december.*

Directory

Further Reference

Books

Art & architecture

Meuris, Jacques
René Magritte
The world of the surrealist painter, in words and pictures.
Rombout, Marc
Paul Delvaux
Excellent selection of colour plates, plus biographical text.
Shinomura, Junichi
Art Nouveau Architecture, Residential Masterpieces 1892-1911
The selection of photographs of the Musée Horta would be a fine addition to anyone's coffee table.
White, Christopher
Pieter Paul Rubens: Man and Artist
A lavishly illustrated look at the Antwerp-born artist.

Fiction, drama & poetry

Baudelaire, Charles
Amoenitates Belgicae
A scathing look at the Belgians and their culture. The poems are rarely published by themselves, but found in collected works. (See p69.)
Baudelaire's Brussels.)
Brontë, Charlotte
The Professor
Brontë's first novel was set in Brussels, and she struggled to find a publisher for it, even after the huge success of her later works.
Villette
Brussels was the model for the town of Villette in her final novel, based on her experience there.
Claus, Hugo
The Sorrow of Belgium
Milestone novel, set during the Nazi occupation, by a major Flemish-language novelist.
Conrad, Joseph
Heart of Darkness
Conrad's masterpiece features early scenes in a corrupt, cheerless Brussels, unnamed but clearly identifiable.
Hergé
The *Tintin* books
Belgium's most famous author needs no introduction.
Hollinghurst, Alan
The Folding Star
Fictional art history and sexual obsession in a dreary city in northern Belgium.
Martin, Stephen (ed)
Poetry of the First World War
An anthology, with poems about the battlegrounds of Flanders.

Maeterlinck, Maurice, et al
An Anthology of Modern Belgian Theatre
Works by Maeterlinck, Crommelynck and de Ghelderode.
Meades, Jonathan
Pompey
Portrait of Belgium's imperial escapades in the Congo.
Royle, Nicholas
Saxophone Dreams
Magical-realist adventures in the landscapes of Belgian surrealist Paul Delvaux, including a role for Delvaux himself.
Sante, Luc
The Factory of Facts
Autobiographical account of growing up in Belgium in the '50s.
Simenon, Georges
Maigret's Revolver
Or just about any other title by the Liège-born master of the crime/detective fiction genre.
Thackeray, William Makepeace
Vanity Fair
The middle section describes the social scene in Brussels on the eve of Waterloo.
Yourcenar, Marguerite
Zeno of Bruges
The wanderings of an alchemist in late medieval Europe. Yourcenar was born in Brussels in 1903.

Food & drink

Hellon, John
Brussels Fare
Recipes from Belgian restaurants.
Webb, Tim
Good Beer Guide to Belgium & Holland
Excellent guide for beer lovers from the Campaign for Real Ale (CAMRA).
Wynants, Pierre
Creative Belgian Cuisine
Anyone who has eaten at Wynants' wonderful Comme Chez Soi (*see p108*) will need no further encouragement.

History & politics

Since Belgium did not exist until 1830, few books deal specifically with its history. Instead, the determined reader will have to search for books about Spain, Austria, the Netherlands, etc.
Glover, Michael
A New Guide to the Battlefields of Northern France and the Low Countries
Covers Waterloo as well as the World War I battlefields.

Kossman, EH
The Low Countries
Dull but informative history of Belgium 1780-1940.
Parker, Geoffrey
The Dutch Revolt
Excellent history covering the demise of the Spanish empire in the 16th century.

Travel

Bryson, Bill
Neither Here Nor There
Belgium and Brussels fill two amusing, if predictable, chapters of Bryson's European travels.
Pearson, Harry
A Tall Man in a Low Land
Entertaining and affectionate travelogue.

Websites

http://pespmc1.vub.ac.be/Belgcul.html
Excellent generic site, containing everything you might want to know about Belgium.
www.geographia.com/belgium/
A generic Belgium site, including a good history section.
http://frenchfood.about.com/cs/belgiancuisine
All about Belgian cuisine, including recipes.
http://vbdw.com/vbdw
Comprehensive Belgian beer site.
www.belgianstyle.com/mmguide
Fun but fact-filled guide to the beers of Belgium.
www.ebrusselshotels.com
Descriptions, reviews, prices and photos of the capital's hotels.
www.visitbelgium.com
Useful website geared towards travellers from North America. Lots of links.
www.belgiumtheplaceto.be
A basic but easy-on-the-eye site, covering everything from health to transport.
www.resto.be
Excellent site with detailed search engine and customer reviews of restaurants around Belgium.
www.alltravelbelgium.com
Handy hotel website, with availability search and option to book.
www.gaydar.co.uk
Gay site, with an ever-growing Belgian room split into Brussels and Belgium-Rest. Messaging is instant and in real time.
www.gay.be
Local gay chat room in French, Dutch and English.

Index

Numbers in **bold** indicate key information on a topic; *italics* indicate photographs

Advertisers' Index

Please refer to the relevant sections for contact details

Place of interest	▨
Hospital or college	▨
Railway station	▨
Park	▨
Métro/pré-métro station	Ⓜ
Métro/pré-métro and tram route	▬ ▬
Pedestrianised zone	▨
Area name	**LOWER TOWN**

Maps

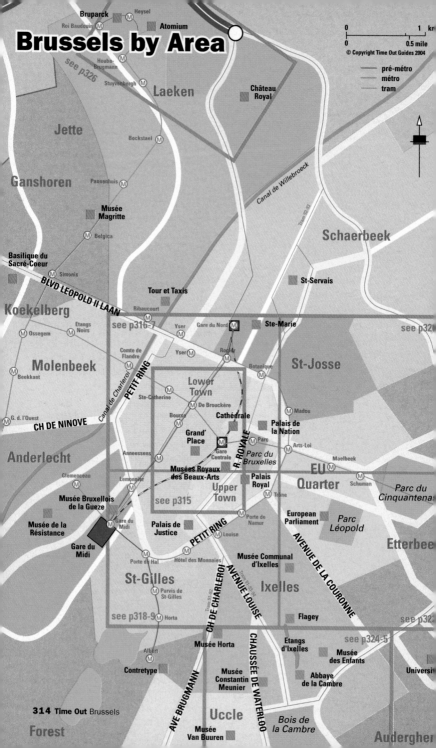

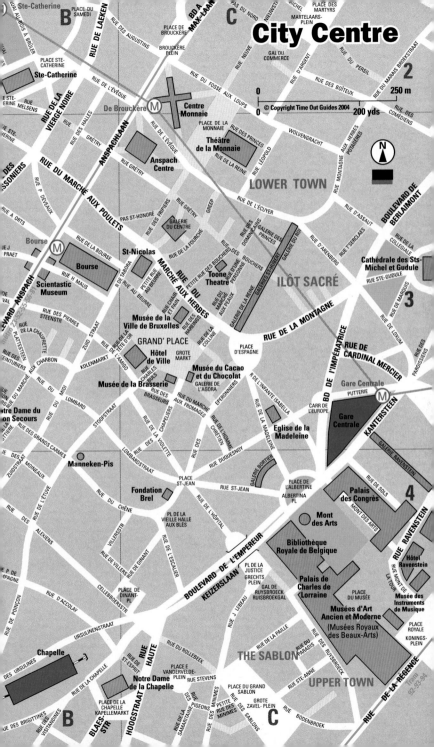

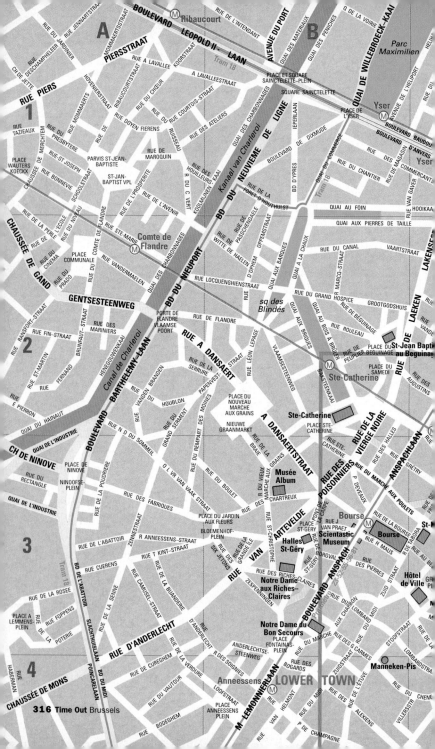

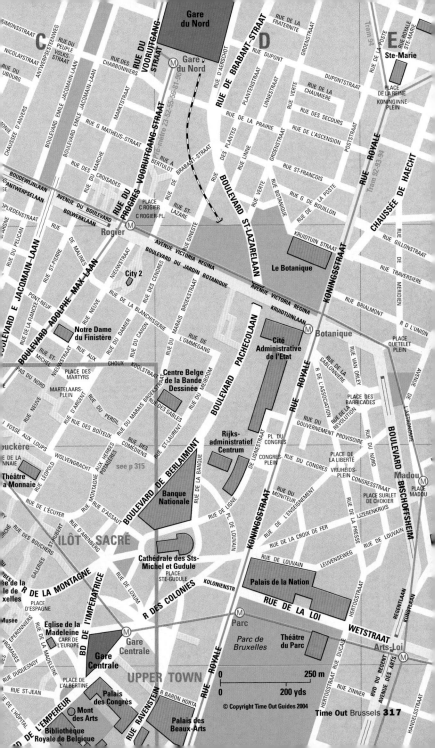

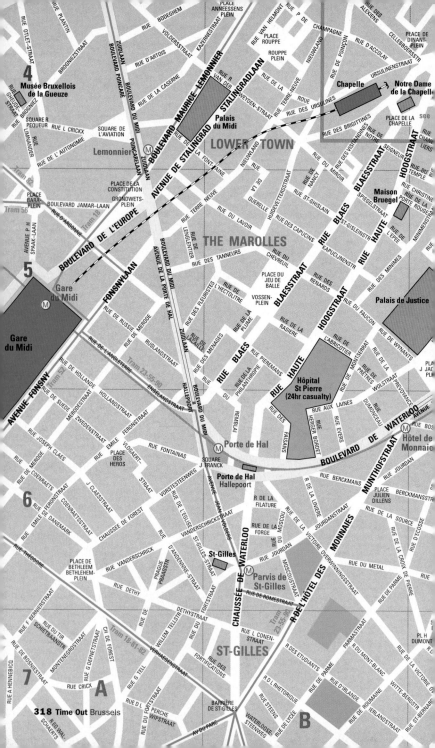

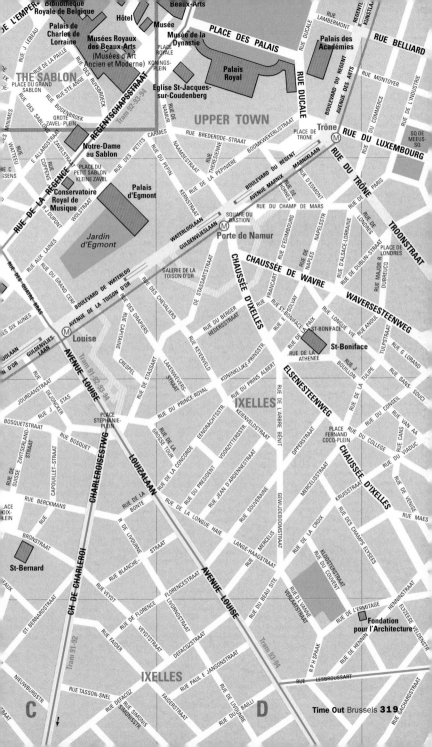

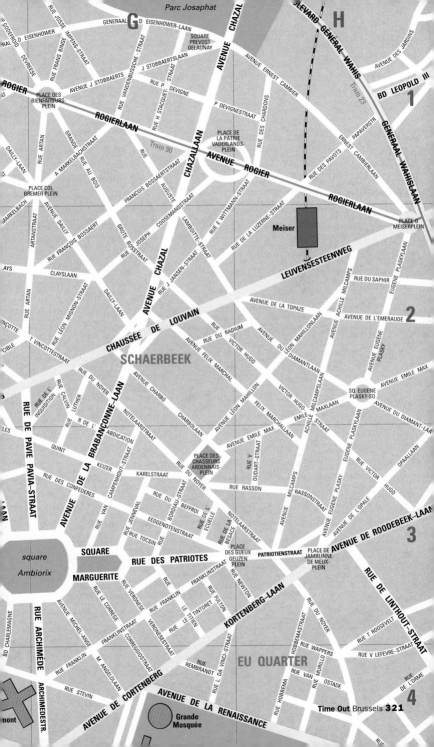

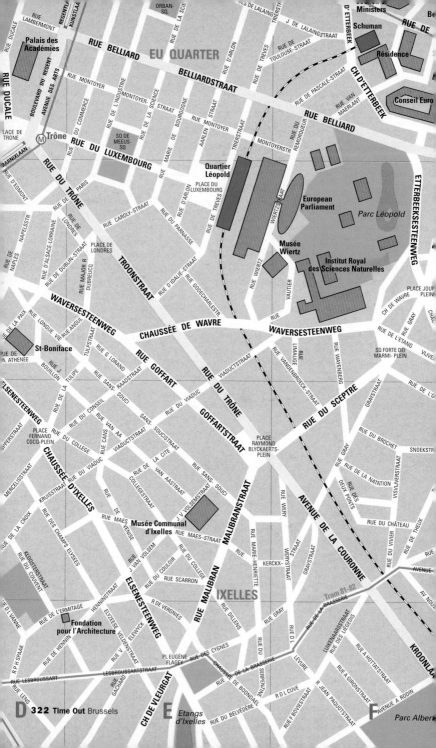

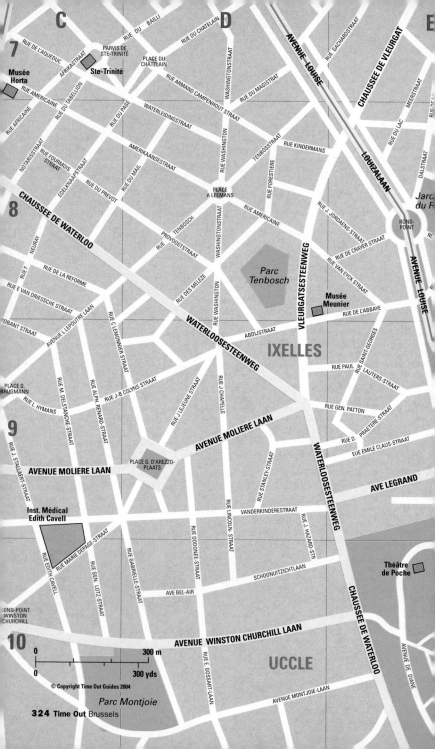

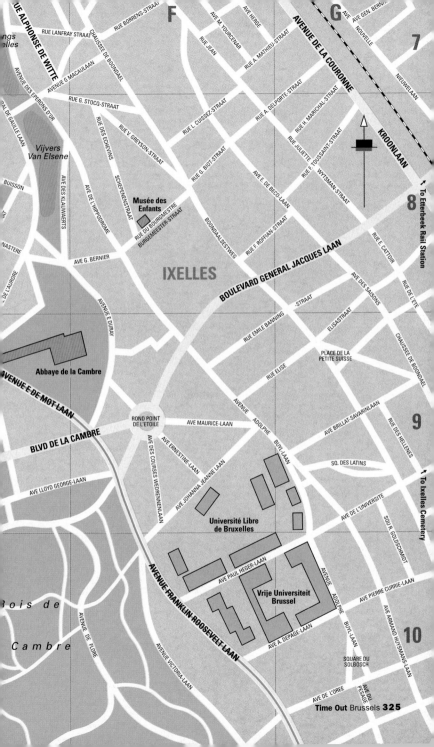

IXELLES

Vijvers
Van Elsene

Musée des
Enfants

Abbaye de la Cambre

BOULEVARD GENERAL JACQUES LAAN

ROND POINT
DE L'ETOILE

PLACE DE LA
PETITE SUISSE

BLVD DE LA CAMBRE

SQ. DES LATINS

Université Libre
de Bruxelles

Vrije Universiteit
Brussel

Bois de

Cambre

SQUARE DU
SOLBOSCH

AVENUE DE LA COURONNE

KROONLAAN

To Etterbeek Rail Station

To Ixelles Cemetery

Laeken

Street Index

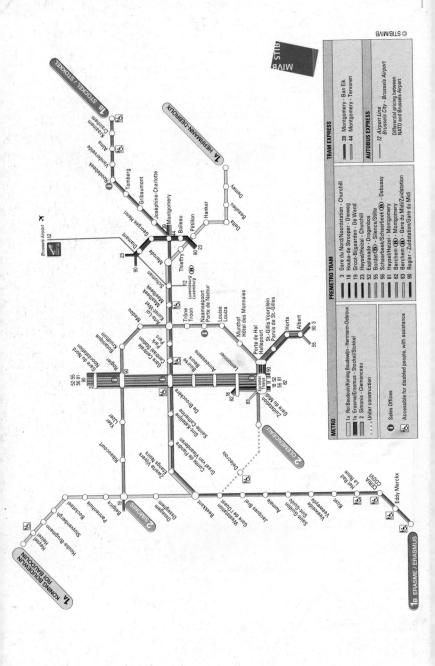

© STIB/MIVB

MIVB
STIB

TRAM EXPRESS
39 Montgomery - Ban Eik
44 Montgomery - Tervuren

AUTOBUS EXPRESS
12 *Airport Line*
   Brussels City - Brussels Airport
   Differential pricing between
   NATO and Brussels Airport

PREMETRO TRAM
3   Gare du Nord/Noordstation - Churchill
18 Houba-de Strooper - Dieweg
19 Groot-Bijgaarden - De Wand
23 Heysel/Heizel - Churchill
52 Esplanade - Drogenbos
55 Bordet ⓑ - Silence/Stilte
56 Schaarbeek/Schaerbeek ⓑ - Debussy
81 Heysel/Heizel - Montgomery
82 Berchem ⓑ - Montgomery
83 Berchem ⓑ - Gare du Midi/Zuidstation
90 Rogier - Zuidstation/Gare du Midi

METRO
1a Roi Baudouin/Koning Boudewijn - Herrmann-Debroux
1a Erasme/Erasmus - Stockel/Stokkel
2   Simonis - Clemenceau
···· Under construction

ⓘ Sales Offices

♿ Accessible for disabled people, with assistance

Brussels Airport ✈ 12

1B STOCKEL / STOKKEL
1A HERRMANN-DEBROUX
2 CLEMENCEAU
1B ERASME / ERASMUS
1A KONING BOUDEWIJN / ROI BAUDOUIN
2 SIMONIS